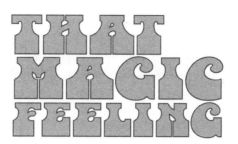

Also by John C. Winn

Way Beyond Compare: The Beatles'
Recorded Legacy, Volume One, 1957–1965

THAT MAGIC FEELING

Volume Two, 1966–1970

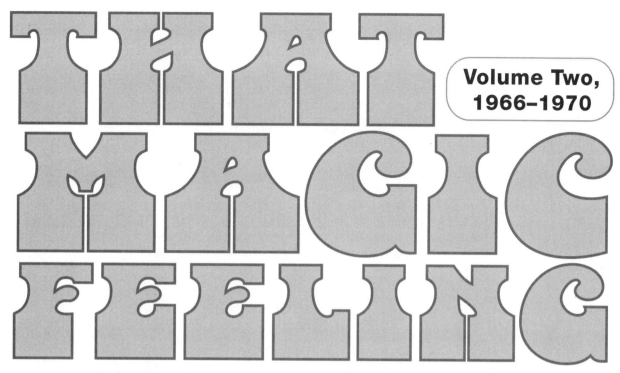

THE BEATLES' RECORDED LEGACY

JOHN C. WINN

THREE RIVERS PRESS
NEW YORK

Published in the United States by Three Rivers Press, an imprint of the Crown Publishing Group,
a division of Random House, Inc., New York.
www.crownpublishing.com

Three Rivers Press and the Tugboat design are registered trademarks of Random House, Inc.

Library of Congress Cataloging-in-Publication
Winn, John C.
That magic feeling / John C. Winn.—1st pbk. ed.
Includes bibliographical references and discography.
p. cm.
1. Beatles—Discography.   2. Beatles—History—Chronology.   I. Title.
ML156.7.B4W547 2009
782.42166092'2—dc22   2008051921

ISBN 978-0-307-45239-9

Printed in the United States of America

Design by Nancy Beth Field

10 9 8 7 6 5 4 3 2 1

First Paperback Edition

To the memory of my grandfathers,
Sterling Winn and William Delorey

CONTENTS

ACKNOWLEDGMENTS

Although I had to do all the dirty work myself, such as transcribing press conferences, this book would simply not exist without the support and help of a lot of other people.

First and foremost are Scott Raile and John McEwen. Scott has given me invaluable feedback on the majority of the manuscript, and has always been there to nitpick over the finer points of arcane Beatle trivia over the last twelve years. Were it not for John McEwen, you'd be reading a guide to audio recordings only—his expertise in the field of Beatles video and generosity in sharing the material are unparalleled.

Other fellow Beatle fans and authors who provided encouragement, recordings, and facts include Mark Ashworth, Chazz Avery, Andrea Bucchieri, Jay Donnelly, Harald Gernhardt, Don Giller, Ted Greenwald, Randy Hall, Chris Hanzl, Walt Janeck, Mike Johnson, LRE King, Katz Kisaki, Tim Kocher, Allan Kozinn, Jason Kruppa, Mark Lewisohn, Chip Madinger, Warren Raab, Tim Riley, Bamiyan Shiff, Doug Sulpy, Dirk Van Damme, and Michael White.

Special thanks to my agent, Matthew Elblonk, for his persistence in getting this revised edition published. A tip of the hat to Andrew Croft for helping to launch my writing career in the pages of his *Beatlology* magazine. Thanks to all my friends who have talked Beatles with me over the years: Oliver Graham, Chris Mirski, Dominic Robillard, Karyn O'Bryant, and especially Abby Dees. Lots of love to my parents, grandparents, and Aunt Cathy and Uncle Jim for helping to raise a fine Beatlemaniac.

Finally, eternal gratitude to my best friend, Janis, for believing in me and giving me the confidence to have faith in myself and my abilities.

This book is meant to be used in conjunction with Volume 1, so I won't rehash the rationale and definitions from the earlier preface. But in case you've been able to acquire only this volume, here's how a typical entry works:

6. Studio session   P, G

The header contains a number (sequential within each chapter—this would be the sixth entry for that year), followed by a categorical designation for the entry. In entries where less than all four Beatles participate in a recording, I've also included the capital letters of their first names (Paul and George in this instance). For this purpose, Pete Best and Jimmy Nicol count as official members, and all studio sessions for Beatle product are exempt from the rule (thus the entry for "Yesterday" is not labeled with a *P*, even though Paul is the only Beatle to sing or play).

Date:	Host:
Time:	Interviewer:
Location:	Broadcast:
Producer:	Length:

These are all fairly straightforward, but note that the date of an entry is the *final* date new sound was added to a recording. For instance, most of the song "Slow Down" was recorded June 1, 1964, but it wasn't completed until George Martin's piano overdub three days later; thus it falls under June 4. Under **Location,** "EMI Studio 2" should be taken to read Abbey Road Studio 2, London; similar shortcuts are used for John's ("Kenwood"), George's ("Kinfauns"), and Ringo's ("Sunny Heights") London homes.

> **[A.] Zip Your Zucchini—takes 2–6 (stereo)**
> (3:55)
> **[B.] Zip Your Zucchini—take 17 (mono)**
> (2:19)
> **[C.] Zip Your Zucchini—RM 8** (2:14)
> **Mixed:** 30 January 1964

Studio session subentries are generally grouped into blocks of raw sessions followed by finished mixes. For the hypothetical song above, we have a continuous stereo recording of five takes, a mono recording of a later take, and a finished mono mix (RM stands for remix mono; RS for remix stereo) created January 30, 1964. For concert recordings and TV/radio performances, the songs are listed in the likely order of performance. "Intro" and "outro" can consist of stage patter or merely audience screaming between songs. All timings in this book are meant to be approximate, not definitive; when faced with different lengths on various sources, I always went with the recording closest to the presumed correct pitch.

RELEASE HISTORY

1964: **C** was released on a single and is available on a CD single of the same title.

1976: **A** and **B** surfaced on the vinyl bootleg *Beatles Tut-Tut Album* in very good quality.

The release history is an attempt to show the genealogy of each recording. It always includes the first appearance, whether on a legitimate or bootleg source, any subsequent upgrades in sound quality or length, and the currently available commercial issues. Sound-quality assessments are obviously subjective, and are meant for comparative purposes only.

Any questions, corrections, comments, or additions? Drop me a line at DinsdaleP@aol.com—I'm always glad to talk Beatle.

1966: TAKE THIS, BROTHER

January 5 John Lennon attends a party at the home of singer P. J. Proby in London.

January 8 While Paul visits his family in Liverpool, the rest of the Beatles attend a party at Mick Jagger's London townhouse.

January 12 John and Ringo fly to Port of Spain, Trinidad, for a vacation with their wives.

George and Pattie nightclub at Dolly's disco with Mick Jagger.

January 21 George marries Patricia Ann Boyd at Esher Register Office; in a reversal of Ringo's wedding, Paul is the only other Beatle in the country and stands in as best man. A reception follows at Kinfauns.

January 23 John and Ringo return to London from their vacation in Trinidad.

January 31 Paul and George, with Jane and Pattie, attend the premiere of the play *How's the World Treating You?* at Wyndham's Theatre in London.

February 3 Paul attends Stevie Wonder's show at the Scotch of St. James nightclub.

February 4 George and Pattie attend the play *Little Malcolm and His Struggle Against the Eunuchs* at the Garrick Theatre.

February 8 Newlyweds George and Pattie fly from London to Barbados for their honeymoon.

February 12 John and Ringo nightclub at the Scotch of St. James.

February 13 John, Paul, and Ringo attend a party at Brian Epstein's house.

February 21 U.S. release of "Nowhere Man"/"What Goes On" single.

February 23 Paul attends a performance of electronic music by Luciano Berio at the Italian Institute.

February 25 George and Pattie return to London from their Barbados honeymoon.

March 4 UK release of *Yesterday* EP.

Maureen Cleave's interview with John is published in the *Evening Standard.* Buried in the middle of the piece is the following quote from John: "Christianity will go. It will vanish and shrink. I needn't argue with that; I'm right and I will be proved right. We're more popular than Jesus now. I don't know which will go first—rock-and-roll or Christianity." Reaction is minimal in Britain; when read within the context of the entire article, the statement is less inflammatory.

March 6 Paul and his girlfriend, Jane Asher, fly from London to Klosters, Switzerland, for a brief ski vacation.

March 20 Paul and Jane return to London.

March 24 The Beatles, their wives, and Brian Epstein attend the premiere of the film *Alfie* (in which Paul's girlfriend, Jane Asher, plays a small role) at the Plaza Haymarket Cinema.

March 25 Robert Whitaker shoots a series of photos of the Beatles at Oluf Nissen's studio in the Vale, Chelsea. Most notably, the group pose in butchers smocks surrounded by raw meat and dismembered baby dolls.

March 26 Paul and his brother Michael watch their father's racehorse win the Hylton Plate at Aintree Race Course.

March 28 George and Ringo attend Roy Orbison's concert at the Walthamstowe Granada Cinema.

April 1 John and Paul visit the Indica Gallery, which opened the previous month with a £5,000 contribution from Paul.

April 6 Sessions for the *Revolver* LP begin at EMI Studios.

April 18 John and George attend the Lovin' Spoonful's concert at the Marquee Club.

May 1	The Beatles give their final British concert, performing at the *New Musical Express* Poll Winners' Concert at the Empire Pool. Though most of the show is videotaped for ABC, the Beatles' set goes undocumented due to contractual disputes.
May 19	John and Paul, along with Keith Moon, spend all night listening to the advance copy of *Pet Sounds,* brought over by Beach Boy Bruce Johnston.
May 20	John and Cynthia attend a party in London with Mick Jagger.
May 27	John and Bob Dylan are filmed in the backseat of Dylan's limo en route from John's Weybridge home to the May Fair Hotel. That night, John and George attend Bob Dylan's concert at the Royal Albert Hall; later, Paul, Bob Dylan, and the Rolling Stones socialize at Dolly's, a nightclub.
May 30	U.S. release of "Paperback Writer"/"Rain" single.
	John's limo is pulled over for speeding while attempting to evade a carful of Beatles fans.
May 31	Ringo is photographed at home for *Beatles Monthly* magazine.
June 1	George attends Ravi Shankar's concert at the Royal Albert Hall; soon afterward they meet for the first time at Peter Sellers's home.
June 10	UK release of "Paperback Writer"/"Rain" single.
June 16	Paul purchases a farm near the Mull of Kintyre in Campbeltown, Scotland.
	The Beatles receive cholera vaccinations (for their upcoming far eastern tour) at BOAC Air Terminal, Victoria Railway Station.
June 20	U.S. release of *"Yesterday" . . . And Today* LP.
June 22	The Beatles attend the pre–opening night celebrations at Sibylla's, a nightclub cofinanced by George.
June 23	The Beatles fly from London to Munich to begin their final world tour.
June 27	The Beatles fly from Hamburg to London Airport to catch a connecting flight to Japan, their next scheduled destination. A decidedly unscheduled typhoon reroutes them to Alaska, where they spend the night at a hotel in Anchorage.
July 3	The Beatles fly from Tokyo to Manila with a stopover in Hong Kong.
July 4	The Beatles offend Imelda, wife of Philippine president Ferdinand Marcos, by missing a ceremonial luncheon at Malacañang Palace.
July 5	The Beatles are harassed by police, government officials, and angry mobs as they make their way to the airport without the promised escorts. They fly from Manila to India via Bangkok, arriving at New Delhi to hundreds of Indian Beatles fans, much to their bewilderment.
July 8	The Beatles return to London Airport in the early morning hours.
	UK release of *Nowhere Man* EP.
July 29	*Datebook,* a U.S. teen fan magazine, publishes Maureen Cleave's March 4 interview with John, under the misleading banner headline "More Popular Than Jesus."
August 2	George visits his mother-in-law's home in Devon.
August 5	UK release of *Revolver* LP.
	UK release of "Yellow Submarine"/"Eleanor Rigby" single.
August 8	U.S. release of *Revolver* LP.
	U.S. release of "Yellow Submarine"/"Eleanor Rigby" single.
August 11	The Beatles fly from London to Chicago (via Boston) for their final concert tour; that night, John explains his remarks about religion, with a pair of remarkable press conferences at the Astor Towers Hotel in Chicago.
August 19	At the evening concert at Memphis's Mid-South Coliseum, a cherry bomb is thrown onstage during "If I Needed Someone."
August 29	The last Beatles concert, at Candlestick Park in San Francisco, is taped by press officer Tony Barrow on a C-60 cassette with a portable recorder pointed toward the general direction of the stage. On the

flight back to Los Angeles after the show, the Beatles agree to cease touring for at least the immediate future.

August 30   The Beatles fly overnight from Los Angeles to London.

August 31   The Beatles arrive back at London Airport.

September 5   John flies to Hanover, West Germany, to the set of *How I Won the War.*

September 6   John has his hair cropped into a crew cut for his role as Private Gripweed; filming begins for *How I Won the War.*

September 14   Shooting of *How I Won the War* concludes at Celle, West Germany.

George and Pattie Harrison fly to Bombay to study yoga and meditation; George also begins sitar lessons under the guidance of Ravi Shankar.

September 15   Paul attends a free-form music concert at the Royal College of Art.

John and Neil Aspinall travel to Paris.

September 16   Paul and Brian Epstein join John and Neil for the weekend.

September 18   John and Neil travel to Almeria, Spain, to continue filming *How I Won the War.*

September 19   George holds a press conference at the Taj Mahal Hotel in Bombay.

Shooting for *How I Won the War* continues on location in Carboneras, in southern Spain.

September 27   Brian Epstein checks in to the Priory Hospital for recuperation and a complete physical following his apparent suicide attempt earlier in the month.

October 4   Ringo and Maureen fly from London to Spain and join John on the set of *How I Won the War.*

October 15   Dressed in an Arabian costume, Paul attends the opening night celebration for the underground paper *International Times,* held at the Roundhouse in London.

October 22   George and Pattie fly from India to London.

October 26   George welcomes Ravi Shankar on the arrival of Ravi's flight at London Airport.

October 31   Donovan arrives at George's bungalow for a week-long visit.

November 6   John's last day of location shooting *How I Won the War.*

Paul flies from Kent to France and spends a week driving through the countryside before meeting up with Mal Evans at Bordeaux.

November 7   John flies from Madrid to London.

November 9   John is formally introduced to Yoko Ono, the artist of Unfinished Paintings and Objects, the day before the avant-garde exhibit opens at the Indica Gallery.

November 11   John and Cynthia attend a Ben E. King performance at the Scotch of St. James nightclub.

November 12   Paul and Mal drive from Bordeaux to Spain, where they had intended to visit John on the film set. Since his part has wrapped early, they drive to Seville, fly to Madrid, have a layover in Rome, and finally arrive in Nairobi, Kenya, for a safari vacation.

November 19   Paul and Mal Evans return to London from their African safari.

November 20   John and George attend a party in honor of the Four Tops at Brian Epstein's house.

November 24   The Beatles reconvene at EMI Studios for new sessions, beginning with "Strawberry Fields Forever," and culminating in the LP *Sgt. Pepper's Lonely Hearts Club Band.*

December 1   Paul attends the Young Rascals show at the Scotch of St James nightclub.

December 2   Paul attends another Young Rascals show at Blaises nightclub in the Imperial Hotel.

December 9   UK release of *A Collection of Beatles Oldies* LP.

December 16   UK release of *Pantomime: Everywhere It's Christmas,* the Beatles' fourth annual Christmas flexi-disc for fan club members.

December 18   Paul and Jane Asher attend the world premiere of the film *The Family Way* at the Warner Cinema. Paul composed the movie's incidental score.

December 31   George, Pattie, Brian Epstein, Eric Clapton, and friends decide to take their patronage elsewhere after George is refused admittance to Annabel's, an upscale nightclub, for not wearing a tie. Instead, the party rings in 1967 at J. Lyons & Co., a small restaurant in southern Soho.

1. Studio session

Date: 5 January 1966
Location: CTS Studios, London
Producer: George Martin
Broadcast: 1 March 1966, 8:00–8:50 p.m.
BBC1
The Beatles at Shea Stadium

[A.] Dizzy Miss Lizzy (2:47)
[B.] Can't Buy Me Love (2:05)
[C.] Baby's in Black (2:07)
[D.] I'm Down (2:07)
[E.] I Feel Fine (2:06)
[F.] Help! (2:19)
[G.] Ticket to Ride (2:14)

Although it wasn't exactly publicized at the time, the Beatles didn't cover up the fact that most of the Shea concert film had to be overdubbed in a studio due to technical limitations. To their credit, they had already refused to release both Hollywood Bowl concerts recorded by Capitol for similar reasons, but with NEMS putting their own money into the Shea project (via Subafilms), the group was persuaded to bring the recordings up to par. This was achieved in a London film-dubbing studio, with George Martin at the helm and the Beatles doing their best to match their new vocals and instrumental tracks to the images on celluloid.

Paul beefed up his bass tracks for **A–D**, with John also fortifying his organ on the latter song, probably having a ball trying to re-create his manic elbow stylings. Both **E** and **F** were completely rerecorded by the whole band, and the studio atmosphere is most evident on these numbers, although they do a good job of investing the songs with concert-level energy. It's not clear whether any overdubbing was done to **G**, and as "A Hard Day's Night" was largely obscured by dialogue, it was left untouched.

There wasn't time to fix up "Twist and Shout" or "Act Naturally," so earlier recordings were added to the soundtrack. In the case of "Twist and Shout," Capitol's 1965 Hollywood Bowl recording was deemed suitable, but "Act Naturally" proved more difficult. A couple of shows into the tour, the group had dropped the song in favor of "I Wanna Be Your Man," and thus no suitable live recording existed. Instead, the original studio version was sweetened with crowd noise and dropped in. Although the record featured acoustic rather than electric rhythm guitar, it's doubtful many viewers noticed the difference.

RELEASE HISTORY

The *Beatles at Shea Stadium* soundtrack has been released on dozens of bootlegs over the years; the earliest titles on vinyl included *Shea, the Good Old Days* and the misleading *Last Live Show.* The best CD source is probably *Shea!/Candlestick Park.*

2. Newsreel footage   G

Date: 22 January 1966
Location: London
Broadcast: 22 January 1966
ITV
Length: 0:59

As Ringo had a year earlier, George consented to meet the press the day following his wedding to Patricia Boyd. This ITV News footage from the press conference captures the newlyweds' entrance, Pattie sporting a knitted beret, as the couple sit on a desk and kiss for the benefit of photographers. As Tony Barrow struggles to control proceedings in the background, George professes his desire to take things slow when it comes to starting a family.

RELEASE HISTORY

This footage was included on the video compilation *Beatles 1962 to 1970.*

3. Interview

G

Date: 22 January 1966
Location: London
Broadcast: 25 February 1966
WABC-AM, New York City
Length: 1:45

One interview from this press conference seems to originate from an ABC-TV report with an unknown American journalist. George doubts that the marriage will have much of an impact on the Beatles' popularity, hoping that the fans are becoming more interested in the music and less concerned with their personal lives. He also refuses to rise to the bait when the reporter presses him to speculate about Paul's marriage plans.

Pattie says she wants to have three children, which prompts George to sing a line from Len Barry's recent hit "1-2-3" (ironically, Barry's follow-up single, which entered *Billboard*'s Top 40 this very day was titled "Like a Baby"!). Pattie patiently answers a couple of patronizing questions before smooching George for the benefit of ABC's cameras.

RELEASE HISTORY

This interview circulates among collectors in good quality from a radio rebroadcast on George's twenty-third birthday.

4. Interview

G

Date: 22 January 1966
Location: London
Length: 1:47

In this interview for a Reuters newsreel, Pattie expresses a wish to remain away from the public eye, much as Cynthia and Maureen were doing. She reiterates her desire to have three children ("Thirty-nine," interjects George), but sadly the couple failed to produce any progeny during their eleven-year marriage. The newlyweds then recount their meeting on the film set of *A Hard Day's Night,* with George revealing that Pattie snubbed him on his initial request for a date.

RELEASE HISTORY

1996: 46 seconds of this interview was released on *Fab Four CD & Book Set.* The full clip circulates on video.

4a. Newsreel footage

G

Date: 22 January 1966
Location: London
Length: 4:37

British Pathe's archive has several minutes of silent footage of the newlyweds' press conference, including shots of George's parents, Brian Epstein, and Tony Barrow watching the proceedings, and Pattie showing off her wedding ring for the cameras. At the end, Mr. and Mrs. Harrison squeeze onto a couch with the new Mr. and Mrs. Harrison and pose for further pictures.

RELEASE HISTORY

This silent footage circulates on video.

5. Newsreel footage

G

Date: 8 February 1966
Location: London Airport
Length: 0:23

George and his new bride decided to wait a couple of weeks before taking off to Barbados for a lengthy honeymoon. Cameras followed the couple through the terminal at London Airport to the steps of their BOAC flight, George in a casual suit and Pattie in a mod black-and-white outfit with stylish shades.

RELEASE HISTORY

This footage circulates on video, and was included in ITV's *Reporting '66: End of Beatlemania.*

6. Speech

Date: ca. 25 February–early March 1966
Location: London
Length: 0:46

At some point early in the year, George agreed to record a brief message of thanks for the readers of *Bravo,* the magazine that would sponsor their upcoming tour of Germany. The message is spoken entirely in German, and George was probably chosen to be the spokesman because he was easily the Beatle most fluent in that language.

RELEASE HISTORY

1966: This recording was issued on a 7-inch flexi-disc, *Die Goldenen OTTO-Sieger 1966,* included with issue 13 of *Bravo* magazine, dated March 21. It's been copied on numerous bootlegs such as *Beatles 4 Ever* and *Live at the Circus Crone.*

7. Interview

Date: 25 March 1966
Time: 3:00–3:30 p.m.
Location: The Vale, London
Interviewer: Tom Lodge
Broadcast: Radio Caroline
Length: 20:52

Once Paul returned from his Swiss skiing holiday, the Beatles could begin convening after a long respite. One of the first such occasions was around this time at NEMS's offices, when the "trunk photo" eventually used on the *"Yesterday"... And Today* album cover was shot. But of course, the alternate picture that initially graced the sleeve was much different, stemming from a March 25 session with photographer Robert Whitaker.

Before donning the butcher smocks and gathering the doll parts and raw meat, however, a somewhat unwelcome publicity task awaited the group. Brian Epstein was half owner in the newly merged *Disc and Music Echo* paper, and to promote its inauguration, a free flexi-disc single would be mailed as a premium to readers who sent in coupons. The disc, titled *Sound of the Stars,* was to feature interviews with a number of British pop stars. With Epstein's involvement, and NEMS's Tony Barrow producing the recording, the Beatles' participation seemed mandatory.

At least that's how it sounds during the unedited interview, with none of the group having anything interesting to say, and Radio Caroline DJ Tom Lodge having no interesting questions to pose. Instead, he tries desperately to fill time, receiving little assistance from his interview subjects. As the tape begins, Lodge asks such inane questions as "What's it like being a Beatle?" and "What do you think of this microphone?" John, just starting to use LSD recreationally around this time, mentions "hallucinations," and Paul knowingly sniggers about "poiple hearts... All them pop groups take 'em." In fact, when Ringo's earnest answer to a question about answering mail induces riotous laughter for no apparent reason, it appears some of the lads may be high, and the tape is switched off.

As we rejoin them, Tony Barrow is heard admitting he has nothing particular in mind for this recording, which is a pity for anyone having to listen to the next fifteen minutes. Such "wacky" jokes as Paul's twins, ages "four and five," and having Gershwin and Trotsky ghostwrite their songs, come across as forced rather than whimsical. In desperation, Lodge even asks Ringo when he first had sex! Even more embarrassing are his attempts to get the Fabs to send greetings to other Radio Caroline DJs; they obviously don't listen to his station and recognize almost none of the names, although John is sure they used to work with Tony Blackburn.

After requesting "Green Door," a 1956 hit for Jim Lowe, and "Priscilla," a hit for Eddie Cooley and the Dimples the same year, they make a dedication to Donny Andrews, bassist for the Liverpool group the Remo Four. Finally, the conversation turns toward politics, and George struggles to make some valid points about military spending and the BBC's monopoly on terrestrial radio. But in the end, only a fraction of this tape was suitable for the flexi-disc.

RELEASE HISTORY

1966: The flexi-disc *Sound of the Stars* contained excerpts from this interview; a bit at the start of side 1 and a further 1:37 to close out side 2.

1996: The unedited source tape was released on the CD *Don't Touch That Dial 2.*

8. Home demo P

Date: ca. late March 1966
Location: 34 Montagu Square, Marylebone

[A.] Eleanor Rigby (0:16)

In March 1966, as Paul was helping Barry Miles set up the Indica Bookshop, the two discussed setting up a recording studio that could be used by poets and experimental musicians. Paul ended up installing a pair of Revox tape recorders in a flat Ringo was leasing, where this demo fragment was most likely recorded. In Paul's authorized biography, *Many Years from Now,* Barry Miles writes: "Paul recorded most of the demo versions of 'Eleanor Rigby' at the experimental recording studio that he had set up in Marylebone."

The tape originally contained Paul's off-air copy of the documentary *The Beatles at Shea Stadium,* aired March 1 on BBC TV. Sometime in the following weeks, Paul erased the tape's first two minutes with a guitar demo of his new composition. According to their chauffeur Alf Bicknell, the Beatles taped demos at George's home on April 10, 1966; this may also come from that session. Following the *Shea* documentary, the tape apparently concludes with an instrumental resembling "I'm Looking Through You," which may mean even more material from 1965 was being taped over.

Paul recalls writing the melody to "Eleanor Rigby" on the upright piano in the Ashers' basement music room (the same piano he and John had used to compose "I Want to Hold Your Hand"), by "vamping an E-minor chord." The demo sounds a half step lower in pitch, with Paul's double-tracked vocal accompanied by his acoustic guitar. The circulating excerpt consists of the refrain "All the lonely people/Where do they all come from?/All the lonely people/Where do they all belong?" The full demo reportedly includes the working lyric "Father McCartney" during the second verse; hopefully the unedited tape will appear someday to verify that fact.

RELEASE HISTORY

2001: This recording turned up out of the blue on a tape being auctioned via the Internet. The sample clip was available on the website www.beatles-auction.com.

2002: **A** was included on the CD-R *As It Happened, Baby!*

8a. Home demo P

Date: ca. 1966
Location: 34 Montagu Square, Marylebone

[A.] tape experiments (4:14)

In the same vein as the "Eleanor Rigby" demo, but far less structured, is this recording of Paul and various friends fooling around with his Revox machines in the basement studio. Playing with the tape echo, Paul babbles in various silly accents (Scouse, Irish, and so on), with his mates chiming in here and there. Although the recording date is unknown, Paul does mention the "Carousel of Light" at one point. While this phrase is fairly close to *Carnival of Light,* the January 1967 festival to which Paul contributed a Beatles sound collage, this is most definitely not that recording.

RELEASE HISTORY

2004: On June 12, BBC Radio 4's series *The Archive Hour* broadcast Barry Miles's documentary *Z Is for Zapple,* which opened and closed with this recording. The entire show circulates on CD-R.

9. Studio session

Date: 6 April 1966
Time: 8:00 p.m.–1:15 a.m.
Location: EMI Studio 3
Producer: George Martin

[A.] Tomorrow Never Knows—take 1 (stereo) (3:13)

[B.] Tomorrow Never Knows—monitor mix of take 1 (mono) (2:02)

The sessions for *Revolver* started off with a bang this evening thanks to a recording that would end up lyrically, melodically, and sonically unlike anything the Beatles had attempted before. It began life with the unassuming working title "Mark I," and John, its author, already had some idea of how he wanted it to sound, although getting it right took some doing.

For this first attempt (**A**), a simple tape loop of slowed-down guitar and resonant percussion was prepared to drone and scrape away in the background. With George Martin's "Here it comes" playback warning, Ringo and Paul added a simple but relentless drum and bass backing on top of this, the result all going on track 1 of the four-track tape. John also sang a guide vocal on track 4, but seems to have been listening to the loop in his headphones rather than what Paul and Ringo were playing, as his vocal lags behind throughout.

A monitor mix of this take (**B**) appears in two segments on the *Anthology* DVD, as George Martin plays back the tape with Paul, George, and Ringo at Abbey Road, occasionally isolating each of the two tracks.

Although the recording as it stood was already revolutionary by their standards, John had something more extreme in mind. By take 3, a satisfactory backing track was laid down on track 1 of the tape. This consisted of Ringo's drums and Paul's bass, this time without any accompanying tape loop. John wanted a more ethereal sound on his vocal than mere double-tracking could give him (something akin to thousands of chanting monks or the Dalai Lama atop a mountain). Presumably, with no Himalayas nearby, the closest thing at hand in Studio 3 was the swirling sound of the Hammond organ's rotating Leslie speaker.

Much to his delight, when John's voice was fed through the Leslie, it produced the desired gyrating tone, and he recorded a lead vocal on track 4 of the tape, with the Leslie effect switched on for the second half of the song. Alongside this, George played a tamboura drone on the same track. There was more work to be done, but that would have to wait for the following day.

RELEASE HISTORY

1996: **A** was officially released on *Anthology 2*.

2003: **B** was released on the soundtrack of the *Anthology* DVD.

10. Studio session

Date: 7 April 1966
Time: 8:15 p.m.–1:30 a.m.
Location: EMI Studio 3
Producer: George Martin

[A.] Got to Get You into My Life—take 5 (mono) (2:52)

Today's afternoon session saw an important addition to "Mark I" as each Beatle arrived with several tape loops of various sped-up and distorted guitars and sound effects such as wine glasses being rubbed. Five of these were placed on different mono machines, the tension taken up by people holding pencils. These signals were all patched into a mixer controlled by the group's new recording engineer Geoff Emerick, who alternated among the signals and fed the results onto track 2 of the "Mark I" tape. Track 3 of the tape would not be filled for a couple more weeks.

This evening session was devoted to Paul's ode to marijuana, "Got to Get You into My Life." By the fifth take, a basic track of acoustic guitar, drums, and George Martin on organ was completed, with added vocals: Paul's lead and some nice harmonies from John and George. The song was lyrically complete at this stage, with the additional words "somehow, someway," after the title line; what would eventually be a guitar break near the end was for now a repeated "I need your love" in rising harmony.

Although take 5 (**A**) was temporarily marked "best," they started again the next day with a slightly different arrangement. With only two tracks of the tape filled this evening, the version released on *Anthology 2* is understandably in mono; if you listen closely, there appears to be a second organ part mixed out (clicking keys can be heard) that duplicates the eventual brass line after each refrain.

In addition, 21 seconds from the end of this take was included in the *Anthology* documentary; although the music overlaps entirely with the CD, the vocal track is left up a bit longer, allowing us to hear Paul's comment "D'you want to do another one, George?" as well as a bit more clowning from John and George.

RELEASE HISTORY

1996: **A** was officially released on *Anthology 2*. The excerpt with extra vocals was also released on the *Anthology* home video the same year; it can be found on the bootleg CD *Abbey Road Video Show*. Its appearance on the *Anthology* DVD has been ruined by aligning the vocal and music tracks out of sync.

11. Studio session

Date: 13 April 1966
Time: 2:30–6:30 p.m.
Location: EMI Studio 3
Producer: George Martin

[A.] Love You To—edit of RM1/RM2/RM3/edit piece (3:03)
Mixed: 16 May 1966

[B.] Love You To—edit of RS1/RS2/RS3/edit piece (2:56)
Mixed: 21 June 1966

[C.] Love You To—RS from takes 6 and 7 (w/edit piece) (2:56)

John and Paul had each contributed a new song, and now it was George's turn. His composition, given the impromptu working title "Granny Smith," incorporated the Indian instrumentation he was growing fonder of, and the lyrics continued in the philosophical vein of "Think for Yourself." Recording began on the eleventh with three takes in the afternoon and three more in the evening session to complete a basic rhythm track. Based on the written and aural evidence, the four tracks filled that day consisted of the following:

A1—George's acoustic guitar and lead vocal, with harmony from Paul on the last word of each verse
A2—fuzz bass from Paul, using the volume pedal to swell the notes during the refrains
A3—sitar, tamboura, and tabla overdub, the latter performed by Anil Bhagwat
A4—second sitar and fuzz guitar overdub

Also, at some point on this first date, a 34-second edit piece was taped for the song's intro, consisting of swarmandal and sitar. At the end of the day, a rough mono mix of take 6 was made for George to take home.

Two days later, this afternoon session completed the song; take 6 was reduced to take 7 by means of combining A1 and A2 above to a single track (let's call it B1), and A3 and A4 to a second (B2). Track B3 of this new tape had a high harmony vocal from Paul (this track was not used on any released mix), and track B4 had a second vocal from George and tambourine played by Ringo. John doesn't seem to have participated in the song at any point, unless he played the fuzz guitar.

The session sheet from this day indicates that take 7, with a length of only 2:44, didn't have the intro edit piece added yet, nor did the three mono remixes done this day. The intro was probably joined during an April 25 session, as John Barrett's tape log has a separate reel from that date (E60604) notated "INTRO. SITAR EDIT PIECE FULL TITLE." With this done, copies of the "best" mono master were made on May 16, one for the United States and one for the UK, which may indicate that George Martin was considering sending this song to Capitol for inclusion on their *"Yesterday"... And Today* LP. As the final stereo mixing and editing was done on June 20 and twenty-first, the song was still being referred to as "Granny Smith"; sometime between then and the transfer order prepared on July 4, George settled on the awkward title "Love You To" (often erroneously listed as "Love You Too").

This mono mix (**A**) lasts several seconds longer during the fade than the other two. The original stereo mix (**B**) makes one of the edit points quite obvious, as a jump in the vocal track can be heard at 2:21. This mix has track B4 mixed in the center, B1 mixed right, and B2 mixed left. By 1999, engineers were able to sync up all four tracks from take 6 (A1–A4) with B4 from take 7 when doing the remix (**C**) for *Yellow Submarine Songtrack*. The result is that A3 is mixed left and A4 to the right, allowing the previously buried second sitar and fuzz guitar to be heard much more clearly than on earlier releases.

RELEASE HISTORY

1966: **A** and **B** were included on mono and stereo pressings, respectively, of the *Revolver* LP. **B** is available on EMI's CD of that title.

1999: **C** was included on Apple's *Yellow Submarine Songtrack* CD.

12. Studio session

Date: 13 April 1966
Time: 8:00 p.m.–2:30 a.m.
Location: EMI Studio 3
Producer: George Martin

[A.] Paperback Writer—take 1 (stereo) (1:23)

After the usual dinner break, the Beatles reconvened to work on Paul's "Paperback Writer," which was destined to be the A-side of their next single. Undoubtedly a lot of rehearsal and discussion took place, for at the end of six and a half hours, they were able to perfect the backing track in two takes. The rhythm consisted of Paul and George on electric guitars, Ringo on drums, and John on tambourine. Ringo tapped his sticks to keep time during the breaks, which would later be filled with multiple vocal harmonies.

The raw tape opens with Paul practicing the intro; as this section is in stereo, with the instruments spread across at least three tracks, it probably comes from the rehearsals, although it does have a "take one" announcement. This is followed by a loud crashing noise, and suddenly everything is on a single track. The first attempt makes it through one verse, but breaks down when George is late changing from a G to a C chord. He is then heard commenting that the others were speeding up, and Paul concurs, saying they are "pressing" too much. George Martin reminds them that the tape is still running, and they begin a second take, which goes off without a hitch.

Although we have both takes on a continuous recording from the multitracks, take 2 as we hear it incorporates overdubs from the following day's session, so it is examined below (entry **13A**)—the timing for that entry begins where the first bit of overdubbed sound is heard.

RELEASE HISTORY

1988: The vinyl bootleg *Ultra Rare Trax, Volume 5 & 6* included a very good, but incomplete, copy of this outtake.

1989: A more complete recording, in the same sound quality, appeared from tape source on the bootleg CD *Unsurpassed Masters, Volume 3*.

1994: **A** was included on the boxed set *The Ultimate Collection, Volume 3: Studio Sessions, 1965–66* in excellent quality, and with an extra second or so at the start (but running too slow).

13. Studio session

Date: 14 April 1966
Time: 2:30–7:30 p.m.
Location: EMI Studio 3
Producer: George Martin

[A.] Paperback Writer—take 2 (stereo) (2:39)

[B.] Paperback Writer—RM2 (2:23)
Mixed: 14 April 1966

[C.] Paperback Writer—RS3 (2:16)
Mixed: 31 October 1966

[D.] Paperback Writer—RS from take 2 (#1) (2:25)

[E.] Paperback Writer—RS from take 2 (#2) (2:20)

Thanks to tape operator Phil McDonald's notes, we can reconstruct some of the work done this afternoon to complete "Paperback Writer." With the rhythm on track 1, Paul overdubbed his main vocal on another track, and a second vocal with backing from John and George on a third track. To fill the remaining track (track 2), numerous overdubs were attempted and discarded, using all the new tricks and toys employed over the previous week. Paul played a bass part, with the signal limited, filtered, and compressed. George Martin tried playing piano through the Leslie speaker for one attempt, and "had a good time" on organ for another. A further idea was to overdub guitar in the gaps after the title phrase was sung. In the end, the only thing not crossed out in the notes is what was used: George and John added further vocals (including the infamous "Frère Jacques" phrase) while Paul played his bass part and George added some lead guitar fills here and there.

At the end of the full take 2 as heard on bootleg (**A**), a couple of seconds of a rehearsal take (rhythm track only) can be heard—this was obviously something taped over by the "proper" takes. Simultaneous to that, as the final track 2 overdub ends, the tail of one of the earlier overdub attempts is audible, as the Leslied piano jangles on.

With the song complete, mono mixing was done that same evening, and as McDonald's notes specify, track 1 was faded out during the a cappella interludes, so that Ringo's tapping wouldn't be audible (although you can hear it on **A**). Also indicated is an instruction to slow down the tape echo on the "die away of 'Paperback Writer'" before each chorus. This was done very deliberately on **B**, but toned down in the stereo mix done some months later (**C**), which also fades the song several seconds earlier. A new stereo mix was done around the time of *Anthology* for the soundtrack of the promo clip for "Paperback Writer." This mix (**D**) has tracks 1 and 2 mixed center, and the two vocal-only tracks split left and right. The remix (**E**) on the *Anthology* DVD, however, is more faithful to the original stereo mix.

RELEASE HISTORY

1966: **B** was released as a single worldwide and can be found on a CD single of the same title. **C** was released later that year in the UK on *A Collection of Beatles*

Oldies; its initial U.S. appearances on the LPs *Hey Jude* and *The Beatles 1962–1966* had reversed channels. Mix **C** is also contained on the *Past Masters, Volume 2: The Beatles 1962–1966;* and *1* CD collections.

1983: The multimedia presentation *The Beatles at Abbey Road* contained a sped-up, fake stereo mix of this song, most likely derived from **A** or **C**; although it's nothing special, this variation can be heard on bootlegs such as *Turn Me On Dead Man: The John Barrett Tapes* (where it's been speed-corrected), and *Abbey Road Video Show* (where the bass has been EQ'd out for some reason).

1984: Most of **A** appeared from the raw studio tape in Westwood One's *Sgt. Pepper's Lonely Hearts Club Band: A History of the Beatle Years 1962–1970* radio special, although the last 31 seconds are obscured by narration.

1988: The bootleg *Ultra Rare Trax, Volume 1* included **A** in excellent quality, although nearly 2 seconds were chopped out near the end of the song. The full recording surfaced later that year on the vinyl bootleg *Ultra Rare Trax, Volume 5 & 6;* it appeared from a tape source the following year on *Unsurpassed Masters, Volume 3.*

1994: An upgraded copy of **A** was included on the boxed set *The Ultimate Collection, Volume 3: Studio Sessions, 1965–66.*

1996: **D** was prepared for use in *Anthology;* it was heard in complete form on an Apple electronic press kit (EPK), and is on the CD *Lost and Found* and the CD-R *Video 1.*

2003: **E** was released on the soundtrack of the *Anthology* DVD.

14. Studio session

Date:	16 April 1966
Time:	2:30 p.m.–1:30 a.m.
Location:	EMI Studio 2
Producer:	George Martin

[A.]	**Rain—RM3** (2:58)
Mixed:	16 April 1966

[B.]	**Rain—RS1** (2:59)
Mixed:	2 December 1969

[C.] Rain—RS from take 7 (#1) (2:54)
[D.] Rain—RS from take 7 (#2) (2:53)

With the A-side of the single finished, the group tackled its equally excellent B-side, John's "Rain." Already in these sessions, they had experimented with new techniques such as tape loops, jangle and fuzz boxes, putting voices through Leslie speakers, messing with filters and heavy tape echo, and trying new ways of miking instruments. Anything to get new and different sounds, and "Rain" would add a couple more twists.

The basic backing was recorded on the evening of April 14 with drums and guitars on one track of the tape, and Paul's bass occupying a second track. To give the song extra weight, the tape was rolled at a slightly fast speed during the recording, giving the rhythm a slower, heavier, more lethargic sound upon playback. John then added his lead vocal on the tape's third track, but this time the tape was slowed down during the overdub, so his voice would sound slightly fast on the finished product. Although it's not documented on the session sheet, John must have taken home a rough mix of "Rain" that night. While trying to play it back at home, he threaded the tape backwards by mistake and (being stoned at the time), loved what he heard.

Two days later, the group reconvened to add more vocals and tambourine to finish the song. John mentioned his moment of reverse-enlightenment to George Martin, and during a break (perhaps while the group went out to dine), the producer prepared a surprise. He copied some segments of John's lead vocal track (the first line of the song, and the words "sun shines/Rain" spanning the second verse and chorus) onto a second reel. This reel was turned around and overdubbed onto the end of the song, and John was pleased with the result presented upon his return.

There is little difference between the released mono and stereo mixes, which is odd as they were made more than three years apart! John's lead vocal was treated to artificial double-tracking (ADT), yet another innovation of these sessions, during the mixing process. A new remix (**C**) was done for the *Anthology* home video, leaving everything centered but the tambourine/backing vocal track, which is panned to the left. On the *Anthology* DVD (**D**), however, the drums and guitars are left, bass and main vocal centered, and tambourine/backing vocals right.

There is also a version of "Rain" released on several bootlegs (best found on *The Ultimate Collection, Volume 3: Studio Sessions, 1965–66*) that sounds identical to **B**, although it may be from the raw studio tape, as it seems to have a split-second extra at the fade compared to commercial stereo pressings.

RELEASE HISTORY

1966: **A** was released as a single worldwide and can be found on the "Paperback Writer" CD single.

1970: **B** was released in the United States on *Hey Jude;* this mix is also contained on the *Past Masters, Volume 2* CD collection.

1983: The version of **B** used in the multimedia presentation *The Beatles at Abbey Road* was slightly sped up and had reversed channels.

1996: **C** was released in the *Anthology* home video documentary.

2003: **D** was released on the soundtrack of the *Anthology* DVD.

15. Studio session

Date:	19 April 1966
Time:	2:30 p.m.–midnight
Location:	EMI Studio 2
Producer:	George Martin

[A.] Doctor Robert—edit of RM4 (2:13)
Mixed: 12 May 1966

[B.] Doctor Robert—edit of RS1 (2:11)
[C.] Doctor Robert—edit of RS2 (2:11)
Mixed: 20 May 1966

[D.] Doctor Robert—edit of RM6 (2:12)
Mixed: 21 June 1966

[E.] Doctor Robert—RS from take 7 (2:10)

Although it wasn't as inspired or innovative as any of the songs worked on so far for *Revolver,* "Doctor Robert" did introduce new subject matter into the Beatles' lyrical canon, being loosely based on a real-life New York physician who allegedly prescribed amphetamine-fueled vitamin injections to "pick you up."

The rhythm track was perfected in seven takes on April 17; it consisted of rhythm guitar, bass, drums, and George on maracas. George then overdubbed lead guitar, John added harmonium, and Paul played piano, although the latter was either buried deep in the mix or unused entirely. They returned two days later to complete the song by overdubbing all the vocals, which would be split via ADT during the mixing process. Although the complete take 7 lasted 2:56, all released versions are edited down.

The U.S. mono mix (**A**) is the longest, allowing a comment from John to be heard after the song ends (often reported as "OK, Herb," but it sounds to me like "OK, er . . ."). As with the tapping stick on "Paperback Writer," the maraca that kept time under the "well well well" segment was lowered on most mixes, but is audible on mix **A**. The UK mono mix (**D**) has a slightly longer delay on the vocals' ADT and seems to be missing a bit of guitar at 1:36. The two stereo mixes sound nearly identical, but one of the edit points, at 1:34, is more audible on mix **C**. A stereo remix, buried under dialogue on *Anthology* (**E**), has the rhythm track moved a bit to the left.

RELEASE HISTORY

1966: **A** was released on mono copies of *"Yesterday" . . . And Today* in the United States; initial stereo pressings included this mix in fake stereo, but later issues used the correct mix, **B. C** was included on UK stereo copies of *Revolver,* and is on EMI's CD of that title. **D** was released on UK mono pressings of *Revolver.*

2003: **E** was released on the soundtrack of the *Anthology* DVD.

16. Studio session

Date:	20 April 1966
Time:	2:30 p.m.–2:30 a.m.
Location:	EMI Studio 2
Producer:	George Martin

[A.] And Your Bird Can Sing—take 2 (stereo) (2:12)

[B.] And Your Bird Can Sing—RS from take 2 (2:20)

An excellent song written mainly by John, and a flawed but entertaining performance, "And Your Bird Can Sing" was first attempted at the start of this session. The arrangement is nearly finalized, being played in the key of D at this point, and having a more Byrds-like feel to the guitar sound. In addition, the third verse comes before the solo here, rather than after the second bridge. Instead, the second bridge is followed by a repeat of the first verse, and a rather impressive bass and drum flurry precedes the coda.

The backing track consisted of two electric guitars and drums. On the second track, John sang his first lead vocal while Paul played bass and Ringo (or perhaps George) shook a tambourine. The third track was filled with a second vocal from John, with Paul and George singing harmonies. This track also had more lead guitar "punched in" for the solo and end of the song; rather than use ADT or even manual double-tracking, this was played by Paul and George on two guitars simultaneously.

For the fourth track of the tape, yet another John/Paul vocal was added, but something caused a giggling fit as they began this overdub, and the resultant singing is less than serious, with many lines missed entirely due to laughter, and one rendered as "When your bike is broken." The *Anthology* CD mix (**A**) has the "giggly" vocals centered, making them easy to

remove via the OOPS process, while a remix for the DVD (**B**) has the "straight" vocals centered. The DVD mix is also artificially extended by 8 seconds by repeating one of the final phrases. The session concluded with the first four takes of George's "Taxman," but this too would be remade, beginning the following day.

RELEASE HISTORY

1996: **A** was released on *Anthology 2*. An OOPSed version included on bootlegs such as *Upgraded Collection—Highlights* eliminates the "giggling" vocal track, allowing us to hear what this arrangement might have sounded like had it been released in 1966.

2003: **B** was released on the soundtrack of the *Anthology* DVD.

17. Studio session

Date: 21 April 1966
Time: 2:30 p.m.–12:50 a.m.
Location: EMI Studio 2
Producer: George Martin

[A.] Taxman—take 11 (stereo) (2:31)

[B.] Taxman—RS from take 11 (0:50)

This long session saw "Taxman" nearly through to completion. Eleven rhythm track takes (electric guitars, bass, and drums) were laid down. George overdubbed two lead vocal tracks, with harmonies from John and Paul, and for the fourth track, Ringo added tambourine, Paul played lead guitar, including a ferocious solo, and John and Paul dropped in a few falsetto "anybody got a bit of money's." The song at this stage (**A**) ended with a sung "Taxman!" in the style of the *Batman* TV series theme. A new stereo remix (**B**) from this take is included on the *Anthology* DVD; it centers the

rhythm track, splits the two vocal tracks slightly, and pans the fourth track to far right.

Although Mark Lewisohn's two books (*Recording Sessions* and *Chronicle*) indicate that Paul's exaggerated "count-in" was only added on May 16, it is present on this take, and was probably spoken during the backing vocal overdub. As Lewisohn's liner notes for *Anthology 2,* written more recently, denote that take 11 from this date is what we're hearing (and John Barrett's tape log has no mention of any May 16 overdub work on "Taxman"), I'm assuming the earlier reference was in error.

RELEASE HISTORY

1996: **A** was officially released on *Anthology 2*.

2003: **B** was released on the soundtrack of the *Anthology* DVD.

18. Studio session

Date: 22 April 1966
Time: 2:30–11:30 p.m.
Location: EMI Studio 2
Producer: George Martin

[A.] Tomorrow Never Knows—RM8 (2:55)
Mixed: 27 April 1966

[B.] Tomorrow Never Knows—RM11 (2:56)
Mixed: 6 June 1966

[C.] Taxman—edit of RM5/6 (2:37)
[D.] Taxman—edit of RS1/2 (2:35)
Mixed: 21 June 1966

[E.] Tomorrow Never Knows—RS6 (2:55)
Mixed: 22 June 1966

[F.] Tomorrow Never Knows—monitor mix of take 3 (mono) (2:19)

The first task this afternoon was to complete "Taxman" with a reduction mix of take 11, combining both vocal tracks onto one track of a new tape, called take 12. The newly freed fourth track was filled with a cowbell overdub, and the "bit of money" vocal was erased and replaced with the notorious "Mr. Wilson/Mr. Heath" part. In addition, some unwanted lead guitar notes during the second verse were wiped from the tape.

Paul's guitar solo was so splendid, they decided to feature it again at the end of the song, so it was mixed separately and spliced onto the end of the main body of the song (and George's final "me" at the end of the song, which overlaps the splice, was presumably lifted back in from the main take). The only real difference between the mono and stereo mixes is that the cowbell track enters at 0:34 on **C** and at 0:46 on **D**.

"Mark I" was finally completed this day with overdubs of organ, tambourine, and piano on track 3 of the tape. At the same time, John manually double-tracked the first couple of verses; apparently he found the non-Leslied first half of his vocal a bit thin-sounding. The tape was then turned around so that someone could overdub a backwards guitar solo (probably Paul, as the tone is similar to his "Taxman" solo); this was "punched-in" and erased part of the track. Note that John's second vocal was not achieved through ADT, as has been previously reported, since it cuts out exactly when the tambourine and organ do; in addition, there is a slight difference in the way "meaning of within" is sung on each vocal track. Mark Lewisohn reports this session as a sitar and vocal overdub, which makes no sense until you substitute "guitar" for "sitar."

The first nine mono remixes were made on April 27, with the eighth chosen temporarily as "best." This mix (**A**) is the only one to have the guitar solo treated with ADT. A tape copy of this mix was made on May 16, and sometime over the following three weeks, John ditched the title "Mark I" in favor of one of Ringo's epigrams, "Tomorrow Never Knows," to "take the edge" off the song's ponderous lyrics. Three more mono mixes were done on June 6, the middle of which (**B**) was selected as a new "best"—this mix leaves out the last phrase of the guitar solo and fades the effects track a tad early, allowing the piano to clank away on its own longer than on any other mix. The stereo mix (**E**) fades in more gradually than the mono mixes, which open at full volume.

For whatever reason, George Martin changed his mind on July 14 and made an eleventh-hour effort to substitute the original "best" mono mix, but a small batch of albums had already been pressed. Thus UK mono copies of the album with the matrix number XEX 606-1 on side 2 contain mix **B**, while XEX 606-2 and all subsequent issues contained mix **A**. A monitor mix (**F**) of this take found in three segments on the *Anthology* DVD has the individual tracks isolated and plays through to the end, as the piano and organ stumble to a halt.

RELEASE HISTORY

1966: As noted above, early mono pressings of *Revolver* in the UK contained **B**, while the majority included **A**; all mono copies also contained **C. D** and **E** were released on stereo pressings of *Revolver* worldwide, and are both on EMI's CD of that title.

2003: **F** was released on the soundtrack of the *Anthology* DVD.

19. Studio session

Date:	26 April 1966
Time:	2:30 p.m.–2:45 a.m.
Location:	EMI Studio 2
Producer:	George Martin

[A.] And Your Bird Can Sing—edit of RM7/RM8 (1:58)
Mixed: 12 May 1966

[B.] And Your Bird Can Sing—edit of RS1/RS2 (1:57)
Mixed: 20 May 1966

[C.] And Your Bird Can Sing—edit of RM9/RM10 (1:59)
Mixed: 6 June 1966

This remake of "And Your Bird Can Sing" was performed, as John put it before the first attempt, at a "quite brisk" tempo, and raised to the key of E. The backing of rhythm guitar and drums on one track, and Paul's bass on another, was taped simultaneously. Eleven takes later, they listened to their efforts and selected take 10 as the best, although they liked the very end of take 6 as well, with Paul's sputtering bass, so this was spliced to the end of the song at the remix stage. Vocals from John, Paul, and George (treated with ADT on the remix) and percussion (tambourine, cymbal, and handclaps) filled the third track, and a dual guitar solo from Paul and George completed things on the fourth track.

The only difference of note among any of these mixes is that the U.S. mono mix (**A**) has the percussion track mixed slightly louder during the guitar solo.

1966: **A** was released on mono copies of *"Yesterday"... And Today* in the United States; initial stereo pressings included this mix in fake stereo, but later issues used the correct mix, **B.** In addition, **B** was included on UK stereo copies of *Revolver* and is on EMI's CD of that title. **C** was released on UK mono pressings of *Revolver.*

20. Studio session

Date:	29 April 1966
Time:	5:00 p.m.–1:00 a.m.
Location:	EMI Studio 3
Producer:	George Martin

[A.] I'm Only Sleeping—rehearsal take (mono) (0:39)
[B.] I'm Only Sleeping—take 1 (mono) (2:57)

On April 27, the Beatles had taped eleven takes of John's new composition "I'm Only Sleeping." These were played in the key of Em, but with the tape machine running fast. As with "Rain," this gave the song a more languid, dreamy quality when played back. Only the rhythm track of bass, drums, and two acoustic guitars was taped that night, and take 11 was temporarily marked "best." However, they returned to the song two nights later, attempting a remake.

As usual, they recorded several of their rehearsals, in this case consisting of drums and vibraphone on track 1 of the tape, and acoustic guitar on track 2; no vocals were attempted during these run-throughs. The first nine minutes of this rehearsal were then erased by five "proper" takes, but the last minute or so of the rehearsal (**A**) survived. This can be heard on *Anthology 2,* mixed into mono (even though two tracks were used).

The first take (**B**) of the remake was the only one seen to completion, and it had acoustic guitars, tambourine, percussion, and John and Paul's vocal duet all taped on track 1. While the rehearsal sounds in Em, these "real" attempts were again recorded with the machine running fast, and they play back a half step lower in pitch. At this point, the structure is the same as the earlier version through the solo break; this is followed by repeats of the first refrain, the bridge, the third verse, the solo break, and the second refrain, fading out on some vamping.

This remake owes quite a bit in style to the Lovin' Spoonful's then-current hit "Daydream," quite apart from the obvious lyrical similarities. The Spoonful were currently touring England, and John and George caught their show on April 18.

They presumably played this new version back to back with the "best" take from the twenty-seventh and preferred the latter, as this remake was quickly abandoned. Instead, to finish up the session, John taped his lead vocal onto track 2 of take 11, this time with the machine running slow (also as with "Rain") to make it sound faster in the final mix. More work would be done to this recording the following month.

RELEASE HISTORY

1996: **A** and **B** were officially released on *Anthology 2.*

21. TV performance

Date:	1 May 1966
Time:	afternoon
Location:	Empire Pool, Wembley
Host:	Peter Murray
Broadcast:	15 May 1966, 3:50–5:00 p.m. ABC-TV *Poll Winners' Concert*
Length:	2:25

For the fourth year running, the Beatles performed at the *New Musical Express* Poll Winners' Concert. Although nobody could have known it, the ten thousand people present were witnessing the group's final live concert in front of a paying British audience. In an impressive display of British pop's breadth and power, on the bill besides the Beatles were the Rolling Stones, the Who, the Yardbirds, the Spencer Davis Group (featuring Stevie Winwood), Small Faces (with Kenney Jones and Ronnie Lane), Cliff Richard, and the Shadows.

Unfortunately, the Beatles' show-closing set was neither broadcast nor filmed, due to contractual squabbles, but they are known to have played "I Feel Fine," "Nowhere Man," "Day Tripper," "If I Needed Someone," and "I'm Down." These five songs had featured in their December 1965 set list and would be carried over to their June–July 1966 tour as well.

Cameras did capture the award ceremonies at the end of the show, with John receiving trophies as runner-up, world musical personality and Britain's top vocal personality, and all four named top vocal group in Britain and the world. The group, dressed all in black with John sporting a pair of shades, accepted the awards from actor Clint Walker, posed with the trophies for the press and the fans, and then walked offstage, their nine-year British performing career effectively over.

RELEASE HISTORY

1999: The audio of this event (although no Beatle can be heard speaking) appeared on the boxed CD boot *Mythology, Volume 2,* taken from a videotape that circulates among collectors.

22. Radio interview

Date:	2 May 1966
Time:	5:00 p.m. (?)
Location:	Playhouse Theatre, London
Host:	Brian Matthew
Broadcast:	4 June 1966, 10:00 a.m.–noon
	BBC Light Programme
	Saturday Club, #400
Length:	3:14

For the first time in over five months, the Beatles consented to a handful of interviews for BBC Radio, all conducted by Brian Matthew. Although they had no specific product or appearance to plug, the 400th edition of *Saturday Club* was a special enough occasion to warrant their participation; as originally aired, their appearance consisted of four segments totaling 6:05, including yet another a cappella rendition of the *Saturday Club* theme song.

Matthew gets right to the point, wondering just why they have been so absent from the public eye lately. After some nonresponses, George finally explains that they prefer being in the studio to appearing in front of their adoring fans, and John points out that they are now spending twice the usual amount of time recording an album. George hopes that their impending album will be done in two or three weeks, so they can get some time off before their next tour (in the end, sessions stretched out for seven more weeks, right up to the eve of the tour).

Somewhat unwisely, Matthew assumes that the new LP won't contain any sitar, now that "everybody's using it." While the others defend its continued use, George states matter-of-factly that he doesn't care what others do, he plays sitar because he likes it. After John explains that the new album will have no cover versions, Matthew inquires about their upcoming North American tour (announced in April). The news that they will revisit Shea Stadium is a cue for some joshing about baseball and partying on the plane during the summer '65 tour. Matthew, who had traveled with them on the first leg of that marijuana-fueled journey, interjects knowingly, "Everybody takes off before you get off the ground, it's a jolly good trip."

RELEASE HISTORY

1972: A portion of this interview, apparently from a rebroadcast on *Top Gear,* was aired in the BBC Radio documentary *The Beatles Story.*

1999: A more complete recording, in two segments, appeared on the boxed CD bootleg *Mythology, Volume 2.* Unfortunately, about 25 seconds are missing from the second segment here that were included in *The Beatles Story.*

2000: A slightly better quality copy of the first segment only was bootlegged on *The Beatles Broadcast Collection Trailer 2.*

23. Radio interview   R

Date:	2 May 1966
Time:	5:00 p.m. (?)
Location:	Playhouse Theatre, London
Host:	Brian Matthew
Broadcast:	*Pop Profile*
Length:	6:28

After John and George were given furloughs, Brian Matthew chatted with the two remaining Beatles not yet interviewed for the BBC Transcription Service's *Pop Profile* series. First up was the drummer. (Mark Lewisohn's *Complete Beatles Chronicle* has the *Saturday Club* interview *and* this one both starting at 5 p.m., which seems unlikely!)

Ringo declares the extra free time the group now has to be beneficial, although he can't exactly say why; unlike his bandmates, he seems to have few interests outside being a Beatle. He happily admits to being "a lump of nothing, just sitting on a chair" raising "a family of blobs."

Even on the seemingly pertinent topic of music, Ringo can't name a single artist whose albums he would make an effort to listen to. He discusses his short attention span, reminiscing about begging for a bicycle in his childhood only to trade it away. Finally he opens up when recounting his origins as a drummer, playing in a hospital ward band and then improvising his first kit from biscuit tins, wire, and sticks of firewood.

RELEASE HISTORY

1988: Portions of this interview were broadcast in the December 17 episode of BBC Radio's *The Beeb's Lost Beatles Tapes*. It appears from this source on the CD-R *Attack of The Filler Beebs, Episode 3.*

1999: A more complete recording was bootlegged on *Mythology, Volume 2* (and in slightly better quality on *The Beatles Broadcast Collection Trailer 2* the following year), although this has music added to link two segments that are heard as a clean continuous recording on the earlier source.

24. Radio interview   P

Date:	2 May 1966
Time:	5:30 p.m. (?)
Location:	Playhouse Theatre, London
Host:	Brian Matthew
Broadcast:	*Pop Profile*
Length:	6:07

Paul's *Pop Profile* proved a bit more illuminating than Ringo's, although where the drummer's was a bit too mundane, Paul's is a bit too pretentious. He complains how "it's a drag" that he is becoming pigeonholed for attending concerts of experimental music (specifically Luciano Berio's on February 23). Matthew wonders whether Paul will simply retire "when the bubble bursts," reasoning that he will be rich enough. Paul, obviously not having heard a word Ringo just said, claims that "like any of the others, I don't like doing nothing, particularly."

A revealing joke slips from Paul's lips when discussing George's new passion for Indian music: "We've been 'round to his house a couple of times, he plays you . . . and, uh . . . so boring! [laughter] No, no! It's— it's good . . ." After enthusing about seeing great plays in London (and dissing the repertory company in his hometown of Liverpool), he names filmmaking as a potential field to conquer; from *Magical Mystery Tour* through *Let It Be,* Paul would try and usually fail to get the other Beatles excited about this medium.

RELEASE HISTORY

1972: A bit of this interview was broadcast in the BBC Radio documentary *The Beatles Story,* including 27 seconds not found on any other source. This includes two "Oh, God" exclamations from Paul, which were apparently censored from the version used elsewhere.

1988: Portions of this interview were broadcast in the December 10 episode of BBC Radio's *The Beeb's Lost Beatles Tapes*. It appears from this source on *Attack of the Filler Beebs, Episode 3.*

1999: A more complete recording was bootlegged on *Mythology, Volume 2* (and in slightly better quality on *The Beatles Broadcast Collection Trailer 2* the following year), although this has music added over the beginning and ending of the second segment, which is clean on the earlier source.

25. Radio interview   P

Date:	ca. May 1966 (?)
Interviewer:	Brian Matthew (?)
Broadcast:	2 July 1972, 5:00–5:55 p.m.
	BBC Radio 1
	The Beatles Story
	Episode 7—"When the Touring Had to Stop"
Length:	0:31

This brief recording may be an excerpt from the *Pop Profile* described in the previous entry; Brian Matthew's narration in *The Beatles Story* implies that he was the interviewer, although his voice is nowhere to be heard on the recording (nor are his trademark "Yeah's" and "Mm-hmm's," which are peppered throughout the rest of his interviews during his subjects' replies). The only other obvious place this would be from is *The Lennon and McCartney Songbook* (see the August 6 entry).

In this short clip, Paul explains that despite its popularity, "Michelle" wasn't considered as a single release because they usually chose more up-tempo material for singles.

RELEASE HISTORY

1972: This interview was broadcast in the BBC Radio documentary *The Beatles Story*. It appears from this source on the CD-R *Attack of the Filler Beebs, Episode 2*, mislabeled as a June 1965 recording.

26. Studio session

Date:	6 May 1966
Time:	2:30 p.m.–1:00 a.m.
Location:	EMI Studio 2
Producer:	George Martin

[A.] I'm Only Sleeping—RM5 (2:59)
Mixed: 12 May 1966

[B.] I'm Only Sleeping—RS1 (2:56)
[C.] I'm Only Sleeping—RS2 (2:56)
Mixed: 20 May 1966

[D.] I'm Only Sleeping—RM6 (2:59)
Mixed: 6 June 1966

[E.] I'm Only Sleeping—RS from take 13 (1:12)

Returning to take 11 of "I'm Only Sleeping," George filled up the tape's two remaining tracks on May 5 by taping two backwards guitar solos, one played through a fuzz box. These overdubs apparently carried on through most of the song, to be faded up in appropriate spots during remixing. At the beginning of the next day's session, two tape reductions were done (the second attempt was best) to combine the two guitar tracks onto one track of a new tape. The newly vacated fourth track was then filled with a final vocal overdub, John double-tracking his lead in places, and Paul and George singing harmonies. Both vocal tracks were treated to ADT during mixing.

The easiest markers to differentiate the four released mixes are the points where the backwards guitar track was faded up. For the U.S. mono mix (**A**), it appears only three times: at 1:22–1:27, 1:33–1:46, and from 2:47 to the song's end. The U.S. stereo mix (**B**) has backwards guitar in four places, at 0:44–0:47, 0:49–0:53, 1:33–1:45, and 2:45 to the end. The UK stereo mix (**C**), done the same day, is similar, with guitar at 0:44–0:47, 0:49–0:53, 1:32–1:45, and 2:45 to the end. By the time the UK mono mix (**D**) was done, it was decided to include guitar at all five spots: 0:45–0:47, 0:51–0:53, 1:25–1:27, 1:33–1:45, and 2:46 through the end. The incomplete remix (**E**) used in *Anthology* centers all instruments and splits the vocals left and right.

RELEASE HISTORY

1966: **A** was released on mono copies of *"Yesterday"... And Today* in the United States; initial stereo pressings included this mix in fake stereo, but later issues used the correct mix, **B**. **C** was included on UK stereo copies of *Revolver* and is on EMI's CD of that title. **D** was released on UK mono pressings of *Revolver*.

1980: **C** was released on Capitol's *Rarities* collection in the United States, with a misleading liner note claiming verses had been "rearranged."

2003: **E** was released on the soundtrack of the *Anthology* DVD.

NOTE:

An often-reported "fifth alternate mix" from the French *Strawberry Fields Forever* EP is actually just a copy of **D**.

27. Studio session

Date:	9 May 1966
Time:	7:00–11:00 p.m.
Location:	EMI Studio 2
Producer:	George Martin

[A.] For No One—monitor mix of takes 1 and 2 (mono) (2:47)

"For No One" was composed by Paul during his March 6 to March 20 ski vacation with Jane Asher in Klosters, Switzerland. It remains one of his greatest accomplishments, with evocative lyrics and a simple but effective melody.

Ten takes of the backing were recorded this evening, consisting of Paul playing piano on one track while Ringo drummed on a second. This off-line tape (**A**) begins with Paul practicing his piano part and counting in for the first take, which breaks down right after the third verse. Take 2 is announced, after which Paul plays a glissando and comments on the echo on his piano. A few more riffs lead into the second take, which stops after the first chorus; it's not clear whether the take broke down at that point or if that's just where our tape happens to end.

The tenth and "best" take had overdubs added to the third track: Paul on clavichord, plus maracas and hi-hat cymbal.

RELEASE HISTORY

1993: **A** was included on the bootleg CD *Control Room Monitor Mixes*. It also appears on the 2002 CD *Complete Controlroom Monitor Mixes* in slightly lesser quality.

28. Studio session

Date: 16 May 1966
Time: 2:30 p.m.–1:30 a.m.
Location: EMI Studio 2
Producer: George Martin

[A.] For No One—monitor mix of unknown takes and take 10 (mono) (6:27)

The fourth track of the "For No One" tape was filled this day with Paul's lead vocal overdub, done with the tape running slow to raise his voice slightly in pitch on playback. A tape reduction was then made, leaving the vocal on its own track and combining the other three tracks to one.

Once again we have an off-line tape from the preparation of the 1983 presentation *The Beatles at Abbey Road,* which features each of the tracks in isolation as they are switched back and forth on the mixing board. It begins with about two minutes of various un-

known piano and drum takes from the May 9 session. The tape is then fast-forwarded to the start of take 10, which opens with Paul giving Ringo drumming instructions. Each track is isolated in turn: piano, drums, clavichord/percussion, and lead vocal (beginning with Paul practicing the opening lines and asking for "silence for the studio, over and out"). The tape is rewound for another listen to take 10, again isolating individual tracks.

RELEASE HISTORY

1993: A 4:03 portion of **A** was included on the bootleg CD *Control Room Monitor Mixes.*

2002: A complete (but slightly worse quality) version of **A** appeared on the bootleg CD *Complete Controlroom Monitor Mixes.*

29. Promo clips/TV performance

Date: 19 May 1966
Time: 10:00 a.m.–6:30 p.m.
Location: EMI Studio 1
Director: Michael Lindsay-Hogg

[A.] Rain—version 1 (2:58)

[B.] Paperback Writer—version 1 (2:19)
Broadcast: 5 June 1966, 8:00–9:00 p.m.
CBS-TV
The Ed Sullivan Show

[C.] Paperback Writer—version 2 (2:23)
Broadcast: 25 June 1966, 5:50–6:35 p.m.
ABC-TV
Goodbye Lucky Stars

[D.] Paperback Writer—take 3 (2:29)
[E.] Paperback Writer—take 4 (2:30)
[F.] Rain—take 1 (3:21)
[G.] Rain—take 2 (2:58)
Broadcast: 3 June 1966, 6:07–6:35 p.m.
Rediffusion-TV
Ready, Steady, Go!

[H.] intro (0:18)
Broadcast: 5 June 1966, 8:00–9:00 p.m.
CBS-TV
The Ed Sullivan Show

With a new single to promote and no desire to interrupt recording sessions with visits to numerous TV studios, the Beatles repeated the successful efforts of the previous November and used InterTel's VTR production team to videotape further promotional clips. Rather than a film studio, Abbey Road's large Studio 1 was used, with Michael Lindsay-Hogg beginning a long association as director of Beatles projects.

After a brief rehearsal, the group took their places for the first two clips, both shot in color. John wore tinted sunglasses, a paisley shirt, and a dark jacket, and played an Epiphone Casino; Paul had on a salmon shirt and dark jacket, and played his Hofner bass; George sported a tan jacket and played his Gibson SG; Ringo, at his kit, wore a coat and tie. After "Rain" (**A**) was taped, the group watched a playback, and then John and Paul removed their jackets for "Paperback Writer." This clip (**B**) begins with Paul peering through some transparencies of the Butcher cover photo session and has all four Beatles wearing shades, John switching to small rectangular yellow-tinted lenses for this clip only. Both these clips would be aired exclusively in the United States on *The Ed Sullivan Show.*

Lunch followed, and then work began on taping monochrome clips for the UK, still without regular color TV broadcasts. For the next take of "Paperback Writer" (**C**), John and George sat atop a grand piano, while Paul perched in front of Ringo's riser. John has put his jacket back on and is the only one wearing sunglasses; this version opens with a close-up of Paul's eyes.

Two more takes of "Paperback Writer" followed in succession (**D** and **E**), with the group standing around Ringo's kit in a similar formation to clip **A**. George has now removed his jacket, but Paul has put his back on; John still wears shades. The second of these clips ends with John turning away and hopping off the riser, and

George removing his guitar. These two takes would be edited together for use on *Ready, Steady, Go!*

Following this, two takes of "Rain" (**F** and **G**) were taped in the same clothes and location. The circulating copy of **F** carries on well past the song's end, showing George unstrapping his guitar, and Paul saluting and doing likewise before the camera zooms in for an out-of-focus shot of nothing in particular. These two takes may also have been edited together for use on *Ready, Steady, Go!* (only the unedited masters are circulating).

The final task was to tape a special introduction (**H**), in color, for *The Ed Sullivan Show;* for this, Paul and George sit atop the grand piano while John stands next to Ringo at a microphone. All four hold up colored lighting gels in front of their faces, remove these and their sunglasses (Paul's stay on), and say hello, before Ringo gives a brief excuse for their not appearing in person.

RELEASE HISTORY

All of these clips circulate on video among collectors. The *Ed Sullivan* promos and introduction (**A, B, H**) were the first to surface, in excellent quality from the original 2-inch color video masters. A red-tinted copy of the *Ready, Steady, Go!* edit of **D** and **E** circulated from an unknown rebroadcast, and the *Lucky Stars* clip (**C**) appeared from a film source in the *Private Reel* compilation, taken from Ringo's private collection. Most recently, what appears to be the raw tape of **C–G** appeared from an excellent-quality video source, complete with InterTel slates. The audio of **H** is available on the bootleg CD *The Ultimate Collection, Volume 1: TV Appearances.*

30. Studio session

Date:	19 May 1966
Time:	7:00–11:00 p.m.
Location:	EMI Studio 3
Producer:	George Martin

[A.] For No One—monitor mixes of take 14 (mono) (3:54)

[B.] For No One—RM8 (1:57)
[C.] For No One—RS1 (1:56)
Mixed: 21 June 1966

[D.] For No One—RS from takes 10 and 14 (1:57)

"For No One" was completed this evening by filling the two remaining tracks on the tape reduction. One overdub consisted of bass and tambourine, and the other featured Alan Civil's exemplary French horn during the solo break and the final verse.

The off-line control room tape (**A**) includes further isolations of the individual tracks. It begins with the presong chatter and continues through the middle of the last verse; the tape is then rewound. The song is then played through to the end, allowing the final chord to ring out longer than either released mix. There are no major differences between the mono and stereo mixes (**B** and **C**), done at the same session. A remix (**D**) for the *Anthology* DVD syncs the four tracks from take 10 (piano left, vocal center, drums and clavichord right) with the overdubs from take 14 (left).

RELEASE HISTORY

1966: **B** and **C** were included on mono and stereo pressings, respectively, of the *Revolver* LP. **C** is available on EMI's CD of that title.

1993: Portions of **A** were included on the bootleg CD *Control Room Monitor Mixes*.

2002: A complete (but worse quality) version of **A** appeared on the bootleg CD *Complete Controlroom Monitor Mixes*.

2003: **D** was released on the soundtrack of the *Anthology* DVD.

31. Promo clips

Date:	20 May 1966
Time:	morning/afternoon
Location:	Chiswick House, London
Director:	Michael Lindsay-Hogg

[A.]	**Rain** (2:57)
Broadcast:	9 June 1966, 7:30–8:00 p.m.
	BBC1
	Top of the Pops

[B.]	**Paperback Writer** (2:22)
Broadcast:	2 June 1966, 7:30–8:00 p.m.
	BBC1
	Top of the Pops

[C.] Rain—*Anthology* edit (2:59)

The previous day's videotaping of promo clips had served its purpose well enough, but failed to stray from the typical "stand around and lip-sync in a studio" format. To this end, the Beatles and Michael Lindsay-Hogg accompanied a film crew this morning to Chiswick House and Gardens in the west of London. The group again sported their psychedelic shades, and all but Ringo brought the same instruments they had employed a day earlier.

Color filming began at the front gate with sequences for "Rain," which then moved to a cedar tree, the group performing as children played on the branches. "Paperback Writer" was filmed in a nearby statue garden and inside the conservatory. Shots from the conservatory were also used in "Rain," and several shots of nonperformance footage (the group hanging out and walking through the grounds) were edited into both finished clips. In addition, the version of "Rain" seen in the *Anthology* documentary (**C**) incorporates outtake footage from the day's filming, also in color, as well as shots from both May 19 video clips, in black and white.

Even though they were filmed in color, the only contemporary airings of **A** and **B** were on the monochrome-transmitted *Top of the Pops*. To make up for this, though, the Beatles made a surprise appearance on that show, lip-syncing both songs in a live broadcast from London's Television Centre on June 16. Sadly, this appearance was not preserved, as with all Beatles appearances from *Top of the Pops* (bar a clip of their April 10, 1965, performance used in a *Dr. Who* episode), despite the BBC's recent efforts to track down a copy.

RELEASE HISTORY

Only a black-and-white copy of **A** was circulating at first, from Ringo's *Private Reel* compilation, but pristine color copies of **A** and **B** turned up in preparation for *Anthology* and are both traded in unedited form. **B** and **C** were included in *Anthology*, and Apple distributed a copy of **B** in 1996 to promote the *Anthology 3* CD, and a copy of **A** in 2003 to promote the *Anthology* DVD.

32. Documentary footage   J

Date:	27 May 1966
Time:	7:00 a.m.
Location:	limo between Kenwood and London
Director:	D. A. Pennebaker
Length:	20:38

Bob Dylan was in England again, braving the occasional boos to bring his own brand of rock-and-roll to the Kingdom. As he had the previous year, Bob invited the Beatles to his shows, and John and George took him up on it, attending this evening's gig at the Royal Albert Hall in London; all four socialized with him in nightclubs and his May Fair Hotel room.

But the night before the concert, Bob paid a visit to John's home in Weybridge, and whatever they got up to, Dylan was the worse for it early the next morning as the pair were chauffeured into downtown London to be dropped off at the May Fair. Also in the limo were film-maker D. A. Pennebaker and his camera, and comrade Bobby Neuwirth operating the boom mike and manning the sound recorder. ABC had commissioned Dylan to produce a one-hour special about the tour for the TV series *ABC Stage 66,* and two ten-minute reels of film were shot during the limo ride.

It's a less-than-inspiring occasion, as the hungover Dylan and the uptight-looking Lennon, both wearing shades, sit in the backseat smoking cigarettes. The two famed lyricists parry weakly, attempting to parody serious documentaries by lobbing joke interrogatives at each other about the Mamas and the Papas (Dylan calls them "terrible"), Barry McGuire ("a great war hero," says John), and the Silkie (Bob says he's taken a few milligrams of Silkie once). Bob does have good words for Johnny Cash, who had already put in an appearance for the documentary, and good-naturedly ribs John about how superior the United States is.

As the second reel begins, Dylan complains of an unspecified ailment and proceeds to remove his shades and rub his eyes, spending the last several minutes slumped forward clutching his head. Pennebaker and Neuwirth make mock retching sounds and suggest he might as well puke on camera, as John sits by silently. Bob pleads with the driver, Tom Keylock, to hurry back to the hotel as the final reel runs out, and indeed, Pennebaker recalls that he and John practically had to carry Dylan up to his room when they arrived.

RELEASE HISTORY

The finished edit by Dylan and Howard Alk, titled *Eat the Document,* used only a small bit of this footage. It was rejected by ABC and eventually screened at the New York Academy of Music on February 8, 1971, with a revival run in 1998. A different edit by Pennebaker and Neuwirth, called *You Know Something Is Happening,* reportedly contains a bit more of the Lennon footage; neither documentary has been released on video. Fortunately, both unedited reels, with a mostly synchronized soundtrack (apparently the sound reel ran out, as the last 2:24 are silent), circulate among video traders in good quality. The complete soundtrack to this footage appears on the Dylan bootleg boxed set *Jewels and Binoculars.*

33. Studio session

Date:	1 June 1966
Time:	2:30 p.m.–2:30 a.m.
Location:	EMI Studio 2
Producer:	George Martin

[A.] Yellow Submarine—take 5 (stereo) (2:46)

[B.] Yellow Submarine—RM5 (2:36)
Mixed: 3 June 1966

[C.] Yellow Submarine—RS2 (2:36)
Mixed: 22 June 1966

[D.] Yellow Submarine—RS from takes 4 and 5 (2:37)

For *Revolver*'s obligatory Ringo track, a verse melody from John was combined with a chorus melody from Paul, to which both authors (with help from Donovan) wrote a set of fairy-tale lyrics. The resulting song, "Yellow Submarine," was probably considered as LP filler but turned out well enough to be pulled from the album as a single, and it topped charts around the world a few months later.

The first session, on May 26, was conducted in George Martin's absence—he was suffering from food poisoning, which probably explains the five-day gap in sessions that followed. Two reels were filled with rehearsals, although these were mostly erased later. The rhythm track was then recorded in four takes, with acoustic guitar, drums, tambourine, and Paul's bass filling up two tracks of the tape. The last of these takes was "best," and was overdubbed with Ringo's lead vocal, joined by his bandmates for the choruses, and a fourth track with further vocals from all four. The vocals were recorded with the tape running slow to play back slightly higher in pitch. At the end of the night, a reduction into take 5 combined both vocal tracks to one and both instrument tracks to one.

For this session six days later, everyone present, including Neil, Mal, studio staff, and guests such as Brian Jones, Marianne Faithfull, and Pattie Harrison, joined in adding sound effects, party atmosphere, and of course the mass vocal choir that ends the recording. The two remaining tracks of the tape were filled as follows (in rough order of appearance):

1. John blowing bubbles, two separate bells, a grinding noisemaker, party chatter, an ocarina, a propeller being cranked and dunked in water, change being spilled, a foghorn, and the final group sing-along

2. Chains swishing in a metal tub of water, clinking glasses, more rattling change and party chatter, a brass band section, a tapping noise, a bunch of

mock naval orders ("full stern ahead"), a submerging *whoosh* effect, John's "life of ease" response shouts, and, finally, a marching band bass drum played by Mal Evans

In addition, an elaborate set of overdubs was prepared for the start of the song (perhaps as an edit piece), but not used at the time. This featured "marching feet" effects (coal shaken from side to side in a cardboard box) and a spoken passage from Ringo: ". . . Yellow submarine. And we will march till three the day to see them gathered there. From Land O'Groats to John O'Green, with Stepney do we tread. To see a yellow submarine! We love it."

A rough mono mix was done at the end of the June 2 session, and five "proper" mono mixes were created the following day. The released mono mix (**B**) is the only version to leave the rhythm track up from the start; all other versions bring it in after the first strummed chord. Conversely, mix **B** fades out the second effects track briefly at 1:44, omitting some of the *whoosh* noise. The original stereo mix (**C**) has the rhythm in the left channel, main vocals right, and effects tracks mostly in the middle; it also mixes out John's spoken "life of ease," which is present on all the other versions.

The "marching/spoken" intro is present only on **A**,

which also allows us to hear both effects tracks without being faded down during the song. One is in each channel (the bass drum is panned around a bit at the end), and the intro and remaining tracks are mixed to the center. Finally, we have the *Songtrack* remix (**D**), which synchronizes the original tracks from take 4 with the effects overdubs from take 5, thus allowing the two vocal tracks to be split (the second is treated with ADT and sent left and right); the sound effects are panned all over the stereo picture.

RELEASE HISTORY

1966: **B** and **C** were included on mono and stereo pressings, respectively, of the *Revolver* LP. **C** is available on EMI's CD of that title, and **B** is on the "Yellow Submarine" CD single.

1967: A tape copy of **B** was made for the production of the film *Yellow Submarine,* probably during the November 7 session. It appears, with Ken Scott's announcement, on the bootleg *The Lost Pepperland Reel.*

1996: **A** was released on Apple's "Real Love" CD single.

1999: **D** was included on Apple's *Yellow Submarine Songtrack.*

34. Studio session

Date:	3 June 1966
Time:	7:00 p.m.–2:30 a.m.
Location:	EMI Studio 2
Producer:	George Martin

[A.] I Want to Tell You—RM1 (2:26)
Mixed: 3 June 1966

[B.] I Want to Tell You—RS2 (2:25)
Mixed: 21 June 1966

George's third contribution to *Revolver* was untitled at the start of the June 2 session, although Geoff Emerick came up with the joke title "Laxton's Superb" (a type of apple and a play on "Granny Smith," still the working title of "Love You To" at this point).

Five takes of the song's rhythm track were recorded that day, with lead guitar, piano, and drums all going onto a single track. Take 3 was chosen as "best," so George added his lead vocal to the second track, with Paul and John backing him up on the third. The final track of the tape was filled with an overdub of extra piano (high notes at the end of each bridge and the off-kilter F and E notes near the end of each verse),

tambourine, and maracas. A tape reduction (called take 4, despite the rhythm track takes 4 and 5 already existing) was made; this combined both vocal tracks onto one track of the new tape, and both instrument tracks onto a second. The third track of the new tape had handclaps added for the final verse, and the session ended there.

The following evening, June 3, Paul overdubbed his bass part onto the remaining track, and mono remixing began immediately thereafter. At one point during this session, the song was designated "I Don't Know" on the recording sheet (another joke at George's expense, as this was his reply when asked what the song was called), and then finally the obvious title "I Want to Tell You" was chosen. Both mixes have the vocals and handclaps treated with ADT, and the mono mix (**A**) is much more compressed-sounding than the stereo (**B**).

RELEASE HISTORY

1966: **A** and **B** were included on mono and stereo pressings, respectively, of the *Revolver* LP. **B** is available on EMI's CD of that title.

35. Studio session

Date: 7 June 1966
Time: midnight–1:30 a.m.
Location: EMI Studio 3
Producer: George Martin

[A.] Eleanor Rigby—RM5 (2:03)
[B.] Eleanor Rigby—RS1 (2:03)
Mixed: 22 June 1966

[C.] Eleanor Rigby—RS from takes 14 and 15 (#1) (2:03)
[D.] Eleanor Rigby—RS from takes 14 and 15 (#2) (3:05)

After coming up with the first few lines and melody, Paul solicited help from his fellow bandmates and friends such as Pete Shotton to complete the lyrics for "Eleanor Rigby," although who contributed what is in dispute. Undeniable is the brilliant arrangement for doubled string quartet, which George Martin scored and conducted on April 28. Although it's not given an entry here because no Beatle appears on it, a stereo mix of take 14, the "best" take of the instrumental backing, can be heard on *Anthology 2* and is worth a listen. At the end of the session, all eight instruments (four violins, two violas, and two cellos) were reduced to track 1 of a new tape, with the result called take 15.

The following day, Paul added his lead vocal on track 4, and then he, John, and George harmonized for the choruses on track 3. The song was presumed fin-ished and given three mono mixes that night. However, George Martin had an idea that proved the icing on the cake when he decided that Paul should sing the chorus in counterpoint to his final vocal refrain. This was overdubbed onto track 2 after a mixing session that began on June 6; since the overdub began at midnight, it's listed above as a June 7 entry.

Paul's lead vocal was split with ADT for the choruses and refrains of both originally released mixes. For the stereo mix (**B**), someone was a bit tardy at the ADT switch after the opening chorus, allowing a bit of the first "Eleanor" to be doubled where it shouldn't have been. The *Songtrack* remix (**C**) synchronizes the four string tracks from take 14 (spread across the stereo image) with the three vocal tracks from take 15 (mostly centered). A similar mix on the *Love* CD (**D**) is extended with an instrumental introduction and guitar from "Julia" at the end.

RELEASE HISTORY

1966: **A** and **B** were included on mono and stereo pressings, respectively, of the *Revolver* LP. **B** is available on EMI's CD of that title, and **A** is on the "Yellow Submarine" CD single.

1999: **C** was included on Apple's *Yellow Submarine Songtrack*.

2006: **D** was released on the *Love* CD.

36. Studio session

Date: 9 June 1966
Time: 2:30–8:00 p.m.
Location: EMI Studio 2
Producer: George Martin

[A.] Good Day Sunshine—RM2 (7) (2:07)
[B.] Good Day Sunshine—RS1 (2:06)
Mixed: 22 June 1966

Like "I'm Only Sleeping," this was Paul's "Daydream"-influenced song, written with John's help at Kenwood. On June 8, numerous rehearsals were taped, along with the first three "proper" takes of the rhythm track: piano, bass, and drums. Take 1 was chosen as "best" and the main vocals were added on a second track (Paul on lead, with John and George's harmonies).

The next day, work continued with overdubs on the third track: cymbal for the intro and choruses, snare drum for the choruses and instrumental break, and more piano (playing in a low register). The break was then filled with a honky-tonk-style piano solo from George Martin on the fourth track, recorded with the tape running fast; handclaps were also added to this track on the final two verses. For a finishing touch, some extra three-part harmonies were punched-in on the cymbal/snare/piano track (this occurs at 1:58). The main vocal track was also treated with ADT during mixing (beginning at 1:45), and both vocal tracks are panned back and forth in the stereo mix to give the effect of harmonizing Beatles everywhere.

Six mono mixes were created on June 9, but none

were used; the seventh mix, done June 22, was erroneously labeled "RM2." The main difference between the released mixes is that the rhythm track is faded out a bit sooner in stereo (**B**), allowing a bit more of the drums to be heard in mono (**A**).

RELEASE HISTORY

1966: **A** and **B** were included on mono and stereo pressings, respectively, of the *Revolver* LP. **B** is available on EMI's CD of that title.

37. Studio session

Date: 16 June 1966
Time: 8:30 p.m.–3:30 a.m.
Location: EMI Studio 2
Producer: George Martin

[A.] Here, There and Everywhere—RS from takes 7 and 13 (2:21)

Inspired by hearing "God Only Knows" from the Beach Boys' *Pet Sounds* on May 19, Paul wrote the final ballad in his trio of *Revolver* classics, "Here, There and Everywhere," finishing it up as the LP's deadline loomed. The first four takes were recorded on June 14, and although vocals were added to take 4, they decided to start over two days later. By take 13, the bass, drums, and electric guitar rhythm track (with a second guitar playing volume pedal "swells" near the end) was perfected. During all these takes, Paul sang a live guide vocal on the second track, which he may have then gone back and redone. The final two tracks were each filled with silky three-part harmonies; one of these tracks was also accompanied by finger snaps.

The version released on *Anthology 2* allows us to hear the unused take 7, with instruments and guide vocal mixed in the center, and the final harmony tracks from take 13 superimposed left and right. At the end of this session, a tape reduction into take 14 combined those two on a single track, and Paul made a first attempt at adding a second lead vocal on the newly vacated track, but he would redo it the following day.

RELEASE HISTORY

1996: **A** was released on *Anthology 2*.

38. Studio session

Date: 17 June 1966
Time: 7:00 p.m.–1:30 a.m.
Location: EMI Studio 2
Producer: George Martin

[A.] Here, There and Everywhere—monitor mix 1 of take 14 (mono) (2:30)
[B.] Here, There and Everywhere—monitor mix 2 of take 14 (mono) (2:28)
[C.] Here, There and Everywhere—monitor mix 3 of take 14 (mono) (2:03)
[D.] Here, There and Everywhere—monitor mix 4 of take 14 (mono) (2:28)

[E.] Got to Get You into My Life—RM8 (2:34)
Mixed: 20 June 1966

[F.] Here, There and Everywhere—RS2 (2:21)
[G.] Here, There and Everywhere—RM3 (2:21)
Mixed: 21 June 1966

[H.] Got to Get You into My Life—RS1 (2:26)
Mixed: 22 June 1966

[I.] Got to Get You into My Life—RS from takes 8 and 9 (0:44)

The evening began with the completion of "Here, There and Everywhere." The final track was filled with a second lead vocal from Paul (harmonizing with himself on the second "love never dies/watching her eyes") and some lead guitar work from George. A rough mono mix was done at the end of the session.

Further control room tapes (**A–D**) from preparation of 1983's *The Beatles at Abbey Road* allow us to hear each track in isolation briefly as levels are being adjusted—three of these attempts also capture some extra guitar strumming prior to the beginning of the song, while **C** begins at the phrase "changing my life." The main difference between the released mixes is that the stereo (**F**) lets the backing vocalists' "ooh" linger over the song's final chord, while the mono (**G**) fades the vocals a bit earlier. The second lead vocal is also mixed out in mono for the phrase "I will be there," leaving just the first vocal track, on which Paul sings "will be there."

Paul's other song completed this day, "Got to Get You Into My Life," stretched across the entire *Revolver* sessions, being the second song started and the second to last song finished. A remake began on April 8; judging from Phil McDonald's notes on the session, this consisted of bass and drums on track 1, two fuzzed guitars on track 2, a second bass guitar (and perhaps backing vocals) on track 3, and Paul's guide vocal on track 4. By the time the song was released, all that remained of this work was the drums and bass from track 1 (although some fuzz guitar leakage can be heard, probably picked up by the drum mikes).

On April 11, an unspecified guitar overdub was recorded, wiping at least a portion of either track 2 or 3. A rough mono mix was created April 25, and after listening to this, Paul decided to add a brass section. This was recorded on May 18, erasing two of the original tracks. The five-piece ensemble consisted of Les Condon, Ian Hamer, and Eddie Thornton on trumpets, and Alan Branscombe and Peter Coe on tenor saxophones. A tape reduction was made into take 9, freeing up two more tracks (leaving only bass/drums and brass). On the new third track, Paul redid his lead vocal, accompanied by tambourine and (near the end of the song) organ. The fourth track had a second lead vocal and electric guitar overdub, and more mono mixes were created.

But one final touch was added on June 17, when George overdubbed a brief but thrilling guitar solo; this was punched in to the vocal/tambourine/organ track from 1:45–2:06 on the tape. The song was mixed into mono several more times that night, with RM7 chosen as best. This was tweaked a bit the following day by copying it onto a new tape with a simultaneous overdub of the brass from take 8 of May 18; the result,

called RM8, was released on *Revolver*. No such trickery was done for the sole stereo mix (**H**) the following day.

At the end of the song, Paul ad-libbed the melody during each vocal overdub, so George Martin and Geoff Emerick chose to alternate between the two when mixing the song, as follows:

Vocal 1: "I was alone, I took a ride, I didn't know what I would find there"
Vocal 2: "Another road where maybe I could see another kind of mind there"
Vocal 1: "Then suddenly I see you"
Vocal 2: "Did I tell you I need you"

At this point the two mixes diverge; in mono, vocal 2 continues with "every single day of my life"; in stereo, we hear vocal 1's "every single day" instead, just before the song fades out.

A remix (**I**) done for the *Anthology* DVD syncs the separate brass tracks from take 8 (split far left and right) with the bass/drums from that take and the overdubs from take 9 (all centered).

RELEASE HISTORY

1966: **E** and **G** were included on mono pressings of the *Revolver* LP. **F** and **H** were included on stereo copies of *Revolver* and can be found on EMI's CD of that title.

1991: A fair-sounding tape of **C** appeared on the bootleg CD *Unsurpassed Masters, Volume 6*.

1993: **A–D** were included (in upgraded quality) on the bootleg *Control Room Monitor Mixes*.

2003: **I** was released on the soundtrack of the *Anthology* DVD.

39. Composing tape   J

Date: September 1965–21 June 1966
Location: Kenwood

[A.] **He Said He Said—take 1 (mono)** (0:21)
[B.] **He Said He Said—false starts (mono)** (0:13)
[C.] **He Said He Said—take 2 (mono)** (0:25)
[D.] **He Said He Said—overdub take 1 (stereo)** (0:10)
[E.] **He Said He Said—overdub take 2 (stereo)** (0:46)

[F.] **She Said She Said—take 1 (mono)** (0:42)
[G.] **She Said She Said—take 2 w/false starts (mono)** (1:41)

As "She Said She Said" was a composition with a long gestation period, it's difficult to date these home demos. Certainly they come from two separate sittings, perhaps months apart. **A–E** are all excerpts from a composing session lasting 10:31, which has yet to be circulated widely. The cassette it's taken from continues with a recording of John on the phone, and has him telling a story about a green bottle on side B.

Inspired by Peter Fonda's comments during a late August 1965 acid trip in Los Angeles, the song took life with the phrase "He said, 'I know what it's like to be dead', I said." **A** is nothing more than that phrase sung twice over acoustic guitar accompaniment (in a key somewhere between F-sharp and G major—perhaps John was out of tune, perhaps the tape is at the wrong speed). After two false starts (**B**), John then tests the recording level with a quick "Hello? OK?" The next segment (**C**) adds the line "I said, 'I must be out of my head' " and modulates up a full step in key near the end. **D** and **E** are both rudimentary two-track recordings; the original vocal and acoustic guitar (with heavy echo) dominates one channel, while John adds some guitar notes and an extra "he said" on the other track. **E** adds the lines "I know what it's like to be sad" and "that's what he said," but the song is clearly far from being completed.

In an interview published in *Melody Maker* on June 25 (perhaps conducted June 16 when they were appearing on *Top of the Pops*), John says he has one more song to contribute to the new album, but has completed only "about three lines so far." If we assume "She Said She Said" is the song in question, the second composing tape must have been recorded between June 16 and June 21, as it is considerably more advanced.

The song is now played on acoustic guitar in the key of B-flat. **F** consists of two verses, with John singing a prolonged "I . . ." in place of "she said." The second segment (**G**) begins with a false start, after which John curses and tunes up. A second false start leads into the first verse, which is now lyrically complete. The second verse is a bit different, with "crap" rather than "things" in your head, and a misguided attempt to rhyme "born" with "feel like my trousers are torn." This leads to the bridge, which has echoes of "Girl" in the line "She said, 'I will love him more when he's dead.' " Rather than going into a 3/4 section, John repeats "no it's wrong" and then the tape ends abruptly, apparently where he later erased over it with an otherwise unheard acoustic demo titled "Hold On I'm Com-

ing." The rest of the cassette contains more of John's omnipresent Mellotron noodlings.

George remembers being at John's house and helping him wrap up the composition by joining the waltz tempo "when I was a boy" section, an unfinished song fragment John had started, to the "she said" verses.

RELEASE HISTORY

1988: These tapes first surfaced on episode 88-11 of Westwood One's *The Lost Lennon Tapes* series; only **A** and a portion of **G** were aired. Both segments were bootlegged on the LP *The Lost Lennon Tapes, Volume 2.*

1990: A later episode (90-26) of *The Lost Lennon Tapes* aired **A–E** as well as repeating the same portion of **G**. These were bootlegged on the vinyl *The Lost Lennon Tapes, Volume 24* and the CD *My Love Will Turn You On.*

1996: A more complete version of **G** was included on an obscure homemade CD-R compilation, *Entomology.* This was copied on the more common *From Me to You* bootleg. **A–E** and **G** are gathered on the CD-R *Vinyl to the Core;* the versions on *Mythology, Volume 2* should be avoided, as **D** and **E** are presented in mono.

2002: John gave a Philips cassette containing 25 minutes of "She Said She Said" demos to Yoko's ex-husband, Tony Cox, in January 1970. The tape was auctioned at Christie's on April 30, 2002, where it sold for £58,750; a portion of the recording (**F**) was included on the CD-R *As It Happened, Baby!* from its airing on news reports. Judging from the sound and content, this tape is also the original source of **G**.

40. Studio session

Date: 21 June 1966
Time: 7:00 p.m.–3:45 a.m.
Location: EMI Studio 2
Producer: George Martin

[A.] She Said She Said—RM4 (2:33)
[B.] She Said She Said—RS1 (2:32)
Mixed: 22 June 1966

[C.] She Said She Said—RS from takes 3 and 4 (0:52)

The pressure was on to record the final song for *Revolver,* and indeed "She Said She Said" was the only song on the LP completed during a single session. In addition, Paul became the first Beatle to walk out on a session when he had an unspecified argument with

the others, although not before contributing to the rhythm track.

The song, still untitled at the start of the session, was recorded in three takes of the backing: bass and drums on one track and two electric guitars on a second. Since the song was inspired by events during an LSD trip John, George, and Ringo had taken, it's tempting to speculate that the others were needling Paul about not having tried acid yet; he might have also been irritated that John had sought George's help in completing the song.

In any case, Paul took a hike, and only two Beatle voices appear on the finished product; John's lead vocal and John and George's backing vocals filled the remaining two tracks. These two were combined to one in a tape reduction, called take 4. The extra track was filled with John's organ and George's lead guitar, and with that, the song and the album were finished, at a quarter to four in the morning. Thirty-two hours later, the Beatles were flying from London to Munich for their final stretch of concerts.

A remix (**C**) on the *Anthology* DVD soundtrack, although buried under dialogue, appears to have the two vocal tracks split slightly, suggesting it's from a synchronization of takes 3 and 4. It also centers the bass/drums track.

RELEASE HISTORY

1966: **A** and **B** were included on mono and stereo pressings, respectively, of the *Revolver* LP. **B** is available on EMI's CD of that title.

2003: **C** was released on the soundtrack of the *Anthology* DVD.

41. Newsreel footage

Date:	23 June 1966
Time:	morning
Location:	London and Munich airports
Length:	2:06

Silent footage of the Beatles' arrival in Germany exists from at least three different sources: BBC News (who also filmed the London departure), Reuters, and color footage from a German police training film. The group and Brian Epstein wave to fans from the steps of the BEA airplane (George has on rectangular sunglasses, a fur hat, and a turtleneck) before entering the white Mercedes, which took them to their hotel in Munich. Separate clips of their hotel arrival also exist.

RELEASE HISTORY

This footage circulates on video among collectors.

42. TV interview

Date:	23 June 1966
Time:	noon
Location:	Hotel Bayerischer Hof, Munich
Length:	1:33

After a brief delay due to a stuck elevator, the Beatles made it from their suite to the hotel press conference. No recording of that event seems to exist, but this brief television interview was filmed after the general questioning. John talks about *A Spaniard in the Works,* Paul says it's too hot to wear the lederhosen they were just presented with, Ringo admits he knows only a few German phrases, and George opts to compete in the three-legged race at the 1972 Munich Olympic Games.

RELEASE HISTORY

1996: This interview was released on *Fab Four CD & Book Set;* it also circulates on video, as does an extra 17 seconds of footage from the press conference itself.

43. Concert

Date:	24 June 1966
Time:	5:15 p.m.
Location:	Circus-Krone-Bau, Munich

[A.] intro (0:25)
[B.] I Wanna Be Your Man (0:49)
[C.] I'm Down (2:02)
[D.] outro (0:06)

The first of two shows in Munich was partially captured in a newsreel lasting 2:23 and containing fragments of "Rock and Roll Music" and "If I Needed Someone." This doesn't exist with the original sound, but has been overdubbed with MC Charly Hickman's intro (**A**) and a full performance of "I'm Down" (**C**), both presumably from this concert. A 1:08 edit of this footage, with British narration, was used for a Movietone newsreel. "I Wanna Be Your Man" (**B**) is taken from a different newsreel and sounds slightly clearer than "I'm Down." In addition, there is 49 seconds of silent footage of "If I Needed Someone" from one of the two Munich concerts in circulation.

RELEASE HISTORY

2000: Both songs appeared on the bootleg CD *Beatles '66: Munich • San Francisco;* the newsreel footage circulates on video.

44. Concert

Date: 24 June 1966
Time: 9:00 p.m.
Location: Circus-Krone-Bau, Munich
Broadcast: 5 July 1966, 8:00–8:45 p.m.
ZDF-TV
Die Beatles

[A.] **intro** (0:42)
[B.] **Rock and Roll Music** (1:30)
[C.] **intro** (0:02)
[D.] **She's a Woman** (0:06)
[E.] **Baby's in Black** (2:15)
[F.] **intro** (0:21)
[G.] **I Feel Fine** (2:08)
[H.] **intro** (0:25)
[I.] **Yesterday** (2:05)
[J.] **outro** (0:05)
[K.] **intro** (0:19)
[L.] **Nowhere Man** (2:10)
[M.] **outro** (0:06)
[N.] **intro** (0:30)
[O.] **I'm Down** (1:36)
[P.] **outro** (0:11)

The second Munich show was videotaped for West German television, and the broadcast included songs from opening acts (Cliff Bennett and the Rebel Rousers, the Rattles, and Peter and Gordon) as well as just over half of the Beatles' set. It truly points out how out of practice the Beatles were at performing live by now. They had played only a single five-song set in the last six months, and a short ten-city tour in the four months previous to that. In the meantime, although they had recorded a nearly flawless album, they hadn't rehearsed playing as an ensemble. Rather than bothering to learn any songs from *Revolver,* they merely worked up a rendition of "Paperback Writer" and added it to a set list replete with stale songs such as "She's a Woman" and "Baby's in Black."

Thus the German fans were treated to sloppy renditions with out-of-tune harmonies and botched lyrics (particularly "I'm Down," which had the verses scrambled and was broadcast with several bars chopped out of the ending, perhaps to cover up further mistakes). The highlight of this show is probably a fairly well-sung "Nowhere Man," which was included in the *Anthology* documentary. The first few seconds of "She's a Woman" are spliced awkwardly onto "Baby's in Black" for some reason; presumably this was true of the original broadcast as well as the circulating copy.

In addition to the video, a German police training film includes four minutes of silent color footage of this concert, including the Beatles walking onstage and clips from their first three songs. Some of this was broadcast February 11, 2001, on ZDF-TV's *History*.

RELEASE HISTORY

This concert initially appeared in mediocre quality from an off-line recording on many 1970s vinyl boots, at first coupled with other TV recordings as *Live in Europe & US TV Casts.*

1983: An August 31 rebroadcast of the performance on ZDF-TV meant that a clean copy began circulating widely on video. This in-line source was used for subsequent bootleg CDs, all with decent sound, such as *Atlanta ∗ Munich ∗ Seattle.*

2000: The CD *Beatles '66: Munich • San Francisco* contains the usual songs, but edits in the superior copy of **L** from the *Anthology* video.

45. Concert

Date: 25 June 1966
Time: afternoon
Location: Grugahalle, Essen

[A.] **intro** (1:27)
[B.] **Rock and Roll Music** (1:34)
[C.] **intro** (0:03)
[D.] **She's a Woman** (2:50)
[E.] **intro** (0:38)
[F.] **If I Needed Someone** (2:28)
[G.] **intro** (0:17)
[H.] **Day Tripper** (2:58)
[I.] **intro** (0:05)
[J.] **Baby's in Black** (2:24)
[K.] **intro** (0:12)
[L.] **I Feel Fine** (2:14)
[M.] **intro** (0:29)
[N.] **Yesterday** (2:07)
[O.] **intro** (0:26)
[P.] **I Wanna Be Your Man** (2:12)
[Q.] **intro** (0:27)
[R.] **Nowhere Man** (2:13)
[S.] **intro** (0:27)
[T.] **Paperback Writer** (2:05)
[U.] **intro** (0:46)
[V.] **I'm Down** (2:12)
[W.] **outro** (0:25)

The Fabs left Munich this morning in style, via a luxuriously appointed train used by Queen Elizabeth the previous year, and arrived in Essen for another pair of concerts. The first performance is available in its entirety from a fair-quality audience tape with plenty of screaming drowning out the music. Several minutes of silent WDR-TV footage also document the afternoon show, mostly showing fans scuffling with police outside, but including just over a minute of concert material (mostly from the first three songs).

RELEASE HISTORY

1999: The audience recording first surfaced on the bootleg CD boxed set *Mythology, Volume 2*. The silent news footage circulates on video.

46. Press conference

Date:	25 June 1966
Time:	evening
Location:	Grugahalle, Essen
Broadcast:	WDR Radio
Length:	9:32

Backstage between shows, the Beatles dined and held a press conference, presided over by Tony Barrow as in 1965. This and the following entry both stem from a female German reporter's tape. The weariness with press conferences that had started to creep in during the summer 1964 tour and their jaded attitude of 1965 had now blossomed into full-blown cynicism and, in John's case, thinly veiled disgust.

It didn't help that the questions were mostly still inane, as heard here by successive inquiries about whether they like German girls, German cities, German fans, and a German river. These were complemented by bizarre questions such as "What's the time?" and hostile questions such as "Do you sing for music or money?" Whereas in earlier years they would have played along or quipped back to such queries, they now limit their responses to one or two words, with only Paul making an effort to sound sincere. When someone asks John what he thinks of the questions being posed, he pointedly says, "They're a bit stupid." His patience would be tried further the following day.

RELEASE HISTORY

1992: This press conference was released on a CD titled *Die Beatles In Essen,* and was later copied on the bootleg CD boxed set *Mythology, Volume 2*.

47. Radio interview

Date:	25 June 1966
Time:	evening
Location:	Grugahalle, Essen
Broadcast:	WDR Radio
Length:	3:15

Following the conference, each Beatle was interviewed in turn by the WDR reporter. George says he likes having more private time now and isn't quite ready to be a father yet; John claims to enjoy some classical music, though he has trouble naming any composers; Paul denies for the umpteenth time that he is engaged; Ringo expresses his distaste for musicals.

RELEASE HISTORY

1992: These interviews were released on a CD titled *Die Beatles In Essen.* They were later included on the bootlegs *Die Beatles In Deutschland 1966!* and *Mythology, Volume 2*.

47a. Radio interview

Date:	25 June 1966
Time:	evening
Location:	Grugahalle, Essen
Interviewer:	Camie McKay
Broadcast:	Radio Canadian Army Europe
Length:	11:12

Also attending the concerts in Essen was Corporal Camie McKay, reporting for Radio Canadian Army Europe. In addition to brief interviews with the Rattles and Peter Asher, McKay captured several minutes of the press conference on tape.

The report begins with his description of the

Beatles' outfits, as they pose for photographs prior to the general questioning. A bit of the conference follows, and then McKay makes his way to the table to interview Ringo, Paul, and George in turn. All three Beatles agree that the quality of questions at the conference was particularly poor (George calls them "idiotic"). Ringo says he enjoys soaking up the sun in Los Angeles and Spain, and Paul says he thinks they'll be playing in Toronto on the upcoming tour. As McKay moves on to

George, you can hear Paul being interviewed by the female WDR reporter (see previous entry). George has time to answer only a single question before the event is over, and McKay moves out into the concert hall to wrap things up.

RELEASE HISTORY

This recording circulates in very good quality.

48. Concert

Date:	25 June 1966
Time:	evening
Location:	Grugahalle, Essen
Broadcast:	WDR Radio

> **[A.]** intro (0:19)
> **[B.]** Paperback Writer (1:37)
> **[C.]** outro (0:09)

While interviewing fans in the audience, the WDR reporter captured most of the Beatles' performance of

"Paperback Writer" from their second show at the Grugahalle. It can be distinguished from the earlier recording by Paul's introduction. Here he calls it a "song," whereas on the audience tape he announces it in German as a *"lied."*

RELEASE HISTORY

1992: This recording was released on a CD titled *Die Beatles In Essen,* subsequently copied on the bootleg *Die Beatles In Deutschland 1966!*

49. Newsreel footage

Date:	26 June 1966
Time:	5:25 a.m.
Location:	Central Station, Hamburg

Leaving Essen via the same train after their final show, the Beatles pulled in to Hamburg in the wee hours for their first shows in the city since New Year's Eve 1962. Thirty-seven minutes of raw newsreel footage of their Hamburg visit (all silent and black and white) is in circulation; these may be offcuts from a 1966 TV documentary *Damals In Hamburg,* which used a lot of the same scenes. These clips are so frag-

mented (and include so much repetition) as to make accurate timings futile, but include the railway arrival and other activities discussed below.

Also circulating is a 34-minute documentary, *The Beatles Am 26. Juni 1966 In Der Ernst-Merck-Halle,* produced by the Hamburg police department and covering the train arrival, hotel, concert, and airport departure.

RELEASE HISTORY

This footage circulates on video among collectors.

50. Newsreel footage

Date:	26 June 1966
Time:	2:30 p.m.
Location:	Schloss Hotel, Tremsbüttel

After being driven to their hotel, an enormous castle some thirty miles from Hamburg, the group slept in and appeared at the balcony to wave to fans before departing for the city again. The raw newsreel footage in-

cludes crowds and police outside the hotel, glimpses of their suite, beds, and bathrooms (filmed before they arrived), and their balcony appearance.

RELEASE HISTORY

This footage circulates on video among collectors.

51. Concert

Date: 26 June 1966
Time: 4:27 p.m.
Location: Ernst Merck Halle, Hamburg

    [A.] **intro** (0:58)
    [B.] **Baby's in Black** (0:30)
    [C.] **outro** (0:16)
    [D.] **I Wanna Be Your Man** (1:46)
    [E.] **Nowhere Man** (0:19)
    [F.] **Paperback Writer** (0:19)

Silent footage from the early show in Hamburg appears in both the TV special *Damals In Hamburg* and the raw newsreel offcuts. These include backstage scenes and snippets from "She's a Woman," "If I Needed Someone," "Day Tripper," "Nowhere Man," "Paperback Writer," and "I'm Down." The Hamburg police documentary *The Beatles Am 26. Juni 1966 In Der Ernst-Merck-Halle* includes further scenes from the concert, as well as poor-quality recordings of **A–D** on its (nonsynchronized) soundtrack.

In addition, when some of this footage was aired on *Weltjournal,* it included audio of two songs (**E** and **F**), presumably from this very concert. The same fragment of "Paperback Writer" was repeated twice in the report.

RELEASE HISTORY

1996: **E** and **F** surfaced on the bootleg CD *Die Beatles In Deutschland 1966!*

2000: **E** and **F** appeared in slightly upgraded quality on *Beatles '66: Munich • San Francisco.*

2003: **A–D** were bootlegged on the CD *Bravo Beatles Britztournee.*

52. Press conference

Date: 26 June 1966
Time: evening
Location: Ernst Merck Halle, Hamburg
Length: 20:18

A near-disastrous event, the press conference between shows in Hamburg should have been a happy affair. They were meeting up with old friends such as Astrid Kirchherr, producer Bert Kaempfert, Star-Club barmaid Bettina Derlien (presumably present here, as John and Paul shout, "Hi, Betty!"), and an unknown comrade in a bow tie whom Paul tells Mal to allow backstage. But John, suffering from a slight sore throat, was in a foul mood and had no patience for the questions, which were admittedly poorer on this occasion than most.

Things begin civilly enough with several minutes of posing for photographers, and then a short TV interview focusing on their prior stints in Hamburg (Paul cheerfully recalls "Lying in the street . . . out of your mind" at "seven o'clock in the morning"). We get an inkling that all is not right with John after the first general question. Someone asks their opinion of birth-control ("antibaby") pills, and John says, "I wish they'd had it a few years ago." Ouch! Don't tell Julian!

After that, the questions get more and more like an interrogation from Dieter of *Sprockets.* Some examples: "Where do you want to dance tonight?"; "What's the matter with Peter Sellers?"; "Ringo, who is better, Cassius Clay or you?" When the latter reporter tries for the penetrating follow-up "What about Ringo?," John replies, "I think you're soft! 'What about this?' and 'What about that?' " A couple of questions later, John freely admits to plagiarizing parts of his last book, and to being lazy.

Someone then seems to ask Ringo in fractured English whether Zak bringing him a spoonful of spinach would make him happy, and wonders if nine-month-old Zak will follow them to Tokyo. This is too much for John, who loudly moans, "What kind of *questions* are these? Come on, anybody from the press here?" Another question about his writing being "great literature like James Joyce" engenders the response "It's nothing to do with James Joyce," John's voice dripping with disgust. Another reporter asks what they dream of, and John interjects, "What do you think we are? What do *you* dream of? We're only the same as you, man, only we're rich!"

Things come to a head as a woman accuses them of being "horrid-snobby," and Paul explains their attitude a bit more eloquently: "You expect sort of nice answers to all the questions. But if the questions aren't nice questions, they don't have to have nice answers. And if we don't give nice answers, it doesn't mean we're snobby. It just means we're natural." This gets a smattering of applause, and thankfully the last few questions relate to their music. But this press conference was just one more nail in the coffin of their touring era.

1996: A bit of this press conference was released on the bootleg *Die Beatles In Deutschland 1966!*

Several minutes of silent footage from this conference appear in the aforementioned *Damals In Hamburg* TV special and the raw offcuts; a basically continuous audio recording of the proceeding is dubbed over the top on the circulating copy, none of it synchronized with the picture.

53. Concert

Date: 26 June 1966
Location: Ernst Merck Halle, Hamburg

[A.] Paperback Writer (0:32)

It's unclear which of the two Hamburg shows this comes from, since it doesn't overlap at all with the other available recording (see earlier entry); it apparently originates in a TV report.

RELEASE HISTORY

1996: **A** surfaced on the bootleg CD *Die Beatles In Deutschland 1966!*

53a. Newsreel footage

Date: 27 June 1966
Time: 4:05 p.m.
Location: Fuhlsbüttel Airport, Hamburg
Length: 1:27

The documentary *The Beatles Am 26. Juni 1966 In Der Ernst-Merck-Halle* includes footage of the Beatles leaving their Hamburg hotel and boarding a Japan Airlines flight in a light drizzle, bound for London and Tokyo.

The mind-numbingly lengthy journey was made even longer when a typhoon forced an unscheduled stop in Anchorage, Alaska. The entourage quickly booked accommodations for the night and continued on to Japan the next day. During the flight, Ringo apparently kept occupied by playing with a cassette recorder—one of the tapes he made documenting the tour went up for auction at Christie's in 1996 and again at Sotheby's in 1998. The lot, which included a second cassette of Ringo running through some unreleased compositions ("Looking for the Lightning" and "Sitting in the Back of My Car"), sold for $2,866.

RELEASE HISTORY

This silent footage circulates on video.

54. Newsreel footage

Date: 30 June 1966
Time: 3:30 a.m.
Location: Haneda Airport and Hilton Hotel, Tokyo
Length: 3:09

When they finally landed in Tokyo, sporting kimonos, the Beatles strained to see through the blinding TV lights and waved from the steps of their plane at what they assumed were fans. As they would discover on the drive to the Hilton Hotel (where they arrived at 4:13 a.m.), the Tokyo police force had spared no effort in keeping the crowds as far away as possible, organizing them into small groups along the route from the airport and nearly outnumbering the fans.

RELEASE HISTORY

A color newsreel in circulation (with sound) captures 30 seconds of their airport arrival and a further 10 seconds as they entered the hotel. Further black-and-white silent film contains 1:03 at the airport and 1:26 of the drive to the Hilton.

55. TV interview

Date: 30 June 1966
Time: afternoon
Location: Hilton Hotel, Tokyo
Interviewer: E. H. Eric
Broadcast: NTV Channel 4
Length: 2:57

Finally emerging from their suite ("at 7:14 and a third," as Ringo later joked), the Beatles made their way down to the press conference. En route, they were intercepted by a camera crew from Nippon Television, and they stopped in a hallway alcove to chat with E. H. Eric (real name Taibi Okada), the master of ceremonies for all their Tokyo concerts.

They admit to ignorance about Japanese culture, and Ringo gently criticizes the overzealous security, which is making it difficult to see their Japanese fans. Queries about meeting the Queen, marriages, and how often they washed their hair must have made them dread the upcoming press conference, in fear that the questioning would be no more intelligent than that in Germany.

RELEASE HISTORY

This clip has circulated on video for many years, although none of the footage is in-sync with the soundtrack. The audio portion is available on numerous vinyl bootlegs and interview discs, but is best found on the 1989 Swingin' Pig CD *Five Nights in a Judo Arena*.

56. Press conference

Date: 30 June 1966
Time: 3:20 p.m.
Location: Hilton Hotel, Tokyo
Length: 49:22

The Tokyo press conference was a somewhat tedious affair, due to the lengthy translations from Japanese to English and then vice versa for the responses. Although Tony Barrow was present, the translator took charge of the event. The Beatles were seated onstage behind a long table, flanked by Barrow, Brian Epstein, and others, with the press relatively far away in the audience. Problems with the PA system made it difficult for the participants to be heard, although everything is captured clearly on the tape.

The translator begins by introducing "Ringo Starr-san" and the others, followed by a photo shoot, with the Beatles standing in front of the table to pose. The first few questions are less than riveting, covering tired issues such as fan reaction and haircuts. We learn that the Beatles' wives socialize with one another, but the Beatles' parents do not. Asked what they seek next, John says, "Peace," and Paul adds, "Ban the bomb."

Kevin Garry of Reuters reads questions from the foreign correspondents. He asks for a reaction to critics who accuse the Beatles' performance at the Budokan, a martial arts arena, of desecrating traditional Japanese culture. Paul replies that nobody condemns Japanese dance troupes for performing in England, and John mutters that singing is better than wrestling.

Someone wonders why they don't wear their MBEs in public, and John counters, "We don't wear all our gold discs, either." Brian is asked if he has taught the group any principles for success, and he replies that artists and manager have influenced each other equally. When the typhoon is mentioned, John quips, "There's probably more wind from the press than from us!" John also speaks for the group in denouncing the war in Vietnam, a topic Brian reportedly warned them against commenting on.

Kevin Garry is then allowed five more minutes for questions and spends most of that time in a futile attempt to elicit thoughtful insight into the reasons for their success. Paul does reveal that at age twelve, he saved up to see a Bill Haley concert; he also feels that crowds at football matches are more violent than those at Beatles concerts. Garry passes on a tongue-in-cheek question about what they will do when they grow up, but John doesn't find it funny: "You look adult enough not to ask questions like that."

RELEASE HISTORY

1996: The complete audio of this press conference was included on the bootleg CD *Japan 1966*. Eleven minutes of black-and-white newsreel pool footage (mostly the questions from Kevin Garry) circulate on video, with sound; a small portion of this was used in the *Anthology* documentary. Brief color clips also appeared in the Japanese TV special *The True Story of the Beatles*.

57. Concert

Date: 30 June 1966
Time: 6:30 p.m.
Location: Nippon Budokan Hall, Tokyo
Broadcast: 1 July 1966, 9:00–10:00 p.m.
NTV Channel 4
The Beatles Recital, from Nippon Budokan, Tokyo

[A.] **intro** (1:12)
[B.] **Rock and Roll Music** (1:32)
[C.] **intro** (0:02)
[D.] **She's a Woman** (2:48)
[E.] **intro** (0:31)
[F.] **If I Needed Someone** (2:27)
[G.] **intro** (0:33)
[H.] **Day Tripper** (3:02)
[I.] **intro** (0:05)
[J.] **Baby's in Black** (2:23)
[K.] **intro** (0:17)
[L.] **I Feel Fine** (2:12)
[M.] **intro** (0:23)
[N.] **Yesterday** (2:07)
[O.] **intro** (0:23)
[P.] **I Wanna Be Your Man** (2:07)
[Q.] **intro** (0:24)
[R.] **Nowhere Man** (2:10)
[S.] **intro** (0:19)
[T.] **Paperback Writer** (2:06)
[U.] **intro** (0:38)
[V.] **I'm Down** (2:09)
[W.] **outro** (1:07)

Opening night nerves? Or four musicians who no longer have their hearts in it? Whatever the reason, this Tokyo concert is infamous for being a truly wretched effort on the Beatles' part. Lamentably, it's also the best existing document of a Beatles concert, videotaped in full color with a decent sound balance in front of a relatively quiet audience. The first two of five Budokan concerts were taped for broadcast on Japanese TV, featuring songs from each concert combined with documentary footage and songs from the opening acts. The group's stage suits (dark green for this show, white on the following day) make it simple to tell the two shows apart.

As for the concert itself, it isn't a good sign when John has to stand sideways during the opening song because his microphone keeps revolving in its stand. This problem would plague all the vocal mics throughout the show, with Ringo having to hunch over to sing "I Wanna Be Your Man." At several points, George stops playing and waves to the audience in the middle of a number. He later revealed that this was to induce a scream to cover up some of the shakier moments in the band's arrangements.

No amount of crowd noise could cover up the lack of care evident in this performance. George's lead singing on "If I Needed Someone" is woefully off-key throughout, and his guitar solo in "Day Tripper" atrocious. In the latter song, John plays a B-flat chord rather than an A at one point and either doesn't notice or doesn't care. Ringo looks bored out of his skull as he plods away on the drums. Only Paul puts energy into his singing and playing, but his stage banter is perfunctory. He doesn't attempt any Japanese other than an occasional *domo,* and introduces "I'm Down" with: "This song is called [mumbling] good-bye, we'll see you later . . ."

RELEASE HISTORY

Both Tokyo shows have circulated for decades in complete form on video; there is also some newsreel footage (monochrome) of the group leaving the Budokan in dark suits, mopping their brows with towels, and entering a limo, which probably comes from this evening. A further 1:40 of silent color amateur footage shows their arrival at the Budokan, followed by excerpts from two of the concerts (one dark green suit and one white suit).

1975: The Beatles' set from this concert was booted on vinyl as *Five Nights in a Judo Arena* in excellent sound. The videotape source was used for a Swingin' Pig CD of the same title in 1989.

1993: This show was released in Japan by Apple on a laser disc, *Beatles Concert at Budokan 1966,* which includes bits and pieces of the opening acts such as Isao Bitoh, Yuya Uchida, and Jacky Yoshikawa and the Blue Comets. This source was used on the 1996 bootleg CD *Japan 1966.*

1996: **B** and **D** were officially released on the CD *Anthology 2.*

58. Concert

Date: 1 July 1966
Time: 2:00 p.m.
Location: Nippon Budokan Hall, Tokyo
Broadcast: 1 July 1966, 9:00–10:00 p.m.
NTV Channel 4
The Beatles Recital, from Nippon Budokan, Tokyo

[A.] intro (1:13)
[B.] **Rock and Roll Music** (1:32)
[C.] intro (0:02)
[D.] **She's a Woman** (2:43)
[E.] intro (0:29)
[F.] **If I Needed Someone** (2:22)
[G.] intro (0:29)
[H.] **Day Tripper** (3:00)
[I.] intro (0:07)
[J.] **Baby's in Black** (2:24)
[K.] intro (0:14)
[L.] **I Feel Fine** (2:11)
[M.] intro (0:19)
[N.] **Yesterday** (2:04)
[O.] intro (0:23)
[P.] **I Wanna Be Your Man** (2:06)
[Q.] intro (0:25)
[R.] **Nowhere Man** (2:08)
[S.] intro (0:31)
[T.] **Paperback Writer** (2:04)
[U.] intro (0:35)
[V.] **I'm Down** (2:06)
[W.] outro (0:14)

The second of five Budokan shows, this Friday afternoon concert was also videotaped, and it went a lot more smoothly than the opening night's performance. The camera cues are more organized, including numerous cutaways to the audience. The microphones stay firmly in place, and Ringo's vocal mic is set to the correct height. "Day Tripper" in particular (introduced by John as "a single record in 1948") is more competently performed. About the only blunder comes when Ringo accidentally repeats the final verse during his number: "I wanna be your lover, baby, I wanna be your man . . . Twice!"

Not that the Beatles are taking things more seriously. George keeps up the cheer-inducing waves, John announces "Nowhere Man" with "We'd like to do a song now that's another song," and Paul finishes up by saying, "And, uh, so, as they say in Runcorn, *'Sayonara.'* "

RELEASE HISTORY

This white-suits concert circulates in excellent quality on video. The soundtrack first appeared on the bootleg LP *Welcome the Beatles,* later upgraded as *Budokan '66.* Most early bootlegs used a scratchy film print, but it's taken from a clean video source on the CD *The Ultimate Collection, Volume 2: Live, Live, Live.*

59. Newsreel footage

Date: 3 July 1966
Time: 10:40 a.m.
Location: Haneda Airport, Tokyo
Length: 1:05

A Reuters news crew captured the Beatles boarding a flight for the Philippines, blissfully unaware of the nightmare that awaited them in Manila.

RELEASE HISTORY

This brief, silent, black-and-white clip circulates on video.

60. Concert

Date: 4 July 1966
Time: 4:00 p.m.
Location: Rizal Memorial Football Stadium, Manila
Length: 1:10

After a stopover in Hong Kong, the Beatles' arrival in Manila was marred by an unexpected detainment wherein they were separated from their narcotics-laden luggage. A quick-thinking Neil Aspinall grabbed the bags and transferred them by car to the Hotel Manila. Meanwhile, the group, having no idea what was going on, found themselves surrounded by military personnel and shepherded to a private yacht, where they were forced to socialize with a Filipino fat cat.

Thus it was understandable when Brian Epstein let them sleep in the next morning, turning down on their behalf an invitation to appear at Malacañang Palace to meet the country's first lady, Imelda Marcos. Unaware of the situation, the Beatles performed two shows to huge crowds, the first of which was fleetingly captured in newsreel footage by Reuters.

By the following morning, the scandalous snubbing was front page news in Manila, and the entire Beatles touring entourage found themselves not only ostracized, but threatened with physical violence from all sides as they made their way to the airport and onto a plane. Although the band members escaped bodily harm, their manager, road managers, and chauffeur all suffered injuries at the hands of both the hostile mob and Manila officials.

RELEASE HISTORY

This silent footage was included in a French TV documentary, *Destinées,* which circulates on video. It also appears in the home videos *The Beatles Story* and *Anthology.*

60a. Newsreel footage

Date:	5 July 1966
Location:	New Delhi Airport
Length:	0:40

Finally permitted to take off from Manila on July 5 at 4:45 p.m., the Beatles looked forward to a few days of recuperation in India before their return to London. The original plan had been for only George and Neil to get off in India, but the others vacillated several times before deciding to join them. Serenity was not to be had, as several hundred fans swarmed around the airport in New Delhi when they arrived, and camped outside their hotel; rather than a furlough, it felt like a continuation of their tour incarceration.

Associated Press cameras filmed their nighttime airport arrival in New Delhi, including a brief glimpse of an impromptu press conference.

RELEASE HISTORY

This silent footage circulates on video in poor quality.

61. Newsreel footage

Date:	8 July 1966
Time:	6:00 a.m.
Location:	London Airport
Length:	0:45

The Beatles' weary arrival back home in the early-morning hours of the eighth was captured by newsreel cameras. But even as they wave cheerfully to the fans, it is clear their hearts are no longer in it. One fan's BEATLES YOUR GREAT banner is grammatically balanced by another's YOU'RE LUVERLY LENNON.

RELEASE HISTORY

This arrival was preserved in a Pathé newsreel titled *Beatles Like Home Best,* which circulates on video.

62. TV interview

Date:	8 July 1966
Time:	6:00 a.m.
Location:	London Airport
Interviewer:	John Edwards
Broadcast:	8 July 1966
	ITV
Length:	2:03

A few days in India had done little to quell the group's bitterness about Manila, and upon their return to London they were eager to complain about the abusive treatment they had received. ITV News dispatched John Edwards to film an interview for that evening's newscast.

Paul relates how they had to carry the equipment up the mysteriously "broken" escalators at the airport, and John wonders facetiously if shoving and kicking is standard supervision for Filipino passengers. Their estimates of the number of officials harassing them range from five to thirty, and John admits he was "petrified" with fear, and declares that they'll "never go to any nuthouses again." George says he didn't even want to go to Manila in the first place, after hearing horror stories about the place beforehand. Paul calls their attackers cowardly, because they knew the Beatles' party would be unable to fight back.

63. Newsreel footage

Date: 8 July 1966
Time: 6:00 a.m.
Location: London Airport
Length: 2:33

This alternate interview for a Reuters newsreel is similar to the previous one, but with a different (unknown) reporter. John says they were assaulted "by some mon-

keys," and George complains that their intimidation at Manila Airport was obviously preplanned. The clip concludes with footage of John and Paul being mobbed by fans, this time friendly, upon leaving the airport.

RELEASE HISTORY

This footage circulates on video.

64. Studio session   P

Date: 9–21 July 1966
Location: EMI Studios
Producers: Paul McCartney, David Paramor

[A.] Got to Get You into My Life (2:31)

Although they had shared a bill at Hamburg's Star-Club back in December 1962, the Beatles' only tour with Cliff Bennett and the Rebel Rousers was the brief German/Far East stint of June–July 1966. Backstage at Essen on June 25, Bennett jokingly asked when John and Paul would write him a hit song. To his surprise, Paul picked up an acoustic guitar and played a number he thought would be perfect for Cliff's group: "Got to Get You into My Life."

Although the song wasn't custom-written for Bennett, it was unusual for the Beatles to "give away" one of their songs before their own version had been released. Paul attended the sessions back in London, as reported in the July 22 issue of *New Musical Express.* On the first day, Paul assisted behind the mixing board

and played the piano glissando heard at 1:48. He left before Bennett recorded his lead vocal that night, but upon hearing the result the next morning, felt the singing could be improved upon. As Paul lived a few blocks from Abbey Road, Bennett arrived at 10 a.m. to find the Beatle wearing bedroom slippers.

Bennett recounted the second day's session to the *New Musical Express:* "He played the number for me on the piano and showed me how to bend the notes. Then I did the vocal with Paul in the control box conducting me by waving his arms about like mad." It paid off, as this cover version has just as much pizzazz as the original, and shot into the British top 10 upon its release.

RELEASE HISTORY

1966: This song was released on a single (Parlophone R 5489) August 5 in the UK, where it reached number 6 in the *Melody Maker* charts. A U.S. release August 29 (ABC 10842) failed to chart. It's also included on the 1990 CD compilation *Lennon & McCartney Songbook.*

65. Radio interview   P

Date: 1 August 1966
Time: 8:30 p.m.
Location: Studio B15, Broadcasting House, London
Host: David Frost
Broadcast: 6 August 1966, noon–1:30 p.m.
BBC Light Programme
David Frost at the Phonograph
Length: 9:10

TV host David Frost made an unsuccessful jump to radio with this short-lived series, which mixed chat and records. Paul put in a pretaped solo appearance on this usually live show, largely because Frost would be overseas on the day of broadcast.

They begin by discussing the Beatles' upcoming tour of America, and Paul says he prefers England, where people aren't as obsessed with money, although he admits that most of the Americans he's met are businessmen. Frost compliments him on "Eleanor Rigby," but Paul expresses disappointment with the string arrangement, agreeing with someone's appraisal of the ending as a "Walt Disney send-up." He goes on to declare that every time they finish an album, they are so sick of hearing the songs that they hate them for a while. Paul seems to have had a particular problem with *Revolver.* While touring Germany, the others had to convince him that the whole LP wasn't out of tune!

He puts it all down to wanting their music to develop, and he claims that Beatles songs from 1963 and 1964 sound corny to him now. On the other hand, he is able to enjoy early Elvis records, corny as they may be, for their nostalgic value. Frost wonders about future plans, and Paul responds vaguely that he wants to spread himself thin, try lots of things, and choose something different. Frost feels (probably correctly) that Paul has the most ambitions of any Beatle, but Paul points out George's love of Indian music.

After Frost relates how a newspaper article once printed his age as seventy-two due to a typo, Paul counters with the tale of a *San Francisco Chronicle* reporter who called the Beatles "John, Paul, George, and Harold" in an August 1964 story. This apparently became something of an inside joke among the group, as Paul can be heard reciting the same names during the *Get Back* sessions while reading another newspaper article aloud.

Frost asks for some tips to improve his radio show and Paul suggests a jingle spelling out Frost's name accompanied by a trumpet fanfare to help win back some of the audience the BBC has lost to pirate radio. The program ends with Frost revealing the prerecorded nature of the episode, adding a "skipping record" effect to poke fun at the "wonderful techniques" of the BBC.

RELEASE HISTORY

This recording circulates in good quality among collectors.

66. Radio interview   J, P

Date:	6 August 1966
Time:	4:00–6:00 p.m.
Location:	7 Cavendish Avenue, London
Producer:	Derek Chinnery
Interviewer:	Keith Fordyce
Broadcast:	29 August 1966, 4:30–5:30 p.m.
	BBC Light Programme
	The Lennon and McCartney Songbook
Length:	11:10

At the end of July, John's remark to Maureen Cleave about the Beatles being "more popular than Jesus" was reprinted in *Datebook,* a U.S. magazine for teens. Within a week, aided by a publicity-starved radio station in Alabama, a crisis was brewing that threatened the group's imminent American tour. To quell the situation, Brian Epstein roused himself from bed in North Wales, where he was recovering from glandular fever, and flew to New York City on August 5. At the same time, a plan was made for John to record a statement of contrition at EMI Studio 3 at 2:30 the following afternoon.

Epstein phoned Lennon from his suite at the Waldorf Towers, and John reportedly refused to record the prepared apology, saying he'd rather they just canceled the tour. That was an unappetizing prospect for all concerned, so Brian wrote up his own statement for the press, and telexed it to NEMS in London. He made a point of stressing that Derek Taylor helped compose the statement, knowing how much John respected Derek.

As their manager held a press conference in New York on the sixth, John and Paul were being interviewed for a BBC Radio special focusing on other artists' renditions of their compositions. The interview was conducted in the sitting room at Paul's new home in London. Not surprisingly, John sounds preoccupied, leaving his partner to do most of the talking.

The tape begins with the Irish Guards' recording of "She Loves You," and host Keith Fordyce asks if they have any resentment toward anyone for covering their songs. Paul feels that most people improve on their songs, but John disagrees vehemently. Paul backpedals by saying that people who just copy their arrangement are wasting their time, and John claims not to mind as long as they get some royalties. Fordyce wonders whether they prefer solo artists' covers as opposed to those by other groups, which leads into the playing of Peggy Lee's "A Hard Day's Night."

Asked to name composers they admire, Paul can come up with only Goffin and King, a team they modeled themselves after (John jokes that they fought over which one would be Carole). They give Matt Monro some backhanded compliments for his cover of "All My Loving," with John muttering, "He did it how people imagine it should be done." While they discuss the strengths of having a partner to bounce ideas off of, Paul's housekeeper arrives and serves drinks. Paul uses "Day Tripper" as an example of a song that would have been two totally disparate concepts if they had each tried to write it separately.

Lena Horne's "And I Love Him" (they undoubtedly

would have preferred Esther Phillips's version) leads Fordyce to ask if the song was written for anyone in particular, and Paul says "most of them are." They may have been talking at cross-purposes; certainly the song was written for or inspired by Jane Asher, but was always intended to be a Beatles performance. Paul says that a song intended for Helen Shapiro ("Misery") ended up being recorded by Kenny Lynch, and John reveals that one Beatles song (he doesn't say which) was originally written for Cliff Richard. John also laughs at the notion that "Wait" was written for Frankie Vaughn, whose rendition follows.

Some howling from Martha, Paul's seven-week-old English sheepdog, interrupts Fordyce's next question about what time of day they write songs. They say it doesn't matter as long as you're not too sleepy, and they use both piano and guitar to compose, although John claims he is running out of guitar chords. Amid the closing pleasantries, Paul invites Fordyce to "pop in" if he's ever in the neighborhood. The Beatles had appeared twice on *Pop Inn,* a BBC show hosted by Fordyce, in 1963.

RELEASE HISTORY

1988: Portions of this interview were broadcast in the December 17 episode of BBC Radio's *The Beeb's Lost Beatles Tapes.*

2000: The bootleg *The Beatles Broadcast Collection Trailer 2* included the portion broadcast in 1988 plus a further segment from an alternate rebroadcast. This show was pressed on a Transcription disc titled "Songwriters Extraordinary," but as that source reportedly lacked music, the original tape must have been preserved. Kevin Howlett's book *The Beatles at the BBC* describes a bit more of the tape's contents that is circulating. (See also May 1966 for a possible further extract from this show.)

67. Newsreel footage

Date: ca. 10 August 1966
Location: Blandford Street, London
Length: 0:25

Brian Epstein's August 5 cable from America had advised the Beatles not to speak to the British press; nevertheless, in the days leading up to the trip, a camera crew caught up with the group as they emerged from a shop in downtown London (the same shop they had walked past in the movie *Help!*).

Most of the entourage strolls straight past the cameras and into the waiting car, but Paul answers a couple of the reporter's questions. He wonders what sort of reception they are expecting "after the odd bonfire" in the United States, and Paul reassures him it will be fine. Trying a different but still polite route, the reporter asks if this is a good time to be going, but Paul sidesteps that neatly by commenting how wonderful the weather is in August.

RELEASE HISTORY

This clip was included on the video compilation *Beatles 1962 to 1970.*

68. Newsreel footage

Date: 11 August 1966
Time: morning
Location: London Airport
Broadcast: 11 August 1966
BBC TV
Length: 0:59

The Beatles spent a nervous morning at London Airport wondering what would be in store for them when they touched down in the United States that afternoon. Already, plans for them to fly on TWA had been canceled due to a strike, so an earlier flight on Pan-Am was hastily arranged. To make matters worse, they were forced to spend a forty-five-minute delay touring the wonderfully exciting control tower.

A BBC News camera captured their tour and eventual emergence onto the tarmac, and they stopped to answer a question or two. John admits that he's worried about the tour, but Paul once again insists that "it'll be fine. You watch."

RELEASE HISTORY

This footage was included in the documentary *Imagine: John Lennon.* An alternate clip circulates on video from a French TV show, *Destinées.*

68a. Newsreel footage

Date: 11 August 1966
Time: 2:30 p.m.
Location: Logan Airport, Boston
Length: 1:37

The Beatles' first stop was Boston, where John must have been heartened by the sight of fans holding aloft banners reading WE SUPPORT JOHN and ALL'S WELL WITH J.W.L. Associated Press and BBC News cameras filmed their brief layover, as they transferred to a flight for Chicago, the first destination on the tour.

RELEASE HISTORY

This footage (some in color) circulates on video.

69. Newsreel footage

Date: 11 August 1966
Time: 4:55 p.m.
Location: O'Hare Airport, Chicago
Length: 0:31

Any hopes John had that his problems would disappear must have evaporated as soon as he stepped from the plane in Chicago. In this clip, the group waves to fans from the tarmac alongside their awaiting limo. After a couple of shouts from the press of "How you feeling, all right?" and "Big loud 'hello,' fellas!," one reporter wastes no time: "John, are you sorry about what you said?" John immediately replies, "Yes, yes I am!" in an "OK, you got me" tone of voice. He knew his biggest test was still to come.

RELEASE HISTORY

This Reuters newsreel clip circulates on video from a French TV show, *Destinées*.

70. Press conference

Date: 11 August 1966
Time: evening
Location: Astor Towers Hotel, Chicago
Length: 17:02

The Beatles were driven directly from the airport to their hotel, where two separate press conferences would be held, such was the demand for immediate clarification of John's remarks. Brian Epstein's statement was only a stopgap solution; the press and public wanted to hear an explanation straight from John's mouth.

The first conference was something of a warm-up, being held mainly for the disc jockeys and reporters traveling on the tour and local newspapers. With no national media present, no footage of this first conference seems to exist, but photos were taken and most of the event was captured on an audio recording.

Unsurprisingly, the first question is directed to John, who makes a lengthy and obviously unrehearsed attempt to explain the circumstances under which his quote was produced, without clarifying the remark itself. He says that when he first heard about the controversy brewing in the United States, he dismissed it as akin to "bad eggs in Adelaide" but grew concerned as he realized how quickly it would snowball. One reporter helpfully points out that the DJ in Birmingham (Tommy Charles of WAQY) has demanded an apology, and John halfheartedly offers one up. ("If he wants one . . . he can have it.")

More sympathetic reporters observe that the American press has covered the affair in a more sensational manner than elsewhere, and that a lot of the trouble really stems from the Bible Belt. Paul defensively replies that John was merely speaking his mind, and that "I thought everyone here . . . believe[d] in free speech." Someone asks if John really believes Christianity will shrink, and he chooses his words carefully: "Only from what my views and from what I've read or observed of Christianity, and what it was, and what it has been, or what it could be, it just seems to me to be shrinking." He then points out the hypocrisy in not pointing this out and pretending religion is as strong as it once was, and Paul implausibly hopes for a resurgence in Christianity.

With the main topic exhausted for the moment, the discussion turns to "Eleanor Rigby." One journalist makes a misguided attempt to perceive Father McKenzie's unheard sermons as a comment on the decline of religion, but Paul insists it's merely about a lonely person who happens to be a priest. More ludicrously, someone invites John to speculate what Jesus would make of the song if he were alive today. John and Paul attempt to downplay the song's significance, but George sums it up thusly: "We had to have another track to fill up the LP." A couple of non-Lennon controversies are touched upon, such as Paul's remark that America was a racist country and an unknown Beatle's claim (not John's) that Britain was becoming a police state. Paul comments sheepishly, "We've really been putting our feet in it lately!"

The mood lightens toward the end. When someone begins a query to John—"I've read something recently that you were"—he interrupts immediately with "Never said it!" George says it'll be nice to have a break from hotel food in Los Angeles, and Paul imagines a banner headline: "Beatles Hotel Food Drama." John is asked how he feels about going to Memphis, the only Bible Belt city on the tour, and he admits he considered hiding out in England and not coming over at all, but is cautiously optimistic that he can clear everything up.

In fact, when someone asks John the starting date for filming *How I Won the War*, he replies, "When I get back from America. I say 'when.'"

RELEASE HISTORY

1966: Excerpts of this recording were released on limited edition LPs such as *Beatle Views* (recorded by DJ Ken Douglas) and *I Apologize* (recorded by *Chicago Tribune* photographer Bill Bender).

1981: A much longer recording was included on the LP *Timeless*, also released on CD but not from tape source. This fades in and out between questions but is the most complete source available, missing only a few seconds captured on *Beatle Views* (the question about Britain being a police state).

71. Press conference

Date:	11 August 1966
Time:	evening
Location:	Astor Towers Hotel, Chicago
Length:	6:13

The second Chicago press conference was covered by all major networks, including ITV News from Britain, and while no continuous recording seems to exist, dozens of newsreel fragments of various lengths are circulating.

It's difficult to assemble the pieces in their original order, but it seems John was initially asked to clarify his statement. His response is a more concise version of the opening remarks from the previous conference, concluding with a cynical "But I said it in that way, which is the wrong way. Yap yap." Told that many teenagers have admitted they do like the Beatles more than Jesus, John launches into the most repeated sound bite of the evening, blinking nervously: "Well, originally I was—I was pointing out that fact in reference to England—that we meant more to kids than Jesus did. Or religion, at that time. I wasn't knocking it or putting it down, I was just saying it, as a fact. And it sort of—it is true, 'spec—more for England than here. Y'know, but I'm not saying that we're better, or greater, or comparing us with Jesus Christ as a person. Or God

as a thing, or whatever it is. Y'know, I just said what I said and it was wrong, or was taken wrong. And now it's all this."

John says the bonfires and death threats worry him, and doesn't seem to find it funny when someone asks if he feels he's being crucified (three years later, he'd have no trouble expressing this sentiment). Nor is he amused by the suggestion that it's all a publicity stunt designed to revive interest in the group. However, when someone asks what they find most enjoyable about the "Godhood on earth" they have achieved as stars, he and Paul can laugh—"Don't say that. It was him—he said it! Now, you all saw that!"

The only fragments not focusing on the matter at hand concern the progression of their music and John candidly discussing his lack of interest in getting to know the father who abandoned him.

RELEASE HISTORY

1996: Portions of this press conference were released on the CD *Rare Photos & Interview CD, Volume 3*. Brief clips appear in documentaries too numerous to list, including *Imagine: John Lennon* and *Anthology*.

72. Concert

Date:	12 August 1966
Time:	3:00 or 7:30 p.m.
Location:	International Amphitheater, Chicago
Length:	6:19

Two silent home movies exist from the first stop on the Beatles' last tour. The first is a color home movie (2:28) of exceptionally awful quality, which usually circulates with an unrelated live version of "I Feel Fine" dubbed over. Somewhere in the fuzzy murk, the Beatles can just be made out performing and then exiting the stage at the end of the show.

Slightly better is a black-and-white film lasting 3:51, which has portions of nearly every song. ("Rock and Roll Music," "I Wanna Be Your Man," and "Long Tall Sally" are absent.) It's not clear whether both films are from the same show or both houses from this date are represented.

RELEASE HISTORY

This silent 8 mm footage circulates on video among collectors.

73. Radio interview

Date:	12 August 1966
Time:	early evening
Location:	International Amphitheater, Chicago
Interviewer:	Ken Douglas
Length:	14:30

Between shows, the Beatles held the first of several "taping sessions" in their dressing room. These were informal gatherings that gave the journalists traveling on the tour (and occasionally local reporters) a chance to interview individual Beatles in a more in-depth fashion than the press conferences allowed.

Ken Douglas, a British DJ then working in Louisville, Kentucky, covered the first half of the tour and was able to chat with all four Beatles this first day. Paul explains that he and John have no formula about who writes which component of their songs, and says he hopes the Jesus controversy is behind them now that John has had a chance to explain himself at great length. Douglas asks about the Indian sounds on *Revolver*, and Paul says they all like the drone, but that George is mainly responsible for those influences. Another reporter inquires about the "weird effects" on "Tomorrow Never Knows," and Paul recounts bringing "a bag full of six tape loops" to the session. Kenny Everett, there to cover the tour for Radio London, wonders if they feel pressure to be less experimental in their music, but Paul thinks they are striking a good balance by progressing slowly on each album and bringing the audience with them. He also claims to have sung "Eleanor Rigby" "very bad" (more of his *Revolver* paranoia).

Douglas then talks to Ringo, who pokes fun at him for reading from a list of prepared questions: " 'How many songs have you and John written?' That's not really for me, is it?" Ringo says their next movie will start filming in January "with any luck," and that although he misses Maureen while on tour, they both understood before marrying that he would have to be on the road from time to time.

John talks about his role in *How I Won the War*, but doesn't seem to know much about the plot beyond his character's name. He lists "Here, There and Everywhere" and "Yellow Submarine" as his listening favorites from the new LP, and seems resigned to an American concert tour every August. Whether he was sincere or not, that attitude would be nonexistent by the end of the month.

Finally, George discusses the Beatles' constant drive to improve their music, hopes that his use of sitar will inspire fans to take an interest in Indian music, and stresses the importance of their apprenticeship in Hamburg's nightclubs.

RELEASE HISTORY

1966: These interviews appeared on the charity LP *Beatle Views*, which was reissued in incomplete form on LPs such as *The British Are Coming* and *The Gospel According To: The Beatles,* but has yet to appear on CD from tape source. An extra 10 seconds at the start circulates from Kenny Everett's report (Paul describes what he did in the hotel the previous night).

74. Radio interview

Date:	12 August 1966
Time:	early evening
Location:	International Amphitheater, Chicago
Interviewer:	Bess Coleman, Jim Stagg
Broadcast:	WCFL-AM, Chicago
Length:	25:01

Another member of the entourage was the Beatles' American press officer, Bess Coleman, writing for *Teen* *Life* magazine and recording daily bulletins from the road for syndication on various U.S. radio stations. DJ Jim Stagg, a veteran of Beatle tours, was also present backstage at Chicago, and he shared Coleman's microphone during the taping session.

The tape begins with Stagg testing the recorder and capturing much of the conversation with Paul discussed in the previous entry. This recording continues past the point where the Douglas version cuts off, with

Paul discussing the French horn in "For No One" and the group's less frenzied demeanor onstage compared with earlier tours. Stagg asks Paul what he's looking forward to in Cleveland, and Paul replies, "Jim Stagg. Can't wait to see him." He jokes that while it's a shame they might lose some fans from the Jesus incident, as long as they steer clear of armed robbery, it won't be a problem. Coleman wonders if "Eleanor Rigby" was inspired by Paul's own loneliness, but he says, "It's just nice writing a sad song instead of a happy one."

The pair moves on to Ringo, who chats first with Coleman about married life and being a father. In a similar vein, he tells Stagg that Zak has been walking since he was eight months old, and that Maureen is walking, too! Ringo claims not to have been worried about how the audience would react during their first concert, and feels that the press conferences the previous day helped clear the air. Knowing Ringo's dislike of Donald Duck, Stagg quacks a brief "Hi, Ringo!"

John talks with Coleman about *How I Won the War,* feeling that he doesn't "stand a chance in hell" of becoming a serious actor, but that he hopes to continue writing poetry, drawing, and painting. Amazingly, Stagg asks whether the recent controversy might be a blessing in disguise, and John says pointedly, "I don't think it'll ever be that." He concedes it could have turned out much worse, but with Memphis on his mind, he adds ominously, "It still could, I s'pose." When Stagg mentions the amplifier troubles in their afternoon performance, John replies, "That's the least of our worries at the moment."

George is more forthcoming, explaining that someone backstage must have unplugged the power supply. He goes on to say that they only rehearse just before beginning a tour, to remind themselves how new songs go. In contrast to the constant nightclubbing of 1964, George describes how the Beatles now stay at home and play board games such as Buccaneer and Risk. He puts the change down to married life creating a comfortable routine, and says he's constantly redecorating their home.

Coleman makes the mistake of asking if George would like to tackle another instrument now that he's "mastered the sitar." George makes it clear that Indian music is no passing fancy, and that maybe in forty years he will have mastered the basics of sitar playing. Stagg attempts to ask a few questions, but George seems more interested in reading about the Beatles' recent visit to Tokyo in a Japanese music magazine.

RELEASE HISTORY

This recording circulates among collectors in poor quality, copied off-line from the raw source tape.

75. Newsreel footage

Date: 13 August 1966
Location: Detroit Airport
Length: 0:08

From Chicago, the Beatles boarded a morning flight to Detroit, where they performed two shows at Olympia Stadium. A few seconds of local news footage captures their airport arrival.

RELEASE HISTORY

This footage circulates on video.

75a. Concert

Date: 13 August 1966
Location: Olympia Stadium, Detroit
Broadcast: Radio London

[A.] intro (0:50)
[B.] Rock and Roll Music (0:10)

One of Kenny Everett's tour reports for Radio London captured the start of one of the Detroit concerts, including a few seconds of the opening number. A supposed audience recording of a complete Detroit show that circulates is a fake, largely constructed from a Tokyo concert.

RELEASE HISTORY

This recording circulates in good quality.

76. Radio interview

Date: 14 August 1966
Location: Cleveland
Interviewer: Jerry G. Bishop
Broadcast: WKYC-AM, Cleveland
Length: 4:22

Although he had followed the Beatles' entire 1965 tour, in 1966, DJ Jerry Bishop was able to travel only to Detroit for their evening concert on August 13. He returned to his home base of Cleveland the following day and interviewed the group before their sole concert that evening.

Paul explains that when he is laughing onstage, it's usually due to a blunder, such as John botching the ending of "Yesterday" in Detroit. Naming Buck Owens, George Jones, Kitty Wells, and Hank Snow among his favorite performers, Ringo says he enjoys country music mainly for the stories it tells.

Bishop warns John that while Municipal Stadium holds eighty thousand people, it might look empty tonight with only thirty thousand, but John doesn't seem to mind: "Try sticking somebody else in there and see how many seats go!" He compares audiences in various countries, describing Japanese fans as high-pitched clappers, and comments on the increasing number of young men at their American concerts.

Finally, Bishop and the boys gather for a farewell photo, inspiring Ringo to sing a line from Dudley Moore's "Goodbye-ee" (theme song for the TV show *Not Only . . . But Also . . .*). Paul takes over with a rendition of "We'll Meet Again," with everyone joining in.

RELEASE HISTORY

1982: The "farewell" segment was released on the LP *The Beatles Talk with Jerry G.*

1983: The remaining segments were included on the LP *The Beatles Talk with Jerry G., Volume 2.* It's possible that this LP includes further extracts from this date, but these are the only ones with identifying features.

77. Radio interview   R

Date: 14 August 1966
Location: Cleveland
Interviewer: Ken Douglas
Length: 3:27

Although no press conference or taping session was held in Cleveland, Ken Douglas found a moment either backstage or at the Sheraton Hotel to tape an interview with Ringo.

In a discussion familiar to those who followed Ringo interviews, he admits to a home life of inactivity, and denies having any plans for his eleven-month-old "big fatso," Zak. The thrills continue as we learn that Maureen cooks a mean lamb dish, and that Douglas and Ringo's gardener share a hometown of Surbiton. Douglas then relates to Ringo some events of the previous evening. The entourage journeyed by bus from Detroit immediately following the concert. Around 2 a.m., they pulled in to the Vermilion Turnpike Plaza in Ohio, where Brian's assistant Wendy Hanson was dispatched to the Howard Johnson's to purchase ice cream bars. Paul and George decided to get out and stretch their legs, to the shock and delight of some passing girls (Ringo had stayed on the bus and missed this excitement). In turn, Ringo relates how a motorist had followed him and Maureen around one day, catching them at a red light only to mistakenly demand autographs from "Paul" and "Pattie"!

RELEASE HISTORY

1966: These interviews appeared on the charity LP *Beatle Views,* which was reissued in incomplete form on LPs such as *The British Are Coming* and *The Gospel According To: The Beatles,* but has yet to appear on CD from tape source.

78. Concert

Date: 14 August 1966
Time: 7:30 p.m.
Location: Cleveland Stadium

[A.] report/intro (2:22)
[B.] I Feel Fine (0:42)

The Beatles' Cleveland concert featured a magnified replay of events from their last concert in that city. This time, rather than a few hundred fans rushing the stage, several thousand fans broke through barriers and swarmed the group as they attempted to play "Day Tripper." Quick thinking allowed the police to hustle the band to a small trailer beside the stage, and it took twenty minutes to calm the crowd down and resume the show.

Ken Douglas recorded some of the mayhem, including WIXY DJ Al Gates pleading with the fans to return to their seats. As Douglas describes the scene, the Beatles retake the stage and, skipping the planned fifth number in their set, "Baby's in Black," begin to play "I Feel Fine."

In addition, several silent home movies documented the occasion. The first of these is a fragmentary 16 mm color film totaling 1:51. This is assembled in a seemingly random order, and features cops, fans, and bits of "I Feel Fine" and "I Wanna Be Your Man." Two minutes and forty-two seconds of further 8 mm color footage is so grainy and dark, only the occasional zoom-in on Paul is of interest.

But there is also a remarkable black-and-white 16 mm silent newsreel, lasting 6:38, that gives a much clearer picture of what happened. It opens with roadies setting up the stage, with several DJs and MCs taking the microphones. The Beatles enter, wave, plug in, and begin their first number, and apart from a girl being carried out in the arms of a policeman, all seems normal. Suddenly the entire crowd moves forward, but it's hardly a chilling sight; in fact, Paul is grinning broadly as they reach the foot of the stage. In the next shot, dozens of cops and other officials are milling around onstage. Once a path is cleared, the Beatles stride quickly but calmly down some steps and into the caravan. Police push the crowd back slowly but surely as Gates appeals for calm.

RELEASE HISTORY

1966: This recording appeared on the charity LP *Beatle Views,* which was reissued in incomplete form on LPs such as *The British Are Coming* and *The Gospel According To: The Beatles,* but has yet to appear on CD from tape source. "I Feel Fine" was copied on the 1999 CD-R compilation *Vinyl to the Core.* The various film clips, often dubbed with irrelevant audio, circulate among collectors.

78a. Newsreel footage

Date: 15 August 1966
Time: afternoon
Location: National Airport, Washington, DC
Length: 0:16

One of the few color newsreels capturing a Beatles airport arrival was filmed in Washington, DC. In this brief clip, George, Paul, Ringo, and John (in that order) descend from the plane and are driven away in limos to the Shoreham Hotel.

RELEASE HISTORY

This silent color footage circulates on video.

79. Press conference

Date: 15 August 1966
Time: evening
Location: DC Stadium, Washington, DC
Length: 16:16

A muggy locker room in DC Stadium was the site for their preshow press conference in the nation's capital. The event gets off to a rousing start when Ringo declares he'd like to be reincarnated as a tree, but eventually they are asked about the "more popular than Jesus" issue. Told of the Ku Klux Klan's protest at that evening's show, John replies, "There's nothing to say about them." Someone points out that the Vatican's official newspaper defended John's remark, and he replies, "If it makes other people feel better, it'll make me feel better." John disagrees that the controversy has had a detrimental effect on ticket sales for their tour, and angrily denies that the whole thing is a publicity stunt.

On other topics, Paul reveals that the idea for "Yellow Submarine" came to him at bedtime, and George and John agree that if the "butcher" cover had been a better photograph (John calls it "unsubtle"), they might have fought against its recall. Asked if they would consider entertaining U.S. troops, John replies, "I wouldn't like to go near Vietnam," and unsurprisingly, he says the biggest drawback of being a Beatle is "interpretations of what you say."

RELEASE HISTORY

1996: A portion of this recording appears on *Rare Photos & Interview CD, Volume 2,* and the complete conference circulates in very good quality. In addition, about a minute of color newsreel footage from the proceedings is traded on video, and 41 seconds of black-and-white footage was released on the compilation video *Beatles 1962 to 1970.*

79a. Radio interview

Date: 15 August 1966
Interviewer: Kenny Everett
Location: Washington, DC
Broadcast: Radio London
Length: 1:26

In this interview with Kenny Everett, George talks about the metamorphoses their career has undergone since Germany, candidly admitting that their live performances have wasted away because of the noise of the fans (and because of the group's lack of interest and preparation, although he doesn't mention those fac-

tors). He feels that the content of the last two albums has begun to increase the ratio of males to females in their audience, and hopes this will diminish the overall noise level at future concerts.

RELEASE HISTORY

1984: Most of this interview was broadcast in the radio documentary *Sgt. Pepper's Lonely Hearts Club Band: A History of the Beatle Years 1962–1970*. The full interview circulates in good quality from an off-line recording.

80. Radio interview

Date: ca. 11–15 August 1966
Broadcast: WMCA-AM, New York City
Length: 0:56

For their upcoming visit to New York City, the Beatles arranged an extra press conference. Unlike the second one in Chicago, this "junior press conference" wasn't for professional journalists, but teenage fans. One hundred fifty lucky teenagers would be selected at random from applicants by the U.S. branch of the Beatles fan club and by WMCA radio.

To plug the event, Paul and Ringo (and probably

the others) recorded brief messages early in the tour that aired on WMCA as the day approached. Paul explains at some length the reasons behind the special occasion, feeling that fans will come up with more interesting questions than professional reporters. Ringo merely reminds the fans to arrive with shiny shoes!

RELEASE HISTORY

This recording circulates from a good-quality off-air tape of WMCA's tour coverage.

81. Radio interview

Date: 16 August 1966
Time: evening
Location: JFK Stadium, Philadelphia
Interviewer: Ken Douglas
Length: 7:20

The Beatles' bus left Washington on the sixteenth for Philadelphia, where they would play a single show that evening, flying directly to Toronto after the concert. Arriving at JFK Stadium, the group was transferred to a floral van and smuggled inside. Rather than a full press conference, representatives of six local media outlets were granted formal interviews. In addition, another taping session was held in the stadium dressing room for the touring reporters. Ken Douglas cornered Paul for a lengthy recorded chat.

With respect to the diminishing crowds, Paul points out that they have only their own attendance

records to match. In fact, they still play to more people than any other artist. Douglas accurately predicts that their records will continue to sell long after they stop touring, and Paul says they're now more interested in writing and recording than performing. He realizes how futile it is to try and communicate to tens of thousands of screaming people at once.

Paul then explains why he bought a house in London rather than out in the suburbs: He prefers being near the city, but it's still close enough to his bandmates that he can go swim at their houses! He wonders if there will be time for a holiday after the tour, assuming that they will be recording a new album for Christmas. After recounting his trip to Paris for John's twenty-first birthday, Paul reflects on the mayhem at the Cleveland concert. In a seeming contradiction of the point he was making a minute earlier, he claims to enjoy the "fan participation" at their concerts, as long as nobody gets hurt. He astutely points out that much of the recent negative publicity is inevitable due to the nature of the newspaper business. After a while, good news is no news, and disparaging articles become the fashion.

RELEASE HISTORY

1966: These interviews appeared on the charity LP *Beatle Views,* which was reissued in incomplete form on LPs such as *The British Are Coming* and *The Gospel According To: The Beatles,* but has yet to appear on CD from tape source.

82. Radio interview   R

Date: 16 August 1966
Time: evening
Location: JFK Stadium, Philadelphia
Interviewer: Bess Coleman, Jerry Leighton
Length: 6:31

Once again, Bess Coleman generously shared her microphone with a fellow reporter, Radio Caroline's DJ Jerry "Super" Leighton.

Ringo greets him as "Jerry Laverne," although it's hard to tell if he's joking. In any case, Leighton gets nowhere with his first two questions: Is there anything you'd like to be asked, and is there anything you feel strongly about? Ringo cheerfully admits, "I don't feel strongly about anything." Coleman tries a different tack and discerns that Ringo doesn't like being asked about personal or financial matters, but otherwise is open to answering anything. She points out that he's down from four rings to two on this tour, and he says the real problem is the gold bracelet, which weighs him down while drumming.

Ringo explains how the amplification is usually so poor that he has to lip-read onstage to keep track of his place in each song, although he praises the sound system in Cleveland. Leighton makes the understandable presumption that if Ringo doesn't care about much, he might not be too keen on the progression the Beatles' music has been taking. Ringo denies that, but says he wishes his playing was progressing at the same rate as their songwriting. Coleman asks if he practices in order to improve, but Ringo says playing on the records is enough to keep him on track. Since they play the same songs every night, and nobody (including himself) can hear them, Ringo logically sees no reason to rehearse while on tour.

RELEASE HISTORY

This recording circulates among collectors in poor quality, copied off-line from the raw source tape.

83. Radio interview   G

Date: 16 August 1966
Time: evening
Location: JFK Stadium, Philadelphia
Interviewer: Jim Stagg
Broadcast: WCFL-AM, Chicago
Length: 0:34

Jim Stagg chatted briefly with George in Philadelphia about the possibility of the Beatles buying their own airplane rather than chartering one for tours. George, who notoriously hated flying, says he's not interested enough to want his own plane, though it might be interesting to "learn how to crash."

RELEASE HISTORY

This recording circulates among collectors in poor quality, from an off-line broadcast.

84. Press conference

Date: 17 August 1966
Time: evening
Location: Maple Leaf Gardens, Toronto
Length: 16:01

The Toronto press conference was held backstage at Maple Leaf Gardens, probably between the 4 p.m. and 8:30 p.m. shows. A complete tape of the event has recently surfaced, recorded by Toronto journalist Graham

Newton. In general, the occasion is a cut above most press conferences, with plenty of thoughtful questions posed and weighty issues tackled.

The early questions are slanted toward religion and the "more popular than Jesus" flap. Asked if he would recommend Christianity to young people, John responds, "I'd recommend it for old people as well. Especially." He says that while his quote wasn't taken out of context, the article was, being meant for a newspaper feature and not a teen magazine. He admits it may have hurt his image in the eyes of certain people, but "I don't mind about them somehow." George says love is more important than popularity, and that most of the Lennon bashers are acting in a very unchristian fashion.

Asked what inspires young people, Paul feels it's anyone who talks honestly, although he realizes the generation gap makes it difficult for parents to communicate to teenagers, no matter how sincerely they try. Someone wonders if "Eleanor Rigby" signals a new trend, but John and Paul quickly point out that violins are actually quite old instruments. Will they go electronic? Paul: "Yes, anything." George: "But not totally." John: "Oh, I could!" It's pointed out that the Beatles got their MBE awards for helping the British economy, and John jokes that perhaps they should return them to help bolster the faltering market. When this quip receives a round of applause and laughter, John grins and says, "It's very friendly here. I think I'll relax."

The lighthearted mood is not long-lived, as a very earnest reporter asks why they don't take a more vocal stance against the United States' involvement in Vietnam. They all denounce war in general, and the U.S. draft specifically, but as John says, "We're not allowed to have opinions, you might have noticed." This was aimed more at Brian Epstein than the media, as their manager had forbidden them on previous tours to make antiwar statements while in the States. Realizing he may have just put his foot in his mouth again, John sighs. "We've had it in Memphis now."

Paul says they've thought about writing a musical, but not one like *My Fair Lady*, because other people can write that style of music much better. John says it's quite possible they will split up, and that they can't go around "holding hands forever"; Paul agrees that it'd be embarrassing to be a thirty-five-year-old Beatle singing "Long Tall Sally" every night (but that didn't stop Paul from doing it as a thirty-one-year-old member of Wings). Finally, Paul relates how being distracted by a full moon caused his moped accident the previous Christmas.

RELEASE HISTORY

2001: This recording was released in excellent quality on the CD *The Beatles Canadian Press Conference*. Poor-quality off-air excerpts had previously circulated as part of the Jim Stagg tour coverage. Twenty-three seconds of silent footage from the conference also circulates on video.

85. Radio interview

Date:	17 August 1966
Time:	evening
Location:	Maple Leaf Gardens, Toronto
Interviewer:	Jim Stagg
Broadcast:	WCFL-AM, Chicago
Length:	3:38

Following the press conference, Jim Stagg taped brief interviews with each Beatle. Unfortunately, the horrendous quality of my copy makes it difficult to decipher all of the conversations, but there seems to be a common theme: aging gracefully as pop stars.

George expresses satisfaction with the growing sophistication in rock lyrics; Paul agrees that they have matured, although it conjures up images of a "very old man with a pipe and slippers" in his mind; John compares their development under the spotlight to bananas being force-grown in a hothouse; Ringo cautions not to take everything they say seriously, as being famous shouldn't give their opinions any more weight.

RELEASE HISTORY

This recording circulates among collectors in poor quality, from an off-line broadcast.

86. Radio interview

Date: 17 August 1966 (?)
Time: evening
Location: Maple Leaf Gardens, Toronto (?)
Interviewer: Bess Coleman
Length: 0:56

This interview clip is a tentative identification based more on its location on the tape than any internal clues. It seems to be the end of a longer chat, as George explains that when one of them starts to get a swelled head, the others will quickly deflate his ego.

RELEASE HISTORY

This recording circulates among collectors in poor quality, copied off-line from the raw source tape.

87. Radio interview

Date: 18 August 1966
Location: Logan Airport and Somerset Hotel, Boston
Interviewer: Jim Stagg
Broadcast: WCFL-AM, Chicago
Length: 2:25

On the morning of August 18, the Beatles flew from Toronto to Boston, where Jim Stagg chatted with George as he deplaned. It seems no press conference was held in Boston, but another taping session gave Stagg a further chance to talk with Paul and George.

Displaying extreme modesty, Paul insists there are "a thousand songwriters" as good as the Lennon and McCartney team, putting down most of their success to serendipity. On the other hand, George feels that people who don't get lucky breaks are mostly people with no talent anyway. He also talks about meeting his uncle and aunt the previous night in Toronto, and staying up until 6 a.m. to talk with them. What George doesn't mention is that after his relatives left, he spent another hour smoking pot and listening to music with members of the Remains.

RELEASE HISTORY

This recording circulates among collectors in poor quality, from an off-line broadcast.

88. Radio interview

Date: 18 August 1966
Location: Somerset Hotel, Boston
Interviewer: Bess Coleman
Length: 13:43

Once again, Bess Coleman spoke individually to each Beatle during the Boston taping session.

Ringo complains how difficult it was to emulate a professional disc jockey when he tried to perform a mock radio show on one of his home tapes. He points out how the press reaction in the first city on any given tour usually sets the tone for subsequent coverage, and gives a wonderfully nonresponsive answer when asked to comment on whether this will be the Beatles' last U.S. tour.

Asked if there's any place new he'd like to visit, George (perhaps thinking of Manila) says he'll go anywhere he won't get arrested! He professes once again not to be satisfied with *Revolver,* because when listening it's impossible for the group to focus on anything but the flaws, and every song could be improved somehow. Another unknown female approaches, saying, "Don't have a tape recorder, I just wanted to chat," and George immediately launches into a parody of a typical pop star listing his fave-raves ("Corn Flakes . . . Mini Minor . . . blue . . . blond . . .").

Asked to define the word *happiness,* John reels off a similar joke list ("A cuddly foot . . . a brown bear . . . and a plate full of Kellogg's . . ."), before admitting that happiness is more a state of mind than something dependent on environment or material goods. He also reveals that George has just given him a haircut, and that the last time he cut George's hair (in Hamburg) was a bit of a disaster.

Paul explains that he bought a farm in Scotland because it was inexpensive and remote, and enthuses about the likelihood of being trapped there one day by a snowstorm. After vaguely describing the property, he admits he's seen it only once, for the grand total of one hour! His priority is moving into the new house in London, but Paul feels by 1967 he'll be able to begin staying at his farmhouse.

RELEASE HISTORY

This recording circulates among collectors in poor quality, copied off-line from the raw source tape.

89. Concert

Date: 18 August 1966
Time: 10:00 p.m.
Location: Suffolk Downs Racetrack, Boston
Interviewer: (B–C) Kenny Everett
Broadcast: (A) WBZ-AM, Boston
(B–C) Radio London

[A.] **She's a Woman** (0:21)
[B.] **Paperback Writer** (0:39)
[C.] **Long Tall Sally** (0:39)

The Beatles' single sold-out show in Boston proved to be wilder than most, borne out by these two recordings of the event. In the first (**A**), a reporter for WBZ Radio describes a fan breaking from the grandstand and being headed off by police before reaching the stage.

"Paperback Writer" (**B**) can be heard in the background of Kenny Everett's interview with a man who helped set up chairs at the concert. Even more remarkable was Kenny's conversation (**C**) with John Labinski, a fan described in the next day's *Boston Globe* as "a

heavy-set young man in a green shirt." As Paul launches into "Long Tall Sally," Labinski nonchalantly discloses that he is about to jump onstage, and seconds later, a disbelieving Everett gives the play-by-play: "OK, there he goes. He's gonna leap up now . . . he's onstage! And he's got hold of John! He's got hold of Paul! Now he's getting George . . . they've got him offstage right now . . . and he's being grabbed by all the police. What an interview! Woo-hoo! I bet this is an exclusive!"

RELEASE HISTORY

1984: C was included in the radio documentary *Sgt. Pepper's Lonely Hearts Club Band: A History of the Beatle Years 1962–1970,* and copied from that source on the CD-R compilation *Vinyl to the Core.*

2004: A was included in fair quality on the CD-R *We'd Like to Carry On.* **B** and **C** circulate from good-quality off-air tapes.

90. Newsreel footage

Date: 19 August 1966
Time: afternoon
Location: Metropolitan Airport, Memphis
Broadcast: 25 August 1966, 6:07–6:30 p.m.
ITV
Reporting '66
Length: 0:45

Leaving Boston on an 11:30 a.m. flight, the Beatles headed south for perhaps the scariest stop on their tour:

Memphis, Tennessee, the destination closest to the Beatle Bonfires in Alabama. On hand to cover events in the city was a crew from Britain's Independent Television News, for the show *Reporting '66.* The first clip from this day shows the band deplaning from their American Airlines flight, looking a tad apprehensive.

RELEASE HISTORY

This footage circulates on video among collectors.

91. TV interview   P

Date: 19 August 1966
Time: afternoon
Location: Memphis
Broadcast: 25 August 1966, 6:07–6:30 p.m.
ITV
Reporting '66
Length: 0:31

The bus ride from the airport to Mid-South Coliseum was harrowing, as the passengers were instructed to keep away from the windows in case any of the roadside protesters decided to exact revenge for John's Jesus re-

mark. Nevertheless, at some stop on its journey, the ITV camera crew was able to film Paul as he signed autographs from the window. A reporter shouted a few questions about their next concert location and the length of the tour, which Paul was able to answer with a little prompting from within the bus.

RELEASE HISTORY

This footage was released on the home video documentary *British Rock: The First Wave.*

92. Concert

Date: 19 August 1966
Time: 4:00 p.m.
Location: Mid-South Coliseum, Memphis
Interviewer: Bess Coleman

[A.] **intro** (1:46)
[B.] **Rock and Roll Music** (1:33)
[C.] **intro** (0:02)
[D.] **She's a Woman** (2:43)
[E.] **intro** (0:43)
[F.] **If I Needed Someone** (2:29)
[G.] **intro** (0:23)
[H.] **Day Tripper** (3:01)
[I.] **intro** (0:09)
[J.] **Baby's in Black** (2:25)
[K.] **intro** (0:34)
[L.] **I Feel Fine** (2:10)
[M.] **intro** (0:14)
[N.] **Yesterday** (1:45)
[O.] **intro** (0:34)
[P.] **I Wanna Be Your Man** (2:11)
[Q.] **intro** (0:34)
[R.] **Nowhere Man** (2:11)
[S.] **intro** (0:35)
[T.] **Paperback Writer** (2:07)
[U.] **intro** (0:48)
[V.] **Long Tall Sally** (2:01)
[W.] **outro** (0:12)

Both Memphis shows survive as audience recordings, taped by teenage fans Gloria Allen and Noreen Prouty. After turning down an offer from EMI in 1996, they auctioned the recordings on eBay in 2003, and the tapes didn't take long to surface on bootlegs.

The afternoon show is relatively uneventful, with the performances being a minor improvement from the Tokyo shows. There's an amusing moment during the introduction (**A**) when the emcee gets the crowd to spell out "B-E-T-L-E-S" [sic]. The tape has a few speed fluctuations, as well as a break in the middle that omits the end of **M** and beginning of **N**; it fades out 34 seconds into "Long Tall Sally."

Also among the ten thousand people at the matinee show in Memphis were Bess Coleman and her tape recorder. As the Beatles finish out their set, she makes several attempts to record a ringside report, struggling to point out over the screams that the notion of the group being unpopular is clearly nonsense. Portions of **P** and **T–W** were captured in the background of Coleman's report. Due to the less than satisfactory conditions and shaky sound, it's unlikely this tape was ever broadcast.

ITV's crew also filmed the group walking backstage just prior to going on (wearing light pin-striped suits); this short clip appears in *Anthology* and numerous documentaries.

RELEASE HISTORY

2001: Bess Coleman's poor-quality report appeared on the CD-R compilation *Live: Make as Much Noise as You Like!*

2007: The nearly complete audience recording (**A–V**) appeared in poor quality on the bootleg CD *From Beatles in Memphis 1966*.

93. Press conference

Date: 19 August 1966
Time: evening
Location: Mid-South Coliseum, Memphis
Broadcast: 25 August 1966, 6:07–6:30 p.m.
ITV
Reporting '66
Length: 0:17

Once again, ITV was on hand to film the press conference between shows, but all that was used in their report was a short clip of the Beatles seated at a long table signing autographs and posing for fans.

RELEASE HISTORY

This footage circulates on video.

94. TV interview

Date: 19 August 1966
Time: evening
Location: Mid-South Coliseum, Memphis
Interviewer: Richard Lindley
Broadcast: 25 August 1966, 6:07–6:30 p.m.
ITV
Reporting '66
Length: 3:01

The ITV camera crew caught up with the Beatles backstage at the coliseum for a sit-down interview. Paul explains that the main difference on this tour is that the press conferences are both more hectic and less frivolous. John says that people are entitled to have negative opinions about the group, and they can dislike those people in turn. The interviewer points out that their past success has hinged on their outspokenness and honesty, and they admit that it's hard to have to bite their tongues.

Paul tries to explain that their controversial comments are meant to be helpful, and that it's actually a good thing for them to be pointing out that the war in Vietnam is wrong. The reporter wonders why anyone should care what an entertainer has to think about politics, and John says that's just a part of showbiz, but that one "can't just keep quiet about anything that's going on in the world, unless you're a monk." Thinking fast to avoid another religious uproar, John adds, "Sorry, monks, I didn't mean it!"

RELEASE HISTORY

1996: Fifty-four seconds of this interview was released on the CD *Rare Photos & Interview CD, Volume 3,* and the complete footage is circulating on video. Excerpts were released on the home videos *Anthology, British Rock: The First Wave,* and *The Beatles Story.*

95. Radio interview   J, P

Date: 19 August 1966
Time: evening
Location: Mid-South Coliseum, Memphis
Interviewer: Bess Coleman
Length: 11:00

Bess Coleman recorded interviews with at least two Beatles backstage in Memphis. Paul explains how difficult it would be to reproduce their newer songs such as "Eleanor Rigby" onstage unless they traveled with supplementary musicians. Even then, the task of amplifying a string quartet to be heard over screeching fans would be a nightmare, which is why they perform "Yesterday" with their usual lineup of instruments.

Coleman points out that the group seems much more open and willing to expound than on earlier tours, and Paul fittingly responds by launching into a two-minute monologue, the gist of which is that when they first played outside of Liverpool, people would mock their appearance and accents, causing them to withdraw and use sarcasm and insults as a defense mechanism. In addition, most of the questions they were asked at early press conferences were less than deserving of thoughtful answers. Paul feels that reporters are now showing an interest in their music, which has led them to open up and discuss things at greater length.

Asked how much of their recording success is due to George Martin, John seems to have trouble giving their producer specific credit, although he says they learned all the technical aspects from him. Coleman wonders if John ever feels like a caged animal, but he reiterates that when they are on tour, they know it's a job and not a sightseeing vacation.

He says that war is the one thing in the world that disturbs him the most, and foreshadowing Paul's statement a year hence, denies that teenagers will take drugs just because their pop star idol does. He feels that instead of banning records with drug themes, the government should be doing more to educate young people about drugs, rather than sensationalizing them.

John admits that while it's hard to differentiate a true friend from a hanger-on, he doesn't mind being conned by people, since he does it himself occasionally! He feels their concerts are now valid as shows, but bereft of any musical quality, and claims to be a voracious reader, but can't name a favorite author or indeed the names of any books he likes.

RELEASE HISTORY

This recording circulates among collectors in poor quality, copied off-line from the raw source tape.

96. Radio interview

Date: 19 August 1966
Time: evening
Location: Mid-South Coliseum, Memphis
Interviewer: Jim Stagg
Broadcast: WCFL-AM, Chicago
Length: 1:20

Since this was Jim Stagg's last night on the tour, he recorded the Beatles' personal farewells (presumably Ringo was occupied at the time). Stagg expresses more than once his suspicion that this may be the last Beatles tour, and the others remain positive about seeing him again but decidedly noncommittal about another visit.

RELEASE HISTORY

This recording circulates among collectors in poor quality, from an off-line broadcast.

97. Concert

Date: 19 August 1966
Time: 10:10 p.m.
Location: Mid-South Coliseum, Memphis

[A.] intro (1:08)
[B.] **Rock and Roll Music** (1:32)
[C.] intro (0:02)
[D.] **She's a Woman** (2:26)
[E.] intro (0:37)
[F.] **If I Needed Someone** (1:42)
[G.] intro (0:29)
[H.] **Day Tripper** (3:02)
[I.] intro (0:07)
[J.] **Baby's in Black** (2:26)
[K.] intro (0:27)
[L.] **I Feel Fine** (2:08)
[M.] intro (0:22)
[N.] **Yesterday** (1:29)
[O.] intro (0:23)
[P.] **I Wanna Be Your Man** (2:08)
[Q.] intro (0:35)
[R.] **Nowhere Man** (2:11)
[S.] intro (0:24)
[T.] **Paperback Writer** (2:07)
[U.] intro (0:42)
[V.] **Long Tall Sally** (2:00)
[W.] outro (0:15)

This was certainly one of the most memorable Beatles concerts, but far from a pleasant memory. A near-capacity crowd packed the Coliseum for the evening show, including Gloria Allen and Noreen Prouty with their tape recorder.

As the band, now wearing dark green suits, finished the second bridge of "If I Needed Someone" (**F**), a sudden loud *bang* (as George sang the word "love") brought a chill to their veins. Once they realized none of them had been shot, instinct told them to keep playing, and the song continued. It turned out to have been a cherry bomb hurled from the balcony, which ended up injuring four crowd members. Two suspects, a teenage boy and girl, were found with fifty firecrackers and cherry bombs in their possession, but at the time, the Beatles had no way of knowing whether it was an adolescent prank or an outraged Klansman with a rifle. Amazingly, John introduces the next song (**G**) with a seemingly nonchalant "Well, thank you, everybody. Thanks for the bang."

Although several cameras were filming the concert, none of them managed to capture the incident clearly. Three minutes and fifty-six seconds of silent color home movie footage circulates, featuring portions of several songs, including "If I Needed Someone." The ITV crew documented 34 seconds of "Baby's in Black," and a second TV report has 15 seconds of concert footage followed by film of a spiritual rally held the same evening at the Memphis Union Mission. Eight thousand people attended the religious event, while 12,500 opted for the Beatles. More popular, indeed!

RELEASE HISTORY

2007: The audience recording (**A–W**) appeared in poor quality on the bootleg CD *From Beatles in Memphis 1966*. The concert footage circulates on video among collectors.

97a. Newsreel footage

Date: 20 August 1966
Location: Cincinnati Airport
Length: 0:14

Out of the frying pan, into the fire. Having escaped Memphis intact, the Beatles probably felt relieved to arrive in Cincinnati in the wee hours of August 20.

This brief news clip captures their airport arrival in darkness (at around 3 a.m.).

RELEASE HISTORY

This silent color footage circulates on video.

98. Concert

Date: 21 August 1966
Time: noon
Location: Crosley Field, Cincinnati
Length: 1:21

Stuck in a hotel with no room service, the Beatles looked forward to playing Cincinnati on the night of the twentieth and moving on. But heavy rain showers arrived just before showtime and soon turned into a deluge. For an indoor show, this wouldn't have posed a problem, but the promoters had failed to provide any kind of shelter for the stage, located in the middle of a baseball stadium.

By 10:25 that night, the decision was made to postpone the show until the next afternoon. Fifteen thousand fans went home wet and unhappy, and about twelve thousand of them returned at noon the next day, ticket stubs in hand, for the rain date.

Some silent color footage of this performance shows the group, in the same pin-striped suits worn in the Memphis afternoon show, taking the stage and playing. A canopy is now present, and of course the sky is clear and sunny.

RELEASE HISTORY

This footage circulates from a broadcast on WCPO, Channel 9 News in Cincinnati, and was partially included in *Anthology*.

99. Amateur footage

Date: 21 August 1966
Time: early evening
Location: Lambert Field and Busch Stadium, St. Louis
Length: 1:50

Hearkening back to the double (and sometimes triple) bookings of 1962, the Beatles flew out of Cincinnati at 4 p.m., bound for their second venue of the day in St. Louis. One fan's black-and-white 16 mm home movie captured their arrivals at both the airport and Busch Stadium, as well as a portion of the concert (the transition from "Rock and Roll Music" into "She's a Woman"). About a minute of black-and-white newsreel footage also exists of their arrival and scenes outside the stadium. See later entry for further home movies of the concert.

RELEASE HISTORY

This silent footage circulates among video collectors.

100. Radio interview   J, P, R

Date: 21 August 1966
Time: 7:00 p.m.
Location: Busch Stadium, St. Louis
Broadcast: KMIN (?), Denver
Length: 10:41

With a limited number of stops on the 1966 tour, radio stations in various nonitinerary cities held contests to send groups of fans to see the Beatles. One such party traveled from Denver to St. Louis, accompanied by a representative of the station who talked his way backstage to interview the group before the concert.

John describes the events that caused them to cancel the Cincinnati show, and says that most of the fans were able to make it back that afternoon for the rescheduled concert. With storm clouds massing, the reporter wonders if that night's show might not be rained out, but John says they don't mind playing in a thunderstorm as long as the equipment is covered. He then fails to get information from John about *How I Won the War*. ("I understand that you and the other three Beatles are under contract to United Artists to do three pictures." "Are we?") Finally, the reporter asks if *Revolver* is any different in England, and amazingly, John is able to name the three tracks pulled for use on *"Yesterday"... And Today* (well, maybe it's not so amazing considering they are all his songs).

Paul is asked about the possibility of the Beatles releasing an album of Christmas songs, and he points out that "White Christmas" is one of the only holiday-themed pop songs to be wildly successful ("You might as well bring out an Easter album . . ."). The reporter unwittingly hits a potential sore spot by asking Paul to explain the meaning of "She Said She Said," and he gives a very literal interpretation of the lyrics, admitting, "I don't know what half of our songs are about."

Ringo reveals that he'll be singing "I Wanna Be Your Man" that night, and Paul jokes that it's a special request for the visiting Denver fans. Asked why he isn't singing "Yellow Submarine" instead, Ringo says they keep meaning to rehearse it, but never get around to it. He feels the crowds have been as good as ever, but might seem smaller now that they are trying to fill larger stadiums. The recording wraps up with further unenlightening chat about security, taxes, and films.

RELEASE HISTORY

This recording circulates among collectors in poor quality, from an off-line broadcast.

101. Concert

Date:	21 August 1966
Time:	8:30 p.m.
Location:	Busch Stadium, St. Louis
Length:	3:30

[A.] **Rock and Roll Music** (0:02)
[B.] **intro** (0:02)
[C.] **She's a Woman** (0:17)

Another rainy evening approached, but this time preparations were in place. Not only was a canopy erected, the order of acts was switched to allow the Beatles to perform in the middle of the bill, just in case the drizzle turned to a torrential downpour. This left the Cyrkle and the Ronettes (backed by the Remains) the ignominious task of following up the act everyone had paid to see, and with the rain still falling, the stadium emptied out pretty quickly.

The Beatles were transported out of the stadium in a pair of police cars. Paul, perhaps combining two events, remembers leaving the show in an "empty chrome van." Already coming down with a nasty flu and terrified of having to play in the rain and face electrocution, Paul was so miserable that he agreed with the others that it was time to put an end to touring.

In addition to the brief footage mentioned earlier, a longer home movie exists from the show, beginning with the introduction from MC Nick Charles. Unfortunately, although it's in color, it's much too dark to see anything, and only the occasional flashbulb reveals that it truly is the Beatles onstage. A poor-quality audience recording of part of the concert (**A–C**) also exists, taken from a news report.

RELEASE HISTORY

2007: **A–C** were booted on the CD *Complete North American Tour 1966*. The silent 8 mm home movie circulates on video, with an unrelated live version of "Rock and Roll Music" dubbed over the top. It's followed by what appears to be a few seconds of footage of John's arrival at Busch Stadium earlier that evening.

102. Radio interview

Date:	12–21 August 1966
Interviewer:	Ken Douglas
Length:	2:57

These interview clips are difficult to tie to specific dates, but were all recorded by Ken Douglas during his tenure on the North American tour (he didn't continue on to New York with the rest of the entourage).

In these brief extracts (eight in all), Ringo talks about his dogs and building company, George talks about his cars, swimming pool, and the nightclub he co-owns (Sybilla's), Paul says he wants them to make better films, and John offers a terse "No comment, no comment!" to an unknown question.

RELEASE HISTORY

1966: These interviews appeared on the charity LP *Beatle Views,* which was reissued in incomplete form on LPs such as *The British Are Coming* and *The Gospel According To: The Beatles,* but has yet to appear on CD from tape source.

103. Press conference

Date:	22 August 1966
Time:	evening
Location:	Warwick Hotel, New York City
Length:	22:48

The Beatles flew from St. Louis to New York City, arriving at LaGuardia Airport around 3:50 a.m. local time on the twenty-second. Most of that day was spent unwinding in their suite at the Warwick Hotel, but that evening they conducted a pair of press conferences, one standard affair and one "junior press conference" for contest winners.

The first one gets off to a roaring start with a question about Vietnam (George: "War is wrong, and it's obvious . . .") and the news of two girls who threatened to jump from the twenty-second floor of a hotel unless Paul visited them. Someone wonders if they were disappointed by the handful of fans who greeted them at the airport and is met with intense sarcasm. (John: "Yeah, we were real brought down about that." Paul: "Three o'clock in the morning. We expected millions.")

Surprisingly, it takes a few minutes before the first question about the "more popular than Jesus" flap, which John dismisses with "a lot of it's just a lot of rubbish, and a lot of it's serious." Another reporter tries to get John to comment on the possibility that America's reaction was less mature than overseas, but he won't take the bait. Paul is happy to, however: "You hear more from American bigots than you do from Russian bigots."

Just when it seems the New York press is more sophisticated, a female reporter asks about their hair, and someone follows up by asking if they wear wigs. Paul merely sighs. "Oh, do you believe that? Do ya?" Someone finally asks George a question, but falls into the usual trap: "Now that you've learned to play the sitar, do you expect to learn any more instruments?" George patiently explains that Ravi Shankar has been playing sitar for thirty-five years and still hasn't learned.

The standard topics shuffle past: John's film and books, Ringo's son, Paul's farm and relationship with Jane Asher. The main angle taken by the press seems to be the group's sagging popularity, and after the fourth time being asked how he feels about this, John replies, "Very rich." About the only other point of interest occurs when a cameraman from one of the U.S. networks has to change reels and holds up the whole proceeding, not wanting to let down his 18 million viewers. John mocks him: "Great. Impressed, eighteen million."

RELEASE HISTORY

1996: Short extracts from this press conference were released on the CD *Rare Photos & Interview CD, Volume 2.* A complete fair quality audio recording of the entire event circulates, as do color film clips of varying lengths. Some were used in *Anthology,* and NBC News has broadcast its archival footage on various episodes of the MSNBC show *Time and Again.* It's likely the NBC footage exists in a fairly complete state (presumably missing the part where the cameraman had to change reels).

104. Press conference

Date:	22 August 1966
Time:	6:30 p.m.
Location:	Warwick Hotel, New York City
Broadcast:	22 August 1966, 7:52–10:37 p.m.
	WMCA-AM, New York City
Length:	7:18

Any hopes the Beatles had that their fans would ask more interesting questions than the press were probably dashed during this junior press conference, although the tone was decidedly more friendly than the cynical and sometimes hostile interrogatives offered up by the real press.

Probably the biggest scoop is Paul's admission that he will one day marry Jane Asher, met with a loud cry of disgust from the fans. Less earth-shattering is the revelation that George doesn't have a cousin named Maggie, although Paul plays along and pretends he knows one Patricia Slater of Cumberland. We also learn that Paul likes chocolate, miniskirts, and the Beach Boys, and thinks the Beatles cartoon series is "fun." Otherwise, the topics are pretty much identical to what the "legitimate" journalists and DJs had covered ad infinitum: John's film, clothes, British versus American girls, even Ringo's rings!

RELEASE HISTORY

A poor-quality off-line tape of this press conference circulates, from bits and pieces (twenty-four separate fragments) broadcast that evening on WMCA radio. In addition, 56 seconds of footage (probably from an AP newsreel) was included on the video *Greatest Rock 'n' Roll Legends Scrapbook*. Both sources are needed, as they don't overlap entirely (and of course, the sound is much better on the video).

105. Radio interview

Date:	22 August 1966
Time:	7:30 p.m.
Location:	Warwick Hotel, New York City
Interviewer:	Bruce Morrow
Broadcast:	live WABC-AM, New York City
Length:	10:58

As usual, New York DJ "Cousin Brucie" Morrow taped exclusive interviews with the Beatles when they came through town. These were apparently conducted immediately following both press conferences, and aired live on the *Cousin Brucie Show*, although the circulating tape is from a rebroadcast.

Beatle number 1 is John and topic number 1 is you-know-what. Morrow wonders why the controversy didn't take hold in Britain, and John replies that "there's no sort of DJs needing publicity in England," referring to the Birmingham, Alabama, bonfire organizers. After describing the chaotic Cleveland concert, John is offered the microphone to say whatever he wants, but demurs: "I'm not a famous ad-libber like they think. And I don't want to take over the show—it's your show Bruce, you do it."

Morrow talks to Paul next, and asks him to classify the nature of his relationship to Jane Asher. Paul responds cheerily, "We're just queer. That's the scene.

But, I mean, I couldn't say that on the air live, y'know." Follow-up questions about dating preferences get nowhere, so the topic shifts to Paul's farm and then John's religious troubles. Paul acknowledges that he was apprehensive about being attacked by people "with masks" (presumably the KKK), but feels it's all been cleared up as well as can be expected. As John had, Paul puts it all down to the Birmingham radio station trying to drum up ratings.

George is in fine laconic form when asked what Indian music is ("It's music that comes from India"). He speaks sincerely about music for a minute, but then Morrow makes the tactical error of asking George about other professional ambitions. "I'd like to be a bricklayer," he responds earnestly.

Ringo chats about his son, Zak, and is beginning to discuss the "butcher cover" when everyone else begins to leave the room. Ringo politely stays behind to answer a few more questions about Shea Stadium and the St. Christopher medal he had lost back in 1964, and which Morrow and WABC had helped him to reclaim.

RELEASE HISTORY

This recording circulates in good quality among collectors from an off-line broadcast.

105a. Radio interview   G

Date:	23 August 1966
Interviewer:	Kenny Everett
Broadcast:	Radio London
Length:	4:00

George chatted with Kenny Everett in New York, primarily about the imminent break from the tour in Los Angeles. George says they hope to hang out with the Mamas and the Papas, the Byrds, and Derek Taylor, and says if they want to get out and see any of the city,

the trick will be not to tell the police. Kenny asks why they don't want to visit any Iron Curtain countries, and George's answer is replete with thoughts of Manila: "It's the sort of thing where you may or may not get back on the plane to come home."

RELEASE HISTORY

This interview circulates in good quality from an off-line recording.

106. Concert

Date: 23 August 1966
Time: 9:20 p.m.
Location: Shea Stadium, New York City

[A.] She's a Woman (0:25)
[B.] If I Needed Someone (0:25)
[C.] intro (0:08)
[D.] I Feel Fine (0:31)
[E.] Yesterday (0:29)
[F.] Paperback Writer (0:25)

Eager to make a quick buck out of the Beatles (presumably before their imminent demise), an enterprising company called Audio Journal sent a roving reporter to Shea Stadium. His mission was to capture the reactions of fans, stadium employees, police, and anyone he ran into before, during, and after the concert. Although a number of Beatles performances were captured far in the background, these are incidental to the voices of the "erupting" fans.

During this segment of the LP, female fans scream on cue, shriek, "I love you, Paul," and ask the reporter how he can just sit there in the presence of Beatles. Some teenage boys estimate the number of police, narrate the exploits of some fans who run onto the field, and declare that the Beatles are obviously on the way out. The only sane voice is a thirty-eight-year-old self-proclaimed "atypical Beatles fan" (presumably the father of one of the screamers), who points to Arthur Fiedler and the Boston Pops' cover versions as proof of the quality of Beatles compositions.

Bits and pieces of silent color footage circulate from this concert, as well as a three-minute color home movie filmed from the upper deck (in which the Beatles may as well be ants). WCBS-TV also sent Leonard Harris to cover the concert, and eight minutes of raw footage from his report survives, consisting mainly of interviews with fans in the stands.

RELEASE HISTORY

This album was apparently released in 1966, under the unwieldy title *Beatles at Shea Stadium Described by Erupting Fans,* although it made no impression on the charts. It was more prevalent after a vinyl reissue in the early 1980s and was transferred to CD in the 1990s. The "musical" portions appeared on the 2001 CD-R compilation *Live: Make As Much Noise As You Like!* The home movie and news footage circulates on video, and some of it appears in the *Anthology* documentary.

107. Press conference

Date: 24 August 1966
Time: evening
Location: Capitol Records Tower, Los Angeles
Length: 22:02

Smuggled out of Shea Stadium in an armored car, the Beatles were taken directly to the airport and flew west to Los Angeles, arriving in the predawn hours of the twenty-fourth. As usual, they rented a private house, this time in Beverly Hills, to decompress a bit. Their sole task this first day out west was to meet the press and receive some awards at the Capitol Tower in Hollywood. In between posing for photos, accepting a gift of branding irons, and schmoozing with Alan Livingstone over the gold record for *Revolver,* the Beatles conducted the liveliest press conference of the tour.

For whatever reason, the group are back in a playful mood, perhaps because they are surrounded by familiar faces. DJ Fred Paul, who had traveled with them on the Summer 1964 tour, is back to ask again "What will you do when the bubble bursts?" At one point, David Crosby, hovering in the background, is pointed out and quickly ducks out of view.

Some highlights:

Q: One of your countrymen was here yesterday or the day before . . . He said he thought that American women were out of style . . . and that because they didn't wear miniskirts, their legs were ugly.

Ringo: Well, if they don't wear miniskirts, how does he know their legs are ugly?

Q: I'd like to direct this question to Messrs. Lennon and McCartney. In a recent article, *Time* magazine put down pop music. And they referred to "Day Tripper" as being about a prostitute and "Norwegian Wood" as being about a lesbian.

Paul: Oh yeah.

Q: Now, I just wanted to know what your intent was when you wrote it, and what your feeling is about the *Time* magazine criticism of the music that is being written today.

Paul: We were just trying to write songs about prostitutes and lesbians, that's all.

John: . . . quipped Ringo.

Ringo: Because we're on tour, people know where we are. That's why we have a crowd.

Paul: Oh! Is that what happens?
Ringo: Yes, yes! I worked that out!
Paul: Oh, you little rascal!
Q: Uh, may I ask about the song "Eleanor Rigby"? What was the motivation or inspiration for that?
John: Two queers.
Q: I'm sure you've all heard of the many Beatle burnings and Beatle bonfires—
John: Well, the photos we saw of them were of sort of middle-aged DJs and twelve-year-olds burning a pile of LP covers.

The mop-tops did not corner the market on wit that evening:

Q: Mr. Lennon, is it true you're planning to give up music for a career in the field of comparative religion?

Of course, it's not all fun and games. A detailed question about their finances is met with a deep sigh from Paul. The obligatory Jesus moment includes a reporter's astute observation "This created quite a controversy and a furor in this country." Paul chimes in facetiously, "Did you know that, John? You created a furor." A British journalist asks them each to name a most memorable and most disappointing moment in their career. Dead silence. John: "No idea." George eventually votes Manila as "most disappointing."

Yet another Beatle quote to Maureen Cleave is dredged up: "Show business is an extension of the Jewish religion." John admits to having said it, but refuses to elaborate. (Paul: "Aww. Come on, John. Tell 'em what you meant.") Ringo had also gotten into trouble in a 1964 *Playboy* interview by joking that Pete Best "took little pills to make him ill." Best was now suing for defamation, and when a reporter asks about the lawsuit and whether Best was really a former Beatle, John cryptically replies, "Uh, I think he's had a few, but we don't bother with those."

RELEASE HISTORY

1985: An excellent-quality copy of most of the press conference was released on the LP *West Coast Invasion,* later reissued on CD. An alternate source tape on the CD *Talkology, Volume 2* contains a few extra seconds here and there (only one line from a Beatle), but is missing parts on the earlier release.

Lengthy black-and-white newsreel excerpts were released on the video *The Beatles Unauthorized,* featuring a few segments (mainly the photo shoots) not on the CDs listed above. KNBC-TV also filmed the event in color, including their arrival in an armored car. Twenty-five seconds of this circulate from a rebroadcast on KNBC, and 45 seconds were included in a 1992 Capitol Records EPK to promote the thirtieth anniversary of "Love Me Do."

108. TV interview   P, G

Date:	24 August 1966
Time:	evening
Location:	Capitol Records Tower, Los Angeles
Length:	2:30

Following the general questioning, there was the usual opportunity for individual TV crews to film Beatle interviews. Cameras for ABC-TV's *Where the Action Is* had been rolling throughout the press conference, and a correspondent (filling in for host Dick Clark) fought his way to the front of the room to corner George for an interview.

After explaining that his voice will be replaced by Clark's and pointing out which of the myriad cameras George should face, the reporter struggles to get a serious answer out of him. George says his favorite music is "honky-tonk," his favorite American country star is Buddy Holly, and that if he could see any American performer, it'd be Len Barry!

A subsequent attempt to interview Paul is even more haphazard. Paul mistakes the name of the show for the name of a group ("the Worthy Actioners") but agrees to answer some questions. The first question is "What time of day do you prefer to write your tunes?" Paul gets up and rambles, "Certainly daytime anyway, or nighttime. Certainly something like that," before walking away. Understandably, none of this footage was deemed suitable for airing on ABC, although they apparently did air clips from the press conference itself on the September 13 edition of *Where the Action Is.*

RELEASE HISTORY

Although it was never aired, this footage circulates in excellent quality among video collectors.

109. TV interview

Date: 25 August 1966
Time: 1:40 p.m.
Location: Sea-Tac Airport, Seattle
Length: 0:21

After their one-day break in Los Angeles, the Beatles flew to Seattle for two concerts on the twenty-fifth. At the airport, a local TV reporter pursued an upbeat Ringo across the tarmac for a few comments.

RELEASE HISTORY

This footage circulates on video from a twentieth anniversary rebroadcast in 1986.

110. Radio interview

Date: 25 August 1966
Time: evening
Location: Seattle Coliseum
Interviewer: Dusty Adams
Length: 8:21

The Seattle taping session was held in a press room at the Coliseum, across the hall from the Beatles' dressing room. Although people such as Jim Stagg and Ken Douglas had left the touring party, there was always someone in each city to talk to, in this case Dusty Adams, who recorded separate interviews with each Beatle.

Asked about the possibility of recording an album in America, Paul says that a Memphis studio wanted an exorbitant fee, but that they would consider it if the price was right. A rather specific rumor was circulating about Jane Asher being flown in to marry Paul that evening in Seattle, and after three years of dealing with such reports, Paul is completely unfazed, putting it down to "occupational hazard."

Adams tells George he was one of the DJs to call a London studio that February to wish him a happy birthday, and the two of them wrack their brains trying to figure out which album the Beatles could have been recording at the time. Presumably George was attending some other artist's session, as the *Revolver* sessions didn't begin until April. George talks about the super-market on Hayling Island John had bought for his pal Pete Shotton in 1965, and says that he has a tape recorder in his car to sing into in case he gets a song idea on the road.

Ringo explains who sings what on "Yellow Submarine," and for the 4,240th time says he does little but "just sit 'round" in his spare time, although he admits to the occasional reading craze. He concedes that airport crowds have been smaller than ever on this tour, but thinks it's because fans have sussed that heavy police protection limits the amount of personal contact the group can have with fans on such occasions. Ringo also gives his account of the Manila incident, although it's "still a mystery" exactly what happened.

John halfheartedly says he's still writing material for a third book, and expresses no interest in attempting to compose songs with anyone but Paul or perhaps George. He declares that his "more popular than Jesus" quote was tossed off so trivially that when it resurfaced, he had to go back and read the original article to remind himself that he hadn't been misquoted.

RELEASE HISTORY

1982: These interviews were released on the picture disc LP *Timeless II*. They have been reissued on the CD *Inside Interviews: Talk Downunder: Sydney to Seattle*.

111. Press conference

Date: 25 August 1966
Time: 8:00 p.m.
Location: Seattle Coliseum
Length: 5:43

Between shows in Seattle, a press conference was held onstage at the Coliseum. A recording of edited highlights exists from what may have been the last joint press conference the Beatles ever gave in America.

Unsurprisingly, the Jane Asher "wedding" is brought up, and at first Paul decides to pull everyone's collective leg: "Tonight, yeah. I couldn't tell you [when and where], that's a secret!" Although reservations for a reception had supposedly been booked at the Edgewater Hotel under the name Mr. Bartholomew, Paul says he knows nothing about it, and George points out that they'll be flying back to California that night anyway. Someone asks if they represent a new type of morality, and Paul jokes that they'll leave the protest music to their support act, the Cyrkle. A female reporter tells John he'll be known as a great author in twenty-five years, and that she'd like to talk to him about it sometime. (John: "See you in twenty-five years, then!")

George explains that they have an idea for their next movie but are waiting to see a completed script before deciding whether to film it. Another female reporter asks Paul what he's doing after the show, and he replies, "I don't know, marrying you, probably!" When someone asks if all Lennon/McCartney songs are true joint compositions, John mutters, "Don't they buy *Datebook*?"

A DJ from Vancouver radio station CFUN, "Jolly" John Tanner, attended the conference dressed as the Jolly Green Giant. He asks if they are coming back to Vancouver (Paul: "Maybe—Brian decides where we go"), wishes John a belated happy wedding anniversary (John: "Well, you thank them, Jolly Green Giant!"), wonders where one can buy a sitar (George: "India"), and wishes Ringo's wife, Maureen, a very belated happy birthday.

RELEASE HISTORY

1978: This press conference was released on the LP *Beatle Talk*, reissued on CD as *Beatles Tapes: The Beatles in the Northwest*. It was also copied on the picture disc *Timeless II*, but with the beginning clipped off slightly.

112. Concert

Date:	25 August 1966
Time:	3:00 or 8:00 p.m.
Location:	Seattle Coliseum
Length:	0:04

A local station was able to capture a whopping 4 seconds of one of the two Seattle concerts before being forced to shut its camera off. Immediately following the evening show, the Beatles caught an 11:30 p.m. flight back to Los Angeles for two days of relative solitude.

RELEASE HISTORY

This silent footage circulates from a twentieth anniversary rebroadcast in 1986.

113. Concert

Date:	28 August 1966
Time:	evening
Location:	Dodger Stadium
Length:	3:10

The Beatles spent a couple of days hanging out with Derek Taylor, Joan Baez, David Crosby, Cass Elliott, Roger McGuinn, Brian and Carl Wilson, and other Los Angeles musicians. On the evening of the twenty-eighth, they performed their penultimate concert before a packed Dodger Stadium crowd.

A home movie, shot from high above home plate, captures the excitement fairly well, despite being silent and fairly distant from the action. It opens with a shot of the stage, a platform near second base draped with curtains, sporting a huge KRLA radio logo. The scoreboard flashes a message: FOR YOUR INFORMATION— THE BEATLES HAVE ARRIVED AND ARE IN THEIR DRESSING ROOM. Finally, a spotlight picks out the four tiny figures emerging from the third base dugout and walking onstage. Along with fragments of the first five songs, the film depicts a handful of fans running across the outfield before being chased down and escorted off by security.

In a display of bad planning, promoters tried to get the Beatles out of the stadium in a limousine through the main exit gate. Of course, hundreds of fans were awaiting just such a vehicle, so after a U-turn, they were transferred to an armored car, which met up with the limo at a nearby gas station. It was the last of dozens of close-call escapes they'd suffered through since 1963. The next night, an armored car would be ready and waiting to whisk them offstage.

RELEASE HISTORY

This silent home movie, transferred from 8 mm courtesy of Fotomat Transfer Service, circulates among collectors in decent quality.

114. Newsreel footage

Date: 29 August 1966
Time: 5:45 p.m.
Location: San Francisco Airport
Length: 1:29

A private jet carried the Beatles from Los Angeles to San Francisco this afternoon for their final concert. This also meant their final group airport arrival in the United States, captured, as usual, on film. After posing briefly on the steps of the plane, John, Paul, George, and Ringo take the short walk to their awaiting M&M Chartered Bus. It lingers in the parking lot just long enough for fans to snap souvenir photos and wave at the windows, before pulling away for the short drive to Candlestick Park.

RELEASE HISTORY

This silent footage circulates on video among collectors.

115. Radio interview   J, G, R

Date: 29 August 1966
Time: evening
Location: Candlestick Park, San Francisco
Interviewer: Lee Darling (?)
Broadcast: WTRY-AM, Albany
Length: 4:06

The final taping session of the tour occurred in the Beatles' dressing room before their Candlestick concert. A disc jockey from Albany, New York, (goodness knows what he was doing in California) was present and taped interviews with three of the Beatles.

John talks for one last time about *How I Won the War* and the possibility of a third book and insists that he reads all the banners hung by fans at each arena. George accepts congratulations on his marriage, and recounts how "Rain" came to have backwards vocals, although he can't remember whose idea it was. Ringo chats about Zak and expresses incredulity at the thought that Paul would want to get married in Seattle.

RELEASE HISTORY

This recording circulates among collectors in poor quality, from an off-line broadcast.

115a. Radio interview   J, G

Date: 11–29 August 1966
Interviewer: Kenny Everett
Broadcast: Radio London
Length: 2:04

These interviews with Kenny Everett were taped sometime during the final tour. In one clip, John describes what it feels like to be hit on the head with a shoe while performing, and does a brief promo for Kenny's radio show. In another, Everett asks John what he would do given his own radio show, and John reveals that he often pretends to be a DJ on his home recordings. He then relates how Paul brought some tape loops from his home studio for use on "Tomorrow Never Knows." There's also a 6-second snippet of George whistling the Radio London jingle.

RELEASE HISTORY

1984: Parts of these interviews were broadcast in the radio documentary *Sgt. Pepper's Lonely Hearts Club Band: A History of the Beatle Years 1962–1970.* The full recordings circulate in good quality from an off-air recording.

116. Concert

Date: 29 August 1966
Time: 9:27 p.m.
Location: Candlestick Park, San Francissco

[A.] intro (0:04)
[B.] **Rock and Roll Music** (1:32)
[C.] **She's a Woman** (2:44)
[D.] intro (0:26)
[E.] **If I Needed Someone** (2:27)
[F.] intro (0:27)
[G.] **Day Tripper** (2:58)
[H.] intro (0:04)
[I.] **Baby's in Black** (2:20)
[J.] intro (0:20)

[K.] **I Feel Fine** (2:11)

[L.] *intro* (0:26)

[M.] **Yesterday** (2:16)

[N.] *intro* (0:23)

[O.] **I Wanna Be Your Man** (2:10)

[P.] *intro* (0:21)

[Q.] **Nowhere Man** (2:13)

[R.] *intro* (0:29)

[S.] **Paperback Writer** (2:08)

[T.] *intro* (0:33)

[U.] **Long Tall Sally** (0:32)

On a windy and cold Monday evening in San Francisco, the Beatles took the stage for the last time. The twenty-five thousand fans in the audience were unaware of this fact, but the four musicians seemed to know it was the end. John brought a camera onstage to photograph the occasion, and press officer Tony Barrow was instructed to grab a cassette tape and record the concert from his position on the field.

A fifteen-year-old fan, Barry Hood, was also documenting the proceedings from the seats with an 8 mm home movie camera on silent color film. Together with a bit of news footage from KRON-TV, we thus have a visual record of the Beatles' arrival by bus and portions of "She's a Woman," "Day Tripper," and "Nowhere Man."

Coming at the end of a long tour, the performances are far more polished compared with the Tokyo concerts, but the vocal harmonies are still generally ragged and out of tune. However, the atmosphere of reckless abandon provides some entertaining moments. John introduces "Day Tripper" as being "about the naughty lady" and "Nowhere Man" as "from our BBC album," while George pegs "I Feel Fine" as a 1959 recording! Not to be outdone, Paul dedicates "I Wanna Be Your Man" to "all the wonderful backroom boys on this tour."

When a couple of fans escape onto the field during "Baby's in Black," Paul's singing provides a running commentary: "Dear, what can I—hey! Hey! Baby's in black, and I'm—whoa yeah! Oh, very good." It apparently happens again before "Paperback Writer," as Paul tells the crowd, "We'd like to carry on . . . I think. Not really sure yet. I'd like to carry on, certainly. Definitely. Well, should we just watch this for a bit?"

After the usual sloppy performance of "Paperback Writer," Paul steps to the microphone. "Thank you very much, everybody. Everybody, wonderful. Frisco. Butchered. Uh, we'd like to say that, um, it's been wonderful being here [crowd screams]. It is wonderful

to see you all. Sorry about the weather. And we'd like to ask you to join in and, uh, clap . . . sing . . . talk. In fact, go on, do anything. Anyway, the song is—good night."

This is a remarkably indifferent stage announcement from the normally cheerful Beatle, and it gives no hint of what is to follow. Hitting a low G note on his bass to find the pitch, Paul screams at the top of his lungs: "I'm gonna tell Aunt Mary! 'Bout Uncle John! He said he got the mis'ry BUT HE'S GOT A LOTTA FUN OH BABY!!"

It's a song he's performed probably two or three hundred times with the Beatles; he'd even sung it onstage with his brother Michael in 1957 before officially joining the Quarry Men. "Well, long tall Sally's built— pretty sweet she's got—everything that Uncle John need oh baby!" But it's never sounded quite like this. Paul is putting everything he has into his vocal. "Yeahheh now baby! WHOO baby! Some fun tonight! WAAAAAAAOW—"

And then Tony Barrow's tape ran out.

We have to rely on written reports for what happened next. The band finished "Long Tall Sally," and John played the opening guitar phrase to "In My Life" for reasons we'll never know. After their synchronized bows, the Beatles set up a camera on an amplifier and took a timed self-portrait of their final moment together on stage. Then they waved good-bye while sprinting to the armored car, which had sat on the field throughout their performance, engine revved and ready to speed them into the night.

RELEASE HISTORY

1984: Most of this concert first surfaced in good quality on the bootleg LP *Candlestick Park, San Francisco '66,* but **U** was missing entirely. The same year, portions of **N** and **O** were broadcast in superior quality in the radio documentary *Sgt. Pepper's Lonely Hearts Club Band: A History of the Beatle Years 1962–1970.*

1989: The full concert appeared from tape source on the bootleg CD *Live in Paris 1964 and in San Francisco 1966.* This version was electronically processed with added reverb on Masterdisc's CD *Candlestick Park: Big Events of '66,* later copied on Vigotone's CD *Shea!/Candlestick Park.*

The home movie and newsreel footage was released on the videos *One Last Time* and *Live in San Francisco;* a bit of it was used in the *Anthology* documentary.

117. Newsreel footage

Date: 31 August 1966
Time: morning
Location: London Airport
Length: 0:59

Not long after their final bows, the Beatles were flying south to Los Angeles, touching down at fifty minutes past midnight on the thirtieth. At 12:25 that afternoon, they flew back to England, leaving Brian Epstein behind to mourn the likely end of their touring days, and landed in London early on the thirty-first.

This short clip of their arrival includes a few words from Paul, who says the American fans still love them, but that the tour was exhausting and his only plan for now is to get some sleep. George, who several hours earlier had declared, "Well, that's it, I'm no longer a Beatle," concurs.

RELEASE HISTORY

1996: A slightly abbreviated copy of this interview was released on the CD *Rare Photos & Interview CD, Volume 3*. The full clip is on the video *Beatles 1962 to 1970*.

118. Newsreel footage   J

Date: 13 September 1966
Location: Celle
Length: 0:49

The first location for *How I Won the War* was West Germany, with filming taking place in the town of Bendesdorf and at a NATO base in Celle. A Reuters camera crew filmed some of the action this first week, as John, in doughboy outfit and National Health spectacles, lined up as "Private Gripweed" and mingled with real NATO soldiers.

RELEASE HISTORY

This silent footage circulates on video. Some of it was used in ITV's *Reporting '66: End of Beatlemania* program, and in the *Beatles 1962 to 1970* collection.

119. Newsreel footage   P, R

Date: 13 September 1966
Location: GPO Tower, London
Length: 0:49

With John busy filming on location and George packing for an imminent trip to India, it was left to Paul and Ringo to perform the more mundane task of accepting an award from *Melody Maker*. The ceremony occurred atop the general post office tower, and was filmed by news cameras. This short clip has Paul accepting the certificate, and holding it up to pose alongside Ringo (who is dressed in a white jacket and polka-dot shirt) for photographers.

RELEASE HISTORY

This silent footage circulates on video among collectors.

120. Studio session   P

Date: early October 1966
Location: Trident Studios, London
Producer: Mickie Most

[A.] Mellow Yellow (3:37)

Paul and Donovan apparently began their close friendship in the spring of 1966, visiting each other often, both at home and in the studio. Donovan remembers helping compose the "Sky of blue, sea of green" verse to "Yellow Submarine" when Paul dropped by his apartment. And, possibly to return the favor, Paul lent a hand to Donovan's studio session for his own "Yellow" song, "Mellow Yellow."

Erroneous reports in the musical press attributed the whispered words of wisdom "Quite rightly" to Paul.

His actual contribution was little more than whooping and hollering (and possibly handclapping) in the background during the instrumental verse. Paul is particularly easy to hear at 1:56, shouting, "Hey!" He can also be heard crooning "Yellooooowww . . ." around 2:16 into the track. From about 3:02 onward, Paul continues to babble through the fadeout.

RELEASE HISTORY

1966: This song was released on a single (Epic 10098) October 24 in the United States, where it reached number 2 on *Billboard*'s chart. It wasn't released until February 1967 in the UK (Pye 7N 17267), where it peaked at number 8. It is readily available on CDs such as *Troubadour* and *Donovan's Greatest Hits*.

121. Studio session   P

Date: late October 1966
Location: Maximum Sound Studios, London
Producer: Paul McCartney

[A.] From Head to Toe (2:27)

The Escorts, one of a multitude of lesser-known Liverpool beat groups, had an interesting Beatle connection: Their original drummer, John Foster, was Ringo's cousin. By late 1966, Foster was gone and the group's original rhythm guitarist was replaced by Paddy Chambers, who had worked in a group with Klaus Voormann. Perhaps at Klaus's request, Paul visited one of the Escorts' final sessions to play tambourine on their Smokey Robinson cover, "From Head to Toe." As so often happened when a Beatle got involved with another artist, Paul was credited as producer for both sides of the single, and is even rumored to have cowritten the B-side, "Night Time," with Chambers.

An interesting note: Elvis Costello and the Attractions released excellent covers of both songs in 1982; Costello had selected the songs not from hearing the original single but a later reissue on his own label, Demon. Although he had recently met Paul while working at AIR Studios on the LP *Imperial Bedroom* (Paul was recording *Tug of War*), and the duo would later cowrite numerous songs, it's not clear whether Elvis knew of Paul's connection with these recordings.

RELEASE HISTORY

1966: This song was released as a single in the UK only (Columbia DB 8061) on November 18. It appears on the 1995 CD *From the Blue Angel*.

122. Radio interview   J

Date: ca. 29 October 1966
Location: Carboneras
Interviewer: Fred Robbins
Broadcast: *Assignment: Hollywood*
Length: 13:52

Toward the end of location shooting in Spain, the entertainment reporter Fred Robbins, who had previously interviewed the Beatles in New York and the Bahamas, visited John on set. Their lengthy conversation is chiefly interesting for capturing John at a crossroads between Moptopia and Pepperland. He exhibits none of the wisecracking of the 1963–64 Lennon and none of the impatience and grouchiness of the 1965–66 Lennon, instead sounding rather subdued, mellow, and hesitant.

The first topic is John's new hairstyle, which Robbins likens to Bob Dylan's; John then describes the desert location, standing in for North Africa in the movie, as "a dump . . . it's like the moon." Even though most of the picture has been filmed, John is still at a loss for words when trying to describe his character and the plot. He praises the cast and particularly Richard Lester, saying he would have been too nervous to act in front of an unfamiliar director.

They talk about George's recent visit to India, and John claims the sitar is "George's own scene" and won't be used on Beatles records with any regularity. Robbins then praises John and Paul's songwriting, using "Michelle" and "Yesterday" as examples. Although he had little input on either, John describes the writing process behind those two songs.

Looking back on the Jesus furor, John says it seems like a bad dream, and he's reminded of it only when he reads in the newspaper every so often that "Cardinal so-and-so says it's OK." Robbins compares the ordeal to the McCarthy era, and John agrees that it was frightening. John then reveals that Paul has signed up to write a theme for the movie *The Family Way*. Although he seems to think it will be a Lennon/McCartney project, Paul would have the task pretty much wrapped up by the time John returned to England.

After saying farewell, Robbins evidently continued

chatting with John off the record, but then switched his tape back on to record an anecdote from John about exploring Paris nearly unrecognized thanks to his new hairdo. Robbins wonders if they've ever purposely traveled in disguise, and John says he's just heard that Paul was in London recently dressed as an Arab (at the October 15 fancy-dress party for the *International Times*). Robbins thinks George will be unrecognizable in his new mustache, and John seems to feel the best way to go incognito is to smash your own face in.

RELEASE HISTORY

This interview can be found on the cassette *Historic Interviews, Volume 2,* sold primarily through the Beatlefest catalog.

123. Composing tape   J

Date: 19 September–6 November 1966
Location: Santa Isabel

[A.] Instrumental (0:24)
[B.] Strawberry Fields Forever—take 1 (0:47)
[C.] Strawberry Fields Forever—take 2 (1:18)
[D.] Strawberry Fields Forever—take 3 (1:28)
[E.] Strawberry Fields Forever—take 4 (1:46)
[F.] Strawberry Fields Forever—takes 5 and 6 (2:12)
[G.] Strawberry Fields Forever—demo fragment (0:12)

Perhaps no other Beatles song is as well documented from conception to finished recording as John's "Strawberry Fields Forever." He began composing the tune in his hotel room in Spain, using a nylon-stringed acoustic guitar and a portable tape recorder to create the basic structure.

These recordings all come from a single cassette taped sometime during the fall of 1966; John begins by playing a short classical-style instrumental (**A**) in F-sharp to warm up. The song itself is performed in the key of A major at this point, and the first take (**B**) consists of two run-throughs of what would become the song's second verse. The working lyric is "There's no one, nobody in life/I mean it's either too high or too low/That is you can't you know tune in, but it's all right/I mean it's not too bad". The second take (**C**) has the first line changed to "There's no one on my way there," and John sings the verse three times, humming through the third time.

By take 3 (**D**), he has hit upon "No one I think is in my tree," and plays the verse through twice before introducing the chord changes for the chorus, without lyrics at this point. He finishes by repeating the sole verse again. The fourth attempt (**E**) is similar, although this time, the chorus has rudimentary words: "Let me take you back/Was it a dream/Nothing is real/Nothing to get mad about."

The ambience switches to a heavily echoed room (perhaps the lavatory or a corridor) for the final demos (**F**). After a breakdown apparently caused by a door slamming, John sings the usual verse, following it up with the new line "I always no sometimes think it's me"—with nothing to follow it, he fills in the rest with a repeat of the "high or low" verse. The title finally shows up in the chorus: "Let me take you down there/Strawberry Fields/Nothing is real/Nothing to get mad about/Strawberry Fields and nothing," and the song ends with another repeat of the "tree" verse. An apparent seventh take (**G**) is probably from a much earlier demo session erased by these takes; it's performed a half step higher and consists of the line "That is you can't you know tune in, but it's all right" repeated twice.

RELEASE HISTORY

1994: **B–D** appeared on the bootleg CD *Revolution*. These were copied the same year on the LP *The Lost Lennon Tapes, Volume 30.*

1996: The limited-circulation CD-R *Entomology* contained a tape of **F,** supposedly in slightly better quality than subsequent releases.

1997: This entire reel (**A–G**) was included on the bootleg *It's Not Too Bad.*

124. Amateur footage

Date: 12–19 November 1966
Location: various, Spain and Kenya
Length: 61:14

After a drive through France, Paul met up with Mal Evans, intending to visit John on the set of *How I Won the War* in Almeria. Informed that John had already returned to London, he spent a day or two exploring Spain with Mal.

Both men had Canon 8 mm home movie cameras, and while Paul's movies (he filmed in France as well) are long gone, Mal's have surfaced. Most of the Spanish footage consists of countryside and architecture, but there are some glimpses of Paul and Mal strolling through a plaza and chatting with local boys, as well as filling up at a petrol station and visiting a farm.

Once arrangements had been made, they journeyed on to Kenya for a photo safari. Two of Mal's reels, labeled "African Safari Oct 1966 [sic]" and "Africa Paul," were sold at auction. Paul and Mal can be seen riding an open-topped Jeep and a safari bus, but most of the footage concentrates on various animals (elephants, rhinos, hippos, giraffes, monkeys, zebra, fish, birds, lions, and a snake).

To travel unrecognized, Paul grew a mustache over the course of this trip. On his flight back to London, Paul would conceive the notion of having the Beatles record a whole album "in disguise." Once home, he would compose "Love in the Open Air" for *The Family Way* (he had already written the film's main theme before leaving for France).

RELEASE HISTORY

This silent color footage was released on the DVD *The Complete Mal Evans Silent Films.*

125. Composing tape

Date: 8–23 November 1966
Location: Kenwood

[A.] Strawberry Fields Forever—guitar overdub (1:02)

[B.] Strawberry Fields Forever—guitar overdub (2:08)

[C.] Strawberry Fields Forever—demo playback (0:15)

[D.] Strawberry Fields Forever—vocal overdub (2:13)

[E.] Strawberry Fields Forever—demo playback (0:30)

[F.] Strawberry Fields Forever—take 1 (0:37)

[G.] Strawberry Fields Forever—takes 2–7 (4:01)

[H.] Strawberry Fields Forever—take 8 (1:55)

[I.] Strawberry Fields Forever—Mellotron overdub on takes 3–7 (4:04)

[J.] "backwards" speech and "swinging flutes" Mellotron (0:38)

Back home, anticipating the next round of Beatles sessions, John perfected "Strawberry Fields Forever" by recording a number of demos with differing instrumentation and arrangements. **A**–**G** (and probably **H**) are taken from side A of a cassette, the flip side of which consists of recordings made at Kenwood on an unknown date: an a cappella "Danny Boy," John fooling around on organ, and an improvised ditty titled "Pedro the Fisherman" (see Appendix B for details). The Mellotron overdubs (**I**) stem from another cassette, which also contains the improvised "Stranger in My Arms" (see Appendix B), a bit of "Hello Dolly," a conversation with Julian, and an otherwise unknown electric guitar demo titled "Who's Your Man."

First (**A**) we hear the hum of a second tape machine and a playback of previously recorded electric guitar, running through the song's chords in the key of B. John plays a few live guitar stabs over this, but doesn't seem to have any clear idea of how to proceed. The next attempt (**B**) is similar, with his live guitar notes getting more and more wretched as the playback proceeds.

On a different occasion, John recorded a guitar and vocal demo in the key of C—this begins with the "tree" verse and continues with the eventual third verse (sung here as "Sometimes no always think it's me"), the now-complete chorus, the "tree" verse and chorus again, and the repeated title refrain as a coda. Although we don't have this demo in basic form, we do have a recording (**C**–**E**) of John playing it back on another machine and adding a live second vocal. **C** and **E** are false starts of the playback, but **D** is a complete overdub take.

The third set of recordings begins with several takes of an electric guitar/vocal demo, also in C. Take 1 (**F**) makes it nearly through a verse before John says, "OK" and shuts off the recorder. Apparently he's unhappy with his guitar accompaniment, as he then tries out several styles (G), each lasting only a few lines. Take 2 is arpeggiated, but John mutters that "it just sorta goes too quiet." Takes 3 and 4 are both unsuccessful attempts to play in a strumming style reminiscent of "Yesterday." (John wonders aloud, "Can I do it?") The next two takes are finger-picked, but John realizes it "doesn't work like that." Changing to a softer guitar tone, John busks his way through take 7, a complete run-through, with the same structure as **D**.

An eighth take on electric guitar (**H**) may not come from this tape, but sounds similar: It begins with a count-in and has the same lyrics, although John doesn't sing during the first half of the third verse, perhaps hoping some words will come to him.

After adding a second vocal track to his composing tape, John played back the result to add Mellotron accompaniment and occasional further vocals. This was captured on a recording (**I**) that begins with playback of takes 3 and 4; John stops the tape and comments, "That's fuckin' near, I must say I don't think much of that." Starting the tape again at take 3, John fiddles around on the Mellotron and makes sarcastic comments as all the previous false starts roll by. ("Please. Have a bit of respect, will ya? Shut up, I'll smash your face in.") When the complete take 7 approaches, John shouts, "It's a ready, it's a be going now!" and plays along on Mellotron, using the "wine glasses" setting for the verses and "pipe organ" chords for the chorus.

One final home tape (**J**) that may have nothing to do with "Strawberry Fields Forever" is included here because it features John babbling in pseudo-backwards Scottish while playing the "swinging flutes" Mellotron tape, which ended up on the record of "Strawberry Fields Forever" (at 3:37 and 3:53 on the U.S. stereo mix).

RELEASE HISTORY

1988: Many of these recordings debuted in the radio series *The Lost Lennon Tapes,* as follows:

> Premiere episode: edited version of **H** (verse 1, verse 2, verse 1 again); bootlegged on the CD *Backtrack 3*.
> Episode 88-08: edited version of **G** (takes 2, 4, 6, and 7); bootlegged on the LP *The Lost Lennon Tapes, Volume 1* and the CDs *Backtrack 3* and *Not For Sale*.
> Episode 88-15: longer edit of **H** (repeating both of the first two verses); bootlegged on the LP *The Lost Lennon Tapes Volume 3*.
> Episode 88-30: **J**; bootlegged on the LP *The Lost Lennon Tapes, Volume 9*.

1991: **G** and an incomplete recording of **I** were aired on episode 91-27 of *The Lost Lennon Tapes*. They were included that year on the LP *Nothing but Aging* and in 1993 on its CD counterpart, *Arrive without Aging*.

1996: A different edit of **G** (take 6, John's comment following take 4, edited take 7) was released on *Anthology 2*.

1997: All of these demos (**A–J**), unedited and adjusted to the presumed correct speed, were included on the bootleg CD *It's Not Too Bad*.

126. Studio session

Date:	24 November 1966
Time:	7:00 p.m.–2:30 a.m.
Location:	EMI Studio 2
Producer:	George Martin

[A.] **Strawberry Fields Forever—take 1 (stereo)** (3:15)

[B.] **Strawberry Fields Forever—take 1 (mono)** (1:19)

[C.] **Strawberry Fields Forever—RS from take 1 (#1)** (1:20)

[D.] **Strawberry Fields Forever—RS from take 1 (#2)** (2:33)

Convening for their first studio session in five months, the Beatles tackled "Strawberry Fields Forever," laying down a single take after much discussion and rehearsal. John had written a new opening verse about how "living is easy with eyes closed," which bumped the other two verses ahead in the song. Otherwise, the structure was similar to his most recent demos, being performed in the key of C.

The backing consisted of Paul playing Mellotron flutes (on the intro and coda), Ringo on drums, and John and George on electric guitars. John sang his lead vocal on a second track, recorded with the tape running fast to sound slowed-down on replay, and accompanied by George playing some Hawaiian-sounding Mellotron slide guitar. John then double-tracked portions of his vocal (the end of the first chorus and all of the third verse), and on the fourth track, he, Paul, and George added some beautiful wordless harmonies. The result was a simple, succinct, and admirable performance, but not satisfactory; the remakes would begin at their next EMI session.

The raw studio tape (**A**) circulates in a mix with the rhythm left and the other three tracks centered. A 1983 remix (**C**) of take 1 has the backing vocals left, second vocal right, and the other two tracks centered. The *Anthology* mix (**D**) omits the backing vocals and John's second vocal entirely.

RELEASE HISTORY

1983: The multimedia presentation *The Beatles at Abbey Road* included **C**. This appears from tape source on the CD *Abbey Road Video Show*.

1986: A very good stereo copy of **A** surfaced from the raw studio tape on the vinyl bootleg *Nothing Is Real*. A slight upgrade appeared two years later on the LP *Ultra Rare Trax, Volume 5 & 6*.

1989: **A** appeared from tape source on the Condor CD *Strawberry Fields Forever* and later on the CD *Unsurpassed Masters, Volume 3*.

1992: **B** was broadcast in the TV special *The Making of Sgt. Pepper*, wherein George Martin played back the original session tape, briefly isolating the Mellotron slide guitar/vocal track. This source was copied on the 2001 CD-R *Strawberry Lane*.

1996: **D** was released on *Anthology 2*.

1997: **A**, speed-adjusted to the (incorrect) key of B major, was bootlegged on the CD *It's Not Too Bad*.

127. Studio session

Date:	25 November 1966
Time:	3:00 p.m.
Location:	Dick James House, London
Producer:	George Martin

[A.] Pantomime: Everywhere It's Christmas—edit of unknown takes (6:38)
Mixed: 2 December 1966

For their fourth annual fan club Christmas message, the Beatles gave up all pretense of trying to sound sincere in thanking the "Beatle people" for all they'd done over the past year. Instead, they recreated the feel of their 1963 and 1964 Hammersmith Christmas Show skits with a twist: Rather than the usual heroic antics, this pantomime featured a collection of short unrelated episodes strung together.

The front cover for the flexi-disc sported a psychedelic logo designed by Paul, and the back listed each "skit" individually, as follows:

- "Song: Everywhere It's Christmas" (a jaunty tune with each Beatle taking a turn singing to Paul's piano accompaniment)
- "Orowayna (Corsican Choir and Small Choir)" (conducted by a bearded man in glasses)
- "A Rare Cheese (Two Elderly Scotsmen)" (wonderful stuff, this)
- "The Feast" (the king overindulges)
- "The Loyal Toast" (aboard H.M.S. *Tremendous*)
- "Podgy the Bear and Jasper" (George and John act out a delightful tale about a shopping list)
- "Felpin Mansions—Part One (Count Balder and Butler)" (starring the eccentric son of Baron Landsberg, the inventor of the rack)
- "Felpin Mansions—Part Two (The Count and the Pianist)" (in which the Count mistakes himself for his father)
- "Song: Please Don't Bring Your Banjo Back" (Paul plays this nostalgic ditty on the piano)
- "Mal: Everywhere It's Christmas" (self-evident)
- "Reprise: Everywhere It's Christmas" (the same take that opens the disc)

One has to wonder what American fans, familiar with neither traditional pantomimes nor *The Goon Show*, made of all this, but it's certainly a creative and refreshing change from their previous Christmas efforts, and probably eased the pain of having no new songs released for the holidays.

RELEASE HISTORY

1966: **A** was released on a flexi-disc titled *Pantomime: Everywhere It's Christmas*, mailed out to fan club members on December 16. It's available on the bootleg CD *The Ultimate Beatles Christmas Collection*.

128. TV performance

Date: 27 November 1966
Time: morning
Location: Broadwick Street, London
Producer: John Street
Broadcast: 26 December 1966, 9:00–9:50 p.m.
BBC2
Not Only . . . But Also
Length: 0:50

Having appeared in its debut episode (see the November 29, 1964, entry), John made a return visit to the Dudley Moore/Peter Cook sketch comedy series *Not Only . . . But Also* for its 1966 Christmas special. His brief contribution was filmed on a Sunday morning outside a public men's room, but the sketch's Beatles content exceeds far beyond John's cameo.

It is presented as an American TV documentary about the Swinging London scene, titled *The Pipesucker Report* and produced by "Idaho Television." Cook hosts it as Hiram J. Pipesucker, and he and Moore poke fun at performance artists and fashion models before turning their sights to the world of pop music.

Pipesucker interviews Moore as Simon Accrington, pill-popping manager of the group the Mothers, who traveled to Lhasa where they fell under the influence of banjo player Ravi Oli. The band is then seen in the studio recording their next smash hit, "The L. S. Bumblebee." Cook and Moore double as the group's lead singers, complete with Eastern garb and Cook's drooping mustache, and accompanied by a bongo player and a seemingly naked man hitting a gong. The song's main target seems to be "Tomorrow Never Knows": The sea-gull effects are provided by a bird perched over a bowl of water, and lines such as "Listen to the color of your dreams" are skewered fittingly with "I hear with my knees/Run with my nose/Smell with my feet/My heart is a rose." Interestingly, the song's title actually anticipates the forthcoming "Lucy in the Sky with Diamonds" controversy.

The sketch ends with Pipesucker visiting a trendy nightclub, the Ad-Lav (an obvious satire of the Ad Lib club). John makes his appearance here, dressed as the club's doorman and allowing Cook entrance only when he reveals himself to be the duke and duchess of Windsor. The closing credits reveal the name of John's character to be Dan, but it should be noted that the club's owner, played by Moore, is named Dan Druff. The real strength of this lampoon lies in Peter Cook's splendid characterizations; it doesn't rise to the level of a *Rutles* or a *Spinal Tap,* but most Beatles fans should enjoy it.

RELEASE HISTORY

Although the majority of this series was sadly scrapped by the BBC, this episode was retained, and the entire fifteen-minute sketch circulates on video. A studio recording of "The L. S. Bumblebee" was released as a single in the UK (Decca F 12551) on January 27, 1967. This song appeared on numerous Beatles bootlegs in the 1970s, purporting to be a Beatles outtake or at least a Lennon-penned composition. In fact, he had nothing to do with it apart from appearing in the TV show where it debuted, although it's obviously partly inspired by Beatles music.

129. Studio session

Date: 28 November 1966
Time: 7:00 p.m.–1:30 a.m.
Location: EMI Studio 2
Producer: George Martin

[A.] Strawberry Fields Forever—take 2 (stereo) (3:09)
[B.] Strawberry Fields Forever—takes 3 and 4 (stereo) (3:36)

The second attempt at recording "Strawberry Fields Forever" used a slightly altered arrangement, lowered to the key of A major, and beginning with a Mellotron flute introduction and the chorus before moving into the usual framework. Take 2 is an attempt to lay down a rhythm track (same instrumentation as take 1, with the addition of maracas). It was probably rejected because the guitar plays some bum notes at the end of the second chorus; although it doesn't break down, it ends cold after the final refrain.

The third take makes it only a few bars into the Mellotron opening before John complains that it's too loud. Take 4 is complete, with George playing a mix of slide and Morse code blips on the Mellotron guitar setting. John added another slowed-down vocal track, and Paul overdubbed a bass part on the remaining track; three rough mono mixes of the finished product convinced John that they should start fresh the next day.

1984: The radio documentary *Sgt. Pepper's Lonely Hearts Club Band: A History of the Beatle Years 1962–1970* included a slightly sped-up version of **A**, lasting 1:38 and used as a bed for a George Martin interview.

1986: The vinyl bootleg *Nothing Is Real* contained **A**, copied from the *Sgt. Pepper* special, and the first appearance of **B**.

1988: A clean version of **A** and a slight upgrade of **B** were booted on the LP *Ultra Rare Trax, Volume 5 & 6*.

1989: **A** and part of **B** (take 4 only) appeared from tape source on the bootleg CD *Dig It!* All three takes were included on *Unsurpassed Masters, Volume 3* the same year, although **B** was still slightly incomplete and suffered from bad distortion in the right channel.

1997: **A** and **B** appeared in excellent quality on the bootleg CD *It's Not Too Bad*.

130. Studio session

Date:	29 November 1966
Time:	2:30–8:00 p.m.
Location:	EMI Studio 2
Producer:	George Martin

[A.] Strawberry Fields Forever—takes 5 and 6 (stereo) (4:12)

[B.] Strawberry Fields Forever—rehearsal takes (stereo) (0:29)

[C.] Strawberry Fields Forever—take 7 (stereo) (3:30)

[D.] Strawberry Fields Forever—RM3 from take 7 (3:20)

Mixed: 29 November 1966

This time, the "Strawberry Fields Forever" remake wasn't for structural reasons—the same arrangement and instrumentation was used—but an attempt to capture a better performance. It paid off, after plenty of rehearsal and a false start (take 5). The sixth take was ideal, continuing with an extra-long coda, so John added a slowed-down vocal and Paul his bass line. After take 6 runs out, the ends of two earlier rhythm track rehearsal passes (with no bass) erased by the proper takes can be heard (**B**)—the first lasts 25 seconds, devolving into busking, and the second a mere 4 seconds. These may actually be remnants of the November 28 session, since the same reel was used both nights.

Take 6 was reduced to two tracks of a new tape, called take 7 (**C**). On one of the new tracks, John doubled his vocal on the choruses. An overdub of Mellotron (guitar and piano settings) finished things off, and three mono remixes were created, the last of which (**D**) was cut onto acetates for the group to take home.

John must have given his copy plenty of listens, as he dreamed up an entirely new slant for the song over the following week.

RELEASE HISTORY

1983: The multimedia presentation *The Beatles at Abbey Road* included about two minutes of slightly sped-up excerpts from **D**. This appears from tape source on the CD *Abbey Road Video Show*.

1985: The vinyl bootleg *Strawberry Fields Forever* contained **D**, taken from an acetate.

1988: A slightly incomplete copy of **A**, as well as **B** and **C**, were booted from the raw studio tape on the LP *Ultra Rare Trax, Volume 5 & 6*.

1989: **A**–**C** appeared from tape source on the bootleg CD *Unsurpassed Masters, Volume 3*.

1992: **C** was broadcast in the TV special *The Making of Sgt. Pepper*, wherein George Martin played back the original session tape, briefly isolating the rhythm track. This source was copied on the 2001 CD-R *Strawberry Lane*.

1997: **A**–**D** appeared in excellent quality on the bootleg CD *It's Not Too Bad*, although **D** was still taken from an acetate.

1999: John Barrett's cassette compilation contained a copy of **D** from tape source, including a false start and count-in. This was bootlegged on *Turn Me On Dead Man: The John Barrett Tapes* in excellent quality. The same year, the CD *More Masters* included a slightly inferior copy of **D**, also from tape source, but including George Martin's "RM3" announcement for the first time.

131. Studio session

Date: 6 December 1966
Time: 7:45 p.m.–1:00 a.m.
Location: EMI Studio 2
Producer: George Martin

[A.] **Christmas Messages (mono)** (0:22)
[B.] **Christmas Messages—monitor mix of various takes (mono)** (3:38)

The previous year, DJs from pirate stations Radio Scotland and Radio Caroline had recorded Christmas greetings from the Beatles from their concert dressing rooms. With no future tours planned and no new holiday product to go out and promote, the group agreed to record a number of seasonal tidings at EMI for broadcast on Radio London and Radio Caroline. These were simple spoken-word items, four of which (**A,** one from each Beatle) were dubbed onto the 1967 outtake of "Christmas Time Is Here Again!" and released on the "Free As a Bird" single.

A lengthy playback of the original session tape (**B**) recently surfaced, from preparation of the 1983 multimedia presentation *The Beatles at Abbey Road*. It begins with each Beatle in turn reading a message, underscored by different Mellotron vamp tapes. They are clearly reading from a script (two different messages per Beatle, presumably one for each station), but try to inject some life into their readings via silly accents. This is followed by the unaccompanied messages heard in **A,** plus an alternate set of greetings. The tape concludes with two takes of John's initial message, as he gives instructions about the Mellotron backing he wants to use.

The main purpose of this evening's session was to record the basic tracks for Paul's composition "When I'm Sixty-Four." The melody of the verse had been written several years earlier, but John helped finish off the lyrics about the grandchildren. A basic track of Paul on bass and Ringo on drums was recorded in two takes, with John or George joining in on electric guitar near the end. On another track, Paul added piano, but that was as far as it went that night—work would continue two days later.

RELEASE HISTORY

1995: **A** was released on Apple's "Free As a Bird" CD single.

2002: **B** was included on the bootleg CD *The Seven Years of Christmas*.

132. Studio session

Date: 8 December 1966
Time: 7:00 p.m.–3:40 a.m.
Location: EMI Studio 2
Producer: George Martin

[A.] **Strawberry Fields Forever—edit of RM3/take 25 (mono)** (4:11)

On December 8, the Beatles decided to approach "Strawberry Fields Forever" from a new perspective. John had already asked George Martin to write a brass and strings score, but first a new rhythm track had to be recorded. This was accomplished in fifteen takes (numbered 9–24 with no take 19), all at a faster tempo than previous efforts and with a cacophony of noise filling the tape. In addition to normal drums, Ringo added some backwards cymbal, and various people contributed tambourine, timpani, maracas, scrapers, bongos, and finger cymbals. The first 2:24 of take 15 was used, and this was spliced onto the latter portion of take 24, which had John free associating fruit-wise with "cranberry sauce," and telling madman Ringo to calm down at the kit. At the end of the session, an attempt was made to reduce this edit into a single track of take 25 on a new tape, but that would be redone the following day.

Anthology 2 includes 2:57 from RM3 of take 7 crossfaded with 1:18 of this rhythm track.

RELEASE HISTORY

1996: **A** was released on *Anthology 2*.

133. Studio session

Date: 15 December 1966
Time: 2:30 p.m.–midnight
Location: EMI Studio 2
Producer: George Martin

[A.] Strawberry Fields Forever—take 25 (stereo) (3:47)

[B.] Strawberry Fields Forever—monitor mix of take 25 (mono) (3:24)

[C.] Strawberry Fields Forever—RM9 (3:21)
Mixed: 15 December 1966

Once the spasmodic rhythm track was successfully combined onto a single track on December 9, track 2 of "Strawberry Fields Forever" was filled with Paul's lead guitar and the previously mentioned "swinging flutes" Mellotron tape (as well as a "piano riff" tape near the very end). Six days later, George Martin conducted his score, in the key of C major, with three cellos and four trumpets filling the two remaining tracks of the tape.

Take 25 as heard on bootleg (A) is a bit misleading, as track 2 is mixed nearly out (a bit of the guitar leaks through). The last 5 seconds, which seem to repeat John's "calm down" instruction to Ringo, are probably just a remnant of the first attempt to reduce the rhythm track from December 8. An off-line recording of this same take (B) from preparations for the 1983 multimedia presentation *The Beatles at Abbey Road* includes a bit of extra Mellotron noise at the end mixed out of A.

Take 25 was reduced to two tracks for take 26, with the rhythm remaining on track 1 and everything else going onto track 2. John recorded his first lead vocal on the third track, and then double-tracked himself during the choruses on track 4 while George added some swarmandal. A mono mix of all the work so far (C) was done the same night, and four acetates were cut of this the next day, but there was more to be done.

RELEASE HISTORY

1986: The vinyl bootleg *Nothing Is Real* contained a very good, but slightly incomplete, copy of A.

1988: An upgraded version of A was included on the LP *Ultra Rare Trax, Volume 5 & 6*. It appeared from tape source on the CD *Unsurpassed Masters, Volume 3* the following year.

1997: A appeared complete, in excellent quality, and speed-adjusted to B major on the bootleg CD *It's Not Too Bad*.

1999: John Barrett's cassette compilation contained a copy of C, which was bootlegged on *Turn Me On Dead Man: The John Barrett Tapes* in excellent quality. The same year, the CD *More Masters* included a slightly inferior copy of C, but contained Geoff Emerick's remix announcement and some presong chatter from take 26 for the first time.

2002: B surfaced on the bootleg CD *Complete Control-room Monitor Mixes*.

134. TV interview

Date: 20 December 1966
Time: evening
Location: EMI Studios
Interviewer: John Edwards
Broadcast: 29 December 1966, 6:08–6:35 p.m.
Rediffusion-TV
Reporting '66: End of Beatlemania
Length: 4:47

While it's now common for top groups to go several years between new albums, in 1966 a lapse of even a few months without releasing new material was cause for concern. With no product out for Christmas, solo projects in the works, and no indication of future tours, speculation was prevalent that the Beatles might be finished.

ITV News put together a remarkably incoherent package on the topic for *Reporting '66*, stringing together archival footage of the group, sprinkled with comments from people such as Richard Lester, but with no narration or editorial point of view. The payoff comes at the end of the show with exclusive interviews of each Beatle, conducted by John Edwards on the front steps of EMI Abbey Road Studios as the group arrived for a 7 p.m. session.

First to arrive is John, carrying an armload of LPs. He says that while they may focus on individual efforts in 1967, they all get along fine and will continue working as a group. He reveals that he wouldn't have accepted the role in *How I Won the War* had the other Beatles been unhappy about it, but that none of them are really interested in film careers. Although he thinks tours are no longer in the cards, John says he and Paul will continue writing songs "forever."

As darkness falls, Paul shows up with Mal Evans and goes into greater detail about why concerts have become so frustrating. Not only has their live performance ability sunk to an all-time low, but they realize nobody is really listening anyway. George arrives in a fur coat and rushes up the steps, uninterested in answering any questions about a Beatles split, apart from a fleeting "no."

Ringo is the last to arrive, accompanied by Neil Aspinall, and chats the longest. He explains that they don't want to simply repeat past successes, and that if they can't find a decent script for the next Beatles film, they may pursue separate projects until they have a reason to work together again. Since John and Paul write songs during their time off and George studies the sitar, Ringo contemplates making a film on his own. He denies several times that he is bored or fed up with being a Beatle, and after wishing the viewers a Merry Christmas, signs a few autographs for waiting fans before joining his mates in the studio.

RELEASE HISTORY

Much of this new footage was used in documentaries such as *Anthology, The Making of Sgt. Pepper,* and *It Was Twenty Years Ago Today.* The complete *Reporting '66* also circulates in good quality among video collectors. A small portion of Ringo's interview was bootlegged on the CD *The Ultimate Beatles Christmas Collection.*

135. Studio session

Date:	21 December 1966
Time:	7:00–9:00 p.m.
Location:	EMI Studio 2
Producer:	George Martin

[A.] When I'm Sixty-Four—RM8 (2:38)
Mixed: 30 December 1966

[B.] When I'm Sixty-Four—RS1 (2:36)
Mixed: 17 April 1967

[C.] When I'm Sixty-Four—RS from takes 2 and 4 (2:36)

During an afternoon session on December 8, Paul had recorded his lead vocal on the third track of the "When I'm Sixty-Four" tape. The fourth track was filled on December 20 with the addition of Ringo playing chimes and the other three Beatles singing backing vocals. A reduction that night combined the bass/drum/guitar track and the piano track into one, freeing up another track for George Martin's clarinet arrangement.

This final overdub—two clarinets and one bass clarinet—was taped on the twenty-first, completing the song. Mono mixes done this night and December 29 were unused after Paul decided the whole song should be sped up, "just to make it more rooty-tooty." Thus the song as heard on disc is raised from the key of C major to C-sharp, although the stereo mix (**B**) is a touch slower. The *Songtrack* remix (**C**) isolates the piano track from take 2 and centers all the vocals but is otherwise identical to the earlier stereo mix.

As separate mixes were done for the United States and UK on December 29, "When I'm Sixty-Four" was probably slated for the flip side of the "Strawberry Fields Forever" single at that point. The situation would change over the next two weeks.

RELEASE HISTORY

1967: **A** and **B** were released on mono and stereo pressings, respectively, of the LP *Sgt. Pepper's Lonely Hearts Club Band.* The latter is on EMI's CD of the same title.

1999: **C** was included on Apple's *Yellow Submarine Songtrack* CD.

136. Studio session

Date:	21 December 1966
Time:	10:00–11:45 p.m.
Location:	EMI Studio 2
Producer:	George Martin

[A.] Strawberry Fields Forever—take 26 (stereo) (3:44)
[B.] Strawberry Fields Forever—monitor mix of take 26 (mono) (3:10)

[C.] Strawberry Fields Forever—RM12 (4:05)
Mixed: 22 December 1966

[D.] Strawberry Fields Forever—RS3 (4:05)
Mixed: 29 December 1966

[E.] Strawberry Fields Forever—RS? (4:05)
Mixed: 26 October 1971

[F.] Strawberry Fields Forever—RS from demo, take 1 and take 26 (4:32)

John was apparently unsatisfied with his lead vocals on "Strawberry Fields Forever" after hearing the acetate of take 26. With that in mind, he erased track 3 during this session, replacing it with a fresh vocal, accompanied

75

by heavy snare drum and occasional piano. This vocal (heard on **A**) can be distinguished from the other because here John harmonizes with himself on the final chorus. In addition, it seems John had already made the decision to join the first part of take 7 with the rest of this take, as he doesn't bother to sing most of the first verse during this overdub (a bit more of John's opening verse vocal can be heard in **B** as compared to **A**).

With both versions finished to John's satisfaction, it was up to George Martin and Geoff Emerick to join them together. Realizing they had a slower recording in A major and a faster one in C major, they decided to let the two meet midway by manipulating the speeds to somewhere around B-flat. For the first 54 seconds, they used the intro, chorus, and opening verse of take 7. The next few words ("Let me take you down, 'cause I'm—") were pasted in from the second chorus of take 7, and from "going to" onward, we hear take 26.

Two stereo mixes were prepared on December 29, one for the United States and one for the UK. The latter was rejected because of "too much vocal," according to the tape box. The former (**D**) was copied on November 7, 1967, for Capitol's *Magical Mystery Tour* LP; this mix has the trumpets and cellos pan abruptly from left to right at the take 26 edit point. A new stereo mix (**E**) was eventually done for the West German release of *Magical Mystery Tour,* identifiable by the panning of swarmandal from right to left. In addition, the "siren" trumpet/guitar blare moves from right to center on mix **D** and all the way from right to left on mix **E**.

George Martin thought the chaotic rhythm track got a bit too far out of sync at one point; to disguise this, he faded the volume down (around 3:32 in the song) and then back up again during mixing. The mono mix released on a single (**C**) fades down but not entirely out, while the 1971 stereo mix (**E**) fades to complete silence. The *Love* remix (**F**) begins with a home demo, segues into take 1 and concludes with take 26. The ending is overlaid with a mashup of elements from "Sgt. Pepper's Lonely Hearts Club Band," "In My Life," "I'm Only Sleeping," "Penny Lane," "Piggies," and "Hello Goodbye."

RELEASE HISTORY

1967: **C** was issued worldwide on a single and is available on the "Strawberry Fields Forever" CD single. **D** was released on Capitol's *Magical Mystery Tour* LP.

1971: A new stereo mix, **E,** was released on West Germany's stereo-only issue of the *Magical Mystery Tour* LP. It's currently available on EMI's CD of the same name.

1983: The multimedia presentation *The Beatles at Abbey Road* included 2:45 of **A,** mixed into mono. This appears from tape source on the CD *Abbey Road Video Show.*

1986: The vinyl bootleg *Nothing Is Real* contained a very good, but slightly incomplete, copy of **A.** This was copied on the 1988 CD boot *Ultra Rare Trax, Volume 1.*

1988: An upgraded but still slightly incomplete copy of **A** appeared on the LP *Ultra Rare Trax, Volume 5 & 6.* This appeared from tape source the following year on the Condor CD *Strawberry Fields Forever.*

1989: **A** appeared complete and from tape source on the CD *Unsurpassed Masters, Volume 3.*

1992: **A** was broadcast in the TV special *The Making of Sgt. Pepper,* wherein George Martin played back the original session tape, briefly isolating the various tracks. This source was copied on the 2001 CD-R *Strawberry Lane.*

1997: **A** and **D** appeared in excellent quality on the bootleg CD *It's Not Too Bad.*

2002: **B** surfaced on the bootleg CD *Complete Control-room Monitor Mixes.*

2006: **F** was released on the *Love* CD.

1967: A LITTLE BIT OLDER

January 7   Ringo is photographed at home after being served a writ by his gardener.

January 8   John and Paul attend a party thrown by singer Georgie Fame at the Cromwellian Club.

January 11   Paul attends the Jimi Hendrix Experience's show at the Bag O'Nails nightclub.

January 13   Paul and Ringo attend the Jimi Hendrix Experience's show at the Bag O'Nails nightclub.

January 15   Paul and George attend Donovan's concert at the Royal Albert Hall.

   John is reportedly involved in a minor car accident.

January 21   Paul attends a party thrown by Julie Felix at a Chelsea art studio.

January 24   Paul meets with playwright Joe Orton at Brian Epstein's home to discuss a proposed script for the next Beatles movie.

January 27   The Beatles sign a nine-year contract with EMI Records.

January 28   Paul and George attend the Four Tops' concert at the Royal Albert Hall.

January 29   John and Paul attend a double bill of the Who and the Jimi Hendrix Experience at the Saville Theatre.

January 30   The Beatles begin filming promo clips for "Strawberry Fields Forever" and "Penny Lane."

January 31   During a break in shooting at Knole Park, Sevenoaks, John purchases the "Mr. Kite" circus poster in a nearby antique shop.

February 5   The Beatles attend Cream's show at the Saville Theatre.

February 7   Paul socializes at home with the Monkees' Mickey Dolenz.

February 13   U.S. release of "Penny Lane"/"Strawberry Fields Forever" single.

February 17   UK release of "Penny Lane"/"Strawberry Fields Forever" single.

February 19   John and Ringo attend a twin-bill concert at the Saville Theatre: Chuck Berry and Del Shannon.

   The London Drug Squad thoughtfully waits until George and Pattie have left to bust a party at Redlands, Keith Richard's house. Mick and Keith aren't so lucky, nor are George and Pattie in March 1969, when the police have worked up the nerve to arrest a Beatle.

March 7   Paul socializes at home with Peter Blake and Jann Howarth, who will help design the *Sgt. Pepper* album sleeve.

March 15   John and Paul dine with Peter Blake and Jann Howarth.

March 30   The Beatles shoot the cover photo for *Sgt. Pepper's Lonely Hearts Club Band* at Michael Cooper's Chelsea Manor Studios.

April 3   Paul and Mal Evans fly from London to Los Angeles (via Paris).

April 4   Paul and Mal fly to San Francisco on Frank Sinatra's private Learjet. Later that day, they attend Jefferson Airplane's rehearsal at the Fillmore West.

April 5   Paul and Mal fly from San Francisco to Denver to visit Jane Asher, celebrating her twenty-first birthday that evening with a party.

April 6   Paul, Mal, and Jane drive into the Rocky Mountains for a day trip.

April 8   John visits J. P. Fallon Coachworks in Surrey and arranges to have his Rolls-Royce painted in a wash of psychedelic hues.

   Paul and Mal drive to the Boodle Mine and visit Paul's Cafe and a bar, the Gilded Garter, in Central City. That evening, they attend Jane's stage performance in *Romeo and Juliet.*

April 9	Paul and Mal visit the Red Rocks Amphitheatre, then fly from Denver to Los Angeles and stay with Derek Taylor.
April 10	Paul and Mal shop at Century Plaza and visit John and Michelle Phillips. Later, Paul attends the Beach Boys' recording session for "Vegetables" and offers tips from the control room.
April 11	Paul and Brian Wilson return to the Phillips house early in the morning and participate in an impromptu jam. After returning to Derek Taylor's house to pack, Paul and Mal fly from Los Angeles to London, formulating the idea for *Magical Mystery Tour* en route.
April 12	Paul and Mal arrive back at Heathrow.
April 24	The Beatles attend Donovan's concert at the Saville Theatre.
April 29	John attends the 14-hour Technicolor Dream multimedia event at Alexandra Palace in London.
May 7	Ringo attends the Jimi Hendrix Experience's show at the Saville Theatre.
May 12	John and Paul nightclub at the Speakeasy.
May 15	Paul meets future wife Linda Eastman at the Bag O'Nails nightclub. The two continue on to the Speakeasy later that night.
May 18	The Beatles hold a joint photo session for *Time* and *The Beatles Book* magazines in Hyde Park.
May 19	The Beatles attend the press launch for the *Sgt. Pepper* album held at Brian Epstein's home.
May 20	Ringo entertains John, Cynthia, George, Pattie, and Brian Epstein at home for tea.
May 24	The Beatles attend Procol Harum's show at the Speakeasy nightclub.
May 28	The Beatles attend a party thrown by Brian Epstein at his new country house.
May 29	Paul greets Jane at Heathrow upon her arrival from the United States.
June 1	UK release of *Sgt. Pepper's Lonely Hearts Club Band* LP.
June 2	U.S. release of *Sgt. Pepper's Lonely Hearts Club Band* LP.
June 4	Paul and George attend the Jimi Hendrix Experience's show at the Saville Theatre. Much to their astonishment, Jimi's opening number is "Sgt. Pepper's Lonely Hearts Club Band." Also on the bill are Procol Harum, the Chiffons, and future Wings sideman Denny Laine.
June 18	Paul begins producing sessions for brother Mike's *McGough & McGear* LP.
June 19	Confirming his just-published press quotes in *Life* magazine and the *Daily Mirror,* Paul (the last Beatle to take LSD) becomes the first Beatle to publicly admit to taking LSD.
June 25	The Beatles perform and record "All You Need Is Love" live on the *Our World* satellite worldwide program.
June 28	George receives a £6 speeding ticket at South Western Court.
June 29	John is photographed at home for *Beatles Monthly* magazine.
July 2	George and Pattie attend a party at Brian Epstein's home; Pattie meets future husband Eric Clapton for the first time.
July 3	John, Paul, and George attend a party at the Speakeasy nightclub.
July 5	John and Cynthia attend Marmalade's performance at the Speakeasy.
July 7	UK release of "All You Need Is Love"/"Baby You're a Rich Man" single.
July 17	U.S. release of "All You Need Is Love"/"Baby You're a Rich Man" single.
July 20	Paul contributes piano and vocals to the Chris Barber Band's recording of "Catcall," a retitling of Paul's song "Catswalk."
	George, Pattie, Neil, and Ringo fly from London to Greece for a vacation/potential island-shopping trip.
July 22	John and Paul (with Mal, Jane, Cynthia, and Julian) join George and Ringo in Greece.
July 26	Ringo and Neil return to London from Greece.
July 30	George and Pattie return from Greece.
July 31	John and Paul return from Greece.

August 1	George, Pattie, and Neil Aspinall fly from London to Los Angeles to spend a week with Derek Taylor. While waiting for a tardy Derek to arrive at the house they are renting, George begins writing a song about being kept up late. The song is named "Blue Jay Way" after the street address of the house.
August 2	George and Pattie visit Ravi Shankar's music school.
August 3	George and Ravi Shankar hold a joint press conference to promote Ravi's upcoming concert.
August 4	George and Pattie attend Ravi Shankar's Hollywood Bowl concert.
August 5	George, Pattie, Neil, and Derek attend Alla Rakha's recording session.
August 8	George, Pattie, Neil, and Derek visit Haight-Ashbury and are besieged by hordes of kids demanding to hear some music from George. Despite having been dosed with LSD, George obliges by playing a bit of "Baby You're a Rich Man" on a borrowed acoustic guitar. George is generally disappointed and disgusted by the hangers-on, junkies, hustlers, and dropouts swarming around the supposedly hip and peaceful district.
August 9	George, Pattie, and Neil return to London from the United States.
August 11	Photo session with Richard Avedon for *Look* magazine at Thomson House photo studios.
August 19	Maureen Starkey gives birth to her and Ringo's second son, Jason, at Queen Charlotte's Hospital.
August 24	At a board meeting attended by John and Paul, "Magic" Alex Mardas is hired as head of Apple Electronics.
	John, Paul, and George attend a lecture by Maharishi Mahesh Yogi at the London Hilton; he invites the Beatles to join him at a seminar beginning the following day in Wales.
August 25	The Beatles, their wives (save Maureen, still at home with the new baby), and Mick Jagger travel by train from London to North Wales for the maharishi's weekend conference at Normal College.
August 26	Just two months after revealing they were LSD users, the Beatles announce they have given up drugs at a press conference with the maharishi.
August 27	Brian Epstein is found dead of a lethal mixture of Carbatrol (contained in Nembutal sleeping pills) and alcohol; though he has attempted suicide previously, the death is ruled accidental by the coroner.
	John, George, and Ringo answer questions about their reactions to Brian's death at a hastily assembled press conference. Paul has already returned to London, and the others soon follow suit.
September 1	The Beatles assemble at Paul's house in St. John's Wood to chart their future career together.
September 11	The Beatles and forty or so passengers head from Allsop Place, London, to parts unknown in a large yellow bus. Filming of scenes for *Magical Mystery Tour* begins on the bus and at lunch in the Pied Piper restaurant in Basingstoke.
September 15	On the way back to London, the Beatles stop and film scenes at Smedley's fish and chip shop. Further scenes are shot onboard the bus, featuring a sing-along led by accordionist Shirley Evans.
September 19	First day of a six-day shoot at West Malling Air Station (various locations) for *Magical Mystery Tour.* Sequences accompanying "I Am the Walrus" and "Blue Jay Way" are filmed during the week.
September 24	The grand finale of *Magical Mystery Tour,* a production number to accompany "Your Mother Should Know," is filmed inside a hangar at West Malling Air Station.
October 14	Paul and George travel to Falsterbohus, Sweden, for a weekend trip to visit the Maharishi Mahesh Yogi.
October 15	Paul and George return to London.
October 17	The Beatles attend Brian Epstein's memorial service at the New London Synagogue on Abbey Road.
	John and Cynthia visit the Annual Motor Show at the Earl's Court Exhibition Building.
October 18	The Beatles attend the world premiere of the film *How I Won the War* (featuring John Lennon as Private Gripweed) at the London Pavilion, followed by a party at Cilla Black's apartment in Portland Place.
October 19	George and Ringo fly to Falsterbohus, Sweden, for a day trip to visit the Maharishi Mahesh Yogi.
October 29	Paul, Mal, and cameraman Aubrey Dewar travel to Nice, France, where they shoot a sequence to accompany "The Fool on the Hill" for the *Magical Mystery Tour* film.
November 1	Paul flies back to London from France.
	John and George attend a private party at Sibylla's nightclub for the group Family.

November 3	Filming the final scenes for *Magical Mystery Tour* at Ringo's home in Surrey.
November 10	Filming a promotional clip for "Hello Goodbye" at the Saville Theatre. The shooting, ostensibly directed by Paul, produces three usable edits.
November 17	The Beatles Limited undergoes a change of name to Apple Music Limited.
November 19	Paul and Jane attend a package show at the Saville Theatre including the Bonzo Dog Doo-Dah Band (featured in *Magical Mystery Tour*) and Tony Rivers and the Castaways (soon to become Grapefruit, Apple Music's first signing).
November 21	The Beatles are filmed by BBC cameras at Norman's Film Productions while editing film footage for *Magical Mystery Tour.*
November 24	UK release of "Hello Goodbye"/"I Am the Walrus" single.
	John and Paul visit Tony Rivers and the Castaways' first recording session at IBC Studios after being signed to Apple Music.
November 27	U.S. release of "Hello Goodbye"/"I Am the Walrus" single.
	U.S. release of *Magical Mystery Tour* LP.
December 3	Ringo flies from London Airport to Rome for a fortnight's shooting of a cameo role in the film *Candy.*
	Paul and Jane retire to Paul's Scottish farm for a vacation.
December 4	John visits the preview of a Lennon/McCartney–sponsored art exhibition by Jonathan Hague at the Royal Institute Galleries.
December 5	John and George attend the opening night party for the first Apple Boutique at 94 Baker Street.
December 8	UK release of *Magical Mystery Tour* EP.
December 15	UK release of *Christmas Time Is Here Again!,* the Beatles' fifth annual Christmas flexi-disc for fan club members.
December 16	John and George attend a UNICEF banquet at the Palais de Chailloy.
December 17	Ringo flies back to London from Rome, as do John and George from Paris.
	John and George host a party for Official Beatles Fan Club Area secretaries (highlight: a sneak preview of the film *Magical Mystery Tour*) at the Hanover Banqueting Rooms.
December 20	Paul and Jane return to London from their Scottish vacation.
December 21	The Beatles and friends celebrate (prematurely) their self-made TV film *Magical Mystery Tour* with a costume party at the Royal Lancaster Hotel.
December 25	Paul finally gets engaged to Jane Asher; it doesn't stick.
December 26	BBC1-TV premieres the Beatles' TV Spectacular *Magical Mystery Tour* in black and white. In retrospect, not such a smart move.
December 29	John, Cynthia, and Victor Spinetti travel to Morocco for a weekend vacation.
December 31	The Beatles attend a New Year's party at Cilla Black's apartment.

1. Studio session

Date:	9 January 1967
Time:	7:00 p.m.–1:45 a.m.
Location:	EMI Studio 2
Producer:	George Martin

[A.] Penny Lane—overdub session (mono)
(13:05)

The recording sessions for Paul's "Penny Lane" proved nearly as complicated and protracted as those of its counterpart, "Strawberry Fields Forever." This was clear from the initial session on December 29, 1966, when Paul played three separate piano parts to create the backing track. On track 1 went six takes of the basic piano rhythm. On track 2 a second piano was added to the last half of each verse. On track 3, Paul added another piano rhythm, supplemented by tambourine, with the signal fed through a guitar amp. Track 4 was filled with various effects (some of them sped up), including staccato percussion (heard at 1:27 and 2:32 on the finished product), harmonium whistles, and extra cymbal (both prominent at the song's end).

The next evening, all four tracks were reduced to track 1 of a new tape, called take 7. Paul and John then sang their main lead vocal track, with the tape running slow, on track 4. On January 4, track 2 was filled with John's piano and George's lead guitar, and track 3 had a second vocal contribution from Paul, but neither of these would be used. On January 5, Paul redid his vocal on track 3, supported again by John, but at a normal speed this time. On January 6, track 2 was wiped and replaced with bass, drums, rhythm guitar, and congas.

Things get confusing at this point: Mark Lewisohn has these four tracks being reduced to two as take 8, the remaining tracks filled with more pianos, hand-claps, and backing vocals from John, Paul, and George. He then says that yet another reduction was done from take 8 into take 9, clearing two more tracks. John Barrett's tape log, however, indicates that takes 8 and 9 are on the same reel, making such a reduction impossible; in addition, none of the aforementioned overdubs seem to have been used. Possibly what occurred was that these overdubs were added to take 8, but they decided to go back to the original take 7 and reduce it again, resulting in take 9.

In any case, by the beginning of this January 9 session, the music was all on track 1 and the vocals were all on track 4. To fill track 3, George Martin had written a score for flutes, piccolos, trumpets, and a flügel-horn. While the hired musicians rehearsed their parts, John was in the control room recording the proceedings **(A)** for unknown reasons, adding plenty of tape echo and using the oscillator to fluctuate the speed wildly.

The first 90 seconds consist of the sounds of flute and piccolo players warming up and discussing their instruments, followed by George Martin calling for a ten-minute break. Paul then plays through the song on piano, admitting it's "kinda confusing to what key it's in" and vocalizing some possible brass parts.

George Martin conducts the flutes in a rehearsal of the chorus, joined by trumpets for the second run-through; the piccolos then play the song's opening bars. The song as it stands (before any orchestral overdubs) is played back, while someone joins in occasionally on piano and the musicians joke from the sidelines. In the final segment, George Martin points out that something is way out of tune, and another playback follows (with more live piano), stopping at the song's final verse. This audio-verité tape was apparently taken home by John, as it no longer exists in the EMI archives.

RELEASE HISTORY

1990: Excerpts from this tape totaling 2:30 aired on episode 90-10 of the radio series *The Lost Lennon Tapes.* These were copied in 1992 on the vinyl bootleg *Arrive without Travelling* and a year later on the CD *Arrive without Aging.*

1994: A more complete tape lasting 6:31 was included on the CD *The Lost Pepperland Reel,* but this was missing 21 seconds of material (the flute/piccolo warm-ups and George Martin's comment "Have a ten-minute break, lads!") compared with earlier releases.

2007: A complete copy of this recording appeared on the CD-R *Sgt. Pepper Deluxe.*

2. Studio session

Date:	12 January 1967
Time:	2:30–11:00 p.m.
Location:	EMI Studio 3
Producer:	George Martin

[A.] Penny Lane—RM8 (3:06)
Mixed: 12 January 1967

The still-vacant track 2 of "Penny Lane" had its first additions on January 10, although there was very little to show for the nearly seven-hour session. On each mention of the fireman, the same chimes used on "When I'm Sixty-Four" were rung (at 1:06 and 2:10). In addition, more vocal harmonies were added this day, but, assuming they went on track 2, they were later erased.

Most of track 2 would instead be filled on this evening with more classical instruments: two trumpets (heard mostly on the choruses), two oboes, and two cor anglais (these contributions largely going unused) and a double-bass (playing at 2:03 as the banker waits for a trim). The song now presumed complete, two mono mixes were done at day's end.

RM8 begins with Geoff Emerick's announcement, a bit of the unused piano/lead guitar overdub from January 4, and then Paul's count-in. It also allows us to hear not only the original trumpet/oboe solo, but also some oboe passages from 2:26 onward, which would be wiped from the session tape five days later. Paul had already seen a TV show the previous evening that would inspire the song's ultimate enhancement.

Mythology, Volume 3. The same year, a slightly inferior-sounding copy was bootlegged on the CD *More Masters,* but this included the "RM8" announcement missing from previous releases.

3. Studio session

Date:	17 January 1967
Time:	7:00 p.m.–12:30 a.m.
Location:	EMI Studio 2
Producer:	George Martin

[A.]	**Penny Lane—RM9**	(3:26)
[B.]	**Penny Lane—RM10**	(3:18)
[C.]	**Penny Lane—RM11**	(2:56)
Mixed:	17 January 1967	

[D.]	**Penny Lane—RM14**	(2:56)
Mixed:	25 January 1967	

[E.]	**Penny Lane—RS?**	(2:58)
Mixed:	30 September 1971	

[F.]	**Penny Lane—RS from takes 6, 7, and 9 (#1)**	(3:10)
[G.]	**Penny Lane—RS from takes 6, 7, and 9 (#2)**	(2:58)
[H.]	**Penny Lane—RS from takes 6, 7, and 9 (#3)**	(2:56)

Having viewed BBC2's *Masterworks* on January 11, Paul was struck by the use of a high-pitched trumpet that featured in the performance of Bach's Brandenburg Concerto no. 2. After consulting with George Martin, Paul requested not only that instrument but that very player, David Mason, be called in to contribute to "Penny Lane." So using a B-flat piccolo trumpet, Mason played a brilliant solo onto track 3. To deliver his reprise for the last chorus, rather than have Mason erase the previous brass and woodwind performance, Paul decided the oboes from track 2 could be sacrificed. The song was capped off with a seven-note coda from Mason, and mono mixing began immediately thereafter.

All three mixes done this day sound nearly identical—the first two (**A** and **B**), coming from unreleased source tapes, feature slate calls, false starts, and count-ins. RM11, however, was considered "best" and duly copied and sent to Capitol, which had been eagerly awaiting the replacement for "When I'm Sixty-Four." A total of twelve acetates were cut at Abbey Road over the next two days, and Capitol went ahead and pressed promotional copies of the single (using **C**), which were distributed to radio stations by the end of January.

Upon hearing the acetates, Paul had second thoughts. On January 25, further mono remixes were created, the best of which, RM14, omitted the seven-note trumpet coda. This mix (**D**) was hastily dispatched to the United States in time to be used on all commercial pressings of the single. "Penny Lane" was not mixed for stereo until 1971; this mix (**E**) includes some brass notes just prior to the solo that had been mixed out of both "best" mono variations. In 1980, this stereo mix had the missing seven notes "restored" (simply dubbed onto the left channel from a copy of the promo single) for release on Capitol's *Rarities* LP.

More recently, digital technology has allowed the original multitracks from each stage of the recording to be isolated and synchronized for new stereo mixes, particularly useful when dealing with a song with so many overdub layers. For *Anthology 2,* all three piano tracks from take 6 are heard spread across the stereo image, and the original solo is used in place of the piccolo trumpet, although the latter is heard in its reprise, including the fabled seven notes. This version (**F**) uses only the normal-speed vocal track for the verses, adding the second vocal for choruses. In addition, the tape also carries on past the song's climax, allowing some silliness from the vocal overdub session and a bit of the wiped lead guitar to be heard.

A similar technique was used to remix the song when it accompanied its promo clip on Apple's EPK to promote the *1* collection. This mix (**G**) has the normal vocals, rhythm track (including much more prominent rhythm guitar), and verse piano centered, with the sped-up vocal track appearing left of center and the other pianos and tambourine mixed left. Otherwise, it resembles the regular stereo mix until the very end, when the shrill harmonium/cymbal is panned across from left to right. A new remix (**H**) for the *Anthology* DVD sounds similar, but centers the piccolo trumpet and tambourine.

RELEASE HISTORY

1967: **C** was issued in the United States and Canada on promotional copies of the single. It has appeared on numerous bootlegs, but never from a tape source, always dubbed from vinyl. **D** was released worldwide on a single and is available on the "Strawberry Fields Forever" CD single. It also appeared on Capitol's *Magical Mystery Tour* LP in "duophonic" stereo.

1971: The first true stereo mix, **E,** was released on West Germany's stereo-only issue of the *Magical Mystery Tour* LP. It's currently available on EMI's CD of the same name.

1980: As described above, the version of this song on Capitol's *Rarities* LP (also included in the UK *Beatles Box* that year) was **E** overlaid with the ending of **C.**

1983: The multimedia presentation *The Beatles at Abbey Road* used a sped-up version of **E,** with the channels reversed. This nonvariation can be heard on the bootlegs *Turn Me On Dead Man: The John Barrett Tapes* (speed-adjusted to match the released mix) and *Abbey Road Video Show.*

1988: A decent copy of **A,** running too slow and missing the false starts, appeared from tape source on the bootleg CD *Ultra Rare Trax, Volume 1.* This was copied on the 1991 CD *Unsurpassed Masters, Volume 7.*

1996: **F** was released on the CD *Anthology 2.*

1999: **B** turned up among John Barrett's cassette material in excellent sound but missing the presong chat, and appeared on bootleg CDs such as *Turn Me On Dead Man: The John Barrett Tapes* and *Mythology, Volume 3.* The same year, **A** and **B** were bootlegged on the CD *More Masters,* including presong chat and false starts previously unavailable. **A** was an upgrade to previous releases, but **B** didn't sound quite as good as earlier issues.

2000: **G** was included on the soundtrack to Apple's EPK for *1* and bootlegged on the CD-R *Video 1.*

2003: **H** was released on the soundtrack of the *Anthology* DVD.

4. TV interview   P

Date:	18 January 1967
Time:	afternoon
Location:	Granada Television, London
Producer:	Jo Durden-Smith
Interviewer:	Jo Durden-Smith
Broadcast:	7 March 1967, 10:25–10:55 p.m. Granada-TV *Scene Special:* "It's So Far Out, It's Straight Down"
Length:	3:33

To spotlight London's flourishing underground scene, Granada TV assembled many of its proponents to comment on the trends and their potential future. With the *International Times,* Indica Bookshop, and its proprietor Barry Miles all contributing, it's not surprising that Paul consented to film an interview for the documentary.

In his four filmed segments scattered throughout the program, Paul walks a line between talking down to and trying to enlighten the general British public, most of whom probably wouldn't have bothered to watch the show in the first place. To make things worse, the show was aired only in the north of England, narrowing its potential audience even further.

Paul opens the show with a plea for understanding for the "weirdos" who produce "psychedelic freakouts," realizing how unorthodox they appear to the average citizen. He then makes England sound like a fascist state, decrying its stifling rules and lack of artistic freedom, although he fails to give any concrete examples. The first breeze of the Summer of Love begins to rustle past as Paul proclaims that he and his peers might have a better answer to how one should live.

After some more exhortations not to prejudge based on far-out sounding language, Paul patronizingly suggests that "If you don't know anything about it, you can sort of trust that it's probably gonna be all right . . . it's human beings doing it, and you know vaguely what human beings do." The show works best as a period piece, but apart from the fact that Pink Floyd performs in it and Paul would be recording "A Day in the Life" the following day (wearing the same tie), few of the subjects featured had a major impact on society.

RELEASE HISTORY

After its initial airing, a brief segment of Paul's interview filmed for this documentary was used in an American TV special, *The Record Makers,* broadcast April 2, 1971, on NBC and hosted by Flip Wilson. This clip, which includes 13 seconds of unique material, circulates on video and was bootlegged on the LP *The Best of Tobe Milo.* More recently, the entire thirty-minute Granada documentary has surfaced and now makes the rounds among video collectors in excellent quality.

5. Studio session

Date: 19 January 1967
Time: 7:30 p.m.–2:30 a.m.
Location: EMI Studio 2
Producer: George Martin

[A.] A Day in the Life—take 1 (stereo) (1:09)
[B.] A Day in the Life—monitor mix of take 1 (mono) (1:20)
[C.] A Day in the Life—take 1 (mono) (0:34)
[D.] A Day in the Life—take 4 (mono) (1:09)

John and Paul's "A Day in the Life," perhaps the greatest achievement of the *Sgt. Pepper* sessions, was born this evening with four takes of the song's basic rhythm. Photos from this day's session show the group rehearsing the song with John at the piano and Paul at an organ, George on acoustic guitar, and Ringo playing congas. Although these rehearsals were later erased, a bit of organ can be heard prior to the start of take 1. After Geoff Emerick's announcement, using the working title "In the Life of . . . ," John gives a "sugar plum fairy, sugar plum fairy" count-in.

The start of the first take is available from two similar documentary clips of George Martin playing back the multitrack tape at Abbey Road. The first is an in-line recording (**A**) from the *Making of Sgt. Pepper* TV special. The second is an off-line excerpt (**B**) from the *Anthology* DVD bonus disc; this is slightly longer, ending just after the second verse. A further mono fragment of the first take (**C**), consisting of the third verse and "turn you on" link, was included in an *Anthology 2* EPK.

For these "proper" takes, John sang his guide vocal on track 4 while his acoustic guitar, Paul's piano, George's maracas, and Ringo's congas all played together on track 1. The fourth take was best, so John added two more vocal overdubs on the remaining tracks, giving him several performances to choose from. In addition, on track 3, Paul added some piano in several spots: over the intro just before John's vocal entrance, a brief lick after the lyrics "lights had changed," dramatic chords after "House of Lords," and single notes during the twenty-four-bar buildup in the middle.

A rough cut of *Anthology* that circulates on video includes George Martin playing back take 4 (**D**), isolating tracks 1 and 4, and including John's count-in.

RELEASE HISTORY

1992: **A** originates from the TV special *The Making of Sgt. Pepper,* wherein George Martin played back the original session tape, briefly isolating the vocal track. The same footage was reused in the *Anthology* documentary. **A** appeared on the vinyl bootleg *Arrive without Travelling* later that year, and from tape source on the CD *Arrive without Aging* in 1993.

1996: **C** was included on the soundtrack of an EPK for the CD *Anthology 2.* It appears on the CD-R *As It Happened, Baby!* in very good quality.

2003: **B** was released on the soundtrack of the *Anthology* DVD.

2004: **D** surfaced in the rough cut of *Anthology,* which circulates on video.

6. Studio session

Date: 20 January 1967
Time: 7:00 p.m.–1:10 a.m.
Location: EMI Studio 2
Producer: George Martin

[A.] A Day in the Life—RM1 (4:20)
Mixed: 30 January 1967

Take 4 of "A Day in the Life" was reduced to two tracks with several tape reductions at the start of this session, keeping the rhythm on track 1 and combining the vocal, double-tracked in places, and extra piano onto track 2. The best of these reductions, take 6, was then overdubbed with Paul's bass and Ringo's drums on track 3 and some brief clavichord from Paul on track 4 (over the song's introduction). In addition, Paul sang his lead vocal section for the first time, "dropping it in" onto track 2. Unfortunately, he botched the words, singing that "everybody" rather than "somebody" spoke, and realized with a laugh and a curse that he'd have to redo them later.

All of this can be heard on the demo remix (**A**) done January 30, including Mal Evans counting out the empty bars following each of John's passages and the alarm clock in the middle of the song; both come from the original take 4 from the nineteenth.

RELEASE HISTORY

1987: **A** made its bootleg debut in the LP *It Was Twenty Years Ago Today;* it originates from an acetate sold at auction and was copied onto many other vinyl bootlegs such as *Foretaste, Classified Document,* and *1967.*

1991: A much cleaner copy of **A** was included on the bootleg CD *Acetates.*

7. Promo clip

Date: 30–31 January 1967
Location: Knole Park, Sevenoaks
Director: Peter Goldmann
Broadcast: 16 February 1967, 7:30–8:00 p.m.
BBC1
Top of the Pops

[A.] Strawberry Fields Forever (4:15)
[B.] Strawberry Fields Forever—*Anthology* edit (3:10)

With touring and personal appearances now out of the question, promoting a new Beatles single was a matter of filming a suitably groovy clip to be aired on various TV shows around the world. The project was produced as usual by Tony Bramwell and funded by the NEMS offshoot Subafilms. Acting on the advice of Klaus Voormann, the Beatles selected Swedish TV director Peter Goldmann to shoot the clips. Voormann was then the bassist for Manfred Mann, and Goldmann had worked with that group early in his TV career. He proved a suitable choice, having been inspired to film pop bands by Richard Lester's pioneering work in *A Hard Day's Night*.

These clips would be particularly important in projecting the group's new image; the public had not seen the foursome in action in five months, and a lot had changed over that stretch. The first objective was to concoct some suitably unconventional images to accompany "Strawberry Fields Forever"; this was achieved over a two-day location shoot at a National Trust property called Knole Park.

The finished product has no attempt to perform the song in question and no plot to speak of. The fuzzy-faced Fabs wander through a field of kettledrums and pace stoically around a huge dead oak tree. Paul is seen (in reverse-motion) "jumping" from the ground to a high branch, and "turning off" the daylight. The balance of the clip was shot at night with the group gathered around an upright piano connected to the tree by a network of strings. They proceed to pour cans of paint all over the piano—1967 being the era of painting their instruments, cars, and houses in psychedelic palettes. The film ends with the Beatles and Paul's sheepdog, Martha, meandering into the gloom.

The edit of this clip seen in the *Anthology* documentary (**B**) incorporates outtake footage, including a scene from the thirty-first that reveals how Paul's "jump" looked in real time. One of the U.S. screenings of **A,** on ABC's *American Bandstand* on March 11, circulates from a black-and-white kinescope. The bewildered reaction of American teenagers to the song and the group's new look has to be seen to be believed.

RELEASE HISTORY

A decent-quality and complete copy of this color promo circulates on video; appearances in the documentaries *Imagine: John Lennon* and *Anthology* both look cleaner but are incomplete. It's a shame Apple hasn't included this promo in any EPK yet; hopefully, it will be included in a home video release of all the Beatles' promos one day.

8. Home demo   J

Date: ca. January–early February 1967
Location: Kenwood

[A.] Good Morning Good Morning (1:04)

This home recording was plucked from the center of fourteen minutes of John and Ringo's usual shenanigans (see Appendix B for further examples) and aired on *The Lost Lennon Tapes*.

The tape opens with John playing an unknown "Penny Lane"–style ditty on piano, filling in the lyrics with plenty of "la la's." After some equipment problems ("Hello? Is anybody there? . . . Stupid bugger"), we come to the familiar bootlegged portion (**A**), which features John playing Mellotron and singing a rough version of his new composition "Good Morning Good Morning," performed in the key of F major.

After running through the first verse, John tentatively sings a single "good morning" and giggles. Perhaps he hadn't yet seen the Kellogg's commercial that inspired the eventual repeating refrain. The second verse is also complete, and the first bridge is nearly finished, the only difference being that everyone you see is "fast" rather than "half" asleep. This may be all he has written at this point, as the playing peters out.

The tape, however, continues with nine minutes of uncirculating material, which seems to consist of John overlaying piano tapes and jet airplane effects (or perhaps it's a real plane flying overhead) on top of the Mellotron. Ringo sings a bit of country ("There's a blue ridge round my heart—take me to them dear old splendid mines"), and buried under a few minutes of annoying Mellotron cacophony, John converses with him (it sounds as though Paul may be present as well).

1988: A slightly incomplete copy of **A,** edited abruptly into the released version of "Good Morning Good Morning," was aired on episode 88-19 of *The Lost Lennon Tapes*. It was bootlegged that year on the LP *The Lost Lennon Tapes, Volume 4* and in 1994 on the CD *Revolution*.

1994: A version of **A** from tape source and with the ending intact was included on the bootleg CD *The Lost Pepperland Reel*.

9. Studio session

Date:	2 February 1967
Time:	7:00 p.m.–1:45 a.m.
Location:	EMI Studio 2
Producer:	George Martin

[A.]	**Sgt. Pepper's Lonely Hearts Club Band—RM1** (2:09)
Mixed:	2 February 1967

On the flight back to London from his November 1966 Kenyan safari, Paul conceived the notion of "the act you've known for all these years," and by February 1, he was ready to record their theme song, which would also serve as the LP's opening title track.

The backing was perfected in nine takes, with Ringo's drums and Paul and George's electric guitars all going onto track 1. Paul then overdubbed his bass guitar on track 2, not amplified and miked but with the signal fed directly into the recording desk. The following evening, the vocals were added, with Paul's lead, joined by John and George on the chorus, going on track 4, and further vocal harmonies on track 3. These were reduced to two tracks with take 10: instruments on track 1 and vocals on track 4.

A demo remix of the result (**A**) was cut onto an acetate, most likely to assist George Martin in scoring the brass parts. Apart from its lack of overdubs, the main point of interest is the fadeout, which continues 20 seconds beyond Billy Shears's eventual entrance with the band vamping on a C major chord.

RELEASE HISTORY

2002: **A** first appeared on the double CD version of Yellow Dog's *Acetates* bootleg. It's taken from a fairly degraded acetate (reportedly owned by John's cousin), which was auctioned by Bonham's in August 2000 and fetched approximately £3,500.

9a. Studio session

Date:	3 February 1967
Time:	7:00 p.m.–1:15 a.m.
Location:	EMI Studio 2
Producer:	George Martin

[A.]	**A Day in the Life—take 6 (mono)** (2:57)

During this session, Paul and Ringo erased their bass and drums on track 3 of "A Day in the Life" with a new performance, Ringo's austere drumming being especially inventive. Paul then corrected his vocal blunder by taping a new vocal on track 2, also adding some soaring "aahs" over the circle-of-fifths segment that linked back to the final verse.

Three segments of take 6 (**A**) can be heard in the *Anthology* rough cut, with George Martin playing the tape back (leaving track 4 muted). This begins with his original take announcement, briefly isolates John's heavy breathing, and concludes with the announcement of take 7.

RELEASE HISTORY

2004: **A** surfaced in the rough cut of *Anthology,* which circulates on video.

10. Promo clip

Date: 5 and 7 February 1967
Time: noon–4:00 p.m. and morning
Location: Angel Lane, London and Knole Park, Sevenoaks
Director: Peter Goldmann
Broadcast: 16 February 1967, 7:30–8:00 p.m.
BBC1
Top of the Pops

[A.] Penny Lane (2:59)

Unlike "Strawberry Fields Forever," the promo film for "Penny Lane" was shot on several different locations. The plot involved John encountering his bandmates, ostensibly in Penny Lane, riding off with them on horses, and having tea by a pond.

In reality, they never traveled to Liverpool and filmed the city sequences in London's Angel Lane early one Sunday afternoon. John strolls down the sidewalk and—lo and behold—runs into Paul, George, and Ringo. After donning some shades (Penny Lane got in his eyes, apparently), he joins the other Beatles, now sporting red hunting jackets, on horseback. Appropriately, only George is riding a dark horse; the others' are white. All this action is intercut with footage shot sep-arately by the crew in Liverpool around the actual Penny Lane. This includes the #46 bus running from Grove Street to Smithdown Road, the "shelter in the middle of a roundabout," the "barber's" pole, and the "fireman" riding a similar white horse.

We then cut back to Knole Park, where the Four Horsemen dismount and sit at a dining table lavishly decorated with candelabras and a lace cloth. The main course at this banquet turns out to be guitars, served up by Mal Evans, but John shows his displeasure by overturning the entire table. The whole clip is not much more sophisticated than an average episode of *The Monkees,* but it served its purpose well enough.

RELEASE HISTORY

Like "Strawberry Fields Forever," this clip also circulates from the monochrome *American Bandstand* broadcast (see January 30–31 entry); the teenagers were more charitable toward this song than its companion. Better-quality color prints emerged over the years, with the best coming from a 1998 Apple EPK. The clip's appearance in *Anthology* is slightly incomplete at either end.

11. Studio session

Date: 10 February 1967
Time: 8:00 p.m.–1:00 a.m.
Location: EMI Studio 1
Producer: George Martin

[A.] A Day in the Life—edit of takes 1 and 2/RM1/orchestra/chat (stereo) (5:03)
[B.] A Day in the Life—take 6, track 1 (4:24)
[C.] A Day in the Life—take 6, track 2 (4:24)
[D.] A Day in the Life—take 6, track 3 (4:24)
[E.] A Day in the Life—take 6, track 4 (4:24)
[F.] A Day in the Life—edit piece take 11 (mono) (0:06)

On February 10, "A Day in the Life" was seen nearly to completion with a grandiose brainstorm. In the kind of move only the Beatles could have gotten away with, a forty-piece orchestra was booked into Studio 1 and told to fill the twenty-four-bar interludes by starting on their lowest notes and ending on the highest, loudest notes they could reach. How they got from point A to point B was up to each individual player. With dozens of invited guests watching, Paul "conducted" the musicians in this task, recorded four times to fill up each track of a separate reel (called take 7), which would be synced with take 6 during mixing.

The orchestral passages were also performed a fifth time, on track 4 of take 6 (**E**), with the punch-in beginning about 19 seconds before the first note is played.

The hodgepodge (**A**) heard on *Anthology 2* begins with the presong chat and count-in from take 1, cuts to take 2 at 0:27, to RM1 from January 30 at 2:45, and back to take 2 at 3:50. This is all mixed in mono, but the orchestral pieces are cross-faded in at 4:16 in stereo. In place of the familiar crashing piano chord, the recording ends with some audio verité, an excerpt from one of four mono reels filled during the February 10 session, as Paul explains to an unknown person why people shouldn't be skeptical about this rather unorthodox method of recording.

Feeling that the orchestral crescendo was too

abrupt a finale for the song and the album, the Beatles attempted to create a suitable edit piece for the ending. The first attempt, on February 10 after the orchestra had gone home, was to fill a tape with four tracks of humming (**F**). A much more fitting solution would be concocted on February 22.

RELEASE HISTORY

1996: **A** was released on *Anthology 2*.

2004: **F** surfaced in the rough cut of *Anthology,* which circulates on video.

2007: **B–E** appeared on the CD-R *Sgt. Pepper Deluxe*.

12. Promo clip

Date:	10 February 1967
Time:	8:00 p.m.–1:00 a.m.
Location:	EMI Studio 1
Producer:	Tony Bramwell

[A.] A Day in the Life (4:58)

Fortunately, seven full-color movie cameras were present in Studio 1 during the celebrated orchestral overdubs for "A Day in the Life." Unfortunately, they were silent handheld cameras, and the result was more a haphazard home movie than a coherent document of the proceedings. The filming, under the supervision of NEMS's Tony Bramwell, was for a proposed TV special to tie in with the album in progress. Brian Epstein told the *New Musical Express* in the February 11 issue that "an outside film crew is working on location." Whether or not that was strictly true, the *NME* reported on April 1 that "No further progress has been made on the Beatles' TV spectacular since the one filming session earlier this year. The group has decided to shelve this project until finishing its LP, upon which the TV show will be based."

Things changed later in April when Paul came up with the idea for a *Magical Mystery Tour* film. By July 1, the *NME* stated that "the original plan to base the show on the 'Sgt. Pepper' LP has been scrapped because the album will no longer be topical by that time." Nonetheless, the idea lingered into the fall with a filming schedule for the other *Sgt. Pepper* numbers from October 21 to November 21 being proposed. As it turned out, the only surviving result of the project was this clip, edited in sync with the finished song, but never screened publicly at the time.

Among the swirling images from the recording session, many of the invited guests can be picked out: Mick Jagger, Marianne Faithfull, Keith Richard, Donovan, Michael Nesmith. All four Beatles, along with Pattie Harrison, are glimpsed, with John getting the most screen time. He is seen wearing a blue velvet coat and chatting to Nesmith and to George Martin. John also sports an ill-fitting bald wig, one of the many novelty props brought in to enliven the proceedings. Orchestra members wear bulbous noses, false teeth, and oversized sunglasses; clothing designer Marijke Koger bangs a tambourine and spreads bubbles with a wand; others blow noisemakers toward the camera lens.

Highlights include shots of both George Martin and Paul "conducting" the orchestral buildups, and an unwanted female visitor being forcibly removed from the premises. Along the lines of the homemade films Paul had been creating for his own amusement, several unrelated images are superimposed or intercut with the studio footage. These include flying birds, rows of electric lights, an effervescent sparkler, film of Julian playing with another child (Zak?), and, most amusingly, a shot of Big Ben when the alarm clock goes off in the middle of the song.

RELEASE HISTORY

The first time this full clip surfaced was from Ringo's 16 mm print, transferred to video and bootlegged in the 1985 *Private Reel* compilation. A different edit, incorporating unrelated home movies from Weybridge, appeared in the 1988 documentary *Imagine: John Lennon*. Most of the original clip can be seen in *Anthology* in very good quality, but with both ends truncated.

13. Studio session

Date: 16 February 1967
Time: 7:00 p.m.–1:45 a.m.
Location: EMI Studio 3
Producer: George Martin

[A.] Good Morning Good Morning—take 8 (stereo) (2:39)

Having polished off the lyrics, John presented "Good Morning Good Morning" as his second candidate for the new LP. The rhythm track was perfected on February 8 in eight takes of drums, tambourine, and rhythm guitar, with John probably singing a guide vocal. Eight days later, Paul added bass and John perfected his lead vocal; the result was a punchy, bare, and hard-rocking recording (**A**). As usual in the *Pepper* sessions, they couldn't leave well enough alone, and the four tracks were reduced to two (music on one, John's vocal on another) to make way for more overdubs. A demo remix was also done this night, presumably to assist George Martin in scoring the horn parts.

RELEASE HISTORY

1996: **A** was released on *Anthology 2*.

14. Studio session

Date: 17 February 1967
Time: 7:00 p.m.–3:00 a.m.
Location: EMI Studio 2
Producer: George Martin

[A.] Being for the Benefit of Mr. Kite!— takes 1 and 2 (stereo) (0:42)
[B.] Being for the Benefit of Mr. Kite!— rehearsal take 7 (stereo) (0:10)
[C.] Being for the Benefit of Mr. Kite!— studio chat (mono) (0:02)

Having purchased the poster advertising Pablo Fanques's Fair on January 31, John wasted no time arranging its sales pitch into rhyming and scanning verses, and setting this to music on his piano at Kenwood. By February 17, the Beatles could begin recording what Geoff Emerick announces prior to take 1 as "For the Benefit of Mr. Kite," although John immediately corrects him.

The backing consisted of George Martin playing harmonium, Ringo on drums, Paul on bass, George on tambourine, and John singing a guide vocal. The first take (**A**) is counted in by Paul at a ridiculously slow tempo, and only lasts a bar and a half before everyone realizes this. Paul practices the tempo a bit on his bass before counting in for the second take, but this too breaks down after a single line. By the seventh take, the backing was perfected; this take can be heard cross-faded with later overdubs on *Anthology 2* (see the March 31 entry).

A snippet (**B**) of the end of a take, with John making a comment and Geoff Emerick announcing "take eight," appears in the *Anthology* video documentary. This is apparently from the rehearsal takes on the reel that were largely erased by the "proper" attempts; according to John Barrett's tape log, rehearsal takes 6 through 8 were preserved at the end of the reel.

A second fragment (**C**) from the same rehearsal session has John declaring jokingly, "Well, we'll have the Massed Alberts on by then." This dialogue snippet is buried in Paul's experimental release *Liverpool Sound Collage,* at 6:38 on track 1, "Plastic Beetle."

Takes 8 and 9 were reductions that combined the bass and harmonium to a single track. At the end of the session, John erased his guide vocal with a better attempt, with Paul harmonizing on the last line of each verse, and a rough remix of the song was made for Paul to take home.

RELEASE HISTORY

1996: **A** was released on *Anthology 2*. **B** was included in the *Anthology* home video set in mono, and was bootlegged from this source on the CD *Abbey Road Video Show;* it appears in stereo on the *Anthology* DVD.

2000: **C** was released on the CD *Liverpool Sound Collage.*

15. Studio session

Date: 21 February 1967
Time: 7:00 p.m.–12:45 a.m.
Location: EMI Studio 2
Producer: George Martin

[A.] Fixing a Hole—edit of RM3/6 (2:37)
Mixed: 21 February 1967

[B.] Fixing a Hole—RS1 (2:34)
Mixed: 7 April 1967

With Abbey Road already booked for the evening, the Beatles and George Martin traveled across town to Regent Sound Studio on February 9 to record Paul's "Fixing a Hole." The backing, consisting of Paul playing bass, Ringo on drums, and George Martin on harpsichord, went onto track 1, while Paul's guide vocal and some rhythm guitar (John or George) went onto track 3. This was perfected in three takes, the second of which was "best." Backing vocals were added to track 4, and someone played a guitar solo on track 2. Mark Lewisohn and George Martin both claim this to be the work of George, but another source suggests it was Paul, playing his Epiphone Casino guitar through his ancient El Pico amplifier.

When they returned to the song on February 21 at Abbey Road Studios, a single take of a remake was attempted but rejected. Instead, the tape of Regent Sound's take 2 was reduced into take 3 (even though a take with that designation already existed), combining the lead guitar and backing vocals into a single track. Paul then erased the original vocal/rhythm guitar track with a fresh lead vocal, and doubled his singing in places on the fourth track.

The final mono master (**A**) is an edit of two mixes, the splice seemingly occurring at 2:06. This version lasts a bit longer at the fade than its stereo counterpart (**B**).

RELEASE HISTORY

1967: **A** and **B** were released on mono and stereo pressings, respectively, of the LP *Sgt. Pepper's Lonely Hearts Club Band*. The latter is on EMI's CD of the same title.

16. Studio session

Date: 22 February 1967
Time: 7:00 p.m.–3:45 a.m.
Location: EMI Studio 2
Producer: George Martin

[A.] A Day in the Life—edit piece take 9 (mono) (0:48)

[B.] A Day in the Life—edit of RM9/edit piece take 9 (5:02)
[C.] A Day in the Life—RS1 (4:55)
[D.] A Day in the Life—RS2 (1:49)
[E.] A Day in the Life—RS3 (4:43)
[F.] A Day in the Life—RS4 (1:57)
[G.] A Day in the Life—RS5 (0:35)
[H.] A Day in the Life—RS6 (2:38)
[I.] A Day in the Life—RS7 (4:41)
[J.] A Day in the Life—RS8 (4:43)
[K.] A Day in the Life—RS9 (4:43)
Mixed: 22 February 1967

[L.] A Day in the Life—edit of RS12/edit piece take 9 (5:03)
Mixed: 23 February 1967

[M.] A Day in the Life—RS from take 7 and edit piece take 9 (4:51)
[N.] A Day in the Life—RS from takes 1 and 7 and edit piece take 9 (5:08)

A suitably dramatic ending for "A Day in the Life" was recorded this evening. Using three pianos and a harmonium, John, Paul, Ringo, Mal Evans, and George Martin all slammed down an E major chord on the count of four as Geoff Emerick sat in the control room capturing every last iota of sound. It took nine attempts to synchronize everyone's fingers, but the best take (**A**) lasted for 48 seconds, and was duly overdubbed with three more tracks (two of pianos, and one of harmonium) to thicken the sonic impact.

The mono mix of the song's main body was then completed, using the syncing of two playback machines as discussed earlier, and the edit piece was joined to create the mono master (**B**). Stereo mixing on the main body of the song also began that night, with nine attempts (**C–K**); problems with synchronizing the tapes of takes 6 and 7 caused many of the mixes to be aborted. Each of the complete mixes ends with studio ambience and a smattering of applause, and no piano edit piece. Many of these mixes have all four tracks centered during the second verse.

A new approach the next day generated the final stereo mix, RS12 (**L**). This time, the instruments stayed where they were but the vocal track wandered across the stereo picture, although the rhythm track does jump abruptly from left to right for the final verse. With the piano edit piece mixed to stereo and added to RS12, "A Day in the Life" was now complete, although for unknown reasons, a piano overdub was attempted March 1 onto take 6. According to the tape log, this had something to do with the "he blew his mind out in a car" verse, but it went unused.

A fresh stereo mix (**M**) for the *Anthology* DVD is nearly identical to RS12, but centers Paul's vocal. The *Love* remix (**N**) is preceded by some chat from prior to take 1 (actually indexed as part of the previous track, "While My Guitar Gently Weeps").

RELEASE HISTORY

1967: **B** and **L** were released on mono and stereo pressings, respectively, of the LP *Sgt. Pepper's Lonely Hearts Club Band*. The latter is on EMI's CD of the same title.

1983: The multimedia presentation *The Beatles at Abbey Road* used a slightly sped-up version of **L**, with the channels reversed but John's count-in left intact. This can be heard on the bootlegs *Abbey Road Video Show* (with some of the bass frequency spliced out), *Turn Me On Dead Man: The John Barrett Tapes* (speed-adjusted to match the released mix), and *Reel to Real Sessions*. Unfortunately, the latter two sources omit the start of the count-in.

1984: The radio documentary *Sgt. Pepper's Lonely Hearts Club Band: A History of the Beatle Years 1962–1970* included **J**. This was copied onto bootlegs such as *Not For Sale* and *Ultra Rare Trax, Volume 3*, both of which tacked the piano edit piece onto the end. Note that the widely pirated copy of the special had reversed channels, and so do the bootlegs derived from it.

1988: The vinyl bootleg *Ultra Rare Trax, Volume 5 & 6* included an excellent copy of **G** and **H**, although the latter segued abruptly into "What's the New Mary Jane"; both appeared from a tape source the following year on the CD *Not Guilty*. Also in 1988, the first release of **L** with a clean intro (no applause effects overlaid) occurred on the *Imagine: John Lennon* soundtrack album. This same version was included on the 1993 CD *The Beatles 1967–1970*.

1989: The bootleg CD *Unsurpassed Masters, Volume 3* contained complete and excellent-quality tapes of **F–H**.

2003: **M** was released on the soundtrack of the *Anthology* DVD. The same year, **E** was booted on the CD *Rare Tracks*.

2004: Excellent copies of **C–K** were bootlegged on the CD *A Day in the Life*. The same year, **A** surfaced in the rough cut of *Anthology*, which circulates on video.

2006: **N** was released on the *Love* CD.

17. Studio session

Date: 1 March 1967
Time: 7:00 p.m.–2:15 a.m.
Location: EMI Studio 2
Producer: George Martin

[A.] Lucy in the Sky with Diamonds—take 6 (stereo) (1:01)

Having borrowed from newspaper articles, TV jingles, and antique circus posters for recent songwriting inspiration, John turned to his son Julian. The three-year-old's description of a portrait of classmate Lucy O'Donnell served as a springboard for John and Paul's sense of whimsy, and they constructed a surreal landscape from such phrases as "marmalade skies," "kaleidoscope eyes," and "newspaper taxis."

Eight hours of rehearsal on February 28 produced no usable recordings of "Lucy in the Sky with Diamonds," and were mostly later erased. *Life* magazine had a reporter present that evening and quoted George Martin as saying, "We are light years away from anything tonight . . . They know it is awful now, and they're trying to straighten it out. It may be a week before they're pleased, if ever."

On March 1, seven rhythm track takes were recorded, with George's acoustic guitar and occasional piano from George Martin on track 1, Paul playing Lowrey organ, including the opening passage, on track 2, Ringo's drums on track 3, and John playing maracas and singing a guide vocal (remaining silent for the refrain) on track 4. This is all heard in take 6 (**A**).

By take 7, the piano part was omitted from the arrangement. Track 4 of this "best" take was erased and replaced with a tamboura drone, and all four tracks were reduced to a single track for take 8, ready for more overdubs the following day.

RELEASE HISTORY

1992: **A** originates from the TV special *The Making of Sgt. Pepper*, wherein Paul and George Martin played back the original session tape, fiddling around with the individual tracks. This also appeared on the vinyl bootleg *Arrive without Travelling* later that year, and from tape source on the CD *Arrive without Aging* in 1993.

18. Studio session

Date: 2 March 1967
Time: 7:00 p.m.–3:30 a.m.
Location: EMI Studio 2
Producer: George Martin

[A.] Lucy in the Sky with Diamonds—RS from takes 6, 7, and 8 (3:04)

[B.] Lucy in the Sky with Diamonds—RM4 (3:26)
Mixed: 3 March 1967

[C.] Lucy in the Sky with Diamonds—RS5 (3:25)
Mixed: 7 April 1967

[D.] Lucy in the Sky with Diamonds—RM20 (3:35)
Mixed: 1 November 1967

[E.] Lucy in the Sky with Diamonds—RS from takes 7 and 8 (#1) (3:26)

[F.] Lucy in the Sky with Diamonds—RS from takes 7 and 8 (#2) (4:10)

The finishing touches to "Lucy in the Sky with Diamonds" were added this evening, all recorded at different slow speeds to sound higher-pitched on playback. Paul added bass and George some lead guitar through a Leslie speaker, all on track 4. John then taped two lead vocal tracks, supported each time by Paul's harmony, on tracks 2 and 3, and the song was wrapped up. Eleven mono mixes done that evening were rejected, possibly because John wanted more "flanging" (ADT with speed manipulation to create a psychedelic wobble), and he got plenty of it in the final mono mix created the following day (**B**); no other mix has nearly as much of that effect.

The *Songtrack* remix (**E**) is similar to the original, but with the drums from take 7 isolated and centered. *Anthology 2* (**A**) offers the complete unused take 6, with the tamboura overdub from take 7 added. In addition, since John hadn't sung on the refrain, the chorus vocals from take 8 are mixed in where needed. The *Love* remix (**F**) incorporates horns and guitar from "Sgt. Pepper's Lonely Hearts Club Band," Clavioline from "Baby You're a Rich Man," and effects from "Tomorrow Never Knows," before cross-fading to a remix of the orchestral backing from "Good Night."

Finally, there is a unique mix (**D**) created by Geoff Emerick for the producers of the *Yellow Submarine* film on November 1. This mixes out John's vocal for the first verse and replaces it with a newly written verse, in similar nonsensical style, sung by Dick Emery, the voice of Jeremy Boob in the film. The new lyrics, penned by scriptwriter Erich Segal, were never used because, according to Segal, John refused to share the songwriting royalties.

RELEASE HISTORY

1967: **B** and **C** were released on mono and stereo pressings, respectively, of the LP *Sgt. Pepper's Lonely Hearts Club Band.* The latter is on EMI's CD of the same title.

1994: An excellent copy of **D,** complete with Geoff Emerick's announcement, surfaced on the bootleg *Secret Songs in Pepperland,* soon copied as *The Lost Pepperland Reel.*

1996: **A** was released on the CD *Anthology 2.*

1999: **E** was included on Apple's *Yellow Submarine Songtrack.*

2006: **F** was released on the *Love* CD.

19. Studio session

Date: 6 March 1967
Time: 7:00 p.m.–12:30 a.m.
Location: EMI Studio 2
Producer: George Martin

[A.] Sgt. Pepper's Lonely Hearts Club Band—take 10 (stereo) (1:23)

[B.] Sgt. Pepper's Lonely Hearts Club Band—RM3 (2:01)

[C.] Sgt. Pepper's Lonely Hearts Club Band—RS8 (2:02)
Mixed: 6 March 1967

[D.] Sgt. Pepper's Lonely Hearts Club Band—RS from takes 9 and 10 (2:00)

[E.] Sgt. Pepper's Lonely Hearts Club Band—take 10, track 1 (2:27)

[F.] Sgt. Pepper's Lonely Hearts Club Band—take 10, track 2 (2:27)

[G.] Sgt. Pepper's Lonely Hearts Club Band—take 10, track 3 (2:27)

[H.] Sgt. Pepper's Lonely Hearts Club Band—take 10, track 4 (2:27)

George Martin's arrangement for four French horns was recorded onto track 3 of the new LP's title song on

March 3. *Beatles Book Monthly* photographer Leslie Bryce captured the proceedings on film and John captured the discussion and rehearsals on tape again (see the January 9 entry), from the control room. Paul's lead guitar was also punched in to track 3 that evening, bringing the song to musical completion.

As with most of *Pepper,* however, the song needed a final layer of icing. As the sergeant's band was ostensibly putting on a concert, why not add applause and other audience effects? This was done on March 6. First the sound of an orchestra warming up, taken from one of the four February 10 reels of the "A Day in the Life" session, was dubbed onto track 2. The other effects, including crowd ambience, laughter, and applause, came from the Abbey Road sound effects library. They were added on track 2 throughout the song and can be heard in isolation on the bootleg *The Lost Pepperland Reel,* from a copy made November 1 for the producers of the film *Yellow Submarine.*

Mono and stereo mixes were both perfected that night; the mono (**B**) has the lead guitar mixed louder on the final verse as well as slightly different audience effects. In the original stereo mix (**C**), Paul's lead vocal is mixed to the right, and the backing vocals begin left and travel across the soundstage. The *Songtrack* remix (**D**) centers Paul's lead vocal and splits the backing vocals from take 9 between the left and right channels. The isolated multitracks that recently surfaced (**E–H**) carry on well past the song's usual ending.

RELEASE HISTORY

1967: **B** and **C** were released on mono and stereo pressings, respectively, of the LP *Sgt. Pepper's Lonely Hearts Club Band.* The latter is on EMI's CD of the same title.

1992: **A** originates from the TV special *The Making of Sgt. Pepper,* wherein George Martin played back the original session tape, briefly isolating the vocal and horn tracks. This also appeared on the vinyl bootleg *Arrive without Travelling* later that year, and from tape source on the CD *Arrive without Aging* in 1993.

1999: **D** was included on Apple's *Yellow Submarine Songtrack.*

2007: **E–H** appeared on the CD-R *Sgt. Pepper Deluxe.*

20. Radio interview   J, P

Date: 20 March 1967
Time: 7:00 p.m.
Location: EMI Studio 2
Interviewer: Brian Matthew
Broadcast: 27 March 1967, 2:00–3:00 p.m.
BBC Light Programme
The Ivor Novello Awards for 1966
Length: 7:07

Beginning in 1965, Capitol Records sporadically distributed a pop music magazine, *Teen Set,* covering artists on all labels but with a healthy dose of Beatles content. Editor Judith Sims traveled to London to cover the *Sgt. Pepper* sessions and was present this evening as John and Paul recorded BBC Radio interviews and then overdubbed lead vocals on "She's Leaving Home." No other Beatles arrived for the session, although John's cousin Stanley was visiting.

The session began with Brian Matthew conducting the interviews, accompanied by two other BBC employees. A reel of EMI tape was used, the interviews being spliced out from the mono reel by George Martin and taken back to a BBC studio for further production. For the fourth straight year, the Beatles had won several Ivor Novello music awards, and only once had any of them bothered to attend the ceremony (in July 1965 Paul made an appearance, and John forgot to show up).

Unsurprisingly, given their much lower profile, none of them accepted the invitation in 1967 to the March 23 festivities, their excuse being that the ceremony was held "too early in the day." Instead, John and Paul consented to accept the awards on tape and talk briefly about each song. The tape was then played back during the ceremony at the BBC's Playhouse Theatre in London, and the whole event was broadcast four days later.

First up is the citation for best-selling single A-side of 1966 for "Yellow Submarine," although as it was a double A-side with "Eleanor Rigby" in Britain, it's not clear how they picked one title over the other. Paul explains how he came up with the idea for the song with Ringo in mind, combining his chorus with John's verse melody. Matthew wonders whether Paul used to play this song on the piano to his nephews, and Paul deadpans, "No, that's all wrong. That was Mozart's Piano Concerto."

"Michelle" is awarded most performed song of 1966, and John reminisces about borrowing an idea for its middle eight from another artist's song (Nina Simone, although they don't reveal this). Paul jokes that most of their songs are pinched from somewhere, but is afraid to elaborate in case the PRS (Performing Rights Society) are listening.

Amazingly, although it was released in July 1965, "Yesterday" had been performed often enough in 1966 by other artists to win runner-up to "Michelle." For not the last time in his life, Paul relates the tale of the working title, "Scrambled Egg," intriguingly stating that John came up with the title "Yesterday." He also claims to have written it "on a medieval guitar" rather than the usual piano. Matthew reveals that four hundred cover versions of "Yesterday" were already released ("We did three hundred versions of it," says Paul), and presses them to pick a favorite. John can only insist Paul's performance is preeminent and complains that Andy Williams's version botched the string arrangement.

In between each of these interview clips, Brian Matthew is heard at the actual ceremony presenting the awards (to Tony Barrow, EMI's Ron White, and Northern Songs' Dick James and Lionel Conway) and introducing the various acts performing each song live, accompanied by the Joe Loss Orchestra.

RELEASE HISTORY

1999: A good-quality off-line tape of this broadcast was included on the CD-R compilation *Vinyl to the Core*. Its subsequent appearance on *Mythology, Volume 3* sounds similar and has some bits missing from the earlier release, but is in turn missing a few words present on *Vinyl to the Core*. Both sources have the complete pretaped Beatle interviews intact.

21. Radio interview   J, P

Date:	20 March 1967
Time:	7:00 p.m.
Location:	EMI Studio 2
Interviewer:	Brian Matthew
Broadcast:	*Top Of The Pops* #127
Length:	5:15

Brian Matthew was still hosting *Top of the Pops* radio programs for BBC Radio's Overseas Transcription Service, and he chose that venue to broadcast this exclusive interview with John and Paul, taped immediately after the Ivor Novello discussions above.

The chat begins with an analysis of the failure of "Penny Lane"/"Strawberry Fields Forever" to top the British charts (although it did achieve this feat according to *Melody Maker*'s calculations). Paul doesn't sound fazed in the least to have been beaten out by Engelbert Humperdinck's "Release Me," hiply proclaiming, "That's a completely different scene altogether." John and Paul then vaguely describe the songs completed so far for *Sgt. Pepper*, including some "happy-go-lucky Northern songs" ("Only a Northern Song"?) and making reference to one with "medieval guitar," which must have confused overseas listeners who hadn't heard the Ivor Novello broadcast. They also praise the recently taped "Within You Without You," calling it "a great Indian one."

Paul makes passing reference to a TV show and a film being their next projects (and denies that he and John are writing a musical); presumably he had the proposed *Pepper* special in mind, as the *Magical Mystery Tour* was still a few weeks from conception. Predictably, Matthew wonders about future tours, and while John bluntly says they're out of the question, Paul diplomatically suggests performing a juggling act in brightly colored suits while five tape machines play Beatle melodies!

RELEASE HISTORY

1988: This interview was broadcast in the December 31 episode of BBC Radio's *The Beeb's Lost Beatles Tapes*. It appears in excellent quality on the bootleg *The Beatles Broadcast Collection, Trailer 2*, and a bit of it was used in the *Anthology* home video documentary. Since Mark Lewisohn reports the original Transcription Disc used only four minutes of chat with John and Paul, we actually have all of it for a change (with the introduction and two segments of "Penny Lane" accounting for the other 75 seconds).

22. Studio session

Date:	20 March 1967
Time:	7:00 p.m.–3:30 a.m.
Location:	EMI Studio 2
Producer:	George Martin

[A.] She's Leaving Home—edit of RM6 (3:24)
Mixed: 20 March 1967

[B.] She's Leaving Home—edit of RS6 (3:33)
Mixed: 17 April 1967

[C.] She's Leaving Home—take 9, track 1 (3:38)
[D.] She's Leaving Home—take 9, track 2 (3:38)
[E.] She's Leaving Home—take 9, track 3 (3:38)
[F.] She's Leaving Home—take 9, track 4 (3:38)

John and Paul had written "She's Leaving Home" after reading the story of real-life runaway teen Melanie Coe in the February 27 edition of the *Daily Mail* (see the October 4, 1963, entry). Paul came up with the verses, and John contributed the chorus lines from the girl's lamenting parents. Although the melody was probably composed on his piano, Paul felt a string arrangement would be more suitable. When he found that George Martin was unwilling to drop prior commitments (to oversee a Cilla Black recording session) at a moment's notice, Paul impatiently turned to independent producer Mike Leander.

To his credit, Martin swallowed his pride and agreed to conduct Leander's score on March 17. This was perfected in six takes, although the initial take was eventually chosen as "best," with the harp going on track 1, the double-bass on track 2, four violins on track 3, and two violas and two cellos on track 4.

On March 20, take 1 was reduced into take 9, with tracks 1 and 3 combined and tracks 2 and 4 combined.

This left two tracks: one for Paul to sing his lead vocal, accompanied by John, their voices overlapping to suitable narrative effect, and one for his and John's doubled vocals (on the refrains). Mono mixing was completed that evening, vari-speeded as usual to raise the pitch from E to nearly F major. They forgot to do this for the stereo mix (**B**), which consequently runs several seconds longer. In addition, each mix had two cello passages chopped out (at 1:17 and 2:30 in **B**), so George Martin did get a touch of revenge on Mike Leander in the end! These excised passages can be heard in the uncut multi-track isolations (**C**–**F**) that have recently surfaced.

RELEASE HISTORY

1967: **A** and **B** were released on mono and stereo pressings, respectively, of the LP *Sgt. Pepper's Lonely Hearts Club Band*. The latter is on EMI's CD of the same title.

2007: **C**–**F** appeared on the CD-R *Sgt. Pepper Deluxe*.

23. Studio session

Date: 21 March 1967
Time: 7:00 p.m.–2:45 a.m.
Location: EMI Studio 2
Producer: George Martin

[A.] Lovely Rita—edit of RM11/14 (2:43)
Mixed: 21 March 1967

[B.] Lovely Rita—RS2 (2:40)
Mixed: 17 April 1967

Paul came up with the idea for "Lovely Rita" after hearing the Americentric term *meter maid* and began composing it while visiting his brother Michael in Liverpool, although the lyrics were unfinished when he brought it into the studio February 23. The backing was recorded that night in eight takes: George and John's acoustic guitars on tracks 1 and 2, Ringo's drums on track 3, and Paul's piano on track 4. These were all reduced to track 1 of a new tape, called take 9, with the tape running at a slow speed. This increased the pitch from C major to D major. Paul added his bass part on a second track, and the vocals were left for the following day.

Beatles Book Monthly photographer Leslie Bryce was present on the twenty-fourth, and a report on the session appeared in its sister publication, *Beat Monthly*. Other visitors that evening included Tony Hicks of the Hollies, David Crosby of the Byrds, NEMS

employee Tony Bramwell, and Ravi Shankar's brother. John and Paul then gathered with Mal and Neil in a corner of Studio 2 to complete the lyrics for "Lovely Rita." In one photo from the session, Paul is seen holding the original manuscript, and a reproduction of that sheet shows that he had only the opening chorus and verse completed, in which Rita filled in a ticket "with her little blue pen." Below that, a couple more rough verses are transcribed in Mal's handwriting, including the unused rhyme "now I go to meet her."

With the words completed, Paul added his lead vocal on track 3, again recorded with the tape running slow to sound higher-pitched. The *Beat Monthly* report claims that David Crosby assisted with the vocals, but any contributions he made were obviously not used. Instead John, Paul, and George added backing vocals March 7, as well as humming through EMI regulation toilet-paper-and-combs, and injecting the moaning and heavy breathing over the song's coda. All of this went onto track 4, and the song was nearly done but Paul couldn't decide what instrument should play the solo in the middle.

This was solved on March 21 when George Martin "dropped in" a piano solo on track 4. This was played in B major, as the tape was slowed way down during the overdub to allow for a more honky-tonk feel, aided by wrapping a bit of adhesive tape around the capstan of the machine to vacillate the sound as it recorded. Mono mixes were completed that night, and stereo mixes nearly a month later. With the backing track, bass, vocals, and piano all being performed in different keys, they must have figured it would make little difference if they sped up the mixes as well, and the result is a song that plays back somewhere around E-flat major, even though none of it was performed that way.

RELEASE HISTORY

1967: **A** and **B** were released on mono and stereo pressings, respectively, of the LP *Sgt. Pepper's Lonely Hearts Club Band*. The latter is on EMI's CD of the same title.

24. Studio session

Date:	23 March 1967
Time:	7:00 p.m.–3:45 a.m.
Location:	EMI Studio 2
Producer:	Peter Vince

[A.] Getting Better—RM3 (2:46)
Mixed: 23 March 1967

[B.] Getting Better—RS1 (2:46)
Mixed: 17 April 1967

"Getting Better" married Paul's optimism to John's cynicism and set the result to a bouncy beat, sounding closer than any other song on *Sgt. Pepper* to 1964-era Beatles. Despite the relative simplicity of its structure, the tale of the song's recording is confusing and involved.

On March 9, the basic rhythm was recorded in seven takes, with Paul's rhythm guitar and Ringo's drums going onto one track, Paul's guide vocal on a second, and George Martin hitting the strings of an electric keyboard called a pianette on a third. Ringo then recorded extra drums on the fourth track of take 7. Three of these tracks (omitting the guide vocal) were reduced to a single track of a new tape, with take 12 being the "best" reduction.

March 10 saw the remaining three tracks filled as follows: Ringo's extra snare and bass drum on track 2, Paul's bass on track 3, and George's tamboura on track

4. These were reduced again on March 21, with the rhythm and tamboura on track 1 and bass and drum overdubs going to track 2. Visitors that evening included Dick James, Peter Brown, and Ivan Vaughan, the mutual mate who had introduced Paul to John ten years earlier. Ex–Beatle engineer Norman Smith even dropped by with a new group he was producing, Pink Floyd.

Attempts to fill the other two tracks with vocals that night were unsuccessful, largely due to John's mistakenly taking a couple of tabs of acid and being led to the roof of the studio by an unsuspecting George Martin. Paul fetched him down, drove him home, and they "stayed up all night, sat around, and hallucinated a lot," as Paul later put it.

The vocals were completed March 23, and amazingly a third reduction was done, combining the two vocal tracks to free space for more overdubs. These included handclaps, congas, a bit of piano, and further electric guitar (all heard in the right channel of **B**). The completed mono and stereo mixes have no noteworthy differences.

RELEASE HISTORY

1967: **A** and **B** were released on mono and stereo pressings, respectively, of the LP *Sgt. Pepper's Lonely Hearts Club Band*. The latter is on EMI's CD of the same title.

25. Studio session

Date:	29 March 1967
Time:	7:00 p.m.–5:45 a.m.
Location:	EMI Studio 2
Producer:	George Martin

[A.] Good Morning Good Morning—take 11 (stereo) (0:33)

[B.] Good Morning Good Morning—RM2 (2:35)

[C.] Good Morning Good Morning—RS5 (2:41)
Mixed: 6 April 1967

When we left "Good Morning Good Morning," the song consisted of a scalding rhythm track and a solitary lead vocal. On March 13, this was supplemented with some horns, played by members of the group Sounds Inc, long-time road mates of the Beatles. Three saxes, two trombones, and a French horn all went onto the third track of the tape, with heavy limiting and compression of the signal.

On March 28, John filled the final track with a second lead vocal, harmonizing nicely with himself in places. A second reduction combined both vocal tracks and freed a track for overdubs of backing vocals and Paul's stinging guitar solo. Listen carefully around

2:10 in the song as the backing vocalists begin singing the title refrain in German!

Perhaps inspired by the Beach Boys' *Pet Sounds,* John then decided to assemble an array of animal noises to be overlaid at the end of the song. The opening rooster crow at least made sense, both in the context of the song's title and the Kellogg's ad that inspired it. But the main effects were akin to someone opening all the cages in a zoo. Beginning with twittering birds, we hear a howling cat, a *meow* transmuting into barking, horses whinnying, sheep bleating, tigers growling, an elephant call, a fox hunt (with some *baa's* and *moo's* mixed in for good measure), ending with a pig grunting. This effects tape, copied intact for the producers of the *Yellow Submarine* film on November 1, 1967, can be heard in isolation on the bootleg *The Lost Pepperland Reel.*

The effects were assembled on March 28 and twenty-ninth and overdubbed onto the lead vocal track of "Good Morning Good Morning" on the latter day. On April 6, mono and stereo mixes were finalized; the mono mix (**B**) has the lead guitar mixed down a bit sooner at the end of the solo. The stereo mix (**C**) has an extra 6 seconds of the effects tape before the edit to the chicken cluck that provided a link to the reprise of the title track.

RELEASE HISTORY

1967: **B** and **C** were released on mono and stereo pressings, respectively, of the LP *Sgt. Pepper's Lonely Hearts Club Band.* The latter is on EMI's CD of the same title.

1992: **A** originates from the TV special *The Making of Sgt. Pepper,* wherein George Martin played back the original session tape, briefly isolating the effects track. This also appeared on the vinyl bootleg *Arrive without Travelling* later that year, and from tape source on the CD *Arrive without Aging* in 1993.

26. Studio session

Date: 30 March 1967
Time: 11:00 p.m.–7:30 a.m.
Location: EMI Studio 2
Producer: George Martin

[A.] With a Little Help from My Friends— RM15 (2:43)
Mixed: 31 March 1967

[B.] With a Little Help from My Friends— RS3 (2:43)
Mixed: 7 April 1967

[C.] With a Little Help from My Friends— RS from takes 10 and 11 (2:43)
[D.] With a Little Help from My Friends— take 11, track 1 (2:51)
[E.] With a Little Help from My Friends— take 11, track 2 (2:51)
[F.] With a Little Help from My Friends— take 11, track 3 (2:51)
[G.] With a Little Help from My Friends— take 11, track 4 (2:51)

The March 29 session was attended once again by Judith Sims, reporting for *Teen Set,* as well as by photographers for *Beatles Book Monthly.* Sims's article describes a jam session with John and Paul on guitars and Ringo on drums, some overdubbing for "Being for the Benefit of Mr. Kite!" (see the following entry), Ringo playing back a home demo on his portable cassette, and Paul running through a new song he had written at home that afternoon for Ringo (aka Billy Shears), with a little help from John and others. At this stage it had the working title "Bad Finger Boogie."

They began by perfecting the rhythm track in ten takes, with Paul's piano on track 1, George's rhythm guitar on track 2, Ringo's drums and John's cowbell on track 3, and George Martin playing organ on track 4. A tape reduction into take 11 combined all this work to track 1 (**D**), and Ringo added his lead vocal to tracks 3 and 4 of the new tape, with John, Paul, and George assisting for the call-and-response passages. With the clock approaching 6 a.m., everyone went home for a few hours' rest.

March 30 was largely occupied shooting the *Sgt. Pepper* album cover, but around 11 p.m., the Beatles straggled over to Abbey Road for more work on Ringo's tune, now officially titled "With a Little Help from My Friends." Camera Press photographer Frank Hermann captured the group having a midnight snack and listening to playbacks. A series of overdubs was performed for track 2 of the tape (**E**). For the song's intro, a snare drum and timpani heralded the arrival of Billy Shears, and for the body of the song, Paul added bass, George lead guitar, and Ringo a tambourine.

Ringo's track 3 vocal was then erased by an overdub (**F**) of John and Paul's vocal harmonies and a guitar fill from George (just before the second verse). Finally, organ and vocal overdubs for the Billy Shears intro were punched in on tracks 3 and 4 (**G**), prior to Ringo's vocal entrance.

Remixing began the next day, doubling Ringo's vocal with ADT, and the final mixes were cross-faded with the LP's title track to help solidify the concept of the "show." The *Songtrack* remix (**C**) separates the piano/organ, drums/cowbell, and guitar tracks from take 10 and syncs them with the overdubs from take 11.

RELEASE HISTORY

1967: **A** and **B** were released on mono and stereo pressings, respectively, of the LP *Sgt. Pepper's Lonely Hearts Club Band.* The latter is on EMI's CD of the same title.

1999: **C** was included on Apple's *Yellow Submarine Songtrack.*

2007: **D–G** appeared on the CD-R *Sgt. Pepper Deluxe.*

27. Studio session

Date: 31 March 1967
Time: 7:00 p.m.–3:00 a.m.
Location: EMI Studio 2
Producer: George Martin

[A.] Being for the Benefit of Mr. Kite!—edit of takes 7 and 9 (stereo) (2:43)

[B.] Being for the Benefit of Mr. Kite!— take 9 (stereo) (0:56)

[C.] Being for the Benefit of Mr. Kite!— RM4 (2:33)
Mixed: 31 March 1967

[D.] Being for the Benefit of Mr. Kite!—RS8 (2:34)
Mixed: 7 April 1967

[E.] Being for the Benefit of Mr. Kite!—RS from take 9 (1:23)

[F.] Being for the Benefit of Mr. Kite!/I Want You (She's So Heavy)/Helter Skelter (3:22)

After sitting on the shelf for more than a month, the multitrack of "Being for the Benefit of Mr. Kite!" was dusted off for further overdubs on March 28, all on the vacant track 3 of take 9. In the first half of the song, John played a few organ chords while George, Ringo, Mal, and Neil contributed on harmonicas of various sizes, and George Martin added some Mellotron. The waltz-tempo middle of the song had an overdub of tambourine, Paul on guitar, John playing an oom-pah-pah organ piece, and George Martin a cascading stream of notes on a second organ, all recorded with the tape running at half speed and sounding dementedly squeaky on playback. Piano chords were also overdubbed for the transition from the waltz back into the final verse.

Judging from photographs and Judith Sims's report, the organ/harmonica sections were thickened up on March 29, with George Martin playing the organ and John and George on harmonicas. This was likely dropped into track 4 between the lead vocals. Organ was added on that track for the last portion of the song, carrying the melody underneath what would be the penultimate overdub.

All these harmonicas, organs, and harmonium were not enough to provide a suitable circus ambience; to this end, George Martin and Geoff Emerick had assembled an effects reel on February 20 consisting of dozens of tape snippets of real calliopes and steam organs playing various tunes. Each section of tape was distorted in some way, either turned backwards or sped up or slowed down to create a random noise but no recognizable tune. This effects tape was added to the end of track 3, and on March 31 the finishing touch of a closing organ and glockenspiel flourish brought the Pablo Fanques Fair to its fruition.

The mono mix (**C**) has the effects tape mixed louder during the waltz but quieter during the end of the song compared to the stereo (**D**). Both mixes are treated with ADT on the vocal. A much less lopsided mix (**E**) was done for the *Anthology* DVD, centering all the organs and vocals that had been shoved over to the right channel on the original stereo mix. The *Love* remix (**F**) includes most of the song before segueing into a mashup comprised primarily of the coda from "I Want You (She's So Heavy)" and vocals from "Helter Skelter," along with more "Kite" effects.

Anthology 2 offers up the basic take 7 (**A**), crossfading at 2:25 to tracks 3 and 4 from take 9. This is all prefaced by some interesting chat that preceded take 7. While Paul exhorts John to sing the lyrics "as though you know about the show," George asks about a glass of water Ringo has and jokingly wonders whether he's put any acid in it!

RELEASE HISTORY

1967: **C** and **D** were released on mono and stereo pressings, respectively, of the LP *Sgt. Pepper's Lonely Hearts Club Band.* The latter is on EMI's CD of the same title.

1992: **B** originates from the TV special *The Making of Sgt. Pepper,* wherein George Martin played back the original session tape, briefly isolating the effects and organ tracks. This also appeared on the vinyl bootleg

Arrive without Travelling later that year, and from tape source on the CD *Arrive without Aging* in 1993.

1996: **A** was released on the CD *Anthology 2*.

2003: **E** was released on the soundtrack of the *Anthology* DVD.

2006: **F** was released on the *Love* CD.

28. Studio session

Date:	1 April 1967
Time:	7:00 p.m.–6:00 a.m.
Location:	EMI Studio 1
Producer:	George Martin

[A.] Sgt. Pepper's Lonely Hearts Club Band (Reprise)—take 5 (mono) (1:25)

[B.] Sgt. Pepper's Lonely Hearts Club Band (Reprise)—take 5 (stereo) (1:22)

[C.] Sgt. Pepper's Lonely Hearts Club Band (Reprise)—RM9 (1:19)

Mixed: 1 April 1967

[D.] Sgt. Pepper's Lonely Hearts Club Band (Reprise)—RS10 (1:18)

Mixed: 20 April 1967

[E.] Sgt. Pepper's Lonely Hearts Club Band (Reprise)—RS from take 9 (1:22)

Longtime Beatles road manager Neil Aspinall came up with the idea of reprising the *Sgt. Pepper* title track. Having watched Paul make his usual "thank you all for coming" announcement prior to several hundred performances of "Long Tall Sally" and "I'm Down," he realized it would be appropriate for the Lonely Hearts Club Band to do likewise before their final number. Paul quickly fashioned up some suitable lyrics and the band's alter egos made short work of recording it.

On April 1, with the rest of the album nearly complete, nine takes of the hard-rocking backing were taped in the cavernous Studio 1. Each Beatle played his standard instrument as an ensemble, for the only time on the album, while someone (probably George Martin) joined in on organ. Paul also sang a rough guide vocal on each take, though this would later be erased. All this can be heard in the unused take 5, mixed to mono (even though it occupied three of the tape's tracks) on *Anthology 2* (**A**), and in stereo (but buried beneath dialogue) on the *Anthology* DVD (**B**). With take 9, fresh vocals from John, Paul, and George went onto track 3, maracas and tambourine were added to track 4, and the song was finished.

During mixing, the vocals were treated with ADT, and some of the audience effects tape prepared March 6 was added to the song's intro; this differs slightly on each released mix. Further cheering from this tape helped to disguise the cross-fade into "A Day in the Life." The mono mix (**C**) has Paul's excited shouting over the final chords mixed much louder than its stereo counterpart. In addition, the latter (**D**) edits out half a bar of rhythm just before the count-in, perhaps to remove a stray but indecipherable comment from John. The *Love* remix (**E**) begins over the orchestral chords from the coda of "Hey Jude" and centers everything apart from the percussion track.

RELEASE HISTORY

1967: **C** and **D** were released on mono and stereo pressings, respectively, of the LP *Sgt. Pepper's Lonely Hearts Club Band*. The latter is on EMI's CD of the same title.

1996: **A** was released on the CD *Anthology 2*.

2003: **B** was released on the soundtrack of the *Anthology* DVD.

2006: **E** was released on the *Love* CD.

29. Studio session

Date:	3 April 1967
Time:	7:30 p.m.–3:00 a.m.
Location:	EMI Studio 1
Producer:	George Martin

[A.] Within You Without You—take 2 (stereo) (1:06)

[B.] Within You Without You—RS from takes 1 and 2 (#1) (5:24)

[C.] Within You Without You—RS from takes 1 and 2 (#2) (1:35)

As February turned to March and the finished recordings began to accumulate, it seemed less and less likely that George's "Only a Northern Song" would make the cut (see the April 20 entry). To replace it, George had written a new song with much weightier lyrics, composed on a harmonium at Klaus Voormann's house. A photo from the March 3 session shows George at a keyboard, presumably playing his new composition for Ravi Shankar's brother.

By March 15, he was ready to record the backing track to the still-untitled song, assisted by several musicians from the Asian Music Circle on traditional Indian instruments. Several tambouras, including two played by George himself and Neil Aspinall, provided a drone on track 1. Track 2 contained tabla and swarmandal, while track 4 had a dilruba playing the melody line. The song was broken up into three distinct parts, the middle improvised section played in ⅝ time sandwiched by the first and last sections of George's written verses. This was all recorded in a single take, lasting 6:25 at this stage.

By March 22, the song was officially titled "Within You Without You" on the recording sheets. That evening, two more dilrubas were added on track 3, recorded with the tape running fast to sound lower in pitch on playback. A reduction into take 2 that night combined all the dilrubas onto track 2 and the other instruments onto track 1. A demo remix was made of the reduction to aid George Martin in scoring the song for Western classical instruments.

On April 3, with George the sole Beatle in attendance, eight violins and three cellos did an excellent job complementing the dilrubas in their overdub (entering at 1:13) on track 3. To wrap things up, George taped his lead vocal, and some sitar in the song's middle, on track 4. Initial remixing began that night but would be perfected the following day.

The new mix presented on *Anthology 2* (**B**) spreads out the instruments from take 1, with tambouras left, tabla centered, and one dilruba track in each channel, with the swarmandal passages panned across the soundstage. Synced up with all this are the latter portion of the violin/cello performance (entering at 2:56) and George's sitar, leaving his lead vocal unrepresented. Another mix on the *Anthology* DVD (**C**) syncs the tambouras (left), the tabla and swarmandal (center), and the dilrubas (right) from take 1 with strings and the vocal from take 2 (centered).

RELEASE HISTORY

1992: **A** originates from the TV special *The Making of Sgt. Pepper,* wherein George Martin played back the original session tape, briefly isolating the various tracks. This also appeared on the vinyl bootleg *Arrive without Travelling* later that year, and from tape source on the CD *Arrive without Aging* in 1993.

1996: **B** was released on the CD *Anthology 2*.

2003: **C** was released on the soundtrack of the *Anthology* DVD.

30. Studio session

Date: 4 April 1967
Time: 7:00 p.m.–12:45 a.m.
Location: EMI Studio 2
Producer: George Martin

[A.] Within You Without You—edit of RM10/12 (5:06)
[B.] Within You Without You—edit of RS3/5 (5:04)
Mixed: 4 April 1967

[C.] Within You Without You/Tomorrow Never Knows (3:08)

In best *Pepper* tradition, all the mixes of "Within You Without You" were sped up, raising the key from C major to C-sharp. In addition, part one of the song was mixed as a separate entity to parts two and three and edited together, resulting in the removal of about a minute from the song's running time. The edit, occurring at 2:23 in each mix, is quite obvious, although it was done much more smoothly on the mono mix (**A**). The lead vocal was treated with ADT, and George decided to add a tape of laughter to the end of the song; this effect sounds slightly different on each mix.

The *Love* CD includes a mashup (**C**) consisting of the "Tomorrow Never Knows" rhythm track overlaid with George's vocal and much of the instrumentation from "Within You Without You," ending with effects from "Tomorrow Never Knows," backwards vocals from "Rain," and organ notes from "Lucy in the Sky with Diamonds."

RELEASE HISTORY

1967: **A** and **B** were released on mono and stereo pressings, respectively, of the LP *Sgt. Pepper's Lonely Hearts Club Band*. The latter is on EMI's CD of the same title.

2006: **C** was released on the *Love* CD.

31. Amateur footage

Date: 5–9 April 1967
Location: San Francisco and Denver
Length: 23:28

Jane Asher was currently touring the United States with the Old Vic Company, performing *Romeo and Juliet*. Paul decided to surprise her with a visit for her twenty-first birthday; he and Mal left London on Air France on April 3, bound for Los Angeles via Paris. In Los Angeles, they were met by a private Learjet (reportedly Frank Sinatra's, but with an NBC News logo), which would shuttle them around for the week.

They spent the fourth in San Francisco, where Paul did some record shopping and sightseeing and jammed with Jefferson Airplane. Paul and Mal had both brought Canon 8 mm home movie cameras and the next few days are documented in Mal's surviving footage (Paul's was reportedly stolen by fans), from a reel labeled "Mal plane trip Paul."

It opens at San Francisco Airport on the fifth as they board the Lear; Paul signs autographs for the pilot and his family. On arrival in Denver, they are met by Bert Rosenthal, who would lend Paul and Jane his house for their stay. As they stand beside a silver limo on the tarmac, Paul lifts his pants leg to reveal his socks for Mal!

From the sixth, we see Paul and Jane in the Rocky Mountains, relaxing by a creek and walking barefoot through the snow. After further adventures (see time line for details), Jane departed to continue her tour on the ninth. The next available footage is from that afternoon, as Paul and Mal travel from the Driftwood Motel (where Mal was staying, in room 15) down I-70 en route to Red Rocks Amphitheatre, scene of the Beatles' 1964 Denver concert.

RELEASE HISTORY

This silent color footage was released on the DVD *The Complete Mal Evans Silent Films*.

32. Amateur footage

Date: 10 April 1967
Location: Los Angeles
Length: 3:30

The journey continued on the evening of the ninth as the Learjet took Paul and Mal back to Los Angeles, where they would be spending a couple of days with their old pal Derek Taylor.

Mal's home movies documented the events of the tenth, probably coming from a reel labeled "Paul & D Taylor," which sold at auction. Paul, wearing a white suit and two-tone shoes, is seen filming Derek's children as they splash about in the Taylor swimming pool. Derek himself makes an appearance smoking a cigarette poolside. That afternoon, Paul and Mal went shopping at the newly opened Century Square Center, where Mal reportedly purchased a talking pillow!

Footage from this excursion shows Paul riding up an escalator and wandering through the plaza.

By the evening of the eleventh, they were ready to return to London. During the flight, Paul occupied himself by sketching out ideas for the next Beatles TV special. Such a project had been mentioned to Brian Matthew back on March 20, and one rejected idea was to assemble a one-hour show based on the *Sgt. Pepper's Lonely Hearts Club Band* album, using the February 10 footage and newly filmed material. That certainly would have been preferable to what Paul came up with.

RELEASE HISTORY

This silent color footage was released on the DVD *The Complete Mal Evans Silent Films*.

33. Studio session

Date: 20 April 1967
Time: 7:00 p.m.–2:15 a.m.
Location: EMI Studio 2
Producer: George Martin

[A.] Only a Northern Song—RS from takes 3 and 12 (2:43)

[B.] Only a Northern Song—RM6 (3:26)
Mixed: 21 April 1967

[C.] Only a Northern Song—RS1 (fake stereo) (3:21)
Mixed: 29 October 1968

[D.] Only a Northern Song—RS from takes 3 and 11 (3:22)

For a song with such humble lyrics, George's "Only a Northern Song" had a lot of work put into its recording, if not its actual performance. It started life as a potential candidate for the *Sgt. Pepper's Lonely Hearts Club Band* LP, and the basic track, including organ, tambourine, and drums, was taped on February 13, under the working title "Not Known." The best of nine attempts that day, take 3, was reduced to two tracks of a new tape the following day. This was done three times, with the final attempt, take 12, chosen as best for George to overdub two lead vocal tracks. At this stage the lyrics included a few lines that would be revised later: The "words" are not quite right, because "I wrote them myself," and the harmony is "off" because "I sing it myself."

In any case, something was definitely off, and the others probably breathed a sigh of relief when George came up with "Within You Without You" a few weeks later, and "Only a Northern Song" sat in this unfinished state until the album had been completed. On April 19, a demo mono mix was created—the producers of the *Yellow Submarine* film project were due to visit the studio the following day, and the Beatles decided this outtake, spruced up a bit, would be a suitable first contribution.

On April 20, the group returned to the original rhythm take 3 and erased two of the tracks, replacing one with a new bass overdub and the other with a cacophony of glockenspiel, whistling, and trumpet. The latter was played, very sped-up and very badly, by Paul, returning to his first instrument and proving he'd never mastered it. He later recalled, "The film producers were wandering around the studio and they had to sort of go along with this—I saw some very sad faces while I'm playing this trumpet."

With all the tracks full, the normal procedure would be to reduce them on a new tape to make room for vocals. Rather than do that, they pulled an unused reduction (take 11 from February 14) off the shelf. To this, George again sang two lead vocal tracks, joined on one by Paul adding still more trumpet, and with plenty of humming and throat-clearing. In place of take 11's drum track, further tumult was overdubbed, consisting of random piano tinklings, booming timpani, Mellotron, and a bit of organ.

Perhaps bitter about his song's rejection, George has shifted the narrative blame from himself to his fellow Beatles. Now it's the "band" who are not quite right, because "they just play it like that," and the harmony is "dark" because "there's nobody there." Near the end, George mocks Paul's horn skills with a "Take it, Eddie!" perhaps referring to the Blue Flames' trumpeter Eddie Thornton, who had played on "Got to Get You into My Life."

Two separate four-track tapes now existed: one with bass, trumpet, glockenspiel, and drums, and one with vocals and assorted noises. Both tapes contained the original organ track. Having successfully synchronized two four-track machines while mixing "A Day in the Life," they repeated the process on April 21 in creating the mono mixes for "Only a Northern Song." This gave the organ a much thicker sound, being doubled, but made a true stereo mix daunting. On November 15, 1967, the "best" of these mixes (**B**) was copied for the producers of *Yellow Submarine* and can be heard on bootlegs in all its monaural glory from that reel, complete with Geoff Emerick's slate call. Interestingly, the song as used in the film is slowed down a half step from the original key of A major for an unknown reason, even though it's at the correct speed on this mix.

When it came time to create the stereo mixes for the *Yellow Submarine* album, Emerick threw in the towel. Instead a "duophonic" mix (**C**) was created with the treble boosted in the left channel and bass frequencies to the right. With all the sonic sludge already present in the session tapes, this sounded bad enough, but the problem was compounded for the UK mono LP; rather than using the clean mono mix, this combined both channels of the "duophonic" to one unlistenable lump.

Time has been kinder to George's song, thanks to advances in digital technology that have made it easier to synchronize multiple tracks. For *Anthology,* three of the musical tracks from take 3 (organ, bass, drums) were synced up with the unused vocals from take 12 to create the song's first-ever true stereo mix (**A**). Even better is the *Songtrack* remix (**D**), which re-creates the elements of the released version, isolating the elements of take 3 (organ left, bass and drums center, and trumpet/glockenspiel right) but adding George's final vocals and the piano/timpani overdubs from take 11.

1969: C was released on stereo copies of the *Yellow Submarine* LP (and reduced to mono on UK monaural copies). It's available on the EMI CD of the same title.

1994: An excellent copy of **B** surfaced on the bootleg *Secret Songs in Pepperland,* soon copied as *The Lost Pepperland Reel.*

1996: A was officially released on *Anthology 2.*

1999: D was included on Apple's *Yellow Submarine Songtrack* CD.

34. Studio session

Date: 21 April 1967
Time: 7:00 p.m.–1:30 a.m.
Location: EMI Studio 2
Producer: George Martin

[A.] "Edit for LP End"—take 1 (0:03)

Not content to end the *Sgt. Pepper* album with an orchestral climax, protracted piano chord, and 15 kilocycle tone for pets, the Beatles wanted to employ the second side's run-out groove. To this end, they stood at the studio microphone and babbled simultaneously, even double-tracking the process, until a suitably meaningless 3 seconds were produced. This was chopped out and added to the master reel and then cut into British copies of the album; for some reason, Capitol was never sent this bit of nonsense. Since it and the high-pitched tone were added at the cutting stage (April 28 for the mono and May 1 for the stereo), U.S. copies of the album lacked both. The fact that the message was gibberish didn't stop fans from playing it backwards in an attempt to discern a hidden meaning, complete with a naughty word.

RELEASE HISTORY

1967: A was released on both mono and stereo pressings of the LP *Sgt. Pepper's Lonely Hearts Club Band* in the UK. It's on EMI's CD of the same title, looped and repeated for 23 seconds to simulate the sound of a turntable with no automatic phonograph arm return.

1980: Capitol finally released **A** on the *Rarities* compilation LP, under the title "Sgt. Pepper Inner Groove."

35. Studio session

Date: 27 April 1967
Time: 7:00 p.m.–12:45 a.m.
Location: EMI Studio 3
Producer: George Martin

[A.] Magical Mystery Tour—RM4 (2:47)
Mixed: 27 April 1967

Official Beatles biographer Hunter Davies was present as the Beatles began to record Paul's title song for the proposed *Magical Mystery Tour* TV special. Although he conflates the first two sessions to a single event, his description provides an instructive glimpse into their recording methods of the time.

On April 25 in Studio 3, Paul played on the piano for the others what he had written so far. The chord progression was complete, but the only lyrics written at that point were "Roll up, roll up for the mystery tour." Paul had also decided the song should open with a trumpet fanfare and include bus sound effects, so the Abbey Road library was plundered and a tape loop of automobiles traveling across the stereo image was prepared.

The rhythm track was taped next, with Paul on piano, Ringo on drums, and John and George playing guitars. Take 3 was best, and Paul supervised its reduction to a single track in five attempts, take 8 being best, while the other Beatles occupied themselves on the studio floor.

To help come up with suitable lyrics, and perhaps inspired by "Being for the Benefit of Mr. Kite!" Paul dispatched Mal to make the rounds of bus stations the next day in search of posters for real-life mystery tours. Mal showed up that evening empty-handed, and several phrases were brainstormed, such as "satisfaction guaranteed" and "trip of a lifetime" (the latter would be used in the film but not on the record). John, Paul, and George added some vocals ("Roll up" and "Mystery trip" calls) on track 4, with the tape running slow to sound sped-up on replay. Paul then added bass to track 2, and various percussion (maracas, cowbell, tambourine, and extra drumming) went onto track 3. A further reduction into take 9 combined the bass and vocals to one track and the rhythm and percussion to a second.

This was supplemented April 27 by a main vocal

overdub on the third track, with John and George supporting Paul's lead. A demo remix (**A**) was prepared at the end of the day and cut onto acetates, presumably to assist the preparation of a trumpet score. This rough mix has Paul's vocal treated with ADT and a much louder entrance of the piano during the coda. Overdubs would continue May 3.

RELEASE HISTORY

2002: **A** appeared from a good-quality acetate (with plenty of surface noise) on the bootleg CD *Another Tracks of "Magical Mystery Tour."* It may originate from an acetate sold at auction by Bonham's on March 22, 1997.

36. Documentary footage   J

Date:	29 April 1967
Time:	evening
Location:	Alexandra Palace, London
Broadcast:	17 May 1967, 8:05–8:35 p.m.
	BBC2
	Man Alive: "What Is a Happening?"
Length:	1:11

The BBC's belated answer to the Granada TV documentary about London's alternative scene (see the January 18 entry), this entry in the *Man Alive* series was subtitled "What Is a Happening?" It included footage of one such happening, the so-called 14-hour Technicolour Dream held at the Alexandra Palace. Cameras captured the fleeting presence of John Lennon, wearing a fur-lined coat and wandering around the presentations while chatting with Indica Gallery owner John Dunbar. One such presentation was Yoko Ono's infamous Cut Piece, in which a young woman was disrobed in stages by participants wielding a pair of scissors. Although footage of this is intercut with footage of John, it's not clear that he witnessed it or was even aware of Yoko's presence; the couple had been introduced by Dunbar five months earlier at his gallery.

RELEASE HISTORY

This footage, intercut with color film of Pink Floyd's performance from the event, was released on a home video titled *Pink Floyd London '66–'67.*

37. Studio session

Date:	3 May 1967
Time:	7:00 p.m.–12:15 a.m.
Location:	EMI Studio 3
Producer:	George Martin

[A.]	**Magical Mystery Tour—RM7** (2:44)
Mixed:	4 May 1967

[B.]	**Magical Mystery Tour—RS from takes 8 and 9** (2:45)
[C.]	**Magical Mystery Tour—RS from takes 7, 8, and 9** (0:47)

Sessions for the song "Magical Mystery Tour" continued this evening with a brass overdub. However, the four trumpeters hired were perplexed to find that no score had been prepared and waited around while Paul tried to work up their parts on the piano, with George Martin's assistance.

As it transpired, one of the trumpeters, Gary Howarth, ended up writing out the score himself and it went onto the fourth track of the tape. As a final touch, the glockenspiel that had been used recently on "Only a Northern Song" was added to the vocal track during the coda. The song was considered finished and seven fresh mono mixes were created May 4. The last of these (**A**) was copied on September 28 for use in the production of the TV special, but the song itself would have further overdubs for record release (see the November 7 entry).

RM7 was used in the *Magical Mystery Tour* special, with several extra sounds added during film editing. These include applause and motor coach effects, as well as John spieling the "step right this way" spoken intro and plugging the "trip of a lifetime" in the middle. A new stereo mix for the *Magical Mystery Tour* home video (**B**) re-creates this, isolating the individual tracks from take 8 and syncing them with the vocal and trumpet overdubs from take 9. This is heard twice in the film, once complete at the beginning and a 1:10 reprise at the very end; the latter is a bit less obscured by effects, although it does include a farewell message from John.

An even more ambitious remix (**C**) appears in part on the *Anthology* DVD, synchronizing elements from all three stages of the recording. From take 7, we have piano (left), drums (center), and guitars (right); from take 8, percussion (left), bass (center), and "roll up" vocals (right); from take 9, main vocals (center) and trumpets (right), all topped off with a fresh application of the bus effects loop.

RELEASE HISTORY

1967: As discussed above, the original print of *Magical Mystery Tour* included a version of **A** with overlaid effects and narration. This appeared on numerous vinyl bootlegs such as *Cinelogue 5, 1967, Dig It!,* and *Rarer Than Rare* in varying sound quality.

1988: The home video release of *Magical Mystery Tour* included **B**. It appears from this source on the CD *It's All in the Mind Y'Know.*

1991: A clean copy of **A,** taken from an acetate, was included on the bootleg CD *Acetates.*

2003: **C** was released on the soundtrack of the *Anthology* DVD.

38. Studio session

Date: 11 May 1967
Time: 9:00 p.m.–3:00 a.m.
Location: Studio 1, Olympic Sound Studios, London
Producer: George Martin

[A.] Baby, You're a Rich Man—RM1 (3:02)
Mixed: 11 May 1967

[B.] Baby, You're a Rich Man—RS? (2:58)
Mixed: 22 October 1971

[C.] Baby, You're a Rich Man—RS from take 12 and reduction take 2 (2:59)

"Baby, You're A Rich Man" was a combination of John's verses and Paul's chorus, recorded to fulfill the *Yellow Submarine* film quota. Although it did appear fleetingly in the movie, its release on a single B-side in July meant that it went no further in completing the requirement of exclusive soundtrack songs. It was recorded at Olympic Studios in Barnes, an independent studio used often by the Rolling Stones that year. Indeed, Mick Jagger was in attendance this evening, although his vocal contributions (if any) are not conspicuous.

One whole reel was filled with rehearsal takes, and by the twelfth "proper" take, a backing track of piano, drums, maracas, and tambourine was perfected. To fill up the tape, Paul added bass and John sang a main vocal, joined by Paul and others with singing and handclaps on the choruses. This was reduced to two tracks of a new tape; rather than carry on with take 13 as per Abbey Road policy, the reductions began afresh at take 1. The second reduction was best, and the third track was occupied by George's lead guitar and John playing Olympic's Clavioline, a presynthesizer keyboard invented in the 1940s and used on the Tornadoes' hit "Telstar." On the final track, more vocals for the choruses were added, along with some backwards piano on the final verse, and a single note of vibraphone played by that night's tape operator Eddie Kramer.

The mono mix (**A**), created that same night and released on a single, brings up the piano track with heavy reverb between the last stanzas of each verse; this effect is absent from the other mixes. The *Songtrack* remix (**C**) isolates the piano from take 12 and moves the second vocal track slightly to the right to spread out the chorus a bit.

RELEASE HISTORY

1967: Mix **A** was released worldwide as the B-side of the single "All You Need Is Love." It can be found on the CD single of that title. This same mix appeared in fake rechanneled stereo that year on stereo pressings of Capitol's *Magical Mystery Tour* LP. Later U.S. pressings of the single include a strange noise before the song begins that has been interpreted as the end of the word "seven" or "eleven," neither of which make sense considering the take, mix, and matrix numbers involved; this oddity is included on the CD-R *Vinyl to the Core.*

1971: The first true stereo mix, **B** was released on West Germany's stereo-only issue of the *Magical Mystery Tour* LP. It's currently available on EMI's CD of the same name. Strangely, when Parlophone compiled the UK version of this album in 1976, they used the "duophonic" mix of this song. The correct mix was finally issued in the UK in 1980 on *The Beatles Box* and a year later on an EP titled *The Beatles,* but these releases faded the track 2 seconds early.

1999: **C** was included on Apple's *Yellow Submarine Songtrack* CD.

39. Studio session

Date: 12 May 1967
Time: 7:00 p.m.–12:30 a.m.
Location: EMI Studio 2
Producer: none

[A.] All Together Now—RM6 (2:14)
Mixed: 12 May 1967

[B.] All Together Now—RS1 (2:07)
Mixed: 29 October 1968

[C.] All Together Now—RS from take 9 (2:07)

Given its nursery-rhyme qualities, "All Together Now" was most likely written by Paul specifically for inclusion in the *Yellow Submarine* film. It stands out as an anomaly in the year of psychedelia, wordplay, and overdubs, being recorded in a single evening with no tape reductions and no hired musicians or studio trickery. George Martin's presence wasn't even required!

The skiffle-style backing track was perfected in nine takes, with Paul and George playing acoustic guitars (one played on the high frets and sounding like a banjo), Ringo on drums, sundry percussion (a honking horn and a whirring ratchet), and John wheezing away on harmonica for the first time on a Beatles recording in two years.

Paul overdubbed a bass guitar track and then sang his lead vocal, backed by John and George for the choruses. On the final track, John sang the "bom-pa-bom" bridges, accompanied by a bass drum and finger cymbals, and everyone joined in for the singalong, adding handclaps, which dissolved into a round of applause at the song's climax. Given such a simple four-track recording, all three mixes sound fairly similar, but the remix for *Songtrack* (**C**) has Paul's verse vocals in the center and pans the calls and responses of the bridge and chorus around the soundstage. An edited version of this remix (1:12) appears on the soundtrack of the *Anthology* DVD.

RELEASE HISTORY

1969: **B** was released on stereo copies of the *Yellow Submarine* LP (and reduced to mono on UK monaural copies). It's available on the EMI CD of the same title.

1994: An excellent copy of **A,** complete with Geoff Emerick's announcement, surfaced on the bootleg *Secret Songs in Pepperland,* soon copied as *The Lost Pepperland Reel.*

1999: **C** was included on Apple's *Yellow Submarine Songtrack* CD.

40. Interview   G

Date: mid-May 1967
Location: *International Times* office, London
Interviewer: Barry Miles
Length: 46:38

In addition to supporting the Indica Bookstore and Gallery, Paul was a great champion of the *International Times,* quite literally an underground paper, as it was run from a basement office in the Indica building. One of its founders, Barry Miles, remained a lifelong friend of Paul's, writing his authorized biography, *Many Years from Now.* In that book, Miles recounts interviewing Paul for the paper's sixth edition, published in January 1967: "Rather than do a conventional interview, [I] just taped an afternoon's conversation at Paul's house, during which [we] discussed fame, spiritual matters, drugs and electronic music."

Paul suggested interviewing George next, and Miles did so in a similarly loose fashion around the second week of May, presumably at the *International Times* office at 102 Southampton Row in London. The long rambling conversation was preserved on tape,

punctuated by Miles's stoned-sounding giggles and occasionally competing with two employees' discussion in the background.

As the tape begins, George is enthusing about the concept of universal love and communication, saying it "buzzes you into the astral plane." However, the buzz of all buzzes is God, and to achieve that permanently, he says you need to forswear drugs, something he wouldn't be able to bring himself to do for a few more months. Miles expresses regret that George couldn't make it to the 14-hour Technicolour Dream (see the April 29 entry). George is skeptical, but Miles insists everyone there had a wonderful time. George relates that John had been hassled by autograph seekers during his visit, but managed to convince a few of them to just relate to him as a human rather than a Beatle.

Miles says the police didn't raid the event thanks to the use of Michael X's black Muslims, there as private security. George quotes Muhammad Ali as saying there are only Muslims, not "black" Muslims, and describes the pathetic sight of the four or five KKK members who had picketed their Washington, DC, concert only to be laughed at by arriving fans. Asked if he found it easy to communicate with people in India, George explains that Ravi Shankar was educated in Paris and is "hip to the West." Shankar's students made a huge impression on George, not only through their talent but their humility.

Miles wonders why music is a more effective means of communication than other art forms, and George thinks it's because sonic vibrations express pure energy, equating mantras with prayers and hymns as a tool for achieving divine unity through sound. Miles describes a sixteenth-century-school of Japanese painting wherein the artist meditates on a subject and then draws on that energy later to paint it. He encourages George to explore Zen Buddhism, and recommends a macrobiotic restaurant. George agrees that staying free of stimulants such as caffeine is a worthy objective, which leads them to laugh at the thought of little old ladies going through coffee withdrawal.

We also get the first of innumerable instances of George quoting Gandhi's "Create and preserve the image of your own choice," although here he attributes it to Nehru. He likens the Beatles' music to an exhaust pipe that disseminates all the information and ideas they are receiving. Realistically, George admits records such as "Strawberry Fields Forever" will probably cause a lot of fans to lose interest, but may gain them a whole new audience.

A lightbulb seems to go on in George's head, and he excitedly proclaims that people are too hung up on the meanings of words rather than the sound of them, chanting "Krishna" several times to illustrate his point. He stresses that Miles should emphasize the notion of karma to his readers, although he feels that on some level, everyone understands the concept. He laments that they'll all have to be reincarnated repeatedly until it truly sinks in.

They ponder where things went wrong for mankind, and George feels it was the development of ego and organized religion, particularly in the West, where people are indoctrinated to shut up and do as they're told. He marvels at his mother-in-law's belief in a holy trinity and feels the only difference between Christ and anyone else is that he realized that he was God, when in fact everyone is. George also says he doesn't feel part of "the young generation" because that sets up an "us versus them" dichotomy; being young does not automatically make one right.

Further talk about the cycles of civilization and the nonfinality of death close out the recording. At times the philosophizing gets almost parodical, but it's fascinating to hear how far George had come from the young man who a year or two earlier showed interest in nothing deeper than cars, guitars, and Motown artists. If this conversation was typical of those Paul and his acquaintances were holding, it's quite easy to see where his inspiration for the lyrics of "The Song We Were Singing" came from.

RELEASE HISTORY

1991: This interview was released in the UK on a picture disc LP confusingly titled *George Harrison Welcome to Japan 1967 Interview*. It's been traditionally dated as being recorded in mid-August 1967, but Miles refers to the Technicolour Dream as occurring "a couple of weeks ago."

41. Radio interview   J, P, R

Date:	19 May 1967
Time:	evening
Location:	24 Chapel Street, London
Producer:	Geoff Hayden
Host:	Chris Denning
Interviewer:	Kenny Everett
Broadcast:	20 May 1967, 4:00–5:30 p.m.
	BBC Light Programme
	Where It's At
Length:	3:01

Numerous journalists were present at Brian Epstein's flat this evening for the *Sgt. Pepper's Lonely Hearts Club Band* press launch. This was the likely date of recording for the interviews conducted by Kenny Everett for BBC Radio's *Where It's At,* broadcast the next day in a special episode largely devoted to the album. John sounds particularly stoned on his segments of these interviews.

The broadcast opens with Paul's introduction of host Chris Denning. John gives a narrative lead-in to the LP's title track ("We're sitting in the hushed semi-circular theatre and waiting for the Sgt. Pepper's Lonely Hearts Club Band to come on . . .") but complains that he's not about to do that for each song on the album! After the opening medley is played, Ringo speaks about what he's been doing since the last tour (not much, apart from recording), and the LP's "psychedelic" content.

John proffers a prelude for "Lucy in the Sky with Diamonds" ("Picture yourself on an old-fashioned elephant"), and after the song is played, Everett humorously re-creates the scenario that gave rise to its title. After skipping ahead to "Fixing a Hole," John enthuses about the studio trick of phasing (Paul reminds him they call it "double-flanging"), offering a Sgt. Pepper badge to anyone who can pick out a song on the LP that doesn't employ the effect. "Being for the

Benefit of Mr. Kite!" closes out the first half of the feature, leaving two songs from the LP's first side unheard for the moment.

These were moved to part two of the package to make up for the omission of "Within You Without You" and "A Day in the Life" (the latter song had been banned from airplay by the BBC; the former was presumably too long). Following "When I'm Sixty-Four," Paul chats about the evolution in their recording process since 1963, admitting they spend a lot of studio time working out arrangements rather than bringing in finished compositions.

"She's Leaving Home" and "Lovely Rita" are next, then it's back to Paul, who is obviously describing the orchestral session for "A Day in the Life" ("We had a lot of people there, y'know, 'cause it was a big session and we wanted to make a happening . . ."). With the ban, that song and its companion, the reprise of "Sgt. Pepper," both went out the window, so the show closes with "Getting Better," "Good Morning Good Morning," and some words of praise for Kenny from Paul.

RELEASE HISTORY

1998: A very good-quality recording of this broadcast is chopped up into segments and scattered throughout the CD *Pepperland,* including abbreviated versions of the songs as aired.

1999: The boxed set *Mythology, Volume 3* reconstructed this show, using a mix of decent- and atrocious-sounding tapes. This is the only place to find the complete sentence from Paul that closed the show: "And I'd just like to say . . . thank you."

2000: An excellent-quality recording of much of this broadcast, apparently from a Kenny Everett retrospective, was booted on *The Beatles Broadcast Collection Trailer 2.* It includes a recording of John talking about "When I'm Sixty Four" taken from an unrelated interview. This is the only place to find Paul's introduction at the top of the show, but is missing segments heard in earlier releases.

42. Studio session

Date:	2 June 1967
Time:	7:00 p.m.–2:15 a.m.
Location:	De Lane Lea Recording Studios, London
Producer:	George Martin

[A.] It's All Too Much—RM1 (8:15)
Mixed: 12 October 1967

[B.] It's All Too Much—RS1 (6:22)
Mixed: 16 October 1968

[C.] It's All Too Much—RS from takes 4 and "2" (6:23)

In composing "It's All Too Much," George ensured that *Yellow Submarine* would be the only Beatles project in which his new songs outnumbered those written by John or Paul. The song, which began with the working title "Too Much," had vaguely philosophical lyrics in keeping with most of George's recent compositions, and was inspired by both meditation and acid trips.

The first two sessions for the song took place without George Martin at the helm and in unfamiliar territory at De Lane Lea Studios amid a string of directionless sessions in the wake of *Sgt. Pepper*'s completion. Apart from the songs used in the *Magical Mystery Tour* and *Yellow Submarine* films, the Beatles attempted to record John's "You Know My Name (Look Up the Number)," wasting four sessions experimenting

with different sounds and arrangements, only to reject the results. Even worse were whole days (May 9, June 1, and most of June 2) when the Beatles did nothing but fill reels with haphazard jam sessions; it's little wonder that George Martin was staying away whenever possible!

The backing track of "It's All Too Much," recorded in four takes on May 25, was comprised of organ, bass, heavily distorted lead guitar, and drums. These were reduced to a single track on May 31; under EMI's protocol, these reductions would have been labeled takes 5 and 6, but instead they became takes 1 and 2. Take 2 was then overdubbed with George's lead vocal, backed by John and Paul and with handclaps, on the second track, and cowbell and tambourine on a third track.

No demo mixes were prepared for scoring purposes, so when George Martin joined them for the June 2 session, it was up to George Harrison to instruct the four trumpet players and bass clarinetist what to play. One of the trumpeters, David Mason, recalls that the composer didn't seem to know what he wanted, and George later complained, "I am still annoyed that I let them mess it up with those damn trumpets." With these overdubs on the fourth track of the tape, "It's All Too Much" was finished, and sat for four months awaiting mixing. This may indicate that it wasn't being considered for use in the film yet.

That changed when "Baby, You're a Rich Man" was released in July, which may have led to the resurrection of George's number. A mono and a stereo mix were completed on October 12 at De Lane Lea where the tapes had apparently been kept all this time. The first of these mixes was copied on November 15 back at Abbey Road for the film producers. This unedited mix (A) allows us to hear which segments were chopped out by later participants who felt eight minutes really was "too much." For instance, the version used in the film hacks this mix down to 2:31 by including only the following pieces: the intro, first verse, second chorus, trumpet solo, fourth verse, fifth chorus, and beginning of the long coda.

When it came time to compile a soundtrack album, the original take 2 was transferred over to a fresh four-track tape, perhaps to account for differences in the brand of tape and machines used at each studio. This occurred October 16, 1968, at Abbey Road, and the new tape was jokingly labeled "take 196" (too much, indeed!). Fresh mono and stereo mixes were done from this; while the mono was never used, the stereo (B) went onto the LP. It was also an edit, though not as severe as the one in the film. The portion from 3:06–3:41 in the original song is excised, removing the third chorus and fourth verse; in addition, an early fade deleted the final minute of the coda. The vocal/handclap track was split with ADT during mixing and sent to both channels.

The remix on *Yellow Submarine Songtrack* (C) is nearly identical, but isolates the organ track from take 4 in the left channel. When the movie was first released on VHS with a stereo soundtrack, the abbreviated "It's All Too Much" appeared in fake stereo (bass left, treble right), but the 1999 reissue does mix the unique film edit into a discrete 5.1-channel format.

RELEASE HISTORY

1969: **B** was released on stereo copies of the *Yellow Submarine* LP (and reduced to mono on UK monaural copies). It's available on the EMI CD of the same title.

1992: A fair-quality tape of **A,** purportedly from a summer 1968 radio broadcast on WABC in New York City, was bootlegged on the LP *Arrive without Travelling,* and from tape source on the CD *Arrive without Aging* in 1993.

1994: An excellent copy of **A,** complete with Geoff Emerick's announcement, surfaced on the bootleg *Secret Songs in Pepperland,* soon copied as *The Lost Pepperland Reel.*

1999: **C** was included on Apple's *Yellow Submarine Songtrack* CD.

---

43. Studio session   J, P

Date: ca. 14 June 1967
Location: Olympic Sound Studios, London
Producer: Andrew Loog Oldham

[A.] We Love You (4:18)

Contrary to what many fans wanted to believe, the Beatles and the Rolling Stones had been mutually supportive colleagues right from 1963, when John and Paul donated "I Wanna Be Your Man" for the Stones' second single. Various members of the Stones were guests at Beatles sessions throughout the first half of 1967 ("A Day in the Life," "Baby, You're a Rich Man," "You Know My Name (Look Up the Number)," and "All You Need Is Love"), and George had been present at Keith Richard's house the evening he and Mick were busted in February, but left before the raid took place.

Mick and Keith came up with "We Love You," a number to say thank you to the fans who supported them throughout the negative publicity and court battles that resulted from the drug bust. Although John would later claim the song was a rip-off of his own "All You Need Is Love," it was actually recorded earlier. Bassist Bill Wyman reports in his book *Stone Alone* that the backing track was recorded June 12 and thir-teenth at Olympic Studios. John and Paul agreed to add backing vocals on the song, which Wyman claims were overdubbed in July. As the Beatles were in Olympic June 14 to lay down a rhythm track for "All You Need Is Love," it seems more logical to assume their contribution was taped that evening. Further overdubs may have continued into July, however.

Mark Lewisohn dates the session as May 18, which was actually the recording date for "She's a Rainbow"; this may be the recording date for the original discarded backing track of "We Love You." Take 4 from this early session appears on the Stones bootleg CD *Time Trip, Volume 4.* Several more instrumental outtakes (15–19) are on the boxed set *Satanic Sessions, Volume 1,* and probably stem from the June sessions.

RELEASE HISTORY

1967: This song was released as a single in the UK on August 18, reaching number 8 on the charts. In the United States, the sides were reversed and it became the B-side of "Dandelion," issued August 28. It's available in mono on the CD boxed set *Singles Collection (The London Years)* and in stereo on the CD *More Hot Rocks 2.*

Date:	19 June 1967
Location:	7 Cavendish Avenue, London
Broadcast:	19 June 1967, 8:55 p.m.
	ITV
Length:	2:12

The June 16 issue of *Life* magazine carried a feature on the Beatles with the following quote from Paul regarding LSD: "After I took it, it opened up my eyes. We only use one-tenth of our brain. Just think what we could accomplish if we could only tap that hidden part! It would mean a whole new world. If the politicians would take LSD, there wouldn't be any more war, or poverty or famine."

Pretty startling stuff coming from someone whose second-ever acid trip had been on March 21 of that year (the quote originated in an earlier article in Britain's *Queen* magazine). This was the first time any Beatle had spoken in public about LSD, although three of them had been using it since the summer of 1965. Unsurprisingly, the admission, buried in the middle of *Life*'s story, was plucked out and recycled for headline fodder. One day after his twenty-fifth birthday, Paul agreed to an interview with Independent Television News, filmed in his backyard for broadcast in that evening's bulletin.

The clip begins with Paul stating he's taken the drug only four times, and the reporter brazenly asks where he obtained it. Naturally, Paul refuses to reveal his contact and says he considers it a personal issue, but makes it sound as though it was the *Queen* reporter's fault for having asked him about it in the first place. Paul's claim that he wasn't "trying to spread the word about this" seems disingenuous given the fervent tone of his earlier statement.

An interesting moral argument follows, with the reporter trying to pin the blame for anyone who chooses to experiment with the drug on Paul, and Paul blaming the media for spreading his remarks in a sensationalist fashion. In so doing, both men fail to give the public credit for being able to make up its own mind about whether to experiment or not, making the world's youth sound like a flock of brainwashable sheep.

RELEASE HISTORY

1996: This interview was released on *Fab Four CD & Book Set;* it also circulates on video in compilations such as *Beatles: Then and Now* and *The Beatles Story.*

45. TV performance/Studio session

Date:	25 June 1967
Time:	2:00 p.m.–1:00 a.m.
Location:	EMI Studio 1
Producer:	George Martin
Director:	Derek Burrell-Davis
Host:	Steve Race
Broadcast:	(B only) live
	Our World

[A.] **All You Need Is Love—unknown take (stereo)** (0:26)

[B.] **All You Need Is Love—take 59 (mono)** (6:50)

Even though they hadn't released a new album in nine months and rumors of their imminent split were rampant, the BBC knew they could count on the Beatles to deliver. Thus in early May, they signed the group to represent all of the United Kingdom in *Our World,* the first worldwide television broadcast, to be seen by people in twenty-seven countries thanks to satellite technology.

The Beatles' contribution would be to compose a new song for the show and perform it live from Abbey Road as upward of 350 million viewers looked on. As May turned to June and the broadcast approached, John and Paul must have been disheartened looking around at the less-than-inspiring batch of recordings they had been accumulating since April. They each agreed to try and come up with a suitable tune, and John's "All You Need Is Love" won handily.

Apparently unable to book Studio 2 on short notice, they assembled at Olympic Studios in Barnes on June 14. Keen as ever to experiment (and remaining self-indulgent), they chose odd instruments for the rhythm track: John played harpsichord, Paul a double-bass, and George a violin. Poor Ringo was stuck on drums. This was perfected in thirty-three takes, with the tenth being judged "best" after playback. Take 10 was copied onto a new four-track tape, with all instruments going onto track 1, and the result perplexingly called take 10 (again, converse to Abbey Road protocol). A rough mix was made of the result for the group to take home and enjoy. (*Note:* An instrumental acetate, presumably cut from this rough mix, was sold at a Christie's auction on May 26, 1994).

June 19 saw the Olympic reduction copied over to a fresh reel of EMItape at Abbey Road Studio 3. The three empty tracks were then filled, with piano, banjo, and percussion going on track 2. Vocals went on tracks 3 and 4, including the "love love love" refrains and John singing lead for the choruses. Sessions scheduled for June 20 and 22 in Studio 2 were canceled, meaning that none of the song was recorded in those familiar surroundings.

Instead, two rough mono mixes were done in Studio 3 on June 21, one of which was cut onto an acetate and given to BBC director Derek Burrell-Davis to show that a song would indeed be ready in time. On the twenty-third, also in Studio 3, the orchestra gathered for the first time to rehearse the song. Four violins, two cellos, two saxophones, two trombones, two trumpets, a flugelhorn, and an accordion played George Martin's score in ten run-throughs. These were done as four-track to four-track reductions with simultaneous overdub, but were mainly for reference purposes.

The next day in Studio 1, after plenty of morning photo opportunities and press interviews, the BBC camera crew joined in the afternoon rehearsals, blocking the camera angles with the Beatles and the orchestra. The evening saw four more rehearsal takes taped in the same manner as the previous day.

On June 25, the momentous occasion arrived and everyone took their places back in Studio 1 for the final crucial run-throughs. These included four-track to four-track reductions with not only orchestral but vocal overdubs; one such vocal rehearsal take (**A**) has John singing the first verse with Paul inserting asides ("I believe you, Johnny!"). This cuts to John and Paul laughing (with heavy tape echo) because they aren't hearing the rhythm track playback in their headphones.

Such potential nightmare problems were ironed out with rehearsal takes 44–58 being recorded on four-track and some of these proceedings captured on two reels of the mono signal that would be fed live to the BBC control van. The introductory sequence was actually pretaped during these rehearsals, and thus the first two minutes or so of the Beatles' segment wasn't actually going out "live."

This began with a staged glimpse of the group "recording a second vocal track" (actually they are miming to the work already done) with BBC narrator Steve Race describing the action. George Martin, in the control room, then pretends to order in the session musicians, who enter as Race facetiously claims, "The Beatles get on best with symphony men." In actuality, the orchestra was seated comfortably as the live broadcast got under way. Tape operator Richard Lush is then seen "winding back" the rhythm track (again, it would have been cued up well in advance of the live telecast).

On the studio floor, John sings a bit of the Kinks' current hit "Waterloo Sunset," and Paul jokingly calls his producer "Uncle George."

All of this was played back at 9:36 p.m. local time when the BBC began transmission. By 9:38 the feed was truly live, and for better or worse, take 59 (unannounced) of "All You Need Is Love" began. The existing material went onto track 1, and the live performances on the other tracks—John's lead vocal on track 4 (Paul and George sing along, but their vocal mikes are not plugged in), the orchestra on track 3, and Paul's bass, George's lead guitar, and Ringo's drums all on track 2. In addition, everyone present joined in on vocals for the chorus. The crowd included Beatle friends and family, as well as musicians such as Eric Clapton, Graham Nash, Mick Jagger, Keith Richard, Keith Moon, and Gary Leeds.

Everything went smoothly, and the raw tape of the BBC feed (**B**) reveals that after the director signaled cut, someone yelled, "Happy New Year, everybody!" obviously inspired by the festive atmosphere. George then attempted to reprise "La Marseillaise" on his guitar, but failed badly. Once the party had wrapped up, John stayed around to fix a bit of his lead vocal, and some more tinkering would be done the next day, but the Beatles had indeed come through and delivered a memorable performance. It would be one of their last such unified efforts.

RELEASE HISTORY

The entire Beatles segment of the *Our World* broadcast has been circulating on video for many years, and was even colorized for use in the *Anthology* project. The soundtrack appeared on bootlegs such as *LS Bumblebee* and *The Beatles vs. Don Ho* in fair quality throughout the 1970s.

1984: **B** finally surfaced from the original studio tape in Westwood One's *Sgt. Pepper's Lonely Hearts Club Band: A History of the Beatle Years 1962–1970* radio special, although only 4:24 of the tape was used, and it was partly obscured by narration.

1988: A complete and excellent-quality copy of **B** appeared on the vinyl bootleg *Ultra Rare Trax, Volume 5 & 6*. This appeared from tape source on the CD *Unsurpassed Masters, Volume 3* the following year. Both releases run slightly slow, but subsequent CD issues such as *Pepperland* have speed-corrected the tape.

1996: **A** was included in the *Anthology* home video set in mono, and was bootlegged from this source on the CD *Abbey Road Video Show;* it appears in stereo on the *Anthology* DVD.

46. Studio session

Date: 26 June 1967
Time: 4:00–8:00 p.m.
Location: EMI Studio 2
Producer: George Martin

[A.] All You Need Is Love—RM4 (3:57)
Mixed: 26 June 1967

[B.] All You Need Is Love—RM11 (4:30)
Mixed: 1 November 1967

[C.] All You Need Is Love—RS6 (3:46)
Mixed: 29 October 1968

[D.] All You Need Is Love—RS from takes 10 and 59 (#1) (3:44)
[E.] All You Need Is Love—RS from takes 10 and 59 (#2) (3:39)

In a final bit of garnish on June 26, the tambourine that opened "All You Need Is Love" was replaced with a drumroll from Ringo. The song was mixed into mono (**A**) later that night, with John's lead vocal treated with ADT. With "Baby, You're a Rich Man" hastily chosen as a B-side, the single was in shops in eleven days and atop the charts two weeks after that.

The song was also chosen to appear in the *Yellow Submarine* film, but the producers must have requested a slightly longer version. To this end, Geoff Emerick prepared a new mono mix on November 1, announcing the remix with tape echo on his voice and giggling. This mix (**B**) opens with George Martin's count-in and continues as normal through the fourth chorus. At that point, Emerick spliced in an extra chorus, with the saxophone riff mixed out. Although the entire song may have been animated at this length (indicated by outtakes in the film's trailer), by the time the movie was released, the "All You Need Is Love" sequence had been scaled back to a mere 2:42, somewhat defeating the purpose of extending the song in the

first place. The film edit uses the following segments from this mix: intro/first verse/first chorus/third verse/fourth chorus/"extra" chorus/coda, fading early. When *Yellow Submarine* was released on VHS in stereo, this edit was re-created pretty faithfully, although they forgot to mix out the sax riff on the repeated chorus.

The song was not mixed into stereo until 1968 for the film's soundtrack LP; this mix (**C**) has track 1 mixed left, tracks 2 and 4 centered, and track 3 right; it also fades a bit earlier than the mono mix. The *Songtrack* remix (**D**) is similar, but splits the two vocal tracks from take 10, and pans the orchestra around in various places. The *Love* remix (**E**) synchronizes the Olympic backing track (John's harpsichord left, George's violin right) with later overdubs, and mixes in elements from "Baby, You're a Rich Man," "Sgt. Pepper's Lonely Hearts Club Band," "Good Night," and "The Beatles' Third Christmas Record."

RELEASE HISTORY

1967: **A** was issued worldwide on a single and is available on the "All You Need Is Love" CD single. It also appeared on Capitol's *Magical Mystery Tour* LP in "rechanneled" stereo.

1969: **C** was released on stereo copies of the *Yellow Submarine* LP (and reduced to mono on UK monaural copies). It's available on the EMI CD of the same title, as well as the CD version of *Magical Mystery Tour.*

1994: An excellent copy of **B,** complete with Geoff Emerick's announcement, surfaced on the bootleg *Secret Songs in Pepperland,* soon copied as *The Lost Pepperland Reel.*

1999: **D** was included on Apple's *Yellow Submarine Songtrack* CD.

2006: **E** was released on the *Love* CD.

47. Radio interview   P

Date: 26–30 June 1967
Interviewer: Kenny Everett
Broadcast: 1 July 1967, 4:00–5:30 p.m.
BBC Light Programme
Where It's At
Length: 1:17

Six weeks after the *Sgt. Pepper's Lonely Hearts Club Band* feature, BBC Radio's *Where It's At* spotlighted the

Beatles' follow-up single, airing "All You Need Is Love" twice and its B-side, "Baby, You're a Rich Man" once over the course of the program. In addition, Kenny Everett recorded a brief interview with Paul about how the song and *Our World* appearance came to be.

Paul quips that they "went away and played Monopoly" rather than come up with a tune, but when prodded by Derek Burrell-Davis, he and John each wrote a song. Apparently they "just decided" to record

John's first, but it was obviously perfect for the occasion. Paul's composition is said to be ready "for the next one [project]" and that it's "of a similar nature in its simplicity, but with a different message"; this may have been "Your Mother Should Know."

RELEASE HISTORY

1972: This interview was included in the radio documentary *The Beatles Story.* It appears on the CD-R compilation *Vinyl to the Core,* copied from the 1984 series *Sgt. Pepper's Lonely Hearts Club Band: A History of the Beatle Years 1962–1970.*

48. Speech   P

Date: 12 July 1967
Time: afternoon
Location: 7 Cavendish Avenue
Length: 33:37

Amazing as it may seem, in the Summer of Love meeting a Beatle was still as simple as ringing one's doorbell and hoping he was home. This was the method New York fans Leslie Samuels and Donna Stark employed, although they had to travel a long way to reach their goal. They were ostensibly taking a course at Oxford University, but this was just a ruse to pay homage at various Beatles shrines. The girls arrived at Paul's house first, armed with a camera, tape recorder, and bag of goodies.

The recording begins with Paul being presented with a list of seventeen fans' names; he complies and greets them all individually on tape (throwing in a "Hello, Martha" when his pooch interjects with a bark). He is then presented with a gift of a LOVE button, and the girls describe their journey from New York to London via Paris, revealing that they are cutting classes on only their second day. Paul doesn't seem concerned, and relates the true story of a runaway girl that had inspired "She's Leaving Home." Leslie (who does most of the talking for her companion) asks whether *Sgt. Pepper* was meant to be a concert, and Paul says, "It's anything you wanna make it."

At this point, Jane Asher appears and greets the girls (also present is a fan from New Jersey named Beverly). Paul confirms that an LP by one "Lord Sitar" is not George playing under a pseudonym, despite Murray the K promoting it as such. Leslie wonders why Capitol's versions of Beatles records often differ from Parlophone's (using "I'm Only Sleeping" and the missing run-out groove on *Sgt. Pepper* as examples). Paul seems unaware of these anomalies but insists they are out of his control. As the fans take pictures, Paul introduces his black cat, Thisby, and her two-month-old kittens.

Jane arrives with drinks for everyone, and Paul explains that the "noise in the middle" of "Baby, You're a Rich Man" is a keyboard called a Clavioline. He says they have a couple of songs in the can, including one for

a TV show ("Magical Mystery Tour"). Leslie says she doesn't approve of the Monkees, but Paul defends them, saying he enjoys their TV show and "imitation is the sincerest form of flattery." He says it's too soon for them to look objectively at their new LP, since they hear only the flaws when they play it.

We also learn that Paul has a recording session scheduled that night with his brother Mike (presumably for the McGough & McGear LP; see the April 1968 entry). They talk about the Beatles' public image, with Leslie describing her fear that they were breaking up when their "new look" was revealed in January. She wonders whether George will be "packing it in" and going to India, but Paul emphasizes that there is nothing to "pack in." Any work they do now as a group is not for money, but because they are friends. He admits they probably won't do any more tours, but may use more electronic effects on their next album.

The girls want to take more photos, so Paul holds the mic for them and does a mock announcement for radio station "W-I-N-N-E-R": "We're sitting here in the Bel Air home of a young successful steel magnate." Paul then gets an exhaustive tour of the bag's contents, including descriptions of the items that were too unwieldy to carry (a painting and a "butcher cover" *"Yesterday" . . . And Today* LP). Seeing a copy of John's *In His Own Write,* Paul reads aloud the poem "On This Churly Morn."

The lucky fans repack their belongings and ask Paul if they could make it to Surrey, where the other three Beatles lived. He feels it's too late to make it out there and back to Oxford before their curfew, but that they should try their fortune another day. "I came, I saw, I conquered Seven Cavendish!" exclaims Leslie, and the girls thank Paul and Jane for their hospitality before departing.

RELEASE HISTORY

This delightful slice of history has been preserved and circulated among collectors on CD-R. The sound quality is decent enough given the circumstances, with the biggest distraction being an unknown clanking noise that intrudes in places.

Date: 12 July 1967
Time: evening
Location: Kinfauns
Length: 22:35

Given the chance, wouldn't you have broken curfew to try and see a few more Beatles? That's what Leslie and Donna decided to do, making their way to Esher by nightfall and encountering George at Kinfauns, his bungalow.

As first, George appears delighted to welcome them and accept their gifts, although he is less enthusiastic than Paul about recording individual greetings for the list of fans, reading out the names rapid-fire. He signs a photo for Leslie's friend in Chicago and is baffled when presented with the Lord Sitar LP they had obtained in Paris. George denies that he and John were at the Monterey Pop Festival, but acknowledges giving an interview to the *International Times* (see the mid-May entry). Leslie offers a compliment on its contents: "You're deep!," but George refutes this and tells her, "You are, too!," causing the girls to giggle.

But George is serious; he stresses that the Beatles are no more special than anyone and pleads for the cessation of fan mail, which must have hurt Leslie's feelings, as George recognized her name from the many letters she had sent. He stresses it's nothing personal that none of them respond, since their answers can now be found in the music: "Do you want me to be me or to be a shorthand typist?" George's polite but blunt attitude toward his fans is quite a contrast to Paul's accommodating charm.

Asked whether he still plays guitar, George replies hesitantly, "Well . . . slightly. I'm trying to do it all." In fact, he wouldn't fully shift his focus from sitar back to guitar until the following spring. He jokes that he's learning "Guitar Boogie Shuffle" on the sitar but admits he's really just studying scales and exercises. Leslie wonders whether his latest song "in the bag" will be Indian influenced, and he describes it as a pop song called "It's All Too Much."

Once again, the girls want to take pictures, and George holds the mic while they dig through their bag in search of flash cubes (George calls them "ice cubes"). They seem surprised to find he is smoking, and George confesses that he cut it out but "cut it back in again," claiming that he will shortly be giving up smoking, coffee, tea, and food! Leslie worries he'll get too thin but he deadpans, "As long as you can see me, I'm not thin enough."

After clarifying a line from "Baby, You're a Rich Man," George explains why touring is an inefficient way of communicating and says there will "definitely" be a third Beatles film. Klaus Voormann wanders over and is introduced to Leslie and Donna. In turn, they show him a snapshot of George and Klaus painting the exterior of Kinfauns with psychedelic scribbles, which one of their friends had taken a few months earlier. As the tape ends, George advises the girls to speak to NEMS employees Peter Brown and Tony Barrow for assistance if they are thinking of moving to England.

RELEASE HISTORY

As with the previous entry, this recording circulates on CD-R. It's of similar sound quality but the latter portion of the tape is disrupted by frequent dropouts and loss of signal.

50. Studio session   P

Date: 20 July 1967
Location: Chappell Recording Studios, London
Producers: Chris Barber, Giorgio Gomelsky, Reggie King

[A.] Catcall (3:02)

Among Paul's repertoire of unused songs was a jazz instrumental titled "Catswalk," which probably dated back to the Quarry Men days (a Beatles rehearsal of the song was recorded circa October 1962 at the Cavern; see the entry for details). Paul was acquainted with Chris Barber, trombonist and leader of a trad jazz combo, from meetings at the Bag O'Nails and other nightspots, and offered him the chance to record this rejected tune.

It had obviously been unsuitable for a Beatles release, but proved to be just the ticket for the Chris Barber Band. The first version they taped, at London's Marquee Club in a session Paul attended, was a straight performance of the melody probably akin to the Beatles' rendition. But Paul could sense the potential in a slightly more over-the-top arrangement, complete with a chorus of catcalls (thus the title change).

The remake was completed at Chappell Studios with Paul and Jane attending and joining in with the howling and applause. Paul is also heard calling out, "Please play it slower!" before the half-tempo coda and joining in a chorus of "For he's a jolly good fellow" shortly thereafter. It's not clear what instrument he played on the song, if any. A photo from the session shows him seated alongside keyboardist Brian Auger playing an organ, and other reports have him sharing a piano with Auger. I don't hear any piano on the song, and the three organ passages don't really sound like Paul's style, although it's possible he played the first two. Certainly the frantic organ solo in the middle was beyond his capabilities.

RELEASE HISTORY

1967: This song was released on a single in the UK only, on October 20, 1967, and failed to chart. It appeared on the UK album *Battersea Rain Dance* in 1970 and has been reissued on the compilation LP *The Songs Lennon and McCartney Gave Away* but doesn't seem to have been officially released on CD yet.

51. Amateur footage

Date: 22–30 July 1967
Location: Greece
Length: 1:57

Fed up with living in a country that ate up most of their earnings in taxes, closed down pirate radio, and harassed pop stars for taking drugs, the Beatles suddenly decided to buy an island of their own. Spurred on by "Magic" Alexis Mardas, a Greek expatriate soon to be named head of the newly formed Apple Electronics, they sent Alistair Taylor to scout out and negotiate the purchase of a suitable island in the Aegean.

The plan was to build homes for each Beatle and their families and associates, plus a recording studio, and for the group to live there during the cold English winter months. By mid-July, they were ready to inspect the chosen property in person and flew out with home movie cameras in tow. The surviving silent footage seen in *Anthology* begins with John and Paul's arrival on July 22 in Athens. As the yacht that was to transport them to their paradise was held up by storms, they stayed in the capital until the twenty-fifth; clips from this period include Paul and Ringo sitting under a tent, George peering through a camera, and various members of the party dancing in a circle to the strains of a local bouzouki band.

On July 26, the yacht arrived and George was filmed boarding it at the dock in Piraeus; further boat footage includes Paul and George swimming in the sea and the group on deck drawing colorful pictures, from the twenty-seventh. Julian Lennon is also there, playing on the boat and on the beach with Paul and Jane Asher. Ringo did not accompany them on the yacht voyage, having flown back to England on the twenty-sixth with Neil Aspinall.

Presumably the others enthused to him about the island on their return, but the fervor waned quickly when they realized the potential legal hassles required to purchase land abroad, and the matter was dropped within a matter of weeks.

RELEASE HISTORY

1996: This color footage from the Beatles' private collection was seen for the first time in the *Anthology* home video documentary, in a montage set to their recording of "Baby, You're a Rich Man."

52. Newsreel footage   J, P

Date: 31 July 1967
Location: London Airport
Broadcast: 31 July 1967
BBC-TV
Length: 0:14

Neither Ringo's (July 26) nor George's (July 30) returns to London from Greece were deemed newsworthy, but apparently the "two Beatles" rule kicked in this after-
noon when John and Paul touched down. A BBC News crew dutifully captured the electrifying sight of the duo deplaning, along with Cynthia and Julian Lennon and Jane Asher. Perhaps it was just a slow news day.

RELEASE HISTORY

This silent footage circulates on video in fair quality.

53. Radio interview

R

Date: 31 July 1967
Location: Radio London office, London
Interviewer: Philip Birch
Broadcast: 5 August 1967
Radio London
Length: 0:11

With the passage of a Marine Offences Act in the summer of 1967, pirate radio stations began to fold, ostensibly replaced by the still-monopolizing BBC's Radio One on September 30. Radio London's last day would be August 5, and with John and Paul on their way back from Greece, and George home for less than twenty-four hours, Ringo was chosen as spokesman to deliver the Beatles' condolences. He visited the station's London office to show his support, pose for a photo, and tape a short message of farewell. It's likely the tape was aired several times over the station's waning days.

RELEASE HISTORY

2000: An excellent-quality recording of this message appeared on the bootleg *The Beatles Broadcast Collection Trailer 2,* seemingly from the last day of transmission. This source is missing a word each at the start and end of Ringo's speech that are present on a circulating tape of slightly inferior quality taken from an earlier broadcast.

54. Radio interview

G

Date: 9 August 1967
Location: New York City
Interviewer: Murray Kaufman
Broadcast: WOR-FM, New York City
Length: 12:57

On August 8, George and company flew from San Francisco to New York City for a one-day stay before returning to London. On his last day in the States, George dropped by the studios of WOR-FM to visit the "fifth Beatle," Murray the K. To give him credit, Murray was progressing with the times, having recently hosted a series of concerts giving American audiences their first glimpse of artists such as Cream and the Who. And he seemed eager to converse about Indian music and philosophy, which must have put George instantly at ease.

George begins by praising Ravi Shankar's Hollywood Bowl concert, singling out Bismillah Khan's shehnai playing. Murray seems to think the Beatles' first deliberate use of sitar was on the *Help!* soundtrack album, but George admits that was a total fluke due to the picture's nominal Indian themes. In fact, composer Ken Thorne incorporated Eastern instruments into the score without the Beatles' contribution. But George relates how being given a book on yoga during *Help!* location filming in the Bahamas marked the start of his own interest in Indian culture.

After some discussion about the differences in religion between the East and West, George singles out two gurus who have traveled to America to spread the word: Maharishi Mahesh Yogi and Meher Baba. The latter would have great influence on musicians such as Pete Townshend and Ronnie Lane, and of course the maharishi would count the Beatles, the Beach Boys, and Donovan among his disciples after crossing paths with the rock world later that month.

Scarcely letting Murray get a word in edgewise (a feat unto itself), George continues to pontificate about his realization that all religions stem from the same source, and that belief in Christ's resurrection is an ultimate example of having faith. In a bit of philosophy he would eventually spin into the lyrics of "The Inner Light," he enthuses, "The more you learn, the more you know that you don't know anything."

Returning to more earthly matters, Murray asks about some *Sgt. Pepper* rumors: "Lucy in the Sky with Diamonds" standing for LSD and the "man from the motor trade" in "She's Leaving Home" representing an abortion doctor. George sensibly points out that such speculation merely underscores "what's going on in people's twisted minds." He similarly denies there is any message other than the obvious stated one in "All You Need Is Love."

Murray wonders if a Beatles breakup is imminent but is reassured, "We'll never split up." As George makes several attempts to exit gracefully for his impending flight, Murray compliments Pattie's appearance and the lyrics of "Within You Without You" ("It's just an idea, y'know," George mutters impatiently).

RELEASE HISTORY

Although it's been circulating among collectors for many years in fairly good quality, this interview has never been released or bootlegged.

55. Newsreel footage

Date:	20 August 1967
Location:	Queen Charlotte's Maternity Hospital, London
Broadcast:	20 August 1967 ITV
Length:	1:58

On August 19, Maureen Starkey gave birth to Jason, her second son with Ringo, at Queen Charlotte's Hospital. The following day, as the news broke, Ringo arrived and spoke briefly to the gathered press.

The ITV footage begins with Ringo getting out of a car and amusingly pretending to shoot photos of the cameramen who are busy snapping and filming his image. Wearing oval sunglasses and a button reading I MISS YOU LIKE HELL, Ringo poses for the press with his mother-in-law, Florence Cox. He then chats about his new son, revealing that since he'd gotten to pick Zak's name, Jason was Maureen's choice, and that the new baby looks just like his first one. Ringo cheerfully confesses he doesn't care how many kids he ends up with, what sex they are, or what they end up doing for a living. The clip ends with Maureen emerging through a revolving door, followed by a nurse who hands her Jason, making his first public appearance.

RELEASE HISTORY

1996: A slightly incomplete copy of this interview was released on *Fab Four CD & Book Set*. The full clip circulates on video.

56. Studio session

Date:	22 August 1967
Time:	7:00 p.m.–?
Location:	Chappell Recording Studios, London
Producer:	George Martin

[A.] Your Mother Should Know—take 8 (mono) (2:29)

For their first recording session in two months, the Beatles tried out yet another new studio, Chappell, on George Martin's recommendation. Paul's composition "Your Mother Should Know" was the focus of these two days of work, beginning with eight takes of the basic rhythm on August 22. These were played by Paul on piano and Ringo on drums, and the "best" take had a pair of lead vocals added by Paul before the end of the day. Although it's undocumented, a rough mix (**A**) must have been made at this point, as it appears on the batch of *Magical Mystery Tour* acetates used during production of the film.

The next evening would see the vocals combined to one track and the piano and drums to another on a new tape, called take 9, and two further tracks of backing vocals added to this, plus a splash of rhythm guitar on the choruses. The song would be picked up again in September during the *Magical Mystery Tour* sessions proper.

RELEASE HISTORY

1981: Lot 116 in the December 22 auction at Sotheby's consisted of a shooting script for *Magical Mystery Tour* and four "pre-release Beatles pressings on Emidisc" of film songs; in other words, production acetates. The lot sold for £495, and all four acetates have appeared on bootlegs: "Magical Mystery Tour" (RM7 from May 3), "Blue Jay Way" (RM1 from September 7), "Ariel [sic] Instrumental" (RM4 from September 8), and this rough mix of "Your Mother Should Know." See individual entries for further information on these recordings.

1984: **A** first appeared in Westwood One's *Sgt. Pepper's Lonely Hearts Club Band: A History of the Beatle Years 1962–1970* radio special, where the intro and ending were both obscured by dialogue. It was copied on the bootleg LP *Not For Sale*, which chopped out the obscured intro and spliced on the very end from the commercially released take.

1991: The complete recording surfaced on the bootleg CD *Acetates*, running a touch fast. It has been speed-corrected on *Upgraded Collection—Highlights*.

57. Newsreel footage

Date: 24 August 1967
Time: 8:00 p.m.
Location: London Hilton Ballroom
Length: 0:38

According to Paul, the Beatles first became aware of Maharishi Mahesh Yogi sometime in the early 60s after seeing an episode of Granada's *People and Places* about the guru's ongoing travels to spread the word about spiritual enlightenment. Pattie Harrison began to study Transcendental Meditation in 1967, and she probably informed her husband about the maharishi's latest round of lectures (see the August 9 entry). When they learned of his visit to the London Hilton, George and Pattie enthused to the others about attending the lecture; George was particularly keen to be given a personal mantra to chant during meditation.

Ringo was still with his wife and newborn son in the hospital, but John, Cynthia, Paul, his brother Mike, and Jane Asher all joined George and Pattie at the Hilton. Newsreel cameras captured them occupying most of one row near the front of the ballroom, and a new era in the Beatles' legend was about to take flight. After the lecture and a press conference, the pop stars met the guru privately. He invited them to follow him down to Bangor, North Wales, the following day for a week-long conference at Normal College. They accepted, rounded up their drummer, and made hasty arrangements to travel to Bangor by train the following day.

RELEASE HISTORY

This silent footage was included on the video compilation *Beatles 1962 to 1970*.

58. Newsreel footage

Date: 25 August 1967
Location: Euston Station, London
Length: 1:17

The Beatles' trip to Bangor got off to an inauspicious start. Despite less than a day's notice, the fans and press descended on the train station as the group and their entourage arrived. The mayhem is well documented by news footage: The maharishi awaits his followers peacefully, holding flowers. The Beatles race across the platform, George lugging a sitar and the others carrying bags. After fighting through the crowd, the last Beatle boards, the door is shut, and the train begins to pull away. Still outside the door is Cynthia Lennon, held back by a helpful policeman. Peter Brown tries in vain to halt the runaway express and is seen consoling a tearful Cynthia and escorting her across the platform. Although Neil would drive her to Bangor to reconvene with her husband, she had a premonition at that moment that John would soon be leaving her life for good.

RELEASE HISTORY

This footage, including shots from two different angles, was included on the video compilation *Beatles 1962 to 1970*. It appears in numerous documentaries, along with footage of fellow travelers Mick Jagger and Marianne Faithfull.

58a. Newsreel footage

Date: 25 August 1967
Location: Bangor Railway Station
Length: 1:04

The party's arrival at Bangor station was also filmed by newsreel cameras, along with brief glimpses of the group being whisked away to the college in black cars.

RELEASE HISTORY

This silent Reuters newsreel footage circulates on video.

59. Newsreel footage

Date: 26 August 1967
Location: Normal College, Bangor
Length: 0:12

The Beatles were watched closely by the media during their first full day of meditation. A joint press conference with a flower-clutching Maharishi Mahesh Yogi was held on a stage at the college. As newsreels whirred, the group delivered the bombshell reporters had hoped for: Now that they had a new path to self-realization, they no longer needed to take illicit drugs!

Any potential this story had to spread new goodwill for the group would be wiped out by developments the following day.

RELEASE HISTORY

This brief silent footage of the maharishi onstage with his newest disciples appeared in videos such as *The Compleat Beatles* and *Greatest Rock 'n' Roll Legends Scrapbook.*

60. Newsreel footage   P

Date: 27 August 1967
Location: Normal College, Bangor
Length: 0:18

The Beatles' newfound peace was shattered by grim reality in the form of a ringing dormitory phone. Jane Asher answered and fetched Paul to take the call from Peter Brown. Brian Epstein had been found dead in his bedroom of an apparent drug overdose. After a short

audience with the maharishi, Paul and Jane were designated to travel back to London immediately. The news had leaked out by then, and news crews were on hand to register the couple's departure via limousine.

RELEASE HISTORY

This silent clip was included in the video compilation *Beatles 1962 to 1970* and used in *Anthology.*

61. TV interview   J, G, R

Date: 27 August 1967
Time: evening
Location: Normal College, Bangor
Length: 2:32

The three remaining Beatles gamely faced the waiting press to express their initial reactions to Brian's death. At least two interviews were filmed that evening, probably with ITV and BBC news reporters, respectively (both were filmed and combined in a Reuters newsreel, from an alternate angle).

The first begins with John calling Brian "a beautiful fella" and, looking thoroughly lost, he and Ringo admit that they have no immediate plans other than returning to London later in the day. George discusses Brian's plan to have arrived in Bangor the next day to join them, revealing that their manager was just as interested in spiritual regeneration as they are, adding preachily, "As everybody should be."

George relates that Brian seemed in a great mood when they last spoke (August 23 at the Beatles' Chappell Studio session) and that the group now won't have time to return to Bangor before the conference concludes on the thirty-first. Finally, John relays the advice the maharishi gave them to think positively and "not to get overwhelmed by grief."

RELEASE HISTORY

1996: Most of this interview was released on *Rare Photos & Interview CD, Volume 3,* more or less matching a 2:08 clip in the video compilation *Beatles 1962 to 1970.* Twenty-one seconds missing from the start are included in the *Anthology* home video. And the final 3 seconds were included in a 1998 *Arena* TV documentary about Brian Epstein. (Q: "Tomorrow?"; J: "Yes.")

Date: 27 August 1967
Time: evening
Location: Normal College, Bangor
Length: 1:05

The second interview was conducted in the same location as the first, but only John and George spoke (although Ringo was still present).

They both claim to be at a loss for words when asked to pay tribute, but John comes up with a simple and fitting sentiment: "We just loved him, and he was one of us." The same questions about plans and the maharishi's advice are asked, with similar but slightly more lucid responses. John unconvincingly claims that their two days' experience with meditation gives him

enough confidence to weather such a tragedy. George takes the approach of "Within You Without You" and expresses comfort in knowing that Brian still exists, just not in a physical state.

RELEASE HISTORY

1984: Most of this interview was broadcast in the radio documentary *Sgt. Pepper's Lonely Hearts Club Band: A History of the Beatle Years 1962–1970.*

1996: This interview was released on *Fab Four CD & Book Set* in inferior quality and missing a bit at the beginning and end. It also circulates on video from various sources.

63. Studio session

Date: 5 September 1967
Time: 7:00 p.m.–1:00 a.m.
Location: EMI Studio 1
Producer: George Martin

[A.] I Am the Walrus—monitor mix of takes 7–9 and rehearsal (mono) (7:51)

John's sole contribution to the *Magical Mystery Tour* soundtrack was a song that drew from myriad lyrical sources and recording tricks to conjure up a darker version of the nonsensical world of "Lucy in the Sky." Recording of "I Am the Walrus" began this evening with a basic rhythm track, although the complex chord changes and shifts in tempo caused some problems.

John played electric piano, George electric guitar, Ringo drums, and on the initial takes, Paul played bass. The "monitor mix" tape from this session (**A**) begins with take 7 already in progress (cutting in right at the first verse). John seems to be singing a faint guide vocal to help everyone keep track of the song, but there is an awkward extra bar of transition into the fourth verse ("yellow matter custard") that throws everyone off, and Ringo seems unsure where to come back in. They carry on regardless, but when the "English garden" section arrives, there is total chaos and the performance breaks down.

After some tuning and doodling, take 8 begins but is a false start, making it only one line into the first verse. They start take 9 right away and things go a lot more smoothly. This take reaches a full ending, although that extra bar is still a bit tricky (it will continue to be a source of confusion right through final mixing). Take 9 is followed by about a minute from another performance, apparently a remnant of rehearsals taped over by the "proper" takes. The group perfected the backing track by take 16, by which point Paul had switched to tambourine, preferring to overdub his bass later.

RELEASE HISTORY

1989: A portion of **A** (take 9 only) appeared on the bootleg CD *Unsurpassed Masters, Volume 3,* running almost a half step too high in pitch.

1991: A different segment of the tape (take 7) was bootlegged on the CD *Unsurpassed Masters, Volume 6.*

1993: Most of the tape (still missing the rehearsal take) surfaced on the boot CD *Control Room Monitor Mixes.*

2002: The complete tape appeared in very good quality on the CD bootleg *Complete Controlroom Monitor Mixes, Volume 2.*

64. Studio session

Date: 6 September 1967
Time: 7:00 p.m.–3:00 a.m.
Location: EMI Studio 2
Producer: George Martin

[A.] I Am the Walrus—RS from takes 16 and 17 (4:00)
[B.] The Fool on the Hill—take 1 (mono) (2:46)

[C.] I Am the Walrus—RM4 (4:34)
Mixed: 6 September 1967

The previous day's work on "I Am the Walrus" was reduced to take 17 to make room for further embellishments. Paul overdubbed his bass guitar, while Ringo played some extra snare drum. Then John recorded an outstanding lead vocal, spitting out the words into his microphone, with the signal heavily filtered to give it an extra wallop. When the notorious extra bar arrived, John came in early and immediately caught himself: "Yellow . . . ooh!"

DJ Kenny Everett was present that night and described in his autobiography the reason for John's raspy singing: "George Martin, their producer, was working with John on the vocal track and he said: 'Look, you've been singing now for about seven hours, you're beginning to sound hoarse, why don't we do it tomorrow?' John wanted to get it done that day and that's why he sounds so raucous on that track."

The song was then mixed into mono for demo purposes; the best of these (**C**) was used for miming on the film set later that month. This mixes out John's vocal flub and edits out a four-beat passage leading into the "English garden." The version heard on *Anthology 2* contains both of these anomalies as well as some chat before the song starts and a full seven-beat piano intro. This mix (**A**) synchronizes the instruments from take 16 with the vocal overdub from take 17.

The first *Magical Mystery Tour* song written was Paul's "The Fool on the Hill"; he had the melody as early as March, although the lyrics were far from complete. In a few spare moments during this session, Paul laid down a studio demo (**B**), playing piano and singing the still-unfinished lyrics. The first verse and chorus are composed, and the second verse is nearly ready (missing the first line and with some other amendments). In place of further verses, Paul sings nonsense syllables, wrapping the whole thing up with a music-hall piano riff. This demo take was apparently recorded in mono for reference purposes only and was cut onto acetates.

Kenny Everett presumably managed to get tape copies of both acetates (**B** and **C**); in his book, he describes "feeling privileged beyond belief and listening to 'I Am A Walrus' [sic] and 'Fool On The Hill' before anyone else in the world . . . I decided to be extremely naughty and I pinched the tape." He misremembers this as occurring at the late Brian Epstein's house, but the basic story must be true, as it explains the appearance of these two tracks on bootlegs, neither of which were in the batch of acetates sold at auction in 1981. Everett continues: "I took the tape home and made a copy of it, then slipped the original back into Eppy's cupboard."

RELEASE HISTORY

1977: **B** and **C** first surfaced, from a fair-quality radio broadcast, on the bootleg LP *Indian Rope Trick* and EP *Studio Outtakes*. Unfortunately, both songs were excerpts, edited with the finished versions. The DJ who played the tracks, Bob Harris, may have acquired them directly from Kenny Everett.

1980: **C** appeared, nearly complete and in excellent quality, on the vinyl bootleg *Casualties*.

1985: A complete version of **B**, in very good quality, was booted on the LP *Strawberry Fields Forever,* along with **C**. Both songs were copied from this source on the 1988 CDs *Ultra Rare Trax, Volume 1* (**B**) and *Volume 2* (**C**).

1991: Excellent copies of **B** and **C** were included on the bootleg CD *Acetates;* **C** is a few seconds longer on this release than on any previous.

1996: **A** and **B** were released on the CD *Anthology 2,* both from tape sources.

65. Studio session

Date: 7 September 1967
Time: 7:00 p.m.–3:15 a.m.
Location: EMI Studio 2
Producer: George Martin

[A.] Blue Jay Way—RM1 (3:47)
Mixed: 16 September 1967

Most of George's compositions in 1967 ended up on film soundtracks, and "Blue Jay Way" would be his contribution to *Magical Mystery Tour*. This rather dreary tune was composed during the evening of August 1 while waiting for Derek Taylor to arrive at the house George was renting in Los Angeles. The original manuscript, on Robert Fitzpatrick Associates stationery, reveals the original opening line to be "There's a fog on Blue Jay Way," but he must have realized rhyming "Way" with "way" wasn't too clever, and the last four words are amended to "upon LA." There is also an unused fourth verse, thankfully cut as the song turned out to "be very long" without it.

George had composed what little melody "Blue Jay Way" possessed on a Hammond organ in the rented house, and opted to play EMI's Hammond on the song's rhythm track. This was perfected in a single take on September 6, with John playing a second organ, Paul on bass, and Ringo on drums filling out the rest of the tape. The next evening, this was bounced down to two tracks on a new tape to make space for George's doubled lead vocals. These would be treated to heavy phasing during mixing, and it also sounds as though his vocal is put through a Leslie speaker during the choruses.

Another reduction into take 3 consolidated both lead vocal tracks and both instrument tracks, and then John, Paul, and George added some Leslied backing vocals on the third track. The fourth track would be left empty for the time being, but a rough mix (A) was made of the work so far on September 16. This was copied for use during filming, and George mimed to it during the week of the nineteenth for the cameras, playing an "organ" drawn on the pavement with chalk.

RELEASE HISTORY

1991: **A** was included on the bootleg CD *Acetates,* running slightly fast and taken from an acetate sold at auction in 1981 (see the August 22 entry for details).

66. Studio session

Date: 8 September 1967
Time: 7:00 p.m.–2:45 a.m.
Location: EMI Studio 3
Producer: George Martin

[A.] Flying—RM4 (2:01)
Mixed: 8 September 1967

In addition to acting, writing, directing, editing, and recording songs for *Magical Mystery Tour,* the Beatles took on the responsibility of creating an instrumental score for the soundtrack. As with most of the project, this was not composed per se, consisting mainly of brief links of Mellotron noises and other homemade tape loops. One proposed scene was to feature the coach flying up into the clouds to visit the "five magicians." In the end, this was pared down to a sequence of passengers "looking out the window" and watching psychedelically tinted sky and landscape (reportedly outtake footage from *Dr. Strangelove*) rush past.

As background music for this scene, Paul led the others in a twelve-bar instrumental in C, provisionally titled "Aerial Tour Instrumental," on September 8. With John on organ, Paul on bass, George on heavily tremoloed guitar, and Ringo on drums, this 1:33 jam was perfected in six takes. Three organ pieces were then overdubbed backwards onto the remaining tracks and the recording was reduced to two tracks of a new tape, with take 8 being the best reduction. A half-hearted melody was then worked out and added to the song, first played by John on a Mellotron with the trumpet setting and then sung in wordless "la la" fashion by all four Beatles.

The song was then mixed into mono, with RM4 being cut onto an acetate for use in the film production. This acetate (**A**) contains a few elements ultimately mixed out of (or erased from) the song, including some slide whistle and Mellotron flutes. Most notably, it features a "stock ending" taken straight from a Mellotron tape, which extends the length of the song to just over two minutes. This consists of a Dixieland band playing a jaunty tune and ends with a "yeah" from Bill Fransen, one of the Mellotron's creators.

RELEASE HISTORY

1984: **A** first appeared in Westwood One's *Sgt. Pepper's Lonely Hearts Club Band: A History of the Beatle Years 1962–1970* radio special, taken from an acetate auctioned in 1981 (see the August 22 entry). Unfortunately most of the song was obscured by dialogue and narration, with only the Dixieland ending left intact.

1988: A clean copy of the acetate was aired on episode 88-36 of the radio series *The Lost Lennon Tapes*. It was copied from this source on the bootleg LP *The Lost Lennon Tapes, Number 9* and the CDs *Back-Track* and *Unsurpassed Masters, Volume 3,* running a bit slow on all releases.

67. TV interview

Date:	12 September 1967
Time:	afternoon
Location:	Grand Hotel, Plymouth
Interviewer:	Hugh Scully
Broadcast:	13 September 1967, 5:55–6:15 p.m.
	BBC1
	Spotlight South West
Length:	0:51

The first full day of shooting for *Magical Mystery Tour* was something of a disaster, with the bus being pursued by a convoy of journalists and fans. En route to filming at a fairground in Widecombe, the coach got stuck halfway across a bridge and was forced to turn around, but not before backing slowly off the bridge amid an enormous traffic snarl.

To appease the media, a lunchtime stop in Plymouth became an impromptu photo session, and a BBC TV reporter managed to get a few words from John and Paul as they greeted fans and wandered between the bus and the Grand Hotel.

In the extract that circulates, Paul explains why they chose Devon and Cornwall as a location and claims not to mind the horde of reporters on their trail. This black-and-white report also includes some silent footage from inside the bus and of the photo shoot on the grass. There is also 22 seconds of silent footage circulating, shot inside a room at the hotel. The camera pans from George to Paul (who waves vigorously) to Ringo, all seated at a table, then to John, lounging on a bed.

RELEASE HISTORY

This footage circulates in excellent quality as part of a compilation titled *At the Movies,* and in slightly more complete form, but poor quality, from a rebroadcast (introduced as *Southwest at 6,* perhaps from a later incarnation of the same newsmagazine). The original report lasted four minutes. The silent interior footage also circulates on video.

68. Radio interview   G

Date:	13 September 1967
Time:	afternoon/evening
Location:	Atlantic Hotel, Newquay
Interviewer:	Miranda Ward
Broadcast:	30 September and 7 October 1967,
	6:32–7:29 p.m.
	BBC Radio 1
	Scene and Heard
Length:	10:54

One of the new series on BBC's upcoming Radio 1 service, *Scene and Heard,* dispatched reporter Miranda Ward to Newquay while the Beatles and crew were filming there. George consented to a lengthy interview for use on the program's debut episode, conducted at the hotel while his bandmates were busy directing and acting in various scenes for *Magical Mystery Tour.*

He begins by describing the terms of their film contract with United Artists, explaining that the lack of a follow-up feature to *Help!* is due to lack of decent material. He seems eager to make a movie with some statement of purpose, which perhaps explains why he's sitting in the hotel rather than participating in the current project. In any case, he gives a likely schedule of February 1968 for shooting the next Beatles feature film; this was just one more in an ongoing string of postponed starting dates.

Interestingly, Ward asks how it feels to be "on the road again as the Beatles"—even though this was far from a concert tour, it was the first chance most people had to see the group together in public in more than a year. George once again goes into detail about his passion for Eastern spiritualism, naively expecting to see people levitate and dematerialize, and describing the Brahmin sect as "groovy people." Realizing just how superfluous his own affluence is, George also yearns to have the same peace and contentedness as the Indians he's met who hold few material possessions.

In part two of the interview, aired the following week, George describes the process and purpose of Transcendental Meditation, using the phrase "No time or space" (later to become the title of an experimental

LP track). He says he believes firmly in reincarnation and karmic law, comparing the latter to the biblical concept of reaping what you sow. George also says the Beatles plan to open a Transcendental Meditation academy in London, an idea never followed to fruition by Apple.

RELEASE HISTORY

1988: Part one of this interview was broadcast in the December 31 episode of BBC Radio's *The Beeb's Lost*

Beatles Tapes. All broadcast material is included on the bootleg CD *The Beatles Broadcast Collection Trailer 2*, although Kevin Howlett's book *The Beatles at the BBC* describes a bit more of the tape's contents (the full segment lasted 6:22). The original show was not pressed on a Transcription Disc and survived only because Miranda Ward salvaged it from the trash. Part two circulates from a fair-quality off-air recording of the original broadcast.

---

69. Radio interview   R

Date:	14 September 1967
Location:	Atlantic Hotel, Newquay
Interviewer:	Miranda Ward
Broadcast:	14 October 1967, 6:32–7:29 p.m.
	BBC Radio 1
	Scene and Heard
Length:	1:14

Miranda Ward also taped an interview with Ringo on location, with the topics decidedly more lighthearted than George's discussion. Ringo talks about having recently been to see a movie for the first time in ages at a public cinema with John. He says they saw the last half of one movie and the first half of another and found both "useless," but refuses to divulge their titles. Presuming this was the same outing John described to

Hunter Davies in their authorized biography, one of the films would have been a Morecambe and Wise feature, *The Magnificent Two*.

Ward asks if Ringo's doing any writing on the quiet, and he counters, "Not even in the loud!" He also talks about one of his favorite pastimes, playing billiards at home with John, George, or "whoever's around."

RELEASE HISTORY

This recording circulates from a rebroadcast circa 1969, apparently on New Zealand radio. The BBC doesn't seem to have retained a copy, as it hasn't appeared in any of their Beatles radio specials.

---

70. Amateur footage

Date:	13–15 September 1967
Location:	Holywell and Atlantic Hotel, Newquay
Length:	4:23

Mal Evans was along on the *Mystery Tour* and captured some of the activity in home movie footage. From the afternoon of September 13, John is seen directing a sequence featuring Nat Jackley as "Happy Nat the Rubber Man" pursuing several bikini-clad ladies. The location is a cliff overlooking the sea at Holywell, and the unfortunate extras are seen shivering in the cold (all for naught, as none of the sequence was used in the finished product). Also on hand are Neil and George,

who does a few dances for the camera. Paul puts in a brief appearance on his way to film with Ringo on the beach at Porth.

The balance of the footage seems to be from the morning of the fifteenth, as the Beatles and company check out of the Atlantic Hotel. The cast is seen posing alongside the bus in front of the hotel before departing for London.

RELEASE HISTORY

This silent color footage was released on the home video *The Magical Mystery Trip*.

71. Documentary footage

Date: 12 or 15 September 1967
Time: evening
Location: coach between Newquay and London

[A.] You Made Me Love You (0:36)

Returning to London from a working week on the road, the *Mystery Tour* coach party loaded up on liquor and had a group sing-song, accompanied by accordionist Shirley Evans. The proceedings were filmed and included in the TV show, and an apparent outtake appears in *Anthology*. This clip, from slate 56, take 9, features Ringo's "Aunt Jessie" (Jessie Robbins) leading the passengers in a rendition of "You Made Me Love You." As Shirley Evans is not present, and 56 is a relatively low slate number, it's possible this was actually filmed earlier in the week, perhaps on the evening of the twelfth en route to Newquay.

Although this is the only available outtake with sound, other home movies and rushes from the *Magical Mystery Tour* shoot appear in *Anthology*. These include the Beatles in costume filming "I Am the Walrus," dancers rehearsing for the "Your Mother Should Know" sequence, and Paul, in a white jacket and holding up an orange, on location in Nice at the end of October to direct scenes for "The Fool on the Hill." These silent outtakes may all stem from an unreleased promo film for "Hello Goodbye" (see the November 10 entry for details).

RELEASE HISTORY

1996: This footage was included in the *Anthology* home video documentary, with the other outtakes mentioned above incorporated into the finished sequences for each song. The soundtrack of **A** can be heard on the bootleg CD *Fanthology*.

72. Studio session

Date: 16 September 1967
Time: 7:00 p.m.–3:45 a.m.
Location: EMI Studio 3
Producer: George Martin

[A.] Your Mother Should Know—take 27 (stereo) (3:00)

Unsatisfied with the Chappell Studios recording, Paul instigated a remake of "Your Mother Should Know" back at Abbey Road on this evening. With the numbering starting at take 20, a further eleven takes were attempted, none of which ultimately proved suitable. Instead of piano, Paul played harmonium for these takes while singing his guide vocal ("with ciggie in mouth"). He was accompanied by drums, bongos, and piano played through a Leslie speaker.

The take heard on *Anthology 2* (**A**) was chosen as temporary "best," later supplanted (also temporarily) by take 30, the last take from this session. Take 27 begins with Paul asking George Martin if he's ready for them to begin another performance and needs a while to get started, as Paul mistimes his vocal entry. Ringo plays some snare drum rolls, and the ending isn't worked out (they vamp until Paul says "it should fade out"), but the structure is basically similar to the August recording. When it came time to film the scene accompanying this song on September 24, the earlier version had been chosen as superior and was used for playback on the set.

RELEASE HISTORY

1996: **A** was officially released on *Anthology 2*.

73. Studio session

Date: 25 September 1967
Time: 7:00 p.m.–3:00 a.m.
Location: EMI Studio 2
Producer: George Martin

[A.] interviews/The Fool on the Hill—rehearsals (mono) (15:11)
[B.] The Fool on the Hill—take 4 (stereo) (3:43)

The first three "proper" takes of backing for "The Fool on the Hill" were recorded this evening, in the presence of visiting Japanese journalists: reporter Rumiko Hoshika and photographer Koh Hasebe. Several photos from this session have been published, showing the group wearing checkerboard coats and gathered around the piano rehearsing Paul's song (he plays a recorder and John strums acoustic guitar). In addition, a long tape (**A**) was recorded by Rumiko (which has come to be known as the "Rumi tape"), capturing brief interviews and ongoing rehearsals for the song. Unfortunately, most of the music is obscured by Hoshika's narration and the awful quality of the circulating tape.

Documentation of the song's recording is ambiguous, but take 3 was bounced down to take 4 for further overdubs, and by the end of the day, "The Fool on the Hill" included several flutes and recorders, two pianos, drums played with brushes, a cymbal, acoustic guitar, and Paul's lead vocal. All of this can be heard on **B**, playing back somewhere between the key of C and C-sharp, so perhaps the reduction was done with varispeed (the natural key should be D major).

Paul is still working on the lyrics at this stage: The "man with the empty mind" would become the "man of a thousand voices." The other partial verses have variant words as well. Although take 4 was marked "best," mixed to mono, and cut onto an acetate, the Beatles would start from scratch the following day.

RELEASE HISTORY

1993: **A** surfaced on the bootleg CD *Rumitape and More* in horrendous sound quality, seemingly from a radio broadcast. Hopefully, an improved tape will surface one day.

1996: **B** was officially released on *Anthology 2*.

74. Studio session

Date:	28 September 1967
Time:	7:00 p.m.–3:00 a.m.
Location:	EMI Studio 2
Producer:	George Martin

[A.] Flying—take 8 and overdub takes 1–5 (mono) (9:37)

[B.] Flying—edit of RM6 (2:12)
Mixed: 28 September 1967

[C.] Flying—edit of RS1 (2:12)
Mixed: 7 November 1967

The group returned to the "Aerial Tour Instrumental" this evening to finish it off with a few more overdubs, probably erasing elements heard in the previous "best" mix. Ringo shook maracas, George added some licks on acoustic guitar, and John added further Mellotron flutes. To replace the Dixieland ending, John and Ringo prepared several tapes consisting of Mellotron, organ, and chimes.

Mark Lewisohn indicates that these tapes were assembled in five "takes," with the last of these being overdubbed onto track 4 of the song. John Barrett's tape log and the aural evidence reveal otherwise. In fact, all five "takes" appear on the same multitrack reel as the body of take 8, labeled as part two of the song, and we can hear each one play through on the raw studio tape (**A**). "Take 1" comes in at about 1:24 and is played backwards; this fades to silence at 2:48. The next two takes are played forward: "Take 2" lasts from 2:51–5:14, while "take 3" runs from 5:25–6:09. Two more backwards takes appear at 6:16–7:01 and 7:06–9:35. To round the whole thing off, George Martin's voice appears, exclaiming, "That's it!"

It's likely that these were never meant to be part of the song (now titled "Flying") for record release, but rather to be used generally in the film soundtrack (and indeed they pop up throughout as incidental music). Both released mixes fade the song well before the first overdub "take" has ended, with the effects coming in a bit earlier in mono (**B**). In stereo (**C**), the effects are panned from the center to the left of the soundstage. This song was apparently not remixed for the *Magical Mystery Tour* home video, although the channels are reversed.

RELEASE HISTORY

1967: **B** and **C** were released on mono and stereo pressings, respectively, of *Magical Mystery Tour* (an LP in the United States and an EP in the UK). **C** is on EMI's CD of the same name and **B** is on the *Magical Mystery Tour* CD-EP.

1994: An excellent-quality recording of **A** surfaced on *The Ultimate Collection, Volume 1: Miscellaneous Tracks;* this appears twice on the CD, first forward, then backwards!

Date: 29 September 1967
Time: 6:00–7:00 p.m.
Location: Studio 1, Wembley Studios
Host: David Frost
Broadcast: 29 September 1967, 10:30–11:15 p.m.
Rediffusion-TV
The Frost Programme
Length: 22:00

Although they had to cut short their training in Bangor, the Beatles met up with Maharishi Mahesh Yogi again in the first week of September back in London and continued a course of meditation throughout the month. On the morning of the twenty-ninth, the maharishi flew out of London Airport, filming an interview for that evening's *Frost Programme* before boarding his flight. That afternoon, prior to an Abbey Road session, John and George videotaped an appearance for the same show, chatting to David Frost about their experiences with Transcendental Meditation. The show opened with the maharishi interview, and after the first commercial break, Frost introduced John and George's pretaped discussion.

He begins by asking whether they have found more serenity and energy through meditation, and both Beatles claim that positive energy has been within them all along but they now have a way to tap into it more easily. George describes the purpose behind the mantras they were given, the idea being to replace conscious thought with the mantra until you reach a level of deeper awareness. They admit that it's tricky to get your mind to stop thinking of mundane things, but that once you do, time and space cease to have meaning. John compares it to not being aware you're in a sleeping state until you wake up.

Frost wonders if they can relay what they experience during meditation, but George says it'd be like trying to describe what it feels like to be drunk—it's something the individual needs to observe firsthand. Although they are novices, John and George enthuse about how much better they feel, but it's obvious they approach the matter with different aims. John seems to have practical reasons (wanting more energy to tackle work) while George hopes to attain a permanent state of bliss.

Frost asks them to compare the revelations with those experienced while on drugs, and John claims they had gotten all they could from LSD and abandoned it "long before Maharishi" (not exactly true, they tripped constantly during their late-July visit to Greece). He goes on to say acid was more about discovering yourself (he would later say it destroyed his ego), and George points out that your "true self" isn't on a physical level anyway.

Frost's main worry seems to be that the process is too self-centered as compared with Christianity's more charitable tenets. John and George dispute this, insisting that all religions have basically the same message. George is excited over the prospect of being able to personally experience God-consciousness, and John wishes he'd been taught Transcendental Meditation at age fifteen, because by now he'd be really groovy! Asked what the word "God" means to them now, George says, "Every aspect of creation is part of God," and John compares God to a sort of spiritual power plant. Frost belabors the idea of helping others, but George figures that if everyone could sort out their own problems, the world would be a much nicer place.

They conclude with some discussion about reincarnation: George feels people are here to fulfill all desires, and that everyone will keep coming back until they are ready to "become one with the Creator." Returning to earth for a moment, he admits that "it sounds far out, but it's what I believe," and John adds that if it all seems daunting, just use Transcendental Meditation to improve your life in the present, and the future will take care of itself. Frost ends the show by announcing that discussion of the topic will continue next Wednesday night, and indeed John and George would return for a second appearance.

RELEASE HISTORY

It's not clear whether this entire show has survived, but bits and pieces of the original videotape have been used in various documentaries (including *Anthology* and *It Was Twenty Years Ago Today*). A fair-quality offline tape of the complete audio portion circulates among collectors.

76. Studio session

Date: 29 September 1967
Time: 7:00 p.m.–5:00 a.m.
Location: EMI Studio 2
Producer: George Martin

[A.] **I Am the Walrus—RM23** (4:33)
[B.] **I Am the Walrus—edit of RM23** (4:31)
Mixed: 29 September 1967

[C.] **Your Mother Should Know—RM25** (2:24)
Mixed: 2 October 1967

[D.] **Your Mother Should Know—RS2** (2:24)
[E.] **I Am the Walrus—edit of RS6/7** (4:31)
Mixed: 6 November 1967

[F.] **I Am the Walrus—edit of RS25/7** (4:32)
Mixed: 17 November 1967

[G.] **Your Mother Should Know—RS from take 52** (2:24)
[H.] **Your Mother Should Know—RS from takes 8, 9, and 52** (1:33)
[I.] **I Am the Walrus—RS from takes 16, 17, 20, and 25 (#1)** (4:32)
[J.] **I Am the Walrus—RS from takes 16, 17, 20, and 25 (#2)** (4:28)

George Martin had come up with a magnificent score for "I Am the Walrus" that suited the mood of the song perfectly. In addition to strings, clarinets, and horns, this included a vocal arrangement for the Mike Sammes Singers, a professional session group who were asked to chant such phrases as "Everybody's got one!" and "Stick it up your jumper!"

All of this was recorded on September 27, first the orchestra during simultaneous reduction mixes of take 17, with take 20 being best. Another reduction was done to free up a track for the choral overdub, with take 25 being the keeper. All four tracks were now full, but the rhythm, bass, and lead vocal were squeezed onto one of them, so George Martin went back to take 17, which still had a spare track, and added the new orchestral/choral overdubs to it, directly from take 25. All mixing would be done from take 17.

John had another brainstorm two days later: In keeping with the anything goes spirit of the project and the year in general, he decided to incorporate a direct feed from BBC Radio into several of the mixes. What he ended up with, on RM22, was a prerecorded (August 24) performance of *The Tragedy of King Lear* (specifically act IV, scene VI), which would provide excellent fodder for "Paul is dead" clue hunters.

For now, though, it was just a groovy sound, and so a clean mono mix (RM10) was edited to the last half of RM22 (the edit occurs at 2:03 right in the middle of the string passage) to create RM23, the mono master (**A**). This mix trims the piano intro to four beats and mixes out the rhythm track after each mention of "I'm crying." The extra bar of music before "Yellow matter custard" is still present.

Stereo mixing didn't occur until November 6, and with the radio feed being on the mono mix rather than the multitracks, a bit of cheating was called for. RS6 contains the first half of the song in true stereo; halfway through, the stereo mix (**E**) switches to RS7, which is a fake "rechanneled" mix from RM22 (bass in the left channel, treble in the right). To wrap things up, at around 3:48 the mono signal is merely panned back and forth. This mix also has a four-beat piano intro, but edits out the extra bar of music before "Yellow matter custard" and does not mix out the rhythm track after each "I'm crying."

The next day, Capitol Records' Voyle Gilmore visited Abbey Road to procure copies of **A** and **E,** which ended up on a single and stereo LP, respectively, in North America. However, in the next few days, someone must have realized that the songs didn't match up length-wise, and that pesky extra bar was excised from the mono master to create **B** for use on the British single. This was done by November 13, by which time Capitol had started pressing singles using their unedited tape (**A**). Word reached them in time to make their own edit for the mono *Magical Mystery Tour* LP.

Presumably, editing of the sequence in question for the film was going on simultaneously to all this, as the film print does not contain the extra bar either, and they certainly would have been working from the mono mix. On November 17, the day stereo copies of the British EP were cut, a last-minute substitution was made, using a fresh stereo mix of the first half of "I Am the Walrus" (RS25), which accidentally includes a six-beat piano intro. This variation (**F**) was edited into the master reel and has since become the standard stereo version.

Perhaps the greatest accomplishment of the *Anthology* DVD remixing team was their creation of the first complete true stereo mix of "I Am the Walrus" (**I**). This allows the song to breathe by spreading out the previously clustered rhythm track (electric piano left, drums and tambourine centered, guitar right), splitting the orchestra to far left and right, and recreating the *King Lear* excerpts from a disc of the original broadcast, complete with faux radio static! The *Love* remix (**J**) also spreads out the orchestra (and includes George Martin's count-in for their overdub) and adds bits of *King Lear* and other radio noises.

The final objective of the September 29 session was to polish up "Your Mother Should Know" for record release. Too lazy to check how many takes had been attempted, John and Paul reduced take 9 into takes "50" through "52," and added further instruments to the last of these. The original vocals were now all on one track and the piano and drums still occupied their own track. Paul added his bass to the third track, and then shook a tambourine while John played an organ part for the final track. A rough mono mix was done that night that would have slowed the song down considerably from its natural key of C major.

One of the remixes done the next day (RM23) is labeled "gimmick" and may also have employed some varispeed, but the mix chosen for release (**C**) did not, although the signal was heavily compressed. The stereo mix (**D**) sounds much more natural in comparison, although it resorts to the "gimmick" of panning the vocal track from left to right. It also splits the vocal on the final verse and choruses with ADT, placing it in both channels. Both mixes also have ADT applied to the opening "ooh's."

The remix for the *Magical Mystery Tour* home video (**G**) keeps the vocals mostly centered, but retains the ADT splitting trick at the end. Another mix on the *Anthology* DVD (**H**) isolates the piano track from take 8 (left) and splits the two backing vocal tracks from take 9.

RELEASE HISTORY

1967: **A** was released on promotional and commercial copies of the "Hello Goodbye" single in the United States and Canada only. **B** and **C** were included on mono copies of the UK *Magical Mystery Tour* EP and are on the CD-EP of that title. Stereo pressings of that EP included **D** and **F,** both available on EMI's *Magical Mystery Tour* CD (regular and EP versions). In the United States, the mono *Magical Mystery Tour* LP contained **C** and a version of **A** edited to resemble **B**. U.S. stereo copies included **D** and **E**.

1980: Capitol's *Rarities* LP contained a composite recording made from **F** with the extra bar from **A** spliced in and mixed to "rechanneled" stereo (treble left, bass right).

1988: The home video release of *Magical Mystery Tour* included **E** and **G**. They appear from this source on the CD *It's All in the Mind Y'Know*.

2003: **H** and **I** were released on the soundtrack of the *Anthology* DVD.

2006: **J** was released on the *Love* CD.

77. Studio session

Date: 2 October 1967
Time: 10:00 p.m.–2:30 a.m.
Location: EMI Studio 2
Producer: George Martin

[A.] Hello Goodbye—take 1 (mono) (5:05)

Paul had written "Hello Goodbye" too late for inclusion in the *Magical Mystery Tour* film (although its coda appears over the end credits) and decided it would make a good Christmas single instead. It was apparently inspired by a songwriting exercise he and Alistair Taylor had done, seated at Paul's home harmonium and calling out antonyms to each other.

The basic track was laid down this evening in fourteen takes of piano, drums, organ, and tambourine. The first of these (**A**) begins with Paul and Ringo running through the chords in a slow tempo before engineer Ken Scott announces take 1 (under its working title "Hello Hello"). This makes Paul realize the tape is running, and he tells Ringo to keep quiet before counting in. The first take is similar in structure to the finished product, with an extra verse and chorus thrown in, which may indicate that Paul hadn't finalized the lyrics yet or had an extra verse in mind that was later discarded.

Take 14 turned out best, and with the addition of maracas (and perhaps bongos or congas on the coda, although they are buried if present), it was ready for the first of many reductions. This was done twice before the session was through, with all the instruments going onto track 1 of take 16.

RELEASE HISTORY

1988: **A** first surfaced on the vinyl bootleg *Ultra Rare Trax, Volume 5 & 6*. This appeared from tape source on the CD *Not Guilty* the following year, running nearly a half step too slow.

1989: A slightly slow tape source was included on *Unsurpassed Masters, Volume 3,* including a split-second more at the start, but unfortunately, that CD fades out to silence for a couple of seconds, expunging Paul's count-in.

2005: The bootleg CD *Miscellaneous Tracks* included a minor upgrade of **A**, with an extra exclamation from John at the very end.

Date: 4 October 1967
Time: 6:00–7:00 p.m.
Location: Studio 1, Wembley Studios
Host: David Frost
Broadcast: 4 October 1967, 10:30–11:15 p.m.
Rediffusion-TV
The Frost Programme
Length: 38:18

When John and George returned to discuss Transcendental Meditation on *The Frost Programme,* they faced a much harder sell than the genial host had given them previously. This time, among a panel of invited guests, the decidedly unsympathetic writer John Mortimer was there to square off against anyone showing the slightest bit of belief in the maharishi's methods. An audio recording of the complete show exists, and reveals the differences in John and George's degrees of conviction. George is at times patronizingly self-assured in his faith, while John is at the opposite end, sounding genuinely irritated and defensive for someone who is trying to argue he's found a new path to inner peace.

The tape begins with the opening theme and Frost's monologue before John and George recap and expand upon some of the topics from their previous appearance. Frost wonders how their lives have changed since beginning Transcendental Meditation, but George feels life is just one continuous process of alteration and self-improvement. He claims he'd be happier if all his money were taken away, because he wouldn't have to deal with all the headaches revenue brings (income tax, for example). He's learned that spiritual wealth helps to put the material wealth in proper perspective.

Some letters from viewers are read, including a woman who reports that meditation has made her so impatient with life's hassles that she has become withdrawn and antisocial. George dismisses this by assuming she's using the wrong technique: "Obviously hers isn't much cop." Asked to explain the ultimate goal of Transcendental Meditation, George talks about attaining a state of permanent bliss, and beyond that, acquiring supreme knowledge, which enables one to do miracles. Quite straight-faced, he relates the tale of one yogi who conquered cancer of the mouth at age 112 by smoking and lived to be 136, and another who has been living in the Himalayas "since before Christ, in the same physical body."

At this point, the other guests are asked to chime in, including a pair of Transcendental Meditation believers, John Allison and Nick Clark. John Mortimer's pessimism about the state of the world naturally clashes with the maharishi's followers, unshakable in their espousal that if everyone meditated, peace would be attainable. Mortimer is concerned that the universe will go to hell while people sit alone and achieve bliss. John Lennon, sounding quite upset, insists that you only need to do twenty minutes of meditation each morning to give yourself more energy for going out and solving tangible problems.

Someone compares this to the philosophy of Quakers, and George agrees: "I'm a Quaker, I'm a Christian, I'm a Buddhist, and I'm a Hindu. And it's all the same." He says the problem with Mortimer's argument is that it's based in ignorance and needs to be tested with first-hand experience. After a commercial break, John complains bitterly that Transcendental Meditation is not a selfish proposition, otherwise they wouldn't be on television (a place he'd rather not be) trying to help spread understanding about it.

Mortimer concedes that if the process is a scientific or psychological technique of self-examination, he can agree to its usefulness, but has a problem with it being a "mystical" way of revealing hidden laws. George snaps that laws are hidden only by people's ignorance. John Allison describes Transcendental Meditation as both conceptual and perceptual because it's a literal experience but not one easily verifiable by nonparticipants. George agrees that it's hard to put into words, and Allison compares it to trying to explain to someone what a strawberry tastes like.

As the show wraps up, Frost asks again about the aftereffect and John says he's just a better person, adding: "I wasn't bad before!" George seconds that, and the program ends with none of the participants having shifted their positions. At least the studio audience and viewers were able to hear both sides of the issue at some length, assisting them in making up their own minds.

RELEASE HISTORY

1999: A very good copy of this recording was bootlegged on the boxed CD set *Mythology, Volume 3.* Although it doesn't circulate, I have it on good authority that at least some of this show survives on video.

79. Studio session

Date: 6 October 1967
Time: 7:00 p.m.–2:00 a.m.
Location: EMI Studio 2
Producer: George Martin

[A.] Blue Jay Way—edit of RM27 (3:48)
[B.] Blue Jay Way—edit of RS12 (3:50)
Mixed: 7 November 1967

[C.] Blue Jay Way—RS from takes 1 and 3 (3:45)

The remaining empty track of "Blue Jay Way" was filled with a cello and tambourine overdub this evening, although there seems to be no record of who played the cello. It is almost amateurish enough to have been played by a Beatle, but documents indicate someone got paid £27 for scraping their way through the song. On October 12, the first eight mono mixes were created, and two of them were edited together to produce a temporary master, but there was something missing.

Of course! This was 1967 and none of the song was backwards! This heinous error was corrected with fresh stereo mixing on November 7—a separate reel of the song running backwards was fed into the board during mixing and faded up between vocal lines. The problem with this method, like feeding the radio into "I Am the Walrus" during mixing, was that the mono mix could not duplicate the process exactly. They considered merely collapsing the stereo to mono, but in the end used a fresh mono mix (**A**) with no backwards tapes added. Since the song matches the length of the unedited RM1, it's hard to say where the edits would be on each released mix, or what their purpose is.

The remix for the home video of *Magical Mystery Tour* (**C**) similarly ignores the reversed effects, and isolates the various elements of take 1 (organ left, second organ and bass right, drums panned around) and syncs them with the vocals and overdubs from take 3. This mix also has the cello passage at 1:10–1:27 mixed much louder than previous versions.

RELEASE HISTORY

1967: **A** and **B** were released on mono and stereo pressings, respectively, of *Magical Mystery Tour* (an LP in the United States and an EP in the UK). **B** is on EMI's CD of the same name, and **A** is on the *Magical Mystery Tour* CD-EP.

1988: The home video release of *Magical Mystery Tour* included **C**. It appears from this source on the CD *It's All in the Mind Y'Know*.

80. Newsreel footage

Date: 17 October 1967
Time: 6:00 p.m.
Location: New London Synagogue, London
Broadcast: 17 October 1967
ITV
Length: 0:26

Having been persuaded not to wear their usual colorful accoutrements, the Beatles paid final respects to their manager by showing up at his memorial service in appropriately dark suits, even donning black yarmulkes once inside. An ITV News film crew captured their separate arrivals that evening as their cars pulled up and they crossed Abbey Road to the synagogue: first John and Cynthia, then Paul (solo), George with Pattie and Neil, Peter Brown with Lulu, and finally Ringo and Maureen.

RELEASE HISTORY

This footage was included in the video *Beatles 1962 to 1970* and also appears in the documentary *Imagine: John Lennon*.

81. Newsreel footage

Date: 18 October 1967
Time: evening
Location: London Pavilion
Length: 1:19

Nearly a year after completing principal photography, the film *How I Won the War* opened at the London Pavilion, site of the *Help!* and *A Hard Day's Night* premieres. As always, TV and newsreel cameras were on hand to film the celebrity arrivals.

John makes quite an impression pulling up in his psychedelically pigmented Rolls-Royce, accompanied by Cynthia, Alexis Mardas, and Pete Shotton. The other Beatles are seen fighting their way through the crowd, alongside Pattie, Maureen, and Jane. Other familiar faces glimpsed in the footage are director Richard Lester, star Michael Crawford, and Jimi Hendrix and bandmate Noel Redding.

RELEASE HISTORY

Thirty-eight seconds of silent color footage was included in the contemporary featurette *The Man behind the Beatles,* an overview of Richard Lester's films to date with particular emphasis on *How I Won the War.* This circulates on video along with an additional 41 seconds of black-and-white footage from ITV News coverage.

The Man behind the Beatles also includes a 7-second color clip of Richard Lester chatting with John at an unknown outdoor location sometime around this date. Lester was acting as an unofficial "technical adviser" on the *Magical Mystery Tour* project.

82. Studio session

Date: 19 October 1967
Time: 7:00 p.m.–3:30 a.m.
Location: EMI Studio 1
Producer: George Martin

[A.] Hello Goodbye—take 16 (stereo) (3:16)

The Beatles returned to "Hello Hello" this evening, filling up track 2 with a pair of lead guitar parts and some clever counterpoint vocals, and lead vocals from Paul on tracks 3 and 4. Also added on one of the latter were handclaps and the "hela" vocals for the song's end. All of this can be heard on the outtake (**A**), including several guitar passages that would later be mixed out or erased.

A second reduction at the end of the day into take 17 combined tracks 3 and 4 to make room for more instruments.

RELEASE HISTORY

1996: This outtake was officially released on *Anthology 2.*

83. Studio session

Date: 20 October 1967
Time: 7:00 p.m.–3:45 a.m.
Location: EMI Studio 3
Producer: George Martin

[A.] The Fool on the Hill—edit of RM12 (2:56)
Mixed: 25 October 1967

[B.] The Fool on the Hill—edit of RS5 (2:55)
Mixed: 1 November 1967

[C.] The Fool on the Hill—RS from takes 5 and 7 (1:26)

As suggested earlier, the existing documentation is unclear about the recording process of "The Fool on the Hill." On September 26, a fresh backing track called take 5 was recorded. Paul's piano occupied one track, Ringo's drums and finger cymbal a second, and acoustic guitar and maracas a third. The fourth track was then filled with celeste, more piano, and recorder.

This was all reduced to a single track as take 6. Paul recorded a pair of lead vocals (one of which included a recorder solo), and John and George played bass harmonicas to fill the fourth track. A tape loop of slowed-down guitar was also added on this track; it can be heard skittering across the stereo image at 2:39 on **B**.

Nearly a month went by until the final addition on October 20 of three flutes, played by session musicians. With all four tracks full, these were recorded on a separate tape as take 7, along with a sync tone and a mixdown (for reference purposes only) of the take 6 ingredients. The tapes of takes 6 and 7 were then played back in sync during final mixing.

The completed song was mixed into mono on October 25 and edited down from an initial length of 4:25. It's not entirely clear where the edits are, although it sounds like the intro may have been longer (the piano and flutes cut in abruptly on **B**).

The stereo mix used in a 1993 EPK to promote the CD *The Beatles 1967–1970* is said to be an alternate mix, but it sounds identical to the mix heard on the *Magical Mystery Tour* home video, which in turn sounds the same as **B** to my ears. A remix on the *Anthology* DVD (**C**) is nearly identical, but has the maracas and guitar from take 5 isolated from the rest of the rhythm track.

RELEASE HISTORY

1967: **A** and **B** were released on mono and stereo pressings, respectively, of *Magical Mystery Tour* (an LP in the United States and an EP in the UK). **B** is on EMI's CD of the same name, and **A** is on the *Magical Mystery Tour* CD-EP.

2003: **C** was released on the soundtrack of the *Anthology* DVD.

84. Location recording

Date: ca. October 1967

[A.] Jessie's Dream (stereo) (3:27)

One of the most memorable scenes in *Magical Mystery Tour* is a dream sequence wherein Ringo's Auntie Jessie dreams of gorging on a mound of spaghetti served up by John, playing a sinister-looking waiter. To accompany this scene, a composition credited jointly to McCartney/Starkey/Harrison/Lennon and titled "Jessie's Dream" was overdubbed on the soundtrack during the editing process in November.

It's not entirely clear what this encompasses, as the musical cue in question is comprised of two distinct elements. In the version remixed for the stereo home video, the left channel contains a series of electronic noises, including Mellotron and slide whistles, which runs throughout. This is most likely the copyrighted portion and was probably taped at one of the Beatles' home studios rather than Abbey Road.

In the right channel, during the portion from 0:23–2:58, a jazz trio (piano, upright bass, and drums) is heard vamping in C#m. This is certainly amateurish enough to have been played by the Beatles, but is more likely taken from a Mellotron rhythm tape.

RELEASE HISTORY

1988: The home video release of *Magical Mystery Tour* included **A**. It appears from this source on the bootleg CD *Back-Track, Part 2*. The original mono film soundtrack, booted on the LP *Cinelogue' V,* uses an alternate mix with some different effects.

85. Studio session

Date: 2 November 1967
Time: 2:30–6:00 p.m.
Location: EMI Studio 3
Producer: George Martin

[A.] Hello Goodbye—RM6 (3:23)
Mixed: 2 November 1967

[B.] Hello Goodbye—RS2 (3:26)
Mixed: 6 November 1967

[C.] Hello Goodbye—RS from takes 14, 16, 17, and 22 (3:34)
[D.] Hello Goodbye—RS from takes 14, 16, and 22 (3:32)

The next step for "Hello Hello" was to add a pair of violas to its remaining free track. This was done October 20 in Studio 3; during this same session, Paul wiped the guitar solo and replaced it with his deeply echoed "Why why why why why why, do you say goodbye goodbye?"

A third tape reduction on the twenty-fifth combined the violas with the guitar track, and Paul overdubbed bass on the "best" reduction, take 21. This should have wrapped up the song and indeed accounts for everything heard in the released mixes. But Mark Lewisohn reports that an unprecedented fourth reduction was made on November 1, to which Paul added a second bass part on November 2. There seems to be only one bass in the finished song, and if Paul wanted to redo his performance, it was on its own track, so replacing it would have been simple enough.

Interestingly, John Barrett's tape log indicates that these mystery reductions were for "Parts Two and Three" of "Hello Goodbye." And for what it's worth, I can hear edits or changes in ambience at 1:36 and 2:13 in the stereo mix. But there is no record of any editing during mixing. During the so-called Maori finale, the stereo mix (**B**) splits the rhythm track with ADT left and right and moves everything else to the center.

A very ambitious remix used for the soundtrack of various Apple promotional videos (**C**) syncs together elements from practically every stage of the recording. Thus we have isolated organ, drums, maracas, and piano (from take 14), separated vocal tracks (take 16), violas (take 17, independent from the guitars), and the bass overdub (take 22).

A newer stereo mix for the *Anthology* DVD (**D**) appears to sync the rhythm from take 14 (drums centered, the rest at far left) with the remaining elements of the final take (lead guitar, violas, and backing vocals right, lead vocals and bass centered). Over the coda, we can also hear the split "hela" vocal tracks from take 16. Both remixes are slowed down a full half step, presumably to line up better with the images in the promo clip.

RELEASE HISTORY

1967: **A** was issued worldwide as a single and is available on the "Hello Goodbye" CD single. **B** appeared on Capitol's *Magical Mystery Tour* LP and is included on EMI's CD of that title, as well as the CD compilations *The Beatles 1967–1970* and *1*.

1983: A copy of **B** was used in the multimedia presentation *The Beatles at Abbey Road;* apart from reversal of the stereo image, this seems to be identical to the released mix, perhaps sounding a bit drier. It's booted on the CD *Turn Me On Dead Man: The John Barrett Tapes*.

1993: **C** was included on the soundtrack of an EPK promoting the CD release of *The Beatles 1967–1970*. It can be heard on the CD-R *Video 1,* and speed-corrected to match the original key on the CD *Lost and Found*.

2003: **D** was released on the soundtrack of the *Anthology* DVD.

86. Newsreel footage

Date:	1–7 November 1967
Location:	TVC Studios, London
Length:	0:22

As work continued on *Magical Mystery Tour,* animators were working hard to pull together the film *Yellow Submarine* from an ever-changing script and storyboards. Most of the Beatles songs to be used in the film were copied at Abbey Road this month for use by King Features. Early in the month, the group made a morale-boosting visit across Soho from their editing suite to the offices of TV Cartoons.

In addition to inspiring the animators, the visit was filmed for promotional purposes, and fleeting clips ended up in the movie's trailer and a behind-the-scenes featurette, *Mod Odyssey*. In the latter, the Beatles pose with life-size cutouts of their characters and a cartoon minisubmarine. For the trailer, they are filmed sitting in a screening room, ostensibly watching the finished product. The group laughs and points at the screen, acting greatly amused by their Lonely Hearts Club Band counterparts.

In both sources, these clips are intercut with footage from their January 25, 1968, cameo shoot at Twickenham, but it's easy to tell which scenes are from which date, since George shaved off his mustache in mid-January.

RELEASE HISTORY

1999: The DVD release of *Yellow Submarine* included all this footage, including the complete *Mod Odyssey* short, although better-quality prints of the featurette circulate on video.

87. Studio session

Date:	7 November 1967
Time:	9:00 p.m.–4:30 a.m.
Location:	EMI Studio 1
Producer:	George Martin
[A.]	**Magical Mystery Tour—RS6** (2:46)
[B.]	**Magical Mystery Tour—RM10** (2:45)
Mixed:	7 November 1967

During editing of the *Magical Mystery Tour* special, John had added a spoken barker's call over the title song: "Roll up, roll up for the Magical Mystery Tour! Step right this way! Hurry, hurry, hurry!" At the eleventh hour, it was decided to incorporate this into the song for record release.

This was added during a lengthy mixing session on November 7, along with the bus effect loop prepared April 25. With John most likely absent, Paul stepped in and re-created the spiel, leaving out the "Hurry, hurry, hurry!" line. A previously prepared stereo mix (RS4 from November 6) was copied onto a fresh tape with the new overdubs added simultaneously; the same was then done with RM7.

The final mono mix (**B**) adds phasing to the lead

vocal and mixes out the trumpets' held E chord (at 1:26) a couple of seconds earlier than in the stereo mix (**A**). Copies of both "best" mixes were taken away by Capitol's Voyle Gilmore at the end of the session.

RELEASE HISTORY

1967: **A** and **B** were released on stereo and mono pressings, respectively, of *Magical Mystery Tour* (an LP in the United States and an EP in the UK). **A** is on EMI's CD of the same name, and **B** is on the *Magical Mystery Tour* CD-EP.

88. Promo clips

Date:	10 November 1967
Location:	Saville Theatre, London
Director:	Paul McCartney
Broadcast:	(**A** only) 26 November 1967, 8:00–9:00 p.m. CBS-TV *The Ed Sullivan Show*

[A.] **Hello Goodbye—version 1** (3:20)
[B.] **Hello Goodbye—version 2** (3:20)
[C.] **Hello Goodbye—version 3** (3:19)

With the decision to release "Hello Goodbye" as a single separate from the *Magical Mystery Tour* project, the Beatles needed to assemble a film clip to promote the song on television. Unsurprisingly, Paul took charge of this, acting as director and employing the same editor (Roy Benson) and camera crew used on the *Tour.* The group assembled onstage at the NEMS-leased Saville Theatre and lip-synced several versions of the song, accompanied by hula dancers for the coda.

The most commonly seen version (**A**) features the Beatles dressed as Sgt. Pepper's band in the Day-Glo satin uniforms they had worn on their last LP cover. The backdrop is a floral painting, and Ringo is playing his absurdly small "toy" drum kit, with no logo on the bass drum head. In all clips, Paul plays his repainted Rickenbacker bass, George his Epiphone Casino electric guitar, and John (seen without glasses for one of the last times) a Martin D-28 acoustic guitar. Brief inserts feature the group posing in their gray collarless suits, made famous in Dezo Hoffmann's photos, and waving quizzically at the camera.

The second variation (**B**) was performed in front of a painted farmland backdrop and has the group dressed in their civilian clothes, with John in black apart from a white sports coat, Paul wearing his patchwork sweater vest, and the others in more psychedelic garb. This time Ringo plays his regular-size kit with the familiar Ludwig Beatles logo.

A third clip (**C**) incorporates outtake footage from all the above and combines it with film of a rehearsal in front of a lighted and glittery pastel backdrop. This is by far the most entertaining version, showing the group flirting with the dancers, running across the stage, and dancing frenetically (John does the Charleston and the twist). Ringo bashes the front of an oversize bass drum (again, with no logo) and George even does a brief striptease, slipping his jacket provocatively off his shoulders!

Although version **A** was used in the United States on both *The Ed Sullivan Show* and *Hollywood Palace,* in Germany on *Beat Club,* and in several other countries, all the hard work went to waste in England. A Musicians Union ban on mimed TV appearances was in effect at the time, and they went to great lengths to circumvent this. Since no viola players had been filmed, a special mono mix of the song was created for the BBC's copy of the promo. This mix, done November 15 at EMI Studio 2, eliminated the viola track, but the ruse fooled no one.

A planned airing on *Top of the Pops* November 23 was denied on the twentieth, officially because "a minor portion of the film contravened the Musicians Union regulations concerning miming on television." Since the whole thing was clearly mimed, it's not clear what the "minor portion" would have been; perhaps it's the moment in **A** when Paul's lip sync is obviously late (on the word "goodbye-bye-bye-bye"). On the twenty-first, BBC cameramen filmed the group in a Soho film editing suite, working on *Magical Mystery Tour.* Their understanding was that the new footage would be inserted to cover the offending portions.

The BBC had other ideas. The initial quashed airing on the twenty-third was replaced at the last minute by some footage from *A Hard Day's Night.* A screening in color on *Late Night Line-Up* the same evening was canceled entirely. The song was missing from *Top of the Pops* on the thirtieth, and by December 7, a compromise version was shown, consisting entirely of the editing suite footage and still photographs, with no sign of the Saville performance. This BBC clip hasn't surfaced; nor has a fifth alternate prepared by John and Roy Benson and comprised of outtake rushes from *Magical Mystery Tour.*

The Benson clip did turn up at a Fleetwood Owen auction in September 2001 as a 16 mm copy (presumably Benson's own) struck from the original negative. The contents were described as follows: "The Beatles and the crowd from the bus entering the restaurant to sit down and eat—the sequence has many optical effects that are intercut with a variety of scenes from 'I Am The Walrus' including Ringo as a wizard, the crowd from the bus running through many balloons in the hangar, John on the bus, George as a wizard, the stripper with the Bonzo Dog Doo Dah Band, John as a wizard carrying a tray of tea, Paul, Ringo, and George in a garden with a ball, John and Ringo as Wizards dancing, John and Ringo asleep on the bus, The Beatles coming down stairs in white tails from 'Your Mother Should Know,' John, Paul and Ringo in a Fish & Chip shop, Paul on the sea front in Nice running up to the camera and throwing his coat over it, long shot of Paul standing on a sunset lit hill, a car chase sequence at an aerodrome, Paul as a wizard, George on the bus, Paul throwing up an apple whilst walking through Nice market, finishing with an end sequence of an empty hangar. Edited with still frames dissolving through each other to fade out into blue." The footage went unsold, but will hopefully see the light of day

eventually (it may be the source of the "outtakes" used in *Anthology*).

RELEASE HISTORY

The Ed Sullivan Show version (**A**) was first to circulate, complete with Ed's introduction from a kinescope, and later on its own from an excellent-quality color print. In 1985, the compilation *Private Reel,* an illicit transfer from Ringo's archive, included all three variations (**A**–**C**). In 1993, to promote the CD issue of *The Beatles 1967–1970,* a blue-bordered copy of **B** was distributed.

The edit appearing in *Anthology* is mostly from **A,** but the coda consists of footage from all three versions (this also includes Sullivan's intro and outro). It should be noted that the clips circulate at two different speeds: Those on *Private Reel* are in the proper key (matching the timings listed above) and other versions are slowed down considerably, extending the length to 3:30.

89. Home demo   P

Date: ca. mid-November 1967
Location: 7 Cavendish Avenue, London

[A.] Step Inside Love (2:14)

Before he died, Brian Epstein had negotiated with the BBC to sign Cilla Black for a nine-episode TV variety series, to be aired in early 1968. Paul was approached "backstage somewhere" (presumably at the Saville Theater during filming on November 10 or during the show he attended there on the nineteenth) to compose a theme song for her new show, and the result was the bossa nova–influenced ballad "Step Inside Love."

This demo features acoustic guitar and vocal, both double-tracked, and was recorded at his home studio. The first and third verses are complete but no lyrics are written for the second verse yet, so Paul hums his

way through it. The only source for this demo is a poor-quality off-line radio airing by DJ Kenny Everett, presumably playing an acetate (he apologizes for "the hiss and the rumble and the crud") that may have been obtained from Paul along with the "All Together on the Wireless Machine" jingle (see the entry below).

RELEASE HISTORY

1973: This recording surfaced on the vinyl bootleg *Abbey Road Revisited* in dismal quality and has never really been upgraded.

2002: The off-air source tape appeared on the CD-R *As It Happened, Baby!* (including Kenny's spoken outro about it being a "collector's item"); the only improvement it offers is lack of surface noise.

90. Studio session   P

Date: 21 November 1967
Location: Chappell Recording Studios, London
Producer: George Martin

[A.] Step Inside Love—rehearsal and demo take 1 (10:59)
[B.] Step Inside Love—rehearsal and demo take 2 (10:18)
[C.] Step Inside Love—demo takes 3 and 4 (3:22)

After finishing off the second verse of "Step Inside Love," Paul joined Cilla Black and George Martin in the studio to record a more polished demo. These rehearsals were also filmed, and the uncut soundtrack from this shoot has recently surfaced (a whirring camera can be heard throughout). The recordings offer an excellent look into the collaborative give-and-take between Paul and George Martin in a non-Beatle context.

As the tape begins (**A**), Paul is playing through the song on acoustic guitar, stopping occasionally to discuss the arrangement with Cilla and Martin. She sings along in places, trying to learn the phrasing, and seems pleased with the song's intimacy, noting that she won't have to use her "big voice." She and Paul then run through the number more formally, with Paul making suggestions: swoop down on the word "shoulder," and hold the note on "stay" longer going into the final verse.

George Martin decides they should record a take, although he realizes it will just be a demo, as Paul is playing in a key too low for Cilla's optimal range. Take 1, with Cilla's voice and Paul's guitar accompaniment, would eventually be released on a Cilla Black boxed set. When it finishes, Martin tells them over the talkback to come up to the control room for a listen, and the tape is wound back.

The session continues (**B**) with another rehearsal, joined in progress. From here on out, George Martin is joining in on piano, and Paul stops several times to teach him the chord structure. A complete rehearsal pass follows, and then a second demo take (recorded by the engineer upstairs), during which Cilla stumbles over the lyric a bit. The final piece of tape (**C**) captures take 3, a false start, and the complete take 4, after which Paul admits, "I made a goof in the middle." The footage shot during this session is discussed in the following entry.

RELEASE HISTORY

1997: A 2:50 excerpt of **A** was released on the CD boxed set *Cilla 1963–1973 The Abbey Road Decade*.

2006: A mediocre-quality tape of **A**–**C** surfaced on the CD-R *The BZ Auction Tape*.

91. Promo clip

Date:	21 November 1967
Location:	Chappell Recording Studios, London
Director:	Tony Bramwell (?)

[A.] Step Inside Love (2:32)

The footage of the "Step Inside Love" rehearsal features Cilla standing at a mic running through the song and holding a lyric sheet. Paul removes his jacket and plays along on his acoustic guitar while seated next to her, and George Martin listens in. The clip ends with Paul putting his guitar on a music stand and walking out with Cilla and George, perhaps to listen to playbacks.

It's not clear what the purpose of this filming was; Mark Lewisohn says the clip was produced by the BBC, but the footage features a shot of Paul playing the piano, filmed with a "star filter/kaleidoscope" effect. This same shot was reused in one of the edits of the "Lady Madonna" promo, which also employs the filter effect on some shots of John and Paul singing. Since the "Lady Madonna" clip was produced by Tony Bramwell and ends with some unused footage from this November 21 shoot (Paul getting up from the piano, grabbing his coat and guitar, and exiting the studio), it seems likely Bramwell, who worked for NEMS and Apple Films, not the BBC, had some involvement in the Cilla footage.

In any case, this clip doesn't seem to have been aired anywhere to promote the "Step Inside Love" single, although the circulating copy is synced to Cilla's finished recording of the song (taped February 28, 1968, and released March 8).

RELEASE HISTORY

This clip circulates in decent quality among video collectors.

92. Radio jingle   P

Date:	ca. mid-November 1967
Host:	Chris Denning, Kenny Everett
Broadcast:	25 November 1967, 2:00–3:00 p.m.
	BBC Radio 1
	Where It's At

[A.] All Together on the Wireless Machine (0:57)

Paul recorded this special jingle for Chris Denning's BBC Radio series *Where It's At,* accompanying himself on piano. He begins by playing the verse chords from "Hello Goodbye" and crooning, "While sitting at my piano one day/A magical thought came my way/To write a number for the BBC." Some whistling leads into a bouncy number reminiscent of "Please Don't Bring Your Banjo Back," as Paul sings "Kenny Everett and Chris Denning/All together on the wireless machine" repeatedly, with Everett assisting by singing along and adding various effects.

There's no solid evidence about when or where the jingle was taped, although Mark Lewisohn assumes

Paul recorded it at his home studio. Could this have been what Paul is seen playing on the piano at Chappell Studios (November 21)? Or was Kenny present at one of the Abbey Road sessions for "Hello Goodbye"? Only the second half of this jingle was played following John's interview on the November 25 edition of *Where It's At,* although the show may have opened with the full version.

RELEASE HISTORY

1973: Interestingly, this recording first appeared on the vinyl bootleg *Abbey Road Revisited* along with the demo of "Step Inside Love," in similarly poor quality. This might mean the "Step Inside Love" demo comes from an episode of *Where It's At.* This inferior-sounding version was booted on the CD *Attack of the Filler Beebs, Episode 3.*

2000: The best-sounding copy of the jingle can be found on the bootleg CD *The Beatles Broadcast Collection, Trailer 2* (this source is slightly superior to that on *Mythology, Volume 3*). This version, from a rebroadcast (perhaps the 1983 special *The History of Pop Radio*), unfortunately has dialogue overlapping the first couple of seconds.

93. Radio interview   J

Date:	mid-November 1967
Host:	Chris Denning, Kenny Everett
Broadcast:	25 November 1967, 2:00–3:00 p.m.
	BBC Radio 1
	Where It's At
Length:	8:09

Following up the *Sgt. Pepper* preview special, Chris Denning's *Where It's At* (a show increasingly being appropriated by cohost Kenny Everett) set its sights on the next major Beatles project, *Magical Mystery Tour.* To accompany the debut airings of all six tracks from the forthcoming EP, the duo recorded an interview with John sometime around the third week of November. The location is unknown, but may have been in the film editing suite in Soho; the group gave an interview to the *New Musical Express* there on the weekend of November 18 and were filmed by the BBC there on the twenty-first. Mark Lewisohn postulates that it was recorded at Abbey Road, and John did hold a session in Studio 2 on the twenty-fourth to compile tapes for his stage play *Scene Three, Act One.*

The interview begins with John talking in general about how boring the editing process is and then giving a vague synopsis of the film's equally vague plot. This leads into the playing of the title track, "Magical Mystery Tour." Denning asks if they are truly doing the editing themselves and John insists they are, "to see how it's done." In reality, Roy Benson was employed as editor, but all four Beatles took an interest in the process to one degree or another. John says they'd scheduled three weeks for editing and postsync work but that editing has already taken eight weeks (it began September 25) and they've just started working on the sound.

John assures them that the film will be finished in time to be broadcast on TV at Christmas, although he doesn't know yet on which channel (in early December, it was finally announced that the BBC had the rights). Kenny then reminisces about visiting the "I Am the Walrus" session (see the September 6 entry) and wonders why the finished single doesn't have the "guitars or organ" he heard that day (and on the tape of the rough mix he purloined). John says the song has no organ, but that electric piano can be heard at the beginning. Referring to a proposed BBC ban because of the word "knickers," he asks Everett whether they'll play it, suggesting they insert a *cuckoo* sound effect to censor the offending word. The song itself was played in full but remained unofficially prohibited on BBC playlists for the time being.

Everett inquires about the heavy amount of editing he hears on "I Am the Walrus," but John explains how it was all done with overdubs and mixing, similar to how the tape loops were mixed in live for "Tomorrow Never Knows." Mention of loops leads to some confusion, and John clarifies that the only new song with a "little teeny loop" is "The Fool on the Hill"; presumably this is the source of the strange noise heard at 2:39 in that song, which is played next.

Denning then challenges John about a quote he made proclaiming that the Beatles won't be around when they reach thirty, a mere three years off in John's case. What John actually meant was that they won't be singing the same type of songs at age thirty (Paul had talked about "being old men singing 'From Me to You'" as far back as 1963). Everett then asks for a description of "Blue Jay Way," which John calls "a moaning thing that George has done," leading into the airing of that track.

John then describes how a "flanging," or phasing, works, and Everett gives a demonstration courtesy of some postproduction. The cohosts encourage John and his bandmates to do their own radio show or a spoken-word LP, and John admits he's "got a lot of that lying 'round the house," as would be proven by the numerous ad-lib comedy tapes to surface from his Kenwood archives. He also confirms that the Beatles are trying to start their own studio; the initial idea was to have a joint studio with the Rolling Stones but the result would be the largely unused Apple basement studio. John complains that EMI's recording equipment is antique, and that they are just getting around to buying eight-track decks. The Beatles wouldn't even be permitted to use one until September 1968!

RELEASE HISTORY

1988: The vinyl bootleg *Tragical History Tour* contained 6:33 from the original off-air broadcast in fair quality. That same year, 2:48 of this interview, apparently from the unedited prebroadcast tape, was aired on the December 31 episode of *The Beeb's Lost Beatles*

Tapes. This was bootlegged on the CD-R *Attack of the Filler Beebs, Episode 3.*

2000: The same 2:48 segment was included from a different rebroadcast (possibly a Kenny Everett retrospective) on the bootleg CD *The Beatles Broadcast Collection, Trailer 2.*

A good-quality recording of the original broadcast also circulates, lasting 7:17 and including Kenny and Chris introducing a truncated version of "All Together on the Wireless Machine"; this is missing material found on the prebroadcast tape, however. Kevin Howlett's book *The Beatles at the BBC* also describes a bit more of the interview's contents than is currently circulating.

94. Studio session

Date: 28 November 1967
Time: 6:00 p.m.–2:45 a.m.
Location: EMI Studio 3
Producer: George Martin

[A.] Christmas Time (Is Here Again)—take 1 (mono) (6:42)
Mixed: 23 April 1976

[B.] Christmas Time (Is Here Again)—take 1 (stereo) (2:23)

[C.] Christmas Time (Is Here Again)—edit of unknown mono mixes (6:08)
Mixed: 29 November 1967

The Beatles' fourth annual fan club Christmas disc was probably their most entertaining—a good balance of words and music, sincerity and cynicism, surrealism and satire. It's structured in a similar fashion to the 1966 message, with a theme song interwoven among several skits, but the material is sharper and faster-paced.

The session began with the theme song "Christmas Time (Is Here Again)" being recorded in a single take, with Paul pounding the piano, George strumming acoustic guitar, Ringo keeping the beat on his kit, and John adding some thumps on timpani. All four Beatles then overdubbed two sets of lead vocals, consisting of the title phrase sung over and over, with Ringo crooning "O-U-T spells 'out'!" at the end of each stanza. In addition, there seems to be an effort to trade off the line "It ain't been 'round since you-know-when," with Paul singing it the first time, then John, then George. The song winds its way through ten identical verses, nine sung and one instrumental, before ending with a drum/timpani roll accompanied by piano glissandos.

The skits were then recorded in ten takes, overlaid with sound effects, and edited with portions of the theme song. The finished product (**C**) opens with the first verse of the song and cuts to a sketch poking fun at BBC policy, featuring a cameo by Victor Spinetti. The actor, a veteran of all three Beatle films thus far, was in the studio that evening to assist John in preparing tapes for *Scene Three, Act One,* which Spinetti would direct the following year. Another brief snatch of the song links to the Fluffy rehearsal rooms, with tap-dancing and Mal Evans's brilliant "13 Amp" appearance. A jingle for miracle product Wonderlust precedes a spoof public-affairs show with host "Michael" (Paul) failing to communicate with "Sir Gerald" (John).

Another riff from the theme song, overlaid with echoed snorting and laughing, leads into George as a BBC announcer, reading a request for "Plenty of Jam Jars," followed by the highlight of the disc: John as quizmaster and George as idiotic contestant winning "a trip to Denver and five others." A reprise of the Wonderlust jingle follows, and then Ringo performs a quickie mystery in *Theatre Hour.* More of the theme song (an edit of the fifth through seventh verses) plays underneath an echoed repeat of lines from the game show and applause. George Martin helps the boys thank you for a wonderful year, and John is heard admonishing listeners to "look after yourself." Finally, John recites a Scottish Yuletide verse over windswept moor effects and "Auld Lang Syne" organ. The whole thing plays like a condensed episode of *Monty Python's Flying Circus.*

A rough mono mix of the full take of the theme song (**A**) comes from an off-line recording of tapes played for EMI executives in 1976, one of whom is heard making the astute comment "Lyrically not the most inventive one!" The recording begins with John's comment: "Interplanetary remix—thr—page four hundred and forty-four!" John's brief slip up ("thr-") was spliced from the song as used in the flexi-disc.

The song was mixed into stereo for the *Sessions* project in 1984, since the LP was originally to have been released around Christmas of that year. The final track on that unreleased album was a 1:08 edit, including 4 seconds of piano and guitar warm-up at the start not present on the rough mono mix. In addition, the proposed single from that album, "Leave My Kitten Alone," featured a cross-faded medley of "Ob-La-Di, Ob-La-Da/Christmas Time (Is Here Again)" on its B-side. This contained about a minute of the song, but with no unique material compared with the LP edit.

Finally, in 1995, the song was used for a Christmas release: the "Free as a Bird" single. This track included the first 2:19 of the song, using the same stereo mix as *Sessions,* but overdubbed with some Christmas greetings for pirate radio stations (see the December 6, 1966, entry); this cross-fades with John's Scottish poem described earlier. The 2:23 timing listed above (**B**) takes into account the extra 4 seconds of intro heard only on the *Sessions* LP.

RELEASE HISTORY

1967: **C** was released on a flexi-disc titled *Christmas Time Is Here Again!* and mailed out to fan club members on December 15.

1983: **A** first appeared on the vinyl bootleg *File Under: Beatles.*

1985: The 1:08 edit of **B** surfaced on the bootleg *Sessions,* which appeared from tape source on Spank's 1993 CD of that title.

1986: The single edit of **B,** after circulating on tape for a year or so, was pressed on the boot LP *Ob-La-Di, Ob-La-Da.* It was included from tape source on the 1989 Condor CD *Dig It!*

1995: 2:19 of **B** was released on Apple's "Free as a Bird" CD single.

1998: All variations, apart from the "Ob-La-Di, Ob-La-Da" single edit, were compiled on the bootleg CD *The Ultimate Beatles Christmas Collection.* **A** was copied from vinyl.

1999: The bootleg *Another Sessions . . . Plus* contained a unique hybrid of **B:** the "Free as a Bird" single mix with the extra 4 seconds from *Sessions* spliced onto the beginning.

2002: **A** appeared from tape source for the first time on the CD-R *As It Happened, Baby!*

95. Newsreel footage   J

Date: 4 December 1967
Time: evening
Location: Royal Institute Galleries, London
Length: 1:17

John and Paul agreed to fund an exhibition of paintings by one of John's former art college classmates, Jonathan Hague. With Paul vacationing on his Scottish farm, Pete Shotton accompanied John to the opening. BBC newsreel footage shows John and Pete strolling through the gallery, drinks and ciggies in hand. John also chats with Hague in front of one of his works, one of which depicts the Beatles in their Sgt. Pepper's Band uniforms.

RELEASE HISTORY

This silent BBC footage circulates among collectors, taken from NBC News archives.

96. Newsreel footage   J, G

Date: 5 December 1967
Time: 8:16 p.m.
Location: Apple Boutique, London
Length: 2:50

Only half of the Beatles were able to attend the opening night festivities for Apple's first shop at 94 Baker Street (on the corner of Baker and Paddington). Ringo was busy filming in Rome, and Paul was on holiday in Scotland, so John and George stepped up to bat and hosted a packed house of celebrities and journalists. John and shop manager Pete Shotton had come up with the idea of holding the party at sixteen minutes past the hour, just to be different.

Newsreel cameras captured the occasion and the arrival of such guests as Cilla Black, Alan Freeman, Keith Moon, Eric Clapton, Kenneth Tynan, Victor Spinetti, and Richard Lester. A clown is seen juggling apples and distributing them to visitors, and John is filmed munching on one (an apple, not a visitor); other guests sip apple juice. George takes a rest on a translucent inflatable chair, presumably one of the shop's initial offerings, while clothing designers the Fool provide background music.

Over the weekend of December 2–3, and in blatant defiance of the Westminster Borough Council's objections, the Fool had overseen the painting of an enormous and suitably colorful mural for the outside of the building. This lasted as long as May 18, 1968, before it was reluctantly whitewashed over.

RELEASE HISTORY

Two separate black-and-white newsreels exist from this evening; Pathé's coverage lasts 1:20 and circulates as part of a Pathé compilation reel. The second, lasting 1:13, was included as a bonus on the *Magical Mystery Tour* DVD and is seen in part in the *Anthology* documentary. In addition, the *Greatest Rock 'n' Roll Legends Scrapbook* includes 17 seconds of color footage from the occasion (probably from an AP newsreel).

97. TV interview   G

Date:	early December 1967
Location:	London
Interviewer:	Alan Freedman (?)
Broadcast:	10 December 1967
	Channel 13, New York
	Public Broadcasting Laboratory (?)
Length:	11:22

December 10, 1967, was Human Rights Day, and to mark the occasion a concert was held in the General Assembly Hall of the United Nations building in New York City. Ravi Shankar performed several numbers alongside violinist Yehudi Menuhin, accompanied by Alla Rakha on tabla. The concert was broadcast live on the local PBS station, WNDT, as part of a new series, *Public Broadcasting Laboratory (PBL)*. This may be the source of a George Harrison TV interview that has survived only in audio form. George's segment was reportedly filmed in London a few days earlier.

George begins by describing Indian music as a stepping-stone to the spiritual world, depending upon the performer and the raga being played. He recounts having been introduced to Ravi Shankar's music by a friend in America (probably David Crosby) and how when he first played Shankar's music, although he'd "never heard it before in this life," it sounded familiar. Asked to compare it with pop music, he recites the notes of the Indian scale, but isn't sure how many different scales there are, suggesting the interviewer "ask Yehudi about that" (presumably Menuhin was another guest interviewed on the show).

George then talks about how much discipline is needed to learn sitar, beginning with proper handling of the instrument through exercises until "eight years into it" when you can start to improvise and express yourself through the music as Shankar can. He feels that despite having met dozens of famous artists, noted politicians and even royalty, he never totally respected anyone until meeting Ravi.

Whereas people may have an image of Eastern music akin to "smoke a bit of opium and you can play like that," George stresses the opposite is true. It's only through purity of mind, body, and spirit that someone like Shankar has become a great performer. Although he is addicted to nicotine and can hardly deny using illicit substances, George understands Ravi's admonition to his audiences not to smoke while watching him perform: Shankar has respect for the music and they should show him equal respect. George says this isn't a problem in India, where citizens readily pay homage to artists, doctors, and other achievers.

Asked if Eastern themes will continue to play a large role in his songs, the Beatles' lead guitarist admits he's been so obsessed with learning sitar, he's forgotten how to play chord changes, having neglected his guitar playing for the past year or two. He seems less certain how much his bandmates are affected by Indian music: "Yeah . . . maybe . . . yes, I think it is a lot." Ringo was apparently "scared" when confronted with learning to play the tabla in the winter of '65/'66, but George thinks he may be more open to it now.

The interviewer wonders why Ravi is having such a big impact now in the West, and George responds that the time is ripe, with so many swamis and yogis around the United States. He feels the next generation will be even more aware, and that "it's all part of a plot" that may take another two thousand years, but that eventually a golden age of peace and enlightenment will be reached and "Earth will be Heaven!"

RELEASE HISTORY

This interview, from a fair-quality off-line tape, circulates among collectors. The corresponding footage has yet to surface, and may be lost.

Date: 27 December 1967
Time: 6:00–7:00 p.m.
Location: Studio 1, Wembley Studios
Host: David Frost
Broadcast: 27 December 1967, 10:30–11:15 p.m.
Rediffusion-TV
The Frost Programme
Length: 23:15

The airing of *Magical Mystery Tour* on Boxing Day was a magnet for criticism from the British press and public, many of whom had been waiting for years for an opportunity to get the boot in. To his great credit, rather than slink away from the barrage of criticism or spread the task to his bandmates, Paul, the Beatle chiefly responsible for the project, agreed to come on David Frost's TV show the following day to face the music.

Paul's hastily arranged appearance opened the show, and Frost wasted no time probing the matter at hand, saying he'd enjoyed the show but wondered why Paul thought it had been so badly received. Paul cops to the lack of plot and indeed the aimlessness of the film, and seems to have assumed the word "magical" in the title would be enough to explain its incoherence. Frost compares it to merely looking through a kaleidoscope while listening to the soundtrack EP, and Paul gets in a plug for the second showing (in color on January 5, 1968), hoping it will grow on the audience with repeated viewings. Frost jokingly says the BBC will have to air it seventeen times to get through to everyone.

He makes a futile attempt to get Paul's true feelings about whether the project was a failure, but the diplomatic Beatle does bluntly admit that if reviews had been great, he wouldn't have been on Frost's show that night! Paul compares the criticism to the reproach that songs such as "Strawberry Fields Forever" and "I Am the Walrus" had faced, and predicts that the show was merely ahead of its time. Frost wonders whether the film had any message, and Paul enigmatically says most things he does have a deep but unintended message.

Talk turns to the Beatles' personalities, and Paul says he can't see them splitting up because they all have such similar attitudes about the maharishi and projects like *Magical Mystery Tour*—in hindsight this is obviously not true, but says bundles about the lack of

honest communication among the group at the time. In reality, John and George allowed themselves to be dragged into the film project and Ringo was half-hearted at best when it came to Transcendental Meditation. Frost runs through the stereotypes of Ringo the clown, George the mystic, and John the rebel, and wonders where Paul fits in. "I keep hearing that I'm the cute one," he replies, and Frost suggests he put that on his passport under "occupation."

The conversation takes a serious turn as Paul says the human race is fantastic, but after five years of meeting people around the world, he's disappointed in what they do. Frost presses for specifics, but Paul can refer only vaguely to violence and "the myth of war" (people think it's necessary to start a fight to avoid losing a fight), admitting that he often just changes the channel when he sees depressing news rather than try to affect any change. He doesn't like media tags such as "Mersey Beat" or "flower power" but doesn't mind "make love not war" because he realizes slogans need to be simple to get across to a wide number of people.

Paul discusses the LSD debacle of the summer, again abrogating responsibility for the influence he has over young people. Nonetheless, Frost asks if he has any advice to give, and Paul says the best way to be successful is to be yourself. Frost points out that this works fine in a creative field such as entertainment but might not be good advice for a more conformist occupation. Paul concedes, and relates the issue back to *Magical Mystery Tour*. He paints a picture of a show that might have been successful (five thousand dancing girls and the Beatles hanging from a Christmas tree) but wouldn't have been true to the group. He concludes by optimistically saying the next film will be better because they've learned from their mistakes. Frost leads into the commercial break by inviting Paul to stick around for the next segment: cockroach racing! Perhaps mercifully, the circulating tape ends there.

RELEASE HISTORY

Unlike most of the other Beatles/Frost TV ventures, this one has not surfaced yet on video and all we have is a fair-quality off-line recording of the audio portion, as yet unbootlegged.

Date: ca. December 1967
Location: EMI Studios
Producer: George Harrison

[A.] In the First Place—original Abbey Road mix (3:20)

[B.] In the First Place—movie mix (2:29)
Mixed: 16 November 1997

During the sessions for his *Wonderwall* film score, George employed Liverpool contemporaries Remo Four as a backing group for most of the non-Indian songs. "In the First Place," composed by band members Colin Manley and Tony Ashton, was also recorded during these sessions and produced by George, although it's not entirely clear whether this was for the film or a potential Remo Four single. It was probably taped during an Abbey Road session on December 11, 20, or 31, and went unheard for nearly thirty years.

In 1997, George sent a copy of his original score to *Wonderwall* director Joe Massot, who was preparing to reissue the movie in a restored edition with stereo sound. At the end of the reel was a completed take of "In the First Place," and George gave the go-ahead to use the long-lost recording in the new director's cut of *Wonderwall*. The song was also released on a CD single containing two versions, the original stereo mix from 1967 (**A**) and a newly mixed edit for the restored film (**B**).

In addition to producing the song, George probably plays the acoustic guitar on it, as the original tape reportedly includes his spoken count-in (which was unfortunately omitted from both released versions).

RELEASE HISTORY

1998: **A** and **B** were released on a CD single.

1968: YOU BECOME NAKED

January 2   Ringo and Maureen fly from London to Liverpool.

January 4   George, Paul, and Jane attend the premiere of the film *Here We Go Round the Mulberry Bush* at the London Pavilion.

January 5   BBC2-TV broadcasts *Magical Mystery Tour* in color for the first time; a case of too little too late.

January 7   George flies from London to India (via Paris, Frankfurt, and Tehran) to continue recording sessions for *Wonderwall* in Bombay.

January 12   Apple Music Limited changes its name to the punning Apple Corps Limited.

January 17   John, Paul, and Ringo attend a luncheon at RCA House in honor of Apple Music's first signed band, Grapefruit.

January 18   George flies back to London from India.

January 19   A launch party is held at the soon-to-open Apple HQ for Grapefruit, attended by all four Beatles, the Jimi Hendrix Experience, and Brian Jones.

January 20   Paul produces sessions for his brother Michael's album *McGough and McGear;* Jimi Hendrix participates in the day's recordings.

January 22   Apple Corps opens its first headquarters at 95 Wigmore Street.

January 25   John and George attend a Mayfair fashion show.

February 3   Brief sessions for a new single ("Lady Madonna"/"The Inner Light") begin at EMI Studios.

February 5   Paul attends a press conference at the Royal Garden Hotel, announcing Leicester University's Arts Festival and denying that he will contribute financially.

February 10   Paul and Jane attend the Scaffold's concert at Queen Elizabeth Hall.

February 15   John, George, Cynthia, and Pattie fly from London to India.

February 16   Half of the Beatles arrive at Maharishi Mahesh Yogi's Transcendental Meditation ashram.

February 18   Paul, Ringo, Maureen, and Jane fly from London to India.

February 20   The other half of the Beatles arrive at Maharishi Mahesh Yogi's Transcendental Meditation ashram.

March 1   Ringo and Maureen leave Rishikesh, after sticking it out for only ten days at the maharishi's Transcendental Meditation camp.

March 7   Ringo presents Geoff Emerick with his Grammy for best engineer for his work on the *Sgt. Pepper's Lonely Hearts Club Band* LP.

March 15   UK release of "Lady Madonna"/"The Inner Light" single.

March 18   U.S. release of "Lady Madonna"/"The Inner Light" single.

March 23   Ringo attends a private screening of the film *Around the World in 80 Days* at the Coliseum Cinerama, followed by a party at the Dorchester Hotel.

March 26   Paul and Jane return (with Neil Aspinall) from India.

April 12   John and George become the last Beatles to leave Rishikesh, two weeks earlier than scheduled. John flies to London Airport, and George spends a couple of weeks in Madras and the south of India.

April 18   John and Ringo attend a luncheon thrown by Bell Records at Le Prince nightclub.

April 20   Publication of Apple Corp's first ad soliciting tapes, photos, films, and manuscripts leads to an unimaginably massive deluge of (mostly) amateurish submissions to Apple offices, 90 percent of which are never looked at.

May 9	John and Ringo (the only two Beatle parents) attend an Apple board meeting to discuss opening a school for the children of Apple's employees.
May 11	John and Paul fly to New York for a promotional blitz to hype Apple Corps.
May 12	John and Paul hold a business meeting aboard a Chinese junk in the harbor surrounding the Statue of Liberty.
May 13	John and Paul entertain newspaper and magazine reporters most of the day at the St. Regis Hotel.
May 14	John and Paul hold an afternoon press conference at the Americana Hotel. In the evening, they appear on *The Tonight Show,* videotaped shortly before broadcast on NBC at Studio 6B, Rockefeller Center, and guest-hosted by Joe Garagiola.
May 15	George, Pattie, Ringo, and Maureen fly from London to Cannes, France.
	John and Paul catch a late-night flight back to London, arriving early the next morning.
May 17	George and Ringo attend the premiere of *Wonderwall* at the Cannes Film Festival.
May 18	John calls an Apple board meeting to announce that he is Jesus Christ.
May 19	George, Ringo, and their wives return from France to London.
	The Beatles attend a housewarming party thrown by playwright Harold Pinter.
	John and Yoko make recordings that would form the basis of their first album, *Unfinished Music No. 1: Two Virgins,* entirely on John's home recorders.
May 21	It's Andy Williams Day! Paul and Jane have lunch with him, attend his concert at the Royal Albert Hall, and follow it up with a party in his honor.
May 22	John, Yoko, George, and Pattie attend a luncheon at the Club dell' Aretusa to celebrate the imminent opening (the following day) of Apple Tailoring, the second boutique owned by the Beatles.
May 26	At Kensington Gardens, Paul directs a promo film clip for "Elevator," the latest single by Grapefruit, the first group signed to Apple Publishing.
May 30	First of the marathon sessions for the LP *The Beatles* (aka the "White Album") at EMI Studios.
June 7	George, Ringo, Pattie, and Maureen fly from London to California, staying initially in Monterey.
	In Wales, Paul acts as best man at his brother Michael's wedding to Angela Fishwick.
June 10	On this and the following day in Big Sur, George films scenes with Ravi Shankar for the film *Raga.*
June 15	As their contribution to the National Sculpture Exhibit, John and Yoko plant acorns for peace in a ceremony on the grounds of Coventry Cathedral.
June 18	George and Ringo return to London from the United States.
	John, Paul, and Ringo attend a press reception for Apple Publishing artists Grapefruit, at the Hanover Banqueting Rooms.
	John and Yoko attend the opening night performance of *In His Own Write,* a play based on Lennon's writings, at the Old Vic Theatre.
June 20	Paul flies from London to Los Angeles to promote Apple Records.
June 21	Paul screens the *Apple* promotional film short for Capitol Records sales execs at the Century Plaza Hotel.
June 24	George begins producing sessions for Apple artist Jackie Lomax's first single.
June 25	Paul flies back to London from Los Angeles.
June 30	Paul produces the Black Dyke Mills Band's recording session for an Apple single at Victoria Hall. Returning from Saltaire, Paul, Derek Taylor, Peter Asher, and *NME* reporter Alan Smith stop at a pub in Harrold where Paul gives an impromptu piano performance.
July 1	John and Yoko officially open their exhibition *You Are Here* at the Robert Fraser Gallery by releasing 365 white helium-filled balloons.
July 2	Paul lunches with EMI chairman Sir Joseph Lockwood at Lazard Brothers & Co.'s merchant banking headquarters.
July 8	Paul, George, and Ringo attend the press preview of the film *Yellow Submarine* at the Bowater House Cinema.

July 9	Ringo attends Solomon King's recording session and contributes to the song "A Hundred Years or More."
July 11	John and George attend the wedding of Apple Electronics' would-be boy genius, "Magic Alex" Mardas, to Eufrosyne Doxiades at St. Sophia's Church.
July 15	Apple Corps' new headquarters at 3 Savile Row officially opens for business as the employees begin moving into their new offices.
July 17	The Beatles attend the world premiere of the film *Yellow Submarine* at the London Pavilion, and the postpremiere party at the Royal Lancaster Hotel's newly christened Yellow Submarine nightclub.
July 26	John and Paul finish composing "Hey Jude" at Paul's house in St. John's Wood. John inadvertently subjects Beatles fans to an interminably repeated anecdote from Paul's lips by making him keep the line "The movement you need is on your shoulder."
	Paul reportedly ruins Mick Jagger's twenty-fifth birthday party/Stones' *Beggars Banquet* album unveiling/Mick and Keith's coowned Vesuvio Club opening night festivities by playing an advance copy of "Hey Jude" and stealing the Stones' spotlight. However, the Beatles have not even recorded the song yet! Thus the true date of this event must be at least a week later, and not on Mick's actual birthday.
July 28	The Beatles spend the day in a massive series of photo sessions at various locations around London.
July 30	The Beatles plunder their own Apple Boutique the day before closing and spirit away the best items for their personal wardrobes.
July 31	Apple's Baker Street Boutique closes forever and gives away its remaining inventory to customers on a first-come, first-served basis.
August 3	Paul and girlfriend Francie Schwartz socialize at Revolution, a nightclub in Mayfair.
August 6	John attends a fashion show at Revolution.
August 7	Figuring a way to milk some free advertising space out of the otherwise unused Apple Boutique, Paul writes the titles "Hey Jude" and "Revolution" (their next single) in huge letters on a coat of whitewash across the storefront windows.
August 10	The Beatles and visiting Capitol Records president Stan Gortikov have morning tea at Apple Corps headquarters, followed by lunch at the Ritz Hotel.
	John and Yoko escort Stan Gortikov to the Queen's Theatre for the evening's production of *Halfway Up the Tree*.
August 11	John and Yoko attend an Ossie Clark fashion show in Chelsea.
August 17	George, Pattie, and Mal fly to Greece for a short vacation.
August 21	George returns to London from his Greek vacation.
August 22	Feeling underappreciated and thinking his playing has been substandard, Ringo quits the Beatles prior to this evening's session, becoming the first member to leave voluntarily. As if that wasn't enough bad news for one day, John is also served with divorce papers from Cynthia on the grounds of adultery.
August 26	U.S. release of "Hey Jude"/"Revolution" single.
August 27	Paul attends a Liverpool vs. Everton soccer match.
August 30	UK release of "Hey Jude"/"Revolution" single.
	Paul and Ringo attend the wedding of Neil Aspinall and Suzy Ornstein at Chelsea Register Office, followed by a celebratory luncheon at a nearby restaurant.
September 3	Ringo's return to the studio after quitting the group eleven days earlier. Also the first EMI Beatles session to use an eight-track tape recorder.
September 4	The Beatles videotape promotional clips for their first Apple single at Twickenham Film Studio Stage 1. An introduction by David Frost is shot first, followed by several takes of "Hey Jude" and at least two of "Revolution."
September 30	*The Beatles,* Hunter Davies's authorized biography, is published in the UK by Heinemann.

October 14	Ringo and Maureen fly to Sardinia for a fortnight's vacation. Ringo begins to compose "Octopus's Garden" during this trip.
October 16	George flies to Los Angeles to continue producing sessions for Apple Records artist Jackie Lomax.
	Working in the control rooms of studios 1, 2, and 3, plus rooms 41 and 42, John, Paul, and George Martin compile, cross-fade, edit, tidy up, and band the near-final mono and stereo masters for *The Beatles* double album in a marathon twenty-four-hour session concluding at 5 p.m. on October 17.
October 18	John and Yoko, staying temporarily at a flat sublet to them by Ringo, are busted by Sgt. Pilcher of the drug squad, who discovers traces of cannabis resin in an envelope and a binocular case. They are briefly detained at Marylebone Lane station.
October 19	John and Yoko are formally charged with possession of cannabis resin and obstruction at Marylebone Magistrates' Court.
November 1	UK release of George's *Wonderwall Music* LP.
November 4	Yoko checks in to Queen Charlotte's Hospital and is joined by John.
November 5	Paul and Linda travel to Paul's farm in Scotland where they hibernate for most of the month.
November 8	Cynthia is granted a divorce from John at London divorce court.
November 11	Planned U.S. release date of John and Yoko's *Unfinished Music No. 1: Two Virgins* LP delayed until January due to distribution problems.
November 12	On this or the following day, George and Mal Evans attend a Frank Sinatra recording session and dine with him afterward at a local restaurant.
November 19	Ringo and Maureen move out of Weybridge and into Brookfields, a house in Elstead they purchased from Peter Sellers.
November 21	Yoko and John's first child is lost to miscarriage at Queen Charlotte's Hospital.
November 22	UK release of *The Beatles* LP.
November 25	U.S. release of *The Beatles* LP.
	Yoko checks out of Queen Charlotte's Hospital. John and Yoko move back into Kenwood, staying a month or so until it goes on sale and then moving to Sunny Heights, Ringo's former house in Weybridge.
November 28	John pleads guilty to possession of cannabis resin at his Marylebone Court hearing and is fined £150 plus court costs. By copping a plea, John avoids the obstruction charges against him and Yoko, but creates unforeseen future problems with entering and staying in the United States.
November 29	UK release of John and Yoko's *Unfinished Music No. 1: Two Virgins* LP.
November 30	After visiting Bob Dylan in Woodstock, New York, for Thanksgiving, George and Mal stop off at the apartment of Brian Epstein's former business partner Nat Weiss and tape a portion of the Beatles' sixth Christmas record with the help of Tiny Tim.
December 2	U.S. release of George's *Wonderwall Music* LP.
December 6	George and Pattie fly back to London from New York.
December 10	John and Yoko participate in the two-day videotaping of the Rolling Stones' TV special *Rock and Roll Circus* at Stonebridge House. The rehearsing and simultaneous audio- and videotaping doesn't wrap up until early in the morning on the twelfth, all for naught as the Stones decide against releasing any of it.
December 11	Paul and Linda fly to Algarve, Portugal, for a three-week vacation.
December 12	Paul holds a press conference on the beach in Portugal.
December 18	John and Yoko appear at the Royal Albert Hall in Celebration in December, a benefit art event; their contribution, titled "Alchemical Wedding," is to writhe around inside a white bag onstage.
December 20	UK release of *The Beatles' 1968 Christmas Record*, the Beatles' sixth annual Christmas flexi-disc for fan club members.
December 23	John and Yoko, dressed as Father and Mother Christmas, distribute presents at Apple Corps' first Christmas party.

1. Newsreel footage   G

Date: 7 January 1968
Location: London Airport
Broadcast: 7 January 1968
BBC-TV
Length: 0:20

A fur-hatted George (alias "Mr. Brown" for the occasion), accompanied by Neil Aspinall, is seen boarding a flight to India in this very brief clip. He would arrive in Bombay the following day to produce a week of sessions for his *Wonderwall* film score, as well as what ended up being the backing track for his next Beatles song, "The Inner Light."

RELEASE HISTORY

This footage, from two separate sources (BBC News is one), circulates on video.

2. Newsreel footage   G

Date: 10 January 1968
Location: EMI Studio, Bombay
Broadcast: 11 January 1968
BBC-TV
Length: 1:00

Sessions for *Wonderwall* took place in the poorly soundproofed EMI Bombay studio from January 9–13. On the second day, George allowed a camera crew in to film a bit of studio rehearsal. Reuters shot 45 seconds of color footage with natural sound, although only a silent copy seems to be circulating. BBC News also filmed 27 seconds of mute footage.

Although the footage is silent, the song being worked on is clearly "Fantasy Sequins," as not only the instrumentation but even the stereo image is replicated exactly! On the left is a sarangi player, behind George in the center is a percussionist (jingling the khas, a type of bell), and on the right is a harmonium player.

RELEASE HISTORY

This footage circulates on video.

3. Documentary footage

Date: ca. 25 January 1968
Time: afternoon
Location: Twickenham Film Studios, London
Length: 1:05

Although they declined to provide voices for their animated counterparts, the Beatles did consent to film a cameo appearance to wrap up *Yellow Submarine*. This fleeting 43-second scene is charming, if a bit superfluous: Ringo displays the "hole in his pocket," George the sub's motor, and John spies Newer and Bluer Meanies through a telescope. The group are dressed in matching shirts against a black background. The idea was to superimpose some animation behind them, but time and budgetary restraints made this impossible; in the end, only Paul proffers an animated "LOVE."

Further footage from this day appeared in the *Mod Odyssey* featurette about the making of the film. These extra 22 seconds (all color but silent) include Paul listening through headphones to a playback, Ringo peering through a camera viewfinder, and George running across the studio with a tape measure. One problem with the traditional dating of this footage is that George still had his mustache on the evening of January 25 (see entry below). He had shaved it off by February 8, so this may have been filmed in the interim.

RELEASE HISTORY

1999: The DVD release of *Yellow Submarine* included all this footage, including the complete *Mod Odyssey* short, although better-quality prints of the featurette circulate on video.

4. Newsreel footage   J, G

Date: 25 January 1968
Time: evening
Location: Revolution Club, London
Length: 1:03

After marrying George, Pattie Boyd had basically given up her modeling career, but she did accept the odd assignment. One such occasion took place this evening at the Revolution nightclub when she took part in a show highlighting designs by Alice Pollock and Ossie Clarke.

Pathé's newsreel of the event features Pattie sporting ensembles such as "African Queen" and "Powder Puff" as well as a glimpse of her table, where George, John, and Magic Alex sit smoking and drinking.

RELEASE HISTORY

This silent Pathé newsreel (with overdubbed narration) circulates among video collectors.

5. Radio interview   J

Date: 27 January 1968
Time: morning
Location: Kenwood
Interviewer: Kenny Everett
Broadcast: 4 February 1968, 10:00 a.m.–noon
BBC Radio 1
The Kenny Everett Show
Length: 1:08

Although he had nothing in particular to promote, John agreed to appear on Kenny Everett's new self-titled BBC Radio series. Everett brought his tape recorder to John's house for the occasion and apparently caught John in a stoned or sleepy state (perhaps both), judging from the tone of his voice. The original broadcast doesn't seem to have survived, but I've tentatively identified two fragments as being likely excerpts from this recording.

In the first segment, John wishes the listeners good morning and welcomes them to the show, praising it as "one of the most swinging of the swinging England set today" with "none of your FBI playing in the background." In the second, John is attempting to explain the meaning behind "Strawberry Fields Forever" (clearly one of Everett's favorite songs) but can barely remember the lyrics and melody. Everett tries to prompt him by asking if it's a random collection of thoughts, but John says it's straightforward: "bit of messing, then let's get away to Strawberry Fields." He admits that after working on it so long, he kind of lost perspective and that it's taken him about a year to realize what the song was really about: his own confused state of mind at the time he wrote it.

RELEASE HISTORY

1972: The second segment of this interview was rebroadcast July 9 in part eight of the BBC Radio documentary *The Beatles Story*.

1999: The first segment was included on the bootleg CD boxed set *Mythology, Volume 3*.

2000: Both segments appeared on the bootleg CD *The Beatles Broadcast Collection, Trailer 2*. The first is a slight upgrade, but the second has a few seconds excised and is overdubbed with portions of "Strawberry Fields Forever," which tend to drown out the dialogue.

6. Composing tape   J

Date: ca. December 1967–January 1968
Location: Kenwood

[A.] **Cry Baby Cry—guitar** (0:52)

[B.] **Cry Baby Cry—piano take 1** (0:48)
[C.] **Cry Baby Cry—piano take 2** (0:48)
[D.] **Across the Universe/Cry Baby Cry—piano/Mellotron** (0:41)

[E.] **Hey Bulldog—piano** (1:23)
[F.] **Hey Bulldog—piano/Mellotron** (1:53)
[G.] **Across the Universe—piano/Mellotron** (1:29)

[H.] **You Know My Name (Look Up the Number)—piano** (2:31)

The bulk of these demos feature John playing piano in his music room at home sometime during the winter of

'67–'68; many of them have strange whistling sounds in the background, as though they'd been recorded in an aviary. They mainly consist of unfinished fragments that would later be polished into full songs.

A nineteen-minute tape from John's archive yielded a mere 52 seconds worthy of airing on *The Lost Lennon Tapes*. It opens with six minutes of electric guitar riffs, as John fiddles with the equipment, altering the tone, feedback, delay, and amount of distortion. It becomes apparent that the guitar is on a prerecorded tape, on top of which John plays some organ notes.

The guitar segues into the chorus of "Cry Baby Cry," with its original "make your mother buy" lyric. The bootlegged portion of this (**A**) consists of two fragments from the performance. The first is played in F-sharp, with John shouting the melody an octave too high; after he strums along with the tape for a bit, the second fragment has him playing a chorus in the standard key of G major.

A few more guitar riffs (including one reminiscent of Wings' "Old Siam Sir") are followed by seven minutes of John and Ringo presaging *Two Virgins* with an audio collage of their own. Apart from Yoko's vocal gymnastics, all the elements are present: tinkling piano, random interjections from John ("hit a policeman's daughter"), and even the spinning of a vintage tune ("Girl of My Dreams"), which sounds as though it comes from the same disc as "Together" and "Hushabye Hushabye" used in John and Yoko's debut opus. Ringo's role is a smooth presenter on "your all-play music station," introducing "The Palm Court Orchestra with Albert Arkwright."

A second recording from this period (it may even be side 2 of the same cassette) lasts fourteen minutes, but includes a great deal more in the way of structured music. The first two minutes are mostly guitar strumming, feedback, whistling, and dead air, but John cues up one of his piano composing tapes. The first circulating segment (**B**) is a pair of false starts of the first verse of "Cry Baby Cry." After a few more unbootlegged false starts, the next portion (**C**) has the first verse, chorus, and first verse repeated (John sings along, singing "queen" instead of "king").

John continues with another chorus (unbootlegged) and segues straight into a familiar melody: the "jai guru dev" section of "Across the Universe" (**D**). John accompanies his piano tape with Mellotron strings; this flows right into a chorus of "Cry Baby Cry," perhaps indicating that they were originally part of the same song. An interesting section follows, as John plays a bouncy tune (akin to "Mean Mr. Mustard") with inaudible lyrics. After a minute of this, he stops and plays a melody that would become the chorus to "Hey Bulldog."

The first take (**E**) is mostly false starts and a run-through of the "she can talk to me" passage, with a tentative verse of "lonely sitting Sunday in my room, I'm a lonely." The second pass (**F**) is a bit more developed, with lyrics about "nothin' doin, something she can say." This take has a bit of Mellotron overdubbed near the beginning, and both have John double-tracking his vocal.

The playback continues with a bit of work on the verse, followed by an unfamiliar song. Phrases such as "never changes" and "it is the road that set me free" indicate that it may have been cannibalized for use in "Child of Nature" and "Across the Universe." After a minute or so, John slows down the arrangement, leading to the bootlegged portion (**G**), which ends with the "jai guru" melody repeated several times. The tape fades out with John playing a piano riff not unlike "Imagine."

Yet another unfinished song (**H**), not on either of these raw tapes but sounding very much like it's from the same era, begins with slow piano riffs as John sings, "She's walking past my door, and I'm trying to keep away." Suddenly it hits him that the chord pattern is recycled, and going into double-time rhythm, he pounds out "You Know My Name (Look Up the Number)," trying his best to remember the changes while singing along.

RELEASE HISTORY

1988: An incomplete version of **H** was broadcast on episode 88-13 of the radio series *The Lost Lennon Tapes;* this source was booted on the LP *The Lost Lennon Tapes, Volume 3*.

1991: Incomplete versions of **E** and **G,** along with **A–D,** were broadcast on episode 91-26 of the radio series *The Lost Lennon Tapes;* this source was booted on the LP *The Lost Lennon Tapes, Volume 30,* later issued on CD; the same songs appear on the bootleg CD *Arrive without Aging*.

1994: Complete versions of **E–H,** from tape sources but running too slow, surfaced on the bootleg CD *The Lost Pepperland Reel*.

7. Studio session

Date: early February 1968
Location: EMI Studios
Producer: Peter Asher

[A.] And the Sun Will Shine (3:03)
[B.] The Dog Presides (2:44)

This session was sort of a preview of how Apple might work: Peter Asher, soon to be that label's head artist and repertoire man, was producing a single for ex–Manfred Mann vocalist Paul Jones. Asher was able to acquire Paul's assistance for both sides on the drum kit, an instrument Paul was always eager to dabble with.

Featuring an A-side written by the brothers Gibb, and playing from top musicians Jeff Beck and Nicky Hopkins, the single should have been a surefire hit, even though Paul's contribution was largely unpublicized at the time. Unfortunately, the song itself (**A**) is quite awful, sounding reminiscent of David Letterman's spoof anthem, "It's a Late Night World of Love." The B-side (**B**) is an acid rock tune composed by Jones, with Spinal Tap–style lyrics, full of barking dog effects. The latter may have given Paul McCartney a brainstorm a few days later when recording a much better song by his partner John.

RELEASE HISTORY

1968: **A** and **B** were coupled on a single (Columbia DB 8379), released in the UK only, which failed to chart. Both songs were included on the British CD *The Paul Jones Collection, Volume 3: Come Into My Music Box.*

8. Studio session

Date: 3 February 1968
Time: 7:00 p.m.–midnight
Location: EMI Studio 3
Producer: George Martin

[A.] Across the Universe—monitor mix of take 2 (mono) (4:12)
[B.] Across the Universe—take 2 (stereo) (3:26)

In the wake of the *Magical Mystery Tour* fiasco, the Beatles wanted to release a strong follow-up single to fill the public void left by their imminent departure to study with the maharishi in India. John, Paul, and George each had a new composition to offer, and after working on the basic track of Paul's "Lady Madonna" the first night, they turned to John's "Across the Universe." The song had taken full shape, with the tentative chorus melody from the earlier demos set to a spiritual refrain, and a series of stream-of-consciousness verses of irregular lengths.

It was clearly a beautiful song, but John had difficulty translating the sounds in his head to a finished recording. He should have quit while he was ahead, for in a mere two takes, a suitably celestial and delicate backing track was perfected. The choice of using all acoustic stringed instruments (two guitars, a table harp, and tamboura) was effective, particularly when overlaid with a flanging effect. John's breathless and exquisite lead vocal floated above it all, and as they left the studio that night, take 2 was marked "best"—it would have made a superb release as is.

John didn't see it that way and would start afresh the next day, but luckily, take 2 was chosen for release on *Anthology 2*. It was also considered for inclusion in the 1983 multimedia presentation *The Beatles at Abbey Road*. A monitor mix (**A**) from preparation of this show has some extra warm-up material at the start, including John making a comment about Leslie Bryce (a *Beatles Book Monthly* photographer who would document the February 8 session). This mix isolates the harp and guitar tracks briefly and also carries on past *Anthology*'s fade to the take's true ending.

NOTE

This take is noted in both of Mark Lewisohn's books as being from February 4, but a specific correction in his *Anthology 2* liner notes (he even mentions it was a Saturday) indicates that more accurate information must have turned up in the interim. John Barrett's notes show tape E67494 as containing takes 1–3 of "Lady Madonna" (marked February 3) and takes 1–2 of "Across the Universe" (marked February 4). Tape E67495 has "Across the Universe," with no take numbers noted, also from February 3. Presumably these would be takes 4–7 (there was no take 3). It's possible that John was undecided at the end of the day whether he preferred take 2 or 7 and added overdubs to both the next day.

RELEASE HISTORY

1993: Most of **A** was included on the bootleg CD *Control Room Monitor Mixes.*

1996: **B** was officially released on *Anthology 2.*

2002: A more complete version of **A**, including a very faint take announcement, appeared on the bootleg CD *Complete Controlroom Monitor Mixes, Volume 2.*

9. Studio session

Date: 4 February 1968
Time: 8:00 p.m.–2:00 a.m.
Location: EMI Studio 3
Producer: George Martin

[A.] **Across the Universe—rough mono mix from take 7 and FX** (3:51)
Mixed: 4 February 1968

[B.] **Across the Universe—RS3** (3:29)
Mixed: 5 January 1970

[C.] **Across the Universe—RS from take 7** (3:34)

Having decided to concentrate on take 7 of "Across the Universe," John added his lead vocal this evening (with the tape running slow to raise the pitch of his voice). This joined the basic track of his acoustic guitar, Ringo's tom-tom, and George's tamboura to produce a simple and satisfying recording. It was at this point that John's later charges of Paul's "sabotaging" the song with experimentation perhaps began to have some merit.

For whatever reason, Paul felt it would be a grand idea to invite in two young ladies from among the fans congregating outside the studio to sing backing vocals. The lucky teenagers, Lizzie Bravo and Gayleen Pease, warbled "nothing's gonna change my world" tentatively on the tape's fourth track and were then escorted back outside. It's likely none of their friends believed the anecdote of their good fortunes, as the song didn't see release for almost two years, and then only on an obscure charity LP—the mix released on *Let It Be* in 1970 omitted their efforts.

In the meantime, more of that experimentation conspired to clutter the song unnecessarily. A reduction into take 8 freed up space for an overdub of backwards bass and drums on track 4. Three separate effects tapes were also prepared, of guitar and harp, both "to be played backwards," and four tracks of humming, titled "Hums Wild." At some point on this day, a rough mono mix (**A**) was apparently prepared for John to take home. This must be from take 7, as it doesn't include any backwards bass or drums, but it does incorporate the backwards guitar and harp, as well as "Hums Wild" during the "om" chant sections, and right near the end.

On February 8, the backwards track was erased and replaced with wordless three-part harmony from John, Paul, and George. After discarding organ and Mellotron overdubs, John settled on final adornments of electric guitar (with volume pedal swells), maracas, and piano. With Paul and George's songs now selected for the upcoming single, Spike Milligan came to the rescue of "Across the Universe." In the studio visiting old *Goon Show* producer George Martin, as well as *Cilla* costar Ringo (see next entry), Milligan asked John if he would donate the song to a projected album to benefit the World Wildlife Fund. John, not satisfied with the recording but unwilling to let such a good composition go unheard, agreed.

And there the matter sat for many months. A mono mix incorporating animal effects was prepared sometime later that year (an acetate is played back during the January 1969 Twickenham sessions), but the charity LP failed to surface. In March 1969, the mix was copied for inclusion on a mooted *Yellow Submarine* EP, but that was aborted as well. Finally, the Wildlife album surfaced in December 1969, by which time John must have felt the recording was cursed.

Since the song was featured in the *Let It Be* documentary, Glyn Johns wanted to add it to the soundtrack LP he was preparing in January 1970. To differentiate it from the Wildlife version, he went back to the original four-track of take 7 and mixed it into stereo: guitar, tom-tom, and vocal centered, tamboura right, and the girls' vocals left. This mix (**B**) ignored any backwards effects and animal noises, as well as the February 8 overdubs, but ended up unreleased when Phil Spector was brought in to helm the *Let It Be* project. A remix (**C**) for *Let It Be . . . Naked* pares the song down to John's vocal and acoustic guitar, plus unobtrusive tom-tom from Ringo, with George's tamboura gliding in halfway through and hovering over the song, which fades out in a heavy-handed wash of echo.

RELEASE HISTORY

1987: **B** appeared from an acetate on the vinyl bootleg *Dig It!*, a title later issued on CD.

1988: A slightly incomplete copy of **A** was aired on episode 88-17 of *The Lost Lennon Tapes*. It was bootlegged on the LP *The Lost Lennon Tapes, Volume 3*, and CDs such as *Ultra Rare Trax, Volume 3* and *Unsurpassed Masters, Volume 4*, always with surface noise.

1994: **A** was included on the CD *Revolution* from a tape source that is slightly longer at the end than the broadcast version.

1999: An excellent copy of **B** from tape source surfaced along with the rest of Glyn Johns's January 1970 assembly. It's been booted on CDs such as *Get Back 2nd Mix* and *Get Back: The Glyn Johns Final Compilation*.

2003: **C** was released on the CD *Let It Be . . . Naked*.

10. TV performance

Date: 6 February 1968
Time: 8:00–8:50 p.m.
Location: Television Theatre, London
Host: Cilla Black
Broadcast: live
BBC1
Cilla

[A.] **viewer mail** (2:16)
[B.] **ventriloquism/Nellie Dean** (4:42)
[C.] **Do You Like Me?** (3:13)

Ringo once referred to himself as "Mr. Showbiz," and apart from his solo scenes in Beatles films, his first chance to shine as an all-around entertainer occurred this evening on BBC TV. He was a guest star on the second episode of Cilla Black's self-titled variety series, and after three days of rehearsals, he was more than up to the task. While his bandmates toiled in EMI Studio 1, Ringo spent the day in dress rehearsals and a live broadcast, which went off flawlessly.

If the original show still exists on video, it's never seen the light of day in any form; Mark Lewisohn's description in the book *The Complete Beatles Chronicle* seems to indicate that he has viewed a copy, although he may be working from still photos and a comparison with later episodes (he mentions that Ringo is seen during the opening credits, but this may have been standard procedure for guest stars). An off-air audio recording does circulate, including all of Ringo's contributions.

In the first skit, he assists Cilla in sorting through her fan mail and ends up introducing one of her num-bers, "I'm Playing Second Fiddle to a Football Team." A more elaborate skit involves Ringo interacting with ventriloquist Peter Brough and performing an act with his own "dummy," Ariadne (Cilla in schoolgirl costume). The team duets on "Nellie Dean" a cappella while Ringo swigs a pint of beer. Finally, Ringo and Cilla sing and dance their way through a ridiculously corny oldie, "Do You Like Me?"

Overall, Ringo proved a charming and affable foil for Ms. Black, and his fellow Beatles must have been proud as they took a one-hour break from their session to watch their drummer step into the spotlight.

NOTE

A recording of Ringo and Cilla duetting on "Act Naturally," long assumed to be from this show, is actually from Ringo's second appearance on *Cilla,* taped October 1, 1970.

RELEASE HISTORY

1989: A fair-quality copy of **C** surfaced on the 7-inch EP *1989 Beatleg News Christmas Record,* taken from a longer tape circulating for several years.

1999: The full tape of **A–C** was included on the CD-Rs *Telecasts Four* and *Vinyl to the Core;* both releases are in comparable quality and run at different speeds. Another circulating strain of the tape is of worse quality but has a few extra seconds of (non-Ringo) material.

11. Studio session

Date: 6 February 1968
Time: 9:00 p.m.–2:00 a.m.
Location: EMI Studio 1
Producer: George Martin

[A.] **Lady Madonna—rough mix from take 4 (stereo)** (2:08)
[B.] **Lady Madonna—take 4 (stereo)** (2:16)
[C.] **Lady Madonna—monitor mixes from take 4 (mono)** (9:53)
[D.] **Lady Madonna—take 5 (stereo)** (3:17)
[E.] **Lady Madonna—RS from takes 3, 4, and 5** (2:20)

[F.] **Lady Madonna—RM10** (2:15)
Mixed: 15 February 1968

[G.] **Lady Madonna—RS1** (2:14)
Mixed: 2 December 1969

[H.] **Lady Madonna—RS from takes 4 and 5 (#1)** (2:13)
[I.] **Lady Madonna—RS from takes 4 and 5 (#2)** (2:57)

Paul's contender for the new single's A-side was "Lady Madonna," a boogie-based piano composition harking back to Fats Domino but with tongue-in-cheek contemporary lyrics. The documentation is fuzzy about the exact order of overdubs, but recording began February 3 in Studio 3 with three takes of a basic track. Paul played piano, with the signal squashed to sound more primitive, and Ringo played a swing drum part using brushes.

After a break, the session continued with overdubs onto the "best" take: on tracks 2 and 3 went a heavier drum track, accenting the off-beat, Paul's Rickenbacker bass, and John and George duetting on two electric guitars fed through the same amplifier. Track 4 was reserved for Paul's main vocal, with John and George adding some faint scat vocals during the middle eight solo; this vocal overdub concluded with John singing "Lady Madonna-ha-ha-ha" in a mock-operatic style, which can be heard on many of the outtakes. Apparently at the beginning of this overdub, George and Ringo are heard munching on a bag of crisps; George suggests that Ringo write to the company and request they make Marmite-flavored ones, but that's not to the drummer's taste.

On February 6, this recording was reduced into take 4 by combining the bass, guitars, and drums to a single track. Various overdubs came next: Paul thickened his piano part (notably during the intro), handclaps were added in spots, and for the second "see how they run," Paul doubled his vocal, backed by an organ. In addition, to fill the middle eight solo, John, Paul, and George sang an imitation brass combo through cupped hands while someone (Ringo was absent) shook a tambourine. During these overdubs, Paul sang a loud "Lady Madonna" at the beginning and laughed at his silliness, and he and John joked around at the end with the song's final word: "meet! eet! eet!"

All of this can be heard in the two variant rough mixes of take 4. Version **A** begins abruptly after the piano intro and has the bass, drum, and guitars mixed left, piano and main vocal right, and the new overdubs centered. This overdub track is left down apart from the intro, middle eight, and outro. Version **B,** used in the 1983 *The Beatles at Abbey Road* presentation, includes the Marmite comment faintly underneath Paul's count-in. It mixes the piano/brush track right and everything else center, and generally leaves all four tracks open throughout. However, a monitor mix tape (**C**) from the preparation of this 1983 mix allows us to hear even more of the silliness on the overdub track as it's isolated. This includes more handclaps, tambourine rattling, a bit of Mellotron, and Paul discussing what the song's promotional film should look like.

At this point, Paul decided a mock-brass section was no match for the real thing, and hastily arranged to have two tenor and two baritone sax players brought in to finish off the song. This was done with a simultaneous reduction from take 4 into take 5, and as usual with Paul's brainstorm parts, was created on the spot, recorded "101 times" (as one of the musicians joked) until it sounded right. Ronnie Scott played the tenor solo for the middle eight.

One final touch was to refine the backing vocal track further. The "see how they run" lines were harmonized, more handclaps were added, and a second section of "vocal brass" (with no tambourine accompaniment this time) was dropped in behind the final bridge. A rough mix of take 5 (**D**) begins with the sound of Paul and Ringo warming up on piano and brushes from the basic track. The Marmite conversation is then heard up-front (obscuring Paul's count-in somewhat), and the tape is stopped after the first verse and wound back. Another couple of false tape starts follow before the song plays through, sounding much as released but with reversed channels.

The song was mixed twice for mono that evening, but perfected in seven further attempts on the fifteenth (**F**) for single release. The sole stereo mix (**G**) was created over a year later for use on the U.S. album *Hey Jude;* both released mixes clip the decay of the final piano chord. That can be heard coming to an end on the *Anthology 2* remix (**E**), which is comprised of the piano/brush and main vocal tracks of take 3 synced with the "vocal brass/tambourine" overdub from take 4's first bridge (but spliced in here during the second bridge), and the sax solo from take 5 plus some extra sax riffs at the end unheard elsewhere. The *Love* remix (**I**) incorporates elements from "Why Don't We Do It in the Road?," "I Want You (She's So Heavy)," "Hey Bulldog," and "While My Guitar Gently Weeps."

RELEASE HISTORY

1968: **F** was released on a single worldwide and is available on EMI's CD single of the same title.

1970: **G** was released in the United States on the LP *Hey Jude;* it was eventually included on the CD *Past Masters, Volume 2* as well as the compilation CDs *The Beatles 1967–1970* and *1.*

1983: **B** was used in the multimedia presentation *The Beatles at Abbey Road,* vastly sped up to accompany its promo film. It appears in excellent sound on the bootleg *Abbey Road Video Show* and speed-corrected on *Turn Me On Dead Man: The John Barrett Tapes,* although both fade a bit early to omit narration, under which the song's fade continues on the original source.

1988: An excellent copy of **A** surfaced on the vinyl bootleg *Ultra Rare Trax, Volume 5 & 6.* This appeared later from tape source on the CDs *Not Guilty* and *Unsurpassed Masters, Volume 7,* running a half step too slow in both cases.

1990: **D** was bootlegged in excellent quality on the CD *Unsurpassed Masters, Volume 4.*

1996: **E** was officially released on *Anthology 2.*

2002: **C** appeared in very good quality on the bootleg CD *Complete Controlroom Monitor Mixes, Volume 1.*

2003: **H** was released on the soundtrack of the *Anthology* DVD.

2006: **I** was released on the *Love* CD.

12. Studio session

Date: 8 February 1968
Time: 2:30–9:00 p.m.
Location: EMI Studio 2
Producer: George Martin

[A.] The Inner Light—RM4 (2:33)
Mixed: 8 February 1968

[B.] The Inner Light—RS1 (2:33)
Mixed: 27 January 1970

Among the many ragas George produced in the Bombay sessions for *Wonderwall* was this haunting track, untitled on the day it was recorded, January 12. The song, perfected in five takes, featured a harmonium drone, tabla and pakavaj percussion, and alluring sarod and flute work, all performed by EMI Bombay studio musicians.

The finished two-track stereo tape was brought back to London, and George copied it over to four-track on February 6 during sessions for the new Beatles single. At that point, it seemed likely "Lady Madonna" and "Across the Universe" would occupy both sides of the disc, but George persisted and overdubbed a lead vocal on one of the vacant tracks. He had written a simple but effective melody and philosophical lyrics borrowed from a poem titled "The Inner Light."

In addition, it's likely the shehnai, a wailing reed instrument that matched his new melody in places, was added during this session by an unknown musician from London's Asian Music Circle. For one thing, it appears in the center of the stereo mix, separate from the two tracks likely on the original Bombay tape. There is also a variant performance of the first shehnai passage on the mono mix (**A**), suggesting more than one overdub attempt. A splice at 0:22 in the mono mix makes it clear this used an edit piece; the stereo mix (**B**) seems to play through uninterrupted and probably comes from a single overdub take.

Although a mono mix was created on the sixth, one final overdub was added on the eighth—George doubled his vocal for the final "arrive without traveling" and was joined by John and Paul for a harmony on "do all without doing." The best mono mix from that day was chosen for the B-side of the new single, marking the first Harrison composition to be included on a British Beatles 45. A stereo mix wasn't attempted until January 1970, for unknown purposes (perhaps for inclusion on the U.S. *Hey Jude* album, although that master tape was completed a month earlier). Besides the edit piece, the main difference between the released mixes is a much heavier delay on George's vocal on the mono mix, sounding almost like ADT.

NOTE

A so-called instrumental monitor mix of this song on various bootlegs appears to be nothing more than an OOPSed version of the stereo mix. George's vocal can still be heard faintly in the background, notably on his final "arrive without traveling."

RELEASE HISTORY

1968: **A** was released on a single worldwide and is available on the "Lady Madonna" CD single.

1981: **B** was included on *The Beatles,* an EP compiled for EMI's boxed set of EPs. It's also on the CD release of that title as well as *Past Masters, Volume 2.*

13. Promo clips

Date: 11 February 1968
Time: 4:00 p.m.–2:00 a.m.
Location: EMI Studio 3
Director: Tony Bramwell

[A.] Lady Madonna—version 1 (2:18)
Broadcast: 30 March 1968, 9:30–10:30 p.m.
ABC-TV
The Hollywood Palace

[B.] Lady Madonna—version 2 (2:15)
Broadcast: 9 March 1968, 4:30–5:15 p.m.
Radio Bremen/WDR-TV
Beat Club #29

[C.] Hey Bulldog (3:17)

Sessions had gone better and faster than expected; a studio date booked for the tenth was canceled and this one might have been, too, were it not for the desire to shoot a promotional film to accompany "Lady Madonna." Rather than try to re-create a performance of that song, the Beatles were filmed recording a totally different number: John's "Hey Bulldog," which turned out well enough that it became his only new contribution to the *Yellow Submarine* soundtrack.

In addition to the recording of the song's first three tracks (see the following entry), Tony Bramwell's camera crew captured various rehearsals (John running through the song on piano while Paul follows on bass) and a jam session (Paul on drums, John and George on guitars). Ringo is seen listening to a playback, and George even devours a plate of beans for the benefit of the cameras!

Various tricks such as filters, double exposure, and even inserting leftover footage from Paul's "Step Inside Love" session (see the November 21, 1967, entries) could not disguise the disjointed nature of the clips. None of the visuals really matched up to the soundtrack, and thus it was a delight some thirty years later when the original raw footage was discovered and re-edited to create a new promo for "Hey Bulldog." The highlight of this clip (C) is the long extended shots of John and Paul recording their lead vocals, including their comical dialogue from the end of the released take.

All three clips share a number of mutual shots; the easiest way to tell apart the first two is that the most common clip (A) opens with an overhead shot of Ringo on drums, and ends with Paul (in Chappell Studios at the "Step Inside Love" session) getting up from the piano, picking up his coat and guitar, and leaving the room. The rarer alternate (B) opens with Ringo in a coat and tie and is the only clip to include George's bean feast.

It's not clear which versions were aired in the UK; four separate monochrome screenings occurred on various BBC shows. In the United States, version A was definitely broadcast in color on *The Hollywood Palace*. Version B was aired on Germany's *Beat Club* in black and white. Note that the *Anthology* documentary edits together footage from both promos, plus clips from the "Hey Jude" session (see the July 30 entry), to create a new hybrid.

RELEASE HISTORY

The first two clips have circulated for several years in decent quality, notably A, which was included in the *Private Reel* compilation. The prints used in the *Anthology* home video assembly are generally superior. Apple distributed C to promote the reissue of *Yellow Submarine* in 1999; it debuted on ABCs *20/20* September 17 of that year (with annoying graphic overlays) and VH-1 two days later. It also circulates from a pristine EPK along with some sound bites from Paul, George, and Ringo praising the song.

14. Studio session

Date: 11 February 1968
Time: 4:00 p.m.–2:00 a.m.
Location: EMI Studio 3
Producer: George Martin

[A.] Hey Bulldog—RM2 (2:58)
Mixed: 11 February 1968

[B.] Hey Bulldog—RS3 (3:08)
Mixed: 29 October 1968

[C.] Hey Bulldog—RS from take 10 (3:09)

In the vein of the other new songs, "Hey Bulldog" was a relatively simple recording compared with most of the Beatles' 1967 releases. The basic track was perfected in ten takes, with John pounding on the piano, Ringo at the drums, Paul shaking a tambourine, and George playing rhythm guitar. On a second track went Paul's bass, accompanied by George doubling the main riff on a fuzzed guitar and Ringo playing a snare drum off-beat on the choruses and coda. John and Paul then laid down the main vocal track, standing and sharing a mic while reading from John's handwritten lyrics. This overdub ended in inspired goofiness with the duo bantering and howling into the fade.

All of the above is documented in Tony Bramwell's footage, but unfortunately the cameras were shut off for the final overdubs. In addition to double-tracking the vocal refrains, John apparently recorded the biting guitar solo himself: At one point in the footage, he can be seen borrowing George's Gibson SG Standard, and the finished solo has all the trademarks of a Lennon performance in its jaggedness.

The completed song was hastily mixed into mono that evening, with the playback machine running fast to raise the pitch. This mix (A) was dispatched to King Features, who promptly animated a sequence for it in *Yellow Submarine*. It was a less than inspired addition to the film, and was an obvious choice for excision when the producers decided to trim some fat; thus it was never included in U.S. prints and has only recently been restored on the home video reissue. The stereo mixes for the original soundtrack LP (B) and the 1999 *Songtrack* (C) are similar; the latter has an extra layer of echo and swaps the placement of the main vocal and bass tracks. All releases contain a glitch around 3:05 into the song, apparently present on the master tape.

RELEASE HISTORY

1969: B was released on stereo copies of the *Yellow Submarine* LP (and reduced to mono on UK monaural copies). It's available on the EMI CD of the same title.

1996: A copy of A, dubbed from a video source complete with sound effects from the film, was included on the bootleg CD *It's All in the Mind Y'know*. A purported "true mono mix" of the song is on the CD *The Lost Pepperland Reel,* but it's not clear whether this is anything other than a collapsed stereo copy.

1999: C was included on Apple's *Yellow Submarine Songtrack* CD.

14a. Newsreel footage   J, G

Date: 15 February 1968
Location: London Airport
Broadcast: 15 February 1968
ITV
Length: 0:20

Mal Evans had flown out to India early to smooth the way for the Beatles' imminent arrivals. By the fifteenth,

John, George, their wives, and Pattie's sister Jenny were ready to make the journey east. Their departure from London Airport was filmed by ITV News inside the terminal building (Peter Brown can also be glimpsed).

RELEASE HISTORY

This silent footage circulates on video.

15. Newsreel footage   J, G

Date: 16 February 1968
Time: 8:15 a.m.
Location: New Delhi Airport
Length: 0:43

Two brief silent clips circulate of John and George's arrival in New Delhi early the next morning. Color film shows the party walking across the tarmac, being greeted by Mia Farrow, and boarding a bus. Reuters' black-and-white footage takes place inside the bus and

then during the transfer to cars, as the celebrities pose for photographs.

RELEASE HISTORY

The color footage circulates from a rebroadcast in a French TV show, *Destinées*. Thirty seconds of the Reuters footage circulates from its use in a Swedish newsreel.

16. Newsreel footage   J, G

Date: 17 February 1968
Location: Rishikesh
Length: 0:27

On their first day at the retreat, John and George ignored the world's press, clamoring outside the gates for a glimpse of the pop stars' mystical trappings. Instead, they carried on with meditating and enjoying a vegetarian lunch (rice, chapatis, curried vegetables, and salad) while a Reuters camera crew filmed what they

could: scenic shots of the Himalayas and Ganges, the camp's WELCOME sign, and the exterior of the buildings. Their patience paid off with the fleeting appearance of the musicians, walking in the distance, accompanied by their wives and Mal Evans.

RELEASE HISTORY

This silent color footage circulates on video.

17. Newsreel footage

Date: 17–18 February 1968
Location: London Airport and Rishikesh
Broadcast: 19 February 1968
ITV
Length: 2:03

On February 18, Paul, Jane, Ringo, and Maureen departed for India to join the others. This ITV News report begins with the quartet posing for photographers at the foot of the plane's steps. As they climb the stairs, Paul decides to imitate a bird and flaps his "wings."

In footage taken at the ashram the previous day,

John (cloaked in white), Pattie, and George can be seen in separate shots strolling down a path. The maharishi is then interviewed about what his new disciples have been up to since their arrival. Finally, John, Cynthia, and Mike Love are seen exiting a building, and one of the maharishi's lectures is glimpsed from a great distance.

RELEASE HISTORY

This footage (silent apart from the interview) circulates on video.

18. Newsreel footage

P, R

Date: 19 February 1968
Time: 8:15 a.m.
Location: New Delhi Airport
Length: 0:49

More news footage, this time of Paul, Jane, Ringo, and Maureen deplaning and being met by Mal Evans and a representative from the ashram, who both place garlands around the necks of the new arrivals. After clearing customs, they would remain in New Delhi overnight, the delay caused by Ringo's inflammatory reaction to his travel inoculations.

RELEASE HISTORY

This silent color footage, filmed by Reuters, circulates on video.

19. Newsreel footage

P, R

Date: 20 February 1968
Location: New Delhi
Length: 0:35

Reuters managed to be on the spot again as Ringo was given the all-clear at Willingdon Hospital in New Delhi. Paul also decided to document the occasion on his 8 mm movie camera: He can be seen filming Ringo and Maureen, and pulling an orange from a paper bag as he walks alongside Jane. A couple of long and bumpy car rides later, the four Beatles would be united once again at the Academy of Transcendental Meditation.

RELEASE HISTORY

This silent footage circulates in color from a rebroadcast in a French TV show, *Destinées,* and in black and white from its use in a Swedish newsreel.

20. Newsreel footage

Date: 21 February 1968
Location: Rishikesh
Length: 0:52

Although the maharishi's retreat was relatively secluded, a number of intrepid journalists hovered outside during the first few days of the Beatles' stay. Understandably, there was a lot of curiosity (and skepticism) about what the group was getting up to. Paul remembered: "The camp compound had a wire fence all around it, which was handy later, for the press decided they wanted to have pictures of everything that we did. They would catch us walking past the gates so we started to avoid that area and they didn't get in much."

This footage is an excellent illustration of Paul's recollections: Pathé's cameraman caught 52 seconds of action from afar, shooting through the aforementioned wire fence. George is first to stroll down the shaded path, and he gives a quick wave. Pattie, John, Ringo, and Maureen follow, and after the insertion of some stock Beatle footage, all four Beatles are seen returning in the opposite direction (John has a blanket draped over his head). The following month, an Italian TV crew would have slightly better luck, but the group's own home movies would provide the only real intimate glimpse of life at the ashram.

RELEASE HISTORY

The Pathé newsreel (untitled but screened March 3) circulates among collectors.

21. Newsreel footage/Location recordings

Date: 1–14 March 1968
Location: Rishikesh
Broadcast: 15 March 1968
RAI 1
tv 7

[A.] **When the Saints Go Marching In/You Are My Sunshine** (1:56)
[B.] **natural sound** (1:50)
[C.] **Jingle Bells/She'll Be Comin' Around the Mountain** (1:17)
[D.] **She'll Be Comin' Around the Mountain/Happiness Runs** (2:13)
[E.] **instrumental/Blowin' in the Wind** (1:35)
[F.] **Hare Krishna Mantra** (1:24)
[G.] **O Sole Mio/It's Now or Never** (0:42)
[H.] **Catch the Wind** (1:13)

Soon after Ringo had left Rishikesh, an Italian TV crew was permitted to film the maharishi and his students as they strolled down to the banks of the Ganges and assembled for a sing-along. Although the footage was silent and fragmented, it was accompanied by a soundtrack obviously captured on the occasion (Mia Farrow is seen singing "You Are My Sunshine" very clearly at one point).

The footage begins with the party assembling outside the ashram: John and Paul have acoustic guitars, and George, Pattie, Jane, Cynthia, Mike Love, Paul Horn, Donovan, and Mia Farrow are among those in evidence. A short trek later, everyone gathers on the beach and poses for a Farrow snapshot. The guitars are shared among John, Paul, George, and Donovan, and everyone joins in the singing, although no Beatles numbers, new or old, are attempted.

As the audio portion begins, George is leading a run-through of "When the Saints Go Marching In." Some dialogue follows, with John contemplating getting a tan, and the maharishi exhorting the others to "fathom the infinity" and "dive in the Ganges." George gently pokes fun at him: "We don't really exist!" After a few uninspired campfire songs, punctuated by the sounds of water birds, Maharishi requests a Donovan tune, "Happiness Runs." The performance is pleasant, although Donovan has a hard time arranging it as a round with George taking the other part. Unsurprisingly, some chanting of "Hare Krishna" follows, with guitar accompaniment. Perhaps because of the Italian crew, a bit of mock opera is crooned, leading Paul to sing a line from "It's Now or Never." Mia Farrow requests "100 Miles," but instead Donovan plays his own composition, "Catch the Wind," with John singing along in places.

Although it gives a bit of insight into life at the retreat, the tape is generally disappointing. Imagine how much more interesting it would have been to hear one of the dozens of songs John, Paul, and George had been working on in the past three weeks.

RELEASE HISTORY

1982: Brief excerpts of **A** and **C** accompanied some of this footage in the home video documentary *The Compleat Beatles.*

1992: An 8:38 edit of this recording (omitting **D**) was included on the vinyl bootleg *Nothing but Aging,* and copied the following year on the CD *Arrive without Aging.*

1997: An alternate edit lasting 5:24 appeared on the CD-R *Another Flaming Pie.* This included the first appearance of **D,** as well as portions of **C** and **F–H.**

2001: A composite containing all the musical portions (but omitting much of the ambient sounds of birds and water) totaling 9:25 appeared on the CD-R *Live! Make As Much Noise As You Like.* Two separate video sources also circulate with nonsynchronized sound; these last 8:51 and 8:09.

22. Location recording

Date: 15 March 1968
Location: Rishikesh

[A.] **Spiritual Regeneration** (1:30)
[B.] **Happy Birthday to You/Spiritual Regeneration** (1:00)

Birthdays were a time for ample celebration in Rishikesh. On February 25, George had turned twenty-five and was feted with fireworks; a dual party for his wife, Pattie, and Paul Horn would be held on March 17. And two days earlier, Beach Boy Mike Love turned twenty-seven. To mark the occasion, Paul, George, Donovan, and others whipped up a song and performed it in a Chuck Berry fashion on acoustic guitars with Beach Boys–styled harmonies.

The lyrics pay tribute to Guru Dev, the maharishi's teacher and founder of Transcendental Meditation, who was also mentioned in "Across the Universe." Here the reference is a bit more tongue-in-cheek, à la "All

Together Now": "A-B-C-D-E-F-G-H-I-Jai Guru Dev." After a brief guitar solo, there is a break in the tape, which continues with the traditional birthday song, transposed over the same shuffling rhythm. This piece has appeared on bootlegs under numerous titles, including "Happy Birthday Mike Love," "Thank You Guru Dai," and "Indian Rope Trick."

RELEASE HISTORY

1976: These recordings were originally broadcast on a Beach Boys radio special, *The Best Summers of Our Lives,* hosted by Wolfman Jack. They appeared a year later on the vinyl bootleg *Indian Rope Trick,* including the Wolfman's narration bridging the two pieces; this source was copied on the CD-R compilation *Vinyl to the Core* in 1999.

1985: A slightly superior-quality tape of **A** and **B** was used on the bootleg LP *Strawberry Fields Forever* (also issued on CD by Condor), but this splices out the narration, losing some of the music in the process.

23. TV interview   P

Date:	26 March 1968
Location:	London Airport
Interviewer:	Richard Whitmore
Broadcast:	26 March 1968
	BBC TV
Length:	2:28

Having decided that five weeks of meditation were enough, Paul returned to London from Rishikesh (via Tehran) to work on moving the Apple project forward. At the airport, he and Jane Asher consented to an interview for the BBC (both radio and TV, apparently).

The interview begins with Paul strumming a ukelele and singing the title to "Bye Bye Blackbird" and then describing the meditation process, seeming a bit embarrassed about the whole affair: "It sounds daft." Paul goes on to explain Maharishi's plan to tackle Indian poverty by motivation and encouragement rather than simply pouring money into the country. Told that an Indian member of Parliament alleged that the ashram was actually an espionage center, Paul jokingly admits that the Beatles are secret agents. A bit condescendingly, the reporter wonders if Jane was really there to meditate or just for a holiday, and she explains the calming effect meditation had.

RELEASE HISTORY

Footage containing the majority of this interview (lasting 2:05) was included on the home video *The Beatles 1962 to 1970;* oddly, the reporter's question to Jane has been dubbed in and differs slightly from the radio broadcast described below.

1972: An excerpt from this interview was broadcast in part nine of the BBC Radio documentary. *The Beatles Story,* including portions not seen in the video.

1996: The soundtrack of the video clip was included on the CD *Rare Photos & Interview CD, Volume 3,* but with Paul's one-line rendition of "Bye Bye Blackbird" omitted, presumably for copyright reasons. The song can be found on the CD-R *Unbootlegged 1.*

24. Amateur footage

Date:	16 February–12 April 1968
Location:	Rishikesh

In addition to composing songs and meditating, the Beatles and company spent a lot of time in Rishikesh, particularly early on, playing with their home movie cameras. When they ran out of 8 mm Kodak color film, Mike Love would be dispatched to New Delhi to restock their supply. Although some of the footage was assembled as early as January 1969 (John joked that they should call the result "What We Did on Our Summer Holiday"), it was rarely viewed by the public until *Anthology.*

In a sequence set to "Across the Universe," life at the retreat is illustrated with images of the Ganges, the outdoor discussion groups, the shaded dining hall, and a huge group photo of the maharishi and all the happy campers (taken in late February, before Ringo's departure). A segment accompanied by "Dear Prudence" follows, including Prudence herself, plus Paul

Horn showing off his "Jai Guru Dev" robe, a birthday gift from Paul and Jane. As "I Will" plays, Paul is seen in various settings strumming an acoustic guitar (occasionally right-handed, suggesting some of the film may be reversed). Finally, there is a priceless scene of John being chosen for a helicopter ride with the maharishi, in hopes of being "slipped the answer."

RELEASE HISTORY

This footage, all color and silent, circulates among collectors. The *Anthology* home video includes about five minutes of Rishikesh home movies, some of them slowed down considerably. Other home movies from Rishikesh, mostly shot by Mal Evans, have been broadcast in various venues.

25. Studio session   P

Date: June 1967–April 1968
Location: De Lane Lea Studios, London
Producer: Paul McCartney, Roger McGough, Mike McGear, Andy Roberts

[A.] **So Much** (3:54)
[B.] **Little Bit of Heaven** (1:47)
[C.] **Basement Flat** (2:43)
[D.] **Frink, a Life in the Day of/Summer with Monika—prologue** (8:58)
[E.] **Frink, a Life in the Day of/Summer with Monika—epilogue** (1:51)
[F.] **Come Close and Sleep Now** (2:18)
[G.] **Yellow Book** (2:14)
[H.] **House in My Head** (3:32)
[I.] **Mr. Tickle** (3:20)
[J.] **Living Room** (2:46)
[K.] **Do You Remember?** (3:16)
[L.] **Please Don't Run Too Fast** (1:33)
[M.] **Ex Art Student** (6:29)

Paul was not the only McCartney to enter the music business in the 1960s. His younger brother Mike, under the stage name "Mike McGear," was a member of a three-man outfit called the Scaffold. The trio, comprised of McGear, Roger McGough, and John Gorman, all hailed from Merseyside and performed a mixture of poetry, comedy, and music, which stood them apart from the pack of Liverpool pop bands of the day.

Their initial chart success came with a catchy song called "Thank U Very Much," written by Mike after a phone call to his brother. Paul was present in the control room during the July 1967 Abbey Road session for that single, but did not play on it. He did, however, play a significant role in an album of music and poetry begun around that time, featuring two-thirds of the Scaffold.

Sessions for the album *McGough & McGear* commenced June 18, 1967, at Dick James's studio, and although Andy Roberts was the chief producer, Paul assisted with many of the sessions, not only helping in the booth, but adding vocal and instrumental contribu-

tions. Exact recording dates are unknown, but most of the LP seems to have been worked on during the summer at De Lane Lea Studios. **A** and **M** reportedly feature Jimi Hendrix on guitar: One source has a recording date of June 20, 1967 for both tracks, but Hendrix was playing in San Francisco that night. Another source dates Hendrix's participation as January 20, 1968 (the previous day, he had attended Apple's launch party for Grapefruit), so perhaps his contribution was an overdub. July 12, 1967, is another likely LP date, and sessions were probably wrapped up, apart from mixing, by the time Paul left for Rishikesh in February 1968.

Detailed session credits have never been published, but along with Paul and Jimi Hendrix, guest musicians included Zoot Money, Graham Nash, John Mayall, Dave Mason, and Spencer Davis. Jane Asher and her mother, Margaret, were on hand to sing in some of the choruses as well. Paul's voice is evident several times: On **A** he gives a count-in, suggesting he may be behind the drum kit (it's not far removed from his Scouse-funk style of playing). He speaks to Roger McGough over the talkback at the beginning of **D**. ("D'you wanna do it then?" "Yes, please." "Go.") And he can be heard during the intro ("Oh, swingin' swingin' swingin' London") and outro (some operatic crooning) of **J**.

Various "Beatles '67" production tricks surface throughout: **F** has backwards tapes, **J** has a false ending, and **M** concludes with a lengthy Indian passage. The tracks are linked with the sounds of waves crashing on the shore. Paul even throws in some of his patented raga-style vocalizing during **J** (similar to "I Want to Tell You" and live versions of "If I Needed Someone"). The faint rambling piano in **I** is highly reminiscent of some of Paul's playing during the January 1969 Twickenham sessions, and it's likely Paul plays keyboards on a few of the other songs. The only verified contribution is his piano part on "Do You Remember?" (**K**), on which he also harmonizes with Mike. This song was rerecorded in mid-January 1968 for release as a Scaffold single, without Paul's involvement.

The *McGough & McGear* album holds up remarkably well today, and although it failed to chart, stands as Paul's most impressive extra-Beatle project to that date. It's just as experimental as the work the Beatles were turning out at that stage, and far more eclectic than the average pop album of the era. When Apple kicked into high gear a few months later, Paul would lend his production and performing skills to a wide range of artists.

RELEASE HISTORY

1968: The *McGough & McGear* LP was released May 17 on Parlophone in the UK, and has been reissued on CD. The album was never released in the United States, where the Scaffold remained primarily unknown.

26. TV interview   J, P

Date: 13 May 1968
Location: St. Regis Hotel, New York City
Interviewer: Larry Kane
Length: 10:44

What better spokesmen for a burgeoning company than the most celebrated songwriting team of the decade? Luckily, Apple had such a pair on their board of directors, so John and Paul were dispatched from London to New York on May 11, accompanied by Alexis Mardas, Derek Taylor, Neil, and Mal. Their mission was unclear, other than to spread the word and generate buzz about the new company, and perhaps to remind America of the Beatles' stature. Their latest single, "Lady Madonna," had stalled at number 4 on the U.S. *Billboard* chart, and their aborted involvement with the maharishi hadn't helped matters.

Sunday the twelfth was spent out of the public eye: an unrecognized visit to Central Park, a business lunch in New York Harbor, and an evening at the Scene nightclub. The next two days would be their busiest in America since the 1966 tour, with the thirteenth devoted to interviews for individual media outlets. From a suite in the St. Regis, John and Paul entertained queries from a number of reporters, including their old pal Larry Kane.

Kane's interview was filmed in color and has been excerpted in numerous documentaries; the complete footage was eventually released with Kane's book *Lennon Revealed* (the occasion was also skewered accurately in *The Rutles*, with Nasty and Dirk announcing the formation of Rutle Corps).

Paul's attempt to describe Apple is unsettlingly vague: "It's just trying to mix business with enjoyment. But like all the profits won't go into our pockets. It'll go to help people. But not like a charity." John is more direct, saying applicants won't be "shown into the wastepaper bin."

Kane wonders how the trip to India went, and John replies cryptically, "The journey was terrible. But the trip was all right." He insists somewhat inaccurately that "We were there four months, or George and I were." In fact, they both stayed in Rishikesh for just under two months. Kane then attempts to ask Paul about the previous summer's LSD controversy and is interrupted by a classic Lennon quip. (Kane: "It seemed to me from what I read that you had endorsed it, then condemned it—"; John: "We were manufacturing it at the time.")

Being a newsman, Kane tries to get John and Paul's reaction to various current events (campus rioting and Martin Luther King Jr.'s assassination). John reacts with surprising defensiveness ("What do you think we are, deadbeats?") and Paul noncommittally. ("It's a drag, y'know. People . . . seem to be messing it up.")

The interview concludes with a nod to the past and the future as Kane asks what they will do "when the bubble bursts" and whether they could envision separate careers. John points out that they have already each done solo projects, but Paul is reassuring: "We are the Beatles . . . that's what we are." Asked what he remembers most from the Beatle days, John says, "Escaping from Memphis," then reminisces about the group's first visit to New York four years earlier. Asked about the current music scene, John correctly notes a trend away from psychedelia toward simpler music (citing "Young Girl" as an example). After the interview, Kane's cameraman filmed about a minute of silent cutaways and reverse-angle shots.

RELEASE HISTORY

Several clips from this interview circulate on video, from documentaries such as *Imagine: John Lennon* and *Anthology,* as well as various TV specials (including "All My Loving"; see the May 23 entry). In addition, a more continuous audio recording from a CHUM-FM radio broadcast makes the rounds in good quality; this edits out a single word from John ("viewers") to disguise the tape's origin as a TV broadcast. The complete footage was released on a DVD included with Kane's book *Lennon Revealed.*

27. Press conference J, P

Date: 14 May 1968
Time: 1:30 p.m.
Location: Americana Hotel, New York City
Interviewer: Bob Lewis
Broadcast: 19 May 1968, 10:00 a.m.–4:00 p.m.
WABC-AM, New York City
The Bob Lewis Show
Length: 6:28

John and Paul were out of practice at holding press conferences, and it showed during this buffet lunch reception at the Americana Hotel. For many reasons, it should have gone smoothly: Derek Taylor was fielding the questions and Capitol footed the bill. Among the familiar faces in the crowd was photographer Linda Eastman, whom Paul was meeting on her home turf for the first time. But as he later admitted, Paul was suffering from a "personal paranoia" that day caused by the drugs he was taking. Consequently, John did most of the talking in this and the rest of the day's appearances.

Despite the heavy press attendance, no complete film record of the event has surfaced yet, and the best document is a rebroadcast of highlights on WABC radio on *The Bob Lewis Show* a few days later. This tape is broken up into about eight segments, not presented in strict chronological order. One of the first questions concerns meditation, and when John casually reveals that he thinks "Maharishi was a mistake," the reporters pounce on this, pressing for clarification. "We're human" is about as far as John will elaborate, though he and Paul both stress that they still find meditation useful.

A curiously hostile exchange follows, when some-one asks just why they are there. John responds, "What's it look like?" and various journalists shout out "a circus" and "kinda silly." John throws the question back in their faces ("What are *you* doing here?"), but proceeds to explain the purpose of Apple. "We want to set up a system whereby people who just want to make a film about anything don't have to go on their knees in somebody's office. [pause] Probably yours." His comic timing is exquisite, and draws a round of applause and laughter and a "Sock it to 'em, Johnny!" from Paul.

Otherwise, the questioning is a bit dull, touching on *Magical Mystery Tour,* future projects, student protests, and even the buttons pinned to John's lapels! After the main questioning, Bob Lewis takes the opportunity to ask Paul a few questions. Asked how unsigned groups can get an audition with Apple, Paul says to send tapes to Apple at Baker Street, London, and they'll not only get a listen but receive a reply (with the heavy volume of submissions, both promises would go unfulfilled before long).

RELEASE HISTORY

1982: About a minute of black-and-white newsreel footage from this press conference was included in the home video *The Compleat Beatles.* An audio excerpt from this was released on the CD *Inside Interviews: In My Life: John Lennon & Paul McCartney* in 1995.

1996: Some of the same footage, plus a new 13-second color clip, appeared in the *Anthology* documentary. A good-quality off-air recording from a WABC radio broadcast circulates, which lasts nearly ten minutes (including speech from DJ Bob Lewis).

28. TV interview J, P

Date: 14 May 1968
Time: afternoon
Location: WNDT, New York City
Interviewer: Mitchell Krause
Broadcast: 15 May 1968, 10:00–11:00 p.m.
Channel 13, New York
Newsfront
Length: 27:58

John and Paul's first joint appearance on U.S. network television would be for *The Tonight Show,* but this local public TV appearance was taped earlier in the day. In retrospect, it may have been too serious a forum for the songwriting team: Although John was beginning to develop an articulate social conscience, aided by his blossoming relationship with Yoko Ono, Paul seemed reluctant to explore weighty topics in any depth.

Both men clam up over the first several questions from host Mitchell Krause. Open-ended queries about success, pop culture trends, and the widening of the generation gap elicit monosyllabic responses and disinterest. Paul tries to joke nervously about the stilted atmosphere: "Wrap up, ad-lib, close to script." But Krause persists, steering the conversation to a more personal level. This seems to work, as John and Paul open up about having reached success at such a young age. They reveal that it's saved them wasting their lives chasing the empty goals of wealth and fame.

Krause, noting their soberness, wonders if all the fun has gone out of their musical career, but Paul insists it's the line of questioning that is keeping the mood ponderous. John manages to lighten the atmosphere with a glib reply to an earnest question about "heavy" issues such as war, peace, and family. "War and vegetables. It's all just relative, y'know. So there's relativity . . . and absolute." This line of Lennon bullshit cracks Paul up, and he snickers, "That's great, Johnny." Paul mocks Krause and asks John, "But what do you think about the young people?" John's reply: "I think they're young."

Surprisingly, the topic of Apple is never broached, except tangentially when Paul suggests they use their power to help people, "like charity." John perks up when the topics of anarchy and supplanting the establishment are raised. Paul decries "phony institutions telling you what to do," and John implores people to subvert the system from within, but neither of them has any substantial solutions to the problem. It may have been this line of conversation that inspired John to write "Revolution" around this time.

Dissatisfaction with the maharishi and belief in the power of meditation are covered, with John honestly admitting their false worship of him as a person was probably similar to the awe many Beatles fans felt when meeting their idols. Krause asks if they are still forswearing drugs, and John is reluctant to give a definitive statement either way, although Paul is careful to assert that they don't take them at the moment. In truth, John had resumed taking LSD soon after returning from Rishikesh, and would shift from acid to heroin over the course of the summer. Paul's LSD flap of the previous summer is recounted, with John backing up his partner again.

This gets John on a press-bashing jag, which he takes to extremes, claiming the only truth printed in most newspapers is the name of the paper! He says TV is a bit better because of its immediacy, but still suffers from self-imposed censorship. Krause tries to defend his industry, then attempts to turn the tables, pointing out the racist immigration policies proposed by Enoch Powell and supported by a number of Britons: "Is this the kind of government you want?" This backfires when John and Paul agree that it's a disgraceful situation, only disagreeing with each other on whether the problem is worse in the United States.

They go on to defend their own industry, with Paul saying it doesn't matter to musicians what color hands someone uses to play the guitar; John points out that it shouldn't matter to carpenters and bricklayers, either. John is similarly dismayed by people with prejudice against long hair: "To make haircuts that important is insanity." Krause, sensing he's finally hit an antiauthority streak, tries to get them to condemn the British monarchy, but John and Paul express sympathy with the royals, since they can identify with trying to stay human in the face of adulation and isolation.

After condemning the Vietnam War, John and Paul are asked whom they'd vote for in the U.S. presidential election. They admit to total ignorance about the candidates, but John says he'd choose whoever was a dove, although it might be "an insane dove." As the conversation closes, John points out that "the Establishment" is an abstract concept, and he's just as much a part of it as anyone. In other words, rather than smashing the system, "you better free your mind instead."

RELEASE HISTORY

1988: A good-quality copy of this interview was included on the vinyl bootleg *The Little Red Album;* it also circulates among collectors from a very good tape source. The tape exists with two slightly different introductions, probably accounted for by the show's rerun a week after the initial broadcast.

29. TV interview   J, P

Date: 14 May 1968
Time: evening
Location: Studio 6B, Rockefeller Center, New York City
Host: Joe Garagiola
Broadcast: 15 May 1968, midnight–1:00 a.m. NBC-TV *The Tonight Show*
Length: 23:22

History has been unfairly harsh in appraising John and Paul's visit to *The Tonight Show*. John later called it "the most embarrassing thing I've ever been on,"

and even the generally nonpartisan author Mark Lewisohn describes it as "somewhat disappointing." The conventional wisdom has guest host Joe Garagiola asking inane, uninformed questions and actress Tallulah Bankhead desperately trying to steal the musicians' thunder.

Perhaps it played differently when viewed (the original videotape was erased and no longer exists), but a surviving audio recording paints a considerably different portrait. True, the first few minutes are a bit awkward; however, Garagiola's questions are no worse than those submitted at most Beatles press conferences, and he displays some knowledge of their music and spiritual pursuits. Tallulah Bankhead wavers between mild confusion and apparently genuine enthusiasm for her copanelists.

The tape begins with Ed McMahon's familiar introduction (for some reason, he announces this Tuesday night/Wednesday morning broadcast as "Thursday from New York") and cuts to John and Paul's entrance, with Paul joining Ed on the couch and John seated next to Joe and Tallulah at the desk. Asked how they made it through the crowd, John jokes that "Officer Krupske" (a corruption of a *West Side Story* character) got them through. The reference apparently eludes Garagiola, and there are a few moments of embarrassing silence until the ice is broken by Tallulah. She jokes that her friends have always told her to learn meditation so they can "get a word in edgewise." John suggests she find out for herself, saying "you can't learn to swim if you keep inland," and she retorts, "Oh honey, I can float sitting up, don't be silly." Bankhead 1, Beatles 0!

Paul recounts the similarly stilted *Newsfront* interview from earlier in the day and suggests Joe tell them a joke to lighten the mood. Tallulah interrupts again with a rambling comment about a phone call from London by "Andrews" (John's repeated attempts to confirm if this is Eamonn Andrews go ignored). Garagiola finally interjects some competent questions about whether the Beatles socialize outside of work, and what they would have been if not musicians. John and Paul reassure Joe (perhaps facetiously) that he's "doing great" and a commercial break comes to their rescue.

When they return from the station break, Tallulah is apparently trying to determine whether "whom" or "who" is correct. "Whom-osexual," mutters John, but apart from a lone titter in the audience, this goes unnoticed. Before Paul can finish answering the next question, the musical cue intrudes yet again for advertisements (it's not clear whether material is missing from the beginning of this segment).

Back in the studio, John is unaware that they are on the air until prompted by Garagiola. Discussion of John and Paul's stroll in Central Park follows, and Garagiola wonders if they got to see anything other than stadiums and hotels on their concert tours. Poor Tallulah, hearing the word "stadium," assumes Joe is berating them for not following baseball, and says she lived in England for eight years without watching a cricket match. Once that is cleared up, John and Tallulah find a common bond, commiserating over journalists' penchant for misquoting.

John and Paul then go into their Apple song and dance, somewhat unenthusiastically, considering the huge audience they were now speaking to. Perhaps the novelty of explaining their ideas for two straight days had worn thin (a much-reported quote from Paul about Apple being "Western communism" is often attributed to this broadcast, but does not appear on the existing tape). John reveals that their life is a lot calmer now that they have stopped performing live, and agrees with Paul that New York is hectic enough on its own, Beatlemania or no. Tallulah asks if they find appearing on TV as nerve-wracking as she does, and to the host's surprise, they admit to feeling anxious.

The next segment begins with discussion of the maharishi, who had already appeared on *The Tonight Show* while Garagiola was hosting, and even Tallulah shows some familiarity with the guru ("Does he giggle as much . . . ?"). John and Paul are both careful not to discourage anyone from taking up meditation, but express obvious disappointment with the holy man's earthliness. A mention of *Sgt. Pepper* draws applause from the audience, but John insists "it's only another LP really. It's not that important." This leads to a discussion of songwriting, with Paul telling the "Scrambled Egg/Yesterday" story to a skeptical Garagiola. From the perspective of forty thousand subsequent retellings, it's hard to believe anyone would question the tale.

Despite the audience's protestations, John and Paul depart at the beginning of the following segment, having made a fruitful impression at the very least on those who remained. (Tallulah: "I'm just as sorry [to see them go] as you all are, darlings!" Joe: "Delightful, huh?" Ed: "What a big deal I'm gonna be at home—I was on a couch with Paul McCartney!") Watching the broadcast that night from the New York apartment of Nat Weiss, John, Paul, and friends were reportedly mortified, but they had nothing to be ashamed of, given the circumstances. Time seems to have clouded their memory even further; in *Anthology,* Neil Aspinall confuses this appearance with the Larry Kane interview, and Joe Garagiola with Joe DiMaggio!

RELEASE HISTORY

A decent-quality off-line copy of this interview circulates among collectors. Although the original videotape seems to be long gone, about four minutes of silent 8 mm amateur footage exists, shot off a TV screen. This circulates among video collectors, often partially synced to the audio track.

30. Newsreel footage   J, P

Date: 16 May 1968
Location: London Airport
Broadcast: 16 May 1968
BBC TV
Length: 0:18

At 8:00 p.m. on the fifteenth, John and Paul flew back to London from New York, arriving early the next morning to the clicks of still photographers' shutters and the whirring and lights of a BBC News film crew.

This short clip follows the two chief Beatles through the arrivals lounge, dressed in sparkling white jackets (Paul sports a badge reading "If no one claims me in 30 days I'M YOURS") and carrying vivid red apples. Mal Evans, Derek Taylor, and "Magic" Alex Mardas are in tow.

RELEASE HISTORY

This color BBC News footage circulates on video.

31. Location recording   J

Date: ca. 19 May 1968
Location: Kenwood
Producer: John Lennon, Yoko Ono

[A.] Two Virgins—outtake (mono) (1:47)

[B.] Two Virgins—side one (mono) (14:13)
[C.] Two Virgins—side two (mono) (15:11)

Within days of his return from New York, John was at a crossroads. With Cynthia vacationing in Greece, he invited longtime pal Pete Shotton over to drop acid, but even a day-long messianic kick couldn't fill the void left by his crumbling marriage and spiritual disillusionment. What he needed was Yoko Ono, and after their first artistic collaboration this evening, nothing would be the same in John's life.

Things began tentatively in John's home studio, as an apparent warm-up tape (**A**) from that night reveals. Yoko attempts to instruct John in a simple vocal exercise: Each is to hold a single note as long as possible. John coyly asks whether she'll walk out of the room, leaving him to warble alone. That breaks the ice, and Yoko reassures him happily before beginning her note. John immediately interrupts: " 'Scuse me, do I wait for you to finish?" and shows off nervously with several goofy and elaborate count-ins. This causes Yoko to break into a giggling fit, and they are unable to coordinate a duet for more than a second or two. John adopts the voice of a flamboyant director: "Take that from the top, will you, love? Now, look—lean over, y'know, a bit more sweep as we come round the side wing." Of course, this causes further mirth and John delivers a final aside to the mic: "She's going through a stage. It's all right. We'll wait for her, ladies and gentlespoons." It's a charming bit of tape and has all the atmosphere of a first date or at least a first collaboration.

Their experimentation continued on tape through the night, becoming less inhibited as dawn approached. Two lengthy excerpts from these verité recordings were chosen for issue on John and Yoko's first Apple album. The actual content would be ignored in light of the album's cover photos, front and rear nude shots of the happy couple, but for what it's worth, here is a summary.

Side 1 (**B**) opens with John complaining about having to superimpose sounds to create audio collages. He initiates some tape loops of whistling and radio static, and tells Yoko to "turn the knobs," perhaps to increase the recording level. The two main instruments throughout are John's Mellotron and Yoko's voice, which begin to play off each other, John using piano notes and speed-manipulated rhythm tapes to counterpoint Yoko's shrieks and moans. John bangs on the cabinet and claps, and then starts an extremely slowed-down tape of an unknown singer crooning the standard "Together."

As a samba rhythm plays on the Mellotron, Yoko bleats and John goes into MC mode: "Good afternoon, good afternoon, welcome one and all. Come on, you son!" John moves to piano and accompanies Yoko's cries with random chords, first dramatic, then jaunty. The tape loops and Mellotron continue throughout in the background as then the pair launch into an improvised dialogue.

Y: What's that?
J: It's me, honey, putting the fire in!
Y: What's that?
J: Look who's come over for tea, honey!
Y: Eeeeeee!
J: Who's that?
Y: Joooooooooooooooohn!
J: Owwwwwww owww fuck.
Y: Who's thaaaaaaaaaaaaaaaaat?
J: Meeeeeeee. Bloody daft.
Y: Is that you? That you? Hey there!

J: Fuckin' tin opener, you see?

Y: Who's thaaaaaaaaaaaat?

J: It's just me, Hilda, I'm home for tea.

Y: Tea's ready. Help yourself.

J: Thank you kindly.

Y: Tea's never ready! Neeeeeeeeeehehehehehehever!

John then blows into what sounds like a harmonica or kazoo, chuckles, and stops the tape machine with a final "Thank you."

Side 2 of the album (**C**) begins in midsession with a distorted low-pitched hum and faint organ chords. More shrieking from Yoko is soon obliterated by a foghorn-sounding noise. "That's nothing!" Yoko counters. John launches another slowed-down tape of an oldie, "Hushabye Hushabye," and returns to his Mellotron. Various trumpet and organ sounds are played in intermittent bursts along with snatches of Latin rhythms, and as Yoko begins to chatter in Japanese, the cacophony builds. John sings a single line ("We'll see you in the . . . no tomatoes!"), and Yoko begins to yell "Nooooooo!"

John inserts a comment about Wiltshire in a brief moment of calm, but Yoko emits an extremely intense high-pitched scream, matched by John on the keyboard. He switches frantically among instruments and backings on the Mellotron and teases Yoko: "Here she is . . . spastic from Leeds, singing for you, having had no training whatsoever. That's right dear, spit it out!" The whole thing dies down with John back on piano, and after a final "Amen," John says he's had enough and turns off the tape deck.

As a dress rehearsal for "Revolution 9," these recordings were instructional, and as a liberating force for John's dormant creativity, they were invaluable. As a commercial album, they remain basically unlistenable and should never have been released.

RELEASE HISTORY

1968: **B** and **C** were released on an Apple LP, *Unfinished Music No. 1: Two Virgins,* distributed in the UK by Track Records and the United States by Tetragrammaton (EMI refused to handle it because of the sleeve). Only the first batch of British copies was mastered in true mono; all other copies feature a fake stereo mix created by panning the mono signal across the stereo image. The album was counterfeited, pirated, and bootlegged numerous times over the next twenty-five years on vinyl, eight-track, and CD.

1991: **A** was broadcast on episode 91-29 of the radio series *The Lost Lennon Tapes.* This is reportedly excerpted from a six-minute tape that circulates, but I haven't had a chance to hear the full recording.

1994: **A** was bootlegged on the LP *The Lost Lennon Tapes, Volume 30,* later issued on CD.

1997: Rykodisc reissued *Two Virgins* for the first time officially on CD. Although taken from a master tape, **C** has been truncated by 2 seconds at the start and 30 seconds at the end; **B** is intact. This issue is also presented in fake stereo.

32. TV interview   P, R

Date:	23 May 1968
Location:	EMI Studios
Producer:	Tony Palmer
Interviewer:	Tony Palmer
Broadcast:	3 November 1968, 10:40–11:35 p.m. BBC1 *Omnibus:* "All My Loving"
Length:	2:44

In the same vein as *The Mersey Sound* and "It's So Far Out, It's Straight Down" came this documentary look at the British rock scene circa spring 1968. Originally scheduled for broadcast on BBC1 in September, Tony Palmer's "All My Loving" was an incongruous mix of exciting stage performances, interviews, and distracting camera tricks intercut with violent news footage, presumably in order to make a statement and look important.

Although quite dated in parts, it's worth viewing for the performances from Cream, the Jimi Hendrix Experience, the Who, Donovan, Pink Floyd, and the Animals, along with illuminating comments from Frank Zappa. The Beatles are represented in a six-minute segment near the start of the program featuring extracts from the "Lady Madonna" promo shoot, a glimpse of John walking down the path in Rishikesh, a clip from the May 13 Larry Kane interview, and new interviews with Derek Taylor, Louise Harrison, and George Martin.

In addition, Paul and Ringo filmed short interviews this day in an Abbey Road control room. Paul, wearing a mustard coat and black shirt, gives Palmer the pretentious sound bite he's looking for: "Pop music is the classical music of now." He goes on to complain about people overanalyzing their music, but admits that in some ways, he is too subjective to give it a frank appraisal. Ringo sits behind a mixing board and explains the Beatles' recording process in his own inimitable fashion: ". . . something happens on here. Y'know, I couldn't tell you what, 'cause we have a special man who sits here and goes like this [twiddles knobs furiously]."

RELEASE HISTORY

This documentary circulates in excellent quality among video collectors. Palmer reused much of this footage in his 1977 TV series, *All You Need Is Love*.

33. Home demos

Date: late May 1968
Location: Kinfauns and Kenwood

[A.]	**Julia** (3:59)
[B.]	**Blackbird** (2:36)
[C.]	**Rocky Raccoon** (3:00)
[D.]	**Back in the USSR** (2:58)
[E.]	**Honey Pie** (2:00)
[F.]	**Mother Nature's Son** (2:35)
[G.]	**Ob-La-Di, Ob-La-Da** (3:07)
[H.]	**Junk** (2:40)
[I.]	**Dear Prudence** (4:46)
[J.]	**Sexy Sadie** (2:26)
[K.]	**Cry Baby Cry** (2:39)
[L.]	**Child of Nature** (2:36)
[M.]	**The Continuing Story of Bungalow Bill** (2:58)
[N.]	**I'm So Tired** (3:10)
[O.]	**Yer Blues** (3:35)
[P.]	**Everybody's Got Something to Hide Except Me and My Monkey** (3:07)
[Q.]	**What's the New Mary Jane** (2:40)
[R.]	**Revolution** (4:14)
[S.]	**While My Guitar Gently Weeps** (2:37)
[T.]	**Circles** (2:14)
[U.]	**Sour Milk Sea** (3:53)
[V.]	**Not Guilty** (3:06)
[W.]	**Piggies** (2:05)
[X.]	**Happiness Is a Warm Gun** (2:11)
[Y.]	**Mean Mr. Mustard** (1:56)
[Z.]	**Polythene Pam** (1:24)
[AA.]	**Glass Onion** (1:48)

The respite in Rishikesh opened up the floodgates, inspiring John, Paul, and George to compose a wealth of new material. Some of the songs had been started prior to the trip ("Cry Baby Cry") and some after the return home ("While My Guitar Gently Weeps"), but nearly thirty-five titles were available before the album was even begun, with more to follow as the sessions progressed.

Home demos were taped of most of these, the bulk of which (A–W) come from a tape in John's home archive. The majority were recorded at George's home in Esher (and are usually referred to as "Kinfauns demos" after the name of his bungalow) on a four-track Ampex machine. However, it's likely John and Paul also brought privately taped solo demos to contribute to the overall compilation. All songs feature acoustic guitar (sometimes two or three) and vocals, while some have rudimentary percussion, handclapping, and even organ accompaniment.

Certainly **X–AA,** which feature only John, were recorded at Kenwood. At other points between songs, George can be heard instructing Mal to start the playback, and there is plenty of background chatter during the songs. These clues, along with the strict Paul-John-George order, suggest that John's tape is compiled from various reels. In addition, some of John's demos ("Dear Prudence," "Sexy Sadie," "Mean Mr. Mustard," "Polythene Pam," "Glass Onion") play back in a key a half step lower than the released versions, suggesting different sources, if not sittings.

George spoke many times over the years of his preference for this demo version of "Revolution," yet when it came time to compile *Anthology 3,* he reportedly turned over all the multitrack demos he still possessed, all of which were used on the CD (one edited and one mixed into mono), with "Revolution" nowhere in sight!

Taking these song by song and comparing them with the finished versions (all feature two acoustic guitars and two vocal tracks by the composer unless otherwise noted):

"Julia" (**A**) opens with John asking for the microphone level to be turned down, and is carried by two guitars and two overlapping vocals from John, with Paul adding high harmonies in spots. The arrangement is extended, with all four verses sung before the bridge, followed by repeats of the first two verses, an instrumental verse, the intro reprise, and a whistling verse.

"Blackbird" (**B**) has extra instrumental verses inserted and a few lyrical alterations. There's what sounds like an edit near the end that may be the original demo playback being halted. "Rocky Raccoon" (**C**) has no spoken introduction and is missing the third verse; it also features maracas. When it ends, Mal suggests the song be called "Rocky Checked Out," but George feels "Rocky Raccoon" is more sensible (it actually began life as

"Rocky Sassoon"). "Back in the USSR" (D) has the usual two guitars and vocals, plus handclaps and tambourine. The third verse hasn't been written yet, so Paul repeats the first two verses in lieu of a solo and final verse.

"Honey Pie" (E) was released on *Anthology 3* in a stereo mix that chops out the middle (from 0:54–1:30) of the song. The left channel has acoustic guitar, maraca, tambourine, percussive thumps, Paul's first vocal, and John's brass band vocalization. The right channel has a second acoustic guitar, slapping percussion, and further scat singing from Paul. The spoken intro and first verse have yet to be written, while the first bridge has filler lyrics.

"Mother Nature's Son" (F) is basically identical to the finished arrangement, but fades out rather than coming to a musical conclusion. "Ob-La-Di, Ob-La-Da" (G) has tambourine in addition to Paul's two guitar/vocal tracks, which get way out of sync at times (although this may have been an intentional trick to produce echo). The arrangement is complete, although the Jamaican influence isn't evident in the rhythm yet. "Junk" (H) may have been called "Jubilee" at this point. This demo consists of two guitar and vocal tracks, and was released in a narrow stereo mix on *Anthology 3,* with some of the second vocal mixed out in places. Paul would add a few lyrics prior to recording the song in 1970 for the *McCartney* album.

"Dear Prudence" (I) has a repeat of the bridge inserted after the third verse, and a vocal goof by John on the last verse ("let me see you sm—oops!"). More important, it has a tongue-in-cheek narration over the coda explaining Prudence Farrow's situation that inspired the song: "No one was to know that sooner or later, she was to go completely berserk under the care of Maharishi Mahesh Yogi. All the people around her were very worried about the girl because she was going insane. So we sang to her."

"Sexy Sadie" (J) has maraca and tambourine and ends with an organ blast, as does "Cry Baby Cry" (K). The latter has been completed since John's earlier piano demos; it ends with several repeats of the chorus in waltz tempo. "Child of Nature" (L) has lots of chatter in the background, plus tambourine, maraca, and various thumps for percussion. John would abandon the Rishikesh-inspired lyrics but retain the melody for his 1971 song "Jealous Guy." As the demo ends, George comments, "That's one of the last ones," and John responds, "No, I'm just getting ready to—." George interrupts him: "But they're all the same."

John's demos that follow feature plenty of vocal contributions from his bandmates, beginning with the massed choruses on "The Continuing Story of Bungalow Bill" (M). This also contains thumps, handclaps, maracas, and various animal imitations. "I'm So Tired" (N) has tambourine and high vocal harmonies from Paul, as well as a comment to Derek Taylor ("I'll give you everything I've got, Derek"), who had recently moved back to London from California to work as Apple Corps' press officer. John also interjects an Elvis-style spoken verse ("When I hold you in your arms . . . I wonder should I get up and go to the funny farm"), which he would reshape for "Happiness Is a Warm Gun."

"Yer Blues" (O) includes tambourine and percussive thumps and has a few lyrical alterations ("feel so insecure now" instead of "feel so suicidal") compared with the final version. "Everybody's Got Something to Hide Except Me and My Monkey" (P) has shaker percussion and a basically finalized arrangement, culminating with a repeated "make it, make it." "What's the New Mary Jane" (Q) has tambourine and everyone joining in on the demented choruses. John's rambling at the end ("But I can't speak no loudness! What are you saying? Speak up, I'm not hearing you! Oh my God!") contains the only known rendition of the title phrase, which is absent from the studio recording.

"Revolution" (R) is probably the highlight of the entire batch of "White Album" demos, including the best elements of both released versions ("shooby doo wop's" from the album coupled with the faster tempo of the single) and adding a fantastic Beach Boys–style wordless verse. The only flaw is that the two tracks get badly out of sync on the final verse.

George's songs appear last on the Kinfauns tape, beginning with "While My Guitar Gently Weeps" (S), which fades up already in progress (more evidence of copying). George accompanies his guitar and vocal tracks with organ on the bridges, and the lyrics are in an embryonic state ("the problems you sow are the troubles you're reaping" in verse 1 would be rewritten by July).

"Circles" (T) has two organ tracks in place of guitar, and is a depressing number that makes "Blue Jay Way" sound like a Little Richard freakout. George would revisit the song in 1982 when he was desperate for material to fill his *Gone Troppo* LP. By contrast, "Sour Milk Sea" (U) is an excellent, lively composition written in Rishikesh that he would donate the following month to singer Jackie Lomax. This demo has contributions from the whole band, including tambourine, maracas, and percussive thumps.

When it ends, George discusses "a jazz number" that he could hear as "a good rocker"; this is evidently "Not Guilty" (V), which follows on the tape. Although the Beatles spent many hours recording the song in August, it went unreleased until George's remake for his 1979 LP *George Harrison.* "Piggies" (W) appears in a mono mix on *Anthology 3,* and has John chiming in on the lyric "damn good whacking" (a line contributed by George's mum, believe it or not!).

The Kenwood demos don't seem to contain any contributions from Paul, George, or Ringo. "Happiness Is a

Warm Gun" (**X**) consists of the "I need a fix" and "Mother Superior" sections of the song. John apparently never added a second track to his initial vocal/guitar performance, which appears in mono on *Anthology 3*. The remaining three songs have one track in each stereo channel, allowing a closer listen at John's entertaining asides.

In "Mean Mr. Mustard" (**Y**), one John comments "dirty dirty man—we could almost have him put away for the bad things he's doing!," while the other mumbles something about "grippy eye grippy eye guy." "Polythene Pam" (**Z**) has alternate lyrics ("you may think it's absurd but she's a nice class of bird"), and John's complaint after trying to match his second vocal to his first: "It's too hard, that." "Glass Onion" (**AA**) has tambourine on one track and plenty of nonsense mutterings to fill in for unwritten lyrics ("me and my buddies," "by permission of the United Council and all the friends . . . ," and "Gene Vincent Fan Club"!).

Although they don't all play on every song, these "White Album" demos are one of the last opportunities to hear the Beatles working together as a musical unit rather than as four dissociating forces. They also offer a chance to hear some of the heavier rock numbers in a lighter and more relaxed setting.

RELEASE HISTORY

1988: **A, I–M,** and **P–R** were broadcast on the radio series *The Lost Lennon Tapes.* The same year, the bootleg LP *Off White* included **A** and **I–R,** all from tape source but interspersed with various sound effects. The same songs all appeared on various volumes of Bag's *Lost Lennon Tapes* vinyl bootleg series.

1990: **D, F, W,** and an incomplete version of **V** were broadcast on *The Lost Lennon Tapes* and were bootlegged on a double-EP set, *The Beatles.* They also appeared on the 1991 CD *The 1968 Demos.*

1991: The bootleg CD *Unsurpassed Demos* included **B–W,** all from decent quality but noncontinuous tape sources.

1996: The CD *Anthology 3* included an edited stereo version of **E,** a stereo remix of **H,** a mono dub of **W,** and the first releases of **X–AA,** all from excellent tape sources.

1999: The complete running tape of **A–W** was included on the bootleg CD *From Kinfauns to Chaos* in very good quality. A better source tape reportedly circulates among collectors.

34. Speech/Studio session

Date: 4 June 1968
Time: 2:30 p.m.–1:00 a.m.
Location: EMI Studio 3

[A.] **Revolution 1—take 20 playback** (10:04)
[B.] **Revolution 1—take 20 playback** (4:41)
[C.] **jamming** (0:44)
[D.] **jamming** (4:46)
[E.] **tuning/dialogue** (1:29)
[F.] **jamming/Revolution 1—rehearsal** (8:05)
[G.] **jamming** (0:10)
[H.] **Revolution 1—take 20 overdub** (1:11)
[I.] **Revolution 1—take 20 playback** (3:35)
[J.] **Revolution 1—take 20 playback** (1:29)
[K.] **jamming** (2:18)
[L.] **jamming** (0:48)
[M.] **jamming** (0:11)
[N.] **jamming** (0:05)
[O.] **jamming** (2:24)
[P.] **Revolution 1—take 20 playback** (0:44)
[Q.] **Revolution 1—take 20 playback** (1:05)
[R.] **Revolution 1—take 20 playback/overdub** (7:32)
[S.] **Revolution 1—take 20 playback** (1:11)
[T.] **Revolution 1—take 20 playback** (1:42)
[U.] **Revolution 1—take 20 playback** (1:13)
[V.] **jamming** (0:57)
[W.] **jamming** (0:11)
[X.] **jamming** (0:13)
[Y.] **Revolution 1—take 20 playback** (0:34)
[Z.] **dialogue** (0:56)
[AA.] **dialogue** (0:41)
[BB.] **dialogue** (0:25)
[CC.] **Revolution 1—take 20 playback** (0:18)
[DD.] **Revolution 1—take 20 playback** (0:26)
[EE.] **dialogue** (0:16)
[FF.] **dialogue/tape loop** (2:41)
[GG.] **tape loop** (0:15)
[HH.] **dialogue** (1:16)
[II.] **Revolution 1—RM1** (2:31)

[JJ.] **Revolution 1—RM1** (4:50)

When they assembled back in Studio 2 on May 30, the Beatles chose to begin sessions with one of the strongest songs from the Kinfauns demos, John's "Revolution." On that first evening, they perfected the backing in eighteen takes, with piano, drums, and acoustic guitar all going on a single track of the tape. While most takes matched the format of the demo, the final performance lasted twice as long, running a full 10:17 with an extended jam on the "all right" coda.

The following day, Paul added bass and John double-tracked his lead vocal. A reduction mix made room for "shooby doo-wop" backing vocals from Paul, George, and Paul's new girlfriend, Francie Schwartz. It was John's new love who had a greater impact on the song, however. John and Yoko began to build up a collage of effects and noises over the extended ending of "Revolution," including many items familiar from the *Two Virgins* session: static, piano tinkling, whistling, and even someone crooning an unidentified standard along the lines of "Together" and "Hushabye Hushabye." When John began to consider releasing "Revolution" as a single, this extra musical material would be chopped off to form the basis of "Revolution 9," but for the moment it was considered part of the song.

On June 4, work continued with John redoing some of his lead vocal, particularly a line he wrestled with before deciding to be equivocal. (A change in vocal timbre makes the drop-in obvious: "Don't you know that [EDIT] you can count me out . . . in.") As legend has it, and a snapshot by Tony Bramwell seems to prove, John sang his vocal lying flat on his back with a microphone suspended above his mouth, giving it a breathy quality. Another vocal overdub, for the end of the song, featured Paul and George singing "mama . . . dada" over and over. Two tape loops were also created to be added to the increasingly chaotic recording during mixing: One had a high-pitched vocal "aaaah" and the other featured a frenzied guitar lick.

As engineers Peter Brown and Phil McDonald prepared the song for a second reduction mix into take 20, Yoko Ono switched on a portable tape recorder and began to record an audio diary; luckily for us, this has escaped and documents the rest of the session, albeit as background to Yoko's discourse. The first segment (**A**) opens with the end of a playback of take 20, with many elements familiar to listeners of "Revolution 9" prominent. Meanwhile, Yoko recounts the events of the day, and reveals that plans are already underway to release the first *Unfinished Music* album with the artists pictured nude, taken "with a fish-eye lens" (the photo wouldn't be taken until around August). She feels that if they aren't allowed to release the album under their own names, it should be a private pressing given to fifty close friends (if only . . .). As Yoko confesses feeling insecure in her new relationship, another playback begins, and John comes over to ask if she has made a phone call to Italy.

In the next segment (**B**), the playback continues, Mal offers Yoko a pear, and she discusses that day's assassination attempt on Andy Warhol in New York. Realizing that Cynthia is supposed to return to Weybridge soon, Yoko expresses apprehension about where she and

John will be staying. Over the next few segments (**C–E**), the Beatles tune up their instruments for further overdubs, lapsing into the occasional jam. Paul asks if John wants to overdub anything besides organ and drums, and neither of them can think of anything else to add.

Paul takes over on the organ, Ringo drums, and John plays along on guitar (**F–G**) as they rehearse their overdub parts. Yoko psychoanalyzes herself and John, and John requests a microphone for his amp, indicating that he will join in with the overdub. A first attempt at this is captured in **H** and played back in **I** and **J** as Yoko analyzes John's handwriting. John then gets behind the drum kit and jams with the guitar, organ, and Yoko contributing vocals (**K–O**). John apparently injures himself with the drumstick and complains about this in a sing-song conversation with Yoko. ("Smasharoonie the stick . . . I have been stabbed in the brass vertebrae." "Who did that?" "I did it myself!" "You mustn't do anything without me!")

George Martin adjusts the levels and the previous overdub is played back (**P–R**); John tells Paul to come in earlier on organ, and they begin a more successful overdub pass. While this is going on, Yoko praises Paul for communicating with her as an equal, and even feels he's like "a younger brother." The playback stops, and Paul plays a brief "Lady Madonna" riff on organ before they launch into the final overdub take; this time Paul enters at the end of the first verse.

The song is played back for inspection (**S–U**) as Yoko reports Ringo's and George's bemused reactions to the sight of her presence in the studio. At this point, it sounds like side 1 of Yoko's cassette runs out, suggesting a 120-minute tape. Random doodling, jamming, and playback carries on through the next brief segments (**V–Z**), and Yoko wavers between examining John and feeling guilty about it; in fact, when John goes up to the control booth, she wonders whether she should even be present in the studio.

Paul sings a bit of "Stairway to Paradise" (**AA**) and John tells George Martin they have ten minutes of song to make interesting (**BB**). Various playbacks and preparation of tape loops follow (**CC–GG**); Yoko claims to be "the most insecure person in the world right now"—she is clearly afraid John will abandon her and return to his family at any moment. The tape is wound back one last time as John instructs the engineers to add a flanging effect on tracks 2 and 3 (**HH**). George Martin sings a bit of "Let's Twist Again," and the song is roughly mixed into mono, including a drop-in of the "aaaah" loop after the first chorus. This last segment (**II**) ends just prior to the second chorus.

This lengthy cassette is certainly instructional with respect to the process of recording "Revolution 1," but it also paints a much clearer and more sympathetic picture of Yoko's attitude in the early days of her relationship with John. Not only does she stay out of the way and express doubts about her right to attend the session, she emphasizes how vulnerable her position in John's life was, if only in her mind.

An acetate of RM1 of "Revolution 1" (**JJ**) has recently surfaced. It begins with engineer Peter Bown announcing " 'Revolution,' RM1 of take . . ." As Bown searches his brain for the correct take number, John leaps in with "Take your knickers off, and let's go!" This has both the "aaaah" and electric guitar loops mixed in at various points, particularly over the final minute of the song, as well as John mumbling, "It's gonna be all right," and Paul and George's "mama . . . dada" vocal overdub.

RELEASE HISTORY

1994: 23:36 of "highlights" from this tape were included on the bootleg CD *Revolution.*

1999: An upgrade on the CD *From Kinfauns to Chaos* included most of the tape (**A–G** and **I–II**), but omitted segment **H** for some reason, which had been included on *Revolution.* The 2000 CD-R *The A.M. Tape* combines both sources to create a composite.

2007: **JJ** was bootlegged on the double LP *Sessions,* running noticeably slow.

35. TV interview   J

Date:	6 June 1968
Time:	5:00 p.m.
Location:	EMI Studio 3 (?)
Interviewer:	Peter Lewis
Broadcast:	22 June 1968, 10:05–10:45 p.m.
	BBC2
	Release
Length:	11:57

John's two books had been adapted for the stage late in 1967 by Adrienne Kennedy and longtime Beatles comrade Victor Spinetti. John's participation was limited to approving the scripts, attending a few rehearsals, and preparing tapes of music and sound effects for the production. While he undoubtedly used some tapes from his home studio, Abbey Road was also used, first in November 1967 and again in June 1968. On June 6, while the others worked on Ringo's "Don't Pass Me By" in Studio 2, John and Victor sat down in front of a sound baffle, probably in Studio 3, to be filmed for a BBC TV feature about the project. (The control room of Studio 2 is a short walk from Studio 3, and the distant sound of "Don't Pass Me By" playbacks can be heard occasionally during the interview.)

In addition to twelve minutes of interview footage, the feature included close-ups of various poems and drawings from John's books, and a glimpse of the play's premiere (see the June 18 entry). According to Mark Lewisohn's *Complete Beatles Chronicle,* the original broadcast also included specially staged scenes from the play, filmed June 21 in a BBC studio; these do not appear in the circulating video copy, however.

The segment begins with a brief clip of John, dressed in white and chewing gum, and Spinetti, smoking a cigarette, unaware that the camera is rolling. After Peter Lewis's introductory narration, we return to EMI for the remainder of the story. John praises the production for bringing out truths that were already inherent in the source material, and Spinetti says it was easy for him to identify with the protagonist, a young boy who escapes the humdrum world through daydreaming and wordplay, not unlike the young John Lennon. John runs through a list of things that influenced his childhood, but omits music, which "didn't hit me until I was sixteen."

Lewis notes the script's unique use of the English language, and John admits that getting across an idea or story has always been more important than using precise spelling. Although he eventually bought *Finnegan's Wake,* John denies yet again being influenced by James Joyce, instead citing Lewis Carroll's "Jabberwocky" and the drawings of Ronald Searle as major inspirations. He also describes how the "Shamrock Wombs" parody evolved from reading a Sherlock Holmes anthology during his May 1964 vacation in Tahiti.

Asked if he still writes, John explains that most of his creative energy goes into songwriting and making home tapes for his own enjoyment. He says that Bob Dylan helped him realize that writing song lyrics shouldn't be a segregated concept from writing poetry or prose, although when the tune comes to him first, he sometimes has to use "sound" words as filler, to fit the rhythm. Lewis points out an antiauthority streak running through John's books, and John agrees, although he claims to have softened his animosity of late.

Seconds later, he is declaring that society is being run by "insane people" and "maniacs" and that he's known this all his life, but nobody else will own up to it (although Lewis and Spinetti agree). They tie this into the play's main character, who hasn't been able to escape from life's insanity the way John did by becoming a Beatle (which came with its own special brand of insanity). Victor then helps John explain the play's concept of "brummer striving," whiling away one's life in an unfulfilling dead-end job, and does a humorous impression of trying to explain the idea to Sir Laurence Olivier.

RELEASE HISTORY

1996: Extracts totaling 10:35 from this interview were released in the *Fab Four CD & Book Set,* omitting the introduction and most of Victor Spinetti's replies. The entire segment also circulates on video in average quality.

36. Radio interview

Date:	6 June 1968
Time:	8:00 p.m.
Location:	EMI Studio 3 (?)
Producer:	Tony Olivestone
Interviewer:	Kenny Everett
Broadcast:	9 June 1968, 10:00 a.m.–noon
	BBC Radio 1
	The Kenny Everett Show
Length:	13:40

Of all the Beatles/Kenny Everett interviews, this one was easily the most whimsical and nonsensical—no small feat given the participants involved! Everett's weekly BBC radio show was about to go off the air, and although he would be soon given a daily slot, he wanted to go out with a bang. Luckily, the Beatles were back together in the studio, so Kenny borrowed his friend Tony Olivestone's tape recorder, and his friend Tony Olivestone, who knew how to work it, and visited Abbey Road to see what would happen.

As the tape begins, Tony is attempting to set the levels on the recorder as John blasts his fretless guitar. None of the other Beatles are around, presumably off working on "Don't Pass Me By" in Studio 2. This leads to the question of which studio John and Kenny are in—Olivestone remembers it as Studio 1, but the presence of a sleigh-bell (see following entry) suggests Studio 3. The latter also makes sense as John would use it over the next three sessions to assemble sound effects for the play *In His Own Write* and the audio-collage "Revolution 9." Although Victor Spinetti seems to have gone home, Yoko Ono's presence is evident through an occasional giggle.

John begins the informal chat by explaining that two incomplete songs have been recorded thus far, with one ("Revolution 1") ready for session musicians to add their parts, and the other being Ringo's first composition, written "in a fit of lethargy" (true enough, as "Don't Pass Me By" took nearly five years to write!). Kenny requests a farewell jingle for his final show, and John complies with an ad-libbed ditty, sung in both his normal voice and an American twang. Asked to pick a record request, John selects Harry Nilsson's cover of "River Deep, Mountain High" (which John amends to "Mountain Dew"). This leads into John's celebrated perversion of the Leadbelly classic, "Cottonfields," in which the cradle-rocking becomes cradle-smashing.

Some mock-Italian babbling puts Kenny in the mind of Rishikesh, and he compliments John on the "sheet" he was photographed in (a burnoose purchased in Morocco during his December 1967 visit). An exasperated Everett implores John to say something comprehensible, and laments that the first five minutes of conversation have yielded about thirty seconds of usable material. "There's an LP out of this, Ken," John insists, no doubt thinking of his own *Two Virgins* project. He goes on to complain that the fun bits always end up on the cutting-room floor, and Kenny promises to air the entire tape. He asks how Apple is coming along, and John smirks, "I couldn't ask for any more tapes or bits of paper."

Everett wonders whether the success of *Sgt. Pepper* has set the bar too high to be topped, but John dismisses this with a throwaway double-entendre: "It only got high 'cause everybody said how high it was. It's no higher than it was when we made it." Paul is then summoned over to accompany John in an improvised good-bye jingle. The literal-minded duo comply, with John crooning "Good-bye to Kenny Everett, he is our very pal" and Paul inserting "Jingle, jingle" refrains, leading to a rousing crescendo. Paul's high-pitched giggle at the conclusion leads to a discussion on the merits of singer Tiny Tim, with Kenny's skepticism countered by John and Paul's effusive praise.

George and Ringo arrive at this point and give their own good-bye greetings, with Ringo providing yet another jingle. Paul follows this with a lounge-singer rendition of "Strawberry Fields Forever," and then picks up the sleigh-bell and launches into "Christmas Time (Is Here Again)." John excitedly asks to hear the tape immediately, but Everett is unsure whether EMI has the right equipment to play it back. A break in the tape suggests this was accomplished, and the recording concludes with an interesting 50-second fragment unused in the broadcast. Presumably as a thank-you, Tony Olivestone took the mic and described the scene around him as Paul strummed a guitar, John beat on a drum, someone (perhaps George) pounded on the piano, and

Ringo walked around "thinking up new ideas." A suitably anarchic ending to an absurd recording.

RELEASE HISTORY

1968: A six-and-a-half-minute edit of this raw tape was released on an Italian Apple promo EP, *Una Sensazionale Intervista Dei Beatles*. Bits of this release, notably John's rendition of "Cottonfields," made fodder for numerous bootlegs over the next decade.

1985: The LP *The Golden Beatles* contained the complete interview, taken from an acetate; this title was later issued on CD. CD-Rs such as *Attack of the Filler Beebs, Episode 3* and *Acetate Collection* also included the full interview.

1988: A fair-quality off-air tape of the original broadcast was included on the vinyl bootleg *Tragical History Tour*. This included Everett's edits, sound effects, and narration, and is the only tape source for the interview, albeit in altered form. Four minutes and thirty-six seconds of this 9:44 tape was rebroadcast later that year in the radio series *The Beeb's Lost Beatles Tapes;* this cleaner source can be found on the CD *The Beatles Broadcast Collection, Trailer 2*.

37. Studio session

Date:	6 June 1968
Time:	2:45 p.m.–2:45 a.m.
Location:	EMI Studio 2
Producer:	George Martin

[A.] **Don't Pass Me By—take 3 (mono)** (0:15)
[B.] **Don't Pass Me By—RS from takes 3 and 5** (2:39)

After five years of being passed by, Ringo was finally given the chance to record his country-and-western composition for a Beatles album. As the first session began in Studio 3 on June 5, the song was documented as "Ringo's Tune (Untitled)" and then given the unusual working title of "This Is Some Friendly." Ringo laid down a basic drum track in three takes, accompanied by Paul on piano.

As the third take comes crashing to a halt, Paul exclaims, "I think that's got it!" Ringo concurs, calling out to the control booth, "I think we've got something there, George!" This fragment (**A**) can be heard in the "White Album" outtake medley on the *Anthology* home video. More percussion was added on top of this take, including further drums, a sleigh-bell, and a cowbell. Paul also overlaid his original keyboard part by playing piano through a rotating Leslie speaker. This filled the tape's four tracks, and a reduction mix into takes 4 and 5 freed up two of them.

Take 5 was overdubbed with Ringo's initial lead vocal attempt, recorded with the machine running slow to raise the pitch of his voice. Paul then recorded two separate bass tracks, presumably to have a choice of performances; one of these erased Ringo's rough vocal. Another reduction into take 6 was created at the end of the session, but the next day they returned to take 5 itself.

Turning the tables, Ringo replaced both of Paul's bass parts with two lead vocal tracks. The remix on *Anthology 3* (**B**) syncs these vocal overdubs with all four tracks of take 3 (pianos left, main drums centered, percussion right). This mix reveals some vocal parts mixed out of the final song, including an extra "don't make me blue" in the first chorus and a bunch of spoken ad-libs: "I'm waitin' for ya honey. Hurry up to me, I don't want you to pass me by, I don't want you to make me cry, I want you to make me happy!"

At some point this day (not noted on session sheets), the instrumental track was edited to remove an erroneous extra bar of C major in the second chorus. As heard in **B**, the backing soon afterward gets out of sync with the vocal and doesn't go into the familiar "counting" break, instead fading early. A second reduction into take 7 freed two more tracks, one of which Paul filled with a new bass overdub. To conclude the session, a rough mono mix was done and copies were made for the Beatles to take home and ponder further additions.

RELEASE HISTORY

1996: **A** was included in the *Anthology* home video set and was later bootlegged on the CD *Abbey Road Video Show*. **B** was officially released on *Anthology 3*.

38. Studio session

Date: 11 June 1968
Time: 3:30 p.m.–12:15 a.m.
Location: EMI Studio 2
Producer: George Martin

[A.] **Blackbird/Congratulations—rehearsal** (1:53)

[B.] **Blackbird—rehearsal** (4:28)

[C.] **Helter Skelter/Blackbird—rehearsal** (4:12)

[D.] **Blackbird—rehearsal** (2:06)

[E.] **tuning** (0:07)

[F.] **Blackbird—rehearsal** (0:27)

[G.] **Blackbird—rehearsal** (2:19)

[H.] **Blackbird—rehearsal** (1:06)

[I.] **Mother Nature's Son/Blackbird— rehearsal** (4:56)

[J.] **Blackbird—rehearsal** (1:11)

[K.] **Blackbird—rehearsal** (1:45)

[L.] **Blackbird—rehearsal** (1:24)

[M.] **Blackbird—rehearsal** (2:14)

[N.] **Blackbird—rehearsal** (1:37)

[O.] **Blackbird—rehearsal** (0:41)

[P.] **Blackbird—rehearsal** (0:03)

[Q.] **Blackbird—rehearsal** (2:00)

[R.] **Blackbird—rehearsal** (2:49)

[S.] **dialogue** (0:21)

[T.] **dialogue** (1:12)

[U.] **Blackbird—rehearsal** (4:02)

[V.] **Blackbird—take 4 (stereo)** (2:14)

[W.] **Blackbird—RM6** (2:23)
Mixed: 11 June 1968

[X.] **Blackbird—RS1** (2:18)

[Y.] **Blackbird—RM10** (2:17)
Mixed: 13 October 1968

[Z.] **Blackbird/Yesterday** (2:32)

With George and Ringo out of the country from June 7–18, group sessions were officially on hold. Since the Beatles had prebooked Abbey Road's Studio 2 for every weekday through July 26, John and Paul took advantage of the situation. The pair would soon be temporarily living under the same roof, at Paul's Cavendish Avenue house. With Cynthia and Julian returning from an Italian trip to occupy Kenwood, John and Yoko were invited to stay with Paul and his new girlfriend, Francie Schwartz; all four future housemates were present at the studio on the evening of June 11.

John's main task was to continue assembling sound effects for the play *In His Own Write* and the audio collage "Revolution 9." While John discussed these matters with George Martin, Paul sat with his Martin D-28 acoustic guitar and played "Blackbird" for the benefit of an Apple film crew (see the following entry for full details). An excellent-quality forty-one-minute reel (A–U) from the soundman's feed follows the process of recording "Blackbird," from informal run-throughs to serious performances. Note that each of the subentries are segmented according to breaks in the tape and don't necessarily correspond to track divisions on the bootleg CD.

As the tape begins (A), Paul is completing a performance for the benefit of George Martin's stopwatch. Martin informs Paul that the song lasts just under two minutes and suggests he make more of the break before the final verse. Paul then goes into a half-time rendition of "Blackbird," segueing directly into the Cliff Richard hit "Congratulations." By this time, George Martin has climbed the stairs to the control room, and he interrupts to tell Paul to start over.

Segment **B** opens with the end of the song and an immediate repeat of the opening verse. After a false start, Paul plays the whole thing, but obviously has no ending worked out. Paul comments that he's forgotten the format as George Martin returns to the studio floor to suggest taping further rehearsals, "just as a demo." John suggests dimming the lights to improve the atmosphere, and Paul complains of feeling like he's in a factory. Martin thinks a rough demo would help them decide on an arrangement, but John suggests that voice and guitar are enough. Apparently the previous performance was taped (a total of thirty-two unannounced takes would be recorded that evening), since Geoff Emerick starts to play it back as the tape cuts.

George Martin and John are then heard (C) discussing various recordings for *In His Own Write*. John apparently wants to send the audience home in terror with a chilling "Look after yourselves!" Martin enthuses about a tape he and assistant Chris Thomas had prepared, playing piano and organ, respectively. At this point there is a bit of material missing on the raw tape compared with the finished film, as John talks about the upcoming Capitol sales conference. Meanwhile, Paul is running through "Helter Skelter" in falsetto; he soon switches to an ad-libbed song with the lyric "gone tomorrow, here today." John wants to know at what point the full ten-minute "Revolution 1" becomes boring, feeling that his voice at the end is worth keeping. This problem would be solved by preserving the interesting bits as part of "Revolution 9"; Paul seems to make fun of that track's signature "number nine" by intoning: "This is a stereo ambiophonics take fifty-nine." This is more likely a comment on the microphone setup for "Blackbird": separate tracks for his voice, guitar, and tapping-foot percussion.

Paul is still goofing around (**D**), making up a blues song and running through various parts of "Blackbird," as John and Yoko discuss hearses. Yoko admits that sometimes riding in John's limo feels like riding in a coffin car, and John is baffled: "What are we talking about?" John tunes his own guitar and confirms the key of "Blackbird" (G major) with Paul. John plays along for the next few segments (**E–H**) as Paul continues rehearsing, lapsing into an Elvis voice and a talking blues at various points.

John makes his way to the control room and the song's arrangement is discussed (**I**). Paul imagines a string quartet after the second verse and John suggests a bit of brass band. Running through "Mother Nature's Son" briefly, Paul realizes brass would be a perfect addition for that song. Several attempts to record "Blackbird" follow (**J–M**), mostly ending up as false starts ("take these broken wings and learn to biscuits"). At one point, Paul mutters "take twenty," but proper takes probably haven't begun yet.

One performance (**N**) ends with a repeat of the song's final line. George Martin exclaims that Chris Thomas finds the new ending "all right," and this reminds Francie and Paul of the refrain in "Revolution." John continues to offer Paul encouragement from the booth (**O–Q**), and the two enact a humorous dialogue as sleazy producer and spaced-out rock star. ("We're gettin' it up here for you." "Groovy. Groovy." "Okay, well, if you'd like to go now one more time, Charles." "That's where your head's at, is it?") After butchering one line as "take these suckin' eyes" (**R**), Paul realizes it's time to take a break.

When the tape resumes (**S**), John and Paul are chatting with the film crew about possibly dimming the lights. As a harmonium plays in the background (**T**), George Martin discusses microphones with an unknown person. In the final segment, Paul is back at work taping "Blackbird" (**U**). After a breakdown and full take, he asks for a critique from the control room. John says it wasn't as good as a previous take, and offers to play it back, but Paul feels he'll get it eventually.

The fourth official take (**V**) was released on *Anthol-*ogy 3 and sounds a bit more polished than the previous rehearsals (and Paul's voice sounds a bit more ragged). It has an extra repeat of the first verse and fades out, but otherwise it resembles the finished version. The thirty-second and final take was chosen as "best," so Paul double-tracked his voice on the bridges, filling the tape's fourth track. At the end of the session, six mono mixes were created from this take; the last and temporary "best" of these (**W**) has some additional bars of guitar at the beginning that would be lopped off for release, and extra echo on Paul's voice.

After living with this mix for four months, the only adornment Paul decided upon was to have an actual blackbird warbling along near the end of the song. This was added during remixing on October 13, with the effects tape entering 2 seconds sooner in mono (**Y**) than stereo (**X**). The *Love* CD (**Z**) includes the first 26 seconds of the guitar and foot tapping in "Blackbird," joined to a remix of "Yesterday."

RELEASE HISTORY

1968: **X** was released on stereo copies of the LP *The Beatles* worldwide and is on EMI's CD of that title. **Y** was included on mono copies, released in the UK only.

1990: A very good-quality tape of **W** was booted on the CD *Unsurpassed Masters, Volume 4.*

1993: A sonic upgrade of **W** surfaced on the CD *The Peter Sellers Tape,* issued first on the Masterdisc label and then copied by Spank.

1994: The bootleg *The Ultimate Collection, Volume 1: Miscellaneous Tracks* included excerpts of **B** and **C,** taken from the soundtrack of the Apple promo film (see following entry). A poorer quality copy of "Helter Skelter" from **C** had previously appeared on the 7-inch EP *1989 Beatleg News Christmas Record.*

1996: **V** was officially released on the CD *Anthology 3.*

1997: **A–U** appeared in excellent mono on the bootleg CD *Gone Tomorrow, Here Today,* issued on both the Midnight Beat and Repro-Man labels.

2006: **Z** was released on the *Love* CD.

39. Documentary footage   J, P

Date: ca. 11 June 1968
Location: EMI Studio 2 and Apple Corps, London
Director: Tony Bramwell
Length: 10:25

One of Apple Films' more obscure productions was a ten-minute promotional short titled simply *Apple*. This was a sort of groovy industrial film to give Capitol and EMI executives some idea of what the Beatles and company were up to in their new enterprise. With George and Ringo out of the country, it was left to John and Paul to put in appearances; as always, Tony Bramwell directed the 16 mm footage, which was hastily assembled in time for Paul to bring on his Los Angeles trip June 20. (Some of this film may have been aired on Dutch station VARA-TV's *Puntje* September 27.)

The film opens with crude title cards and some shots of London, including Apple's office building. An American narrator describes the Apple concept in simplest terms as music from *Wonderwall* plays. Meanwhile, inside Apple Corps, Paul is arguing business matters with Dick James while John sits at a desk with his head down, doodling. The attractive Apple Records Granny Smith label is then shown off and we cut to EMI for Paul's performance of "Blackbird" (see previous entry).

The second half of the film opens with further narration and several quick shots, including brief glimpses of Alistair Taylor, the Apple Boutique, and Apple Tailoring. Mary Hopkin, one of Apple's first "discoveries," is then highlighted. Sitting in Paul's yard, she performs a Barry Gibb song, "In the Morning," on acoustic guitar, as Paul's sheepdog, Martha, rolls around in the grass. According to Mark Lewisohn's *Complete Beatles Chronicle,* a scene of Mary and Paul listening to playbacks at EMI was shot on June 11; however, this does not appear in the circulating copy of *Apple.*

Paul provides a link from Hopkin to Apple Electronics, represented in hilarious fashion by Alexis Mardas, who says hello to "all the girls around the world." Back at Apple Corps, John and Paul tease Dick James with what is presumably a Magic Alex creation, a telephone that plays music through its receiver. Finally, we see John at Studio 2 chatting with George Martin about Capitol's sales conference (as noted in the previous entry, this bit of dialogue is missing from the raw sound reel presented on bootleg). The camera pans across to Paul, performing an acoustic rendition of "Helter Skelter."

Apart from the novelty of unreleased McCartney tunes and Hopkin's sweet performance, it's hard to say what attraction this rather disjointed film would have held. However, it would have needed to be truly atrocious to dissuade Capitol and EMI executives from distributing the Beatles' new label.

RELEASE HISTORY

A decent-quality copy of *Apple* with rather washed-out color circulates among collectors (usually with the two reels in the wrong order); excerpts in much better quality were released in the *Anthology* home video, including "Blackbird" and Magic Alex's segment. The circulating edit is presumably the one shown to EMI executives in London August 26, since the exterior shot of Apple Corps shows Savile Row. The office's move from Wigmore Street, where the interior scenes take place, did not occur until July 15, well after the film was completed and shown in Los Angeles, so it would seem a bit of reediting was done to reflect the new location. The complete soundtrack to this film was included on the CD-R *Blackpool Night Out '64—Upgraded.*

40. Amateur footage   J

Date: mid-June 1968
Location: Kenwood
Length: 2:44

John and Yoko's first joint film projects were also the last projects John worked on from his Kenwood home before Cynthia and Julian moved back in. Agreeing that it would be a better home for his son, John lived out of a suitcase for a while, staying with Yoko at the homes of Paul, Peter Brown, and Neil Aspinall temporarily. By late July they had moved into Ringo's former flat in Montagu Square, where they would remain until early November.

In their waning days at Kenwood, the couple spent one sunny afternoon shooting a pair of experimental films, *Film No. 5 (Smile)* and *Two Virgins.* The proceedings were documented in a color home movie, taken by an unknown crew member. The silent footage begins in John's morning room, with glimpses of a Sgt. Pepper drumhead and other psychedelic furnishings. Plucking an acoustic guitar, John (sans spectacles) poses for the *Smile* film, shot with a white 16 mm camera mounted on a table. John and Yoko are then seen conversing while crouched beneath the table. The action moves outside to the swimming pool, where John strolls with his guitar as a white-clad Yoko directs proceedings. John and Yoko then embrace and kiss for a *Two Virgins* sequence.

A short clip of *Smile* would debut on the TV show *Frost on Saturday* (see the August 24 entry), but both completed films had their world premiere at the Chicago Film Festival in October.

RELEASE HISTORY

This excellent-quality silent footage circulates on video in a compilation entitled *At the Movies;* a bit of it was included in the documentary *Imagine: John Lennon.* It originates from a three-and-a-half-minute 8mm reel auctioned at Sotheby's September 12, 1988. *Smile* and *Two Virgins* also make the rounds, usually in fair quality.

41. TV interview

P

Date: 16 June 1968
Location: Stonebridge House, Wembley
Producer: David Frost
Interviewer: Frankie Howerd
Broadcast: 23 February 1969, 6:00–7:00 p.m.
syndicated (United States)
David Frost Presents . . . Frankie Howerd
Length: 5:25

The Apple promotion machine rolled on, with Mary Hopkin remaining in the spotlight. Paul appeared on this TV show to introduce her to American audiences, although by the time it aired, the job was already done; Hopkin would have a number 2 U.S. hit in November 1968 with "Those Were the Days." While technically a David Frost show, comedian Frankie Howerd had the honor of interviewing Paul on the occasion, though it was hardly an in-depth affair.

Paul plays along patiently with Howerd's bumbling but self-deprecating ribbing and is eventually asked to explain the purpose of Apple. He is curiously careful to describe its objective as supporting rather than discovering talent. Howerd correctly predicts that the company will be swamped with mail from would-be stars, but Paul insists that if someone in the audience had a great idea for a film, Apple would be willing to sign them up. After a bit more tomfoolery, Paul introduces Mary Hopkin, who performs "House of the Rising Sun."

RELEASE HISTORY

A good-quality off-line audio recording of this interview circulates among collectors. The video itself has yet to surface, but may be lurking in Frost's archives.

41a. Newsreel footage

G, R

Date: 18 June 1968
Location: London Airport
Length: 0:03

This very short news clip captures George (wearing a hat and toting a sitar), Pattie, Ringo, and Maureen walking down the steps of their flight from America.

RELEASE HISTORY

This silent footage circulates on video.

42. Newsreel footage

J

Date: 18 June 1968
Location: Old Vic Theatre, London
Broadcast: 22 June 1968, 10:05–10:45 p.m.
BBC2
Release
Length: 0:45

This brief color footage stems from BBC TV's *Release* feature (see the June 6 entry) about the National Theatre's production of *In His Own Write,* a play based on John's books. John and Yoko are seen arriving at the premiere, along with glimpses of Neil Aspinall and the director, Victor Spinetti. Since the footage is silent (overlaid with music and narration), we can't hear the cries of "Where's your wife, John?" allegedly shouted from the crowd at the newly public couple.

RELEASE HISTORY

This footage circulates on video along with the rest of the *Release* segment.

43. Studio session

Date: 20 June 1968
Time: 7:00 p.m.–3:30 a.m.
Location: EMI Studio 1, 2, and 3
Producer: George Martin

[A.] Revolution 9—master take (mono)
(7:46)

[B.] Revolution 9—edit of RS2 (8:20)
Mixed: 25 June 1968

On June 4 and eleventh, John could be heard discussing ways to make the lengthy take of "Revolution" more interesting. After adding a number of overdubs, loops, and other effects, John decided to split the song in half—the first half, eventually retitled "Revolution 1," was a more conventional Beatles track. The second half would be combined with a more avant-garde assembly of sounds, along the lines of not only *Two Virgins,* but also an experimental track from January 1967 (for the "Carnival of Light"), and even parts of the group's Christmas fan club discs.

With the insertion of a peculiarly intoned "number nine" borrowed from a Royal Academy of Music audio exam, the collage was given the title "Revolution 9." The master reel was largely assembled on June 20, utilizing Studios 1, 2, and 3, dozens of tape snippets and loops, sound effects discs, and a new spoken-word track from John and George, spouting seemingly random phrases.

A mono version of this recording, taken from an acetate (**A**), turned up on bootleg and is usually referred to as "RS1," the first of two mixes from June 21. I think it's more likely this reflects a rough mix of the master take at the end of June 20, based on what is absent. Apart from a few effects here and there, the main thing missing is all the material known to be from the end of

"Revolution 1": John's cries of "right!" and "all right!" for instance.

In fact, this mix ends just after John's interjection "Take this, brother, may it serve you well!" (And after George's reply: "Thank you. I'd just like to say . . .") The material that follows that point in the released version (**B**) seems to come entirely from the end of "Revolution 1" ("you become naked"), with the exception of the "block that kick" football chants, reportedly taken from an Elektra Records sound effects LP. This suggests that rather than being on the "Revolution 9" master tape itself, this material was simply fed in from the "Revolution 1" session tape during stereo mixing. Or perhaps it was all on a separate tape all along, and was overdubbed from that source on both "Revolution 1" and "9."

Two stereo mixes were created June 21, with the second attempt chosen as "best" and edited down from a length of 9:05 on June 25. Rather than try to re-create the process in mono, the stereo mix was simply copied and combined on a mono tape on August 20 and improved on August 26. Various attempts to "transcribe" this recording have been made. Rather than re-hash all the sonic elements, I'll point you to pages 174–178 of Walter Everett's book *The Beatles as Musicians: "Revolver" through the "Anthology"* and an article in the October 1996 issue of *Mojo* magazine. Read along and see if you can pick up what they missed!

RELEASE HISTORY

1968: **B** was released on the LP *The Beatles* worldwide (collapsed to mono on UK mono copies) and is on EMI's CD of that title.

1994: **A** first surfaced on the bootleg CD *Revolution,* supposedly from a two-sided acetate, although there is no obvious break.

44. Studio session

Date: 21 June 1968
Time: 2:30–9:00 p.m.
Location: EMI Studio 2
Producer: George Martin

[A.] Revolution 1—RM? (4:14)
[B.] Revolution 1—RS12 (4:13)
Mixed: 25 June 1968

On June 21, as Paul was meeting with Capitol Records executives in Los Angeles, John and George polished up the first recording in the "Revolution" trilogy. An

overdub of two trumpets and four trombones on "Revolution 1" replaced the track previously occupied by tape loops. A third reduction combined most of the instruments on one track, leaving the voices and brass on separate tracks. George then added a distorted lead guitar part to the newly freed fourth track, including the stinging chords preceding the opening verse.

The song was mixed into both mono and stereo that night; neither John Barrett's notes nor Mark Lewisohn's *Recording Sessions* book indicate how many mono mixes were prepared. For some reason, John decided on a last-minute edit (also undocumented) to give the crashing

E major chord before the coda a tripled effect. He also panned the brass, vocal, and lead guitar tracks around the image of the stereo mix (**B**) near the song's end. Although a bit of the intro is clipped on the mono mix (**A**); it fades out a tad later, accounting for its greater length.

In the July 6 issue of *New Musical Express,* "Revolution" was reported as being the Beatles' likely first Apple single, to be released August 11. Within days of that report, and to John's consternation, the group would be rerecording the song in an attempt to make it more "commercial."

RELEASE HISTORY

1968: **B** was released on stereo copies of the LP *The Beatles* worldwide and is on EMI's CD of that title. **A** was included on mono copies, released in the UK only.

45. Amateur footage   P

Date: 23–24 June 1968
Location: Los Angeles
Length: 0:32

Although they had left an impression on each other, Paul McCartney and Linda Eastman didn't see each other for a year after their initial meeting in London in May 1967. On his trip to New York in May 1968, Paul spent some time with Linda and her daughter Heather, and they got along well enough for him to invite her out to the opposite coast on his California visit.

Paul was staying at the Beverly Hills Hotel along with Apple's Tony Bramwell and longtime mate Ivan Vaughan. Presumably one of them shot these color home movies of Paul and Linda splashing around in the hotel pool and (on the twenty-fourth) sailing on the yacht of Warner Bros. executive John Calley. Within three months, Linda would fly to London, remaining at Paul's side for the next thirty years.

RELEASE HISTORY

2001: This silent footage was included in the TV documentary *Wingspan,* later released on DVD.

46. Radio interview   P

Date: 20–25 June 1968
Location: Los Angeles
Interviewer: Bobby Dale (?)
Length: 5:55

At some point during his Los Angeles visit, Paul was interviewed for an unknown (presumably local) station. With only an audio recording surviving, it's not clear whether this was for radio or TV, nor is the identity of the interviewer certain. He is traditionally identified as Bobby Dale, and Paul refers to him only as "Robbie"; certainly it's not the same Bobby Dale who covered the Beatles' 1965 San Francisco concert for KEWB-AM. For one thing, the latter has an American accent, while this reporter is decidedly British.

His first question is about Apple Films, and Paul says the company's first film will be called *The Jam.* He already seems to be backing away from Apple's charitable image, describing it as an organization to help the Beatles first and foremost, with assistance to other artists being "incidental." Paul names some of his current favorite musicians (the Beach Boys, Harry Nilsson, the Lovin' Spoonful) and reveals that the next Beatles album will consist of songs written in India and should be released later in the year.

After covering old ground about the maharishi split, Paul is asked about the voting age and suggests it be lowered "to six." In a more serious vein, he questions the need for having an army, since bombs will wage war just as well as "little men with guns." The interviewer suggests that enlistment might foster self-discipline, but Paul points out that being told what to do by superiors hardly constitutes self-discipline.

Although he concedes it'd be easy to rest on their laurels and bank accounts (something John and Ringo seemingly wouldn't have minded), Paul feels the Beatles have been taking it too easy of late and need to put in a solid year of work to get Apple up and running. Within a year, Allen Klein would be in charge of the show, and soon after that Paul would go into seclusion, abandoning his dreams for Apple amid a nightmare of legal and financial squabbling.

RELEASE HISTORY

This interview circulates among collectors from a fair-quality off-air recording.

Date: 24–26 June 1968
Location: EMI Studio 3
Producer: George Harrison

    [A.] Sour Milk Sea (3:52)
    [B.] The Eagle Laughs at You (2:23)

Jackie Lomax's group, Lomax Alliance, was already managed by NEMS before Apple existed. The Beatles knew him best as the lead singer of a Liverpool group, the Undertakers, in the early '60s and signed him up as a solo artist to their fledgling label in the spring of 1968. Somewhat by default, George agreed not only to produce Lomax's first single, but to donate his own composition, "Sour Milk Sea," knocking it from the list of contenders for the next Beatles LP.

Perhaps George thought the song was more suited to Jackie's vocal style; certainly he had no qualms about the Beatles' ability to perform it, since he drafted Paul to play bass and Ringo to drum on the track. Their contribution can be heard in the right channel of the stereo mix (**A**) alongside George's acoustic guitar and distant guide vocal. To this, Jackie added a double-tracked lead vocal (centered), and further overdubs (in the left channel) included Nicky Hopkins's piano, Eric Clapton's lead guitar, and an organ break. As Paul was

out of the country on the first two days of these sessions, and the bass seems to be on the rhythm track, the song was probably started on the twenty-sixth.

For the B-side, Lomax's own composition, "The Eagle Laughs at You," was taped with Clapton again providing lead guitar and George playing rhythm guitar alongside Lomax. No other Beatle plays on this track, but the basic track for another Lomax tune, "You've Got Me Thinking," probably stems from the June sessions. Not only does the drumming sound like Ringo, but he and Paul seem very familiar with the song when Paul busks it during the January 1969 Apple Studio sessions. The horns and backing vocals on "You've Got Me Thinking" were probably overdubbed much later, though (see the December 1968 entry).

RELEASE HISTORY

1968: **A** and **B** were coupled for release as one of the first Apple singles, released worldwide. Both sides "bubbled under" the *Billboard* top 100 in America, but the single failed to chart in the UK.

1969: **A** and **B** were included on the LP *Is This What You Want?,* reissued by Apple on CD in 1991.

48. **Studio session**

Date: 28 June 1968
Time: 7:00 p.m.–4:30 a.m.
Location: EMI Studio 2
Producer: George Martin

    [A.] Good Night—unknown take (stereo)
    (0:22)

Often mistaken for a Paul McCartney composition, the sentimental lullaby "Good Night" was actually written by John for his son Julian. Rather than sing it himself, John decided the song would be more universal if kindly Uncle Ringo crooned it to "everybody, everywhere."

Most of this first session for the then-untitled tune was taken up with rehearsals, some of which were captured on the multitrack tape. One such run-through was released on *Anthology 3,* where it is cross-faded with a remix of the final orchestral overdub (see the

July 22 entry for further details). Five "proper" takes were also recorded, with Ringo's vocal accompanied by softly strummed electric guitar. Each take was prefaced by Ringo's gentle admonition from "Daddy" to his "toddlers" to get tucked in and await the sandman.

The excerpt heard in the *Anthology* outtake medley (**A**) highlights this section, with A, D, and E chords rotating beneath Ringo's speech. Unfortunately, he's unable to squeeze in his last sentence in time to make his musical entrance.

RELEASE HISTORY

1996: **A** was included in the *Anthology* home video set in mono and was bootlegged from that source on the CD *Abbey Road Video Show;* it appears in stereo on the *Anthology* DVD.

49. Studio session

Date: ca. early July 1968
Location: Trident and EMI Studios, London
Producer: Paul McCartney

[A.] Those Were the Days (5:07)

Eighteen-year-old Mary Hopkin was the first prominent discovery signed to Apple Records, and Paul wasted no time in taking her under his wing. Having first seen her on the TV talent show *Opportunity Knocks* on May 4, he phoned her in Wales, and with her parents' permission, she was off to London to audition and record several demos in Dick James's basement studio.

Her specialty was folk songs, and Paul had the perfect tune in mind for her first single: a Lithuanian folk melody set to lyrics by an American cabaret team, Gene and Francesca Rankin. Paul had seen the duo perform the song at the Blue Angel nightclub several years earlier and kept it filed away in his memory, certain that the right singer could make it a hit. By July, he was ready to produce Hopkin's rendition of "Those Were the Days," probably at Trident Studios.

Although he didn't write the fantastic arrangement himself, Paul did play the acoustic guitar heard during the verses, including a doubling of the D/C-sharp/B/ C-sharp motif that dangles tantalizingly in front of the refrain. He also produced the single's B-side, a first-take rendition of Pete Seeger's "Turn! Turn! Turn!" but left the guitar playing to Mary.

"Those Were the Days" proved to be a worldwide smash, helped by Mary's redoing the lead vocal in several languages for foreign markets ("Quelli Erano Giorni" in Italy, "Les Temps Des Fleurs" in France, "An Jenem Tag" in West Germany, and "En Aquellos Dias" in Spain). As these multilingual discs were issued two months after the English versions, the new vocals were probably added well after the initial July sessions.

RELEASE HISTORY

1968: **A** was released on a single worldwide, peaking just behind "Hey Jude" at number 2 in the United States, but knocking "Hey Jude" from the top spot in the UK. It was added to U.S. copies of Hopkin's debut LP *Post Card* the following year, but didn't appear in stereo in the UK until the 1972 compilation LP *Those Were the Days*. The stereo mix was included on the Apple CD of *Post Card* in 1991, along with the Italian- and Spanish-language versions. The English version also appears on the 1995 CD issue of *Those Were the Days*.

50. Newsreel footage

Date: late June–1 July 1968
Location: Robert Fraser Gallery, London
Length: 2:23

John and Yoko's first joint public appearance had also been their first artistic venture displayed to the world. On June 15, they planted a pair of acorns at Coventry Cathedral, their living contribution to the National Sculpture Exhibition. Finding each other on the same creative wavelength, they hastily assembled a joint exhibition to be held the following month at Robert Fraser's London art gallery.

The show, titled "You Are Here," opened on the first of July and was attended by puzzled guests, bemused reporters, Derek Taylor, and the two artists, visions in sparkling white. As this newsreel footage shows, white was the theme of the day, from the 365 ivory helium balloons released to the barren white walls and immense circular canvas marked only by a small "you are here" in the center. Scattered throughout are various charity collection boxes ("please help a homeless dog") and an upturned white hat labeled by John "FOR THE ARTIST. THANK YOU."

The items on display were incidental—what John and Yoko were interested in was the reactions of the patrons, and they duly hired a hidden camera to film the event (a film apparently never completed or screened in public). Color footage of John (in a striped shirt) setting up the various exhibits and writing "you are here" on the canvas was probably filmed in the days prior to the opening. More notable are the newsreel shots from July 1 of John gently brushing the hair from Yoko's face as the two share a drink and beam with the glow of a couple deeply in love.

RELEASE HISTORY

The silent Reuters newsreel footage circulates on video among collectors. Color footage from this day has appeared in documentaries such as *Imagine: John Lennon* and *Anthology*.

51. Studio session

Date: 5 July 1968
Time: 5:00 p.m.–1:30 a.m.
Location: EMI Studio 2
Producer: George Martin

[A.] Ob-La-Di, Ob-La-Da—take 5 (stereo) (2:57)
[B.] Ob-La-Di, Ob-La-Da—edit of take 5 (stereo) (2:53)

Life goes on, and so did the sessions for Paul's "Ob-La-Di, Ob-La-Da," stretching over seven working days and three remakes. Things began simply enough on July 3 with Paul on acoustic guitar and guide vocal, and Ringo, on drums, laying down seven takes of the backing. The last of these was chosen as best, and had a lead vocal and acoustic guitar added before Paul, in a sign of things to come, changed his mind and transferred his allegiance to take 4. Before the session ended, he added a second, much hotter acoustic guitar track to that take, attempting to distort the signal slightly to make it sound like an electric.

The next day, two sets of vocals were added, with Paul harmonizing to his own lead on the last verse, and John and George adding falsetto "la la la's." A reduction into take 5 freed up room for more additions on July 5. On track 3 went a trio of saxophones as well as a conga drum played by none other than the "ob-la-di" man himself, Jimmy Scott. When the record was released, Scott complained in the papers that "you can't hear" his contribution—no surprise, since this take was never used! Starting with the second chorus, additional percussion (maracas, marimba, and claves) also went on this track, and Paul's bass on track 2 (wiping an aborted piccolo overdub) completed the recording. Paul took home a rough mono mix of the result to listen to over the weekend and didn't like what he heard.

The raw studio tape of this take (**A**) begins with a snippet of John rehearsing his falsetto vocal, followed by Paul's count-in. It concludes with George Martin's gleeful comment "That's it, you've done it!" A version prepared by Geoff Emerick for *Sessions* omits the studio chat, replaces the first chorus with a spliced-in later chorus, and is mixed in pseudostereo at best. Its ending originally cross-faded with a reprise of "Christmas Time (Is Here Again)" When this mix (**B**) was eventually released on *Anthology 3,* the song's ending was left intact and some goofy dialogue from John was appended to the start and finish. These exclamations ("Yes sah! Take one, and de Magic Jumbo Band!"; "Oobladi-blada, brutha!") may come from a later session (see the July 9 entry).

RELEASE HISTORY

1986: Originally slated to close out the *Sessions* LP, by the time the lineup was finalized, **B** had been dropped to go on the accompanying single. This single mix floated around on tape for a while before being booted on the LP *Ob-La-Di, Ob-La-Da.*

1991: The bootleg CD *Unsurpassed Masters, Volume 6* contained a mono copy of **B,** running too fast and with the ending faded early to delete the segue into "Christmas Time (Is Here Again)" The same year, **A** made its first appearance, in mediocre quality, on the CD *Unsurpassed Masters, Volume 7.*

1993: Spank's CD issue of *Sessions* included the single mix of **B** from tape source as a bonus track, but with the final chord tacked on from a copy of **A** to omit the cross-fade.

1996: **B** was officially released in excellent sound (but a crummy mix) on the CD *Anthology 3.*

2001: An upgraded copy of **A** was booted on the CD *Abbey Road Tape, Volume 1.*

52. Newsreel footage/Interview   P, G, R

Date: 8 July 1968
Time: afternoon
Location: Bowater House Cinema, London
Length: 2:28

Nine days before its world premiere, *Yellow Submarine* was previewed by the press at the Bowater House Cinema in Knightsbridge. After the screening, 75 percent of the Beatles were available for photos and interviews, with John choosing to miss the proceedings. Deputizing for Mr. Lennon was a cardboard blowup of his car-toon counterpart, which the other three duly posed alongside.

Two film clips document the occasion: 17 seconds of silent color BBC News footage of their separate arrivals (George, then Ringo, then Paul) and a 38-second interview for ITV News. The reporter ("Pete") asks whether the *Magical Mystery Tour* fiasco has soured them on the idea of self-made films. George quips that thanks to that critical lashing, they'll appear only in animation from now on. A question about whether their relationship with the maharishi is finished seems to make

George uncomfortable; rather than respond, he turns his attention to a life-size Blue Meanie. Paul steps in and calls their involvement with the guru a "phase," joking that "we don't go out with him anymore."

In addition, an audio recording sourced from an unknown TV show also seems to be from this date, with interview excerpts totaling 1:33. Paul expresses hope that Apple's expenses won't exceed its profits (ironically, it would take Allen Klein to achieve that feat), and says that although they were too busy to provide voices for *Yellow Submarine,* they considered dubbing their lines on afterward. George reassures the reporter that although the songs for the new album were written in India, they are "just Beatle music," not Indian tunes. He then reveals that they have many more songs to get through when they began *Sgt. Pepper,* but Paul thinks the album should be finished in a couple of months.

RELEASE HISTORY

1995: The audio portion of the ITV interview was released on the CD *Rare Photos & Interview CD, Volume 1.* This is missing a word or two at the start compared to the film clip, which is included on the video compilation *Beatles 1962 to 1970.* The color BBC footage also circulates on video, and the unknown TV interview exists in good quality, complete with video buzz.

53. Studio session   R

Date: 9 July 1968
Time: afternoon
Location: EMI Studio 2 (?)

[A.] A Hundred Years or More (2:55)

Arriving early for the Beatles' EMI Studio 3 session this day, Ringo dropped by an adjacent studio to visit U.S. crooner Solomon King. King was working on a rather trite ballad called "A Hundred Years or More," and perhaps out of sheer boredom, Ringo agreed to contribute some handclapping for the song's instrumental break.

His contribution is prominent beginning about 1:18 into the song, at least on the mono mix used as a B-side on Columbia Records in the UK. Author Kristofer Engelhardt reported that the song contained "no audible hand clapping," but he was working from a U.S. copy, issued on the Capitol label circa August 1969. Since we know Capitol was issuing stereo Beatles singles by the spring of 1969, it's possible the stereo mix of this song omits or buries the handclapping (I was able to examine only a Columbia copy).

To explain the tale of Ringo's assistance, Engelhardt theorized that the drummer might have participated on a different King single, "Somewhere in the Crowd"/"Hava Negila." This seems unlikely, given the evidence (Mark Lewisohn was able to confirm a session for "A Hundred Years or More" on this date using Abbey Road documentation).

RELEASE HISTORY

1968: **A** was released on the B-side of the single "Goodbye My Old Gal" (Columbia DB 8505) in the UK. It was issued in the US as a single A-side the following year (Capitol 2622), possibly in an alternate mix. The song failed to chart in either country.

54. Studio session

Date: 9 July 1968
Time: 4:00–9:00 p.m.
Location: EMI Studio 3
Producer: George Martin

[A.] Ob-La-Di, Ob-La-Da—take 21 (?) (stereo) (0:26)

Paul decided to start afresh with "Ob-La-Di, Ob-La-Da," abandoning the previously completed take 5. The remake began on July 8, and by take 12, a backing of drums, fuzz bass, acoustic guitar, and piano was perfected. The latter was played by John, whose memorable ivory-pounding intro was borne from his impatience with Paul's perfectionism on the song. All four instruments were reduced to track 1 of take 13, initial vocals went onto tracks 3 and 4, and maracas and bongos on track 2. Paul took home a rough mono mix that night and everyone kept their fingers crossed.

Alas, he demanded a second remake the following day, and five hours of work produced two new takes, numbered 20 and 21. The latter of these was temporarily marked "best" and is probably the one heard in the *Anthology* video during an outtake medley (**A**). This is actually a composite of several elements, not all of which may stem from this session. At first, we hear

John complaining of getting cramps (from playing the piano on so many takes?), and then he calls out, "Yes sah, dat's my baby!" in a voice very similar to that used on the *Anthology 3* mix of take 5 (see the July 5 entry). As Paul counts in the song, a voice mutters, "Jones," and the song's intro is heard, with acoustic guitar, drums, piano, and bass audible, as well as some percussion and a lead vocal. This cuts to the ending of a take, with Paul babbling in mock-German, and George commenting that the F-sharp minor chord (in the chorus) sounded out of tune. Since this fragment matches none of the other finished versions, but does have a vocal, I've placed it here.

After an hour's break, Paul ditched this new remake and went back to take 13 from the previous evening, which would form the basis of the master. Some of the vocals were rerecorded, a reduction brought the song to take 22, and handclaps and "vocal percussion" were added, along with some piano licks for the song's final verse. Work would continue two days later.

RELEASE HISTORY

1996: **A** was included in the *Anthology* home video set in mono and was bootlegged from that source on the CD *Abbey Road Video Show;* it appears in stereo on the *Anthology* DVD.

55. Studio session

Date: 10 July 1968
Time: 7:00 p.m.–1:30 a.m.
Location: EMI Studio 3
Producer: George Martin

[A.] Revolution—take 15 (mono) (3:27)

The Beatles all agreed that "Revolution" would be a perfect song for the group's next single. John would have been happy to release the version already completed, but the others convinced him it wasn't lively enough for radio play (perhaps wanting it to resemble the more up-tempo Kinfauns demo). The remake began July 9, with several rehearsal takes being recorded.

These were rejected and erased the next night with ten takes of a stripped-down backing track. Gone were the "shooby-doo-wop" backing vocals and brass of the previous rendition. Onto tracks 1 and 2 went two mightily distorted electric guitars, played by John and George, with Ringo delivering a walloping drum performance, the signal squashed to midrange, on track 3. An overdub on track 4 doubled the already heavy drum part (it gets slightly out of sync at 1:21 into the song). Three reduction mixes followed, putting both guitars on track 1 and both drum performances on track 2.

John then taped a lead vocal on track 3, this time opting "out" of the destruction. Track 4 was filled with a second lead vocal, complete with throat-rending scream intro, and handclaps. Ringo also added a resounding drum thwack at the song's third bar, marking time until his entrance with a "click track" of tapping sticks. Take 13 was reduced again, combining tracks 3 and 4 to track 3 of a new tape, and John took home a mono copy of the "best" reduction, take 15. The copy from his archives (**A**) begins with the hum of the open guitar amps, followed by a count-in.

RELEASE HISTORY

1988: **A** was aired on episode 88-20 of *The Lost Lennon Tapes*. Since the intro was stepped on by dialogue, most bootleg issues such as the LP *The Lost Lennon Tapes, Volume 4* and the CD *Unsurpassed Masters, Volume 7*, spliced in the released stereo mix for the first 7 seconds.

1994: **A** was included on the CD *Revolution* from a clean tape source that is slightly longer at both ends than the broadcast version.

56. Studio session

Date: 12 July 1968
Time: 3:00–11:00 p.m.
Location: EMI Studio 2
Producer: George Martin

[A.] Don't Pass Me By—RM4 (4:11)
Mixed: 12 July 1968

[B.] Don't Pass Me By—RS1 (3:50)
[C.] Don't Pass Me By—RM1 (3:45)
Mixed: 11 October 1968

Who better to do a little fiddling than one of the Beatles' old booking agents? Jack Fallon had promoted the group at five shows from March 1962 through June 1963, and they were surprised when he turned out to be the session violinist booked by EMI on July 12 for "Don't Pass Me By." After the violin overdub concluded at 6:40 p.m., all four tracks of the tape were full, but the bass track was erased yet again, replaced by a new performance from Paul and further Leslied piano from Ringo.

It's also likely that the so-called tinkling piano intro was added during this session. Mark Lewisohn indicates that this was taped on July 22, and this seems to be corroborated by the tape log, which indicates that four takes of "Don't Pass Me By (intro)" were recorded that day, on the same tape as "Good Night." However, the "tinkling piano" appears on the rough mix (**A**) given by Ringo to Peter Sellers. This is almost unquestionably RM4 from July 12, of which Ringo took home a copy that night.

So what is the mysterious "intro" recorded on the twenty-second? Most likely it's the orchestral track released on *Anthology 3* as "A Beginning." This lasts just more than 47 seconds, and Lewisohn claims that the piano edit piece was trimmed down from 45 seconds to 8. It's difficult to imagine that piano rambling on for 45 seconds, let alone needing four takes to perfect.

In the *Anthology 3* booklet, Lewisohn surmises that "A Beginning" was intended to open "Don't Pass Me By." In fact, it had already been used as "a beginning" for the film *Yellow Submarine,* where it's heard right after the opening credits. Since that film had already premiered, it's anyone's guess what George Martin was doing rerecording the piece five days later, unless he was trying to get a head start on the soundtrack album (his film score had been taped at Olympic

and would be remade for LP release at EMI October 22 and twenty-third).

Whatever the case, there are some major differences among the mixes of "Don't Pass Me By." The mono mixes both raise the song's pitch from C to C-sharp major, speeding things up considerably. Mix **A** has some extra bass notes during the piano intro and includes an entire repeat of the first verse—this section, from 2:49–3:16, was chopped out of the released mixes. In addition, all three mixes cross-fade to a tape of the violin overdub right near the end (the backing track can be heard faintly in the background, probably leaking through Fallon's headphones). The stereo mix (**B**) uses a different take of this fiddling compared with the mono mixes.

RELEASE HISTORY

1968: **B** was released on stereo copies of the LP *The Beatles* worldwide and is on EMI's CD of that title; the song's first 8 seconds are mistakenly indexed as part of "Rocky Raccoon" on the CD. **C** was included on mono copies, released in the UK only.

1980: Capitol officially released **C** on the *Rarities* compilation LP.

1990: A very good-quality tape of **A** was booted on the CD *Unsurpassed Masters, Volume 4.*

1993: A sonic upgrade of **A** surfaced on the CD *The Peter Sellers Tape,* issued first on the Masterdisc label and then copied by Spank.

57. Studio session

Date: 13 July 1968
Time: midnight–4:00 a.m.
Location: EMI Studio 2
Producer: George Martin

[A.] Revolution—RM21 (3:21)
Mixed: 15 July 1968

[B.] Revolution—RS1 (3:22)
Mixed: 5 December 1969

[C.] Revolution—RS from takes 10 and 16 (3:23)

On July 11, an afternoon session saw the fourth track of "Revolution" filled by Nicky Hopkins's electric piano during the solo and coda. A third reduction combined tracks 3 and 4 yet again onto track 3 of take 16. Paul recorded a bass overdub that evening on track 4 but

redid it the following day, this time with John playing some fiery lead guitar over the solo and ending (the session actually began at midnight on the morning of the thirteenth).

Mark Lewisohn writes that the guitar overdub went onto track 1, but given the stereo mix, it has to be on the track with the bass. The original guitar track is mixed right, the drums left, and the previously recorded vocals and piano are centered. Since the new guitar, also centered, overlaps with the vocal and piano in places, but couldn't have been added to that track without erasing them, that leaves the bass track as the only suspect.

Four mono remixes, numbered RM10–RM13, were completed at the end of the session but would be improved upon by RM20 and RM21 on the fifteenth. The mono mix (**A**) has the guitars and drums mixed "in your face" and was much preferred by fans (and John himself) for that reason. A stereo remix done for the *Hey*

Jude LP in 1969 (**B**) tones the distortion down somewhat and isn't helped by the extreme separation of guitars and drums. The mix released on *Past Masters, Volume 2* makes the problem even worse, with almost no bleed-through whatsoever between channels. This differs from the vinyl issues by leaving up both channels throughout the intro, allowing the "click track" to be heard. I count this as a mastering variant, not a remix, since only one stereo mix was created in 1969 and I doubt the song was remixed from the session tape in 1988 to make it sound worse! The stereo mix also runs a tad slower than the mono. The *Love* remix (**C**) isolates the guitar tracks from take 10, one in each channel.

RELEASE HISTORY

1968: **A** was released on a single worldwide and is available on the "Hey Jude" CD single.

1970: **B** was released in the United States on the LP *Hey Jude;* it was eventually included on the CD *Past Masters, Volume 2* as well as the compilation CD *The Beatles 1967–1970.*

2006: **C** was released on the *Love* DVD; the CD has a 2:15 edit of the same mix.

58. Studio session

Date:	15 July 1968
Time:	3:30–8:00 p.m.
Location:	EMI Studio 2
Producer:	George Martin

[A.]	**Ob-La-Di, Ob-La-Da—RM21** (3:17)	
Mixed:	15 July 1968	

[B.]	**Ob-La-Di, Ob-La-Da—RS4** (3:07)	
[C.]	**Ob-La-Di, Ob-La-Da—RM10** (3:07)	
Mixed:	12 October 1968	

Work continued on "Ob-La-Di, Ob-La-Da" July 11, with a trio of saxophones added to the remake, and a reduction mix into take 23. Paul then doubled his fuzz bass line, now buried deep in the rhythm track, with a fresh bass performance (beginning about 6 seconds into the song). Mono mixes were prepared that evening and again on the twelfth, but Paul was still unsatisfied with his lead vocal.

On the fifteenth, with John's lifelong pal and ex–Quarry Man Pete Shotton present, the group spent a few hours nailing down the main vocal, adding various mumbled asides (John spelling out "H-O-M-E"), echoing ("ring!" "sing!") or parodying ("lend a hand," "arm!" "leg!") certain words, ending with a somewhat forced-sounding bit of laughter. No doubt this was due to everyone but Paul being sick of the song by now; they must have been relieved when after an otherwise flawless take, he agreed to retain a lyrical goof in the final verse that swapped Desmond's and Molly's identities.

The best mono mix from that night (**A**) was included on Ringo's sampler tape for Peter Sellers. It opens with some indecipherable chatter and conga rattling, plus a false start of John's piano intro. The ending carries on past John's "thank you" comment and reveals that he followed it up with "damn sure!" Stereo mixing took place three months later, and the mono mix was also redone for record release. In stereo (**B**), the main vocal track is doubled left and right via ADT, with everything else centered, making this mix a prime candidate for OOPSing. In mono (**C**), the vocal track is mixed down for the first few seconds, omitting the handclaps heard on the earlier mixes. The other main difference among all three versions is the level of the percussion track.

Although the demo and all outtakes of the song are performed in the key of A major, these finished versions are all in B-flat. It's not known if it was performed in the higher key or if the speed was altered at some stage during the reduction mixing.

RELEASE HISTORY

1968: **B** was released on stereo copies of the LP *The Beatles* worldwide and is on EMI's CD of that title. **C** was included on mono copies, released in the UK only.

1990: A very good-quality tape of **A** was booted on the CD *Unsurpassed Masters, Volume 4.*

1993: A sonic upgrade of **A** surfaced on the CD *The Peter Sellers Tape,* issued first on the Masterdisc label and then copied by Spank.

59. Studio session

Date: 16 July 1968
Time: 4:00–9:00 p.m.
Location: EMI Studio 2
Producer: George Martin

[A.] Cry Baby Cry—take 1 (stereo) (2:43)

Rehearsals for John's "Cry Baby Cry" began on the evening of July 15, with the Beatles filling four reels of tape. Most of these run-throughs were erased in the following two sessions by proper takes and reductions of the song, and by the three marathon takes of "Helter Skelter."

It's odd that such a simple song needed so much rehearsal, and the first July 16 take (**A**) doesn't differ too much from the earlier home demo. An introductory passage has been added (consisting of the title refrain), but the structure and lyrics are otherwise identical. This take begins with John's lead vocal and acoustic guitar, joined by Paul's bass and Ringo's drums from the second verse onward. The backing track was perfected by take 10 and reduced to takes 11 and 12 (retaining John's lead vocal only on the choruses). After an hour's break, an overdub of piano (John) and harmonium (George Martin) occupied one of the two newly vacated tracks. The fourth would be filled two days later.

NOTE

The atmosphere in the studio was so sour that Geoff Emerick, who had engineered most Beatle sessions since April 1966, handed in his notice after this session. He wouldn't return as their regular engineer until July 1969. More casualties would follow before the album was completed.

RELEASE HISTORY

1996: **A** was officially released on the CD *Anthology 3*.

60. Newsreel footage/TV interview

Date: 17 July 1968
Time: evening
Location: London Pavilion
Broadcast: (interview only) 19 July 1968
BBC1
How It Is
Length: 2:27

For the third and final time, all four Beatles attended the premiere of one of their films at the London Pavilion. As usual, it was a major event, with hundreds of fans crowding Piccadilly Circus to get a glimpse of the stars, even though most of *Yellow Submarine* featured neither their images nor voices. Silent black-and-white newsreels shot by AP and Reuters depict the mayhem, with police and a fire engine on hand to control the mob. John, Yoko, and Paul arrive together in a taxi. Other arrivals (Ringo with Maureen and George with Pattie) are seen fighting their way through a lobby packed with reporters and photographers.

Director Tony Palmer, still working on his "All My Loving" special for the BBC (see the May 23 entry), was given the chance to produce a pop/current affairs TV series for the Beeb. Initially titled *My Generation,* it was to have featured a regular slot for the Who, but ended up being retitled *How It Is.* Hosted by Chris Denning and Peter Asher, the debut episode included excerpts from John's *In His Own Write* play as well as a feature about *Yellow Submarine.*

All that seems to have survived is an off-line audio recording of this segment, which begins with 10 seconds of an interview from the premiere. The reporter mentions the show's title, and John quips, "How is it?" Paul says he hasn't seen it yet, but it's not clear if he's referring to the show or the movie. After a brief description of the film's plot, a clip of the "Only a Northern Song" segment is shown.

RELEASE HISTORY

The AP newsreel footage (1:18) was released on the video compilation *Beatles 1962 to 1970,* and the Reuters footage (0:59) also circulates on video. The audio portion of the TV interview circulates in fair quality.

61. Studio session

Date: 18 July 1968
Time: 2:30–9:30 p.m.
Location: EMI Studio 2
Producer: George Martin

[A.] Cry Baby Cry—RS3 (2:33)
[B.] Cry Baby Cry—RM1 (2:33)
Mixed: 15 October 1968

With a single empty track to use, the Beatles crammed on as much as they could to complete "Cry Baby Cry" without a further reduction mixdown. John retaped his lead vocal (for the verses only), assisted by Paul for high harmonies in places. George Martin added a cascading harmonium line for the intro, and Ringo shook a tambourine. During the Duchess of Kirkcaldy's verse, George played some stinging electric guitar licks and "tea party" effects were added.

Interestingly, although the four-track master was transferred to eight-track tape on September 17, nothing more was added to the extra tracks. In fact, the October 15 remixing was done from the four-track tape. There is little difference between the mono and stereo mixes, both of which feature heavy phasing on the acoustic guitar/drum track.

RELEASE HISTORY

1968: **A** was released on stereo copies of the LP *The Beatles* worldwide and is on EMI's CD of that title. **B** was included on mono copies, released in the UK only.

62. Studio session

Date: 18 July 1968
Time: 10:30 p.m.–3:30 a.m.
Location: EMI Studio 2
Producer: George Martin

[A.] Helter Skelter—edit of take 2 (mono) (4:35)

After wrapping up "Cry Baby Cry," the group spent the rest of the night erasing the first two rehearsal reels of that song, filling the tapes with one of Paul's works-in-progress. What had started out as a "ridiculous" acoustic ditty (as heard in the June 11 "Blackbird" session) was on its way to becoming an all-out thrash rocker. At this midway stage, "Helter Skelter" was merely a plodding blues-based jam in E, with Paul throwing in choruses and verses at random.

Takes 1 and 2 lasted 10:40 and 12:35, respectively, and filled one reel; take 3 rambled on for a full 27:11 on the second reel, ensuring its legendary status as the longest continuous Beatles studio performance. All three takes consisted of the backing (two electric guitars, bass, and drums) on one track, and Paul's vocal on a second track.

If the edited highlights of take 2 (**A**) are anything to go by, the Beatles' legend would hardly be enhanced by a release of the full take 3. The back of the recording sheet documented the "structure" of take 2: "Mut-

ter, guitars 2/4, verse OK, 1 line vocal, chorus, verse, verse good, verse, george solo, dancer dancer (good), scream good, guitars, middle OK, helter skelter ×3, guitar good, do you don't you want me, end." It's not clear which portions of this were used to make the *Anthology 3* composite, which begins with Ken Scott's "take two" announcement, followed by two verses, the bridge, another verse, and two choruses. The only point of excitement is when Paul breaks into a scream at the end of the bridge, and the music's intensity peaks briefly.

Author Walter Everett speculates that John may be playing the bass and Paul the lead guitar in these takes, and that would explain the amateurish quality of the guitar playing and the fact that the bass stays glued to E throughout. Two months later, the group would return to "Helter Skelter," pouring a ton of energy into the remake.

RELEASE HISTORY

1996: **A** was released on the CD *Anthology 3*. Mark Lewisohn, knowing of the track's notoriety, implored George Martin and Geoff Emerick to give take 3 a listen when compiling the track list, but they wisely opted not to waste one-third of one disc's playing time on it. Paul didn't need to be reminded, having copied take 3 October 9, 1968, for his home listening pleasure.

63. Studio session

Date: 19 July 1968
Time: 7:30 p.m.–4:00 a.m.
Location: EMI Studio 2
Producer: George Martin

[A.] **Sexy Sadie—take 6 (stereo)** (4:05)
[B.] **studio chat (stereo)** (0:17)
[C.] **Sexy Sadie—monitor mix of various takes (mono)** (7:30)

The first session for John's "Sexy Sadie" was a dispirited occasion. Just over three reels of tape were filled with basic track rehearsals, but nothing usable was produced. With John on lead vocal and acoustic guitar, George on tremeloed electric guitar, Paul on organ, and Ringo on drums, the group slogged through twenty-one takes before giving up for the night. None of the takes were marked "best," even temporarily.

Although the structure is basically complete, the tempo of these takes drags and John seems at a loss to how the song should sound. An early take used on *Anthology 3* (**A**) has a few chord clashes, a lackluster vocal from John, and Paul feeling his way through the organ part. A handful of decent drum fills from Ringo inject some life into the recording. At this stage, stuck for an ending, John repeated the first half of the song again after the second bridge, and although the CD fades the song at 4:05, Mark Lewisohn reports that the completed takes from this day all exceeded 5:36.

A bit of studio chat apparently from this evening was used in the *Anthology* home video during an outtake medley (**B**). It reveals how tense things were getting in the studio. Three days after Geoff Emerick's defection, Georges Martin and Harrison are now squabbling. As John plucks on his acoustic, the following conversation takes place over the studio intercom.

Ken Scott: Sorry, George, what did you say?
George Harrison: I said it's no point in Mr. Martin being uptight.
Paul (?): Right.
George Harrison: Y'know, we're all here to do this, and if you want to be uptight . . .
George Martin: I don't know what to say to you, George.
George Harrison: I mean, you're very negative!

This argument is referred to on a "Beatles chat" reel (E106141) from this session, noted as "Various Jamming—Recorded from J.L.'s Vocal Mic Only" in the tape log. Apparently John had a separate feed running from his vocal microphone to a mono machine to capture various bits of dialogue this evening. Our source for this is a monitor mix tape (**C**) of the reel being played back (and skimmed through) during preparation of the 1983 presentation *The Beatles at Abbey Road*.

The first segment consists of a jam with John tossing out random lyrics ("Fuck a duckie—hey, Pluto, how's it goin'?"), followed by a bit of sluggish "Sexy Sadie" rehearsal. This leads into a few minutes of Chuck Berry–like improvisation, this time with John making up a tale about Brian Epstein and his family members. He sings, "I saw Mary sitting on the dairy," and the jam starts up again, with John exhorting, "Go, little Ringo!" The tape is wound back and forth a few times and lands on a section where John is demonstrating some extremely crude alternate lyrics to his song about the maharishi: "Who the fuck do you think you are? Oh, you cunt!" John jokingly asks if he should sing it like that, and Paul responds, "With a little more sympathy."

The final section of the tape consists of John, Paul, and Yoko on the studio floor listening to a playback of the last two minutes of a take. It opens with Paul asking if they should go up to the control room to hear "the bit when all that happened." John asks if he means on the take they're hearing, but he replies, "No, where George Martin was talking to George over the intercom. I think it's probably—might be recorded." (Presumably he's referring to the incident in **B**.) Paul wants to listen to that and to the take before it when "they kept sort of interrupting it, and we kept on." Yoko suggests they could do the song better, and John agrees that his vocal needs improvement, and considers adding it afterward, or dropping in segments. In the end, they decide that a lighter approach is needed; the remake would begin July 24.

RELEASE HISTORY

1990: The "Brian Epstein Blues" portion of **C** was bootlegged on the CD *Unsurpassed Masters, Volume 4,* running slightly fast.

1993: Various excerpts of **C** (four segments totaling 4:20) appeared on the bootleg CD *Control Room Monitor Mixes,* at the correct speed.

1996: **A** was released on the CD *Anthology 3*. **B** was included in the *Anthology* home video set and was later bootlegged on the CD *Abbey Road Video Show.*

2002: A complete version of **C** appeared on the bootleg CD *Complete Controlroom Monitor Mixes.*

64. Studio session

Date: 22 July 1968
Time: 7:00 p.m.–1:40 a.m.
Location: EMI Studio 1
Producer: George Martin

[A.] Good Night—edit of rehearsal take and take 34 (stereo) (2:34)

[B.] Good Night—RM6 (3:04)
Mixed: 23 July 1968

[C.] Good Night—RS1 (3:10)
[D.] Good Night—RM2 (3:09)
Mixed: 11 October 1968

Before beginning proper takes on June 28, the Beatles had recorded many of the rehearsals for "Good Night." A segment of this tape was used on *Anthology 3,* in mono, but cross-faded with a stereo mix of the eventual orchestral ending (minus Ringo's whispered "good night, everybody"). This run-through (A) begins with John's approval of the newly arranged intro. Rather than beginning with a verse, the "dream sweet dreams" bridge serves as an opening. George Martin tells George to count in, and after Paul reminds himself of the new beginning, they are off. Ringo croons the melody sweetly, with Paul playing the chords on piano and George adding a shaker to keep time.

This performance is quite effective, but John wanted a much cornier, over-the-top arrangement. After the rehearsals, five takes were recorded, with vocal overdubs on the last of these July 2. Recording continued that day, with takes 6 through 15 going on a fresh reel, and George Martin taking home copies of take 15 to prepare a suitably lush orchestral score. According to John Barrett's tape log, even more "outtakes," probably through take 22, went onto another reel that night, but they may have been erased by reductions of "Ob-La-Di, Ob-La-Da."

On July 22, the orchestra assembled in Studio 1 to lay down the backing track. Twenty-six musicians, plus a chorus of eight vocalists from the Mike Sammes Singers, participated in the session. Judging from the stereo mix, flutes, violins, violas, and a horn went on one track, and the cellos and string bass on a second. The vocal chorus, harp, and extra flutes for the ending were taped as an overdub on the third track. This left a track free for Ringo's lead vocal onto take 34, with support from the Mike Sammes Singers. This overdub was documented on the "Beatles Chat" reel (see previous entry). The song's beautiful melody and a competent vocal performance from Ringo are somewhat lost in the wash of echo and syrupy strings.

The first mono mixes for "Good Night" were prepared on the twenty-third, with the "best" of these (**B**) editing out a bar of music prior to Ringo's "humming solo." This mix ended up on Ringo's sampler tape for Peter Sellers and has some extraneous talking during Ringo's whispered ending. The released mixes were created October 11 and leave the transitional bar of music intact. The main difference between the two is that the stereo (**C**) begins very softly and fades in, while the mono (**D**) starts at nearly full volume.

RELEASE HISTORY

1968: **C** was released on stereo copies of the LP *The Beatles* worldwide and is on EMI's CD of that title. **D** was included on mono copies, released in the UK only.

1990: A very good-quality tape of **B** was booted on the CD *Unsurpassed Masters, Volume 4.*

1993: A sonic upgrade of **B** surfaced on the CD *The Peter Sellers Tape,* issued first on the Masterdisc label and then copied by Spank.

1996: **A** was released on the CD *Anthology 3.*

65. Studio session

Date: 23 July 1968
Time: 7:00 p.m.–2:30 a.m.
Location: EMI Studio 2
Producer: George Martin

[A.] Everybody's Got Something to Hide Except Me and My Monkey—RM5 (2:31)
Mixed: 23 July 1968

[B.] Everybody's Got Something to Hide Except Me and My Monkey—RS1 (2:24)
[C.] Everybody's Got Something to Hide Except Me and My Monkey—RM1 (2:24)
Mixed: 12 October 1968

[D.] Everybody's Got Something to Hide Except Me and My Monkey—RS from takes 6 and 12 (0:58)

Sometimes all the rehearsing paid off; an eight-and-a-half hour session on June 26 yielded no usable takes of John's then-untitled song. But by the following evening, what had been a somewhat rambling demo was transformed into a tightly played backing track, complete with complex counter-rhythms. Very much in the vein of "Revolution," this consisted of heavily compressed drumming and two distorted electric guitars. While the demo had been played in A major, these takes brought the key up to D major, and a varispeeded reduction mix would raise the pitch even further to E major. Mark Lewisohn reports that six takes were needed, with the last of these reduced into takes 7 and 8. John Barrett's tape log tells a different story, with all eight takes appearing on the same reel.

Either way, by July 1 take 8 of "Everybody's Got Something to Hide Except Me and My Monkey" contained the drums, guitars, a main bass track, and a percussion track alternating between a handbell and chocalho (an instrument first used on "She's a Woman"). A reduction that night into take 10 cleared room for John's main vocal, but he would erase it with a new performance July 23. One final reduction created take 12, and a second vocal track was added, including plenty of shouting, handclapping, and some snare drum raps following the title. At some point, Paul also added a second bass line for the end of the song, over the repeated D major chord. It sounds as though there is an edit immediately following this (at 2:11) that takes us back to the main body of a performance (the bell reenters abruptly). While no editing is noted in the logs, it seems unlikely that varispeeding alone would be enough to shorten the song from 3:07 to 2:24 as Lewisohn relates.

The best mono mix prepared that night (A) included some vocal gimmickry, with John's vocal being single-tracked on the opening verse, and alternating between single- and double-tracked thereafter ("The deeper you go/THE HIGHER YOU FLY"). It also has the second vocal track mixed higher near the end, allowing some extra screaming and snare drum to be heard. Ringo's copy of this mix ended up on his sampler tape for Peter Sellers and includes John's original count-in. An acetate of this mix adds John's comment "Yes, on the intro" and Ken Scott's "RM5" announcement, both from the mix session, plus a stray word and guitar note prior to the count-in. Both released mixes (B and C), done three months later, have John's vocal double-tracked throughout.

A new stereo mix included in two parts on the *Anthology* DVD (D) has the rhythm guitar far left and lead guitar far right (isolated from take 6) synced with everything else in the center (from take 12).

RELEASE HISTORY

1968: B was released on stereo copies of the LP *The Beatles* worldwide and is on EMI's CD of that title. C was included on mono copies, released in the UK only.

1990: A very good-quality tape of A was booted on the CD *Unsurpassed Masters, Volume 4*.

1993: A sonic upgrade of A surfaced on the CD *The Peter Sellers Tape,* issued first on the Masterdisc label and then copied by Spank.

1995: A copy of A from acetate was included on the CD *Primal Colours.* Despite having surface noise, this is slightly better fidelity than previous copies, as well as having the extra material at the start.

2003: D was released on the soundtrack of the *Anthology* DVD.

66. Studio session

Date:	24 July 1968
Time:	7:00 p.m.–2:30 a.m.
Location:	EMI Studio 2
Producer:	George Martin

[A.] Sexy Sadie—take 28 (stereo) (0:18)

The remake of "Sexy Sadie" was no more productive than the original session. Beginning with take 25, a further twenty-three takes were committed to tape, with the last of these, take 47, marked "best" for the time being. An excerpt from this session (A) shows how uncertain John still was about the song's direction. As a take breaks down after the line "you'll get yours yet," George tells John they should start again. Ken Scott calls for take 29, and John asks his bandmates to "reach for this one. Were any of them [the first four takes] any good?" A second remake, beginning August 13, would do the trick.

RELEASE HISTORY

1996: A was included in the *Anthology* home video set and was bootlegged from that source on the CD *Abbey Road Video Show.*

67. Studio session

Date: 25 July 1968
Time: 7:00 p.m.–3:15 a.m.
Location: EMI Studio 2
Producer: George Martin

[A.] While My Guitar Gently Weeps—take 1 (mono w/stereo echo) (3:12)

[B.] While My Guitar Gently Weeps— monitor mix of take 1 (mono) (3:16)

[C.] While My Guitar Gently Weeps— monitor mixes of take 1 (mono) (6:14)

[D.] While My Guitar Gently Weeps—take 1 (stereo) (0:27)

[E.] While My Guitar Gently Weeps—RS from take 1 w/orchestra overdub (3:47)

Thirty-one sessions into the project, George was finally given a chance to record one of his new songs. Two reels were filled this evening with "odd takes" of "While My Guitar Gently Weeps," but as these were taken away by George at the end of the night, it's unknown what instrumentation they consisted of. Luckily, he did leave behind a single take, performed even more simply than the Kinfauns demo.

Singing to his own acoustic guitar accompaniment, George turned in a lovely performance, joined from the second bridge onward by harmonium. The latter may have been played by Paul or overdubbed by the author himself. After the final strum, George is heard calling for a playback. The most complete mix of this take (**A**) was created for *The Beatles at Abbey Road* in 1983. This has everything centered, with vocal echo sent to the right and very faint harmonium. A few monitor mixes from the preparation of this 1983 mix (**B–C**) have also surfaced; these include isolation of the various tracks, plus chat and a count-in not available on other sources.

In 1984, Geoff Emerick prepared a fresh mix for the proposed *Sessions* LP, extended to 3:23 by looping and fading the final guitar phrase (thus omitting the "Let's hear that back" comment). This version has a longer delay on the vocal echo and mixes the harmonium louder. Unfortunately, this same mix ended up officially released on *Anthology 3*, although a medley heard on the *Anthology* DVD (**D**) does include the song's original ending (in true stereo, with prominent percussion and the harmonium in the right channel). The *Love* remix (**E**) is overlaid with an orchestral accompaniment, scored by George Martin in 2006.

It would take four further sessions and a special guest guitarist for the Beatles to complete this song to George's satisfaction.

RELEASE HISTORY

1983: The multimedia presentation *The Beatles at Abbey Road* included a complete version of **A**. It was included from tape source on the bootleg CDs *Abbey Road Video Show* and *Another Sessions . . . Plus.*

1985: Geoff Emerick's remix/edit of **A** created for *Sessions* began to appear on vinyl bootlegs; it can be heard on Spank's CD of that title.

1996: Emerick's remix/edit of **A** was officially released on *Anthology 2*. The alternate mix of the final 27 seconds was included in the *Anthology* home video set and was later bootlegged on the CD *Abbey Road Video Show.*

2002: **B** and **C** appeared in very good quality on the bootleg CDs *Complete Controlroom Monitor Mixes Volumes 1* and *2,* respectively.

2003: **D** was released on the soundtrack of the *Anthology* DVD.

2006: **E** was released on the *Love* CD.

68. Studio session   P

Date: ca. 27 July 1968
Location: Chappell Recording Studios, London
Producer: Paul McCartney, Gus Dudgeon

[A.] I'm the Urban Spaceman (2:21)

Based on subsequent events, George would seem the most likely candidate to have produced a single for the Bonzo Dog Band, as he later worked with band members "Legs" Larry Smith and Neil Innes on various projects. But it was Paul, using the pseudonym Apollo C. Vermouth, who agreed to coproduce what would become their biggest hit, "I'm the Urban Spaceman."

Composer Neil Innes would go on to perform the song on his own TV show and on Monty Python stage shows, but his biggest Beatle connection would be as the musical force behind the Rutles, writing all of the Prefab Four's numbers and taking the vocal role of

Ron Nasty. During this Bonzo session, Paul played a bit of his newly completed song "Hey Jude" to the band; Neil would later write pastiches of its epic finale for his "Village Rolls" song on Monty Python's *Matching Tie and Handkerchief* LP and later for the Rutles' "Shangri-La."

Vivian Stanshall, who had asked Paul to produce the song in the first place, found his main role on the record usurped. He later griped, "And to my utter chagrin, he played ukelele on it because he said that I didn't cut it. I was deeply pissed off about that." Paul's ukelele performance pops up in the right channel about halfway through the song.

Innes recalled a more welcome contribution from Paul: "Viv got out his garden hose with a trumpet mouthpiece and wanted to whirl it around his head. The engineer said, 'You can't record that thing!' And Paul said, 'Why not? Just put a microphone in each corner of the studio.' It was wonderful to have the power he had over convention." The twirling hose effect can be heard whizzing across the soundstage near the song's conclusion.

RELEASE HISTORY

1968: **A** was released on a single that peaked at number 4 in the UK but failed to chart in the United States. It has appeared on numerous compilation LPs as well as on the CD collection *Cornology Volume 2— The Outro.*

69. Amateur footage

Date: 28 July 1968
Time: afternoon
Location: photo studio, Thomson House, London
Length: 0:12

Just as they had stopped performing live on TV in favor of sending out promotional clips, the Beatles no longer held regular group photo shoots. This made it difficult for outlets other than *Beatles Book Monthly* to keep up with their current look. With a new record label and upcoming single to promote, they decided it would be best to get it out of the way with an all-day multilocation shoot.

Several photographers were invited to the so-called Mad Day Out, which took place at seven London sites from late afternoon through evening. The first of these was a penthouse studio where they posed against various backdrops, their mop-tops being blown by a fan, for an image that would appear on the cover of *Life* magazine in September. Someone present was shooting color home movies of the event, a few out-of-focus seconds of which appeared in MPL's *Wingspan* documentary.

RELEASE HISTORY

2001: This silent footage was included in the TV documentary *Wingspan,* later released on DVD.

70. Studio session

Date: 29 July 1968
Time: 8:30 p.m.–4:00 a.m.
Location: EMI Studio 2
Producer: none

[A.] Hey Jude—take 2 (stereo) (4:18)

George Martin missed out on the genesis of a masterpiece when he failed to attend this evening's session. On a single reel of tape, the Beatles laid down six takes of Paul's brand-new composition "Hey Jude." Written to console both himself (on a July 20 BBC TV chat show, Jane Asher had announced the dissolution of their five-year relationship) and particularly Julian Lennon (on his parents' divorce), the song took on a more universal meaning after becoming one of their biggest hits.

On this first day, the mammoth anthem was a bit more modest. These takes had Paul's live vocal on track 1, his piano on track 2, John's acoustic guitar and George's electric on track 3, and Ringo's drums on track 4. One take from this day (**A**) was released on *Anthology 3*. Although Mark Lewisohn's liner notes don't specify which take this is, he's confirmed that it is take 2, which lasted 4:30 according to the tape box.

As the tape begins, John makes a joke announcement: "From the heart of the Black Country!" and Paul ad-libs a brief tune about being a robber in Boston Place (the location of Apple Electronics in London). The opening verse is sung with only a piano accompaniment. John and Ringo join in at the second verse, and George sneaks in with a few licks about halfway through, but has no prominent role in the song. At this point, Paul does not sing the "na na na na" transition after each bridge, although he does play the riff on piano. The only major lyric difference is a pronoun switch in the third verse: "She has found you, go out and get her."

Work would continue the following night, with their producer and a film crew present.

71. Studio session

Date: 30 July 1968
Time: 7:30 p.m.–3:30 a.m.
Location: EMI Studio 2
Producer: George Martin

[A.] **Hey Jude—take 7 (?) (stereo)** (4:59)
[B.] **"Las Vegas Tune" (stereo)** (0:15)
[C.] **St. Louis Blues (stereo)** (0:56)
[D.] **Hey Jude—takes 8 and 9 (stereo)** (5:52)
[E.] **Hey Jude—unknown take (stereo)** (0:07)

[F.] **Hey Jude—RS1 (?)** (6:16)
Mixed: 30 July 1968

Despite the distraction of a film crew in the studio (see following entry), work continued on "Hey Jude," now inching toward perfection with each take. The instrumentation is the same as the previous evening, with the omission of George's guitar. He had wanted to play "answering" licks after each phrase of the verse, but Paul disallowed this, so George spent most of the night in the control room instead.

According to the session sheet, take 7 lasted 5:00, and I've tentatively identified this as **A;** certainly it's the roughest of the three full takes available from this session. As it begins, rather than keeping quiet and waiting for his entrance, John fiddles around on his guitar during the opening verse. Ringo now enters at the bridge, and Paul vaguely sings along with the "na na na na" bridge/verse transition. When they reach John's favorite line, "The movement you need is on your shoulder," he bellows the last four words happily. The coda features plenty of clowning around, with John singing "goo goo ga Jude," and Paul's exclamation of "Here come the Jude!" Paul even throws in a slurred Elvis Presley impression; ironically, this would be one of the few Lennon/McCartney songs Elvis would cover.

A cabaret-style ad-lib (**B**) follows. ("Put the powder on your hands, singin' Las Vegas Jude. Don't think I missed you . . .") And then Paul sings a bit of the W. C. Handy oldie "St. Louis Blues" (**C**). As he and John tune up, Paul calls to mind the Hamburg days when they would take requests in exchange for alcohol: "Crate of beer, you're on, lad!" George Harrison's response from

the booth isn't captured on the multitracks (the others are wearing headphones), but was caught on film: "And two crates if you do 'Twist and Shout'!" John agrees, hits a chord, and mumbles a line from "Revolution."

Most of take 8 is unavailable, but **D** cuts in as it's winding down and Ken Scott calls for take 9. After a few arpeggios, they begin a take quite similar to take 7, but performed more seriously. The entire coda of this take, plus some dialogue afterward not heard in **D,** was captured by the film crew.

The final take (**F**) available from this session is an anomaly: The other outtakes all have Paul's voice and piano in one channel, the drums in the other, and John's guitar and voice centered. This one has a lopsided mix of Paul's vocal at far left and everything else to the right. The final take from this day was take 23, which was then reduced twice to make room for more overdubs, and it seems logical that this would have consisted of one track for vocals and one for instruments. A rough mix of the best reduction, take 25, was done at the end of the day and taken away by George Martin to compose a score.

Whether this take or mix is what's heard on bootleg is debatable (it lasted 5:53 according to the session sheet), but it does seem to be a more polished take from this session. Paul now sings the "na na na na" transition both times coming out of the bridge and delivers a nice scream going into the coda. After some piano pounding (similar to "Let's Dance") and glissandos, the song crashes to a halt, but John carries on strumming for a few more bars. Eventually he yells, "Stop!" and does just that.

1988: The vinyl bootleg *Ultra Rare Trax, Volume 5 & 6* included **C** and an incomplete copy of **D** in very good quality. These were copied on CDs such as *Not Guilty* and *Back-Track, Part 2,* usually running too slow.

1990: **A–C** appeared from an excellent-quality tape source on the CD *Unsurpassed Masters, Volume 4,* at basically the correct speed.

1991: The bootleg CD *Unsurpassed Masters, Volume 6* contained an excellent copy of **D,** from a tape source but at a slightly slow speed.

1997: **F** appeared in excellent quality (but a bit too fast) on the bootleg CD *Gone Tomorrow, Here Today,* issued on both the Midnight Beat and Repro-Man labels.

72. Documentary footage

Date:	30 July 1968
Time:	7:30 p.m.–3:30 a.m.
Location:	EMI Studio 2
Producer:	James Archibald
Broadcast:	22 February 1970, 4:30–6:00 p.m. NBC-TV *Experiment in Television: Music!*
Length:	5:47

Britain's National Music Council was preparing a documentary film about that country's music, cleverly enough titled *Music!* They lucked out when the Beatles allowed them to film an Abbey Road session—for "Hey Jude," no less—and almost six minutes of color footage was used in the production.

It's preceded by an odd 24-second clip of a printer spewing out a list of Lennon/McCartney song titles. Inside Studio 2, a take is in progress, with Paul scat singing some Little Richard lyrics and John throwing in a refrain from "Drive My Car." John apologizes for snapping a string, and while Mal rectifies the problem, Paul announces, " 'Jude' in A minor." He counts in for a brief rendition of "St. Louis Blues," and John returns to his seat. Another take of "Hey Jude" begins, and partway through, we cut to George in the booth discussing various forms of music with George Martin (Ken Scott is also glimpsed in these shots).

Later, John asks how the session is going, and George Martin praises the singing but feels "it wasn't the one." John agrees that only one out of every three takes is "the one," and George Martin asks if they want to hear any playbacks. At that stage, they may have

been laying down unnumbered rehearsal takes, as the next scene is a 30-second excerpt of what I've identified as take 7, the first "proper" take of the day.

The following segment opens with Paul climbing the scale with "hey's," and the aforementioned "crate of beer" dialogue that probably preceded take 8. The rest of the film consists of the complete coda of take 9, with Paul encouraging his "children" to sing along, à la Ray Charles, and Ringo complying. After the take, Ringo complains of getting his pants caught in his bass drum pedal, and John suggests he remove them. It seems likely that the film crew wrapped things up pretty soon after take 9, leaving the group to concentrate on the recording.

RELEASE HISTORY

The completed film debuted in British cinemas October 1969, as the opening act for *The Producers;* it was seen on American network TV the following spring as part of Alistair Cooke's *Experiment in Television.* A fairly battered print of the Beatles' portion has circulated for years on video. Apple clearly has a pristine copy, but used only silent excerpts from it in *Anthology,* including some outtake footage unavailable elsewhere.

The soundtrack has been bootlegged in mediocre quality since the early 70s, with *LS Bumblebee* being the best vinyl source. It's more easily found on the CD-R compilation *White Sessions.* The CD-R *Down in Havana* attempts to reconstruct this session from the multitrack outtakes and film soundtrack, in a different order than listed here.

73. Studio session

Date:	2 August 1968
Time:	2:00–11:30 p.m.
Location:	Trident Studios, London
Producer:	George Martin

[A.] Hey Jude—RM4 (7:13)
Mixed: 8 August 1968

[B.] Hey Jude—RS21 (7:06)
Mixed: 5 December 1969

[C.] Hey Jude—RS from take 1 (3:59)

The remake of "Hey Jude" began July 31 in fresh surroundings, at the independent Trident Studios. Although

EMI had purchased an eight-track recording machine for Abbey Road, it wasn't installed yet. Trident's was fully operational, and so, fittingly, this epic became the Beatles' first eight-track recording. Four takes of the basic track were recorded the first night: Paul on piano and guide vocal, John on acoustic guitar (entering on the second verse), Ringo on drums (entering just prior to the bridge, with Ringo reportedly returning from the loo just in time to hit his mark), and George on electric guitar (during the bridges).

The first take was chosen as "best," and over the next two days, further overdubs were added. These included tambourine, bass guitar, and a redone lead vocal, with John harmonizing in places and some smooth, wordless three-part backing vocals. The massive overdubs for the coda were taped August 1, with a thirty-six-piece orchestra joining in section by section, and everyone present singing and clapping along over the slow extended fade.

Three stereo mixes were done at Trident on the second, plus a rough mono mix (from RS3 rather than the multitrack) on the sixth, which was copied back at Abbey Road the next day. After acetates were cut of this mix, three further mono mixes were completed on the eighth, with the last of these (**A**) chosen for release as the next Beatles single. On the CD single, this mix lasts a couple of seconds longer than the traditional 7:11 timing (heard on the vinyl single and noted on the session sheet). The stereo mix of "Hey Jude" (**B**), done in 1969 for the LP of the same name, fades a few seconds earlier. The *Love* remix (**C**) has everything but vocals and percussion drop out near the end, along with a bit of Paul's bass line, borrowed from later in the song.

RELEASE HISTORY

1968: **A** was released on a single worldwide and is available on the "Hey Jude" CD single.

1970: **B** was released in the United States on the LP *Hey Jude;* it was eventually included on the CD *Past Masters, Volume 2* as well as the compilation CDs *The Beatles 1967–1970* and *1*. It's also been released in truncated form in various places, usually by fading the ending early.

2006: **C** was released on the *Love* CD.

74. Studio session

Date:	9 August 1968
Time:	7:30 p.m.–2:00 a.m.
Location:	EMI Studio 2
Producer:	George Martin

[A.] Mother Nature's Son—take 2 (stereo) (3:14)

[B.] Mother Nature's Son—unknown take (mono) (0:14)

The first part of this session was devoted to overdubbing George's "Not Guilty," but Paul at least stayed afterward to record another of his Rishikesh-inspired ballads. Like its Kinfauns demo, and like "Blackbird," the initial takes of "Mother Nature's Son" were simple "sing it and pick it" performances, as Paul later described them. Singing to his acoustic guitar accompaniment, and tapping his foot to keep time, Paul laid down twenty-five takes, the penultimate of which was chosen as "best."

After the first take, Paul instructs the engineers to remove an effect from his voice, then changes his mind. Take 2 (**A**) opens with some vamping in D major; according to Mark Lewisohn, early takes featured a double-length guitar intro, but that doesn't seem to be the case here. Eventually, a unique descending riff would be used to open the song. The ending also differs: After the hummed verse, in place of the brief coda, there is another instrumental chorus, which slows down gradually and ends with some lingering hammer-ons. Paul then gives a mock nightclub intro to "Londonderry Air" and continues to strum as the recording fades out. A snippet from an unknown take (**B**) consists of the line "All day long I'm sitting singing songs for everyone," at which point Paul stops and says, "And this is one of them."

It's likely that a rough mix was made of take 24 for George Martin to arrange the brass quartet score, which would be added along with further overdubs August 20.

RELEASE HISTORY

1996: **A** was officially released on the CD *Anthology 3*. **B** was included in the *Anthology* home video set and was later bootlegged on the CD *Abbey Road Video Show*.

75. Newsreel footage

Date: 11 August 1968
Location: London
Length: 0:04

John and Yoko spent a rare weekend "on the town" in London: On Saturday the tenth, they accompanied visiting Capitol exec Stan Gortikov to a Peter Ustinov–penned play at the Queen's Theatre. Sunday night, they put in a visit to a fashion show, and a newsreel fragment from the event shows the couple observing passively, with John forcing a weak smile. The narrator comments wryly, "John Lennon and friend Yoko Ono managed to restrain their enthusiasm."

The location of this show is unclear: One source reports it was in Chelsea, another as being at the Revolution Club in Mayfair, although the latter might be confused with a show John attended there August 6. It's often dated August 12, but John was in the studio that night recording with the Beatles.

RELEASE HISTORY

This brief clip was broadcast in the E! TV special *True Hollywood Story: Beatles Wives,* which circulates on video.

76. Studio session

Date: 12 August 1968
Time: 7:00 p.m.–4:15 a.m.
Location: EMI Studio 2
Producer: George Martin

[A.] Not Guilty—take 102 (4:19)

[B.] Not Guilty—RM1 (4:11)
Mixed: 12 August 1968

After ten weeks of sessions, George had nothing to show but a single demo take of one of his new compositions. Thus he must have been disheartened by the way "Not Guilty" was cast aside, although the group turned in plenty of work. On August 7, forty-six takes of a drums, bass, electric guitar, and electric piano backing were recorded and rejected. The next night, it took a further fifty-one takes before they nailed it down with take 97. These recordings featured Paul's bass on track 1, Ringo's drums on track 2, George's electric guitar on track 3, and a harpsichord on track 4, probably played by Chris Thomas (whoever does the count-in heard on **B,** it's neither a Beatle nor George Martin).

Mark Lewisohn, apparently relying on John Barrett's tape log, reports that takes went as far as 101 that night, with 99 being chosen as "best." The session sheet tells a different story: Take 97 is the last to appear on reel E69829 and lasts 4:16. Takes 98–101, on E69830, all have a length of 4:16 and are thus probably reductions of take 97. Take 99 was indeed temporarily marked as a "best" reduction, but a new reduction was done at the start of the August 9 session. This combined the bass and drums to one track and the guitar and harpsichord to a second.

That evening, overdubs of further electric guitar and drums filled the third track. The new guitar overdub was played by George, seated in the control room while his amp was miked from the far end of an echo chamber. A second bass performance was supposedly also added, but if so, it's undetectable.

On August 12, reporter Allan Hall of the *London Sun* newspaper was present as George completed the song with his lead vocal overdub. Hall sat in the control room with the other Beatles while George sang the lyrics over and over, "in a box on the studio floor." John and Paul then joined George and experimented with adding some harmonies on a few passes, but George was still unhappy. Eventually, he hit upon the novel idea of recording his vocal from the control room, while the backing track played live through the studio monitors.

A single mono remix (**B**) was created that night, but the song was dropped from the LP's lineup by the time stereo mixing was being done in October. Ringo's copy of RM1, made August 27, was included on his sampler tape for Peter Sellers. It opens with the aforementioned count-in, mixes out a bit of the harpsichord track at 2:32, and fades out early, only to have a sudden jump in volume at 3:24.

A rough stereo dub of the original take (**A**) has escaped and reveals how much damage was done to the song for its eventual release. Geoff Emerick, not present at any of the song's original sessions, created a new version for the proposed *Sessions* LP in 1984, and sadly, this same mangled mix was used on *Anthology 3.* It opens normally enough, only differing from **A** by having the harpsichord/guitar and bass/drum track swap places. But after the first chorus, things start to go awry: The first solo break and the lines "not guilty/ for being on your street/getting underneath your feet" are chopped out. Even worse, at 1:06 the mix switches from true stereo to a murky dense pseudostereo mush, with heavy phasing effects added, presumably to make it sound more psychedelic. Superfluous edits repeat a tripleted bar in the solo and a drum fill in the coda.

A "restored complete version" tries to edit together the Emerick version with the session tape, but ends up being distracting as instruments jump around the stereo image. It's available on the CDs *Upgraded Collection—Highlights* and *Mythology, Volume 3,* both with an early fade.

RELEASE HISTORY

1985: Geoff Emerick's remix/edit of **A** created for *Sessions* began to appear on vinyl bootlegs; it can be heard on Spank's CD of that title.

1986: A copy of **B,** taken from an acetate, appeared on the vinyl bootlegs *Not Guilty* and *Nothing Is Real,* in mediocre quality.

1988: The vinyl bootleg *Ultra Rare Trax, Volume 5 & 6* included a slightly incomplete copy of **A** in excellent quality. It was copied on CDs such as *Not Guilty* and *Back-Track, Part 2,* usually running too slow.

1990: A decent-quality tape of **B** was booted on the CD *Unsurpassed Masters, Volume 4.*

1991: The bootleg CD *Unsurpassed Masters, Volume 7* contained an excellent copy of **A** from tape source, incomplete at both ends and a half step too slow.

1993: A major upgrade of **B** surfaced on the CD *The Peter Sellers Tape,* issued first on the Masterdisc label and then copied by Spank.

1996: Emerick's remix/edit of **A** was officially released on *Anthology 3.*

1999: The most complete and best-sounding version of **A** surfaced among John Barrett's cassettes; it appears on the bootleg CD *Another Sessions . . . Plus* at the correct speed.

77. Studio session

Date:	13 August 1968
Time:	7:00 p.m.–5:00 a.m.
Location:	EMI Studio 2 and annex
Producer:	George Martin

[A.] untitled jam (stereo) (1:12)

With George's song completed by an overdub taped in the control room, John felt he could do one better by recording a whole song in the control room's tiny annex, a former storage room with no soundproofing of any kind and no space for baffles. As it happened, the song was "Yer Blues," a perfect candidate for close-quarters wailing, and the result was a unique-sounding rhythm track. The only separation was afforded by facing the guitar amplifiers toward the walls and placing the mics between amp and wall. With John and George on distorted lead guitars, Paul on plodding Rickenbacker bass, and Ringo on thunderous drums, the group cranked out fourteen takes, with John singing a guide vocal.

After take 8, Paul apparently took a break while the other three jammed in E; some of this was captured on the multitrack (**A**) and later spliced from the reel and added to an "Ad-Lib" tape (E70549) alongside some ad-libs from the September 16 session. It's an energetic but sloppy bit of jamming, with particularly amateurish lead guitar playing.

Take 6 was a good performance, but so was take 14. Unable to choose between the two, John naturally decided to use them both. Reductions were made of each "best" take (6 becoming 16 and 14 becoming 17), combining the two guitar tracks to one. For the first 3:16 of the master, we hear take 17; after the guitar solo, there is an abrupt splice to the start of take 16. Overdubs on this edit would continue the next day.

RELEASE HISTORY

2000: **A** surfaced in very good quality (and a lopsided stereo mix, panned too far left) on the CDR *Down In Havana.*

78. Studio session

Date:	14 August 1968
Time:	7:00 p.m.–4:30 a.m.
Location:	EMI Studio 2
Producer:	George Martin

[A.] What's the New Mary Jane—take 2 (stereo) (0:33)

[B.] What's the New Mary Jane—take 4 (stereo) (6:40)

[C.] What's the New Mary Jane—RS2 (?) (3:09)
Mixed: 14 October 1968

[D.] What's the New Mary Jane—RS4 (6:40)
Mixed: 26 November 1969

John, Yoko, and George had been the only ones to contribute to the overdubs for "Revolution 9," and the same lineup, with the addition of Mal Evans, teamed up this evening for a (slightly) more orthodox song. "What's the New Mary Jane" was silly enough as a demo, but in John and Yoko's hands, the studio version became a haphazard rock/avant-garde crossover.

The first couple of takes were conventional enough, with George on acoustic guitar and John on vocal and piano. An excerpt of take 2 (**A**), punctuated by giggles, reveals how difficult it was for John to keep his composure. He later described the song as "Me, George, and Yoko . . . out of our minds on the floor of EMI one day . . ."

The real chaos comes with take 4, which stretches out for six and a half minutes. Unfortunately, John has only about two minutes' worth of song, so the rest of the recording consists of anything that comes to mind, using any materials at hand, until finally John calls out for a playback: "Let's hear it, before we get taken away!" Overdubs included more piano and guitar, a second vocal track (with John making no attempt to match his original vocal), and plenty of cacophonous percussion (drums, handbell, vibes, tambourine, cowbell, ratchet).

A rough mix from the original session tape (**B**) omits much of the second vocal track, but lets us hear the basic structure of the song. After three verses and choruses, Yoko begins screeching, joined by a wheezing accordion. The melody is completely lost, as the piano begins pounding away. Things calm down for some whispered "Maaaary Jaaaaane's," and the piano ascends, pounds some more, and develops into atonal jazzy improv. Someone blows a slide whistle, and John starts striking and strumming the strings of the piano. The noise builds again with a wolf call, handbell, random piano notes, and shouting, before slowly dying out in a wash of echo.

At the end of the day, a rough mono mix of take 4, pared down to a reasonable 3:15, was taken home by John. As far as he was concerned, the song was going on the album, and to that end, two fresh mono mixes were prepared September 25, and two stereo mixes October 14. Given its length, **C** is probably one of these mixes: It includes the first 2:42 of the song, followed by the portion from roughly 4:58–5:24 in the original take. When George flew to the United States October 16, he apparently carried a rough assembly of the album, which included "What's the New Mary Jane" as part of the lineup.

But that night and into the next morning, the final LP masters were being compiled at Abbey Road by John, Paul, and George Martin. Perhaps in a compromise to save "Revolution 9" from extinction, or just a change of heart, John agreed to ax the song. He didn't forget it, though, and when he was looking for suitable material for a Plastic Ono Band single in September of the following year, he had three fresh stereo mixes made. A fourth stereo mix (**D**) comes from the November 26, 1969, session (see entry for details). It contains the complete song with both vocal tracks and ends with John in mid-comment: "Let's hear it—"

The song remained unreleased until 1984, when Geoff Emerick tried to work some magic on it for the proposed *Sessions* project. Working from the original session tape, he prepared a six-minute version that uses plenty of trickery to bounce sounds from speaker to speaker and overlays vocals from the opening verse and final chorus at later points in the song. It also chops off half of the introduction, and, most dishearteningly, fades early, leaving John's pithy "taken away" remark unheard! Thankfully, the remark was tacked on when Emerick's mix was used for official release on *Anthology 3.*

RELEASE HISTORY

1972: An incomplete version of **C**, the first Beatles studio outtake to be bootlegged, surfaced on the LP *Mary Jane.* Tape logs indicate that four-track copies of this song and "Not Guilty" were made June 26, 1971, at Abbey Road, which may or may not be related to its appearance. A complete dub surfaced the following year on *Spicy Beatles Songs.*

1973: **C** appeared in true stereo for the first time on the vinyl boot *Live at the Shea Stadium 1964.* It's been copied from vinyl on the CD *Real Stereo Album 2.*

1980: An acetate containing **D** was bootlegged on the 12-inch single *What a Shame Mary Jane Had a Pain at the Party.* It was copied on the CD-Rs *Vinyl to the Core* and *Acetate Collection,* running nearly a half step too fast.

1985: Geoff Emerick's remix/edit of **B** created for *Sessions* began to appear on vinyl bootlegs; it can be heard on Spank's CD of that title as well as *Unsurpassed Masters, Volume 6* (with heavy noise reduction) and *Turn Me On Dead Man: The John Barrett Tapes.*

1988: The vinyl bootleg *Ultra Rare Trax, Volume 5 & 6* included **B** in excellent quality. It was copied on CDs such as *Not Guilty* and *Back-Track, Part 3,* usually running too slow. An incomplete copy (5:43) of this mix turned up from John Barrett's cassette dubs and is found on the CD *Another Sessions . . . Plus* from tape source.

1990: **B** appeared from tape source on the bootleg CD *Unsurpassed Masters, Volume 4.* This version had reversed channels and a narrower stereo image than previous issues.

1996: Emerick's remix/edit of **B** was officially released on the CD *Anthology 3,* with John's comment appended to the end. **A** was included in the *Anthology* home video set in mono and was bootlegged from that source on the CD *Abbey Road Video Show;* it appears in stereo on the *Anthology* DVD.

79. Studio session

Date: 15 August 1968
Time: 7:00 p.m.–3:00 a.m.
Location: EMI Studio 2
Producer: George Martin

[A.] Rocky Raccoon—take 8 (stereo) (4:09)
[B.] Rocky Raccoon—take 9 (stereo) (0:12)

[C.] Rocky Raccoon—RM1 (3:48)
Mixed: 15 August 1968

[D.] Rocky Raccoon—RS1 (3:32)
Mixed: 10 October 1968

Hearkening back to a 1965 recording schedule, the Beatles managed to rehearse, record, reduce, overdub, and remix a complete song in a single eight-hour session. It helped that the song, "Rocky Raccoon," had an easily digested chord pattern, basically Am7/D7/G7/C repeated ad nauseum.

While the Kinfauns demo had opened with the first verse, on each of these takes, Paul introduced the song by way of an ad-libbed cornball "horse opera" narration. While George watched from the control room, the others ran through nine takes of a rhythm track: Paul on acoustic guitar and vocal, Ringo on drums, and John alternating between rudimentary bass and harmonica. Take 8 (**A**) is performed at a sluggish pace and begins with John's nasal comment, "He was a fool unto himself." This leads into Paul's monologue, in which the song's hero hails from Minnesota, not Dakota. Things proceed as normal until the doctor arrives, and Paul stumbles over the phrase "stinking of gin": "Sminking?" The rest of the verse is a shambles, lyrically speaking.

But the very next take was good enough for Paul to call out for a playback before the last chord had finished: "I wanna hear that, boy! I wanna hear that!" This comment was probably mixed out during a tape reduction, but is evident in the *Anthology* video medley (**B**). Before that reduction, John's bass track was erased by a fresh bass duet from him and Paul, along with harmo-nium and an extra snare drum *thwack* to emphasize Daniel's gunshot.

The reduction into take 10 combined bass and drums, making room for a series of overdubs on the newly freed track. John added some anarchic harmonica during the "showdown" (some of his harmonica from the original rhythm track is heard earlier in the song). George Martin played a pair of honky-tonk piano solos, probably recorded using the same method as his solo in "Lovely Rita" (see the March 21, 1967, entry). A bit of harmonium for the doctor's verse and some three-part harmony vocals thereafter wrapped up the recording.

At the start of the song's one and only mono remix (**C**), John and Paul can be heard singing a bit of something in pseudo-French. This chatter and Ken Scott's "RM1" announcement were retained on the copy made August 23 for Ringo and used on his sampler tape for Peter Sellers. The main difference in the sole stereo mix (**D**) is that the drum track enters 5 seconds earlier than in mono.

RELEASE HISTORY

1968: **D** was released on stereo copies of the LP *The Beatles* worldwide and is on EMI's CD of that title. **C** was included on mono copies, released in the UK only.

1990: A very good-quality tape of the "Sellers sampler" variation of **C** was booted on the CD *Unsurpassed Masters, Volume 4.*

1993: A sonic upgrade of the "Sellers sampler" variation of **C** surfaced on the CD *The Peter Sellers Tape,* issued first on the Masterdisc label and then copied by Spank.

1996: **A** was officially released on the CD *Anthology 3.* **B** was included in the *Anthology* home video set in mono and was bootlegged from that source on the CD *Abbey Road Video Show;* it appears in stereo on the *Anthology* DVD.

80. Studio session

Date: 20 August 1968
Time: 5:00–5:30 p.m.
Location: EMI Studio 3
Producer: none

[A.] Yer Blues—RM3 (4:14)
Mixed: 20 August 1968

[B.] Yer Blues—RS5 (3:59)
Mixed: 14 October 1968

[C.] Yer Blues—RS from takes 6 and 16 (0:37)

"Yer Blues" was virtually completed August 14 with a series of overdubs on the tape's fourth track. John recorded a lead vocal, with harmonies from Paul in spots. Also added on the vocal track was some extra snare drumming to accentuate the beat during the solo, and to double the transition fill at the edit point. John's scratch vocal from the thirteenth leaks through in places because of the lack of mic separation, as do the original guitar solos, replaced by fresh overdubs and heavily flanged during mixing.

Four mono mixes were created that night, the third of which was "best"—copies were made for John, and a day later for George and Ringo. This brings up a puzzle: According to Mark Lewisohn, the "two, three" count-in wasn't recorded until August 20, as an edit piece. However, it's certainly present on Ringo's sampler tape for Peter Sellers, which presumably would have been made from his August 15 copy of RM3. In John Barrett's tape log, the edit piece is labeled "RM1" rather than "take 1," and is on a mono reel. Perhaps it's merely the original count-in, remixed louder to sound a bit more emphatic.

This "Sellers mix" also seems to be preceded by calls for takes 16 and 17, although they're buried under Ringo's homemade effects (see the late August entry). The most complete variation of the mono master (**A**) comes from an acetate, which starts with Ken Scott's "RM3" announcement, and continues a couple of seconds past the mono LP's fade. The stereo mix (**B**) fades out considerably earlier, and the mono LP apparently uses a last-minute copy of RM3, done October 18. A stereo remix (**C**) for the *Anthology* DVD syncs the two guitar tracks from take 6 (John far left, George far right) with the remaining instruments and vocals (centered).

RELEASE HISTORY

1968: **B** was released on stereo copies of the LP *The Beatles* worldwide and is on EMI's CD of that title. **A** was included on mono copies, released in the UK only.

1990: A very good-quality tape of the "Sellers sampler" variation of **A** was booted on the CD *Unsurpassed Masters, Volume 4.*

1993: A sonic upgrade of the "Sellers sampler" variation of **A** surfaced on the CD *The Peter Sellers Tape,* issued first on the Masterdisc label and then copied by Spank.

1995: A copy of **A** from acetate was included on the CD *Primal Colours.* This includes the remix announcement at the start and a longer fade.

2003: **C** was released on the soundtrack of the *Anthology* DVD.

81. Studio session

Date:	20 August 1968
Time:	8:00 p.m.–4:00 a.m.
Location:	EMI Studio 2
Producer:	George Martin

[A.]	**Mother Nature's Son—RM8**	(2:53)
[B.]	**Wild Honey Pie—RM6**	(1:07)
Mixed:	20 August 1968	

[C.]	**Mother Nature's Son—RS2**	(2:46)
[D.]	**Mother Nature's Son—RM2**	(2:46)
Mixed:	12 October 1968	

[E.]	**Wild Honey Pie—RS2**	(0:52)
Mixed:	13 October 1968	

With George enjoying a five-day weekend in Greece, this was basically a solo Paul McCartney session, and he made good use of the time, playing all instruments except the brass and completing three numbers. "Mother Nature's Son" consisted of two tracks at this point: vocal and acoustic guitar. To this, Paul added bass drum on a third track (with heavy natural echo from a stairwell near the song's end), and book-tapping percussion and extra vocal on the fourth.

At the end of the reel of "Mother Nature's Son" takes, perhaps while waiting for the studio musicians to arrive, Paul taped a demo of a song called "Etcetera," although it's not clear for what purpose. He later remembered it had been written for Marianne Faithfull, who turned it down and covered "Yesterday" instead; this would date its composition to 1965. In any case, the demo was spliced from the reel onto a 5-inch spool and taken away by Chris Thomas, George Martin's new assistant; this may indicate Paul wanted Martin to arrange a score for the song. No copy seems to have survived, but Paul recalls it wasn't much of a song.

A reduction of "Mother Nature's Son" combined the bass drum and the percussion to make room for an overdub of two trumpets and two trombones, plus Paul's brief acoustic guitar solo near the end. With the song complete, eight mono mixes were done that evening; the last of these (**A**) appears on Ringo's sampler tape for Peter Sellers. It opens with Ken Scott's "RM8" announcement and a couple of extraneous taps. The percussion is mixed very low and the acoustic guitar overdub is missing entirely. There's also a trombone line mixed out before the line "swaying daisies."

The third McCartney ditty taped this evening was a minute-long bit of filler first noted on the session sheet as "Ad-Lib" but renamed "Wild Honey Pie." In a single take, Paul screeched the "lyric" while playing acoustic guitar. This performance was tripled, with one of these tracks being flanged during mixing to give it a heavy wobble. The fourth track contained a booming bass drum, also probably recorded in the corridor. The session concluded with six mono mixes of "Wild Honey Pie," the last of which (**B**) also appears on the Sellers compilation, complete with "RM6" announcement and foot-tap count-in, plus an extra comment at the end.

During final LP mixing in October, "Mother Nature's Son" was redone for mono (**D**), but the August mix of "Wild Honey Pie" was deemed sufficient for release (minus the studio chatter and count-in). Stereo mixes of both songs (**C** and **E**) differ very little from their released mono counterparts.

RELEASE HISTORY

1968: **C** and **E** were released on stereo copies of the LP *The Beatles* worldwide and are on EMI's CD of that title. **B** and **D** were included on mono copies, released in the UK only.

1990: Very good-quality tapes of **A** and the unedited **B** were booted on the CD *Unsurpassed Masters, Volume 4.*

1993: Sonic upgrades of **A** and **B** surfaced on the CD *The Peter Sellers Tape,* issued first on the Masterdisc label and then copied by Spank.

82. Studio session

Date:	21 August 1968
Time:	7:30 p.m.–7:15 a.m.
Location:	EMI Studio 2
Producer:	George Martin

[A.] Sexy Sadie—RM5 (3:55)
Mixed: 21 August 1968

[B.] Sexy Sadie—RS3 (3:14)
Mixed: 14 October 1968

For "Sexy Sadie," the third time was the charm. This second remake began August 13 with take "100," a humorous comment on the number of rejected attempts and the number of takes for the just-completed "Not Guilty." By take 107, a backing track was perfected, with John's lead vocal on one track, his and George's electric guitars on a second, Paul's piano with delay effect on a third, and Ringo's drums on a fourth. Four reduction mixes made that night went unused.

Instead, take 107 would be reduced threefold on August 21, with each reduction clearing a single track. Judging from the stereo mix, this was the likely order of events:

1. reduction to take 112, combining piano and guitar tracks
2. simultaneous overdub of organ (Paul), tambourine (Ringo), and second lead vocal (John)
3. reduction to take 115, combining new overdub with original vocal track
4. overdub of backing vocals
5. reduction to take 117, combining new overdub with piano/guitar track
6. overdub of bass guitar (Paul)

Although George spent most of this day returning from Greece, it does sound like he arrived in time for the backing vocal overdubs. Five mono mixes were prepared that night, and the last of these (**A**) appears in unedited state from Ringo's August 23 copy. Included on the sampler tape for Peter Sellers, this variation contains a long instrumental passage from 2:56–3:34 (another bridge and partial verse), which would eventually be chopped out of both released mixes. The stereo mix (**B**) fades in the vocal and bass tracks a bit earlier than the mono, allowing some extra tambourine and bass to be heard.

RELEASE HISTORY

1968: **B** was released on stereo copies of the LP *The Beatles* worldwide and is on EMI's CD of that title. An edit of **A** was included on mono copies, released in the UK only.

1990: A very good-quality tape of the "Sellers sampler" variation of **A** was booted on the CD *Unsurpassed Masters, Volume 4.*

1993: A sonic upgrade of the "Sellers sampler" variation of **A** surfaced on the CD *The Peter Sellers Tape,* issued first on the Masterdisc label and then copied by Spank.

83. Studio session

Date: 23 August 1968
Time: 7:00 p.m.–3:00 a.m.
Location: EMI Studio 2
Producer: George Martin

[A.] Back in the USSR—RM1 (2:59)
Mixed: 23 August 1968

[B.] Back in the USSR—RS1 (2:46)
Mixed: 13 October 1968

[C.] Back in the USSR—RS from takes 5 and 6 (2:33)

A day after George returned from his Greek vacation, Ringo decided to take one of his own, although he didn't go any farther than home. Fed up with the hostile atmosphere of the protracted sessions, and reportedly upset one too many times by Paul's criticism of his drumming, the normally easygoing drummer took a hike, vowing not to return. This occurred August 22 during rehearsals for Paul's "Back in the USSR," and, astonishingly, the others decided to simply carry on without him, perhaps assuming it would all blow over in a day or two.

For the five backing track takes, Paul filled in on drums, John took over on six-string bass, and George played electric guitar. Ringo remained absent the next night as the group added overdubs on take 5: Paul's piano and George's drums (erasing John's bass track), and a track of electric guitar. This was all reduced to a single track as take 6. On two of the new tracks, Paul sang a lead vocal, backed by John and George, with all three adding handclaps. The fourth track was filled with Paul's bass, George on six-string bass, and John whacking a snare drum, which meant every Beatle but Ringo ended up playing some drums on the song! One final touch was the sound of a Viscount jet plane, added during the sole mono mix that evening.

An acetate of this mix (**A**) opens with a false start of the jet noise and Ken Scott's "RM1" announcement. Those items are omitted from Ringo's copy of RM1, made the same night and used on the sampler tape for Peter Sellers. When the song was released, it was cross-faded with "Dear Prudence"; thus the jet effects at the ending differ slightly on the released version of **A**. The stereo mix (**B**) has the jet effects in different places throughout and leaves open the vocal track during the solo, allowing various shouts and handclaps to be heard. The *Love* remix (**C**) spreads out the elements from take 5 and synchronizes them with the take 6 overdubs.

RELEASE HISTORY

1968: **B** was released on stereo copies of the LP *The Beatles* worldwide and is on EMI's CD of that title. A version of **A** with new effects for the cross-fade was included on mono copies, released in the UK only.

1990: A very good-quality tape of the "Sellers sampler" variation of **A** was booted on the CD *Unsurpassed Masters, Volume 4*.

1993: A sonic upgrade of the "Sellers sampler" variation of **A** surfaced on the CD *The Peter Sellers Tape,* issued first on the Masterdisc label and then copied by Spank.

1995: A copy of **A** from acetate was included on the CD *Primal Colours*. This includes the extra material at the beginning.

2006: **C** was released on the *Love* DVD; the CD includes a 1:54 edit of the same mix.

84. TV interview   J

Date: 24 August 1968
Time: 6:45–7:30 p.m.
Location: Studio 1, Wembley Studios
Producer: Geoffrey Hughes
Host: David Frost
Broadcast: live
London Weekend Television
Frost on Saturday
Length: 21:59

With nothing in particular to promote, apart from their relationship and artistic philosophy, John and Yoko made their first joint TV appearance on David Frost's latest chat show, on the brand-new independent station London Weekend Television.

After Frost's introduction praising their recent You Are Here exhibition, the couple enter, dressed entirely in black apart from white badges left over from the event. As he sits down, John acknowledges the show's earlier guest, Stan Freberg, who makes a joke about the studio's lack of air conditioning. John laughs and says the comment deserves a badge; Frost, also wearing one, asks Yoko to explain the idea behind You Are Here. She describes her artwork as "unfinished," illustrated by a broken cup on a white pedestal that patrons are to mend as a piece of living sculpture.

In lieu of the gallery's white canvas, studio assistants bring out a blackboard on which John has written "you are here" in chalk. He recounts how people's reactions to the original work ranged from bemusement to enthusiasm (and imitates patrons taking more than their share of badges when they think nobody is looking). A two-minute extract of their *Smile* film is then shown (still lacking a soundtrack), and the audience laughs at the punch line: It continues on a single shot of John's face for more than an hour. John compares the film to a moving portrait and insists that a lot can happen to a face in the span of three minutes.

Yoko enthuses about the positive vibrations dispersed by John's celluloid smile, and Frost asks for a definition of "vibrations." John likens them to sound waves and says that whatever a person's disposition, it will affect those he comes in contact with. He perceives the audience's vibe as interested but skeptical, and Yoko suggests it might change if they participate in the "Hammer-a-nail" piece. As John sets it up atop the blackboard, Yoko describes the piece as a way to channel aggression constructively. Two audience members volunteer to hammer nails in the block of wood and declare the action to be "satisfying" and "unbelievable." Frost warily joins in and says that he merely feels like "a man hammering in a nail." As the audience applauds this comment, John gapes nonplussed and raises Frost's arm like a referee, shouting, "The winner!"

The slightly chagrined host assumes that his reaction was reactionary, but John and Yoko insist that it's the means, not the end, that is important. Yoko displays a similar piece, "Built Around" (John's idea), taking an object and having visitors add to it. John recounts the tale of their meeting at Indica Gallery, when he hammered in an imaginary nail. Frost doubts whether imaginary deeds can be as satisfying as real ones, but John feels that fantasy is just as valid as reality.

Asked to summarize their art, he and Yoko call it an attempt to communicate. The credits begin to roll, and "Hey Jude" (described by Frost as "the newest Beatle song") begins to play. John asks for it to be turned up and exhorts the audience to "communicate" and sing along. This relatively orthodox appearance probably bolstered John and Yoko's public image, although events over the next couple of months (a drug bust and nude LP cover) would largely negate this. It would be rebroadcast as *The Best of Frost* May 18, 1969, when the now-married couple were in the thick of a peace campaign.

RELEASE HISTORY

1999: The audio of this appearance, minus the show's intro, was bootlegged in the boxed set *Mythology, Volume 3*. The video circulates from a slightly worn film print, and parts of it were rebroadcast July 26, 1998, in David Frost's *Interviews I'll Never Forget* cable special.

85. Studio session

Date:	29 August 1968
Time:	7:00 p.m.–6:00 a.m.
Location:	Trident Studios, London
Producer:	George Martin

[A.] Dear Prudence—vocal overdub (mono) (0:09)

[B.] Dear Prudence—take 1 (mono mix #1) (3:47)

[C.] Dear Prudence—take 1 (mono mix #2) (4:07)

[D.] Dear Prudence—RS1 (3:53)
[E.] Dear Prudence—RM5 (3:51)
Mixed: 13 October 1968

[F.] Dear Prudence—RS from take 1 (0:58)

With the success of "Hey Jude," the Beatles Minus One were happy to return to Trident Studios August 28 to use its eight-track machine. After fourteen hours of work, the result was a single take of John's "Dear Prudence," with John and George's fingerpicked guitars, and Paul behind Ringo's kit again, turning in his best performance ever on the skins.

Having twice as many tracks to work with as usual, no reductions were necessary during overdubbing. By the end of the August 29 session, the song included a pair of Lennon lead vocals, tambourine and various percussion, bass guitar, more electric guitar, piano, and two sets of backing vocals. The latter included contributions from Mal Evans and studio visitors Jackie Lomax and Paul's cousin John McCartney.

In contrast to the bucolic and tranquil song being recorded inside, a nasty incident occurred that evening outside the studio. Trident was located in a rather seedy section of Soho, and during the session a knife fight broke out between two men in the street. When one of the combatants was wounded and bleeding, fans waiting outside alerted Mal to call an ambulance.

Rough mono and stereo mixes were done at Trident August 30, and one or both of these may be represented by the two alternate versions available. The first of these (**B**) comes from John's tape archive and concludes with a round of applause and John's comment "Should I just do the last verse?," followed by a burst of flügelhorn and a drum roll. The second (**C**) has a clean intro, some extra bass notes at the start and ending, and mixes out everything but the vocals during the final "won't you come out to play?" It ends with a bit of the applause/horn/drum roll, followed by some extra guitar and a voice (presumably engineer Barry Sheffield) calling, "OK, rolling!" The latter may be a remnant of rehearsals erased by the master take.

Both alternates have some things in common: heavy reverb on the vocal, the fuzz guitar on the "look around" section mixed very low (particularly on **C**), and both "Dear Prudence's" missing entirely from the last verse. There is also a 9-second fragment of the isolated backing vocal track (**A**) circulating, perhaps from a mixing session.

A second unused mono mix was done at Trident October 5, and final mixing occurred eight days later back at Abbey Road. Both released mixes (**D** and **E**) sound similar, while a partial remix for the *Anthology* DVD (**F**) centers the drums.

RELEASE HISTORY

1968: **D** was released on stereo copies of the LP *The Beatles* worldwide and is on EMI's CD of that title. **E** was included on mono copies, released in the UK only.

1988: **B** was aired on episode 88-24 of *The Lost Lennon Tapes*. It was copied on the vinyl bootleg *The Lost Lennon Tapes, Volume 6*.

1997: **C** surfaced in excellent quality on the Midnight Beat CD *Gone Tomorrow, Here Today,* running nearly a half step too fast; the Repro-Man edition of that CD included a copy of **B** as a bonus track.

1998: After circulating on tape for several years, **A** was bootlegged on the *White Sessions* CD-R compilation.

1999: A speed-corrected copy of **C** was included in the boxed set *Mythology, Volume 3.*

2003: **F** was released on the soundtrack of the *Anthology* DVD.

86. Location recording   R

Date: ca. late August 1968
Location: Sunny Heights

    [A.] **applause/effects tape** (0:53)
    [B.] **music/effects tape** (1:40)

While on leave of absence from the group, Ringo had something to look forward to: He had been signed to costar opposite Peter Sellers in a film adaptation of Terry Southern's novel *The Magic Christian.* Sellers had at least a passing acquaintance with the Beatles, through mutual acquaintances such as George Martin and Richard Lester. Filming was due to start in the late fall of 1968, but production problems (mostly innumerable rewrites of the screenplay) delayed this until February of 1969. In October, Sellers would offer Ringo and family a chance to use his private yacht for a two-week Sardinian vacation.

In the meantime, Ringo busied himself at home compiling a tape for his new mate, consisting of rough mixes of many of the songs for the Beatles' upcoming album. This two-sided reel was auctioned in 1988 by Phillips, sold for £2,300, and a copy appeared on bootleg within two years.

Side 1 opens with the five songs copied for all four Beatles by Mal Evans August 23 and ends with RM4 of "Don't Pass Me By," copied for Ringo July 12. Concluding the first side, Ringo whipped up a special message for Sellers (**A**), applauding and cheering wildly ("What a show! More! Wonderful! Bravo!") as one of his dogs barked in the background. This is followed by his instruction to the listener to turn the tape over for "more crazy music," first spoken, then shouted.

Having flipped the tape, Ringo opened the second side with a mélange of "world music," overlaid with mumbling, bubbling, and thumping noises, plus a cry of "It's a raid!" (**B**); this segues directly into RM3 of "Yer Blues," copied August 15 for George and Ringo. This is followed by RM6 of "Good Night" and RM5 of "Everybody's Got Something to Hide Except Me and My Monkey," both copied July 23 for John and Ringo. The tape wraps up with three of the four songs copied by Mal Evans (one copy of each, presumably meant for Ringo) August 27; Ringo evidently decided to spare Sellers from sitting through the fourth song, "Revolution 9."

RELEASE HISTORY

1990: A very good-quality tape of **A** and the last 25 seconds of **B** was booted on the CD *Unsurpassed Masters, Volume 4.*

1993: Sonic upgrades of **A** and **B,** both complete, surfaced on the CD *The Peter Sellers Tape,* issued first on the Masterdisc label and then copied by Spank.

87. TV performance/Promo clips

Date: 4 September 1968
Time: 1:30 p.m.
Location: Stage 1, Twickenham Film Studios, London
Director: Michael Lindsay-Hogg
Host: David Frost
Broadcast: (**A** and **D**) 8 September 1968, 9:00–10:00 p.m.
London Weekend Television
Frost on Sunday
(**E** and **H**) 6 October 1968, 9:00–10:00 p.m.
CBS-TV
The Smothers Brothers Comedy Hour

[A.] **By George! It's the David Frost Theme/It's Now or Never—take 1** (0:49)
[B.] **By George! It's the David Frost Theme—takes 2 and 3** (0:59)

[C.] **Hey Jude—take 1** (7:06)
[D.] **Hey Jude—take 2** (7:05)
[E.] **Hey Jude—edit of takes 1 and 3** (7:10)
[F.] **Hey Jude—edit of takes 1, 2, and 3** (5:58)

[G.] **Revolution—take 1 (audio)** (3:20)
[H.] **Revolution—take 2** (3:34)
[I.] **Revolution—off-line fragment** (0:15)

From *London Palladium* and *Ed Sullivan* through *Shea Stadium* and *Our World,* The Beatles had excelled at using the medium of television to promote and perform their music. Their final hurrah occurred this afternoon as they videotaped spectacular promotional clips for both sides of their first Apple single.

New mixes of both songs were made, with the lead vocal tracks omitted, for Paul and John to sing on top of; a set was built at Twickenham Studios and a crew hired, helmed by Michael Lindsay-Hogg; Mal Evans rounded up an audience of fans to participate in "Hey Jude" (along with a thirty-six-piece orchestra), and David Frost was called upon to introduce the group.

Frost's introductions were taped first, on the "Hey Jude" set, with Paul seated at a piano, Ringo at his kit, John playing his Epiphone Casino guitar, and George the group's Fender VI six-string bass. Paul, George, and Ringo all sport frilly shirts, with Ringo particularly resplendent in a lime-green jacket. Between takes, they reportedly took advantage of the amplified instruments to jam a few oldies for the crowd.

After Paul asks if the orchestra can join in, he is cut off by John's count-in, and the quartet plays a haphazard version of Frost's TV theme song (**A**), composed "By George!" Martin. Frost calls them "the greatest tea-room orchestra in the world," and the camera zooms in on him for the introduction. When he finishes, John launches into a demented "It's Now or Never," and Frost asks for "one more while we're running." A second and third take (**B**) followed, beginning with the camera still zoomed in on Frost and the band attempting to play the theme again, no more successfully.

Three takes of "Hey Jude" followed, each begun by the band alone but with the audience surrounding them and joining in singing, clapping, and playing tambourine on the coda. During take 1 (**C**), John gives Paul an apologetic smile when he forgets to harmonize over the third verse, a problem rectified with take 2 (**D**).

Take 2 was aired complete on *Frost on Sunday* in the UK, prefaced by **A**. In the United States, *The Smothers Brothers Comedy Hour* broadcast an edit of takes 1 and 3 (**E**); the splice comes at 4:34, just before a close-up of John. The complete take 1 was issued by Apple as a promotional video in 1996, while the *Anthology* documentary contains an edit of all three takes (**F**), including a few glimpses of take 3 unavailable elsewhere.

In addition to the usual "Judy Judy" exclamations, the extended codas give Paul a chance to throw in plenty of ad-libs: "I should coco," "when you're smiling, the whole world smiles with you," "good night, ladies and gentlemen," "you must be joking, Jude" (all from take 1), "it's so nice to be here this evening" (from take 2), and "singing it loudly, Jude" (from take 3).

Paul also sings a snatch of the Band's "The Weight" (based around the line "take a load off, Fanny") on each take, which is the easiest way to tell them apart. The coda contains eighteen repeats of the "na na na na" chorus, and "The Weight" pops up at chorus 11 in take 1, chorus 13 in take 2, and chorus 14 in take 3. The best visual cue is the appearance of the crowd at the coda: They enter gradually in take 1, are already in place in take 2, and make a mad rush to the stage in take 3 (seen only in **F**).

"Revolution" is an exciting performance, with John singing live and Paul and George adding harmonies and "shooby-doo-wah" vocals. The band are dressed more casually, and the audience has departed; Paul is now playing his Hofner bass and George a Gibson Les Paul. The first take (**G**) has a couple of flubs: John sings "we'd all love to see the world" in the first verse, and Paul and George fail to sing during the chorus that follows. A second take (**H**) corrects these flaws, although it's marred by feedback and some sloppy singing from Paul in places. There's also an odd off-line extract (**I**) which claims to be the first few seconds of the Beatles playing along with the opening bars; it's anybody's guess what this truly is.

Take 2 was aired on *Top of the Pops* in the UK and

Smothers Brothers in the United States; Apple released a promo video of this take in 1998 with a clean intro and outro. (Paul mocks the count-in voice at the start, and John sings a bit of "It's Now or Never" at the end.) The *Anthology* documentary contains most of take 1, but cuts to take 2 toward the end (although the audio is entirely from take 1). It's obscured by narration in the middle, but a rough cut of *Anthology* that has the untouched audio of take 1 circulates.

RELEASE HISTORY

Initially, all that circulated on video were kinescope copies of **A, D,** and **H. E** and **H** appeared from video sources in the '80s and were upgraded from the *Smothers Brothers* masters in 1993, complete with the original introductions. Apple has issued several of these from clean video sources in various EPKs that circulate among collectors (**C** and **H** in 1996, a longer upgrade of **H** in 1998, and **D** in 2000). **B, F,** and **G** are available on the *Anthology* DVD, leaving only **A** unrepresented from a pure video source (plus **I,** assuming it's legitimate).

1972: The soundtracks to **E** and **H** were bootlegged on the LP *Live in Europe & US TV Casts* in decent quality.

An upgrade of **H** appeared on a bootleg single a few years later.

1985: The vinyl bootleg *Strawberry Fields Forever* contained very good copies of **A** and **D.**

1988: The vinyl bootleg *First Crazy Stretch* included a very good copy of **I.**

1994: The bootleg CD *Revolution* included excellent copies of **E** and **H,** from a video of *Smothers Brothers* with audience applause over the intros and outros of each song.

1996: The *Anthology* home video included **B, F,** and **G.** The bootleg CD *Anthropology* contains **B** and **G,** but the latter removes the second chorus voice-over by splicing in a repeat of the final chorus. The same year, **C** was issued on an Apple EPK; its soundtrack is best found on the bootleg CD *Lost and Found.*

1998: The *White Sessions* CD-R compilation contained the soundtracks to **A–E** and **G–I. H** is copied from *Revolution,* but splices in the intro and outro from a kinescope copy to omit the applause. **I** is slightly truncated.

2001: The CD-R *Video 1* included excellent copies of **D** and **H,** from the soundtrack of Apple's EPKs.

2004: A complete version of **I** appeared on the CD-R *We'd Like to Carry On.*

88. Studio session

Date: 5 September 1968
Time: 7:00 p.m.–3:45 a.m.
Location: EMI Studio 2
Producer: none

[A.] Lady Madonna/While My Guitar Gently Weeps—monitor mix of take 40 (mono) (2:15)

It's little wonder that George found the "White Album" sessions frustrating. His complaints about getting to record one song for every ten of John and Paul's seem justified, as three months into the sessions there was only one completed Harrison recording, "Not Guilty," which would end up in the reject pile. Another of his compositions, "While My Guitar Gently Weeps," was receiving just as little respect.

A full day of rehearsals July 25 yielded only a demo take. George tried again August 16, recording fourteen more takes of an acoustic guitar/organ/bass/drums rhythm track. This was reduced into take 15 but then

set aside during his trip to Greece and Ringo's absence. It was picked up again September 3 during a rather auspicious session: Although George Martin was now gone, on a well-deserved month-long vacation, Ringo was back. Having cheered up thanks to the encouragement and reassurance of his bandmates, Ringo was given a hero's welcome, his drum kit bedecked by George and Mal Evans with an abundance of flowers.

Also now present at the sessions was EMI's eight-track tape machine; having their appetites whetted at Trident was too much for the Fabs, who demanded Abbey Road's engineers stop fiddling with the damn thing and hook it up already. The reduction of "While My Guitar Gently Weeps" was copied over to eight-track tape, giving them six rather than two empty tracks to work with. It mattered little; after adding a backwards guitar solo that night and vocals, maracas, drums, and guitar two days later, George abandoned the remake.

Three more reels of rhythm tracks were taped September 5, running through take 44. Although he was less than happy about the lack of support the others had been giving this tune, George eventually settled on take 25 as the "best" of the new batch. These takes featured George's guide vocal and acoustic guitar, Ringo's drums, John's electric guitar, and Paul on either piano or organ.

On the "best" take, Paul plays piano, but in an outtake from this session (**A**), he is on organ. This comes from one of the "Beatles Chat" ad-lib tapes recorded throughout the "White Album" sessions, although our source is a monitor mix tape from the preparations for the 1983 presentation *The Beatles at Abbey Road*. It features Paul singing and playing "Lady Madonna" on the organ, followed by a verse of "While My Guitar Gently Weeps."

RELEASE HISTORY

1993: A 1:13 excerpt of **A** surfaced on the bootleg CD *Control Room Monitor Mixes* in good quality.

2002: A complete version of **A** appeared on the bootleg CD *Complete Controlroom Monitor Mixes, Volume 2*.

89. Studio session

Date:	6 September 1968
Time:	7:00 p.m.–2:00 a.m.
Location:	EMI Studio 2
Producer:	none

[A.] While My Guitar Gently Weeps—RM11 (4:44)

[B.] While My Guitar Gently Weeps—RS12 (4:43)

Mixed: 14 October 1968

Still annoyed by the lack of progress on "While My Guitar Gently Weeps," George had a brainstorm on the afternoon of September 6. While giving his pal Eric Clapton a lift to London from Surrey, George invited Clapton to join the session that night and play guitar. After some reluctance, Eric agreed, and according to George, his mere presence made the other Beatles suddenly enthusiastic about the song again.

Using the Gibson Les Paul electric guitar that he had presented to George as a gift a month earlier, Clapton erased John's original guitar track with a suitably weeping and moaning performance. Paul added bass, played through a fuzzbox, George overdubbed organ and a pair of lead vocals (with Paul harmonizing in spots), and Ringo shook tambourine and castanets. The result was a recording that George could at last contribute proudly to the album.

Mono and stereo mixes were created October 7, but then redone a week later, perhaps to increase the level of flanging on Clapton's guitar track (at his insistence, to give it a "more Beatley sound"). This effect is more marked on the mono mix (**A**), which also has the vocal tracks reduced in volume near the end, particularly the "yeah yeah's," which are prominent only in stereo (**B**).

RELEASE HISTORY

1968: **B** was released on stereo copies of the LP *The Beatles* worldwide and is on EMI's CD of that title. **A** was included on mono copies, released in the UK only.

90. Studio session

Date:	10 September 1968
Time:	7:00 p.m.–3:00 a.m.
Location:	EMI Studio 2
Producer:	Chris Thomas

[A.] Helter Skelter—RM1 (3:39)
Mixed: 17 September 1968

[B.] Helter Skelter—RS5 (4:29)
Mixed: 12 October 1968

With the schoolmasterly George Martin on sabbatical, it was left to substitute Chris Thomas to oversee the four unruly Scouse pupils. September 9 was his first official night in the producer's chair, and it was a literal trial by fire. Wanting to outdo not a Who record, but a written review of one, Paul had the notion to remake "Helter Skelter" as a savagely clamorous hard rock recording.

All the building resentments and pent-up tensions of the long summer of work were unleashed in a vicious backing track. The last and "best" of these, take 21, starts with Paul's count-in and his opening electric guitar riff. Once the verse begins, he abandons any attempt to play melodically, providing a distorted backwash of amplified racket to John and Ringo's sluggishly monstrous bass and drums accompaniment. Once the beast is finally slain, John inquires, "How's that?" and Ringo laments painfully, "I've got blisters on my fingers!"

Overdubs were completed the next night and included George's searing lead guitar, a second drum track, piano (only audible at the end of the stereo mix), backing vocals, and various noises (Mal Evans "playing" trumpet and John squawking through a sax mouthpiece). When Paul came to record his outlandish lead vocal, George spurred him on by running around the studio with an ignited ashtray raised over his head. This probably explains Paul's barely decipherable comments toward the song's end. ("Come here, son! I saw you do that, you little bugger. Get yer bloody hands on yer head, c'mon!")

The song's sole mono mix on September 17 is available from an acetate (A) that opens with a bit of stray guitar and Paul's count-in. "Helter Skelter" probably has the most disparate mono and stereo mixes of any Beatles song. It might even be that RM1 was meant to be a rough mix that they later forgot to improve upon for release. How else to explain the omission of the last minute of the song, including Ringo's infamous "blisters" comment? In addition, the stereo mix (B) uses Ringo's second drum track sparingly, largely burying it in the left channel, whereas it's prominent in mono. Some of the "horn" noises heard during the solo in mono are also mixed out in stereo.

RELEASE HISTORY

1968: **B** was released on stereo copies of the LP *The Beatles* worldwide and is on EMI's CD of that title. **A** was included on mono copies, released in the UK only.

1980: Capitol officially released **A** on the *Rarities* compilation LP.

1995: A copy of **A** from acetate was included on the CD *Primal Colours,* including the false start and count-in.

91. Studio session

Date: 16 September 1968
Time: 7:00 p.m.–3:00 a.m.
Location: EMI Studio 2
Producer: Chris Thomas

[A.] I Will—take 1 (stereo fragment) (0:06)
[B.] I Will—take 1 (stereo) (1:52)
[C.] I Will—take 19 (Can You Take Me Back) (stereo) (1:56)
[D.] I Will—take 30 (Down In Havana) (stereo) (0:37)
[E.] I Will—take 34–36 (Step Inside Love/Los Paranoias/The Way You Look Tonight) (stereo) (6:35)

[F.] I Will—take 19 (Can You Take Me Back)—RM? (0:27)
[G.] I Will—take 19 (Can You Take Me Back)—RS? (0:27)
Mixed: 16–17 October 1968

Paul began composing the melody for "I Will" back in Rishikesh (it's noted simply as "Ballad" in a list of song titles in his ashram notebook). He and Donovan tried to write some lyrics based around a lunar theme, but Paul started fresh in London with John's help. George was apparently absent September 16 as the other three recorded the song, using four-track tape for the basic takes.

Right from the first of these, "I Will" had a simple arrangement, with Paul singing and playing acoustic guitar, and Ringo and John adding various percussive instruments (drum, cymbals, maracas, and skulls). The snippet of take 1 (A) heard in the *Anthology* video outtake medley includes Paul's count-in and Ringo's subsequent request for the volume in his headphones to be lowered. The former is omitted and the latter mixed way down on the mix used for *Anthology 3* (B). Only a few vocal stumbles and rearranged words ("endear me to you") mar this performance.

In a playful mood, Paul launched into numerous improvisations, joined enthusiastically by John and Ringo, throughout the three reels of tape. Several of these were copied onto another "Beatle Chat" reel, E70549, and have made their way onto bootlegs.

Take 19 (C), better known as "Can You Take Me Back," was even good enough to make it onto the album. While it originally lasted 2:21, only 1:56 is available in bits and pieces. The first version to surface contained the portions from 0:00–0:25 and 1:08–1:56; the *Down In Havana* edit consists of roughly the first 1:09. A reconstruction on the bootleg *Studio Collection* attempts to combine the two, but omits about 18 seconds found on the earlier version.

As the second reel of "I Will" starts up (D), Paul is in the middle of another impromptu tune (something about ashes?). Ken Scott announces take 30, but this turns into a ditty about señoritas in Havana; the tape cuts just as Paul is counting in for take 31.

A few takes later, Paul performs a much longer series of unrelated tunes (E); our tape fades in as he's running through take 34, a loose version of "Step Inside

Love." As take 35 is announced, John calls out "Los Paranoias," which was apparently an in-joke fake band name. This sets the trio off into a mariachi lampoon, complete with mouth trumpet and guitar body percussion solos from Paul. John calls out "Mangoes, papayas, chestnuts from the fires," and Paul responds with a barrage of nonsense syllables ("besame" and "tikki tavi" pop out unexpectedly). When this dies down, Ken Scott calls for take 36, but they aren't quite ready to get back to business. Instead, Paul leads them through a few bars of slushy samba, reinterpreting lyrics from "I Will" and the standard "The Way You Look Tonight."

A severely edited version of takes 34 and 35 was released on *Anthology 3,* using the first 2:08 and the portion from 2:31–2:50 in **E.** While bootlegs of this material have guitar and vocal centered and percussion mixed left, this remix has guitar left, vocal centered, and percussion in the right channel.

By the third reel of tape, sixty-seven takes had been completed, and Paul chose take 65 as the "best" of these. To make room for embellishments, a four- to eight-track copy was made and called take 68. Overdubs would be completed the following night.

During final cross-fading and master tape assembly for *The Beatles* in October, two items were chosen from the many "Beatles Chat" reels assembled during the sessions. Twenty-eight seconds from the end of **C** and a bit of studio dialogue with George Martin and Alistair Taylor discussing a bottle of claret (taping date unknown) were inserted as a prelude to "Revolution 9."

RELEASE HISTORY

1968: **G** was released on stereo copies of the LP *The Beatles* worldwide and is on EMI's CD of that title, indexed as part of "Cry Baby Cry" on the first pressing. **F** was included on mono copies, released in the UK only.

1996: **B** and an edited version of **E** were released on the CD *Anthology 3*. **A** was included in the *Anthology* home video set in mono and was bootlegged from that source on the CD *Abbey Road Video Show;* it appears in stereo on the *Anthology* DVD.

1999: An edited version of **C** and a complete version of **E** surfaced in excellent quality from John Barrett's cassettes and were included on bootlegs such as *Turn Me On Dead Man: The John Barrett Tapes* and *Mythology, Volume 3.*

2000: **D** first appeared on a website and was copied on CDRs such as *Sink in the Can* and *Mything Pieces.* It appeared from tape source later that year, along with a different edit of **C,** on the bootleg *Down In Havana.*

92. Studio session

Date:	17 September 1968
Time:	7:00 p.m.–5:00 a.m.
Location:	EMI Studio 2
Producer:	Chris Thomas

[A.]	**I Will—RM2** (1:43)
Mixed:	26 September 1968

[B.]	**I Will—RS1** (1:44)
Mixed:	14 October 1968

[C.]	**I Will—RS from take 68** (0:34)

Paul probably completed the overdubs for "I Will" on his own this evening, adding a harmony vocal, second acoustic guitar, maracas, and a vocalized bass line. The latter is heard from the start in stereo (**B**) but starts only 17 seconds into the mono mix (**A**). Both mixes use ADT on the main vocal for the final verse. The *Anthology* DVD remix (**C**) centers both acoustic guitars, where the original stereo mix had split them slightly.

RELEASE HISTORY

1968: **B** was released on stereo copies of the LP *The Beatles* worldwide and is on EMI's CD of that title. **A** was included on mono copies, released in the UK only.

2003: **C** was released on the soundtrack of the *Anthology* DVD.

93. Studio session

Date: 18 September 1968
Time: 5:00 p.m.–4:30 a.m.
Location: EMI Studio 2
Producer: Chris Thomas

[A.] Birthday—RM1 (2:56)
Mixed: 19 September 1968

[B.] Birthday—RS1 (2:42)
Mixed: 14 October 1968

Whether it was the proto-punk of "Helter Skelter" or the cheesy lounge act parodies of the "I Will" session, the fun had definitely returned to Abbey Road since Ringo's return and George Martin's departure. On September 18, rather than labor over unfinished tracks or unrecorded demos, the Beatles opted for some spontaneity.

Paul arrived first with a simple guitar riff in his head and gradually developed it into a finished song by jamming with his bandmates, calling out chord changes off the top of their heads. They threw in a long drum break for good measure, during which Paul can be heard screaming to count off each of the eight bars. George's lead guitar played the main riff alongside Paul's bass, and the two duetted for a concise solo.

Within a few hours, twenty backing track takes were completed, and the party moved a few blocks east to Paul's house for further inspiration. The 1956 rock musical *The Girl Can't Help It* was being screened on BBC2 that night at 9:05, and two hours later, the Beatles returned to Abbey Road with Little Richard and Fats Domino pumping through their veins.

The "best" take (19 according to the session sheet) was copied from four-track to eight-track tape; meanwhile, John and Paul whipped up a set of birthday-related lyrics. John and Paul sang lead, with everyone supporting (including Yoko Ono and Pattie Harrison) and adding handclaps. Tambourine and piano (heavily distorted through a Vox amplifier) completed the

song, and the result was a minor classic, created from scratch.

Sometime after 4:30 a.m., the song was mixed into mono (**A**), with John commandeering the control room mic from Ken Scott to announce: "This is Ken Macintosh and the roving remixers. Take farty-one." The following day, permission was acquired to have four single acetates of this mix and four long-playing acetates of various completed songs cut for the group. One of these LP acetates has apparently survived, as the last five songs from it appear on the bootleg *Primal Colours:*

> "Everybody's Got Something to Hide Except Me and My Monkey" (RM5)
> "Yer Blues" (RM3)
> "Back in the USSR" (RM1)
> "Birthday" (RM1, including John's remix announcement and Paul's count-in)
> "Helter Skelter" (RM1)

The stereo mix of "Birthday," done October 14, is less than impressive. In mono, the drums are tight and the vocals are clean and up-front. In stereo (**B**), the instruments are all squeezed into the center of the image and the vocals are doubled with ADT, sent to far left and right. What sounds like an edit piece from 2:08–2:12 in the song has the vocal mixed out in mono, but sloppily left in ("daaaaan/aaance") for the stereo mix.

RELEASE HISTORY

1968: **B** was released on stereo copies of the LP *The Beatles* worldwide and is on EMI's CD of that title. **A** was included on mono copies, released in the UK only.

1995: A copy of **A** from acetate was included on the CD *Primal Colours,* including the studio chat and count-in.

94. Studio session

Date: 19 September 1968
Time: 7:15 p.m.–5:30 a.m.
Location: EMI Studio 1
Producer: Chris Thomas

[A.] Piggies—unknown takes (stereo) (0:12)

This session began as usual in Studio 2 with rehearsals of George's "Piggies," but when Chris Thomas spotted a harpsichord in Studio 1, he suggested they take advan-

tage of it. In turn, George suggested Chris should play the instrument, so they moved into the larger studio and taped eleven takes of a backing track on four-track tape. (Abbey Road's only eight-track machine was in Studio 2.) Although John was present, he didn't participate: In addition to Thomas's harpsichord, George sang a guide vocal and played acoustic guitar, Paul played bass, and Ringo tambourine.

The *Anthology* video's outtake medley includes two snippets of this session (**A**), not necessarily from the same take. George announces, "I'll just be singing to guide you," and Paul replies, "Fair enough" (presumably this preceded take 1). We then hear a breakdown of the bridge, as George makes a mistake and curses. Overdubs would continue the next day and be completed October 10.

RELEASE HISTORY

1996: **A** was included in the *Anthology* home video set in mono and was bootlegged from that source on the CD *Abbey Road Video Show;* it appears in stereo on the *Anthology* DVD.

95. Studio session

Date: 25 September 1968
Time: 7:30 p.m.–5:00 a.m.
Location: EMI Studio 2
Producer: Chris Thomas

[A.] Happiness Is a Warm Gun—rough mix of take 65 (mono) (2:41)

[B.] Happiness Is a Warm Gun—RM12 (2:41)
Mixed: 26 September 1968

[C.] Happiness Is a Warm Gun—RS4 (2:41)
Mixed: 15 October 1968

[D.] Happiness Is a Warm Gun—RS from take 65 (1:14)

John's "Happiness Is a Warm Gun," a song much admired by the other Beatles, was similar to "I Am the Walrus" in being a patchwork of several song fragments. Section A used the fingerpicking style John had learned in Rishikesh, also employed on "Dear Prudence" and "Julia." Section B was based on images and phrases supplied by Derek Taylor. Section C, the bluesy "I need a fix" portion, and section D, with Mother Superior, had both featured in the earlier Kenwood demo. Section E combined a spoken passage lifted from the Kinfauns demo of "I'm So Tired" with a doo-wop tune inspired by the headline in an American firearms magazine ("Happiness Is a Warm Gun in Your Hand," used as the song's working title until being shortened during the September 26 mixing session).

The result was certainly schizophrenic, but the group worked hard to make it a cohesive recording, and it paid off. Playing their standard instruments, and with John singing a guide vocal, they taped forty-five takes on September 23 and twenty-five more the next

day. In the end, take 53 had the best performance of the bulk of the song, but section E was better in take 65.

These takes were duly spliced together September 25 (the edit occurs at 1:34). In the manner of "Yer Blues," the eight-track session tapes were physically joined, rather than copies thereof, and the result was called take 65. Overdubbing could now begin, and a rough mix tape (**A**) isolates what is apparently one of the overdub tracks. It contains organ for sections A and B, distorted electric guitar for section C, hi-hat and tambourine for section D, and piano for section E. All of these can be heard in the released mixes (centered in stereo), although the organ and piano are somewhat buried.

Other overdubs included John's lead vocal, backing vocals, further bass guitar, and reportedly a tuba, although it's inaudible if present. During mixing ADT was added to John's vocal in spots, and the first half of his "I need a fix" vocal was mixed out, although it's brought in unintentionally early in stereo (**C**). The mono mix (**B**) has the spoken portion mixed far louder, plus an extra chuckle before the final drumbeat. A partial stereo remix (**D**) for the *Anthology* DVD centers the bass and drums.

RELEASE HISTORY

1968: **C** was released on stereo copies of the LP *The Beatles* worldwide and is on EMI's CD of that title. **B** was included on mono copies, released in the UK only.

1991: **A** was bootlegged on the LP *Nothing but Aging* and from tape source on its 1993 CD counterpart, *Arrive without Aging,* running a half step too slow. It's also on the bootleg CD *Control Room Monitor Mixes,* at a slightly slow speed.

2003: **D** was released on the soundtrack of the *Anthology* DVD.

96. Studio session

Date: 26 September 1968
Time: 7:00 p.m.–1:30 a.m.
Location: EMI Studio 2
Producer: Chris Thomas

[A.] Glass Onion—RM2 (?) (2:05)
Mixed: 26 September 1968

John's demo for "Glass Onion" consisted of the opening verse repeated three times, but the theme was already clear: to poke fun at the Beatlologists who scoured the lyrics of their songs for hidden meanings. With help from Paul during a visit to Cavendish Avenue, John added two more verses referring to "I Am the Walrus," "The Fool on the Hill," "Fixing a Hole," and "Lady Madonna."

The basic track (acoustic and electric guitars, bass, and drums) was recorded September 11 in thirty-four takes, the penultimate of which was "best." Overdubs began with tambourine and a lead vocal, manually double-tracked in spots, on the twelfth. Piano and more drums were added the next day, and on the sixteenth,

Paul threw in a double-tracked burst of recorder to illustrate the Fool's appearance.

A few days later, John assembled a sound effects tape for "Glass Onion," probably while messing around in the Abbey Road library September 20 to look for grunting noises for "Piggies." This tape had the following looped sounds: a ringing phone on track 1, an organ note on track 2, BBC sportscaster Kenneth Wolstenholme's cry of "It's a goal!" on track 3, and a window being shattered on track 4.

A mono remix from the twenty-sixth (**A**) incorporates these effects, mostly at the end, although the phone pops up at the beginning and in the middle. This unused mix also has John's "yeah" screams brought to the fore and allows the song's true ending to be heard (a final bass note at 1:49). String overdubs would complete the song October 10.

RELEASE HISTORY

1996: **A** was released on the CD *Anthology 3*.

97. Studio session

Date: 4 October 1968
Time: 4:00 p.m.–4:30 a.m.
Location: Trident Studios, London
Producer: George Martin

[A.] Honey Pie—RM1 (2:39)
[B.] Honey Pie—RS1 (2:39)
Mixed: 5 October 1968

With the addition of a few extra lyrics, "Honey Pie" had a smooth transition from demo to finished recording. The backing track was recorded October 1 at Trident: Paul on piano, Ringo on brush-and-cymbal work, George playing bass, and John's ukelele-flavored electric rhythm guitar. Two reels were filled with rehearsals and takes, and the best of these was labeled take 1. A rough mix of the result was given to George Martin, now back at the helm, to assist in composing a score.

In the meantime, overdubs continued on the second, with Paul's main vocal and a guitar solo from John

(later described by George as "like Django Reinhardt or something. It was one of them where you just close your eyes and happen to hit all the right notes . . ."). The studio musicians, five saxophonists and two clarinetists, performed Martin's dance-band arrangement on October 4. The final touch was Paul's rendition of the line "now she's hit the big time!" filtered and overlaid with vinyl surface noise to give the impression of a megaphone-amplified 78 RPM crooner.

The song was mixed into mono and stereo at Trident October 5 and copied over to EMItape two days later at Abbey Road. The main difference between the two mixes is that in stereo (**B**), the guitar solo enters a bit sooner but then exits early, omitting a few notes.

RELEASE HISTORY

1968: **B** was released on stereo copies of the LP *The Beatles* worldwide and is on EMI's CD of that title. **A** was included on mono copies, released in the UK only.

98. Studio session

Date: 5 October 1968
Time: 6:00 p.m.–1:00 a.m.
Location: Trident Studios, London
Producer: George Martin

[A.] Martha My Dear—RM1 (2:26)
[B.] Martha My Dear—RS1 (2:27)
Mixed: 5 October 1968

"Martha My Dear" began life as an exercise in keyboard counterpoint, probably composed by Paul early in 1968. A list of works-in-progress from his Rishikesh notebook includes two song titles, "Martha My Dear" and "Silly Girl," which were evidently merged into one. That gave him and George Martin plenty of lead time to work out an arrangement, and all was settled as they arrived at Trident October 4.

Paul sang a guide vocal and played piano, and drums were overdubbed for the song's middle portion. To the sole completed take was added a track of violins, violas, and cellos, and a track of trumpets, trombone, French horn, tuba, and flügelhorn. Once the hired musicians had departed, Paul retaped his vocal, adding handclaps over the instrumental break.

The next day, he added bass and electric guitar to complete the recording, which was then mixed into mono and stereo with ADT applied to the vocal track. Both mixes, copied over to EMItape on the seventh, sound basically identical.

RELEASE HISTORY

1968: **B** was released on stereo copies of the LP *The Beatles* worldwide and is on EMI's CD of that title. **A** was included on mono copies, released in the UK only.

99. Studio session

Date: 8 October 1968
Time: 4:00 p.m.–8:00 a.m.
Location: EMI Studio 2
Producer: George Martin

[A.] I'm So Tired—edit of takes 3, 6, and 9 (stereo) (2:08)
[B.] I'm So Tired—take 14 (stereo) (0:13)
[C.] I'm So Tired—rough mix 1 of take 14 (mono) (2:06)
[D.] I'm So Tired—rough mix 2 of take 14 (mono) (2:08)
[E.] I'm So Tired—rough mixes 3–5 of take 14 (mono) (7:22)

[F.] The Continuing Story of Bungalow Bill—RS2 (3:14)
[G.] The Continuing Story of Bungalow Bill—RM1 (3:14)
Mixed: 9 October 1968

[H.] I'm So Tired—RS5 (2:03)
[I.] I'm So Tired—RM3 (2:02)
Mixed: 15 October 1968

This overnight session was especially productive, resulting in two more completed John Lennon tracks for the album. First up was "I'm So Tired," perfected in fourteen takes with Paul's bass on track 1, Ringo's drums on track 2, John and George's rhythm guitars on track 3, and John's lead vocal on track 4. *Anthology 3* contains a collage of three of these takes (**A**); the edits seem to be at 0:08 (between the first "I'm" and "so") and 0:54 (before the first bridge). Apart from John's count-in and a few extra guitar phrases, there is little difference between this assembly and the final performance.

Overdubs on take 14 included John's second vocal, with harmony from Paul (track 5), shuffling drums, guitar fills, and electric piano (track 6), a snare drum backbeat for the middle eights (track 7), and organ and lead guitar (track 8). The snippet in the *Anthology* video (**B**) is a remix of the song's ending, with John's muttering (you know, "mih ssim, mih ssim, nam daed si luaP") entering earlier and the guitar from track 8 more prominent.

What seem to be extracts from the mixing session have survived on a rough mix tape, although these are not finished mixes, just attempts at balancing levels. The first (**C**) isolates tracks 7 and 8 and ends with the tape being wound back. After scrutinizing those tracks, John opted to include only the organ from track 8 at certain points and basically ignore the guitar from that track. **D** is a first attempt at timing the appearances of track 8; also prevalent are tracks 2, 3, 4, and 7. This begins with John's count-in and ends with George's comment from the session tape: "... that going into the second time of so—"

Several more attempts, all basically identical to **D**, follow in **E**. This includes two playbacks, each preceded by a false start, and a breakdown. The final released mixes sound similar to each other, with Paul's harmony vocal being mixed a bit louder in mono (**I**).

"The Continuing Story of Bungalow Bill" was a much more cheerful recording, harking back to earlier sing-alongs such as "Yellow Submarine" and "All You Need Is Love." The basic track, completed in just three takes, probably consisted of bass, drums, and a pair of acoustic guitars. John added his sarcastic lead vocal, joined by Yoko on the final verse. A second vocal track featured John's exhortations of "all the children sing!" followed by an en masse rendition of the chorus, with singing, whistling, clapping, and a tambourine.

Once again, Chris Thomas was called in to add some keyboard parts; this time a Mellotron imitating mandolin for the verses and trumpet for the coda. Another stock Mellotron tape was joined to the front of the song as an edit piece (either during mixing or final LP assembly). This virtuoso Spanish guitar run was reportedly originally performed by Australian session man Eric Cook. The song's final mono and stereo mixes, created back to back on John's twenty-eighth birthday, sound nearly identical.

RELEASE HISTORY

1968: **F** and **H** were released on stereo copies of the LP *The Beatles* worldwide and are on EMI's CD of that title (with the Mellotron intro to **F** indexed as part of "Wild Honey Pie"). **G** and **I** were included on mono copies, released in the UK only.

1991: A tape of **C–E** began to circulate; all tracks from this source run a half step too fast. Later that year, **C** was bootlegged on the LP *Nothing but Aging*.

1992: **D** was bootlegged on the LP *Arrive without Travelling*.

1993: **C** and **D** appeared from a tape source on the bootleg CD *Arrive without Aging*. Soon afterward, **C–E** were bootlegged on the CD *Control Room Monitor Mixes*, still running way too fast.

1996: **A** was released on the CD *Anthology 3*. **B** was included in the *Anthology* home video set and was later bootlegged on the CD *Abbey Road Video Show*.

100. Studio session

Date:	9 October 1968
Time:	7:00 p.m.–5:30 a.m.
Location:	EMI Studio 2
Producer:	George Martin

[A.]	**Long Long Long—RS4** (3:02)
Mixed:	10 October 1968

[B.]	**Long Long Long—RM3** (3:02)
Mixed:	14 October 1968

George's love song to God had the working title "It's Been a Long Long Long Time." He apparently composed it around the middle of August, borrowing heavily from Bob Dylan's "Sad-Eyed Lady of the Lowlands" for the melody.

John was absent October 7 as the basic tracks were recorded (there's no evidence of John attending any sessions from October 3–7). These featured George's acoustic guitar and delicate vocal, Paul on Leslied organ, and Ringo playing alternatively discreet and accentuated drum passages. After four reels and sixty-two takes, they reused the first reel to save tape and hit on the master by take 67. The infamous "Blue Nun wine bottle rattling on organ speaker" that ends the song was a happy accident at first, but they emphasized the effect by redoing it and adding a snare roll, some Yoko-like wailing, and sharp acoustic guitar strumming.

The next day, George double-tracked his vocal and added more acoustic guitar, then Paul overdubbed his bass part. The song was finished on the ninth with Chris Thomas playing piano on the middle eight and Paul tossing in some harmony vocals. Unusually, the song was mixed first for stereo; in mono (**B**) the volume is generally higher, with less of a contrast between quiet and loud sections. The second lead vocal also enters slightly earlier, and the wailing at the end is much softer.

RELEASE HISTORY

1968: **A** was released on stereo copies of the LP *The Beatles* worldwide and is on EMI's CD of that title. **B** was included on mono copies, released in the UK only.

101. Studio session

Date: 9 October 1968
Time: 7:00 p.m.–5:30 a.m.
Location: EMI Studio 1
Producer: none

[A.] Why Don't We Do It in the Road—take 4 (mono) (2:12)

At some point during the "Long Long Long" session, perhaps when Chris Thomas was occupied with his piano overdub, Paul and engineer Ken Townsend stole across to Studio 1. Using its four-track machine, Paul recorded a song inspired by his observations of monkey mating rituals in Rishikesh.

Singing and playing acoustic guitar on track 1 of the tape, Paul taped five takes of the basic rhythm. According to Mark Lewisohn, each of these takes began with thumps on the guitar body; this seems to have been chopped off from take 4 (**A**) on *Anthology 3*. Instead it opens with a verse sung in relaxed falsetto followed by a verse in agitated shouting. The third verse is a mix of the two styles, and for the last verse, he returns to falsetto, altering the lyric to "People won't be watching us." After he shouts the title line again, Paul stops and asks Townsend, "What did you think of all that, d'you think I could do it better?"

The fifth take was decidedly better, and Paul added a piano to track 2, leaving further overdubs for the next session.

RELEASE HISTORY

1996: **A** was officially released on *Anthology 3*.

102. Studio session

Date: 10 October 1968
Time: 7:00–10:30 p.m.
Location: EMI Studio 2
Producer: George Martin

[A.] Glass Onion—RS2 (2:17)
[B.] Glass Onion—RM11 (2:16)
Mixed: 10 October 1968

[C.] Piggies—RM4 (2:03)
[D.] Piggies—RS3 (2:04)
Mixed: 11 October 1968

[E.] Glass Onion—RS from take 33 (1:21)

The day after the initial session for "Piggies," the four-track recording of take 11 was transferred to eight-track and called take 12. George then added his lead vocal, heavily filtered for the bridge, and he, John, and Paul harmonized on the last verse in bombastic fashion. John then assembled a tape loop of some real pigs grunting, taken from a sound effects tape (transferred originally from a 78 RPM disc). This probably wasn't added to the tape until the mixing stage, however.

The other effects assembled that day were for "Glass Onion," but despite their use in a rough mono mix (see the September 26 entry), John discarded them in favor of George Martin's string arrangement. On October 10, a string octet added parts to "Piggies" (one track for violins and violas, one for cellos) and "Glass Onion." The latter included "Walrus"-like glissandos, in keeping with the song's self-referential theme.

Each song had a string coda tacked on; for George's it was a sort of reverse "Good evening, friends!" and for John's a rising and falling of diminished chords (the edit at 1:48 clips Paul's final bass note). The mixes on "Glass Onion" differ mainly in the level of vocal tracks: In mono (**B**) a squeak at 1:00 and the yelling after the bridge are omitted. "Piggies" was raised from the key of G to G-sharp during mixing and differs in the placement of pig noises. In mono (**C**), the first grunt (0:15) is louder; in stereo (**D**) there is an extra grunt at 1:30, and the ending grunts are slightly different.

The *Love* remix of "Glass Onion" (**E**) includes elements from "Things We Said Today," "Hello Goodbye," "Magical Mystery Tour," "Penny Lane," "Only a Northern Song," and "Eleanor Rigby."

RELEASE HISTORY

1968: **A** and **D** were released on stereo copies of the LP *The Beatles* worldwide and are on EMI's CD of that title. **B** and **C** were included on mono copies, released in the UK only.

2006: **E** was released on the *Love* CD.

103. Studio session

Date: 10 October 1968
Time: 7:00 p.m.–7:15 a.m.
Location: EMI Studio 3
Producer: none

[A.] Why Don't We Do It in the Road—RS from takes 4 and 5 (0:20)

[B.] Why Don't We Do It in the Road—RM1 (1:39)

[C.] Why Don't We Do It in the Road—RS1 (1:39)

Mixed: 16–17 October 1968

Paul's stealth recording continued in Studio 3, while strings for John and George's songs were being recorded in Studio 2. Once again, Ken Townsend worked the board, and this time Ringo joined the fun. Still using four-track tape, the duo added bass and drums, probably on track 3 of the tape. On track 1, Paul redid his lead vocal (retaining only the acoustic guitar thumping, and thus erasing the rest of the original guitar performance). On track 2, he added some handclapping preceding the piano's entry; track 4 was filled with a second lead vocal performance. A reduction into take 6 combined tracks 1 and 4, making room for Paul's final overdub, electric guitar.

John later claimed to be hurt by his noninvolvement in the recording, saying he could have sung it better. Presumably he wasn't as jealous of other songs such as "Long Long Long" and "Martha My Dear," neither of which he bothered to participate in. "Why Don't We Do It in the Road" was the last song to be mixed for the album; in mono (**B**) the handclapping is omitted.

The *Anthology* home video has a curious variation of this song (**A**) during the "White Album" outtake medley. The first portion appears to be a mélange of takes 4 and 5, playing simultaneously. Paul is heard testing his microphone—"Hello? Yeah, okay."—but it's not clear which take that comes from (perhaps the vocal overdub on take 5). The last 7 seconds are apparently from the end of take 5, with the second vocal mixed prominently and no electric guitar added yet.

RELEASE HISTORY

1968: **C** was released on stereo copies of the LP *The Beatles* worldwide and is on EMI's CD of that title. **B** was included on mono copies, released in the UK only.

1996: **A** was included in the *Anthology* home video set in mono and was bootlegged from that source on the CD *Abbey Road Video Show;* it appears in stereo on the *Anthology* DVD.

104. Studio session

Date: 13 October 1968
Time: 7:00 p.m.–6:00 a.m.
Location: EMI Studio 2
Producer: George Martin

[A.] Julia—take 2 (fake stereo) (1:54)
[B.] Julia—take 3 w/dialogue (stereo) (0:15)

[C.] Julia—RS1 (2:52)
[D.] Julia—RM1 (2:52)
Mixed: 13 October 1968

John had already settled on how "Julia" should sound: fundamentally like his guitar and voice demos. So it's no surprise that he used four-track tape and worked simply, beginning with a basic acoustic guitar performance. The second of these takes (**A**) has John singing a bit of vocal to guide himself. A flubbed note in the second verse is overlooked, but in the third verse, he suddenly pauses and tries to continue playing as though nobody would notice. Paul, in the control booth, does, and the two have a reversed-role replay of their conversation during the "Blackbird" session (see the June 11 entry). Paul plays the "too hip" producer and John the befuddled rock star, asking if he couldn't just pick up where the last take left off. Paul plays along and says John can just "drop in" the rest of the song.

Instead, he opted for a third take, which was flawless. A pair of lead vocal tracks, overlapping in places, and a second acoustic guitar track were all it took to wrap things up. A slightly alternate mix of the end of take 3 (**B**) appears in the *Anthology* video's outtake medley. This is overlaid with a comment from John that seems to refer to the cause of take 2's breakdown. ("The last mistake was entirely when I just took me mind off it for a second.") There is no appreciable difference between the released mixes, both prepared later that same night.

1968: **C** was released on stereo copies of the LP *The Beatles* worldwide and is on EMI's CD of that title. **D** was included on mono copies, released in the UK only.

1996: **A** was released on the CD *Anthology 3*. **B** was included in the *Anthology* home video set and was later bootlegged on the CD *Abbey Road Video Show*.

105. Studio session

Date:	14 October 1968
Time:	7:00 p.m.–7:30 a.m.
Location:	EMI Studio 2
Producer:	George Martin
[A.]	**Savoy Truffle—RM6** (2:53)
[B.]	**Savoy Truffle—RS2** (2:53)
Mixed:	14 October 1968

George decided to pay tribute to his pal Eric Clapton with a song poking fun at the Cream guitarist's love of Creme Tangerine and other sweets. A manuscript reproduced in George's book *I Me Mine* shows the song nearing completion. Both verses are finished, borrowing heavily from the names of real chocolates in Mackintosh's Good News assortment (to which George added pineapple heart, cool cherry cream, nice apple tart, and coconut fudge). The first bridge is also included, with the sweat filling your "brow" (crossed out and replaced with "head"). Derek Taylor's suggestion of "You know that what you eat you are" was the catalyst for the second middle eight.

"Savoy Truffle" was recorded at Trident October 3, resulting in a basic take of rhythm guitar, bass, and drums. Two days later, George added his lead vocal, with Paul harmonizing in places. Back at Abbey Road on the eleventh, a saxophone sextet added the peppery distorted brass score, a terrific Chris Thomas arrangement. The final overdubs for the song (and indeed, the entire LP) were taped on the fourteenth: Chris Thomas played electric piano and organ, George added his lead

guitar parts, and someone (not Ringo, who had already departed for Sardinia) shook a tambourine and beat a set of bongos.

The song was mixed into mono and stereo that same day (early on the morning of the fifteenth, most likely), using ADT to double the vocals and saxophones. In mono (**A**), the organ is absent from the final verse and there is a strange gargling noise as the guitar solo begins. In stereo (**B**), there is extra lead guitar during the second chorus (one note of this peeks through in mono) and the solo ends differently.

The fruits of nearly twenty weeks of work were ready for harvest. Having done his part, George took off for America on the sixteenth, leaving the dirty work (picking a song order, preparing cross-fades and effects, doing last-minute edits) to John, Paul, George Martin, and the Abbey Road staff. This process would take twenty-four solid hours of labor, from 5 p.m. on the sixteenth to 5 p.m. the following day. On the seventeenth, a copy tape of the stereo master only was taken by George Martin to ship off to Capitol (EMI no longer released monophonic Beatles LPs in the United States). By the twenty-first, both mono and stereo "mothers" had been cut at Abbey Road and the "White Album" was born.

1968: **B** was released on stereo copies of the LP *The Beatles* worldwide and is on EMI's CD of that title. **A** was included on mono copies, released in the UK only.

106. Newsreel footage   J

Date:	19 October 1968
Location:	Marylebone Magistrates' Court, London
Length:	1:31

Although he had been tipped off well in advance, John was unable to avoid being busted by Scotland Yard's drug squad on October 18. He did his best to remove all traces of illicit substances from the Montague Square flat he and Yoko were borrowing from Ringo, but it seems Sgt. Pilcher was able to track down long-lost portions of cannabis resin lurking in a film canister and in a binoculars case. John and Yoko were taken to Marylebone Lane station and charged with possession and obstruction.

The next day, they appeared in court and were released on bail. Color footage exists of their struggle to get through a hostile throng outside the courthouse to their car, escorted by officers and accompanied by Peter Brown. A photograph of this traumatic event served as the back cover of John and Yoko's second LP, *Unfinished Music No. 2: Life with the Lions.*

RELEASE HISTORY

This black-and-white footage circulates as part of the Austrian TV documentary *John Lennon & Yoko Ono.* Some color news footage appears in the documentary film *Imagine: John Lennon,* and 10 seconds of silent ITV News footage capturing their arrival with Neil Aspinall circulates.

107. Studio session   P

Date: July–October 1968
Location: Trident Studios, London
Producer: Peter Asher

[A.] Carolina in My Mind (3:34)

Who says nepotism doesn't pay? Paul's brother-in-law-in-waiting, Peter Asher, had been hired by Apple to sign new talent in early 1968. His prize discovery was a young Boston-born singer and songwriter, James Taylor, who had arrived in London that spring. By July, as Peter Asher was ready to begin producing Taylor's first album (working title *James Taylor and Son*), things had fallen apart irreparably between Paul and Jane Asher.

Perhaps that explains why Paul's contribution to the album was limited to playing bass on one song, the excellent "Carolina in My Mind." It sounds as though Paul played his new Fender Jazz Bass, used extensively on the "White Album" in August and September. (The book *Many Years from Now* claims that Paul plays drums on the song, but this is undoubtedly an error.)

Taylor's association with Apple was fairly miserable. Perhaps due to the friction between McCartney and Asher camps, Taylor's releases received minimal publicity. "Carolina in My Mind" was released as a single, but only in the United States. It struggled up to number 118 in the charts for a single week; the LP didn't chart at all. It was only after Asher, now managing Taylor, took him to Warner Bros. in 1970 that Taylor tasted success with his second LP, *Sweet Baby James.* Suddenly, the Apple LP was in the U.S. charts, racking up a respectable twenty-eight weeks in the top 200. In a cynical move, Apple tried to cash in by reissuing "Carolina in My Mind" as a single (edited to 3:06), this time in both the United States and UK. It bettered its previous U.S. chart position, riding the coattails of "Fire and Rain" all the way to number 67.

RELEASE HISTORY

1968: This song was released on the LP *James Taylor,* reissued on CD by Apple in 1991.

108. Radio interview   G

Date: ca. 4 November 1968
Location: KPPC Studios, Pasadena
Interviewer: Don Hall, Charles Laquidara
Broadcast: KPPC-FM, Pasadena
Length: 24:05

In the midst of producing songs for Jackie Lomax's debut LP in California, George attended a Capitol Records press party, during which he was approached by DJ Charles Laquidara, representing underground radio station KPPC-FM in Pasadena. The call letters were derived from its location: The station had begun broadcasting from the basement of the Pasadena Presbyterian Church on November 1, 1967. George agreed to Laquidara's request for an interview, and the pair met at the station a few days later to record it.

Laquidara and Don Hall identify themselves to open the tape, followed by the sounds of George settling in at the mic. He describes *The Beatles* as having "four sides, ninety-five minutes, thirty-one tracks" and offers to play it for the DJs after the interview. Since the finished album has thirty tracks and lasts roughly ninety-three minutes, it's likely he had a rough assembly, which included the 3:11 edit of "What's the New Mary Jane." (We know the extra song can't be "Not Guilty," since George says he's written four songs for the LP.)

He describes running Apple as hard work but worthwhile, and he plugs an upcoming album by "a guy who writes all his own material," James Taylor. Although George says it'll be out in the United States in a couple of weeks, Taylor's illness would postpone its release until the following February (in the UK, it came out in early December). The DJs praise *Magical*

Mystery Tour, which they had seen in May during one of its limited U.S. runs, at the Esquire Theatre in Pasadena. While George considers the film "quite old now," he still blames the British press for ruining America's chance to see it. He reveals that the BBC even tried to censor a quite harmless scene: Buster Bloodvessel's romantic beach-strolling daydream with Aunt Jessie.

A glitch in the tape obscures the next question, about *Yellow Submarine,* which would have its Hollywood premiere in a couple of weeks. (George declined to attend.) George admits that he liked the movie a lot more than he anticipated, singling out the Seas of Holes and Monsters as effective sequences. Someone asks about cartoon Ringo's "born lever-puller [Liverpooler]" pun, which doesn't ring any bells with George, not least because the secondhand quote is mangled to "I just love to pull levers."

One of the DJs, quoting his own Zen Buddhist mentor, disparages Maharishi Mahesh Yogi for his soft stance on military escalation. George halfheartedly defends the guru with a bit of specious, circular logic ("everything in the world is right and wrong . . . but in actual fact, they're both the same thing"), although he does rightly point out that in the modern age, it made sense for Maharishi to try to spread his teachings through modern means of communication, such as appearing on the *Tonight Show.*

This leads to a discussion about the legalities of pot smoking, and George ponders the true meaning of the slogan he'd seen on LAPD squad cars, "To serve and protect." He wonders whether they truly serve all the citizens, and if they protect anything other than their own jobs by blindly enforcing rules (tossing in a quote from "The Weight" for good measure). George goes on to compare the counterculture in the United States and UK, explaining that England has revolutionaries too, just on a smaller scale.

Talk turns to music, specifically the current "British blues boom" epitomized by groups such as John Mayall's Bluesbreakers. George describes the "White Album" as heavier than usual, but says he would hate to be stuck "for the rest of your life playing twelve-bar." He

sings a bit of "Yer Blues," which he jokes is by "T-Bone Lennon," and wonders how it will be received by blues purists. George also recalls how great Donovan sounded writing and playing new songs in Rishikesh accompanied by just his guitar, and he expresses dismay at how the same songs often fell flat when embellished in a studio.

It's pointed out that in the United States, "they're having elections now" (narrowing down the dating of the tape), and George proclaims the entire affair to be "a waste of time," since none of the candidates are to his liking. He opts instead to vote for Pat Paulsen, a comedian on *The Smothers Brothers Comedy Hour* whose tongue-in-cheek TV "campaign" George had evidently been following in the past few weeks. Within a fortnight, George himself would show his support by appearing on the program (see the November 15 entry).

Although he finds presidents and prime ministers to be largely ego-driven positions, George has a soft spot for the royal family, saying that Elizabeth II was chosen to be queen by karma (or as he puts it, "the fickle finger of fate," proving he was also familiar with *Rowan and Martin's Laugh-In*) rather than a desire for power. He also relates the significance of Guy Fawkes Day, fast approaching and later immortalized in John's *Plastic Ono Band* song "Remember."

Asked if there will be a 1968 Christmas record for the Beatles fan club, George says they'll probably record it around the first week of December. Instead, tapes recorded separately over the next month would be patched together by Kenny Everett (see the December 1968 entry). The DJs are curious about the existence of underground radio in England, but George tells them the closest thing would be the now-defunct pirate stations that competed with the BBC until mid-1967. The interview wraps up with George doing a station ID for "Wonderful KPPPPPPC"; his effort is duly proclaimed to be "outta sight."

RELEASE HISTORY

This interview circulates in very good quality among tape collectors.

109. Studio session

G

Date: 12 November 1968
Time: 2:00–5:00 a.m.
Location: Sound Recorders Studios, Los Angeles
Producer: George Harrison

[A.] No Time or Space—RS? (25:04)

Among the benefits of working in California were a new range of musicians and facilities George hadn't en-

countered at Abbey Road. One such modern-day marvel was the synthesizer, just coming into use on rock recordings. On the evening of November 11, synth pioneer Bernie Krause was hired to play his Moog III on five of Jackie Lomax's recordings. Producer George Harrison was intrigued by the machine and asked Krause to demonstrate its full range of capabilities. Early into the next morning, Krause did so as the tapes rolled.

According to Krause, George used this recording (**A**) pretty much verbatim (edited down from thirty minutes) on his experimental LP *Electronic Sound*. As far as the LP sleeve was concerned, it was a George Harrison performance, although at times Apple gave Krause credit for "assistance." Whatever the true case, neither man had anything to be proud of.

The track is a seemingly interminable display of white noise, modulated and adjusted incoherently. At times, it resembles an Atari 2600 video game or the soundtrack to a low-budget sci-fi film. The first 8:26 is mono, after which the signal and echo are panned and ping-ponged between the channels.

Among the effects produced: plenty of static, percussive gunshots/firecrackers, howling wind, bubbles, a siren, a vacuum cleaner, Morse code, a dentist's drill, the rumble and horn of a lorry, an alarm, shrill whistling, beeps and blips, a furious hailstorm, chirping and zapping, and a speeding race car. At one point, it sounds a bit like an electric guitar, but only incidentally does the noise ever approach music, and then for mere seconds at a time.

I'm not sure what's more amazing: that EMI agreed to distribute this album, or that enough Americans bought a copy for it to reach the top 200 for two weeks. (See the February 1969 entry for details of the flip side.)

RELEASE HISTORY

1969: **A** was released on the Zapple LP *Electronic Sound;* U.S. copies inadvertently swapped the titles between the album's two cuts, an understandable error. The LP was reissued on CD in 1996 in the UK and Japan only.

110. TV appearance   G

Date:	15 November 1968
Location:	CBS-TV Studio, Hollywood
Host:	Tommy Smothers, Dick Smothers
Broadcast:	17 November 1968, 9:00–10:00 p.m.
	CBS-TV
	The Smothers Brothers Comedy Hour
Length:	2:38

As noted previously, George was a big fan of the Smothers Brothers' slightly subversive CBS variety show. Tommy Smothers had helped organize the 1967 Monterey Pop Festival, along with Derek Taylor, and it was probably Derek's idea to have the Brothers' show air the U.S. premieres of the promo clips for "Hey Jude" and "Revolution."

George readily agreed to videotape an appearance during his stay in California, and Tommy recalled that "he came over and we spent a lot of time watching some of the old tapes and some of the newer shows together. He was very charming but a little uncomfortable by himself on the show." That pretty much sums up George's cameo appearance, which came at the top of the show.

After announcing the evening's guests (the Committee, Dion, Jennifer Warnes, and Donovan), Dick declares that his brother has a special guest of his own. It turns out to be a Beatle, "not the kind of beetle you would expect it to be," but "the kind of Beatle that . . . you hoped it would be." George strolls out to shrieks of delight from the audience, wearing a leather jacket, frilly yellow shirt, and green striped pants. He flashes a peace sign and gestures for quiet.

The brothers praise the "Hey Jude" clip, and George jokingly introduces Tommy to "my brother, Dick." Finally, George declares that he has "something very important to say on American television." Tommy notes how difficult a task that can be (the series had constant battles with the network censors), a sentiment the audience seems to share. George, quite blatantly reading from a cue card, encourages them to keep trying to speak their minds.

Although it was short on entertainment value, George's appearance was an important show of support, particularly in the wake of Richard Nixon's election. By the end of the season, the show would be yanked from the air for good.

RELEASE HISTORY

1999: The audio portion of this appearance was included in good quality on the CD-R *Telecasts Four*. It also circulates on video thanks to a rebroadcast on the cable channel E!

Date: 20 November 1968
Location: 7 Cavendish Avenue, London
Interviewer: Tony Macarthur
Broadcast: 21 November 1968, 7:30–9:30 p.m.
Radio Luxembourg
Length: 17:07

For the first time, the Beatles failed to make any major BBC Radio appearances upon the release of a new album. With Ringo busy moving house, John in the hospital with Yoko, and George still in the United States, it was left to Paul to promote *The Beatles,* recording a lengthy at-home interview for Radio Luxembourg, to be broadcast on the eve of the album's release.

Although most of the LP was probably aired (the circulating tape omits the music), along with remarks from *Daily Express* columnist Judith Simons, Paul chose to comment only on the songs he had written or sung lead on, plus his personal favorite, "Happiness Is a Warm Gun," and the LP closer, "Good Night" (perhaps to quash any notion that he had written it). As the conversation opens, interviewer Tony Macarthur expresses dismay that the album is not a progression from *Sgt. Pepper,* but Paul calls it "another step, but it's not necessarily in the way people expected." He says they deliberately tried to return to playing as an ensemble, rather than getting lost in a sea of orchestras and effects. Paul agrees that the songs will also be easier to perform live, hinting at a rumored but yet unannounced return to the stage.

"Back in the USSR" is described as the tale of a Russian spy who's returning from a long stint in America, its form inspired by Chuck Berry's "Back in the USA." Mocking overanalytical rock critics, Paul declares that "it concerns the attributes of Russian women—sole element created by George's guitar and heavy brass!" He declares the "Jamaican track," "Ob-La-Di, Ob-La-Da," to be mainly his own composition, since John is "a bit more Nigerian influenced."

Apparently seeing no need to comment on "Wild Honey Pie," Paul moves on to "Happiness Is a Warm Gun," praising the lyrics as good poetry. "Martha My Dear," on the other hand, is described as little more than a series of words to fit the preexisting melody.

Paul goes so far as to claim that he never tries to inject serious social commentary into his songs (what were "Eleanor Rigby" and "She's Leaving Home" about, then?), and concludes that "it's just me singing to my dog."

Illustrating his earlier point, Paul says that if "Blackbird" had been written for *Sgt. Pepper,* they might have ended up cluttering its arrangement with strings or brass overdubs. He relates how "Rocky Raccoon" was composed on a Rishikesh rooftop, and how its protagonist originally had the surname "Sassoon." Macarthur asks what exactly they should be "doing in the road," and Paul replies, "Dance, Tony, dance!"

In discussing "I Will," Paul stresses how diverse the styles of music are throughout the LP, attributing this to the Beatles' need to satisfy requests for everything from rhumbas to rhythm and blues in the nightclubs of Hamburg. After Paul tells the story of the recording session for "Birthday" (see the September 18 entry), Macarthur points out that many of the new songs are centered around acoustic guitar. Paul explains that it's down to the way they were composed in Rishikesh, and that after John's fingerpicking lessons from Donovan, "he sort of stuck it in everything." Paul's only comment on "Mother Nature's Son" is to remind people that he was born in Woolton Hospital, Liverpool, rather than "a poor young country boy."

The well-known tale of the inspiration for "Helter Skelter" is imparted, and Paul explains that his father's playing of "fruity old songs" probably inspired "Honey Pie." To introduce "Good Night," he praises John's melody, Ringo's singing, and George Martin's arrangement. After the final song is played, Paul returns for a final word, thanking the listeners on behalf of himself and the *Beatles Book Monthly* magazine!

RELEASE HISTORY

1999: This interview was included on the bootleg CD boxed set *Mythology, Volume 3,* running noticeably fast. The timing listed above is from a previously circulating copy. Both copies are from the same fair-quality, off-air source, but in-line excerpts do exist, pointing to the possible existence of the full broadcast tape.

Date: ca. 22 November 1968
Location: EMI Studios, London (?)

[A.] **"How Do You Do"** (2:00)
[B.] **Blackbird** (2:52)
[C.] **The Unicorn** (1:03)
[D.] **Laleña** (3:13)
[E.] **"Heather"** (2:16)
[F.] **Mr. Wind** (1:35)
[G.] **The Walrus and the Carpenter** (1:06)
[H.] **"Land of Gisch"** (0:45)

This entertaining tape seems to stem from a session for Mary Hopkin's *Postcard* LP. Paul produced the album, and Donovan contributed a number of his own compositions. According to Hopkin, one Friday night at EMI, Donovan arrived at the studio: "We'd recorded his 'Happiness Runs' earlier in the week and we thought how about asking him if he's got any more. He said how about these, and got out his big book!" The result was two more songs, "Voyage of the Moon" and "Lord of the Reedy River," both of which feature Paul and Donovan duetting on acoustic guitars.

That may be the very session heard on this tape, since Donovan does seem to be running through his catalog of unrecorded songs, and he and Paul both strum acoustics throughout. If it was a Friday night, the fifteenth is ruled out by Donovan's presence in the United States (see the November 15 entry); the twenty-second would be a logical guess.

Although I've broken it down by segments, the tape runs continuously apart from a break between **C** and **D**. As the tape opens, Paul is singing what appears to be a nursery rhyme of his own creation (**A**), although the lyrics about "sucking on a lollipopper" and "sitting on a woody pecker" can be taken more than one way! Donovan harmonizes in spots, and Paul does a double-time impression of the song as Danny Kaye might perform it.

Donovan talks about making simple song sketches with guitar and a bit of organ, and after humming and improvising for a few bars, Paul begins a loose rendition of "Blackbird" (**B**), joined occasionally by Mary Hopkin. Donovan asks if that's the song on the new LP with just guitar, and Paul reminds him there's a blackbird joining in (which Donovan imitates effectively). Paul jokes that when he sang it to Diana Ross (a black "bird") she was offended, then admits that it was inspired by reading about race riots. Donovan recalls how magpies seemed to follow him around after he

wrote a song about them ("The Magpie," on the 1968 LP *Gift from a Flower to a Garden*), and warns Paul that he'll be seeing blackbirds everywhere.

With Paul playing along, Donovan performs an unfinished song, "The Unicorn" (**C**), struggling to remember the chords and humming his way through the latter part. After an edit, someone sounding suspiciously like engineer/producer Glyn Johns has joined them and is trying to recall the name of a Donovan song ("What's that other chick? Oh man, my fuckin' memory's getting so bad . . ."). The song turns out to be "Laleña," Donovan's current U.S. single, and he plays a lovely and fairly complete version (**D**), ruined only by Paul's attempt at playing "lead acoustic." Donovan asks Johns whether the American public "dug" the song and is reassured that they did.

Donovan segues to a samba rhythm, and Paul asks whether they have a decent sound on the guitar yet (presumably they are setting up to record one of Mary's aforementioned covers). The engineer responds from the booth that it sounds nice, and Paul explains that he brought his bass over from Savile Row. Some riffs develop into another McCartney nursery rhyme, apparently written to entertain his girlfriend Linda Eastman's daughter, "Heather" (**E**). Donovan plays along and someone slaps out a rhythm on their legs.

Once Paul stops, Donovan launches into some children's songs of his own (**F–H**). Paul interrupts to ask if he's ever done a whole LP of songs for kids, and Donovan refers him to the second disc of *Gift from a Flower to a Garden*. In 1971, he would release a UK-only album full of fairy tales and poems set to music, another double-LP set titled *HMS Donovan*, which included versions of **C**, **F**, and **G**. The last song on this tape, apparently called "Land of Gisch" (**H**), is cut short and was never heard of again.

Although I've tentatively labeled this as an Abbey Road recording, it should be noted that when the tape was played back to Mary Hopkin years later, she remembered it being recorded at Trident. Donovan himself hazily recalled, "It was around his house at Saint John's Wood or Applewood [sic] in one of the back rooms."

RELEASE HISTORY

1978: **A–H** first surfaced on the vinyl bootleg *No. 3 Abbey Road NW 8* in excellent quality. They appear from tape source on Vigotone's 1994 CD of the same title.

Date: 4–25 November 1968
Location: Queen Charlotte's Maternity Hospital, London
Producer: John Lennon, Yoko Ono

[A.] Mulberry (8:57)
[B.] Song for John (1:26)
[C.] Song for John: Let's Go On Flying/Snow Is Falling All the Time/Mum's Only Looking for Her Hand in the Snow (4:54)
[D.] No Bed for Beatle John (4:41)
[E.] Radio Play (7:59)

[F.] No Bed for Beatle John—RS from mono master (fake stereo) (4:43)
[G.] Baby's Heartbeat—RS from mono master (fake stereo) (5:09)
[H.] Radio Play—RS from mono master (fake stereo) (12:33)
Mixed: 11 February 1969 (?)

On November 4, Yoko Ono, five months pregnant, was rushed to Queen Charlotte's Maternity Hospital for emergency blood transfusions. In immediate danger of losing their baby, she and John settled in for as long as necessary, with John spending each night adjacent to Yoko: at first in a hospital bed, then moving to a sleeping bag on the floor when bed space was needed. Sadly, Yoko miscarried on the twenty-first, and the couple checked out four days later.

During their hospital stay, John brought along his guitar and a portable mono cassette recorder. The result was several more pieces of "Unfinished Music" for their next joint LP, *Life with the Lions.*

Side 2 of the LP would open with "No Bed for Beatle John," a recording of Yoko singing a newspaper article with that headline, and another article apparently titled "The Beatles Win Battle of the Nude LP," about EMI's refusal to distribute *Two Virgins.* This track (**F**) was probably recorded about a week into their stay, since the *Two Virgins* story was reported in the November 9 issue of *New Musical Express* (although that's not the specific source from which Yoko reads). John can be faintly heard singing other Beatles-related articles in the background, and these offer further clues:

- "George Harrison has not renewed his contract with Northern Songs" (reported on the ninth)
- "Miss Ono, age thirty-four, is named in a forthcoming defendant divorce suite [sic] between Cynthia Lennon and Mr. Lennon's wife [sic]" (the divorce was granted on the eighth)

Other topics mentioned by John include his psychedelically painted Bentley (registration no. 222APL) and singer Marc Bolan's wish to publish a book of poems and stories, as well as further negative publicity surrounding *Two Virgins* ("... experimenting to see just how much madness they can get away with").

The next cut was a five-minute recording of their unborn baby's heartbeat (**G**), which opens with a snippet of dialogue (John is ready, but another voice says not to begin recording yet). This was followed on the album by two minutes of silence. The juxtaposition may have been a bit too conspicuous, as some sources (the book *The Love You Make,* for example) claim that the recording actually documents the last five minutes of the baby's life. One hopes the doctors would have been frantically trying to save its life at that point, not capture it on tape!

The LP closed with a lengthy recording (**H**) of someone snapping a radio dial back and forth rather annoyingly for twelve and a half minutes, allowing the signal to come across at about ninety bursts per minute. As it begins, John is heard in the background calling his new assistant Anthony Fawcett (at AMBassador-5973). He instructs Fawcett to keep their possessions relatively separated while moving them from Montague Square back out to Kenwood. ("Don't suddenly pile everything in one big heap. OK?") John and Yoko had been evicted from Ringo's flat thanks to the drug bust and would return to the now-vacant house at Kenwood until a buyer could be found.

After hanging up, John wanders over and takes command of the radio, altering the frequency of the beat just enough that we can make out "Ob-La-Di, Ob-La-Da" being broadcast. It's the only recognizable tune in the whole piece, although at about 9:45 into the track, another bit of melody comes across. The DJ can also be heard to say "OK, good evening" and "Marianne." (Could this be "C'mon Marianne," a July 1968 single for Grapefruit that John helped arrange?) Otherwise, the last seven minutes of this track are maddeningly pointless; it ends with John's query "Talking to me?"

On February 11, 1969, John and Yoko remixed some mono tapes into mock-stereo during a 3:00–5:30 p.m. session in room 53 at Abbey Road. Presumably these were among the recordings, as **F**, the dialogue preceding **G**, and **H** were all initially released in "rechanneled" stereo, with the treble boosted in one channel and the bass in the other (in fact, the "channels" thus created drift back and forth throughout the duration of **H**).

True mono mixes of two of these tracks have also appeared (**D** is identical in content to **F**, and **E** is an edit of **H**). Along with an exclusive recording (**C**), these were released on a flexi-disc included with the spring/summer 1969 issue of *Aspen* magazine (number 7). This special edition, titled "The British Box," included the 33⅓ RPM 8-inch flexi-disc, as well as a copy of John's infamous *1969 Diary*. The disc was prepared in late January 1969 by Malcolm Davies, who transferred John's hour-long cassette to six reels of ¼-inch tape and edited the material down to about eighteen minutes' duration.

C was a medley labeled "Song for John," which turned out to consist of three parts, apparently recorded in one sitting. First were Yoko's a cappella renditions of "Let's Go On Flying" and "Snow Is Falling All the Time." Finally, we have a John and Yoko guitar/voice duet on an early version of "Don't Worry Kyoko." This segment was released with that title on the Rykodisc version of *Wedding Album*, along with a snippet of "Snow Is Falling All the Time."

An alternate take of "Let's Go On Flying" with John providing fingerpicked guitar accompaniment (**B**) also exists; as it ends, John instructs Yoko to "wind [the tape] back or we'll end up with millions of tapes"—prophetic words, indeed!

Probably recorded on the same day is an improvised piece (**A**), whose entire lyrics consist of "mulberries—let's go and find them in the snow." In between bleating and shrieking, Yoko sings variations of these words, while John plays what sounds like his fretless guitar (last heard in the June 6 Kenny Everett interview). And when I say he "plays" it, I mean he rubs and scrapes the strings, twangs and plucks some slide riffs, and plinks numerous high-pitched notes. For nine minutes.

RELEASE HISTORY

1969: **F–H** were released on the LP *Unfinished Music No. 2: Life with the Lions*, which has been extensively pirated. The same year, **C–E** appeared on a flexi-disc included with issue number 7 of *Aspen* magazine.

1977: **C–E** were copied on the bootleg EP *Life with the Lennon's* [sic]. **C** also appears as a bonus track on the CD-R *Night Ride*.

1997: The CD reissue of *Unfinished Music No. 2: Life with the Lions* contained **A, B, D, G,** and **H,** all from tape sources. The same year, portions of **C,** also from a tape source, were released on the CD reissue of *Wedding Album*.

113a. Newsreel footage   J

Date: 28 November 1968
Location: Marylebone Magistrates' Court, London
Length: 0:37

Three days after leaving the hospital, John and Yoko reappeared in court, where John (wearing a white "You Are Here" badge on his lapel) pleaded guilty to possession of cannabis resin and was fined £150. BBC News and Reuters were outside to film the couple being escorted to their car by Peter Brown and Martin Polden, their solicitor.

RELEASE HISTORY

This color newsreel footage circulates on video. Some of the BBC clip is used in *Imagine: John Lennon,* edited together with footage from the October 19 court appearance.

114. Location recordings

Date: late November–early December 1968
Location: various
Producer: Kenny Everett

[A.] Jock and Yono—rough mix (0:57)
[B.] Once Upon a Pool Table—rough mix (0:54)
[C.] The Beatles' Sixth Christmas Record (mono) (7:51)

In years past, the Beatles were together in the studio working on an LP or single when it came time to assemble a Christmas message for their fan club. But even before the "White Album" was completed, George and Ringo had left the country; Paul would soon do likewise, spending the last ten days of October getting to know Linda Eastman better in New York City.

By November, someone had gotten on the ball and the word went out for each Beatle to contribute a tape; the submissions would be edited together back in London by DJ Kenny Everett, already familiar with chopping up Beatles tapes. Paul probably taped his contribution while in London producing Mary Hopkin's LP (he likely didn't have a tape recorder installed at his Scottish farmhouse yet). Ringo taped his after returning from Sardinia, and John and Yoko theirs in Kenwood after Yoko's return from the hospital in late November. George's was recorded November 30 in

New York City, at the apartment of NEMS associate Nat Weiss.

In the November 30 issue of *New Musical Express,* Paul was reported as describing the disc's contents as a "collection of good quality home recordings of unused LP tracks." This brings up the intriguing possibility of a disc including the Esher demos for songs like "What's the New Mary Jane," "Junk," and "Not Guilty."

The finished disc reflects the fragmentation already evident in the group, although that's down as much to Kenny Everett's editing technique as the material at hand. It opens with "footsteps" and "door knock" effects, followed by a greeting from Ringo. The intro to "Ob-La-Di, Ob-La-Da," overlaid with plunking piano, leads into Paul's offering. This acoustic ditty has Paul confused about both the year and the holiday in question. After some applause, a speeded-up copy of "Helter Skelter" is a prelude to John's recitation of his poem "Jock and Yono."

As Yoko plays piano in the background, John gets in thinly disguised shots at "some of their beast friends," in other words the other Beatles and Apple's inner circle who had done their best to ostracize Yoko. A recording of "Baroque Hoedown" (later made familiar as the theme for Disneyland's Main Street Electrical Parade) introduces George's segment. He pokes fun at past messages ("Christmas time is here again, ain't been round since . . . last year!") and somewhat facetiously thanks the "faithful beloved fans who have made our lives worth living." Mal Evans chimes in with "Merry Christmas, children everywhere!"

As "Birthday" and "Yer Blues" play softly in the background, Ringo acts out both ends of a phone conversation, responding to his own voice on tape with satisfyingly nonsensical dialogue. He introduces "one of the most versatile performers in our career," which turns out to be a heavily phased reprise of Paul's earlier song. John recites another poem, "Once Upon a Pool Table," with further effects overlaid to double his voice.

The highlight of the disc is the final portion: Tiny Tim's timeless ukelele version of "Nowhere Man," sung "the exact way" he did it at a 1966 Royal Albert Hall concert. George thanks Tiny, who replies in the spirit of his namesake, "God bless us all." An orchestral "amen" and the final drumbeat from "Happiness Is a Warm Gun" wrap things up.

Unprocessed versions of John's poems turned up in his archives, in slightly better fidelity than on the flexi-disc. **A** has extra piano noodling at the start, and **B** continues on longer, with some extra lines of verse and indecipherable singing from Yoko in the background. It's likely these two recordings were taped as one and split in half by Everett.

RELEASE HISTORY

1968: **C** was released on a flexi-disc, titled *The Beatles' Sixth Christmas Record,* mailed out to fan club members on December 20.

1989: **A** and **B** were aired on episode 89-53 of *The Lost Lennon Tapes.*

1998: **A–C** were compiled on the bootleg CD *The Ultimate Beatles Christmas Collection.*

115. Interview   J

Date:	3 December 1968
Location:	Kenwood
Interviewer:	Maurice Hindle, Daniel Wiles
Length:	16:20

An open letter to John Lennon was published in the October 28 issue of London's radical magazine *Black Dwarf.* The piece, written by Keele University student John Hoyland, was deeply critical of the lyrics to "Revolution," stating that "In order to change the world, we've got to understand what's wrong with the world. And then—destroy it. Ruthlessly . . . There is no such thing as a polite revolution."

John's own pointed defense would be published in the January 10, 1969, issue, but in the meantime he allowed two students, Maurice Hindle and Daniel Wiles, to interview him at home about the topic of social change. The conversation ended up being wide-ranging, lasting several hours over the course of a macrobiotic meal. Two hours' worth of discussion was captured on a Philips C-120 cassette, portions of which have since been made public.

Expanding on the theme of changing people's heads, John insists that ruthless destruction will only lead to having ruthless destroyers in power, using the Russian and French revolutions as examples. He points out that the Soviets are just as ambitious as any capitalist country when it comes to competing in the Olympics or the space race.

He defends the Beatles' decidedly nonradical image, admitting that they had to compromise somewhat to escape being trapped in the system. In a preview of his 1970 "Lennon Remembers" confessional, John reveals that "the most miserable time of our lives was the mop-top MBE cop-out period." He warns readers not to bother chasing fame or material success, and stresses that he couldn't have survived Beatlemania without the support of his bandmates; as long as one of them was in an optimistic mood, they were able to pull through.

It's not clear what he's responding to (the questions have mostly been excised from the circulating recordings), but John berates someone for looking down on popular entertainers like Engelbert Humperdinck merely because they are uncontroversial. He goes on to claim that his friends are ordinary people, and furthermore, he is "the masses." When one of the students tries to point out the built-in flaw in this statement, John switches gears and claims to have always been outside the mainstream, which is why he didn't end up working in an office.

Hoping that society will continue to get more enlightened, John declares that by 2012 he should be "as groovy as Jesus" (you'd think he would have learned not to make that comparison!). Since he believes in reincarnation, John feels that even though history goes in cycles, it's to your own benefit to try and improve the future.

Mentioning that George is in America to meet up with Bob Dylan, John enthuses over a record by songwriter Brute Force, "The King of Fuh," which Apple hopes to issue ("God knows how we'll release it"), singing a line to illustrate the smutty play on words. He also talks about how he could have prevented a lot of headaches, such as getting busted, by not doing things like releasing LPs with nude cover photos.

John goes on to criticize his detractors on the far left, saying that their petty nitpicking about being "extremer than thou" has shown them to be exclusionary snobs incapable of organizing a united movement. Gulping down his food, John exclaims, "But I tell you what, if those people start a revolution, me and the Stones'll probably be the first ones they'll shoot. Y'know, I mean that . . . And it's him—it's the guy that wrote the letter that'll do it, y'know. They'd shoot me just for living here, y'know."

All of the above conversation stems from the Hard Rock Cafe flexi-disc, but further extracts from this conversation were broadcast in various episodes of *The Lost Lennon Tapes* radio series. Topics discussed include the potential divinity within everyone, the beneficial effects of meditation and a macrobiotic diet, subversion from within the system, and Elvis Presley. The original cassette was sold at a Leland's auction in April 2001, along with "a 61 page printed transcript, and additional 15 pages of background material."

RELEASE HISTORY

1991: 12:03 of this interview was released on a double-sided flexi-disc, *The John Lennon Interviews,* distributed by the Hard Rock Cafe. Excerpts had already been broadcast on *The Lost Lennon Tapes* radio series, including episodes 88-19, 89-12, 89-34, and 89-37.

116. Studio session   G

Date: November–6 December 1968
Location: Wally Heider Studios, Los Angeles; IBC Studios, London
Producer: Felix Pappalardi

[A.] Badge (2:41)

Around September, the era of "Savoy Truffle" and the "While My Guitar Gently Weeps" session, George was spending a lot of time with Eric Clapton. Cream had already decided to disband after one final album and farewell tour, and in his first extra-Beatle songwriting collaboration, George helped Eric write his contribution to the LP.

George later recalled the songwriting session: "We were working across from each other and I was writing the lyrics down and we came to the middle part so I wrote 'Bridge.' Eric read it upside down and cracked up laughing—'What's *badge*?' he said. After that Ringo walked in drunk and gave us that line about the swans living in the park."

Eric spent all of October touring the United States with Cream, and when George came over to California, he naturally agreed to contribute to the song's recording. The basic track was recorded in a session at Wally Heider Studios, with George playing the chunka-chunka rhythm guitar that opens the song alongside Jack Bruce's bass riff. Eric played the Harrisound-alike Leslied guitar part in the middle, along with an overdubbed lead guitar solo, and sang an occasionally double-tracked lead vocal. Ginger Baker was on drums, of course, and producer Felix Pappalardi played the piano.

The song appears twice in Atlantic Records' tape logs: as "Eric's Tune" from Los Angeles, November 21, and as "Badge" from IBC Studios, London, December 6 (those aren't necessarily the exact recording dates). The latter session was for Pappalardi's Mellotron overdub and perhaps additional vocal work. The result was an enjoyable and worthy final single for the band. When the LP was released, George was credited as L'Angelo Misterioso, much to his surprise (he assumed Eric chose the name to avoid contractual hassles).

RELEASE HISTORY

1969: **A** was released on the LP *Goodbye,* now readily available on CD (it's also on the boxed sets *Crossroads* and *Those Were the Days*). It was issued as a single, which peaked at number 21 in the UK and number 60 in the U.S. charts.

117. Studio session

Date: November–10 December 1968
Location: EMI and Trident Studios, London
Producer: Paul McCartney

[A.] **The Honeymoon Song** (2:05)
[B.] **Happiness Runs (Pebble and the Man)** (2:01)
[C.] **Voyage of the Moon** (5:52)
[D.] **Lord of the Reedy River** (2:34)
[E.] **The Puppy Song** (2:41)
[F.] **Love Is the Sweetest Thing** (3:42)
[G.] **Lullaby of the Leaves** (2:32)
[H.] **Prince En Avignon** (3:19)
[I.] **Lontano Dagli Occhi** (3:22)

With the mammoth worldwide success of "Those Were the Days," Mary Hopkin's debut Apple LP was hotly anticipated. Producer Paul McCartney chose the material, and unfortunately it was a mixed bag at best. Traditional and new folk songs sit uneasily alongside saccharine standards, although it must be said that Paul's production is largely tasteful, accentuating Hopkin's pure sonorous voice.

The first song recorded, "Young Love," featured backing from the Mike Cotton Sound. It's likely the other songs featuring that group were recorded next, including Paul's old *Pop Go the Beatles* fave, "The Honeymoon Song" (**A**), on which he plays tambourine.

The album's highlights are a trio of Donovan compositions. "Happiness Runs" (**B**) dates back to the Rishikesh era and has Paul playing bass alongside Mary's acoustic guitar. In a later session, Paul and Donovan played acoustics while Mary sang the ethereal "Voyage of the Moon" (**C**) and "Lord of the Reedy River" (**D**). Harry Nilsson's "The Puppy Song" (**E**) also works well, with Paul playing the echoed vaudeville-style piano.

The oldie "Love Is the Sweetest Thing" (**F**) has a dance-band arrangement, but it's possible Paul strums the acoustic guitar buried in the backing (certainly he doesn't play the string bass). He probably also plays the "Michelle"-style acoustic guitar line on "Lullaby of the Leaves" (**G**), and the acoustic guitar, drums, and bass on "Prince En Avignon" (**H**) as well. The non-LP song "Lontano Dagli Occhi" (**I**) would be released on a single in Italy; this possibly features a bass overdub from Paul.

The album was wrapped up by the time Paul departed for Portugal on December 11. By the January *Get Back* sessions, he was designing the LP cover and trying to pick a single. Derek Taylor (as "Max Wax") sent a telegram to Twickenham nominating "The Puppy Song," but in February Paul would compose a standalone single for Hopkin that was better than most of the songs on the album (see the March 1, 1969, entry).

RELEASE HISTORY

1969: **A–H** were released on the LP *Post Card,* reissued by Apple on CD in 1991. **I** was released on a single in Italy only, but was included on the 1972 compilation LP *Those Were the Days* (reissued on CD in 1995) in stereo.

118. Composing tape

J

Date: early December, 1968
Location: Kenwood

[A.] **Oh My Love—take 1** (1:24)
[B.] **Oh My Love—take 2** (1:22)
[C.] **A Case of the Blues** (2:51)
[D.] **Everyone Had a Hard Year** (1:42)
[E.] **Don't Let Me Down—take 1** (2:54)
[F.] **Don't Let Me Down—take 2** (2:08)

Drugs, divorce, and a slipping image. That's what John and Yoko had to contend with as winter set in. Kenwood had been stripped bare by Cynthia and her mother and was up for sale; in the meantime, John and Yoko moved in, occupying only a couple of rooms. Having exhausted his supply of Rishikesh compositions and with Paul making noises in the press about an imminent Beatles concert and TV show, John was able to throw together only a few song fragments, recording his acoustic guitar composing sessions on a cassette.

"Oh My Love" began life as a poem by Yoko, probably titled "John My Love," with lyrics about the loss of their unborn child. The cassette begins with two takes of John attempting to polish up Yoko's melody by singing and finding chords on his acoustic guitar. In the first attempt (**A**), he has trouble making things flow toward the end, admitting, "It's just a bit hard, y'know. To go through it all like that." A second attempt (**B**) is cut short even sooner, as John complains that "it just sort of gets unreasonable." The tape continued with two a cappella renditions by Yoko (both aired on *The Lost Lennon Tapes*) and a fifth take with Yoko singing and John on guitar. Yet another of Yoko's a cappella demos would be aired on the BBC later in the month (see the December 12 entry), but the song would be radically reworked for release on the 1971 *Imagine* LP.

Although he breaks into it from time to time during the January 1969 Twickenham sessions, "A Case of the Blues" was far from ever being finished. In the only known demo (C), John mumbles through what few lyrics he has, centering on "everyone knows that it's a case of the blues," and tossing in phrases such as "albino-colored glasses," "knock-kneed shoes," "cotton pair of knickers," and "alabaster primrose."

John then reflects on his recent troubles, reasoning that "Everyone Had a Hard Year" (D). This repetitious bit of lyric would end up as part of Paul's "I've Got a Feeling." Since the two parts were already joined by the next Beatles session January 2, John and Paul must have gotten together for at least one writing session after Paul's return from Portugal, probably between Christmas and New Year's.

The most promising of these new songs was a ballad that would become "Don't Let Me Down." In the earliest demo (E), John has the first few lines of a verse ("nobody ever loved me like she does") and repeats them over and over, hoping inspiration will strike. At one point, he hits upon the rhythm of what would become the middle eight, singing "oh yeah" on top of a B major chord. At the very end, he plays a riff that anticipates the eventual melody of the chorus.

A second take (F) from later in the cassette opens with his conjecture, "This could be part of that." He weaves in what was apparently a separate piece, the "I'm in love for the first time" bridge, testing out how it flows into the verse section. At the end, he concludes, "That'll do" and switches off the tape. With the addition of the title refrain and a few more lines of lyrics (and the omission of a few chord changes), the song would be ready for Beatles rehearsal the next month.

RELEASE HISTORY

1988: **D** was broadcast in episode 88-19 of the radio series *The Lost Lennon Tapes,* missing the final 18 seconds. This source was used on the vinyl bootleg *The Lost Lennon Tapes, Volume 4* and the CD-R *Vinyl to the Core.* The same year, **C** surfaced in episode 88-34; it was booted on the LP *The Lost Lennon Tapes, Volume 10.*

1989: **E** and **F** were broadcast on *The Lost Lennon Tapes,* in episodes 89-25 and 89-27, respectively; they were bootlegged on the LPs *The Lost Lennon Tapes, Volume 17* (**E**) and *18* (**F**).

1990: **A** and **B** were broadcast in episode 90-12 of *The Lost Lennon Tapes.* They were copied on the vinyl bootleg *The Lost Lennon Tapes, Volume 24.* The same year, a more complete version of **D** was broadcast in episode 90-13, but this was still missing the first 3 seconds.

1991: Episode 91-29 of *The Lost Lennon Tapes* contained a slightly longer version of **A,** which remains unbootlegged. That year, the bootleg CD *The 1968 Demos* contained **A–C, E,** and **F** (with **A** and **B** both incomplete), plus the 1990 airing of **D.**

1994: The bootleg CD *Imagine . . . All the Outtakes* included full versions of the 1990 airings of **A** and **B.**

119. TV performance   J

Date: 11–12 December 1968
Location: Stonebridge House, Wembley
Director: Michael Lindsay-Hogg

[A.] dialogue/Yer Blues (0:41)
[B.] dialogue (1:06)
[C.] untitled jam (mono) (3:58)
[D.] Yer Blues—rehearsal take (mono) (3:58)
[E.] Yer Blues—take 1 (mono) (4:31)
[F.] Yer Blues—take 2 (stereo) (4:34)
[G.] Whole Lotta Yoko (stereo) (4:37)

[H.] Yer Blues—RS from take 1 (4:26)
[I.] Whole Lotta Yoko—RS (4:48)

Not having learned a lesson from the failure of *Magical Mystery Tour,* the Rolling Stones decided to film a TV special of their own to promote their new *Beggars' Banquet* LP. The show was called *Rock and Roll Circus* and had a stellar lineup including the Stones, Jethro Tull, the Who, Marianne Faithfull, classical pianist Julius Katchen, singer Taj Mahal, and supergroup Traffic. Unfortunately, Steve Winwood decided to quit Traffic just before filming was to begin; as a last-minute replacement, Mick Jagger implored John to attend.

He agreed, bringing along Yoko and forming his own supergroup, dubbed the Dirty Mac. Alongside John's vocal and rhythm guitar would be Eric Clapton on lead guitar, Keith Richards on bass, and Jimi Hendrix Experience drummer Mitch Mitchell on the skins. John chose a number that would be relatively easy for everyone to learn, "Yer Blues."

Rehearsals and camera tests commenced December 6 at the Marquee Club and preliminary recording on the eighth at Olympic (probably to record the backing for Faithfull's number), although John didn't attend either. He may have been present at rehearsals, which reportedly took place on the eighth and ninth at the Londonderry House Hotel where Keith Richards and Bill Wyman were staying.

On the tenth, filmed rehearsals began on a closed

set at InterTel's Stonebridge House facility. The visuals were being captured on both videotape (long since destroyed) and film, directed by Michael Lindsay-Hogg. The sound was recorded on Olympic's mobile four-track machine, manned by engineer Glyn Johns and produced by Jimmy Miller.

John and Yoko were also being filmed by Austrian TV for a documentary, *John Lennon & Yoko Ono,* being made to accompany the screening of their film *Rape.* The TV crew accompanied them to InterTel and captured a bit of comedy early on the eleventh (**A**). John is seated in the bleachers alongside Julian and Yoko, with Mick Jagger standing nearby. The cameraman asks John what he'll be doing in the show, and he and Mick sing a chorus of "Yer Blues," with John slowly stripping Mick of his jacket. Mick asks if they should do that as a link, and John concurs.

The actual link (**B**) was filmed soon afterward (John has a pack of cigarettes in his breast pocket in both clips) and is even funnier. Trying to top each other with deadpan sincerity, "Winston" and "Michael" trade quips as John, finishing a plate of Chinese food, runs down the lineup of Dirty Mac.

Rehearsals with Dirty Mac reportedly included oldies such as "Peggy Sue," "Hound Dog," and "It's Now or Never," although no tapes have surfaced. There is a rambling blues jam (**C**), which may be from the tenth, but is more likely a warm-up from the eleventh.

The *Circus* began around noon that day with a photo call; all of the performers, dressed in costumes, assembled under the "big top." John wore a glitter-striped jumpsuit, black hat, and a purple chiffon scarf, Yoko a black cloak and pointed witch's hat. After the audience was admitted, this procession was filmed entering the arena, "playing" various instruments (John blew a trumpet).

The supergroup's performance was filmed in the evening. A rehearsal take of "Yer Blues" (**D**) exists only from a mono Nagra reel located close to the guitar amps (with John's vocal almost inaudible). The first slated take exists in two forms: the mono Nagra mix (**E**) includes some extra studio instructions at the beginning compared with the released stereo mix (**H**), from four-track. During this take, John plays his solo with eyes shut tightly! This take can be seen on the *Rock and Roll Circus* home video.

A second take exists in a stereo mix from the four-track (**F**), and as a bonus feature on the *Rock and Roll Circus* DVD, with a split-screen showing all four camera angles. This take is notable for John's lyrical goof: Even though the words were taped to his mic stand, he transposed "sky" and "earth" in the second verse.

After the last take of "Yer Blues," Yoko emerges from a black bag onstage where she had been throughout, and violinist Ivry Gitlis joins the ensemble. John launches the group into a twelve-bar blues and nods

encouragement in Yoko's direction. After a minute, she hesitantly steps to the mic and launches into her patented vocal improvisations. This one-off performance has been booted from four-track as "Her Blues" in stereo (**G**) and released in a slightly narrower mix (**I**) as "Whole Lotta Yoko."

The Austrian film crew also shot about twenty minutes from these performances, and footage of various takes circulates from this source. In addition to offering different angles, it includes the true ending to take 1, which has a pause before the audience begins applauding. On the official release, the applause is cross-faded much earlier. Note that all these takes play back in the key of E-flat, suggesting that the guitarists had detuned a half step.

John and Yoko traveled across town to participate in a radio show (see following entry) and then returned in time for at least some of the Stones' set, as they can be seen dancing and applauding in the audience. The filming wore on until 6:30 a.m. on the twelfth, by which time the enthusiasm of band and audience alike was flagging (John and Yoko don't seem to have stuck around for the finale, "Salt of the Earth"). For this reason, along with the Who's scene-stealing performance of "A Quick One While He's Away," the Stones kept the show on ice until its 1996 release on home video.

RELEASE HISTORY

Throughout the 1970s and early 80s, various vinyl bootlegs contained mono copies of **F** and **G,** in quality ranging from good to excellent.

1984: The radio series *Sgt. Pepper's Lonely Hearts Club Band: A History of the Beatle Years 1962–1970* included an excellent copy of **F.** This was bootlegged on the 1989 Condor CD *Not For Sale.*

1985: The bootleg LP *Strawberry Fields Forever* included a slightly incomplete copy of **A.**

1988: **C, F,** and **G** were broadcast on episode 88-31 of the radio series *The Lost Lennon Tapes.* **C** was copied on the LP *The Lost Lennon Tapes, Volume 8.*

1989: An incomplete version of **E** was broadcast on episode 89-01 of *The Lost Lennon Tapes;* it was bootlegged on the LP *The Lost Lennon Tapes, Volume 13.* The same year, **A, B,** and **D** were broadcast on episode 89-27; they were bootlegged on the LP *The Lost Lennon Tapes, Volume 18.*

1990: The complete version of **E** was broadcast on episode 90-13 of *The Lost Lennon Tapes;* it was bootlegged on the LP *The Lost Lennon Tapes, Volume 24.* The same year, the Library CD *Yer Blues* included copies of **F** and **G,** in stereo but with reversed channels compared with the 1984 broadcast.

1996: **B, H,** and **I** were officially released on the CD *Rolling Stones* "Rock and Roll Circus," also released on home video; the DVD adds **F.**

1999: The CD-R *Telecasts Four* compiled most of these variations, including **A–E, H, I,** and a mono copy of **F.**

The alternate footage from the Austrian TV crew (including bits of **A, F,** and **G**) circulates on video, in both black and white from the original production, and color from a later German documentary, *John Lennon: A Piece of His Mind.*

120. Radio interview

Date:	12 December 1968
Time:	12:05–1:15 a.m.
Location:	Broadcasting House, London
Host:	John Peel
Broadcast:	live
	BBC Radio 1 and 2
	Night Ride
Length:	24:05

If John and Yoko's 1968 collaborations had a home on BBC Radio, it was the free-form show *Night Ride,* broadcast in the postmidnight Wednesday time slot. A tape of their sole appearance has surfaced recently, including all the music and chat with first-hour host John Peel. Along with various discs, music was provided by folk artists John Martyn, Harold McNair, Jacqui McShee, and John Renbourn, and poet Christopher Logue was in the studio to participate.

After introducing the various guests, Peel asks about *Two Virgins,* which John says has just reached the shops and has already been bought by "seven hundred obscene people." Later, he claims that it won't be available until January 6 in the United States, "in a brown bag, apparently." The traditional release date of November 11 in the United States was obviously not met, due to the difficulty of finding distributors. The January 6 reference squares with reports that police in New Jersey seized several thousand copies on January 3; there would have been little point in impounding an album that had already been on shelves for seven weeks.

Although John admits that he "can't see it being a pop favorite," a 3:41 extract of *Two Virgins* is aired. Assisted by Peel and Logue, John and Yoko then read out a suitably mysterious ad copy plugging the "Alchemical Wedding," an event the couple would attend at the Royal Albert Hall on the eighteenth. Their appearance onstage in a white bag was apparently filmed (a "frame from a video film" is printed in Anthony Fawcett's book, *One Day at a Time*), but doesn't circulate. As a tag for the ad, Peel plays a piece from the Czech Philharmonic Orchestra, and as he scrambles to find the title of the work, John ad-libs, "That was Randy Legmeat and the Incredible Brown Bag."

Yoko describes an idea for another art exhibit, a "sculpture show" featuring "still water" (this may have evolved into her 1971 This Is Not Here show in Syracuse). Then she plays a cassette containing an a cappella home demo of "Oh My Love" (see earlier entry for details), stopping the tape just as another take, with John adding acoustic guitar, begins.

Peel plays a Lonnie Donegan record, which causes John to reminisce about his first guitar, "guaranteed not to split." He describes his contribution to the *Rock and Roll Circus* and mentions plans for a photo book (which never surfaced) depicting the You Are Here exhibit and people's reactions to it. Noting the blatantly racist tone of the hate mail they've received, John spoofs über-Conservative MP Enoch Powell as "Mr. Trowel."

We also learn that John and Yoko already have a title and cover photo picked out for their next album, although they don't seem to know what the content will be. While they would end up filling one side with location recordings from their hospital stay, John says it's more fun to make some new sounds from scratch. Faced with a minute or so to fill before the news, John launches into a version of "It's Now or Never" (which he had just sung with the Dirty Mac group), whistling a verse and intoning, "It's the *Blow Your Mind* show, folks!"

After the top-of-the-hour news, Peel is allowed to stay a few extra minutes, while John reads his poems, "Jock and Yono" and "Once Upon a Pool Table," introducing them as "A Piece of Paper Called Charles." His readings contain even more material than the raw tape used for the Beatles' Christmas flexi, conforming more or less to the text printed in the book *Skywriting by Word of Mouth.*

As the interview wraps, Yoko discusses their film-making career, noting the screenings of *Smile* and *Two Virgins* at the Chicago Film Festival and hinting at an idea of John's (probably *Rape,* which was already in the can). John and Yoko then departed to Wembley in time for the Stones' set.

RELEASE HISTORY

2000: This show appeared on the CD-R *Night Ride,* from a good-quality off-line tape.

Date: 12 December 1968 (?)
Location: Knightsbridge, London
Interviewer: Abram de Swaan
Broadcast: 15 January 1969, 9:25–10:05 p.m.
Nederland 2, VARA-tv
Rood Wit Blauw
Length: 61:03

Soon after their *Night Ride* appearance (perhaps the same day, based on a mention of "yesterday at Inter-Tel"), John and Yoko expanded on many of the same subjects during a lengthy filmed interview for Dutch TV. It was conducted in the waiting room of John's dentist, and while forty minutes were used in the series *Rood Wit Blauw* ("Red White Blue"), a rough cut lasting over an hour circulates. This consists of six 10-minute film reels, in black and white but synced with sound; the title card simply says "An Interview with Yoko Ono and John Lennon."

The first three reels feature Yoko talking with interviewer Abram de Swaan alone while John's teeth are tended to. Yoko expounds on her philosophy of art, which would basically remain constant throughout her years with John: Art is a means of communication, anyone can be an artist, art is functional, not decorative. She recounts in some detail her first meeting with John at Indica Gallery, insisting that while she'd heard of "Beatles," she didn't realize who John Lennon was until someone informed her after the encounter.

With the fourth reel, John enters with a mouth full of anesthetic and jokingly asks for a disclaimer explaining why he's "out of his skull," lest some "freaky people" offer him drugs. Yoko attempts to continue the thread of conversation, saying she'd be disappointed in future civilizations if they had to rely on her preserved artwork rather than creating their own. John plays devil's advocate, pointing out that nobody relies solely on Picasso or da Vinci in the present. After arguing the point further, he grins, "We don't get on at all," then gives Yoko a kiss to show he's kidding. Yoko says they often oppose each other just for the sake of having a dialogue, but often feel like one person sharing two bodies (at this point, John sings a snatch of "It's Now or Never" yet again).

John gives a lengthy account of their narcotics bust, revealing that they'd been tipped off three weeks in advance and thus felt confident about being "clean." He admits that the hash found in a binocular case was "from last year," and he claims to be relieved that it finally happened after worrying for years about an arrest. He and Yoko express optimism about spreading positive vibes through their *Smile* film, calling their artwork a "quiet revolution." Yoko hopes awareness will spread like an epidemic, and John implores young people to wait and infiltrate the establishment rather than try to dismantle it violently.

John is baffled when de Swaan criticizes the song "Taxman," defending it as "an antiestablishment song." It turns out de Swaan is in favor of keeping taxes high for altruistic reasons, and John mumbles something about being able to keep what you earn. We learn the reason for this viewpoint later in the interview, when John complains about being "conned" out of money the Beatles rightfully earned. He is clearly disgusted at how much of his income goes into the pockets of businessmen like Dick James, saying he'd rather throw it down the drain.

Talk of "Revolution" leads John to reiterate many points from his Black Dwarf interview (see the December 3 entry) about the lack of solidarity among the ranks of activists. He says that at college he'd always secretly hoped for anarchy, if only so he could loot, and goes so far as to say he still likes to steal things (shoplifting was one of John and Pete Shotton's boyhood hobbies), although Yoko quickly points out that he doesn't.

He denounces militant protesters as being no better than those they protest against, but de Swaan counters with the example of black Americans' long struggle for equality. John wishes the black power movement good luck, but points out that if there's a total race war and the balance of power shifts, "not all blacks are saints" either. Yoko says she can sympathize because "woman is like the nigger of the world"—before long, John would expand that concept into a song.

RELEASE HISTORY

This footage circulates in decent quality on video.

122. Documentary footage

Date: mid-December 1968
Location: Kenwood
Broadcast: 31 March 1969, 10:25 p.m.
Austrian National Television
John Lennon & Yoko Ono and *Die Verge-waltigung/Rape (Film No. 6)*

[A.] Everybody Had a Hard Year (1:10)

During John and Yoko's hospital stay, they had dispatched cameraman Nick Knowland into the streets of London to film *Rape (Film No. 6)*. To accompany the film's airing on Austrian TV, the ORF film crew shot some color footage at Kenwood.

A tag scene to follow the closing credits, filmed in the backyard, depicts the couple seated on the circular white bench originally installed at Coventry Cathedral in June for their "Acorn Event." Dressed entirely in black (including hats probably lifted from the *Rock and Roll Circus* wardrobe department) apart from white tennis shoes, John and Yoko sing "Everybody Had a Hard Year." John is playing his acoustic guitar, playing C-shapes with a capo at the fifth fret. Ostensibly this would raise the pitch to F major, but the soundtrack plays back in E—perhaps he wasn't in tune in the first place.

In any case, the lyric is similar to the earlier demo, with the change of "everyone" to "everybody," and "got the boot in" switched to "got a soft dream." After a few lines, John stops playing, points enigmatically at the camera lens, and says, "Surprise, surprise." The song resumes, and the camera pans away slowly as John sings "oh yeah, oh yeah, oh yeah"—another fragment that worked its way into "I've Got a Feeling."

Other footage filmed inside Kenwood this day was used in a documentary, *John Lennon & Yoko Ono,* which preceded the airing of *Rape.* John plays the same guitar (the capo is clipped above the neck), while Yoko gives a guided tour of conceptual art pieces, mainly from her 1967 show, sponsored by John as Yoko Plus Me. On exhibit are various objects painted white, including an all-white chess set and a stepladder. Some of these are cut in half, and Yoko proudly displays glass bottles containing "half a wind," "half a letter," and "half a music." The white canvas from the You Are Here show is also in evidence.

RELEASE HISTORY

1986: **A** was bootlegged on the LP *Johnny Moondog* as "Theme from *Rape.*" The full clip was released on the 2003 DVD *Lennon Legend.*

The art exhibit footage also circulates, in black and white from the original *John Lennon & Yoko Ono* documentary with natural sound, and in color from a German TV program, *John Lennon: A Piece of His Mind,* with the commercial recording of "Look At Me" dubbed over the top. On September 20, 2003, BBC2 aired an *Arena* documentary titled *Imagine "Imagine,"* which included 2:31 of the interior footage in color and including some natural sound of John playing the guitar.

123. Studio session

Date: June–December 1968
Location: EMI and Trident Studios, London and Sound Recorders, Los Angeles
Producer: George Harrison

[A.] Is This What You Want? (2:43)
[B.] Speak to Me (3:07)
[C.] Take My Word (3:54)
[D.] Baby You're a Lover (3:01)
[E.] How Can You Say Goodbye (4:10)
[F.] You've Got Me Thinking (2:53)
[G.] Won't You Come Back (4:08)

After producing Jackie Lomax's "Sour Milk Sea" single in June, George continued to work with him throughout the summer and fall, amassing songs for an Apple LP. On October 16, he and Jackie traveled to Los Angeles, along with Mal Evans, to work at Sound Recorders Studios. The sessions resulted in seven songs, and George was delighted to be able to play with a group of renowned session musicians in relaxed, state-of-the-art surroundings.

The core group on each song consisted of George on rhythm guitar, Hal Blaine on drums, Joe Osborne on bass guitar, and Larry Knechtel on piano, organ, and electric piano. Together this unit recorded the backing tracks to **A** (October 22), **B** (October 24), and **C** (October 25). On the twenty-sixth, George sat out the rhythm track session for "Little Yellow Pills."

October 31 saw the addition of strings, arranged and conducted by Allan Capps, to **B** and **C**. The same was done for **A** and "Little Yellow Pills" on November 1, with Hal Blaine joining in at each session. A one-week break followed before the next session on the eighth, for the song "I Fall Inside Your Eyes." This time Paul Beaver was on hand to add synthesizer work, but George didn't contribute instrumentally.

The Harrison/Blaine/Osborne/Knechtel/Beaver combo teamed up on the ninth to record **D** and **E,** with Beaver probably playing the Mellotron flutes on the latter title. On the tenth, more overdubs were added by Beaver to these two titles, plus "I Fall Inside Your Eyes." The final session on the eleventh had Bernie Krause adding further synth work to those three titles, **A,** and "Little Yellow Pills" (see the November 12 entry for details of what transpired).

Sessions continued back in England throughout December, probably at Trident, with backing vocals and horns being added in Lomax's absence (it sounds like George joins in on backing vocals for **D**). "You've Got Me Thinking" (**F**) actually dates from the June single sessions and features George and Eric Clapton on guitars and Ringo on drums, with horns and backing vocals added in December.

An outtake from this project, "Won't You Come Back" (**G**), was recorded in London at an unknown date. It's probable but unverified that George plays either the acoustic or electric guitar on this song, released in 1991 as a CD bonus track.

It's possible that final overdubs and mixing continued into January, but with little assistance from George, who was wrapped up in Beatles rehearsals at the time. During the January 2 session, he can be heard asking his bandmates' opinion of the rough LP acetates he had given them (John admits that he only half-listened to one side of his copy).

RELEASE HISTORY

1969: **A–F** were released on the LP *Is This What You Want?* (U.S. copies omitted **E** in favor of Lomax's upcoming single, "New Day.") Apple's 1991 CD reissue added **G.**

1969: FINANCIAL IMBALANCE

January 2 First day of rehearsals and filming for a new untitled Beatles TV show/concert/documentary film/album at Twickenham Film Studios.

January 6 Long-delayed U.S. release of John and Yoko's *Unfinished Music No. 1: Two Virgins* LP.

January 10 After rehearsing two songs, George walks out during the lunchtime break. The other three pointlessly carry on for a couple more hours without him before packing it in. Having just quit the world's most successful pop combo, George spends the evening at Trident Studios overseeing orchestral overdubs on a potential Apple single, "King of Fuh."

January 12 Paul attends a recording session at EMI Studios for side 2 of Scaffold's *L the P* album.

The Beatles hold a meeting at Ringo's house to discuss the problems in the group and attempt to convince George not to quit. George is not won over and departs early.

January 13 U.S. release of *Yellow Submarine* LP.

Late afternoon rehearsal at Twickenham, very brief, once John finally deigns to grace the others with his presence. George, visiting his parents in Liverpool, is nowhere to be seen.

January 14 A disastrous day of little or no rehearsal: George is still absent; John, wasted from substance abuse the previous night, shows up late; and Ringo is miserable and ill himself. Rather than waste more of Apple's time and money, Paul officially calls a halt to the filming, realizing that with two uncooperative group members nothing can be accomplished.

January 15 At a long group meeting, George and the others agree to ignore their differences long enough to finish up the current recording project.

January 17 UK release of *Yellow Submarine* LP.

January 20 Scheduled commencement of recording sessions at Apple Studios proves impossible when Apple Electronics "wizard" Magic Alex fails to deliver the promised seventy-two-track state-of-the-art recorder and mixing console.

January 21 The Beatles reconvene for filming and serious recording in their own studio in the basement of the Apple Headquarters building, resulting in songs for the film and LP *Let It Be.*

January 27 John and Yoko meet soon-to-be Beatles manager Allen Klein at the Dorchester Hotel. John is mightily impressed with Klein's extensive knowledge of Lennon's body of compositions.

January 28 At Apple, Allen Klein meets Paul, George, and Ringo for the first time.

January 30 Rooftop performance atop 3 Savile Row at lunchtime; nine songs are filmed and recorded by the eight-track machine in the basement.

February 1 The Beatles, Allen Klein, and John Eastman meet to discuss acquisition of NEMS.

February 2 Yoko Ono's divorce from Tony Cox is finalized. Yoko retains custody of their daughter, Kyoko.

February 3 Filming of *The Magic Christian,* starring Ringo and Peter Sellers, begins at Twickenham.

Allen Klein is officially appointed to untangle the Beatles' financial messes.

February 4 Lee and John Eastman are appointed as general legal counsel to Apple.

February 7 George enters University College Hospital with tonsillitis.

Paul is fined £19 for an outstanding speeding ticket issued last July and for failing to pay his auto license fee.

February 8 George's tonsils are removed.

February 12 Paul, perhaps already unhappy with Klein's representation, forms a side company, Adagrose Ltd., with Paul as sole director. This evolves into MPL, Paul's current company.

February 13 Paul and Linda attend Apple's launch party for Mary Hopkin's *Post Card* LP at the Post Office Tower's revolving restaurant.

February 14 John Eastman writes a letter to Clive Epstein warning him of Allen Klein's upcoming audit of all the Beatles' affairs and the possible "improprieties" involving NEMS. The letter, intended to scare Clive into selling NEMS at a low price to the Beatles, backfires.

February 15 George leaves the hospital.

February 17 Clive Epstein, wanting to wash his hands of the financial problems involved in dealing with EMI and Apple, decides to sell NEMS to Triumph Investment Trust.

February 19 Ringo is served with a writ for misuse of property by the landlords of his Montagu Square flat. John and Yoko had been staying there in October 1968 when the flat was raided for drugs.

February 20 Ringo attends the European premiere of *Candy* at the Odeon Theatre in Kensington.

February 24 Triumph Investment obtains full control of NEMS for about £750,000.

February 25 Allen Klein threatens to claim unpaid NEMS royalties from Triumph on behalf of the Beatles.

February 28 Ringo settles with his landlords out of court, agreeing to sell his lease.

George makes a quick trip to Ottawa to attend a performance by folk singer Eric Anderson at the Capitol Theatre.

March 1 Paul produces Mary Hopkin's recording session for the McCartney composition "Goodbye."

March 2 John and Yoko perform "Cambridge 1969," a free-form mélange of feedback and screaming, at Cambridge University's Lady Mitchell Hall. The performance is recorded for release on their second album.

March 4 Princess Margaret visits the set of *The Magic Christian* and socializes with Ringo, Peter Sellers, and the visiting Paul and Linda.

Paul and Linda attend the premiere of the film *Isadora* at the Odeon Theatre.

March 11 George and Paul both play on Jackie Lomax's recording of "Thumbin' a Ride"; Paul produces.

March 12 Paul marries Linda Eastman at Marylebone Register Office; Paul's brother Michael is best man, and no other Beatles are present. A reception at the Ritz Hotel follows the ceremony.

Sgt. Pilcher's drug squad arrives at George's house and plants some cannabis resin, despite Pattie's helpful attempts to lead them to George's real stash. George arrives shortly thereafter and is taken into custody at Esher police station, where he and Pattie are charged with possession.

March 16 Standing at the dock at Southampton, John and Yoko try to get to Holland or France. Unfortunately, a man in a mac says they have to go back, not even giving them a chance.

Newlyweds Paul and Linda fly from London to New York to spend time visiting the bride's family.

March 20 John and Yoko finally make the plane into Paris. While they are honeymooning down by the Seine, Peter Brown calls to say they can get married in Gibraltar near Spain.

March 21 Allen Klein is named business manager of Apple.

March 24 John and Yoko have lunch with artist Salvador Dalí in Paris.

March 25 John and Yoko drive from Paris to the Amsterdam Hilton to talk in their beds for a week. Newspapers ask what they're doing in bed, and John replies, "We're only trying to get us some peace."

March 31 John and Yoko make a lightning trip to Vienna, where they eat chocolate cake in a bag. The press comment, "She's gone to his head! They look just like two gurus in drag."

George and Pattie are found guilty of possession of cannabis and fined £250 each.

April 1 John and Yoko catch the early plane back to London, carrying fifty acorns tied in a sack. The men from the press wish them success and welcome the both of them back.

April 2 John, Paul, and Allen Klein meet at the bank office of Henry Ansbacher & Co.

April 9 In the afternoon, Ringo is excused from filming to participate in the Beatles' next-to-last photo shoot as a group. The session takes place in East Twickenham, just a couple of miles west along the Thames from the film location. The group poses around the riverside Madingley Club and along the river itself on a rowboat.

April 11	UK release of "Get Back"/"Don't Let Me Down" single.
April 12	John and Yoko pay a business visit to Henry Ansbacher & Co.'s main bank offices in central London.
April 14	John and Paul tape the next Beatles' single, "The Ballad of John and Yoko," at EMI Studio 3.
April 17	Another business meeting with John, Paul, and George present, as well as Allen Klein, Lee Eastman, and a representative of Henry Ansbacher & Co.
April 20	Paul pays a business visit to Henry Ansbacher & Co.'s main bank offices in central London.
April 21	In keeping with both the Beatles' financial shuffling and the Lennons' "bagism" concept, John and Yoko announce the formation of Bag Productions. Though it brings the world many films, erotic lithographs, and other projects, its greatest legacy will probably remain as a lyric in John's song "Come Together."
April 22	The second important event to take place on the 3 Savile Row rooftop occurs as John takes Yoko's last name in a formal ceremony. Henceforth he is officially John Winston Ono Lennon, MBE.
April 24	The Beatles and Triumph Investment settle out of court in the dispute over unpaid NEMS royalties.
April 25	John and Yoko fly to Switzerland to attend the Montreux TV festival where their film *Rape* is screened.
May 4	John, Paul, and Ringo attend a private wrap party for *The Magic Christian* held at Les Ambassadeurs nightclub.
	John purchases Tittenhurst, a seventy-two-acre estate in Ascot, for £145,000.
May 5	U.S. release of "Get Back"/"Don't Let Me Down" single.
May 7	John, Paul, George, and Allen Klein meet with EMI executives to try to renegotiate Beatles recording royalties.
May 8	John, George, and Ringo sign management contracts with Allen Klein and his company ABKCO. Paul refuses to sign and eventually has to sue the other three to disassociate himself from the Beatles' joint financial interests.
May 9	UK release of George's *Electronic Sound* LP.
	UK release of John and Yoko's *Unfinished Music No. 2: Life with the Lions* LP.
	Paul sings and plays drums and bass on Steve Miller's recording session for "My Dark Hour."
May 11	George plays guitar on Jack Bruce's recording of "Never Tell Your Mother She's Out of Tune."
May 13	The Beatles return to EMI House's stairwell, site of the front-cover photo for their first LP, to shoot a nearly identical cover photo for the proposed *Get Back* album.
May 15	John visits the U.S. Embassy only to be turned down for a visa thanks to his drug conviction the previous year. This is the origin of lifelong immigration problems for John, but in the immediate future it merely prevents him from traveling with Ringo on the *QEII* to New York and from holding a second "bed-in for peace" in the States.
May 16	Paul and Linda fly from London to Corfu for a vacation.
	John and Yoko watch the *QEII* pull out with Ringo, Maureen, and Peter Sellers aboard, destination New York.
May 20	John and George pay a business visit to Henry Ansbacher & Co.'s main bank offices in central London.
May 22	Ringo and crew finally arrive in the United States to shoot final scenes for *The Magic Christian*.
May 24	John and Yoko fly to the Bahamas, hoping to hold a second bed-in somewhere near the United States, but opt instead for Canada.
May 25	John and Yoko fly from the Bahamas to Toronto, flying on to Montreal the following evening.
May 26	John and Yoko begin their second bed-in at the Hôtel Reine-Elizabeth, lasting eight days. Press interviews are filmed and taped throughout.
	U.S. release of George's *Electronic Sound* LP.
	U.S. release of John and Yoko's *Unfinished Music No. 2: Life with the Lions* LP.
May 30	UK release of "The Ballad of John and Yoko"/"Old Brown Shoe" single.
May 31	George attends a reception for Richie Havens at the Speakeasy nightclub.

June 1	George and Pattie fly to Sardinia for three weeks' vacation. George finishes composing "Here Comes the Sun" during this trip.
June 3	John and Yoko attend an afternoon peace conference in Ottawa.
June 4	U.S. release of "The Ballad of John and Yoko"/"Old Brown Shoe" single.
	John and Yoko spend the day visiting Toronto and Niagara Falls.
June 5	John and Yoko stop over in Frankfurt on their way back to London from Canada.
June 17	Paul and Linda fly back to London from their month-long Corfu vacation.
June 23	George and Pattie return to London from Sardinia.
June 26	John, Yoko, Kyoko, and Julian make a surprise appearance at Holmrook Special School.
June 27	Ringo and Maureen fly to southern France for a brief vacation.
June 29	John and Yoko take their respective children, Julian and Kyoko, for a family car trip across Scotland.

July 1	John runs his car off the road in Scotland, injuring himself and Yoko and her daughter, Kyoko. They are all attended to at Lawson Memorial Hospital, where they spend five days recuperating, and John misses all Beatles sessions through at least July 8.
July 3	Ringo fills in for the hospitalized John and Yoko by hosting a press party for the release of the first Plastic Ono Band single "Give Peace a Chance," held at Chelsea Town Hall.
July 4	UK release of the Plastic Ono Band's "Give Peace a Chance"/"Remember Love" single.
July 6	John and Yoko are airlifted by helicopter from the hospital in Scotland to a private jet, which returns them to London.
July 7	U.S. release of the Plastic Ono Band's "Give Peace a Chance"/"Remember Love" single.

August 2	Paul produces and plays on Badfinger's recording of his composition "Come and Get It."
August 3	Ringo and Maureen attend Hank Snow's concert at the London Palladium.
August 8	The Beatles are photographed six times crossing Abbey Road for their final group album cover by Iain Macmillan. Linda also takes some candid shots during the session.
August 11	John and Yoko move into Tittenhurst, which will be their home for the next two years.
August 17	Paul and Ringo play on two Mary Hopkin songs, both produced by Paul.
August 20	The last Beatles session with all four members present, as the final running order and master tape banding for the *Abbey Road* LP is worked on.
August 21	Sandwiched between the final group recording session and final group photo shoot, the Beatles attend the first annual Apple Corps general board meeting. Probably a dispirited affair, considering the circumstances.
August 22	The Beatles' final photo shoot together takes place on the grounds of John's new estate and is filmed on a home camera by Linda. Photographers Ethan Russell, Monty Fresco, and Mal Evans shoot pictures that serve as the covers for the *Hey Jude* album and many bootlegs of *Get Back* material.
August 27	The Beatles rid themselves of their remaining shares in NEMS Enterprises.
August 28	Linda gives birth to Mary, her first child with Paul, at Avenue Clinic.
	George attends a press reception for the Radha Krishna Temple's new single "Hare Krishna Mantra," which George produced, at Sydenham Hill.
August 31	John, George, and Ringo (and their wives) travel to the Isle of Wight to attend Bob Dylan's performance that evening.

September 1	Following his performance at the Isle of Wight, Bob Dylan returns to John's house to visit with the Fab Three.
September 5	George and Ringo play on Leon Russell's recording of "Delta Lady."
September 8	Ringo checks in to Middlesex Hospital with an unspecified ailment.

September 10	The Institute of Contemporary Arts hosts a John and Yoko film festival. The famous couple don't attend, sending a pair of stand-ins concealed in a white bag. Among the films premiering is *Self-Portrait,* a slow-motion close-up study of John's genitalia, which apparently hadn't gotten enough exposure on *Two Virgins* to satisfy him.
September 11	Ringo checks out of Middlesex Hospital.
September 13	Plastic Ono Band performs at the Toronto Rock and Roll Revival, held at the University of Toronto's Varsity Stadium and recorded and filmed for release.
September 15	John and Yoko fly back to London Airport from Toronto.
September 18	Paul coproduces and plays on Badfinger's recording of "Rock of All Ages."
September 20	At a hectic Apple board meeting, Allen Klein announces the completion of a new contract between EMI and the Beatles, lasting through 1976, with the group's record royalties doubled. Paul, for the moment, is impressed with Klein's negotiation skills. John and Yoko also officially appoint Klein as manager of their company, Bag Productions. Most important, John announces to everyone that he's quitting the group. The others (George is absent, visiting his ailing mother) persuade him not to announce this to the press just yet, perhaps hoping that he'll reconsider.
September 25	ATV now controls 54 percent of the shares in Northern Songs, thereby gaining possession of publishing rights to most Lennon/McCartney compositions.
	John and Yoko visit the launch party for Apple band Trash's cover single of "Golden Slumbers"/"Carry That Weight."
	Paul and Linda attend the British premiere of the film *Midnight Cowboy* at the London Pavilion.
September 26	UK release of *Abbey Road* LP.
October 1	U.S. release of *Abbey Road* LP.
October 6	U.S. release of "Something"/"Come Together" single.
October 7	George reportedly sits in on guitar for a Rick Grech session.
October 9	Yoko enters King's College Hospital, expecting John's second child.
October 12	Yoko suffers her second miscarriage at King's College Hospital.
	WKNR-Radio's Russ Gibb takes calls from listeners claiming to know clues proving Paul McCartney is dead. To add to the fun, Gibb invents several clues himself, which really gets the rumor ball rolling.
October 13	Paul and Ringo attend Mary Hopkin's concert at the Savoy Theatre.
October 14	The *Michigan Daily* publishes Fred LaBour's review of *Abbey Road.* To spice up the review, LaBour weaves in the "Paul is dead" rumors. Unfortunately, putting this in print only serves to arm the supporters of this hoax.
October 15	Ringo and Maureen fly to Los Angeles for a business trip.
October 20	George and Patti attend Ravi Shankar's concert at Royal Festival Hall.
	U.S. release of "Cold Turkey"/"Don't Worry Kyoko" single by the Plastic Ono Band.
	U.S. release of *Wedding Album* LP by John and Yoko.
October 22	Ringo and Maureen return to London from Los Angeles.
	Paul and Linda travel to their farm in Scotland for a few weeks' vacation.
October 24	UK release of "Cold Turkey"/"Don't Worry Kyoko" single by the Plastic Ono Band.
October 27	Work begins on building a recording studio on John and Yoko's estate.
October 31	UK release of "Something"/"Come Together" single.
November 1	John and Yoko fly to Athens for a brief vacation spent cruising the Mediterranean with Alexis Mardas. They also travel to India before returning to London.
November 7	UK release of *Wedding Album* LP by John and Yoko.
November 25	John returns his MBE to Buckingham Palace via chauffeur, along with a note explaining the reasons why: in protest of the Biafran and Vietnam wars, and of the slipping chart position of "Cold Turkey" (although it's actually peaking at number 12 this week).

December 1	George, Pattie, Ringo, and Maureen attend Delaney & Bonnie & Friends' concert at the Royal Albert Hall. George is persuaded by band member Eric Clapton to join the group for the remainder of the tour.
December 5	Ringo and Maureen move into Roundhill, a house near Highgate.
December 11	Ringo, George, Pattie, John, and Yoko attend the Royal World Premiere of *The Magic Christian* along with Princess Margaret at the Odeon Theatre in Kensington.
December 12	UK release of the Plastic Ono Band's *Live Peace in Toronto* LP. UK release of *No One's Gonna Change Our World* LP. U.S. release of the Plastic Ono Band's *Live Peace in Toronto* LP.
December 14	John and Yoko make "A Silent Protest for James Hanratty" (hanged seven years prior for murder) by appearing in a white bag (or did they?) at Hyde Park Speakers' Corner. Following this, they drive to 10 Downing Street to deliver a petition to the prime minister.
December 16	As John and Yoko fly from London to Toronto, billboards sponsored by the couple are unveiled in eleven cities announcing WAR IS OVER! IF YOU WANT IT. They stay at Ronnie Hawkins's farm through December 21.
December 17	John and Yoko hold a press conference at the Ontario Science Center to announce their own version of Woodstock, a free three-day Toronto peace festival to be held the following July; the festival never occurs.
December 19	UK release of *The Beatles' Seventh Christmas Record,* the Beatles' final annual Christmas flexi-disc for fan club members.
December 22	John and Yoko travel from Toronto to Montreal by train and hold a press conference at the Château Champlain Hotel.
December 23	In Ottawa, John and Yoko meet with Canadian prime minister Pierre Trudeau for almost an hour, discussing peace. Later that day, they fly back to Toronto and then on to London.
December 24	John and Yoko participate in a sit-in/fast at Rochester Cathedral for peace and against poverty.
December 29	John and Yoko fly from London to Denmark to visit Yoko's daughter Kyoko (and Kyoko's father, Tony Cox), staying on a farm in Ålborg.
December 31	George, Pattie, Paul, and Linda attend a New Year's party thrown by Ringo and Maureen at Roundhill.

1. Documentary filming/Rehearsal

Date: 2 January 1969
Time: 10:00 a.m.–7:00 p.m.
Location: Twickenham Film Studios, London
Director: Michael Lindsay-Hogg

The last full year of the Beatles' career got off to a rough start with the half-baked "Get Back/Let It Be" project. Having postponed a tentatively announced concert in December, the group arranged to be filmed while rehearsing songs both new and old for a live performance, venue undetermined, which would end the documentary with a bang. If enough new songs were written, an album would be released as well.

Thanks in part to their work on *Rock and Roll Circus,* director Michael Lindsay-Hogg and sound engineer Glyn Johns were chosen to oversee the visual and audio aspects of the film. George Martin popped in now and again to the set at Twickenham, and while Neil Aspinall remained mostly in the Apple offices, Mal Evans was on hand to look after the instruments and equip-

ment. As usual, John brought Yoko to every session, and she never strayed far from his side.

Day one of the filming began pleasantly enough, although there was some grumbling about the cold, cavernous soundstage, ideal for filming but lousy for providing decent acoustics. However, the Beatles had several excellent new compositions to sink their teeth into, and they put in a good day of work on John's "Don't Let Me Down" (similar to his most recent demo with the addition of a chorus), Paul's "I've Got a Feeling" (with John's "Everybody Had a Hard Year" section now incorporated), and Paul's "Two of Us."

RELEASE HISTORY

This session was recorded on Nagra rolls 1–10A. Excerpts seen in the *Let It Be* film included shots of Mal Evans setting up the Beatles' equipment. Footage from this day was also used in the promo clip for "The Ballad of John and Yoko."

NOTE

There is a wealth (some would say an overkill) of material available from the "Get Back" sessions. Each of the two cameras used (only one on the first day and four on the thirtieth) was designated a Nagra brand tape recorder that would pick up sound to be synchronized with the footage during editing. Hundreds of these Nagra rolls still exist and have been bootlegged in excellent sound, with the most complete collection being Purple Chick's *A/B Road.*

An in-depth analysis of the Nagra material can be found in the groundbreaking book *Get Back: The Unauthorized Chronicle of the Beatles' "Let It Be" Disaster* by Doug Sulpy and Ray Schweighardt. The first edition of this book, titled *Drugs, Divorce, and a Slipping Image,* gave rise to the "DDSI" numbering system of cataloging these performances, and I've used these numbers for reference in the following entries. These numbers as used here correspond not with either of those books, however, but with Sulpy's *The 910's Guide to the Beatles Outtakes, Volume 2* (2001 edition), which describes material that surfaced after publication of the two earlier books.

Rather than rehash information from those excellent works, I've concentrated on the two major areas they didn't cover: material captured on the eight-track tapes at Apple, and video outtake footage and promo clips from both Twickenham and Apple. In other words, anything not covered strictly by the Nagra tape rolls.

More specifically:

- Some of Glyn Johns's rough mixes escaped on a two-sided acetate (see the January 30 entry for details) that was subsequently broadcast on U.S. radio and bootlegged. This is referred to in the text as the "WBCN Acetate" due to its airing on that Boston FM station September 22, 1969. That broadcast is best found on the CD *Posters, Incense and Strobe Candles.*
- From March through May, Glyn worked at Olympic Studios cleaning up the "best" takes and banding a master tape assembly May 28. This proposed lineup ("Glyn's first lineup") was due to be released as an album in June or July, but postponed in favor of releasing Abbey Road first and holding the earlier material back to coincide with the documentary film. This first lineup was bootlegged from an acetate in the 1970s and from tape

source in the 1990s. It can best be found on the last disc of the *Thirty Days* boxed CD set.
- To confuse matters further, what appears to be a working version of the above "first lineup" was aired on WBKW in Buffalo beginning September 20. This lineup, which has been booted only on the obscure album *O.P.D.,* contains a slightly longer mix of "Dig It" and uses the raw take of "Get Back" (DDSI 27.63) with a cold ending and comment from John, rather than the single mix (which tacks on the coda from DDSI 28.43).
- As 1970 began, Glyn was called back to revamp the lineup, adding "Across the Universe" and the newly taped "I Me Mine," and dropping "Teddy Boy." He also chopped out bits and pieces and shuffled the song order a bit. Although this version ("Glyn's second lineup") was banded and proffered on January 5, 1970, it too was rejected. It was bootlegged from a tape source in 1999 and is best found on the Strawberry CD *Get Back 2nd Mix.* (Vigotone's *Get Back—the Glyn Johns Final Compilation* does not accurately reflect the contents of the second mix, having some sections that Glyn removed reinstated.) See my book *Lifting Latches* for complete details of all Glyn's various acetates.
- In the end, of course, Phil Spector was asked to remix everything from scratch, and his assembly, drastically different to both of Glyn's, would be issued as the album *Let It Be* in May 1970. The film *Let It Be* was released simultaneously, and though it was available briefly on video in 1981, has long been out of print.
- In the mid-'80s, about 50 minutes of workprint footage (mostly black and white) from these sessions began to circulate on video, heavily fragmented, but largely with synchronized sound. Some of this footage was used in a legitimate documentary, *Yoko Ono: Then and Now,* which explains why 95 percent of it focuses on John and Yoko. A bit of it was even used in the promo video for "Nobody Told Me" in 1984.
- The *Anthology* project naturally included several new recordings from this month on the CDs (mostly "take 1" of each song), as well as pristine remastered footage in the home videos (including several minutes not used in the original film). Other miscellaneous unreleased mixes, promo clips, and film outtakes from these sessions are discussed in individual entries.

2. Documentary filming/Rehearsal

Date: 3 January 1969
Time: 10:30 a.m.–6:30 p.m.
Location: Twickenham Film Studios, London
Director: Michael Lindsay-Hogg

Paul and Ringo spend the beginning of this session huddled around the piano (soon joined by George and his acoustic guitar) as Paul runs through various songs and plays classical-style improvisations. When John arrives, it takes everyone a while to get into the routining of new numbers. A slew of rock oldies and jokey "White Album" covers get the band warmed up.

Serious rehearsal begins with "Don't Let Me Down" and "I've Got a Feeling," at which point nostalgia dominates and they run through a number of early unreleased Lennon/McCartney compositions. The most finished of these, "One After 909," had actually been recorded by the Beatles in March 1963 and would be revived for good by the end of these sessions. After a few more oldies, Paul convinces the others to work on "Two of Us" before splitting for a lunch break.

Nearly all the rest of the day would be spent in a futile attempt (three hours long) to learn George's "All Things Must Pass." John is totally lost at the organ, and even Paul seems disinterested, contributing bass and wretched vocal harmonies. As if George hasn't suffered enough, Paul ends the day by teaching his mates another new number, "Maxwell's Silver Hammer." Despite hours of tortuous rehearsal on this number over the next few days, it would be left until the next album for a proper recording. Despite a fun morning, the afternoon was an inauspicious way to end the working week.

RELEASE HISTORY

This session was recorded on Nagra rolls 11-28A and 50-57B. Excerpts seen in the *Let It Be* film included Paul's morning piano improvisation and Paul teaching the others the chords to "Maxwell's Silver Hammer."

3. Documentary filming/Rehearsal

Date: 6 January 1969
Time: 10:30 a.m.–?
Location: Twickenham Film Studios, London
Director: Michael Lindsay-Hogg

Rather than being refreshed by a weekend off, everyone seemed tired and cranky this Monday, as if being forced to return to the office. George has written a new song over the weekend, "Hear Me Lord," but none of his bandmates take much interest as he presents it to them. Several hours pass with no serious rehearsal, but plenty of jamming and discussion about where to hold the live concert and what kind of audience to invite.

Finally, they try to knock "Don't Let Me Down" into some kind of shape, with Paul taking charge by offering up a number of vocal counterpoints and harmonies. Nobody is very happy with these, and George seems particularly reluctant to cooperate with Paul's suggestions. After an hour of this with little progress, they move on to "Two of Us."

Things get worse as the Beatles' different approaches to rehearsing clash. In exasperation, George blurts out that he will play whatever Paul asks of him, and Paul responds that he isn't trying to boss anyone around. He seems bossy only because of John's apathy and George's unhappiness with the whole project.

Perhaps to appease George, they work on "All Things Must Pass" next, although it shows little improvement over the last batch of rehearsals. "She Came In through the Bathroom Window" is also rehearsed briefly before the session ends, but the day as a whole is an utter washout.

RELEASE HISTORY

This session was recorded on Nagra rolls 29-49A and 61-70B. Excerpts seen in the *Let It Be* film included Paul's morning piano run-through of "Oh! Darling," some of the "Don't Let Me Down" rehearsal, and of course Paul and George's "Whatever it is that'll please you, I'll do it" argument. Footage from this day also made it into the "Don't Let Me Down" promo clip (see the January 30 entry).

4. Documentary filming/Rehearsal

Date: 7 January 1969
Time: 9:30 a.m.–5:30 p.m.
Location: Twickenham Film Studios, London
Director: Michael Lindsay-Hogg

Most of this morning is spent debating whether to even go through with the live concert; Paul is in favor of the idea, but the lack of cooperation from his bandmates is wearing his patience thin. Ringo is amenable as long as it's held in Britain, although Michael Lindsay-Hogg does his best to promote the concept of filming overseas. John offers little opinion one way or the other, and George shoots down practically every idea anyone brings up.

Rehearsal of "I've Got a Feeling" shows some improvement, but then a couple of hours are wasted on "Maxwell's Silver Hammer," with Paul running the song into the ground beyond the tolerance of most mortals. Having no other new compositions to offer, John suggests they resurrect "Across the Universe," but this bears little fruit after nearly an hour of work.

John plays through a half-finished offering, "Dig a Pony," but its sluggish tempo seems to be putting everyone to sleep. He asks if anyone can think of a fast number, and they decide to add "One After 909" to the show. This injects enough life into the proceedings to carry over into the following rehearsals of "Don't Let Me Down," which conclude the day on a somewhat positive note.

RELEASE HISTORY

This session was recorded on Nagra rolls 50–68A and 71–79B. Excerpts seen in the *Let It Be* film included snatches of "Maxwell's Silver Hammer," "Across the Universe," and "Dig a Pony."

5. Documentary filming/Rehearsal

Date: 8 January 1969
Time: 10:30 a.m.–?
Location: Twickenham Film Studios, London
Director: Michael Lindsay-Hogg

George starts this day as he often did, auditioning a song he had composed the previous night ("I Me Mine" in this case) for the others. Once everyone has arrived, a new policy is instituted: Begin the session by running through the list of songs nearest to completion, stopping to iron out problem areas for each individual number, and then work up arrangements for additional songs.

The run-throughs of "Two of Us," "Don't Let Me Down," "I've Got a Feeling," and "One After 909" are successful enough, but the problems begin when they try to work on "All Things Must Pass": Nobody but George seems interested in the song. John moves to piano for these rehearsals, which are followed by a few tries at "She Came In through the Bathroom Window" before breaking for lunch.

Things hardly improve with more than a half hour of mind-numbing work on "Maxwell's Silver Hammer." The rest of the day is devoted to learning "I Me Mine," and although John mostly opts out (waltzing with Yoko while the others play), Paul and Ringo enthusiastically help whip the song into shape. The session ends with further debate about the live show. John is now in favor of an overseas venue, George and Ringo are dead set against performing abroad, and Paul is noncommittal.

RELEASE HISTORY

This session was recorded on Nagra rolls 70–89A and 80–89B. Excerpts seen in the *Let It Be* film included George's morning performance and the later group run-through of "I Me Mine," and rehearsals of "I've Got a Feeling." About nine minutes of fragmented black-and-white workprint footage circulates from this day, consisting of "All Things Must Pass" rehearsals.

A snatch of dialogue from this day's film soundtrack (John's mock headline "Queen Says 'No' to Pot-Smoking FBI Member") was used by Phil Spector on the *Let It Be* LP, preceding "For You Blue."

6. Documentary filming/Rehearsal

Date: 9 January 1969
Time: 10:20 a.m.–5:30 p.m.
Location: Twickenham Film Studios, London
Director: Michael Lindsay-Hogg

A routine is beginning to settle in: Paul arrives first and runs though several of his unfinished songs on the piano ("Another Day," "Let It Be," "The Long and Winding Road," "Her Majesty," "Golden Slumbers," "Carry That Weight," "Oh! Darling"). George shows up and plays another new composition on acoustic guitar (a twelve-bar blues song), ignored by John and Paul, and then serious group rehearsal begin.

The set list begins identically to the previous day: "Two of Us," "Don't Let Me Down," "I've Got a Feeling," and "One After 909" are each worked on, some more thoroughly than others. With less success, "She Came In through the Bathroom Window," "Across The Universe," and George's twelve-bar (eventually titled "For You Blue") are also rehearsed. The day ends with Paul teaching the others the chords to "Let It Be."

The Beatles seem more interested in jamming and improvising this day: A swift rocker based around the lyric "when you get to Suzy's parlor, everybody gets well done" was included in the film *Let It Be* and even copyrighted as "Suzy Parker." Another Chuck Berry–style tune took shape this day, growing out of ad-libbed lyrics about England's immigration policy and evolving gradually into "Get Back." Particularly entertaining was a lengthy stream-of-consciousness piece, "Commonwealth/Get Off!"

With the topic of the live show mostly avoided, the group concentrated on playing music, and everyone's spirits seemed to be improving. Things would take a sudden dramatic turn for the worse the following day.

RELEASE HISTORY

This session was recorded on Nagra rolls 90–106A and 90–102B. Excerpts seen in the *Let It Be* film included performances of "Two of Us" and "Suzy Parker," and rehearsals of "I've Got a Feeling" and "One After 909." About five minutes of fragmented black-and-white workprint footage circulates from this day, consisting of romps through "Tennessee," "House of the Rising Sun," and the "Commonwealth" jam.

7. Documentary filming/Rehearsal

Date: 10 January 1969
Time: 10:30 a.m.–3:00 p.m.
Location: Twickenham Film Studios, London
Director: Michael Lindsay-Hogg

Tensions reached a breaking point this afternoon, although the precise reason is not clear from the surviving tapes. All seems well as the day begins with song publisher Dick James paying a visit to the set, and there is even some whispered talk among the Fabs about a bit of good business news that Neil Aspinall wants to impart at the next meeting.

Lengthy rehearsal of "Get Back" fills most of the morning, and the only moment of friction comes when George wants the strident A chord in the chorus to be a sharp ninth; Paul disagrees, finding it cliché (Jimi Hendrix used the same chord in "Purple Haze," among others). The moment passes though, and work continues with "Two of Us," the first song in the proposed set list, before breaking for lunch.

It was at this point that John and George reportedly got into a heated argument, although the exact cause is probably lost forever. All that's known for sure is that George told the others, "See you round the clubs," and walked out. The only evidence on the Nagra tapes is a fragment of George apparently returning to the soundstage after lunch to hand in his notice:

George: Well, I think I'll be leaving—uh, leaving the band now.
John: What? When?
George: Now. Get a replacement. Or write in to the *NME* and get a few people.

The next thing heard is George talking with Mal about who should pay the musicians for a session booked that night at Trident. George Martin had arranged string players to add overdubs to Brute Force's "King of Fuh" single, and George apparently blew off the rest of that day's session with the Beatles to work on that masterpiece. George is then heard walking out as someone whistles nonchalantly. Michael Lindsay-Hogg gives a concerned "Hmm," someone asks if the camera is still rolling, and then Michael calls, "Cut."

It's clear that nobody knows whether to take George seriously, and given Ringo's departure and swift return the previous summer, a wait-and-see policy is implemented. John, Paul, and Ringo vent their frustrations in a loud and aggressive jam, with Yoko joining in on shrill vocalizations. Some less than serious attempts to rehearse "I've Got a Feeling," "Don't Let Me Down," and "Maxwell's Silver Hammer" quickly degenerate into oldies.

The last hour or so is given over to discussion (although Paul returns to the piano), with the director wondering where the whole project now stands and John doing his best to seem nonchalant, suggesting that if George doesn't return, they take his advice and hire Eric Clapton as a replacement. The meeting Neil had scheduled to impart the business news would take place on the twelfth, although the subject would now be the "state of the group."

RELEASE HISTORY

This session was recorded on Nagra rolls 106–124A and 103–112B. Frustratingly, roll 117A, which would have documented the events immediately after George's departure, is missing in action (only two minutes of it have surfaced). About three minutes of fragmented color workprint footage circulates from this day (with an out-of-sync soundtrack), showing the jam session with Yoko on vocals that followed George's resignation.

8. Documentary filming/Rehearsal — J, P, R

Date: 13 January 1969
Time: 10:00 a.m.–5:00 p.m.
Location: Twickenham Film Studios, London
Director: Michael Lindsay-Hogg

All four Beatles, along with Yoko, Linda, Mal, Neil, and a couple of business advisers, assembled on January twelfth at Ringo's home in Elstead, the closest thing to neutral territory. Once the Apple-related business had been discussed, the financial men departed. Any attempt to then discuss the numerous personal and musical problems within the group was hampered by the presence of both Linda and Yoko, with the others seemingly unable to communicate honestly unless completely alone (Neil and Mal being honorary group members). Once he realized nothing would be accomplished, George decided to leave early and the fate of the band remained undecided.

Nonetheless, Paul and Ringo arrived at Twickenham as usual the following morning. John had also agreed to show up, but attempts to rouse him proved unsuccessful until well after noon. In the meantime, those who had been present at the meeting sat around sharing gossip about the occasion (getting in plenty of jabs at John and Yoko's behavior) with the film crew.

John finally arrived in time to share lunch with the others, and Michael Lindsay-Hogg took the opportunity to eavesdrop on the mealtime conversation by planting a microphone in the Twickenham cafeteria. The resulting tape is of poor quality, with the dialogue obscured by clinking plates and silverware. John expounds at length about what he feels are the roots of the band's predicament, while Paul mostly holds his tongue (Yoko and Linda are both seated at the table). John pleads guilty to conniving to suit his own ends, and Paul admits to having treated George as a sideman at recording sessions. John agrees and says that Paul treats him that way too, sometimes. In the end nothing is agreed upon except that the Beatles need to improve relations or call it a day.

After lunch, the remaining Beatles rehearse "Get Back" for a bit and then agree to come in the following day and see what happens.

RELEASE HISTORY

This session was recorded on Nagra rolls 125–136A and 113–121B. A bit of outtake footage from this day was used in *Anthology*.

9. TV interview — J

Date: 14 January 1969
Location: Twickenham Film Studios, London
Length: 0:20

Toward the end of the January 10 session, John and Yoko could be heard talking with a reporter from Canada's CBC-TV network. He was there to arrange a filmed interview with Yoko for the following week, though he obviously hoped John and perhaps the other Beatles could be persuaded to join. (George had al-

ready walked out, but the reporter seemed to be unaware of this.)

The interview took place in a corner of the Twickenham soundstage around noon on the fourteenth, and John participated, although he was clearly ill (Ringo also flits past in the background at one point). Thirty minutes of footage exist, but all that circulates widely is this short extract used in the documentary *Imagine: John Lennon*. The clip, about thirteen minutes into the interview, has John explaining why he could be "counted out—in" on the LP version of "Revolution." Sitting in a fur coat and mumbling his response, John says he prefers nonviolence but is prone to change, depending upon the circumstance.

This has been labeled the "Two Junkies" interview, and John fidgets uncomfortably throughout the first half, sipping tea and growing paler by the minute. About halfway through, he stamps out his cigarette and seems to be holding back something apart from his responses. "Excuse me, I feel a bit sick," he apologizes, and the camera is shut off, presumably allowing John

to remedy the situation. The remainder of the conversation is much livelier and touches on inspiration, live performances, and John and Yoko's future projects such as the "British Box" for *Aspen* magazine (see the November 4–25, 1968, entry).

RELEASE HISTORY

This brief clip is seen in the documentary film *Imagine: John Lennon.*

---

10. Documentary filming/Rehearsal   J, P, R

Date: 14 January 1969
Time: ?–5:00 p.m.
Location: Twickenham Film Studios, London
Director: Michael Lindsay-Hogg

It's clear that without some resolution to the conflict with George, nothing productive will come of further sessions. Nonetheless, Michael keeps the cameras rolling in hopes that something usable will happen. Paul sits at the piano and expounds on chord theory, joined by Ringo for a bit of Jerry Lee Lewis keyboard pounding. With John and George absent, Glyn Johns noodles away on a guitar in the background.

John and Yoko return from their CBC interview, and everyone sits around drinking and trying to come up with witticisms while avoiding the larger issues. A few of John's quips hit their targets, mainly because he flings them out rapid-fire. Peter Sellers visits, along with Joe McGrath, who will direct Sellers and Ringo in *The Magic Christian* the following month. John's drug-related jokes seem to make Sellers uneasy, and he leaves within a few minutes.

Finally, they try to get some playing in, seemingly for the hell of it, but with John on electric piano and

Paul on lead guitar, it's a doomed enterprise. John plays a couple of unrecorded originals, "Mean Mr. Mustard" and "Madman," and the trio improvises a three-chord tune, "Watching Rainbows." After about an hour of this, Paul asks for the cameras to be switched off, and apart from a few shots of the set being disassembled, the lamentable Twickenham sessions are at an end.

The next day, rather than return to the studio, the Beatles held another summit and patched things up by agreeing to give George more leeway and to abandon the idea of rehearsing or performing in the vast and glacial film studio. The new plush recording studio at Apple's headquarters was nearly ready, and the time seemed ripe to take advantage of its amenities.

RELEASE HISTORY

This session was recorded on Nagra rolls 137–148A and 122–125B. Excerpts seen in the *Let It Be* film included Paul and Ringo's boogie-woogie piano duet (copyrighted as "Jazz Piano Song"). A bit of outtake footage from this day was used in *Anthology*. About two minutes of fragmented black-and-white workprint footage circulates from this day, depicting Peter Sellers's visit.

---

11. Radio interview   R

Date: 21 January 1969
Time: morning
Location: limo between Brookfields and Apple
Interviewer: David Wigg
Broadcast: 25 January 1969, 1:00–2:00 p.m.
BBC Radio 1
Scene and Heard
Length: 3:22

Having made peace with George, the other Beatles agreed to reconvene at their newly constructed studio in the basement of Apple's 3 Savile Row office building.

The documentary filming would continue with no particular end in mind, and Glyn Johns would continue to record rehearsals and completed takes, this time using professional equipment.

On this first day of resumed filming, Ringo consented to tape an interview for BBC Radio's *Scene and Heard* while being driven from his new home in Elstead to London. The interview was conducted by *Daily Express* reporter David Wigg, who would go on to record nearly a dozen interviews with individual Beatles for the program over the next five years.

Reports of Beatles business and personal troubles

were rampant in the press that week. On the eighteenth, an article in *Disc and Music Echo* had quoted John as predicting the financial ruin of Apple, saying that if things didn't change, the group would be bankrupt within six months. This morning's *Daily Sketch* carried a rather sensationalistic article by Michael Housego titled "The End of a Beautiful Friendship?" It reported that John and George had actually come to blows on the tenth, which was probably just thirdhand gossip.

Wigg asks Ringo about all of this, and the drummer candidly admits that like any group of close friends, the Beatles often hurt one another unintentionally by letting problems reach a boiling point. He insists that a split is not imminent, although he stops short of saying they would never consider breaking up.

On the subject of finance, Ringo tries to sidestep the matter of Apple's disorganization, blaming the problem on heavy taxation: "If we earn a million, then the government gets ninety percent and we get ten thousand." (Math was never his strong suit.) He says they're trying to scale back the amount of projects funded by Apple, and Wigg asks if they have been careless with their money. Ringo concedes that while they are rich on paper, their physical assets are far less than most people imagine.

All of these problems led to a "slipping image," as the Housego article put it, and Wigg wonders whether this is a concern. Ringo realizes that it's useless trying to please everyone and declares that they "can't go on forever as four clean little mop-tops, playing 'She Loves You.'" Wigg, who obviously hadn't heard many of Ringo's previous interviews, pegs him as the most industrious Beatle. The drummer admits to being indolent, having few ambitions beyond making LPs and then staying at home and playing "with the kids and the wife. I enjoy playing with the wife!"

RELEASE HISTORY

1976: This interview was released on the LP *The Beatles Tapes with David Wigg,* later reissued on CD.

12. Documentary filming/Studio session

Date:	21 January 1969
Time:	?–7:30 p.m.
Location:	Apple Studios, London
Director:	Michael Lindsay-Hogg
Producer:	Glyn Johns

[A.] She Came In through the Bathroom Window—DDSI 21.78 (stereo) (3:35)

This Apple session only came to light thanks to Doug Sulpy's recent examination of all extant Nagra rolls. In fact, the Beatles had assembled at Apple's new basement studio on the twentieth without the presence of the camera crew. (At one point on the twenty-first, George plays a riff to John and asks, "Remember that thing we did?" John replies, "Yesterday?")

That was probably the day when "Magic" Alex's haphazardly designed recording equipment was found to be unusable. Engineer Dave Harries recalled: "They actually tried a session on this desk, they did a take, but when they played back the tape it was all hum and hiss." A recording of unknown origin, supposedly capturing Alex's attempt to test the equipment, was aired on episode 89-20 of *The Lost Lennon Tapes*. The second voice on the tape was said to be John and Yoko's friend Dan Richter, but he doubted it when I e-mailed him a transcript.

Alex: 1-2-3-1-2-3-1-2-3. Have you made sure that you have recorded with the—

?: Yes.
Alex: You know, because probably something is wrong with the tape, the tape is—
?: Yes, I'm getting it all off the tape.
Alex: You're getting off the tape, and so you make sure that it's all right, the recorder?
?: Yeah.
Alex: 1-2-3-4-5-6-7-8-9-10, 1-2-3-4-5-6-7.
?: This—this is my controller.
Alex: This is my—that's—no, no, you don't have a control, because the right record plays on the left [?] 1-2-3—
?: I see. Right there. 1-2-3-4-5-6-7, 1-2-3-4-5-6. No matter how much I turn this. Doesn't matter.
Alex: It doesn't matter, but we'll figure it out.

Needless to say, they didn't figure it out, and George Martin arranged for an eight-track recorder and mixing console to be brought over from Abbey Road the next day. Ringo's kit was recorded in stereo for one of the first times, with one channel capturing the bass drum and floor tom and a second the snare and rack toms. Most of the twenty-first was spent setting up the new equipment, tuning the studio piano, and jamming various oldies.

The first serious rehearsal is for "Dig a Pony," which occupies most of the afternoon. Glyn Johns is in the control room, and, using reel E90488, he captures several performances of this song, along with brief jokey renditions of "Papa's Got a Brand New Bag" and

"Shout!" Also on this reel are the first takes of "I've Got a Feeling" and "Don't Let Me Down."

During a break in the action, John goes into a corner of the studio to film an introduction for the Rolling Stones' set in the *Rock and Roll Circus*. This snippet ("And now, your host for this evening, the Rolling Stones") was released in the eventual home video, with all but the first two words muted. The complete intro survives on Nagra roll 404A.

At one point after hearing playbacks, John returns to the studio and announces to nobody in particular, " 'I Dig a Pygmy' by Charles Hawtrey and the Deaf-Aids! Phase one, in which Doris gets her oats!" Although the eight-track wasn't running at this point, this comment was captured on Nagra roll 409A and used in the film *Let It Be*. Phil Spector lifted this snippet off the soundtrack to open the *Let It Be* album, preceding "Two of Us."

As the session winds down, the group peruses a list of song titles worked up at Twickenham and selects Paul's "She Came In through the Bathroom Window" to work on next. One very rough take (**A**) is recorded by Glyn, apparently on reel E90489 (running backwards on the tape according to Paul's notation on the box). For this recording John plays the group's new Fender Rhodes electric piano, and George plays his guitar through a wah-wah pedal, as heard throughout the Twickenham sessions.

The song is taken at a very slow tempo, but all the lyrics are complete; John throws in backing vocals here and there. Although this song is labeled as DDSI 21.78, it should actually fall before 21.80, as the dialogue that immediately precedes that version ends this take. Paul discusses how John can vary his keyboard part during the song's different sections, but they wouldn't return to the song again seriously until the July *Abbey Road* sessions.

RELEASE HISTORY

This session was recorded on Nagra rolls 400–411A. Excerpts seen in the *Let It Be* film include John's "I dig a pygmy" comment.

1996: **A** was officially released on the CD *Anthology 3*.

13. Documentary filming/Studio session

Date: 22 January 1969
Location: Apple Studios, London
Director: Michael Lindsay-Hogg
Producer: Glyn Johns, George Martin

[A.] **Dig a Pony—DDSI 22.21 (stereo)** (4:16)
[B.] **Dig a Pony—DDSI 22.23 (mono)** (4:02)
[C.] **I'm Ready/Save the Last Dance for Me/Don't Let Me Down—DDSI 22.58/22.59 (stereo)** (1:56)
[D.] **Don't Let Me Down—DDSI 22.60 (stereo)** (3:55)
[E.] **Dig a Pony—DDSI 22.70 (stereo)** (4:04)
[F.] **I've Got a Feeling—DDSI 22.71 (stereo)** (2:54)
[G.] **Don't Let Me Down—DDSI 22.80 (stereo)** (0:19)

[H.] **I've Got a Feeling—DDSI 22.71 (alt. stereo mix)** (2:46)

After hearing a few playbacks from the previous day, the Beatles settle into another day of rehearsal and recording, which would begin as aimlessly as earlier sessions but would end with the band reenergized.

George has now abandoned his wah pedal in favor of a new Leslie guitar speaker given to him by Eric Clapton. George Martin is present for most of this session, but Glyn Johns is still the de facto producer, since nobody is really sure whether these recordings are for a TV show or record release (or both).

Using reel E90489, another rough take of "Dig a Pony" (DDSI 22.17) is recorded. After a brief playback, the tape is rewound and Glyn commences recording again as Paul runs through a loose rendition of Canned Heat's "Going Up the Country."

Once Paul's bass level is adjusted, the group launches into "Dig a Pony" again; this take (**A**) was released on *Anthology 3*. It has a much longer intro and a couple of different lyrics, but the arrangement is nearly perfected. At the end, Glyn congratulates them on getting the ending right (which they had failed to do on the previous take). John and Paul respond with mock offense: "You're not talking to Rikki and the Red Streaks, y'know!"

The following take (**B**) is basically identical; it circulates from a remix prepared April 23, 1976, one of two reels auditioned by EMI executives considering various unreleased material. Although it was a stereo mix, the circulating tape is mono, taped off speakers.

Back at Apple, the Beatles listen to playbacks of the last two takes of "Dig a Pony" and record one more for good measure before moving on to work on "I've Got a Feeling." After a long rehearsal but no recorded takes, they break for lunch. It was at this point that fortune smiled on the group.

George and Eric Clapton had recently attended a Ray Charles concert at London's Festival Hall; George recognized Ray's organist, Billy Preston, having played alongside Preston in Hamburg. George decided to "put the word out" for Billy to visit Apple while he was in London. During the lunch break, Preston wandered into Apple reception and was quickly drafted by George to join the sessions. He fit in immediately, freeing up the guitarists from having to dream up fills and frills during these "no-overdub" recordings. More important, as Eric Clapton had done the previous year, he helped ease the tensions and relieve the boredom in the studio.

Billy sits down at the Fender Rhodes electric piano and readily picks up the three tunes the group had been concentrating on. When Glyn is ready to tape again, he catches the ensemble jamming Fats Domino's "I'm Ready" (noted as "Rocker" by Paul on the tape box and retitled "Instrumental No. 42" by early bootleggers). After a bit of joking around, they launch into the Drifters' "Save the Last Dance for Me," sliding neatly into the chorus of "Don't Let Me Down" (**C**).

A proper take of "Don't Let Me Down" follows soon afterward (**D**), with Ringo's introductory cymbal crash giving John "the courage to come screaming in." This take shows how much energy Billy Preston is able to inject into the proceedings; and with John's cry of "Hit it, Bill!" the keyboardist throws in a nifty solo over the coda. A clearly delighted John follows this with an exhortation to continue with " 'Dig a Pony' straight into 'I've Got a Fever.' "

That would have to wait until Glyn changed reels, threading up reel E90492. The seeming jump in reel numbers was caused by the order of tapes being shuffled when cataloged back at Abbey Road; in fact, this reel would be misdated in the log as January 24 and later incorrectly amended to January 23 (the date used in *Anthology 3*'s liner notes). Similarly, the order of Nagra rolls got muddled this afternoon when the soundman made some erroneous announcements. The correct order of A-rolls as labeled on bootleg should be as follows: 419, 422, 420, 421, 423.

Reel E90492 begins with a few takes of "Dig a Pony" with Billy sitting in. The last of these (**E**) opens with John's query about Ringo's drum pattern and a false start. After a minimal pause, the quintet swings right into a take of "I've Got a Feeling" (**F**), which breaks down near the end because John "cocked it up tryin' to get loud." This take was released on *Anthology 3* in an alternate stereo mix (**H**) that centers both drum tracks and splits John and Paul's vocal tracks. Naturally, they try taping a couple more takes before returning to the control room to hear playbacks of the new songs with Billy.

With former manager Allan Williams visiting, the group then attempts to perfect "Don't Let Me Down" with fragmented rehearsals and the recording of at least one false start (**G**). This aborted attempt, with Paul accidentally playing his "Dig a Pony" bass line, would be spliced in between **C** and **D** on both of Glyn's proposed *Get Back* lineups.

Detail work on "I've Got a Feeling" concludes the session, with Glyn offering to erase some of the earlier takes and record the rehearsal. John is opposed to the idea, and they depart without any further eight-track recording but with an open invitation to Billy Preston to attend as many of the following sessions as possible.

RELEASE HISTORY

This session was recorded on Nagra rolls 412–429A and 1014–1019B.

D–**F** were included on the "WBCN acetate"; **D** was slightly incomplete at the end. **C**–**G** were included on Glyn's first *Get Back* LP lineup; **D** and **F** were slightly incomplete. **C**–**G** were included on Glyn's second *Get Back* LP lineup; **D** and **F** were slightly incomplete and the opening note of **E** was cleaned up a bit. A large portion of **C** was also excised; Vigotone's issue mistakenly restores this missing material.

1983: **B** first appeared on the vinyl bootleg *File Under: Beatles* from an off-line mono tape of a 1976 stereo mix. Fragments of this appear from tape source on the CD-R *As It Happened, Baby!*

1991: Mono copies of **D** and **E** were included on the bootleg CD *Celluloid Rock* from tape source. **D** runs too fast and is slightly incomplete at the end; **E** is overlaid with a harsh metallic echo.

1996: **A** and **H** were officially released on the CD *Anthology 3*.

14. Documentary filming/Studio session

Date: 23 January 1969
Location: Apple Studios, London
Director: Michael Lindsay-Hogg
Producer: Glyn Johns, George Martin

[A.] Get Back—DDSI 23.78 (stereo) (0:05)
[B.] Get Back/I've Got a Feeling—DDSI 23.79/23.80 (stereo) (2:39)
[C.] Help!—DDSI 23.81 (stereo) (0:02)

This day's session is entirely devoted to Paul's "Get Back," enhanced greatly by Billy Preston's electric piano contribution. Following a number of rehearsals, at least one take is committed to reel E90490 (the only reel used this day) before breaking for lunch. Returning to the studio, the quintet performs a nearly nine-minute instrumental jam, one minute of which was captured on multitrack and labeled "Blues." Further takes of "Get Back" follow (approximately ten altogether), interrupted by another break to view the footage from John and Yoko's July 1968 You Are Here exhibit.

Just over a half hour of silent monochrome workprint footage circulates, documenting the end of this session. It begins with slates 305 and 307 on camera A, followed by slates 306 and 308 on camera B, capturing much of the same action from an alternate angle. The camera B footage concludes with several minutes of the group listening to playbacks in the control booth, along with Glyn Johns, Denis O'Dell, Michael Lindsay-Hogg, and Robert Fraser.

To get into the mood of performing, John, Paul, and George all choose to stand for the final take of "Get Back." It begins with a false start (**A**) caused by Glyn's interruption to instruct engineer Alan Parsons.

Glyn: Go on, Al.
Paul: Wha'? Y'wha'?
Glyn: I said go on, Al, that's all.
John: Look, don't interrupt stars when they're recording!

Paul: Hey son! Hey!
John: We're bloody *stars,* y'know!
Paul: Look, fuckface! Don't come it!
John: Fuckin' cheek!
Paul: All right.
John: —think we are, the Jacaranda?

Most of this dialogue didn't make it onto the multitrack, so the stereo mix cuts directly from Paul's "Wha" to the beginning of the take itself (**B**), which would be marked as "best" of the day. As it ends, Paul begins shaking his head and emitting mop-top "ooh's" as they roll directly into a bit of "I've Got a Feeling." Fragments of this and the jokey rendition of "Help!" that followed (**C**) were included in Glyn's remix. This postsong tomfoolery can all be heard complete and in context on Nagra roll 436A. The aforementioned control room playbacks conclude the day's session.

RELEASE HISTORY

This session was recorded on Nagra rolls 430–437A and 1020–1037B. Some of the "Get Back" rehearsal session is included in the *Anthology* home video. About six minutes of fragmented black-and-white workprint footage circulates from this day, consisting of a jam session with Yoko on vocals, Paul on drums, and John on feedback guitar (this is in addition to the half hour of "Get Back" rehearsal footage mentioned above).

A–C were included on the "WBCN acetate." Note that Yellow Dog's issue shaves off a bit of the beginning of **A** where the DJ had talked over it. It appears intact on Vigotone's release.

1984: Mono copies of **A** and **B,** the latter missing the "I've Got a Feeling" tag, were booted on the LP *Singing the Blues,* running too fast. These appear from tape source on the CD *Celluloid Rock.*

2003: A slight upgrade of **A** appeared on the bootleg CD *Get Back John Barrett's Reel.*

15. Documentary filming/Studio session

Date: 24 January 1969
Time: ?–7:00 p.m.
Location: Apple Studios, London
Director: Michael Lindsay-Hogg
Producer: Glyn Johns, George Martin

[A.] Two of Us—DDSI 24.30 (stereo) (3:24)
[B.] Teddy Boy—DDSI 24.33 (stereo) (5:53)
[C.] Two of Us—DDSI 24.48 (stereo) (0:07)
[D.] Maggie Mae—DDSI 24.49 (stereo) (0:37)

[E.] Two of Us—DDSI 24.69 (stereo) (3:41)
[F.] Dig It—DDSI 24.85 (stereo) (0:12)

[G.] Teddy Boy—edit of DDSI 24.33 (stereo) (3:41)

[H.] Teddy Boy—RS1 (4:34)
Mixed: 25 March 1970

[I.] Maggie Mae—RS 1 or 2 (0:37)
Mixed: 26 March 1970

In Billy's absence, the Beatles begin this session discussing how best to integrate him into the current project, still in limbo between a live performance and simply another studio album. Once they decide to postpone "Get Back" until Billy's arrival, they turn to "Two of Us," with John and Paul playing acoustics and George providing basslike accompaniment on his electric guitar.

All of this day's multitrack performances were recorded on reel E90491. Take 1 of "Two of Us" (**A**) was released on *Anthology 3*. It's marred by plenty of feedback (due to problems with amplifying the acoustic guitars), and the transition to the second bridge is botched. After hearing a playback, the group return to their instruments and Paul leads the others through a rough version of "Teddy Boy," which he had apparently written as far back as Rishikesh but never offered up for recording until now.

About six minutes of "Teddy Boy" were captured on multitrack, with different portions heard on different mixes. Glyn's rough mix from later that night (**B**) is the longest, missing only the opening line but running continuously otherwise. The opening line is heard only in the edit he later prepared for his first *Get Back* LP lineup (**G**); this includes three separate excerpts and has a different stereo image than the rough mix. A third remix (**H**), prepared by Phil Spector but never released, starts about 1:25 in and continues through the end. Yet another remix of portions of this recording was released on *Anthology 3,* edited together with a take from the twenty-eighth (see entry).

Apparently the next song on the multi-track was another take of "Two of Us," as the first couple of seconds of this (**C**) were accidentally included on several sources immediately after "Teddy Boy" (longest on the "WBCN acetate," and a tiny bit on Spector's mix).

After this take of "Two of Us," the skiffle-minded Beatles launch into the traditional "Maggie Mae" (for the third time during this session, but apparently the only one recorded on 8-track), a song the Quarry Men had played on the day John met Paul. This is available in two mixes: Glyn's (**D**) has the drums mixed in stereo, Phil Spector's (**I**) has John and Paul's vocals split, one in each channel. After listening to playbacks of the last couple of songs, it's time to break for lunch.

Back in the studio, a playback of the previous day's "Get Back" takes is followed by more work on "Two of Us." With acoustics in hand, John and Paul are in a 1959 mood, and between takes of the new song, run through a number of highly entertaining Quarry Men classics. In the midst of all this, another usable take of "Two of Us" (**E**) is taped. This begins with a false start and concludes with Paul's comment, "And so we leave the little town of London, England."

John switches to slide guitar for a lengthy improvised jam with the lyric "can you dig it." The end of this (**F**) with John introducing "Ark the Angels Come" was used on both unreleased *Get Back* LPs and, crossfaded with the January 26th "Dig It," on Phil Spector's *Let It Be* album. Billy shows up at this point and the day concludes with a few run-throughs of "Get Back," a double-length take of which is captured on multitrack and labeled merely "Rehearsal."

After the session, Glyn brought several of the multitrack reels (90490, 90491, and 90492) to Olympic Studios, and spent 90 minutes that night selecting some of the "best" takes and mixing these into stereo on a new reel (E69738). These included a take of "Get Back" with false start and related fragments (DDSI 23.78–23.81), the lengthy "Teddy Boy" (DDSI 24.33) and a fragment of "Two of Us" (DDSI 24.48), a full take of "Two of Us" (DDSI 24.69), and the rendition of "Dig a Pony" into "I've Got a Feeling" (DDSI 22.70–22.71).

RELEASE HISTORY

This session was recorded on Nagra rolls 438–453A and 1038–1053B. About two minutes of fragmented black-and-white workprint footage circulates from this day, consisting of dialogue and John practicing his "Get Back" solo.

B, C, and **E** were included on the "WBCN acetate." **D–F** were included on both of Glyn's *Get Back* LP lineups. **E** has been edited to remove a false start. **G** was included only on Glyn's first *Get Back* LP lineup.

1970: **I** was released on the LP *Let It Be* and is on EMI's CD of that title.

1991: Mono copies of **B, C,** and **E** were booted from tape source on the CD *Celluloid Rock*. Unfortunately, these have a harsh metallic echo overlaid and are all slightly incomplete.

1996: **A** was officially released on the CD *Anthology 3*.

1999: **B** and **H** appeared in excellent quality from John Barrett's cassette material and have been booted on the CD *Get Back—The Glyn Johns Final Compilation*. They also appear on *Mythology, Volume 3*, with the identifications flip-flopped. **B** is incomplete compared with its appearance on the "WBCN acetate," fading in 12 seconds late.

16. Documentary filming/Studio session

Date: 25 January 1969
Time: ?–8:00 p.m.
Location: Apple Studios, London
Director: Michael Lindsay-Hogg
Producer: Glyn Johns, George Martin

[A.] For You Blue—DDSI 25.34 (stereo) (2:17)

[B.] For You Blue—DDSI 25.46 (stereo) (3:02)

[C.] For You Blue—edit of DDSI 25.49/25.45 (stereo) (2:45)

[D.] Let It Be—DDSI 25.81 (stereo) (3:46)

[E.] For You Blue—edit of DDSI 25.49/25.45 (alt. stereo mix) (1:40)

With Billy unable to attend this day's session, the Beatles concentrate on three acoustic-based numbers. At this point, all that has been decided is to give a performance of some kind in front of the cameras sometime in the following week, but they still can't agree on a suitable location.

The session begins with Glyn playing back his previous night's rough mixes (reel E69738) for the group's approval. They would each be given a copy to take home and listen to by day's end. As John and Paul strum acoustics in preparation to rehearse "Two of Us," their mind is cast once again back to the skiffle days, and John performs a lengthy rendition of Paul's first-ever composition, "I Lost My Little Girl." Judging from John Barrett's log (which labels it as "I Woke Up Early This Morning"), a bit of this was captured at the start of reel E90493. Curiously, Mark Lewisohn describes this as "a very brief and entirely instrumental piece," but evidently some of the lyrics got through.

Also on this reel are several takes of "Two of Us," and a snatch of Phil Lennon and Don McCartney's harmonized cover of "Bye Bye Love." Following playbacks, it's time for a lunch break, during which a few of the participants make their way to the roof of 3 Savile Row for some fresh air; the seed is now planted for the Beatles' final public performance.

After lunch, they reconvene to tape George's "For You Blue." This song features Ringo on drums, George on acoustic guitar and solo vocal, Paul at the piano, and John playing a Hofner Hawaiian Standard lap-steel slide guitar.

The first take (**A**) was released on *Anthology 3,* and the seventh (**B**) would be chosen for Glyn's ver-

sions of *Get Back* and released (with January 8, 1970, overdubs) on the *Let It Be* album. The film *Let It Be* included an edit of takes 9 and 6 (**C**)—this edit was released as a promo video in 1996 with the soundtrack mixed in stereo; it's also seen in edited form in *Anthology* (with a bit of alternate footage of George near the beginning). The *Anthology* DVD includes a fresh stereo mix (**E**) with slide guitar far left and piano far right.

As usual, playbacks of "For You Blue" follow, with take 7 chosen as best (although George Martin favors editing takes 7 and 12). With John switching to bass and George back to Leslied electric guitar, they conclude the session with lengthy rehearsals of "Let It Be," capturing at least one take (**D**) on reel E90494. This take, released on *Anthology 3,* begins with piano and vocals only, with other instruments entering gradually after the first verse. With everyone growing tired, they agree to pick up recording the song the following day.

As the last Nagra reel of the day runs out, George plays one of his unused compositions from a few years back, "Isn't It a Pity," for John (who fails to recognize it). Apparently after the cameras were switched off, George and Glyn stayed behind a few minutes to tape a 3:03 acoustic guitar and vocal demo of the song on reel E90494.

RELEASE HISTORY

This session was recorded on Nagra rolls 454–476A and 1054–1072B. Excerpts seen in the *Let It Be* film included the performance of "For You Blue." About thirty-three minutes of fragmented black-and-white workprint footage circulates from this day, consisting of rehearsals of "Two of Us," "For You Blue," and "Let It Be," and the group listening to playbacks.

B was included on the "WBCN acetate." **B** was also included on Glyn's first *Get Back* LP lineup with the beginning trimmed. Note that the tape source for this (on *As Nature Intended* and *Thirty Days*) omits the dialogue at the end that is heard on the vinyl source (on *Get Back and 22 Other Songs*).

1996: **A** and **D** were officially released on the CD *Anthology 3.* **C** was included on an Apple promo video and appears on the bootleg CD *Lost and Found.*

2003: **E** was released on the soundtrack of the *Anthology* DVD.

17. Documentary filming/Studio session

Date: 26 January 1969
Location: Apple Studios, London
Director: Michael Lindsay-Hogg
Producer: Glyn Johns, George Martin

[A.] Dig It—DDSI 26.55 (mono) (8:29)

[B.] Rip It Up/Shake Rattle and Roll—DDSI 26.56/26.57 (stereo) (2:12)

[C.] Miss Ann/Kansas City/Lawdy Miss Clawdy—DDSI 26.58 (stereo) (3:52)

[D.] Blue Suede Shoes—DDSI 26.59 (stereo) (2:13)

[E.] You Really Got a Hold On Me—DDSI 26.60 (mono) (3:07)

[F.] Let It Be—DDSI 26.74 (stereo) (3:59)

[G.] The Long and Winding Road—DDSI 26.91 (stereo) (3:44)

[H.] Dig It—edit of DDSI 26.55 (stereo) (3:57)

[I.] Dig It—RS1 (0:49)
Mixed: 27 March 1970

[J.] Rip It Up/Shake Rattle and Roll—mono copy of RS? (2:12)
Mixed: 21 April 1976

[K.] Rip It Up/Shake Rattle and Roll/Blue Suede Shoes (stereo) (3:07)

[L.] The Long and Winding Road—DDSI 26.91 (alt. stereo mix) (3:37)

George and Ringo were the first to arrive this morning, and they probably listened to a playback of the previous night's "Isn't It a Pity" demo. Once the cameras are rolling, George plays the song through on acoustic for Ringo and Mal and then asks Glyn if he can have a rough mix done right away to be cut on an Apple acetate. Glyn says EMI's mobile mixer doesn't have the right effects, but that he'll do some more mixing that evening at Olympic if the studio is free.

George and Ringo work on composing "Octopus's Garden" for a while as John, Paul, and George Martin file in (Paul bringing Linda Eastman and her daughter, Heather); then everyone listens to playbacks of "For You Blue" and "Let It Be" from the previous day. This leads into more rehearsal of the latter song, with John stuck on bass again. Once Billy arrives, they record a handful of takes of "Let It Be," continuing on reel E90494. None of these are very good, and they soon grow tired of the song.

Using the same instrumental lineup as "Let It Be" (bass, piano, Leslied guitar, drums, and organ), a series of jams follows. A loose rendition of "Twist and Shout" soon evolves into the track we all know and love as "Dig It," an improvised three-chord workout with George Martin on shaker and Heather adding occasional vocals. Switching to reel E90495, Glyn captured 12:25 of this; the longest multitrack excerpt (**A**) is unfortunately a mono copy. Glyn would later pare this down to a reasonable 3:58 by joining three extracts (**H**) for his unreleased *Get Back* LP lineups. Phil Spector trimmed it to an even more reasonable 49 seconds (**I**) for release on *Let It Be,* cross-fading the end with John's "'Ark the Angels Come" comment from January 24.

When the interminable "Dig It" finally dies out, George Martin calls for them to return to "Let It Be," but they are having too much fun jamming. Perhaps as a nod to Billy's work with Little Richard, they launch into "Rip It Up," propelled directly into an outstanding version of "Shake Rattle and Roll." The longest version of this medley is heard on the off-line mono "boardroom tape" (**J**); the inline stereo mix (**B**) starts a few seconds later.

George plays the opening riff to "Kansas City," although Paul begins to sing "Miss Ann" over the chords—in the end, they run through both, along with Lloyd Price's "Lawdy Miss Clawdy." This medley was also remixed in 1976 and captured on the "boardroom tape," but the inline stereo mix (**C**) encompasses the whole thing.

Interestingly, John then asks if they should do "Let It Be" but is vetoed by Paul. Instead, they perform Elvis's arrangement of the Carl Perkins classic "Blue Suede Shoes." Paul's vocal is much louder on the Nagra roll compared with the stereo mix (**D**). *Anthology 3* included edited highlights of three of these oldies (**K**) in a fresh stereo mix, which adds a touch of slapback echo to John's voice, à la Presley in "Blue Suede Shoes."

The golden oldies continue with a half-remembered version of "You Really Got a Hold On Me," with John complaining that they never used to perform it in C major. The multitrack mix of this (**E**) fades out, but the complete ending can be seen in the film *Let It Be.* A George-led performance of "Tracks of My Tears" follows, also captured on reel E90495, and a few more oldies and instrumental jams occur before lunch.

Reel E90496 begins with a few takes of "Let It Be," one of which (**F**) is successful enough to be marked as temporary "best." After a playback and another long jam (titled "I Told You Before"), they turn to "The Long and Winding Road," spending more than an hour teaching it to Billy and rehearsing it. (John remains on bass and Billy switches from organ to electric piano.)

Amazingly, everything comes together quite well on the first and only "take" of the day committed to eight-track tape; this would form the basis of the hit single, albeit with a wash of Phil Spector overdubs in April 1970. The uncluttered original can be heard in Glyn's stereo mix (**G**) and a remix for release on *Anthology 3* (**L**), which isolates the electric piano in the left channel.

True to his word, Glyn would spend another ninety minutes that night at Olympic remixing tracks from that day, including the "bests" of "Let It Be" and "The Long and Winding Road," plus an earlier take of "Don't Let Me Down" (DDSI 22.60); these mixes went onto reel E69739. Presumably he also mixed the "Isn't It a Pity" demo for George's private use.

RELEASE HISTORY

This session was recorded on Nagra rolls 477–499A and 1073–1087B. Excerpts seen in the *Let It Be* film included the "Octopus's Garden" composing session, the "Dig It" jam and most of the oldies that followed, plus fragments of the rehearsal for "The Long and Winding Road." About four minutes of fragmented black-and-white workprint footage circulates from this day, consisting of rehearsals of "Let It Be" and a bit of the "I Told You Before" jam. **F** and **G** were included on the "WBCN acetate." **G** and **H** were included on both of Glyn's *Get Back* LP lineups; **G** is slightly incomplete at either end.

1970: **I** was released on the LP *Let It Be* and is on EMI's CD of that title.

1983: **J** and incomplete copies of **C** and **D** first appeared on the vinyl bootleg *File Under: Beatles* from an off-line mono tape of 1976 stereo mixes.

1984: Mono copies of **B–E** appeared on the vinyl bootleg *Singing the Blues*.

1986: **A** was booted on the LP *Ob-La-Di, Ob-La-Da* and copied on the LP and CD *Dig It!*

1991: The bootleg CD *Celluloid Rock* included mono copies of **A–G,** all from tape source, but running too fast (apart from **A**). **A, B, D, F,** and **G** are all slightly incomplete.

1996: **K** and **L** were officially released on the CD *Anthology 3*.

1999: **B–D** appeared in excellent quality from John Barrett's cassette material and have been booted on the CD *Turn Me On Dead Man: The John Barrett Tapes*.

2002: **J** appeared from tape source on the CD-R *As It Happened, Baby!*

2003: Slight upgrades of **A–C** and **E** appeared on the bootleg CD *Get Back John Barrett's Reel*.

18. Documentary filming/Studio session

Date: 27 January 1969
Time: ?–9:15 p.m.
Location: Apple Studios, London
Director: Michael Lindsay-Hogg
Producer: Glyn Johns, George Martin

[A.] **Oh! Darling—DDSI 27.56 (stereo)** (4:05)
[B.] **Get Back—DDSI 27.63 (stereo)** (3:00)
[C.] **The Walk—DDSI 27.83 (stereo)** (0:56)
[D.] **I've Got a Feeling—DDSI 27.84 (mono)** (4:10)
[E.] **dialogue** (0:07)

[F.] **Get Back—RS from DDSI 27.63 (#1)** (2:32)
[G.] **Get Back—RS from DDSI 27.63 (#2)** (2:05)

A later than usual start this day means that everyone, including Billy Preston, is present and accounted for by the time cameras begin rolling. George previews a song he had written the previous night, "Old Brown Shoe" (then untitled), for the others. Glyn then plays back his mixes from the night before, plus the multitrack reel of

oldies from the previous day. Rough rehearsals of "Let It Be" and "The Long and Winding Road" are followed by a break for late lunch.

Recording commences with a lengthy warm-up jam, 10:54 of which is captured on reel E90497. The balance of this reel would be filled with numerous takes of "Get Back," with George Martin again overseeing things along with Glyn in the control booth. Reel E90498 continues with what Mark Lewisohn labels take 9 (DDSI 27.53) of "Get Back."

This is followed by a loose version of "Oh! Darling," played in the same key as "Get Back" and with the same instrumentation (Paul on bass, Billy on electric piano). At least four minutes of this was captured on the multitrack (**A**) and released on *Anthology 3*, including John's spontaneous glee at announcing that Yoko's divorce from Tony Cox was being finalized.

Back to "Get Back," and a handful of takes later, they turn in a solid performance (**B**) that would form the basis of both single and album versions. It opens with the familiar dialogue about "Sweet Loretta Fart" and "Rosetta" before George's count-in. At the conclusion, George comments that they missed the ending, and John notes that it's different on each take. To alleviate this problem, the coda from another take (DDSI 28.43) would be appended for the single, but the original ending can be heard on the "WBCN acetate." This also includes most of the intro chat, but it should be noted that Glyn omitted the "Sweet Loretta Fart" ditty and mixed out some of the other dialogue.

A remix of this take (**F**) on *Let It Be . . . Naked* mixes everything in the center apart from John's (left) and George's (right) guitars; it fades early, prior to Paul's "woo." The *Love* CD uses a mix (**G**) incorporating the opening chord of "A Hard Day's Night," drums and guitars from "The End," and the orchestral climax from "A Day in the Life."

Further takes of "Get Back" carry over to reel E90499 until they realize they've taken the song as far as it can go for one day. For a change of pace, they turn to "I've Got a Feeling," laying down a couple of takes. As Glyn changes reels again, the ensemble jams a loose cover of a 1958 Jimmy McCracklin hit, "The Walk" (**C**). The last minute or so of this is captured at the start of reel E90500, labeled simply "Blues" in the tape log.

After Glyn announces that they are being recorded, the Beatles try for another take of "I've Got a Feeling," complete with a false start due to feedback from John's amp (**D**). Admitting that he "goofed again," John sobs, "I'm so ashamed!" This take is followed by a bit of dialogue from Ringo (**E**), who thwacks his tom-tom and asks Glyn how it sounds. This dialogue was spliced to the end of an earlier take of "I've Got a Feeling" and used on both of Glyn's *Get Back* lineups. After playing back a few of the day's best takes, most of the group called it a night.

Glyn, however, stole some more studio time, presumably at Olympic (although documentation has vanished), to mix further songs into stereo. Picking up where he left off on reel E69739, Glyn mixed the "best" take of "For You Blue" (DDSI 25.46), three takes of "Get

Back" (DDSI 27.63, 27.71, and 27.72) and "The Walk" (DDSI 27.83). With a change of reel to E69742, Glyn also mixed the performance of "I've Got a Feeling," which had followed (DDSI 27.84).

RELEASE HISTORY

This session was recorded on Nagra rolls 500–523A and 1088–1113B. About four minutes of fragmented black-and-white workprint footage circulates from this day, consisting of dialogue and playbacks from the start of the session, plus a bit of "The Long and Winding Road" rehearsal from later. In 2003, Apple issued a promo video for "Get Back" centered around this day's rehearsal of that song, but incorporating unseen footage from throughout the sessions at both Twickenham and Apple.

B and **C** were included on the "WBCN acetate"; note that the last 5 seconds of **B** appeared only on the obscure vinyl bootleg *O.P.D.* and were copied on the CD *The "Get Back" Journals.*

E was included in stereo on both of Glyn's *Get Back* LP lineups, following a different take of "I've Got a Feeling" (DDSI 22.71).

1984: **D** and **E** surfaced on the vinyl bootleg *Singing the Blues,* both in mono and running too fast.

1991: The bootleg CD *Celluloid Rock* included mono copies of **C** and **D,** both from tape source, but running too fast.

1996: **A** was officially released on the CD *Anthology 3.*

2003: **F** was released on the CD *Let It Be . . . Naked.* The same year, a slight upgrade of **D** appeared on the bootleg CD *Get Back John Barrett's Reel.*

2006: **G** was released on the *Love* CD.

19. Documentary filming/Studio session

Date: 28 January 1969
Location: Apple Studios, London
Director: Michael Lindsay-Hogg
Producer: Glyn Johns, George Martin

[A.] Get Back (reprise)—DDSI 28.43 (stereo) (0:38)

[B.] Get Back—edit of DDSI 27.63/28.43 (stereo) (3:09)

[C.] Get Back—RS1 (3:10)
[D.] Don't Let Me Down—RS1 from DDSI 28.45 w/overdubs (3:32)

[E.] Don't Let Me Down—RM1 from DDSI 28.45 w/overdubs (3:28)
Mixed: 4 April 1969

[F.] Get Back—RM5 (3:09)
Mixed: 7 April 1969

[G.] Teddy Boy—RS from edit of DDSI 28.83/24.33 (3:15)

This session begins in familiar fashion, with playbacks of Glyn's remixes from the previous night. Rehearsals continue with "I've Got a Feeling," but these are hampered by Paul's departure to attend a meeting (in his stead, John sings lead and Billy sings Paul's part during the duet verse). Upon Paul's return, they move on to "Dig a Pony," and as usual, break for a late lunch before beginning serious recording.

Reel E90501 contained multiple takes of "Dig a Pony," none good enough for release or remixing. A switch to E90502 captured the last "Dig a Pony," a take of "Get Back," and then an impromptu "Love Me Do" (available from the Nagra roll on the bootleg CD *Love Me Do*).

The next take of "Get Back" would provide the coda for the released single; Glyn would join it to the end of the "best" take from the twenty-seventh and include the result (**B**) on both of his *Get Back* LP lineups. At the point where it fades out, Paul can be heard singing, "Jo-Jo, Loretta . . . get back and get together." Some more of the coda, faded up from this ad-lib, was also used as a "reprise" (**A**) on Glyn's lineups.

Four mono mixes of "Get Back" were prepared at Abbey Road on March 26 but rejected in favor of a last-minute remix (**F**) done by Glyn April 7 at Olympic, which sped up the song slightly. The stereo single mix (**C**), released in the United States only, may in fact be the same mix as **B**.

Clearly on a roll, one false start and full take later, the Beatles record a near-perfect song for the B-side, John's "Don't Let Me Down." About the only flaws in this take are some lyric discrepancies between John and Paul's vocals. In the first verse, where John sings "if somebody loved me like she do me," Paul joins in with, "—body ever really loved me." In the last verse, where John sings "ooh she done me," Paul sings "like she done me."

To tidy up the recording for release, an extra vocal track was overdubbed at an unknown point, perhaps during a February 20 session at Apple. (Mark Lewisohn recently uncovered evidence of such a session, and there are Ethan Russell photos possibly taken that day.) This overdub had Paul correcting his harmony vocal for the first verse (he had failed to sing the whole time on the original take), and John doubling his vocal on the middle eight and ending. On the last verse, rather than add a new harmony, they opted to mix Paul's old vocal out (although it can be heard faintly leaking through John's vocal mic). The only difference between the stereo

(**D**) and mono (**E**) single mixes is the speeding-up of the latter.

The January 28 session continued with a take of "I've Got a Feeling," but unfortunately the tape ran out halfway through. The latter half of the song was captured on reel E90503, followed by take 3 of "Don't Let Me Down." The first three takes of "One After 909," with Billy picking up the song easily, and take 13 of "I've Got a Feeling" were also recorded, at which point George taught the others his new song "Old Brown Shoe." Billy then stepped into the spotlight to sing lead on two songs, noted on the tape box as "Billy's songs"—the second of these was a cover he probably knew from backing Ray Charles: "Sticks And Stones." George also debuted his nearly finished composition "Something," with John and Paul throwing in halfhearted ideas for lyrics.

After the Beatles rehearsed "Get Back" and "Two of Us" for a bit, Glyn threw on reel E90504 and caught a decidedly unserious run-through of "Teddy Boy." *Anthology 3* includes an edit (**G**) comprised of three portions of this take joined to two segments from the January 24 take. The tape continued to roll as the group debated just what the point of the project was—an album, rehearsals for a performance, or both? After some brief work on "All Things Must Pass" and "I Want You (She's So Heavy)," the session wrapped up.

RELEASE HISTORY

This session was recorded on Nagra rolls 524–547A and 1114–1129B. About two minutes of fragmented black-and-white workprint footage circulates from this day, consisting of rehearsals of "I've Got a Feeling" and "I Want You (She's So Heavy)," and yet another "Dig It" jam.

A and **B** were included on both of Glyn's *Get Back* LP lineups.

1969: **C** and **D** were released on a single in the United States only; both are available on the CD *Past Masters, Volume 2*. **E** and **F** were released on a single elsewhere and are on the "Get Back" CD single.

1996: **G** was officially released on the CD *Anthology 3*.

20. Documentary filming/Studio session

Date: 29 January 1969
Location: Apple Studios, London
Director: Michael Lindsay-Hogg
Producer: Glyn Johns, George Martin

> **[A.]** **Cannonball/Not Fade Away/Hey Little Girl/Bo Diddley—DDSI 29.49 (stereo) (3:50)**
>
> **[B.]** **Mailman Bring Me No More Blues—DDSI 29.53 (stereo) (1:30)**
>
> **[C.]** **Mailman Bring Me No More Blues—edit of DDSI 29.53 (stereo) (1:52)**

Having gotten everyone (including a reluctant George) to agree to a lunchtime concert the following day on the rooftop of Apple's 3 Savile Row building, the Beatles decided to run through all the possible candidates for the show, even though Billy hadn't arrived.

The first five numbers would form the set list: "Dig a Pony," "I've Got a Feeling," "Don't Let Me Down," "Get Back," and "One After 909." A few run-throughs of "She Came In through the Bathroom Window" prove that they aren't ready to perform that one live just yet. Moving to acoustic-based songs, they play "Two of Us" and then (with Billy's arrival) "Let It Be" and "The Long and Winding Road," all of which would be performed indoors for the cameras the day after the rooftop gig.

Notably absent from the above are any George Harrison compositions, although he's offered up nearly a dozen over the course of the month. They try out a few of these ("For You Blue," "All Things Must Pass," and "Let It Down") before taking a lunch break.

Having pretty much exhausted their supply of finished numbers, the Beatles turn to those old standbys, jamming and oldies. Captured on reel E90505 are off-the-cuff versions of "I Want You (She's So Heavy)" and "Besame Mucho," followed by one more attempt at "One After 909" (although John rightly protests that they already know that one better than most of the new songs).

As Ringo launches into a Bo Diddley drumbeat, the group plays a medley of oldies (**A**) centering around that rhythm, most of which went onto the eight-track tape. One of these, "Not Fade Away," instigates a Buddy Holly revival, luckily captured on the Nagra rolls. Entertaining versions of "Maybe Baby," "Peggy Sue Got Married," and "Crying, Waiting, Hoping" pass by before Glyn gets on the ball and starts rolling tape again.

Although he misses the first 20 seconds, most of the final Buddy Holly cover, "Mailman Bring Me No More Blues," makes it onto the multitrack (**B**). Despite the less than exciting performance and the missing intro, Geoff Emerick chose to remix and edit this song for inclusion on the proposed *Sessions* LP in 1984. This ill-considered reconstruction has edits at 0:10, 0:18, 1:33 and a particularly sloppy one at 1:23 with John in mid-word. Sadly, this same edit (**C**) was chosen for release on *Anthology 3*.

Truly scraping the bottom of the barrel, Paul leads the others through "Teddy Boy" for a bit (also captured on E90505) before everyone goes home in anticipation of the big day.

RELEASE HISTORY

This session was recorded on Nagra rolls 548–561A and 1130–1145B. Excerpts seen in the *Let It Be* film included Paul's pep talk to a disinterested John about performing live and a rendition of "Besame Mucho." Some conversation about playing on the roof is included in the *Anthology* home video. About a minute of fragmented black-and-white workprint footage circulates from this day, consisting of John tying his shoes while the others work on "All Things Must Pass."

1983: An incomplete copy of **A** first appeared on the vinyl bootleg *File Under: Beatles* from an off-line mono tape of a 1976 stereo mix. This appears from tape source on the CD-R *As It Happened, Baby!*

1985: Geoff Emerick's remix/edit of **C** created for *Sessions* began to appear on vinyl bootlegs; it can be heard on Spank's CD of that title.

1996: **C** was officially released on the CD *Anthology 3*.

1999: **A** and **B** appeared in excellent quality from John Barrett's cassette material. **A** has been booted on the CD *Turn Me On Dead Man: The John Barrett Tapes*, and **B** is on *Another Sessions . . . Plus*.

21. Documentary filming/Concert

Date: 30 January 1969
Time: 1:00–2:00 p.m.
Location: Apple rooftop, London
Director: Michael Lindsay-Hogg
Producer: Glyn Johns, George Martin

[A.] **Get Back—DDSI 30.04 (stereo)** (3:12)
[B.] **Don't Let Me Down—DDSI 30.05 (stereo)** (2:51)
[C.] **One After 909/Danny Boy—DDSI 30.08/30.09 (stereo)** (2:53)
[D.] **Get Back—DDSI 30.17 (stereo)** (3:05)

[E.] **Dig a Pony—RS2?** (3:51)
[F.] **One After 909/Danny Boy—RS3?** (2:49)
[G.] **I've Got a Feeling—RS4** (3:34)
Mixed: 23 March 1970

[H.] **Get Back—RS3** (3:05)
Mixed: 26 March 1970

[I.] **Get Back—DDSI 30.04 (alt. stereo mix)** (2:43)
[J.] **Don't Let Me Down—DDSI 30.05 (alt. stereo mix)** (3:12)
[K.] **Don't Let Me Down—RS from edit of DDSI 30.05/30.16** (3:17)
[L.] **I've Got a Feeling—RS from edit of DDSI 30.06/30.13** (3:29)
[M.] **One After 909—RS from DDSI 30.08** (2:43)
[N.] **Dig a Pony—RS from DDSI 30.11** (3:35)

John, Paul, George, Ringo, and Billy . . . The Beatles' last public performance was unannounced and viewable by nobody apart from friends and technicians assembled on the roof of 3 Savile Row, and a few lucky Londoners with access to the surrounding rooftops. It was certainly heard by a large number of people, mainly startled passers-by and disgruntled businessmen who worked in the area. Fortunately, a camera crew was also present, as well as an eight-track tape machine (manned by Glyn, who communicated with the band via intercom from the basement studio).

The performance was excellent, given the circumstances: The Beatles hadn't performed totally live in two and a half years. Sure, John forgot some of the words to his own songs, but he'd been doing that since the Quarry Men days. They decided to keep it simple and play only the basic rock-and-roll numbers they had perfected over the course of the month. Paul used his classic Hofner bass guitar, adorned with a BASSMAN sticker from his Fender bass amp. George played a Fender Telecaster, eschewing any Leslie effects. John

played his Epiphone Casino guitar, and Ringo his new Ludwig drum kit, the snare and floor tom dampened with towels. Billy, stuck back in the corner on Fender Rhodes electric piano, was largely ignored by the camera crew, but contributed invaluably to the overall sound.

The "concert" begins with a brief warm-up of "Get Back" to test the levels (Ringo also complains that Mal had nailed his kit down in the wrong place, and that needs to be rectified). Glyn cues up reel E90522 and begins recording. With the camera crew needing one of the eight tracks as a sync track (although the Nagras are rolling, it seems they want to use Glyn's more professional mix in the film), Ringo's drums are not recorded in stereo as they had been earlier in the sessions.

The first full take of "Get Back" is labeled "REHEARSAL" on the tape box and is followed by further tuning and adjustments (a few bars of "I Want You (She's So Heavy)" are played). A second take of "Get Back" is an improvement, and labeled "GOOD (except Billy's solo)." As it ends to a round of applause, John pretends he's back at the Cavern: "Oh, thank you! We've had a request from Daisy, Morris, and Tommy." The film *Let It Be* includes this take, with the count-in from the rehearsal take spliced on. A stereo mix of this (**A**), presumably taken from the remastered movie, was used in a video to promote the *1* CD in 2000; a remix (**I**) is on the *Anthology* DVD.

Next on the set list is "Don't Let Me Down," a lively performance marred (or enhanced, depending on your point of view) by John's impromptu gobbledygook lyrics on the final verse. Again, this take was used in the film, and a true stereo mix appeared in the 1988 documentary *Imagine: John Lennon,* in an edit removing the middle eight and chorus. The full version (**B**) was used in the *Anthology* home video release; the DVD has a slightly different mix (**J**), which swaps the positions of John's guitar and Billy's piano. The *Let It Be . . . Naked* mix (**K**) sounds similar to **B,** but has the last verse (2:02–2:29) substituted from the second rooftop take.

As usual, they segue this song straight into "I've Got a Feeling," another excellent performance chosen for both the film and LP *Let It Be*, in a stereo mix by Phil Spector (**G**) that centers John and Paul's solo vocals but splits them left and right for the final verse. *Let It Be . . . Naked* uses a composite (**L**) of this and large chunks of the second rooftop take (0:00–1:03, 1:30–2:04, and 2:27–3:09).

"One After 909" was a natural choice to perform live, since they knew it backwards and forwards, and the sole performance is delivered with gusto by all concerned, including a great solo from George and raucous vocals from John and Paul. This take, including John's a cappella send-up of "Danny Boy" which follows, was used in the film and on all LP variations. Glyn's mix (**C**) has John and Paul's vocals split left and right, and the electric piano centered. Phil's (**F**) centers both vocals and mixes the piano to the left. For *Let It Be . . . Naked* (**M**), everything is centered apart from Billy's piano (left) and George's guitar (right).

After a brief pause in the action, Glyn suggests they do "Dig a Pony" next. John agrees, once the lyrics are fetched for him to use as a cheat sheet, and after a false start, they turn in a reasonable performance. It can be seen unedited in the film, but Phil Spector excised a few bars ("All I want is . . .") from the beginning and end on his mix (**E**) for the *Let It Be* LP. These edits are re-created on *Let It Be . . . Naked,* in a mix (**N**) that omits the false start and brings Billy's piano front and center.

Although Michael Lindsay-Hogg suggests they continue with a few oldies, it's decided to retake a few of the numbers already played, in hopes of capturing superior performances. They jam a very loose instrumental rendition of "God Save the Queen" as Glyn changes reels; the end of this is captured on reel E90524. Second attempts at "I've Got a Feeling" and "Don't Let Me Down" are duly recorded, but offer no improvements.

By this time, the London police department is breathing down their necks, having been alerted by irate businessmen, stalled in Apple's lobby, and then shown to the rooftop. Hoping to be taken into custody in mid-song (for the sake of the cameras), the Beatles carry on with a third take of "Get Back." A nervous Mal Evans begins to disconnect the guitar amps in the middle of this, but Ringo yells, "Don't touch that!" and power is restored. It's a sloppy but amusing rendition, with Paul ad-libbing gleefully: "Loretta . . . you been playing on the roofs again and that's no good, 'cause you know your mommy doesn't like that! She gets angry—she gonna have you arrested!" John comes in too early for the coda, and the timing is thrown off completely, but they soldier on to the end.

As the final public performance by the Beatles concludes, John steps up to the microphone for one last comment: "I'd just like to say thank you on behalf of the group and ourselves, and I hope we passed the audition!" This quip was included on Glyn's LP lineups (following the only rooftop song he used, "One After 909"). The final take of "Get Back" itself, minus comment, was issued in a stereo mix (**D**) on *Anthology 3.*

For the *Let It Be* LP, Phil Spector used the January 27 studio take of "Get Back" (DDSI 27.63) and cross-faded it with the "audition" comment from the rooftop (**H**). The film *Let It Be* includes both song and comment in their original context.

The world got its first glimpse of the rooftop concert in April, when the "Get Back"/"Don't Let Me Down" single was released. Promo clips were assembled of both songs, of which only "Get Back" was aired in the UK (on *Top of the Pops* April 24; Germany's *Beat Club* broadcast the clip April 26). This syncs up the single mix of the song to rooftop footage, including many shots not used in the *Let It Be* film. "Don't Let Me Down" was aired along with its flipside on *The Glen Campbell Goodtime Hour* in the United States (April 30). This promo combines rooftop footage (again, including alternate angles to the movie) with shots of the January 6 rehearsal of the song at Twickenham.

After finishing their set without any arrests, the Beatles went down to the basement to listen to a playback of both multitrack reels. Rather than continue filming, they decided to come back the following day to perform the remaining songs in the basement studio.

That night, Glyn went back to Olympic, and in a 7:30–10:00 p.m. session, prepared some more stereo mixes, probably continuing with reel E69742 and adding "Dig It" and the medleys of oldies from the twenty-sixth. He then cut a batch of two-sided acetates of his earlier work.

On side A went all the numbers from reel E69738.

1. Get Back (false start)—DDSI 23.78
2. Get Back—DDSI 23.79
3. I've Got a Feeling (fragment)—DDSI 23.80
4. Help! (fragment)—DDSI 23.81
5. Teddy Boy—DDSI 24.33
6. Two of Us (fragment)—DDSI 24.48
7. Two of Us—DDSI 24.69
8. Dig a Pony—DDSI 22.70
9. I've Got a Feeling—DDSI 22.71

Side B contained most of reel E69739, although Glyn omitted two redundant takes of "Get Back."

1. The Long and Winding Road—DDSI 26.91
2. Let It Be—DDSI 26.74
3. Don't Let Me Down—DDSI 22.60
4. For You Blue—DDSI 25.46
5. Get Back—DDSI 27.63
6. The Walk—DDSI 27.83

The Beatles were undoubtedly given copies of these acetates the next day, and a tape dub of one disc was passed along by Derek Taylor to California DJ Tom Donahue. The entire tape was aired on WBCN in Boston on September 22, as well as on WBAI in New York and KCOK in St. Louis, and copies multiplied rapidly. Reviews appeared in college newspapers and *Rolling Stone* magazine. Before the year was out, the first Beatles bootleg was born, titled *Kum Back,* using this material.

The rooftop reels were apparently kept at Apple and mixed into stereo there February 5, although Glyn chose only one of these mixes for his *Get Back* LP lineups.

This session was recorded on Nagra rolls 562–563A, 1146–1149B, 4001C, and 5001D. Excerpts seen in the *Let It Be* film included the second and third takes of "Get Back," and the first takes of "Don't Let Me Down," "I've Got a Feeling," "One After 909," and "Dig a Pony." Both the "Get Back" and "Don't Let Me Down" promo clips from April 1969 circulate on video.

C was included on both of Glyn's *Get Back* LP lineups, with John's "passed the audition" comment added to the end.

1970: **E–H** were released on the LP *Let It Be* and are on EMI's CD of that title.

1988: An edited version of **B** was included on the soundtrack of the film *Imagine: John Lennon*. It's been booted from this source on the CD-R *Video 1*.

1996: **D** was officially released on the CD *Anthology 3*. **B** was included on the *Anthology* home video and appears on the CD-R *Anthropology*.

2000: **A** was included on an EPK to promote *1;* it's been booted on the CD-R *Video 1*.

2003: **I–J** were released on the soundtrack of the *Anthology* DVD. The same year, **K–N** were released on the CD *Let It Be . . . Naked.*

22. Documentary filming/Studio session

Date: 31 January 1969
Location: Apple Studios, London
Director: Michael Lindsay-Hogg
Producer: Glyn Johns, George Martin

[A.] Two of Us—edit of DDSI 31.13/31.15 (stereo) (3:28)
[B.] The Long and Winding Road—DDSI 31.40 (stereo) (3:32)
[C.] dialogue (0:03)
[D.] dialogue (0:12)
[E.] Let It Be—edit of DDSI 31.54/31.65 (stereo) (3:57)

[F.] Two of Us—RS2? (3:23)
Mixed: 25 March 1970

[G.] Let It Be—edit of DDSI 31.54/31.65 (alt. stereo mix) (3:58)
[H.] Two of Us—RS from DDSI 31.13 (3:19)
[I.] The Long and Winding Road—RS from DDSI 31.40 (3:31)

If the rooftop concert was the final chapter in the "Get Back" saga, this was its epilogue: a performance directed to cameras of the more acoustic numbers, also taped on eight-track for potential release. All the takes from this day would be numbered consecutively beginning with take 10, regardless of title; this was more for the cameras' benefit than Glyn's. Billy Preston would join in on the final two numbers.

After the usual acoustic warm-up of oldies and skiffle tunes, the Beatles begin with "Two of Us." Although the guitars remain slightly out of tune, these performances are the most polished of this song so far. Take 10 includes a false start, and take 11 is good enough to be chosen for Phil Spector's *Let It Be* album

(**F**). The *Let It Be . . . Naked* remix (**H**) is similar to Spector's, although the guitars are crisper and Ringo's drumming more prominent.

At Paul's insistence, they try for one more performance, but take 12 is no improvement. The film includes an edit of take 11 and the coda from take 12. Apple issued a "promo video" of "Two of Us" in 1996, which was merely excerpted from the remastered *Let It Be* film print; this offered the song in an alternate stereo mix (**A**), with the vocal tracks separated slightly.

It's not clear from the tape log which reel these takes were captured on: It may have been E90508 (labeled as an eight-track tape of "The Beatles Apple Studio Performance" with a notation "(BLANK TAPE!?)" and dated January 31), or perhaps just at the start of reel E90523.

In any case, E90523 captures the next several performances: takes 13 through 16 (complete with unnumbered false starts and breakdowns) of "The Long and Winding Road," none of which are usable. Just before breaking for lunch, Paul makes a comment about "reloading our stomachs"; Glyn would use this snippet on the *Get Back* LP following "Let It Be."

After a late lunch, they return to the studio and jam "Lady Madonna," partially captured on the multi-track tape. Continuing with reel E90574, the quintet makes it through take 19 of "The Long and Winding Road" before throwing in the towel. That take (**B**) would be used in the film; it appears in a true stereo mix (guitar left, electric piano right) on the *Anthology* DVD. A similar mix (**I**) is on *Let It Be . . . Naked,* although this has Paul's spoken interlude mixed out. Both Glyn and Phil Spector would favor the earlier take from January 26 for record release.

Takes 20–22 of "Let It Be" follow. Moving on to reel E90507, take 23 is preceded by John asking Paul, "Are we supposed to giggle in the solo?" This scrap of dialogue (**C**) would be used on Glyn's *Get Back* LP line-ups. Take 24 is a breakdown, although it was noted on the tape box "good first half"—one chorus from this take would be spliced into the day's final take for the film. Although less than serious (Paul began singing "Brother Malcolm"), take 25 is marked "best" for the moment; it is followed by this exchange.

John: I think that was rather grand—I'd take one home with me.
Glyn: Yeah, that was fine.
John: Don't kid us, Glyn. Give it to us straight.
Glyn: Straight.
Paul: What d'you think, Glyn?
Glyn: I think it [inaudible] yet . . .
Paul: Come on.
John: Okay, let's track it. You bounder! You cheat!

The first and last lines of this conversation (**D**) were included on *Anthology 3,* following the January 25 take of "Let It Be."

Take 26 breaks down, and 27 consists of two audio takes. Take 27A is preceded by Paul's mocking the camera crew: "Sync to second clap, please!" The take itself is good enough to form the basis of the eventual album track and number 1 hit single when supplemented with future overdubs (in April 1969 and January 1970).

Take 27B has Paul throwing in a new line in the last verse: "There will be no sorrow, let it be." As noted earlier, an edit of this take and an extra chorus from take 24 was used in the film *Let It Be*—a stereo mix of this sequence (**E**) was included in the *Anthology* home video, and with the sound newly remixed (**G**) on the DVD.

In addition, a film clip was made to promote the "Let It Be" single in March 1970. (It aired on BBC TV's *Top of the Pops* March 5 and Germany's *Beat Club* March 28). This color clip, which circulates on video, is synchronized to the single remix. It uses mostly footage of take 27A (including a close-up of Paul singing "speaking words of wisdom" rather than "there will be no sorrow" as in the film), plus brief clips from the other songs shot that day.

RELEASE HISTORY

This session was recorded on Nagra rolls 564–566A and 1150–1155B. Excerpts seen in the *Let It Be* film included performances of all three songs (take 11 of "Two of Us" with the coda from take 12 added, take 19 of "The Long and Winding Road," and take 27B of "Let It Be" with an extra chorus from take 24 spliced in). The "Let It Be" promo clip from March 1970 circulates on video.

C was included in both of Glyn's *Get Back* LP line-ups, preceding "The Long and Winding Road."

1970: **F** was released on the LP *Let It Be* and is on EMI's CD of that title.

1996: **C** and **D** were officially released on the CD *Anthology 3.* **E** was included on the *Anthology* home video and appears on the CD-R *Anthropology.* **A** was issued as a promo video and is available on the bootleg CD *Lost and Found.*

2003: **B** and **G** were released on the soundtrack of the *Anthology* DVD. The same year, **H** and **I** were released on the CD *Let It Be . . . Naked.*

23. Studio session   P

Date: January–early February 1969
Location: London (?)
Producer: Paul McCartney

   [A.] Rosetta (2:08)

Although it had been five years since John or Paul had donated songs to the Fourmost, they remained on friendly terms. After Brian Epstein's death, the band had abandoned pop tours in favor of the cabaret circuit, and Paul suggested they add the jazz standard "Rosetta" to their act. The song had clearly been on his mind, as he can be heard muttering the title before a January 27 take of "Get Back."

Sometime in the busy aftermath of the "Get Back" sessions, he also found time to produce their recording of the song for a single. Paul played piano on the recording, in the jaunty manner of his "Penny Lane" keyboard stylings. He also produced (but did not play on) the flip side, a number called "Just Like Before" written by Fourmost lead vocalist Brian O'Hara and assigned to Apple Publishing.

The exact recording date and location are unknown, but the session was reported as early as in the February 8 issue of *New Musical Express.* The single was released February 21 and failed to chart.

RELEASE HISTORY

1969: **A** was released on a single in the UK only. It has yet to appear in stereo.

24. Home demo

Date: early February 1969
Location: 7 Cavendish Avenue, London

    [A.] Goodbye (2:19)

Rather than pull a track from the *Post Card* LP, Paul decided to write a song specifically for Mary Hopkin's second single. He came up with the catchy "Goodbye," recording a simple and charming home demo that would be pressed on a Dick James acetate for Mary to learn. The demo is performed on acoustic guitar, with Paul singing in falsetto to approximate Hopkin's voice.

The exact recording date is unknown, but at the *Post Card* launch party on February 13, Mary reported that "Paul has an idea for my next single." In the March 15 issue of *New Musical Express,* she is quoted as saying, "Paul told me he'd written it about four weeks ago."

RELEASE HISTORY

1984: This acetate was sold at auction on December 22, 1981 (see the May 1963 entry for "Bad to Me"). It first appeared on the vinyl bootlegs *File Under: Beatles* and *Not For Sale.* The latter title was also available on CD.

1991: The song was copied on the bootleg CD *Acetates,* with noise reduction to remove scratches, but sounding muffled and running noticeably slow.

25. Studio session

Date: 25 February 1969
Location: EMI Studios, London
Producer: none

    [A.] Old Brown Shoe—take 2 (stereo) (3:04)
    [B.] All Things Must Pass—take 2 (stereo) (3:05)
    [C.] Something—take 1 (mono) (3:16)

    [D.] All Things Must Pass—take 2 (alt. stereo mix) (3:01)

    [E.] Something—RM? (3:17)
Mixed: 25 February 1969

George's growing backlog of songs had been roundly ignored by his bandmates, and he declined to offer any for either the rooftop or basement performances in January. At one point during the Apple sessions, he had talked about recording an album on his own, just to let some of these songs see the light of day.

The Beatles were out of action for most of February as George had his tonsils removed and Ringo filmed *The Magic Christian.* Their sole group session that month occurred at Trident on the twenty-second, when they began recording John's "I Want You (She's So Heavy)." Three days later, George turned twenty-six and celebrated the occasion by taping solo demos at EMI for three of his newer compositions, all of which had been rehearsed with the Beatles in January.

"Old Brown Shoe" (**A**) was performed with a live vocal and piano track, to which George overdubbed two electric guitar tracks: one low and pulsating (proving that he devised the bubbly bass line that Paul would eventually play) and one higher-pitched, including a solo. At the end of the low guitar overdub, he exclaims, "Wow! Very fast!"

Next up was "All Things Must Pass," a luscious rendition with George singing to his live tremeloed guitar accompaniment. He overdubbed a second vocal and plainer guitar track on top of this: These can be heard, along with engineer Ken Scott's take 2 announcement, in stereo (**B**) on the bootleg *More Masters.* The stereo mix released on *Anthology 3* (**D**) mixes out George's second vocal and reverses the positions of each guitar.

Finally, George taped "Something," with a basic track of electric guitar and vocal; this much can be heard in mono on *Anthology 3* (**C**). George sang "dum dum dum" to fill in where the descending piano part would occur. This vocalization would be mixed out on the acetate version (**E**), which includes a subsequent piano overdub. All three songs were mixed that night and cut onto acetates for George to take home.

It's likely that the "Something" acetate was given to Joe Cocker sometime the following month. The Beatles had admired Joe's cover version of "With a Little Help from My Friends," released in 1968. So when Joe arrived at Apple in the early spring, George was glad to offer him an unrecorded original to cover. Joe remembers George playing both "Old Brown Shoe" and "Something"; Paul showed up the same afternoon and donated his own unrecorded song, "She Came In through the Bathroom Window."

Cocker's version of "Something" is similar to George's demo in that both are performed in A major (the Beatles' version is in C), and that a counter-melody ("I need her all the time") is sung over what would become the guitar solo. Joe probably learned the song from this acetate, although he recalls taping his own demos of both this and Paul's song in the Apple basement studio. He recorded proper versions in Los Angeles, prior to the release of *Abbey Road,* but didn't release them until afterward, on his *Joe Cocker!* LP in November.

RELEASE HISTORY

1991: **E** was included on the bootleg CD *Acetates.*

1996: The CD *Anthology 3* included **A** (with an early fade), **C,** and **D.**

1999: Copies of **A** and **B** (the latter in mono) surfaced among John Barrett's cassette material and were bootlegged on the CD *Through Many Years.* Later that year, upgrades of **A** and **B** appeared on the CD *More Masters.* Both were longer than previous issues, and **B** was now in stereo.

26. Location recording   G

Date: 16–28 February 1969
Location: Kinfauns
Producer: George Harrison

[A.] Under the Mersey Wall—RS? (18:40)

Suitably impressed by Bernie Krause's demonstration of the wonders of the synthesizer in Los Angeles (see the November 12, 1968, entry), George immediately purchased a Moog IIIp synth and had it shipped to his home in England.

Krause visited George after the Beatle's release from the hospital (February 15) to help him set up the unwieldy instrument at Kinfauns. George reportedly offended his guest by playing back his mix of Krause's LA demonstration and announcing that it would be released on the Zapple label under George's name. Krause backed out of the endeavor and found his name removed from the LP credits.

In the meantime, George recorded his own track to fill up the LP's flip side. The track's title, "Under the Mersey Wall," was borrowed from the name of a col-umn by George's namesake in the *Liverpool Echo* newspaper. This offering (**A**) is a lot easier on the ears than its companion piece, chiefly because George wasn't running through the gamut of sounds willy-nilly. He stuck to melodic and musical noises and largely steered clear of the more gimmicky and grating effects.

It's still nothing to write home about, and when George can be heard clearing his throat at 12:15 in the recording, it comes as a welcome human relief to all the impersonal automatonic clamor. The whole enterprise would be written off as an experiment: George did nothing to promote the LP upon its release in May and rarely referred to it thereafter.

RELEASE HISTORY

1969: **A** was released on the Zapple LP *Electronic Sound;* U.S. copies inadvertently swapped the titles between the album's two cuts, an understandable error. The LP was reissued on CD in 1996 in the UK and Japan only.

27. Promo clip   P

Date: 1 March 1969
Location: Morgan Studios, London
Director: Tony Bramwell

[A.] Goodbye (2:14)

Apple's Tony Bramwell filmed Paul in action in the studio producing Mary Hopkin's second single, "Goodbye" (see next entry for details). The finished clip alternates between Mary's in-studio mimed performance and shots of her and Paul in the control booth, apparently listening to playbacks. (Paul smokes, sings along, snaps his fingers, and generally twitches.)

According to Mark Lewisohn, a second clip of Mary performing the song in Paul's backyard was produced, but neither clip was aired in the UK. The *New Musical Express* reported April 5 that the song "was issued simultaneously in 28 countries last weekend. In several of these territories a promotional film is being screened by local TV companies, showing Mary and Paul McCartney actually making the disc."

RELEASE HISTORY

A complete black-and-white copy of this promo circulates from an episode of the TV show *Beat Club.* An edited color version (lasting 1:44) also circulates, and a bit of color footage was also released in the *Anthology* documentary.

28. Studio session

Date: 1 and 2 March 1969
Location: Morgan Studios, London
Producer: Paul McCartney

[A.] Goodbye (2:22)
[B.] Sparrow (3:09)

"Goodbye" was an effective production by Paul that elaborated upon his simple demo. Mary sang and played the main acoustic guitar part, changing a few lyrics in the last verse ("sound of lonely drums" becomes "song of lonely love"). The key was raised from C to E to better accommodate Mary's range.

Paul added bass guitar, an acoustic guitar intro and solo (heavy on the treble), lap-slapping percussion (a trick learned from Buddy Holly), and a touch of drums. Backing vocals, horns, and strings (arranged by Richard Hewson) were also overdubbed, the latter reportedly consisting of twelve violas and no violins!

For the B-side, Paul selected a tune by Graham Lyle and Benny Gallagher, a songwriting team signed to Apple Publishing. "Sparrow" is a much less effective production, suffering from an intrusive choir. If Paul plays anything on this song, it's probably maracas. Mary handled the main guitar chores again, and the upright string bass was clearly played by a session musician.

RELEASE HISTORY

1969: **A** and **B** were released on a single worldwide. The A-side peaked at number 13 in the United States and number 2 in the UK, right behind "Get Back." Both songs were included in stereo on the 1972 compilation LP *Those Were the Days,* reissued on CD in 1995.

29. Concert

Date: 2 March 1969
Time: afternoon
Location: Lady Mitchell Hall, Cambridge
Producer: John Lennon, Yoko Ono

[A.] Cambridge 1969—RS? (26:26)

The Beatles hadn't performed onstage in England since May 1966, and with the cancellation of London concerts in December and January, the prospect seemed unlikely. Thus, it must have come as a shock to poet and percussionist Anthony Barnett when he invited Yoko Ono to perform as part of the "Natural Music" concert he was assembling at Cambridge University, and she brought along John Lennon as her "backing band."

Of course, John wasn't there to play pop music. He arrived with his Epiphone Casino electric guitar, and he and Yoko gave the audience of five hundred a taste of the free-form feedback/vocal duets they had perfected during jam sessions at Twickenham and Apple in January.

The performance, recorded in stereo, would be released as side A of their next *Unfinished Music* album in May. It opens with John giving an OK, and Yoko's nonchalant introduction: "Um, this is a piece called, uh, 'Cambridge 1969.'" What follows is nearly a half hour of interplay between Yoko's unflagging cries and moans and John's carefully controlled feedback (largely based around an E major chord). Although he's nowhere near as proficient as Jimi Hendrix or Pete Townshend, John uses the electric buzz effectively as an instrument to counter and complement his partner.

Two jazz musicians who were also on the bill as part of a larger ensemble agreed to participate in John and Yoko's improvisation. About sixteen minutes into the piece, percussionist John Stevens joins in on drums (mostly a wash of cymbals), and about four minutes later, saxophonist John Tchicai adds a repeating three-note motif (C-sharp, G-sharp, C-sharp).

Stevens abandons the drums in favor of castanets and then scrapes the strings of a piano, while Tchicai begins playing melodic runs. Toward the end, John and Yoko drop out completely, leaving the saxophone to carry on into the fadeout (Tchicai recalls performing for quite a while after John and Yoko's departure), which leaves the audience's response to all of this sadly unrecorded.

When "Cambridge 1969" was released, it was registered as a Lennon/Ono composition, despite the other musicians' contributions. Mal Evans was also credited with playing "watch," so presumably it was he who gave John and Yoko the offstage signal to split.

RELEASE HISTORY

1969: **A** was released on the LP *Unfinished Music No. 2: Life with the Lions,* reissued on CD in 1997.

30. Radio interview

Date: 4 March 1969
Location: Apple Corps, London
Interviewer: David Wigg
Broadcast: 8 March and 12 April 1969, 1:00–2:00 p.m.
BBC Radio 1
Scene and Heard
Length: 7:01

"Allen Klein to help Beatles." That was the ironic headline for a blurb in the February 8 edition of *New Musical Express*. This guide isn't the place to recount the long and exasperating series of business dealings that would lead to the unraveling of Apple and ultimately the Beatles (the book *Apple to the Core* is a good place to find that tale), although the basic plot points are woven into the yearly chronologies. Suffice it to say that by early spring, a compromise had been reached wherein Klein would be appointed business manager at Apple, and the law firm of Eastman and Eastman installed as Apple's legal counsel.

With no immediate product to promote, George sat down at Apple for an interview with David Wigg and discussed the group's ongoing financial situation. The interview would be broadcast in two parts, and an off-line recording of the second (aired April 12) exists.

George begins by dispelling the rumors that his departure from the Twickenham sessions was hastened by a fight with John. He is insistent that the story was "glorified" by an unnamed journalist (presumably Michael Housego, who had reported the quarrel), and that he and John hadn't had a physical confrontation since 1960 in Hamburg.

Wigg asks whether the Beatles will make any movies together or tour again. Although he's the Beatle least likely to warm to either prospect, George is diplomatic. He says that once they straighten out the financial situation at Apple, which should take "another couple of months," they might be free enough to do another film. He avoids any mention of touring, but says

that they'll definitely be recording more in the Apple basement studio (they never would as a group).

A variant recording of the start of this interview was broadcast January 1, 1997, on part two of a BBC Radio 2 documentary. It's not clear whether this is from the March 8, 1969, broadcast or just an unedited tape of the original interview. It adds a few lines excised from the April 12 transmission, including a bit where George starts to name the *Daily Sketch* as the source of the brawl tale.

In addition, a 2:49 excerpt evidently from this same interview was released on the 1976 album *The Beatles Tapes with David Wigg*, buried in the middle of a later recording (see the October 8 entry). The change in ambience gives it away: For those of you who have the CD edition, this segment can be found from 1:52–4:43 on track 3 of disc 2.

George begins to make a point about why the tastes of the pop singles market can be so hard to fathom, but lets himself get sidetracked by a chance to rant about the British government. He points out that the BBC has a monopoly on radio that, if practiced by an independent corporation in any other field, would be clamped down on by the government. This launches George into a tirade about taxation, and he bitches and moans about the huge amount of revenue he is forced to pay, claiming that it's not even worth his while to have a steady income.

RELEASE HISTORY

1976: 2:49 of this interview was released on the LP *The Beatles Tapes with David Wigg*, later reissued on CD.

2000: The segment from the 1997 broadcast was included on the bootleg CD *The Beatles Broadcast Collection, Trailer 2*. The off-air tape of the April 12, 1969, broadcast also circulates among collectors in fair quality.

31. Studio session

Date: 11 March 1969
Location: Apple Studios, London
Producer: Paul McCartney, George Harrison

[A.] Thumbin' a Ride (3:56)
[B.] Going Back to Liverpool (3:07)

Jackie Lomax's excellent debut single for Apple, "Sour Milk Sea," had been an inexplicable flop. With the release of his LP *Is This What You Want?* approaching, a

second single was called for. Paul recommended the Coasters' "Thumbin' a Ride" for the A-side, a Lieber-Stoller composition he had sung occasionally at the Cavern and long thought would be a surefire hit if covered by the right artist.

The main session took place the night before Paul's wedding, yet he agreed to produce it in Apple's basement studio. Photos from that evening show Paul playing drums alongside Lomax. Although Lomax has claimed that Paul's drumming didn't make it onto the record (**A**), it certainly sounds like Paul's style. George was also on hand to add lead guitar to the track, although curiously one of the two guitars (in the right channel) sounds a lot like Paul's playing.

Another song recorded around this date was Jackie's own composition, "Going Back to Liverpool" (**B**), presumably as a potential flip side for the single. This one also seems to have Paul on drums (particularly the clumsy fill at 1:42). George was reportedly coproducer of this track with Paul, and he can be heard clearly contributing backing vocals. He probably also plays either the rhythm or lead guitar.

In the March 22 issue of *New Musical Express,* these two titles were reported as being Lomax's next release, but within a few weeks, Jackie would offer up a new song for the A-side, "New Day" (see the April 1969 entry), which would bump "Thumbin' a Ride" to the B-side (U.S. only) and consign "Going Back to Liverpool" to the vaults for twenty-two years.

RELEASE HISTORY

1969: **A** was released on the B-side of the "New Day" single in the United States. In the UK, it was the B-side of "How the Web Was Woven" in 1970.

1991: **A** and **B** were included as bonus tracks on the CD reissue of *Is This What You Want?*

32. Newsreel footage   P

Date: 12 March 1969
Location: Marylebone Register Office, 7 Cavendish Avenue; St. John's Wood Church, London
Length: 1:12

George and Pattie had to spend much of this day dealing with an unexpected police raid on Kinfauns, with Sgt. Pilcher of the drug squad once again "finding" a quantity of cannabis resin. On a much happier note, Paul and Linda were in London tying the knot, accompanied by Linda's daughter Heather, Peter Brown, and Paul's brother Michael acting as best man.

The news had leaked once Linda booked the register office, and Paul had confirmed it the previous night to reporters. Thus press and fans mobbed the couple all day: at their Cavendish Avenue home, at Marylebone, where the wedding took place, and at the church where they had it blessed.

A brief interview was filmed by Reuters on the steps of 7 Cavendish Avenue as the newlyweds, covered in confetti, kissed for the cameras, with Heather tugging at their coats. Paul explains that the wedding was delayed for an hour as they waited for Mike to arrive (wet weather delayed his train), and says they haven't even discussed honeymoon plans yet. Linda, holding a small kitten, is asked how it feels to be "the envy of all the ladies" after marrying "one of the most eligible bachelors in the world." She refuses to take the bait: "Well, it feels great to be married."

This clip ends with 7 seconds of footage from the church steps, showing the couple posing with Rev. Noel Perry-Gore.

RELEASE HISTORY

1996: The audio portion of this interview was released on the CD *Rare Photos & Interview CD, Volume 3.*

The Reuters interview footage was included in the video compilation *Beatles 1962 to 1970.* The *Wingspan* documentary contains a BBC News report from March 12 with similar color footage, including a bit of the same interview. The *Anthology* home video included an additional 57 seconds of Pathé newsreel footage (black and white) of Paul, Linda, Heather, and Mike fighting their way through crowds from the register office to their car.

33. TV interview   P

Date: 12 March 1969
Location: Ritz Hotel, London
Broadcast: 12 March 1969
ITV
Length: 3:08

Paul and Linda's wedding reception was held at the Ritz Hotel, and George and Pattie were able to join the celebration once their police business was concluded. A reporter from ITV News caught up with Paul, Linda, and Heather as they departed, filming a short interview.

After explaining Mike's delay again, Paul reveals that the decision to marry was made only a week earlier. Linda has little to say, except to confirm that despite being a "New York socialite," she'll remain living in London. Paul is asked what it's like to suddenly be father to a six-year-old, and he jokes that it's a terrible burden, to which Heather protests, "You don't mean it!"

Discussion of the unplanned honeymoon is followed by an interesting moment, when the reporter asks about the distressed female fans who had been sobbing in the streets all day. Paul had actually gone out and tried to console some of the "Apple Scruffs" at his home the previous evening after the news broke, and he refers to this obliquely: "No, it's OK, I talked to—I . . . I dunno. It's just difficult, that. What do— what do you say to them?" Given how shabbily most of the Scruffs had been treating Linda, this diplomacy on Paul's part couldn't have pleased her much. The newlyweds are then seen departing in the back of a car with Mal Evans and Peter Brown.

RELEASE HISTORY

1996: This interview was released on *Fab Four CD & Book Set*. The ITV footage circulates on video.

34. Newsreel footage   P

Date: 17 March 1969
Location: Kennedy Airport, New York City
Broadcast: CBS-TV
Length: 0:56

Paul and Linda flew to New York on the sixteenth for a two-week honeymoon/visit with the Eastman family. Upon arrival the next day, they were mobbed by fans seeking autographs and national press seeking photos and interviews.

A clip from the CBS News vault has the newlyweds answering a few questions shouted by various re-porters as flashbulbs pop. Asked why he waited so long to get married, Paul responds dryly, "I was thinking about it." Asked why he chose to marry an American girl, Paul says it wasn't Linda's nationality that swayed him. Linda is asked how she "got" Paul, and she sensibly offers "no comment."

RELEASE HISTORY

This color footage circulates on video among collectors.

34a. Newsreel footage   G

Date: 18 March 1969
Location: Esher and Walton Magistrates' Court
Broadcast: 18 March 1969
ITV
Length: 0:19

George and Pattie's initial court appearance on the possession charge occurred this afternoon. An ITV News crew captured their trip from the courthouse steps into a waiting car, surrounded by photographers, police, and a handful of fans. They would return March 31 for the trial itself.

RELEASE HISTORY

This silent footage circulates on video.

35. Newsreel footage   J

Date: 20 March 1969
Time: afternoon
Location: Le Bourget Airport, Paris
Length: 0:46

Whether by coincidence or not, a few days after Paul had married, John and Yoko decided to do likewise. Once Yoko's divorce from Tony Cox had been finalized at the beginning of February, it was probably inevitable, and with Paul on his honeymoon and Ringo occupied making a film, John had the rest of the month free from Beatles obligations anyway.

John and Yoko flew to Paris on March 16, spent a few relaxing days in the City of Light, and then took a private jet to the island of Gibraltar on March 20 for the ceremony. Peter Brown, who had chosen the location, was best man, and photographer David Nutter documented the occasion. A couple of hours later, the newlyweds flew back to Paris, by which time the news had spread.

Silent color footage exists of their return to Le Bourget, showing John and Yoko deplaning (John trips coming down the steps) and chatting with reporters in the arrival lounge.

This Reuters newsreel footage was included in color in the documentaries *Imagine: John Lennon* and *Anthology* during montages set to "The Ballad of John and Yoko" (it also appears in the black-and-white promo clip for that song).

36. Press conference   J

Date: 25 March 1969
Location: Room 902, Amsterdam Hilton Hotel
Length: 43:29

As John often explained, it was clear that his wedding and honeymoon to Yoko would be given plenty of column inches and broadcast time in the media. So why not use that time and space to promote the cause of world peace? To that end, the couple devoted their honeymoon to a week-long bed-in, remaining in a suite at the Amsterdam Hilton Hotel in their pajamas and encouraging any visitors interested in discussing or spreading the word about peace.

Naturally, a press conference was held to explain this unusual concept, and reporters crammed into room 902, surrounding the bedded peaceniks to get the scoop. Yoko begins by announcing that any parties interested in communicating are welcome to drop by, although John admits that they don't know anyone in particular to invite, being "a very reserved couple." Someone asks about a report that John would be playing Christ in a TV series based on the Gospels; John says he hasn't been offered the role, but would consider it.

It's pointed out that perhaps a Hilton hotel doesn't have the most peaceful vibrations, but John counters that if that's the case, it's their job to bring good vibrations. More realistically, Yoko admits that the Hilton was chosen for practical reasons, to control the access of visitors. John reveals that the original idea was to hold the bed-in onstage at the Albert Hall and invite audiences to watch them grow their hair. John says that "about twelve tracks" are completed on the next Beatles LP, and that when everyone's back in England, they need to continue remixing and record about four more for a summer release. He describes the songs as simple "on the spot" recordings, but says that they may "doctor it a bit" once they listen to the finished mixes.

Someone asks about a report in the British press that morning that the couple would be making love in public. John denies that the report was leaked from Apple, although on second thought, he considers Derek Taylor might be capable of such a comment, albeit tongue-in-cheek. Yoko says that they are conceptually making love, to which John adds, "And some of you ain't so hot at it!" John explains why he doesn't have a wedding ring while Yoko does (most British husbands didn't), and describes how emotional the marriage ceremony was, much to his cynical surprise. Yoko even says the wedding was "the best happening yet."

Talk turns to Apple's recent financial woes, and John admits that the company was in bad shape but will be straightened out by Allen Klein. He has no regrets about revealing that information, going so far as to say Apple should place ads every month asking people to buy more records when they need to refill the coffers (comparing it to Avis's "We try harder" campaign). Someone asks if this is merely a gimmick to plug a new record, and John stresses that it's a sincere effort to promote peace; however, should any journalists want to mention new Beatles or Lennon product, he won't avoid the topic.

After a while, photographers are let in, and John apologizes if any of them who had the idea they would be capturing a lovemaking session are disappointed. Baskets of flowers are placed on the bed, and John and Yoko pose for several minutes holding white tulips until everyone has gotten the shots they need. John says it's time for more talking, but is told there are still forty or fifty photographers waiting outside. He replies that they can come in and continue to take photos if they don't mind the chaos.

An ITV reporter is then heard filming an interview with the couple (see following entry), including portions not seen in the finished footage, and a female journalist asks what John remembers from his 1964 visit to Amsterdam (he recalls trying to escape from the hotel).

RELEASE HISTORY

1995: 9:14 of this press conference was released on the CD *Inside Interviews: In My Life: John Lennon & Paul McCartney.*

1999: The majority of this recording was released on the CD *Man in the Clouds,* lacking a couple of minutes compared with the earlier release.

37. TV interview

Date: 24–25 March 1969
Location: Room 902, Amsterdam Hilton Hotel
Broadcast: 25 March 1969
ITV
Length: 3:40

As described above, after the general press conference, John and Yoko filmed an interview with a British reporter for ITV News. The footage begins with the couple's arrival the previous night with Peter Brown, as they are led into the suite.

John describes the event as having two components: "Bed Peace," the seven days and nights spent in bed (or at least in the same hotel room), and "Hair Peace," a message encouraging people to grow their hair long as a sign of solidarity rather than protesting violently. The reporter points out that the press and public have been saying unkind things about the couple lately, and John says that the criticism used to depress them, particularly the personal attacks on Yoko. But now they treat it as a joke and channel the energy into something positive.

Asked if the Beatles still feel like a group, John claims somewhat implausibly that they are as close now as they ever were. He goes on to say that he stayed in bed for seven days in India and knows how difficult it's going to be.

RELEASE HISTORY

1984: The majority of this interview (1:20) was broadcast in the radio series *Sgt. Pepper's Lonely Hearts Club Band: A History of the Beatle Years 1962–1970,* with "Dig a Pony" playing in the background.

1995: A small portion of this interview was released on the CD *Inside Interviews: In My Life: John Lennon & Paul McCartney.* The full interview circulates on video.

38. Radio interview

Date: 29 March 1969
Location: Room 902, Amsterdam Hilton Hotel
Interviewer: Wim Noordhoek, Jan Donkers
Broadcast: VPRO
Hee
Length: 9:31

Toward the end of the bed-in, John and Yoko appeared on a Dutch radio program called *Hee* ("Hey") that included phoned-in questions from listeners, relayed via VPRO's studio in Hilversum to the Hilton hotel room, and then translated into English (the Dutch questions have been edited out of the circulating copy).

The tape begins with a general interview, with John doing the majority of the talking. He says that although it's been harder work than he anticipated, the bed-in has been enjoyable and worthwhile. Yoko adds that they've been watching the sky through their window, and it hasn't gotten boring yet. It's pointed out that the last time John was seen on Dutch TV, he was in a dentist's office (*Rood Wit Blauw;* see the December 12, 1968, entry). John admits to being "high as a kite" on painkillers that day, and he says he now has some "gold ashtrays" where his back teeth once were.

John is asked a question in Dutch and responds with some double-Dutch of his own, before revealing that they had brown rice for breakfast (part of their macrobiotic diet). He also responds to a priest who criticized their choice of a luxurious hotel suite as an unsuitable location for a peace protest. John insists that they need the security and protection afforded, which is logical given his fame. It's when he adds that room service is a necessity, to cook and bring them food, that it becomes clear how non-self-sufficient he and Yoko were by that time.

The questions from listeners begin to pour in.

Q: Are you smoking hash here?
J: [exaggerated fit of coughing] No!
Q: Did you see the musical *Hair*?
J: I thought it was crap . . . we walked out after the nude bit.
Q: John is against leather, why a car with leather, then?
J: Actually, the car has got plastic on it, but I'm against eating meat for health reasons, not for religious reasons.
Q: Why did John marry Yoko?
J: Because John loves Yoko!
Q: What are your religions and why?
J: Uh, if we have one at all, it might be called Bagism . . . we'll explain it on Tuesday.
Q: Why no more live appearances?
J: George, Paul, and I were talking, I think when Ringo was making his film, about doing some live appearances this year, maybe.

To conclude the interview, John is asked to "hum a small part" of one of the Beatles' new tunes. He grabs his guitar but can't think of a suitable song. Yoko suggests "Don't Let Me Down," and John sings a very rough version of the refrain (which has the only words he can remember). He segues into a demented rendition of "Those Were the Days," with everyone in the room joining in.

RELEASE HISTORY

1973: John's rendition of "Don't Let Me Down"/"Those Were the Days" was bootlegged on LPs such as *Mary Jane* and *Abbey Road Revisited*. It was copied on the CD-R *Vinyl to the Core*. The complete interview circulates among collectors.

39. TV interview   J

Date:	29 March 1969
Location:	Room 902, Amsterdam Hilton Hotel
Length:	5:50

Sometime after the *Hee* broadcast, presumably the same day, a Dutch reporter filmed an interview with John and Yoko.

The reporter begins by asking whether the constant stream of reporters and photographers becomes mind-numbing, but John relates it to Beatles tours, when something lively always managed to break the monotony, such as a photographer missing his shot or falling over. For some reason, the reporter thinks that John's rendition of "Those Were the Days" signaled a sensible, mature attitude. John says he and Yoko are pretty old but have retained a sense of humor.

Asked why they chose Holland as a honeymoon destination, John and Yoko praise it as a center of youth activity, singling out the Provos (a group of anti-establishment, pro-marijuana Dutch youths who had initiated the city's White Bicycle program). The newlyweds reiterate their seemingly conformist belief in the tradition of marriage. Yoko begins to explain how John putting the ring on her finger was also a symbol of sexual activity, but John jokingly tells her to stop as she slides it off and on. John says they hope to conceive a child during the bed-in, and if so, they "might call it Amsterdam, or Peace, or Hair, or Bed or something." John concludes by singing the chorus of "Those Were the Days" (or at least the two lines he knows).

RELEASE HISTORY

1996: The audio of this interview was released on the CD *Man in the Clouds*. A 5:12 segment of the interview circulates on video among collectors, including a second or two extra at the beginning compared with the CD.

40. Radio interview   J

Date:	25–31 March 1969
Location:	Room 902, Amsterdam Hilton Hotel
Interviewer:	Akiva Nof
Broadcast:	Voice of Israel

    [A.] Hava Negila/I Want You (She's So Heavy) (1:24)
    [B.] Yerushalaim (Jerusalem) (0:29)

One of the more interesting people who came to interview the newlyweds in Amsterdam was Akiva Nof, a songwriter who would later be elected to Israeli Parliament. On this occasion he was reporting for the Voice of Israel radio station, and two short extracts from his interview have been bootlegged.

Asked if he knows any Israeli songs, John sings a bit of the traditional "Hava Negila," but admits that he doesn't remember any song all the way through, including his own. He then grabs his guitar and plays the first two verses of "I Want You," the backing tracks of which had already been laid down by the Beatles in February. After a third instrumental verse, John closes with "Hello Israel" and a smooth half step slide down to an A major chord.

Whether coincidentally or not, John's song shares the same chords (A minor, D minor, and E) with Akiva Nof's own composition "Jerusalem"; John, Yoko, and Nof sing a pair of identical verses, again backed by John's guitar.

RELEASE HISTORY

1986: **A** and **B** appeared in good quality on the bootleg LP *Goodnight Vienna*. They were copied from a recent rebroadcast on an Israeli radio documentary, *Magical Mystery Tour: The Beatles' Story*. The full interview reportedly circulates among collectors.

41. Radio interview   J

Date: 25–31 March 1969
Location: Room 902, Amsterdam Hilton Hotel (via telephone)
Interviewer: Larry Kane
Length: 2:58

Among the many journalists who called John in Amsterdam was his old pal Larry Kane, who had last interviewed John and Paul in New York City the previous May. Being most familiar with the 1964-era Lennon, Kane asks whether the whole bed-in isn't just a put-on. John expresses his sincerity in wishing for world peace, and once again explains the two "Peaces" of the event.

Asked what the other Beatles think of all this, John admits that he hasn't heard from any of them yet. (Paul was in the United States with his new in-laws, and Ringo was filming *The Magic Christian*.) Kane wryly muses that this must be the first time anyone's tried to make a baby in public, but John says it's merely "conceptually making love in public." He claims not to mind if all that comes of the bed-in is making people laugh, since that's preferable to having them wage war. Kane signs off by wishing the Lennons' marriage well.

RELEASE HISTORY

1996: This interview was released on the promotional CD *The Fab Four On Tour*.

42. Radio interview   J

Date: 25–31 March 1969
Location: Room 902, Amsterdam Hilton Hotel (via telephone)
Interviewer: Fred Latrimeau
Broadcast: CFUN-AM, Vancouver
Length: 1:40

Around noon one day during the bed-in, Canadian disc jockey Fred Latrimeau phoned the Hilton for a brief interview. Describing the event as a "talk-in," John says they've been speaking with the press from 10 a.m. till 10 p.m. every day, adding that they've spent the morning filming (see entry below). Declaring himself and Yoko "available for functions," John says he'd be open to visiting Yugoslavia or Czechoslovakia to advertise peace.

RELEASE HISTORY

1990: This interview was broadcast on episode 90-31 of the radio series *The Lost Lennon Tapes*.

42a. Interview   J

Date: 25–31 March 1969
Location: Room 902, Amsterdam Hilton Hotel
Length: 4:00

Another joint press interview from the bed-in, with John once again defending their choice of location, calling it "intellectual snobbery" to denigrate the ninth floor of the Hilton. He remembers how impossible it was to get any sleep while on the ground floors of many U.S. hotels, particularly with hundreds of raving Beatlemaniacs camped outside all night.

John admits that he "imposed" "Revolution 9" on the Beatles and thinks that he'll use solo albums as an outlet for freakier material now, as George is doing with his *Electronic Sound* LP. While he prefers to perform simple heavy rock music, John says he likes to record it heavily processed, with doubled guitar lines, "ten basses," and effects to alter or disguise his voice, which he can't stand.

RELEASE HISTORY

1999: This interview was released on the CD *Man in the Clouds*.

43. Press conference J

Date: 31 March 1969
Location: Hotel Sacher, Vienna
Length: 9:52

One evening halfway through the bed-in, John and Yoko hit upon a new concept while talking and watching the night sky. They had already appeared onstage at the Alchemical Wedding in a white bag, and Yoko had been known to make similar public appearances. Their message of peace hadn't been getting through to some people because of the distractions of their fame and unkempt appearance. The ideas collided to form a new one which came to them simultaneously: Bagism.

The initial idea would be to conduct a press conference upon their return to London from within a white bag. It would be "total communication," since the message would be more important than the anonymous messenger. A phone call to the producers of their film *Rape,* which would be shown on Austrian TV March 31, convinced them to fly to Vienna and promote both the show and their peace campaign by holding the Bagism event there.

And so, in the Red Salon of the elegant Hotel Sacher, John and Yoko tied a white bedsheet together and climbed inside. The flabbergasted journalists were shown in while the couple hummed "The Blue Danube Waltz" from within their bag. Presiding over the affair was Hans Preiner, who had coproduced *Rape* and its accompanying TV documentary.

Naturally, there are many requests for John and Yoko to show their faces or otherwise prove their identities, but these are all turned down, although John says they'll be coming out later "for chocolate cake." Clearly not knowing what to make of this, the press toss out whatever questions come to mind. (Are there any holes in the bag? Don't you feel very hot?) At one point, John announces that "this is another peace protest, by the way." In the silence that follows, you can almost hear the reporters exchanging glances of disbelief.

John takes the opportunity to plug *Rape,* but doesn't bother to mention the title or explain the film's concept. Finally, Yoko speaks up: "This is the first an-nouncement to the world of the Bagism. And we decided to make the announcement of Bagism in Vienna."

Pause.

"By God, why?" cries a nonplussed journalist.

John explains how they conceived of the idea, and that by communicating from within a bag, nobody can confuse your message with your skin color or the length of your hair. Someone asks how long their hair is, and John, relishing the moment, replies, "Aha! You have to guess! It's not important, it's only what I say that we're here for." Another journalist points out that they aren't saying anything of great interest, and John blames the line of questioning (hardly fair, since he and Yoko had arranged the whole event without much explanation).

After a few more inane questions (how to prevent pimples, which entertainer deserves to go to hell), someone asks about Ringo's comment, made the previous week, that the Beatles would never perform live again. John chalks it up to miscommunication, revealing that during a Beatles mixing session (probably March 4 at Olympic) while Ringo was busy filming, the others had casually discussed a return to the concert stage, with John now being in favor of the idea of touring.

John concludes a defense of his bed-in with the earliest appearance of a simple phrase he would later make good use of: "Now, a lot of cynics had said, 'Oh, it's easy to sit in bed for seven days,' but I'd like some of them to try it, even if they do it for other reasons than world peace, and talk for seven days about peace. All we are saying is give peace a chance."

RELEASE HISTORY

1995: The audio portion of this press conference was released on the CD *Inside Interviews: In My Life: John Lennon & Paul McCartney.* Silent black-and white footage from this occasion was included in the promo clip for "The Ballad of John and Yoko." The documentary *Imagine: John Lennon* contained 42 seconds of color footage with sound, including a glimpse of John and Yoko climbing into their bag.

44. Documentary footage J

Date: 25–31 March 1969
Location: Room 902, Amsterdam Hilton Hotel and Hotel Sacher, Vienna
Director: Peter Goessens
Length: 40:27

Considering their interest in filmmaking, it was natural that John and Yoko would make a film documenting their Amsterdam bed-in. The film, titled *Mr. & Mrs. Lennon's Honeymoon,* was actually a "Banana" production, using a local film crew comprised of director Peter Goessens, cameraman Mat Van Hensbergen, soundman Wim Van Muyden, and editor Ruud Bernard. The result would be premiered September 10, 1969, at the Institute of Contemporary Arts, but has apparently never been broadcast in full on TV.

It opens with a self-consciously "artistic" montage of various scenes around Amsterdam (an old woman, a scrap of litter, apartment numbers, people smoking in a hash bar), punctuated by John and Yoko in their white bathrobes against a white wall. John strums his acoustic guitar in staccato bursts while he and Yoko interject slogans: "Stay in bed! Grow your hair! Bed peace! Hair peace!" John then plays some arpeggiated chords highly anticipatory of his song "Because." A slow zoom in to the exterior of room 902, with ominous music playing, precedes the title credits.

The rest of the film takes place inside hotel rooms. We begin with two vignettes intercut cyclically. In one, John and Yoko are just waking up (it's 9:30 in the morning). John compares the camera to a fly flitting about, puts on his glasses, and sleepily calls room service to order two teas and some brown toast.

In the second, it's later in the day (or perhaps a different day altogether) and a visitor has brought John and Yoko a dog, but not for keeps. John opens the day's mail and reads out a hate letter ("please stop this nonsense . . . go to a doctor to be normal"), calling it "bloody marvelous." Another nutcase has written claiming to have been contacted by the spirit of Brian Epstein, who apparently told him John would be a willing benefactor.

Another scene has several jazz musicians, presumably members of John Tchicai's quintet (see the March 2 entry), hanging out in room 902. John is on the phone to Vienna and gets the idea to hold the Bagism press conference there the night that *Rape* will premiere on Austrian TV. A bit later, he asks the camera crew if they can follow them to Vienna to cover the event.

In a scene obviously filmed earlier, John explains how he and Yoko thought up Bagism after talking to "you" (presumably the director, Peter Goessens), and says that when they return to London they'll introduce the concept of "total communication" to the press from within a white bag.

Not every visitor was greeted with open arms: Someone who had apparently jumped from a bridge and swum to the Beatles' boat during their 1964 tour of Amsterdam's canals manages to get through on the phone. John patiently explains that they're only there to see the press, and that this is as close as they can get this time. A woman in a wheelchair, Yvonne, is allowed in, but only long enough to secure an autograph from the couple.

Even more unwelcome was *Daily Mirror* reporter Donald Zec, who visited on March 30 and is seen interviewing John and Yoko, along with a Dutch journalist. Zec skeptically interrogates John about the point of the bed-in, saying that maybe if they didn't look like "two chromium-plated nuts," their message would get across. John responds earnestly, and even enthusiastically suggests Zec, the "great English cynic," should hold his own bed-in. In the end, Zec allowed himself to be photographed lying at the very edge of the bed, looking extremely uncomfortable.

This footage is interspersed with scenes of John reading the finished article the following evening in bed at the Hotel Sacher in Vienna. Realizing that it's another hatchet job, John slams Zec as a prima donna, bitterly recalling the Beatles' first interview with him in 1963, when Zec had ignored the fledgling stars and rambled about his own celebrity. This is followed by a brief clip of John and Yoko at Marylebone Court, filmed off a TV screen, evidently during the March 31 broadcast of the *John & Yoko* documentary that preceded *Rape*.

The film concludes with John thanking a visitor for bringing some marijuana, praising the astuteness of some student reporters, and opening a gift of something in a jar. (Struggling to squeeze it from its wrapping, John cries, "It's a boy!")

RELEASE HISTORY

The complete film circulates among collectors in very good quality.

45. Newsreel footage   G

Date: 31 March 1969
Location: Esher and Walton Magistrates' Court
Broadcast: 31 March 1969
BBC TV
Length: 0:09

Meanwhile, back in Esher, George and Pattie's trial for cannabis possession took place this day. Although the actual drugs confiscated by the police were not George's, he decided to plead guilty, as John had done. With the Beatles' drug habits being public knowledge, it would have been hard for either of them to deny the charge and face jail time. George and Pattie were fined a total of £500 plus court costs and given a year's probation. A BBC News crew captured the departure of George, in a navy blue suit, and Pattie, in a crimson velvet jacket, accompanied by the ubiquitous Peter Brown.

RELEASE HISTORY

This silent color footage was included in the documentary *Imagine: John Lennon,* during a montage set to the song "God."

46. Documentary footage

Date: 1 April 1969
Location: London Airport
Length: 0:34

Mr. and Mrs. Lennon flew from Vienna back to London, with the newly hooked British press eagerly awaiting the arrival of the new Ambassadors of Peace. The airport press conference was to have been the debut of Bagism, but the stopover in Vienna altered their plans. Instead, Derek Taylor met them with several envelopes containing a pair of acorns each. One of John and Yoko's first collaborations, the Acorn Sculpture, would now be sent to various world leaders who would be encouraged to install the exhibit by planting the acorns in the name of peace.

Silent color footage documents the Lennons' journey from the press conference to an awaiting taxi, as they ride an escalator and a baggage cart, and John kicks up his heels.

RELEASE HISTORY

This footage was included in the documentary *Imagine: John Lennon* during a montage set to "The Ballad of John and Yoko." Some alternate black-and-white newsreel footage from the arrival and an airport interview is included in the promo clip for that song (see following entry).

47. TV interview

Date: 1 April 1969
Location: London Airport
Broadcast: 1 April 1969
ITV
Length: 0:59

Before leaving the airport, John and Yoko filmed an interview for ITV News, conducted by the same reporter who had interviewed them in Amsterdam (see the March 25 entry). He asks whether the couple is laughing at "us" (whether he means reporters in general or the public isn't clear) during their bed-ins. John admits that the notion of people staying in bed on their honeymoon being front-page news is silly, and delights at the image of microphones being pointed toward a bag, but is careful to add that they are completely serious about wanting peace.

RELEASE HISTORY

1996: The audio portion of this interview was released on the CD *Fab Four CD & Book Set*. The footage also circulates on video.

48. TV interview

Date: 3 April 1969
Time: 11:00–11:45 p.m.
Location: Café Royal, London
Host: Eamonn Andrews
Broadcast: live
Thames Television
The Eamonn Andrews Show
Length: 10:01

The night they returned to London, John and Yoko had appeared on Thames TV's news show, *Today,* to be interviewed by Eamonn Andrews. The host proved a good sport, setting up a bed in the studio to conduct the interview and even posing with the Lennons in a white bag. They accepted Andrews's invitation to appear live on his own talk show two nights later, although it would prove a more challenging occasion.

Among the other guests on the show that evening were Rolf Harris, who knew John from concerts and BBC shows back in 1963, and Jack Benny, who had attended the Beatles' 1965 show at the Hollywood Bowl. The video of this program is probably lost, but ten minutes of John and Yoko's seventeen-minute appearance exists on a poor-quality off-air audio tape.

As they enter the studio, Andrews jokingly apologizes for having only a couch, not a bed, this time. John gives his by-now standard spiel about the purpose of the bed-in and admits that "we're willing to be the world's freaks." Andrews asks if anyone in the audience had thought more about peace after reading of John and Yoko's honeymoon, and one man in the front row puts his hand up.

John, assuming he's found an ally, thanks him, and Andrews arranges for a microphone to get the man's opinion. "Can you tell me how this made you think more about peace, sir?" "Well, I thought it was the biggest piece of rubbish that I'd heard of."

This pun, worthy of Lennon himself, gets a round of applause, but John tries to find out what exactly made the man so upset: "What did you think was wrong with two people staying in bed?" The man replies that there's nothing wrong with it, and "if you stayed there longer, I think it would be better for everybody." John snaps, "OK, don't get insulting. Go and look in the mirror before you get insulting. Now, what offended you about what we do?" The man counters with "Well, I'm sure I don't mind looking in the mirror, I think I'd see something better than looking at you." John responds with "I know you are, but what am I?"

Well . . . no, he doesn't, but the level of discourse is hardly erudite at this point. The man gives a lengthy explanation in which he accuses John of encouraging youngsters to take "cannibals" [sic] and reveals that he did something for peace by volunteering to fight in the last war. John, who must feel like he's in a scene from *A Hard Day's Night,* gives in: "Oh, well, congratulations."

A second audience member sides with John, calling the event "beautiful," and someone else wonders, "What's all this about acorns?" John is exasperated: "The acorn's a symbol. It's a symbol of growth, and if you plant acorns, the tree will grow. If you bomb it, it won't. Can't you see anything beautiful in acorns? D'you like trees? Well, what do you think it comes from? Jam jars?"

Andrews asks what the John Lennon of 1964 would think of himself today, and John insists that he's always thought the same, but wasn't always free to express it as a mop-top. Rolf Harris wonders whether people are taking the couple's message seriously, and John says that even if they get through to five people in the audience, it's better than nothing. He thinks that the press has turned against the Beatles because they are refusing to conform to their once wholesome public image.

There is a gap in the tape at this point, with material missing. When it continues, John is explaining that while other nonviolent protesters such as Gandhi and Martin Luther King Jr. got killed, he hopes having a sense of humor will keep this from happening to him. Just before the tape cuts off, Andrews asks Jack Benny if he ever uses humor to make a moral point, but Benny says he eschews political humor.

RELEASE HISTORY

A poor-quality off-line audio recording of this broadcast circulates among collectors.

49. Location recording

J

Date: 25 March–April 1969
Location: Room 902, Amsterdam Hilton Hotel and Apple Corps, London (?)
Producer: John Lennon, Yoko Ono

[A.] Amsterdam (24:53)

Side 2 of John and Yoko's third album consisted of this lengthy audio collage, documenting the Amsterdam bed-in and its aftermath. It can be broken down into several distinct sections, as follows.

The first 5:14 consists of a long a cappella improvisation, mostly by Yoko, who sings "let's hope for peace" ad infinitum. John joins in from time to time, whispering and then shouting "peace," and the whole thing wraps up with John's *Guten morgen, meine Damen und Herren.*" This seems to come from an interview with a German or Austrian reporter, who then thanks them and shuts off the tape.

It's switched back on for an interview (same ambience), which runs through 12:42 on the track. This and the above were taped sometime in April after the honeymoon, probably in John and Yoko's new private office at Apple. Asked what was the biggest success in the last three hundred years, John hasn't a clue, but Yoko optimistically says maybe it's yet to come. She goes on to make the absurd claim that everyone in the world is equally responsible for any violence that occurs anywhere. John points out that Britain and other countries waited to join World War II until the problem was at their doorstep. He says that every country has had its equivalent of Hitler and admits that he and Yoko can be just as violent as anyone. This segment ends with a fourth voice suggesting they conduct the rest of the interview "in the car."

The next section (12:43–18:51) is lifted directly from the soundtrack of the film *Mr. & Mrs. Lennon's Honeymoon,* edited and rearranged to make a bit more narrative sense. We hear seagulls, ominous music, John's quick "Stay in bed," John waking up and ordering room service, John and Yoko not being given a dog, John reading hate mail, and unwrapping a gift (see earlier entry for details).

This is followed by a section from 18:52–22:13 not seen in the film and apparently taped by a Dutch reporter. John asks for "Robbie" to be brought some tea, and the interviewer congratulates the couple on their marriage. They express glee upon learning that

Amsterdam is the geographic center of Europe and are then filmed waving at fans outside the hotel. "Love, peace, and bed, not forgetting jam, of course," comments the reporter. John concludes this segment playing a twelve-bar blues on his acoustic, singing, "Good-bye, Amsterdam, good-bye."

After a series of beeps, we're back to the film soundtrack, with John and Yoko's song "Stay In Bed" ending at 23:02. This cuts to an apparent outtake from the film, as John sings "Good Night" and discusses the day's events with Yoko. At 24:15, we hear John and Yoko's brief "bed peace" and "hair peace" bits from the beginning of the film, and the track ends with more ominous noises.

RELEASE HISTORY

1969: **A** was released on the LP *Wedding Album,* reissued on CD in 1997 by Rykodisc.

50. Studio session

Date:	14 April 1969
Time:	2:30–9:00 p.m.
Location:	EMI Studio 3
Producer:	George Martin

[A.] The Ballad of John and Yoko—RS5 (2:57)
Mixed: 14 April 1969

[B.] The Ballad of John and Yoko—RS from take 10 (2:37)

John wasted no time in setting his wedding and honeymoon exploits to verse, shaping the events of March 16–April 1 into a pop ballad. The Beatles were due to record at Abbey Road later in the week, but when John and Paul met up there on a Monday afternoon for what would otherwise have been a mixing session, they decided to record John's new song on their own.

George was shopping for a new house (by next March, he would move from the Kinfauns bungalow to the Friar Park mansion), and Ringo was busy on the set of *The Magic Christian,* but the production/engineering team of George Martin and Geoff Emerick was reunited that day. Emerick hadn't worked with the Beatles since the previous July, but was now signed up to be chief engineer for Apple's basement studio.

Throughout the session, and even on the acetate cut at Apple, the song was titled "The Ballad of John and Yoko (They're Gonna Crucify Me)." John was persuaded to drop the parenthetical subtitle for release, obviously aware that it wouldn't help the single's commercial appeal. A backing track was perfected in eleven takes, with take 10 being chosen as "best." John's acoustic guitar on track 2, Paul's drumming on track 3, and John's lead vocal on track 4 were all recorded simultaneously.

Overdubs began with Paul's bass on track 1, followed by John's lead guitar on track 5, his playing heavily reminiscent of that on the Beatles BBC recording of the Johnny Burnette Trio's "Lonesome Tears in My Eyes." On track 6, he doubled the guitar (including some nifty call-and-response licks) while Paul played piano. Paul sang a fragmented backing vocal on track 7, and for track 8, John added percussion by thumping the back of his guitar, while Paul shook maracas for the song's latter half.

It was like 1964 all over again, only more impressive: Half as many Beatles, using twice as many tracks, managed to record and remix for stereo a chart-topping song in a lone eight-hour session! By the end of the week, its B-side would be finished as well, but they held back the single's release until the end of May so as not to compete with "Get Back," which was climbing the charts. The single would be the group's first to be issued exclusively in stereo; thus no mono mixes were prepared. The *Anthology* DVD remix (**B**) moves the acoustic guitar to the left.

RELEASE HISTORY

1969: **A** was released on a single worldwide and is available on the CD *Past Masters, Volume 2* as well as the compilation CDs *The Beatles 1967–1970* and *1.*

2003: **D** was released on the soundtrack of the *Anthology* DVD.

51. Promo clip

Date: November 1968–April 1969
Location: various

   [A.] The Ballad of John and Yoko–version 1
     (2:54)
   [B.] The Ballad of John and Yoko–version 2
     (3:04)

Tradition demanded a promotional film clip for the latest Beatles single, and since John and Yoko were filming every minute of the activities described in the song, it was an easy enough task. According to Mark Lewisohn, two "essentially similar" color 16 mm promo clips were assembled, but he does not describe the differences between them.

Two very different versions are circulating, the roughest of which (**A**) circulates only in black and white. It comes from a rebroadcast on Australia's *Rage* TV show, and if it is one of the original promos, it would be the earliest one, shown on *Top of the Pops* three times in June. This edit includes footage from only four sources: the You Are Here exhibit (see the July 1, 1968, entry), John and Yoko's Marylebone Court appearance (October 19, 1968), the return to Paris after marrying in Gibraltar (March 20, 1969), and the Amsterdam bed-in. The word "Christ" is bleeped out in the soundtrack, accompanied by a visual starburst effect.

The more common version (**B**) illustrates the lyrics much more effectively and includes footage from the following sources, all color except where noted:

- John and Yoko riding in the back of their white limo (filmed in April around England)
- The Beatles rehearsing at Twickenham (filmed January 2)

- John and Yoko by a river (possibly filmed in Paris around March 20)
- John and Peter Brown on the phone at Apple (filmed in April)
- John and Yoko arriving in Amsterdam and holding the bed-in (monochrome newsreel clips)
- John and Yoko's Vienna Bagism press conference (monochrome newsreel clip from March 31)
- John and Yoko dining out at a restaurant (probably filmed in April in London)
- John and Yoko arriving in London and being interviewed (monochrome newsreel clips from April 1)

This promo has a close-up of a traffic sign with an exclamation point inserted at each mention of the word "Christ," although the word is retained in the soundtrack. It's this version that was aired in the United States on ABC's *Music Scene* September 22, with the offending word simply chopped out of the footage entirely. This broadcast also had most of the promo for "Give Peace a Chance" inserted awkwardly halfway through "The Ballad of John and Yoko."

RELEASE HISTORY

A circulates from the *Rage* telecast, while **B** was available for a long time only from a black-and-white airing on Germany's *Beat Club* in 1981. (It originally appeared on that show August 2, 1969, along with the "Give Peace a Chance" promo.) In 2000, a clean color print was distributed by Apple in an EPK promoting the *1* CD. The original *Music Scene* broadcast also circulates in excellent quality, complete with Lily Tomlin's original introduction.

52. Studio session

Date: 18 April 1969
Time: 2:30–10:30 p.m.
Location: EMI Studio 3
Producer: Chris Thomas

   [A.] Old Brown Shoe—RS23 (3:16)
Mixed: 18 April 1969

On April 16, the first full Beatles session at Abbey Road in six months was held in Studio 3, and it was devoted to George Harrison compositions. He had recorded solo demos of three songs back in February, and before the rest of the group arrived that afternoon, he

laid down a second demo of one of these, "Old Brown Shoe."

This second take 1 recording was probably played to the others upon their arrival and then erased as the band recorded the song for real, needing only four takes to perfect a backing track. Ringo's drums went on track 1, George's guide vocal on track 2, his lead guitar on track 3, Paul's jangle piano on track 4, and John's rhythm guitar on track 8 of the tape. Track 5 was filled with backing vocals from John and Paul, and then track 6 had an overdub of Paul's bass, with George doubling up some of the bouncy riffs on electric guitar. George also retaped his lead vocal track, isolating himself in a corner of the room while singing, giving the vocal an artificially distant, claustrophobic sound.

The Beatles moved on to another of George's songs, "Something," recording thirteen takes of an instrumental backing, with Paul's bass on track 1, Ringo's drums on track 2, George's electric guitar on track 3, and George Martin's piano on track 4. These would be abandoned in favor of a remake in May. To conclude the session, the "best" take of "Old Brown Shoe," take 4, was mixed into stereo.

Two days later, George returned alone to Studio 3 for a session presided over by Chris Thomas. George decided to add a Leslied guitar solo to "Old Brown Shoe" on track 7 of the tape, and then played Hammond organ on track 8, erasing John's earlier rhythm guitar contribution.

George and Chris remixed the song into stereo that night, requiring a further nineteen tries to perfect (there was no RS4). A note on the tape box reads "CRACKLES AT ST. TO BE FADED" next to the drum track, but this defect can still be heard at 0:06 in the center as the drums begin. The guitar solo was treated with ADT, mixed into the center to begin with, then split across to either side at the end. The song was chosen as the B-side for "The Ballad of John and Yoko," and likewise was never mixed into mono.

RELEASE HISTORY

1969: **A** was released on a single worldwide and is available on the CD *Past Masters, Volume 2* as well as the compilation CD *The Beatles 1967–1970.*

53. Studio session

Date:	26 April 1969
Time:	4:30 p.m.–4:15 a.m.
Location:	EMI Studio 2
Producer:	The Beatles

[A.] **Oh! Darling—take 26 (mono)** (3:24)
[B.] **Octopus's Garden—take 2 w/dialogue from take 8 (stereo)** (2:47)

Out of the ashes of *Get Back, Abbey Road* was beginning to take shape from the compositions that went unrecorded in January. The Beatles had recorded a basic track for John's "I Want You (She's So Heavy)" during a one-off session in February, and continued working on it throughout April.

April 20 was spent in Studio 3, with Chris Thomas producing again, recording a basic track for Paul's "Oh! Darling." On each of the twenty-six takes, Ringo drummed, John pounded out doo-wop triplets on the piano, George played Leslied lead guitar (stabbing chords on the verses and arpeggiated notes on the bridges), and Paul sang a guide vocal while playing bass. Hammond organ was then overdubbed onto the final and "best" take.

Six days later, they assembled at Studio 2, and although Chris Thomas was present, the Beatles were listed on the session sheet as producers. By this point in their career, the group only needed someone to man the machines and follow their instructions, although George Martin was still useful for writing and arranging musical scores.

The session began with Paul erasing the Hammond organ from "Oh! Darling" and adding new vocals.

His main vocal track was not nearly as raucous as it would become, with the first bridge shouted, but the second sung in quiet falsetto. Paul also manually double-tracked a harmony with himself over the final verse, and low-key "ooh" backing vocals were added in spots. All of this can be heard on **A,** which may be a mono copy of RS4, prepared from this take on May 1. Plenty more work would be done on the song before it was ready for release.

Most of April 26 was spent recording Ringo's second composition, "Octopus's Garden." The Beatles stuck to their standard guitars, bass, and drums lineup for each of these thirty-two takes, with Ringo singing a guide vocal as he played. The second take (**B**), released on *Anthology 3,* has some very tasty country pickin' from George, but Paul's bass playing is rather sloppy. Ringo sings the song's first verse and bridge three times over; perhaps he hadn't completed the lyrics yet, or perhaps he didn't bother to sing all the verses since it was a guide vocal. The song ends with Ringo's facetious comment "Well, that was superb," which actually followed take 8.

RELEASE HISTORY

1978: **A** first surfaced on the vinyl bootleg *No. 3 Abbey Road N.W. 8,* in very good quality.

1991: **A** appeared from tape source on the CD *Unsurpassed Masters, Volume 5;* it's also on the Vigotone CD *No. 3 Abbey Road N.W. 8* in comparable quality, but running a bit fast.

1996: **B** was released on the CD *Anthology 3.*

54. Studio session

Date: 27 April 1969
Time: 3:00–6:00 p.m.
Location: EMI Studio 3
Producer: John Lennon

[A.] John and Yoko—RS7 (22:37)
Mixed: 1 May 1969

What do you get when you cross "Baby's Heartbeat" with Stan Freberg's "John and Marsha"? Well, more filler for John and Yoko's third LP; in fact, one whole side of it. On April 22, John officially changed his name to John Winston Ono Lennon in a ceremony on the roof of 3 Savile Row, which was duly photographed. The photographer, David Nutter, followed the couple to Abbey Road that evening to document their latest avant-garde recording session.

In turn, John and Yoko lay on the floor and recorded their heartbeats using a supersensitive hospital microphone. Then they stood at a microphone each and, occasionally munching what sounds like apples, called out each other's names . . . for twenty-two minutes straight.

The heartbeats were looped and overlaid on the "Yoko! John!" tracks, and the resulting four-track tape was mixed into stereo: John's voice at far left, Yoko's on the right. This took three attempts to mix: on the twenty-second, twenty-sixth, and after rerecording the heartbeats on the twenty-seventh, a final mixing session on May 1.

The recording begins with a few seconds of heartbeats, a pause, and then John's first "Yoko." It ends several hundred variations later, with the cessation of pulses and one final exchange of names. There is some variety in the intonation (pleading, teasing, inquisitive), but not nearly enough to sustain interest for a whole LP side.

RELEASE HISTORY

1969: **A** was released on the LP *Wedding Album,* reissued on CD in 1997 by Rykodisc.

55. Studio session

Date: 29 April 1969
Time: 7:30 p.m.–1:00 a.m.
Location: EMI Studio 3
Producer: Chris Thomas

[A.] Octopus's Garden—take 32 (mono)
(2:47)

Work continued on Ringo's song this evening with the addition of two lead vocal tracks, erasing the previous guide vocal on take 32. Ringo sang the now-completed lyrics for all three verses, even harmonizing with himself in places. Also added to the backing track was a bouncy piano part during the bridge sections, although it's unclear whether this was overdubbed on the twenty-sixth or twenty-ninth—if the latter, Chris Thomas may have played the part, as no other Beatles would have been required in the studio that day. All of this can be heard on **A,** which may be a mono copy of RS4 from that same evening. The song would be completed with further additions in July.

RELEASE HISTORY

1978: **A** first surfaced on the vinyl bootleg *No. 3 Abbey Road N.W. 8,* in very good quality.

1991: **A** appeared from tape source on the CD *Unsurpassed Masters, Volume 5;* it's also on the Vigotone CD *No. 3 Abbey Road N.W. 8* in comparable quality, but running a bit fast.

56. Studio session

Date: 30 April 1969
Time: 7:15 p.m.–2:00 a.m.
Location: EMI Studio 3
Producer: Chris Thomas

[A.] You Know My Name (Look Up the Number)—edit of take 30 (stereo)
(5:41)

[B.] Let It Be—RS? (4:06)
Mixed: 2 May 1969

[C.] You Know My Name (Look Up the Number)—edit of RM4 (4:17)
Mixed: 26 November 1969

Rewind to spring 1967. The Beatles have finished recording *Sgt. Pepper's Lonely Hearts Club Band* and want to rest on their laurels a bit. John, in magpie fashion, spots a London telephone directory while visiting Paul at Cavendish Avenue. On its cover is the slogan "You know their NAME? Look up their NUMBER."

On May 17, the group assemble at Abbey Road Studio 2 with no songs in particular to record. With George Martin absent, Geoff Emerick is left to supervise the session. By now, John has written a basic chord progression to go behind the phrase "You know my name, look up the number," but has taken the idea no further. But in these days of studio experimentation run rampant, who needs a complete song? As Paul later explained, "He brought it in originally as a fifteen-minute chant when he was in space-cadet mode . . ."

A quick arrangement for guitars, bass, and drums was worked up, and fourteen rhythm track takes were recorded, with take 10 tentatively labeled "best." Nothing more was done until June 7, when take 9 was given overdubs of "various bits and pieces" (piano at least). A remake was then attempted, beginning at take 20 and running through take 24, using drums, electric guitar, organ, tambourine, and flute. These takes apparently strayed so far from the original melody as to be unrecognizable.

Meanwhile, Paul had invited Rolling Stones guitarist Brian Jones to show up at EMI and join in the fun. Much to everyone's surprise, he arrived June 8 not with a guitar but an alto saxophone (Jones dabbled in numerous instruments). By this time, the decision had been made to record as many versions of "You Know My Name" as possible, in varying styles and with assorted instrumentation. These would then be edited together, one "part" at a time, to produce a master, although not in order of recording.

Part one would consist of take 9 from the previous session, but four further parts were taped during the session of the eighth. Paul's piano was the common instrument used in all five parts. Jones participated in two of these: a ska section with drums, guitar, and sax, and a jazz combo section with drums, guitar, sax, bass, and vibraphone. A nightclub section featured drums, maracas, and congas playing a rhumba. Part five hearkened back to "Yellow Submarine," with bongos playing alongside various noisemakers (*ding, cuckoo, zip, boing, quack*).

The five parts were stitched into take 30 at the day's end, with the result transferred onto one track of a new four-track tape to allow for further overdubs, and promptly forgotten about.

Fast forward to late April 1969. John is talking with journalist Alan Smith for an interview (published in *New Musical Express* on May 3). John reveals that he's just written a song called "Because" based on a classical chord progression Yoko was playing. Explaining that he's composed with other people as well, John mentions "What's the New Mary Jane," written with

"our electronics genius, Alex . . . it was real madness, but we never released it. I'd like to do it again."

Something is jogged in John's memory. He continues: "There was another song I wrote around *Pepper* time that's still in the can, called 'You Know My Name and Cut the Number' [sic]. That's the only words to it. It just goes on all the way like that, and we did all these mad backings. But I never did finish it. And I must." Title transcription error aside, John's appetite was clearly whetted.

On April 30, the Chris Thomas–helmed sessions continued in Studio 3. Glyn had decided to use take 27A of "Let It Be" from January 31 on the *Get Back* LP. George, unsatisfied with his original solo, replaced track 7 of the tape with a new Leslied guitar part at the start of this session, playing the descending riffs, a new solo, and some licks during the final chorus. Along with some intro chat about "sync[ing] the second clap," this newly overdubbed recording (**B**) would be included in both of Glyn's LP lineups.

George's job done, and Ringo apparently busy on the film set, John brought up "You Know My Name," suggesting they finish it off with vocal overdubs. Paul enthusiastically agreed, having fond memories of the original sessions. George declined, for whatever reason, leaving John and Paul to enjoy what was probably their last-ever stretch of unbridled fun in the studio together.

They recorded vocals across two tracks, tailoring their deliveries to match each style in the song: obnoxious shouting, clipped Caribbean, John's unctuous MC and Paul's crooner "Denis O'Bell" (a poke at *Magic Christian* producer Denis O'Dell), demented Pythonesque falsetto, and guttural nonsense mumbling. Various effects went onto the fourth track: audience ambience and applause for the nightclub segment, and Mal Evans repeatedly scooping a shovel in a bucket of gravel for the noisemaker segment.

It's not clear what the purpose of the session was: With one single out and another in the can, plus one completed LP and a head start on a second, there was little need to plunder the past for material. Three mono mixes concluded the session, and again the song remained in the vault. It was clearly associated strongly with "What's the New Mary Jane" in John's mind, for in November, he decided to pair the two songs for a potential Plastic Ono Band single.

On November 26, he copied RM3 of "You Know My Name," trimming the result down from 6:10 to 4:17. John chose three sections from the original recording: 0:00–0:45, 2:15–3:50, and 4:12–6:10. This mix (**C**) was eventually used as the B-side of the single "Let It Be," using the exact same mono matrix (APPLES 1002-A) as the canceled Plastic Ono Band single.

For twenty-five years, this remained one of the few Beatles songs never released in a stereo mix despite the multitracks existing. The *Anthology* project seemed the perfect opportunity to correct that, and a stereo mix of the complete unedited take 30 was set for inclusion in *Anthology 2* (despite the 1969 overdubs, it was considered a 1967 recording). Sadly, George was still less than enamored of the song, calling it "overindulgent," and reportedly insisted on trimming this new mix (**A**) himself, chopping out the portion from 4:20–4:47 and fading the end a few seconds early.

A reconstruction of the full take 30, lasting 6:10, can be heard on the bootleg *Upgraded Collection—*

Highlights, obviously switching from stereo to mono where necessary.

RELEASE HISTORY

B was included on both of Glyn's *Get Back* LP lineups (see January 1969 for full details).

1970: **C** was released on a single worldwide; it's available on the CD *Past Masters, Volume 2.*

1996: **A** was officially released on *Anthology 2.*

57. Studio session   G

Date: March–April 1969
Location: Olympic Studios, London
Producer: Jackie Lomax, Mal Evans

[A.] New Day (3:12)

Jackie Lomax's second Apple single would use the Paul McCartney–produced "Thumbin' a Ride" as a B-side, but Beatles roadie Mal Evans was somehow roped in to coproduce the A-side. The song was a Lomax original,

"New Day," and George was around to play one of the guitar parts. Reports of Ringo's and Eric Clapton's participation on the session seem unfounded, based on the sonic evidence and corroborated by Jackie's memory.

RELEASE HISTORY

1969: **A** was released on a single worldwide, which failed to chart. It was included on the CD reissue of *Is This What You Want?*

58. Studio session   G

Date: April 1969
Location: Trident Studios, London
Producer: George Harrison

[A.] That's the Way God Planned It— alternate version (4:11)
[B.] That's the Way God Planned It (parts 1 and 2) (5:30)
[C.] Do What You Want (3:39)

Billy Preston's association with the Beatles did not end when the *Get Back* sessions concluded. As early as January 24, Apple was able to buy out Billy's contract from Capitol Records. He continued to sit in on sessions for "I Want You (She's So Heavy)" in February, and "Something" in early May. In the interim, George, who had "discovered" Billy, began producing tracks for his Apple LP, with Glyn Johns engineering.

The first fruits of these labors appeared in June on a single, featuring a fantastic (if slightly familiar— Billy had clearly paid close attention to the verse of "Let It Be" and the bridge of "Something") gospel rocker, "That's the Way God Planned It." An early take (**A**) has a basic track of George's guitar and Billy's piano and vocal, accompanied by drums and bass. The

lyrics are incomplete at this point, the tempo slower and the rhythm looser but still swinging.

The finished recording (**B**) was quite an affair, featuring Ginger Baker on drums and Keith Richards on bass, with George again contributing the main guitar track. Part two of the song is a double-time rave-up spotlighting furious interchanges between Billy's organ and Eric Clapton's lead guitar. The lyrics are fleshed out, with the first two stanzas reversed and a new final stanza added. The mono single trimmed this recording to 3:22, but the full version served as a great title track to the LP.

Also recorded at these sessions was "Do What You Want" (**C**), another Preston composition featuring George on rhythm guitar, plus Clapton on lead, Richards on bass, and possibly Ringo on drums. This song would be held over for the LP's opening track.

The single's flip side, "What About You?" was also recorded around this time, but it doesn't sound like George (or Ringo) plays on it. Some reports state that these sessions took place May 5 and sixth at Trident, which is possible but unlikely as George was busy recording at Olympic with the Beatles both nights.

The single did quite well in the UK charts, peaking at number 7. In the United States, where it only hit number 62, Apple pulled the same trick they had with James Taylor. Billy found success on A&M Records with the number 2 hit "Outa-Space" in May of 1972, prompting a cash-in reissue of the Apple single in June. It failed to improve on its previous position, topping out at number 65, but made a few more dollars for ABKCO.

RELEASE HISTORY

1969: **B** and **C** were released on the LP *That's the Way God Planned It.*

1991: Apple's CD issue of *That's the Way God Planned It* included the first release of **A,** as well as **B** and **C**.

59. Studio session   G, R

Date:	ca. May 1969
Location:	London
Producer:	George Harrison

[A.] She Belongs to Me (4:04)
[B.] It Doesn't Matter (2:37)
[C.] Let Us All Get Together Right Now (4:05)
[D.] This Is It (2:40)

George continued recording with Billy Preston at Trident, Olympic, and Apple studios through the spring; the LP was probably completed by the time George took a three-week vacation in Sardinia beginning June 1.

It's not clear which songs George plays on: three leftovers from Billy's 1968 Capitol sessions can be ruled out, and there's no guitar on "Everything's All Right" or the lovely cover version of W. C. Handy's "Morning Star." One relatively sparse song, "Let Us All Get Together Right Now" (**C**) includes a tamboura drone throughout that, if not played by George, was surely his idea. Billy would later reuse this song's opening chord progression when writing "You Are So Beautiful."

The Bob Dylan cover "She Belongs to Me" (**A**) has George on acoustic guitar, and he probably plays the electric guitars on **B** and **D**. It's also possible that Ringo drums or plays percussion on some of these tracks. The finished LP was released in August to lukewarm reaction, charting in the United States in 1972 only when Billy's career was on an upswing.

RELEASE HISTORY

1969: **A**–**D** were released on the LP *That's the Way God Planned It,* reissued on CD in 1991.

60. TV interview   J

Date:	2 May 1969
Time:	12:30–1:00 p.m.
Location:	Studio G, Lime Grove Studios, London
Interviewer:	Michael Wale
Broadcast:	2 May 1969, 10:55–11:35 p.m. BBC1 *How Late It Is*
Length:	6:42

On April 25, John and Yoko paid a visit to the Montreaux TV Festival, where their film *Rape* was being screened. One week later, they videotaped an appearance on BBC TV's *How Late It Is* to discuss the film with Michael Wale. Although the footage hasn't surfaced, the audio portion was captured by a home viewer and circulates in fair quality.

As a clip from the film is shown, John points out that it's in a different language (the film's sole subject, a Hungarian woman named Eva Majlata, spoke no English), and Yoko counters that "we're all talking foreign language to each other." John translates the gist of the dialogue ("Why are you filming me?") and goes on to describe the genesis of the project. When he and Yoko were in the hospital the previous fall, they had sent a cameraman (Nick Knowland) and a soundman out to Hyde Park to pursue suitable passers-by, filming them but not speaking a word, as some kind of social experiment. John admits that Majlata may have been an actress in "real life" (and was now a model), but had no idea of the reason she was being followed and bothered by the film crew.

Wale brings out a copy of the LP *Unfinished Music No. 2: Life with the Lions* ("which is out tomorrow," John plugs) and asks John about the back cover photo, depicting the scene outside Marylebone Court after the drug bust (see the October 19, 1968, entry). John launches into a fairly humorous narrative of the raid itself, acting out several parts, and blaming Yoko at one point for opening the door out of curiosity. Wale wonders if these pressures led to Yoko's miscarriage, and she responds vaguely that "everything affects our lives, you know. But life is pretty exciting."

x

RELEASE HISTORY

A fair-quality off-line audio recording of this broadcast circulates among collectors.

60a. Documentary footage

J, P, R

Date: 3 February–4 May 1969
Location: various and Les Ambassadeurs, London
Broadcast: 18 December 1969, 9:10–10:00 p.m.
BBC1
Will the Real Mr. Sellers . . . . .
Length: 2:21

While *The Magic Christian* was being filmed, producer Denis O'Dell worked with director Tony Palmer to shoot and assemble a documentary about its star, Peter Sellers. The finished product, titled *Will the Real Mr. Sellers . . . . .,* was aired on TV just in time to promote the movie's December release.

Narrated by Spike Milligan, the program cuts together new interviews with Sellers, scenes from the movie, and location footage shot during production. Naturally, costar Ringo is seen in several sequences, most notably as straight man in an impromptu skit filmed in an unknown restaurant. Sellers plays a baf-fled connoisseur trying to identify what he has just tasted, guessing several varieties of wine, before Ringo fills him in: "In fact, it is half a Scotch egg," holding aloft the plate to demonstrate. "Good Lord!" cries Sellers. "What year is it?"

Principal photography for *The Magic Christian* concluded May 2, and two days later, a wrap party was held at the nightclub Les Ambassadeurs. The documentary includes 41 seconds of footage from this event, including 4 seconds of Sellers chatting with John, and a short interview with the newlywed McCartneys, in which Paul denies that Linda (already five months pregnant) is expecting.

RELEASE HISTORY

The complete 50-minute program circulates on video in very good quality.

61. Interview

J

Date: ca. 5 May 1969
Location: Apple Corps, London
Length: 21:53

This lengthy interview with John and Yoko (apparently conducted by a couple of American reporters) was recorded sometime around the first week of May. One possible clue to the dating occurs when John stops to answer the phone. He tells the unknown caller: "I've heard from the Dorchester [i.e., Allen Klein, who had a suite there] that you were checking it out . . . we want it for the album, as I told you." He then arranges for someone to drive from Apple to Abbey Road and pick up a tape for delivery to Olympic Studios. Most likely this would be reel E91419, the session tape of "Something," which had been recorded at EMI Studio 3 on May 2 and would be overdubbed on the evening of May 5 at Olympic.

In addition to coordinating that bit of business, John and Yoko expound at great length about their bed-in, peace campaign, and various joint artistic proj-ects. Calling the Beatles "sneaky peaceniks," John says that although they were always antiwar, he is now dedicated to overtly attaching that message to all of his work. He credits Yoko for giving him a sense of direction and purpose after the Beatles had stopped touring, and candidly discusses how sudden the change must have seemed to his bandmates: "It appeared like I'd gone mad for a moment, y'know . . . and they suddenly notice there's always this girl sitting next to me."

John runs through the numerous collaborations with Yoko that he feels broke down the barriers between their "pop" and "avant-garde" worlds. The *Two Virgins* album, the *Rock and Roll Circus* appearance, and the Cambridge concert are all examples of their attempts to fuse two disparate styles into a new hybrid. As for future projects, he mentions a set of lithographs (which wouldn't surface until early the following year) and a book based on the You Are Here exhibit, which was delayed due to "all of the shit that's been going on, y'know, with Apple and Northern Songs."

Realizing that the very name "Beatles" has a power

285

that can be used for good, John says none of them are intent on splitting up. Referring to Michael Housego's *Daily Sketch* article, John says that while it was reported that he and George had a fistfight, it was in fact George and Paul who had a "verbal argument." Could this be the specific incident that actually caused George to walk out on January 10, or is John thinking in general terms of the musical disagreements that plagued the entire Twickenham sessions? He admits that they've always argued, particularly when confined in close quarters on tours, and that "poor old Neil and Mal got . . . the brunt of four of us bitching."

Asked about the possibility of Beatles concerts, John explains the miscommunication that led to his and Ringo's conflicting statements on the matter. He doesn't rule it out, particularly if it's arranged to suit their needs, with no grueling and monotonous itinerary. The upcoming *Get Back* album is described as "Apple Skyline," a comparison to Bob Dylan's recent *Nashville Skyline* LP. John doesn't seem to think it's anything special: "Couple of ballads, couple of rockers. The usual meat, y'know." But then he doesn't feel that

Sgt. Pepper was anything more than another group of songs very loosely connected by the packaging and production techniques.

Calling the recent spate of "heavy concept" songs and albums "philoso-rock," John says that with the exception of one song where "I just have fun with the words" ("Dig a Pony," no doubt), the lyrics on the new album are straightforward and unpretentious. John also talks about "The Ballad of John and Yoko," and how George had counseled him to change "crucify me" to "crucify us." As of April 26, the single's title had been announced, but seeing that John insisted in a handwritten note to Tony Bramwell on "NO prepublicity . . . especially the 'Christ' bit," it's possible this segment (track 22 on the CD) comes from a later interview.

RELEASE HISTORY

2000: This interview was released as tracks 10–18 and 21–25 on the CD *Kaleidoscope Eyes*.

62. Radio interview   J

Date:	8 May 1969
Location:	Apple Corps, London
Interviewer:	David Wigg
Broadcast:	11 and 18 May 1969, 3:00–4:00 p.m.
	BBC Radio 1
	Scene and Heard
Length:	12:09

The John and Yoko publicity machine rolled on with interviews ostensibly to promote their second album, *Unfinished Music No. 2: Life with the Lions,* out the following day on the Zapple label. This was their first chat with David Wigg, who had now interviewed every Beatle except Paul for *Scene and Heard.*

The album isn't mentioned once during the interview, which instead focuses on the peace campaign. John says that the bed-in has gotten lots of great feedback, specifically noting a letter from someone who decided to grow his hair instead of joining the Royal Air Force. John feels this is a great way to protest war, because you can't be arrested for it and it doesn't cause further violence. Wigg wonders whether maybe a more proactive approach is needed to bring about peace, but Yoko says these notions are just the catalyst for a "peace competition," and hopes that people will come up with ideas to top theirs.

John paints a picture of the whole world staying in bed: "There'd be peace for a week . . . the tension would be released." Declaring himself a pacifist, he says that in a war, he would defend but not attack, and that he

would rather be remembered for his contributions to the peace effort than for his musical career. Wigg asks what attracted him to Yoko, and John replies, "She's me in drag!" Yoko professes similar astonishment at meeting her soul partner, and John even says that thanks to meeting Yoko, he feels more relaxed than at any time in his adult life.

John claims not to regret any part of his past, including meditation and taking drugs. Asked if he still indulges, John hedges: "Uh, I don't possess drugs . . . depending on the situation, I might take pot, y'know. But I would never carry it again." Yoko says they are so high on love and togetherness, there's no need to take anything (by the end of the summer, they would be struggling to kick a heroin addiction).

Wigg mentions a quote from George about the anti-Beatle attitude (mostly an anti–John and Yoko attitude, truth be told) among the British press and public. John dismisses it as nothing new, explaining that as natives, the first right of insult will always go to the UK. He compares it to a parent with wayward children, which leads to a discussion of corporal punishment, which John is firmly against: "It doesn't help murderers to hang them, or violent people to be violent to them."

After discussing once again his and Yoko's amenability toward being the butt of people's jokes, John discusses his feelings on spirituality, coming up with one of his best-ever metaphors: "God is a power which we're all capable of tapping, we're all lightbulbs that can tap the electricity. You can use electricity to kill people, or to light the room, y'know. And God is that, neither one nor the other, but everything." Because he believes in life after death, John says he doesn't fear his mortality: "I think it's just getting out of one car and getting into another."

RELEASE HISTORY

1976: This interview was released on the LP *The Beatles Tapes with David Wigg,* later reissued on CD.

63. Radio interview   J

Date:	ca. 8 May 1969
Location:	Apple Corps, London (?)
Interviewer:	Pete Drummond
Broadcast:	9 May 1969, 6:00 p.m. (?) BBC Radio 1
Length:	11:21

BBC Radio 1, the corporation's "pop" channel, had only a couple of DJs who played progressive music in early 1969. John and Yoko had appeared on John Peel's *Night Ride* the previous December to promote their *Two Virgins* LP, and for the follow-up release, they appeared on a show hosted by Pete Drummond. The recording and broadcast dates of the show are unknown, but John does mention that the LP is "out today, and don't delay." Since Drummond mentions during the broadcast that the interview was recorded a day earlier, it may have been recorded May 8 (the day prior to the LP's release), along with the David Wigg interview.

Drummond begins by playing "No Bed for Beatle John," and then John explains why he finds the album, traffic noises, and even the ambience of the room they are in to be just as "musical" as any pop single. He attempts to bolster this claim by saying that Apple's disc cutter, Malcolm Davies, "digs" their unfinished music, although the truth is that "he's had to listen, because it's his job."

John relates how "No Bed for Beatle John" was spontaneously recorded on a cassette in Queen Charlotte's Hospital and later transferred to another tape in a studio. He describes "Two Minutes Silence" as "symbolic of a lot of things" (although he doesn't say what, Yoko's miscarriage seems an obvious interpretation) and says that nobody got upset by the Goons' use of silence on their comedy albums. He even finds it a relaxing break from the heavier material that surrounds the lull on the album.

Yoko says that "Cambridge 1969" was similarly unplanned: Apart from a time limit and their voice/guitar roles, the piece was improvised from start to finish. John launches into a rant about how their albums should be just as gratifying as any Beatles work. He points out that relatively simple songs such as "Hey Jude" and "Get Back" weren't instantly accepted by everyone, and that even their third single, "From Me to You," had been reviewed as "below par." It's a long stretch from those songs to "Radio Play," of course, and Yoko is perhaps optimistic when she predicts that by 1990, their experimental recordings will be accessible.

RELEASE HISTORY

This interview circulates among collectors from a fair-quality off-air tape.

64. Radio interview   J

Date:	ca. 8 May 1969
Location:	Apple Corps, London
Interviewer:	Tony Macarthur
Broadcast:	Radio Luxembourg
Length:	26:11

The last in John and Yoko's trilogy of *Life with the Lions* radio interviews was conducted by Tony Macarthur for an unknown program on Radio Luxembourg. The surviving tape comes from a broadcast sometime in late May or June (perhaps on *The David*

Christian Show, from 7–10 p.m. on June 22), as it includes a portion of "The Ballad of John and Yoko." The interview was evidently conducted in John and Yoko's Apple office, as John answers the phone at one point.

As the tape begins, Macarthur is trying to discover why the Lennons feel the need to record and release every event in their lives. Yoko calls it "total communication," and compares it to the *Smile* film, which they tried to infuse with all their energy to send out a positive message. Due to the circumstances surrounding its recording (miscarriage, drug arrest), she admits that the new album will instead convey a sense of sorrow.

A bit of "Cambridge 1969" is played, and Macarthur wonders how this relates to Beatles music, but John says that if you take away the melody and rhythm from songs such as "Tomorrow Never Knows" and "A Day in the Life" and leave only the effects, you end up with something similar. John denies that such recordings are self-involved and hard to relate to, since he puts just as much of his spirit and experience into "Cambridge 1969" as he does into "Strawberry Fields Forever."

Yoko feels that their work is superior to other experimental electronic classical pieces, because it's more instinctual and primitive and not as cerebral. Comparing it to their distant ancestors who used dancing and drumming to express sentiments, John thinks that the cycle of time will eventually make "unfinished music" commonplace again. He relates how the Beatles would often play around with feedback during breaks in recording sessions, "beating hell out of the equipment," and says that if other musicians such as Pete Townshend and Eric Clapton "dig" electric guitar feedback, in a few years, the people will dig it, too.

Macarthur again notes how far removed this all is from the Beatles, and Yoko, while quick to point out that she likes Beatles music, feels that John is versatile enough to express himself in other fashions. John compares their music to the earliest abstract painters, cheerfully admitting that it takes no particular skill, and is similar to the kind of experiments he conducted "as a kid" when he first used a tape recorder.

The next Beatles single was already reported to be "The Ballad of John and Yoko," and John explains how its recording grew out of a mixing session, when he taught the song to Paul and they decided to tape it on the spot. This leads to discussion of their appearance on *The Eamonn Andrews Show* after the Amsterdam bed-in (see the April 3 entry) and the personal nature of an audience member's criticisms. It was this kind of ad hominem attack that led John and Yoko to devise Bagism, and John describes their Vienna press conference before reasoning that if people are going to gawk at them as freaks, they might as well plug peace while they have the public's attention.

Yoko talks about how impersonal and detached from society she finds the current art scene and proposes having the Tate Gallery sell do-it-yourself works that could be exhibited once patrons completed them. John likens the divide between artists and audience to spectators at a football match and invites the world to join them on the field, rather than standing on the sidelines haranguing the referee.

Realizing that *Life with the Lions* appeals to a marginal audience, John says they're plugging it on Radio Luxembourg just as the Beatles promoted their first few singles on *The Friday Spectacular*. Being commercial is not the same thing as compromising, Yoko adds, and John imagines "one groovy guy in Yugoslavia" who purchased *Two Virgins*. Tossing in a plug for George's *Electronic Sound,* he goes on to explain that lyrics and melody have taken on less and less importance in his music compared with the overall sound and atmosphere.

RELEASE HISTORY

This interview circulates among collectors from a poor-quality off-air tape.

65. Studio session   P

Date: 9 May 1969
Time: evening
Location: Olympic Sound Studios, London
Producer: Glyn Johns, Steve Miller

[A.] My Dark Hour (3:08)

What started as a mixing session with Glyn Johns turned ugly this evening as John, George, and Ringo ganged up on Paul. They were effectively trying to force him to sign a contract naming Allen Klein's company as financial manager of Apple. Klein's excuse was that he had to report the next day to ABKCO's board of directors in New York and needed all four signatures. Paul wasn't buying it, and the others, who had all signed the previous day, cursed him and left the studio.

Glyn had been working on an LP with the Steve Miller Band, and when Steve showed up that night, Paul unloaded his troubles, finding a sympathetic ear. The duo decided to make up a tune on the spot, so with Paul behind the drum kit, Miller on guitar, and Glyn at the mixing board, they jammed a song with the suitably pessimistic title "My Dark Hour." Fueled by resentment, Paul's playing is brazenly funky, featuring his trademark eighth notes on the hi-hat.

Paul added bass, backing vocals, and probably one of the three guitars heard on the track; Steve sang lead, the lyrics sounding like a cross between "Good Lovin'" and "Fortune Teller." The result was hastily added to the LP *Brave New World* and even chosen as a single. Paul didn't receive composing credit, but his playing was credited as "Paul Ramon," his earliest stage name from the days of the Silver Beetles.

RELEASE HISTORY

1969: **A** was released on a single, which failed to chart, and on the LP *Brave New World,* reissued on CD in 1989.

66. Studio session   G

Date: 11 May 1969
Location: Morgan Studios, London
Producer: Felix Pappalardi

[A.] Never Tell Your Mother She's Out of Tune (3:38)

After working with Cream on "Badge," George had naturally continued to spend time with his friend Eric Clapton; George had also played alongside Cream drummer Ginger Baker on a Billy Preston single. Thus he gladly accepted an invitation to play on the first solo album by Cream's third member, bassist Jack Bruce.

George reportedly showed up an hour early for the session, guitar in hand. The song in question, "Never Tell Your Mother She's Out of Tune," was a fairly simple slice of British soul. George's accompaniment, largely buried in the mix, was to vamp a series of low-register chords on his guitar, played through a "fuzz" distortion pedal. His "Badge" pseudonym, L'Angelo Misterioso, was reused on the LP's sleeve credits.

RELEASE HISTORY

1969: **A** was released on the LP *Songs for a Tailor,* issued on CD in 1988.

67. Studio session   P

Date: ca. April–14 May 1969
Location: EMI Studios, London
Producer: Norrie Paramor, Tim Rice

[A.] Charity Bubbles (2:40)
[B.] Goose (2:39)

After the *McGough and McGear* album (see the April 1968 entry), Paul's brother Michael went on to have a chart-topping hit in the UK in the fall of 1968 when Scaffold released the single "Lily the Pink." A follow-up Scaffold LP, *L the P,* had one side of songs and one side of poetry and comedy, reflecting the group's diverse talents. Paul was present at Abbey Road on January 12, when the humor side was recorded, but did not contribute.

One of the songs on the music side, "Stop Blowing Those Charity Bubbles," was released as a single to support the album, but in a rerecorded version (with a shortened title). Paul played lead guitar on this and its B-side, "Goose," which also featured Nicky Hopkins on piano.

Both songs were written by the team of Mike McGear and Roger McGough, and neither was particularly memorable, falling halfway between outdated psychedelia and pastiche. Paul's playing is full of bends and pulls, reminiscent of his lead guitar work on "Watching Rainbows" at the Twickenham sessions (see the January 14 entry), as well as his fills on "Another Girl."

RELEASE HISTORY

1969: **A** and **B** were released on a single in the UK only, which failed to chart. They are both included on the 1998 CD *The Scaffold at Abbey Road 1966–1971.*

68. Radio interview   P

Date: 15 May 1969
Location: Rembrandt, Heswall
Interviewer: Roy Corlett
Broadcast: 16 May 1969, 12:31–1:00 p.m.
BBC Radio Merseyside
Light and Local
Length: 16:03

As Ringo would be spending the last half of May abroad (see next entry), the other Beatles took advantage of the break to arrange their own trips. John and Yoko would end up holding a second and more elaborate bed-in in Montreal, and George chose to remain in London until June 1, when he and Pattie flew to Sardinia. Paul took Linda and Heather to Corfu, an island off the coast of Greece, for a month. They stayed in the village of Benitses, where Paul worked on writing "Every Night," a number he had run through briefly during the Apple sessions in January.

Interestingly, the press was given the story that Paul was headed to somewhere in the south of France, and Paul stuck to this cover when interviewed by former Liverpool Institute schoolmate Roy Corlett for a regional BBC Radio program the day before his trip. The interview was taped at Rembrandt, the home Paul had bought for his father in 1964.

After exchanging some pleasantries about his new bride and stepdaughter, Paul reveals that although they haven't been appearing together in public, the Beatles have been extremely busy in the past couple of months. Much of this consisted of headache-inducing business squabbles, but they had also been recording "till four in the morning" (sessions on May 2, fifth, and sixth). One song begun during those sessions was Paul's "You Never Give Me Your Money," and although he claims that the financial side of Apple "seems to be going OK," he's also clearly glad to be "taking a break, get away from it all," admitting that he "still can't stand business."

Corlett reminisces about the Beatles' "homecoming" in July 1964 for the Liverpool premiere of *A Hard Day's Night,* and Paul compares it to the balcony scenes in Adelaide a month prior to that, when they had given the crowd a thumbs-up signal, not realizing that it was a rude gesture in Australia! He explains that after playing to 56,000 people at Shea Stadium, the Beatles realized it was futile to try to top themselves with concerts, instead concentrating on recording from that point on.

Paul also gives a lengthy and halfhearted defense of *Magical Mystery Tour,* trotting out the usual excuses: broadcasting a colorfully psychedelic experimental film in black and white on a day of family-oriented programming was to blame for its failure. Pointing to the more successful recent showings on the American college circuit, Paul predicts that in ten years' time, the film will be regarded more favorably.

Corlett asks about the criticism the Beatles' personal lives have been getting of late, and Paul infers that by "Beatles," he really means "John and Yoko." He sounds torn between supporting Cynthia, "who's a great girl," and John and Yoko, who "look like freaks." But he realizes that the bottom line is that they're in love, and he calls them "two great people" who are very straight. Perhaps to clarify what he was asking in the first place, Corlett asks specifically about the group's attitude toward drugs. This gives Paul the opportunity to paint the "I was only telling the truth" portrait regarding his *Life* magazine quote of two years previous, obviously still a sore spot.

Considering recent events (see the May 9 entry in particular), it's touching to hear Paul refer to his bandmates as "my three best friends." Corlett asks whether he and John have a secret formula for writing good songs, a query that would have found a glib reply in years past. For a change, Paul decides to analyze their songwriting partnership, characterizing it in terms he would later take great pains to quibble with: "I'm sort of a bit more sentimental on the surface, I think. Now John'll write sort of harder songs, so that if we come together, then you get a bit of . . . the sloppy stuff and a bit of the hard stuff, y'know. So then you get a nice combination."

Paul says he'd like a large family, with as many children as he can stand. Linda was in fact more than five months pregnant at that point, and although it hadn't been announced, rumors appeared in the press the following week. The interview concludes with a look into the future, as Paul says he doesn't want to be rocking at "sixty with gray hair," but that he'll be singing and playing music until the day before he dies.

RELEASE HISTORY

1972: Three excerpts from this interview (regarding *Magical Mystery Tour,* being married, and performance ambitions) were included in the BBC Radio documentary *The Beatles' Story.* The full interview circulates in excellent quality among collectors, apparently from a prebroadcast source tape.

69. Newsreel footage   R

Date: 16 May 1969
Location: *Queen Elizabeth II,* Southampton
Length: 0:58

With the completion of principal photography on *The Magic Christian,* the producers treated the film's stars to a luxury cruise aboard the *Queen Elizabeth II* steamship, leaving from Southampton May 16 and arriving in New York on the twenty-second. From there, it was on to the Bahamas for two weeks of well-deserved fun in the sun.

John and Yoko, eager to hold their second bed-in somewhere in the United States, tried to book passage, but the U.S. embassy denied them visas to enter the States. They were forced to watch from the dock as Ringo, Maureen, Derek Taylor, Peter Sellers, director Joe McGrath, and producer Denis O'Dell embarked on the voyage.

An Associated Press newsreel camera was on board to film an interview with Ringo while the ship was still ashore. The footage begins with Ringo and Peter Sellers doing an impromptu bit of soft-shoe before Ringo explains the reason for John and Yoko's delay, still assuming that permission will be given once their papers are stamped. Ringo also talks briefly about his teenage job as a waiter on a pleasure steamer that traveled between Liverpool and North Wales.

RELEASE HISTORY

1996: The audio portion of this interview was released on the CD *Fab Four CD & Book Set.* The AP footage circulates on video.

69a. Interview   J

Date:	ca. 24 May 1969
Location:	Apple Corps, London (?)
Length:	8:40

If he couldn't get into the United States legally, John was determined to do it through the airwaves. Perhaps recalling the number of U.S. journalists who had made their way to Nassau in 1965 when *Help!* was filmed, and wanting to meet up with Ringo in any case, John decided to fly to the Bahamas with Yoko, Kyoko, and Derek Taylor. They arrived on the twenty-fourth, intending to hold a second bed-in there.

Shortly before departing, John and Yoko were interviewed by an unknown journalist, probably in their Apple office before heading to the airport (Derek is also present). John explains that they've spent the last ten days failing to obtain U.S. visas, so have chosen to hold what they are calling a "second honeymoon" in the Bahamas. They plan to stay in bed there for a week, and then see where the visa situation stands, with their ultimate goal being a presentation of acorns to President Nixon.

Lamenting the new slogan of the radical youth, "Kill the pigs," Yoko offers up the alternative "Remember love," and John adds "Give peace a chance"—two sentiments that would form the titles of their next single. John says they don't mind "being Abbott and Costello" in the eyes of the press or public, comparing society to a party that has gotten tense and unpleasant and needs an injection of happiness from a newcomer. Derek Taylor adds that the impact of their actions may be felt in the absence of violence, such as a riot that never has a chance to get started.

RELEASE HISTORY

1999: This interview was released on the CD *Man in the Clouds.*

70. Documentary footage   J

Date:	25 May 1969
Location:	Sheraton Oceanus Hotel, Freeport
Length:	0:34

Unfortunately, the hotel John and Yoko chose was inhospitable, and the prospect of spending a week in bed in sweltering heat was unappealing. A bit of black-and-white film from their brief stay at the Oceanus Hotel shows John on the phone attempting to arrange for a hotel in more temperate Toronto: "One of them that the Beatles and Elizabeth Taylor and Burton usually stay at." Derek then announces that he's booked a direct jet flight from Freeport to Toronto at 5 p.m. that very day. Strumming his acoustic guitar, John sings, "Good old Air Canada!"

RELEASE HISTORY

This footage was included in the 2000 CBC-TV special *The Passionate Eye: John & Yoko's Year of Peace,* which was released on DVD in 2002. It originates in CBC's bed-in episode of *The Way It Is* (see entry number 81).

71. Amateur footage

J

Date: 26 May 1969
Time: morning
Location: King Edward Sheraton Hotel, Toronto
Length: 0:28

While in Toronto, John and Yoko held a single press conference in the late afternoon and talked with journalist Ritchie Yorke of the Toronto *Globe and Mail*. They also snuck out to the local U.S. embassy, escorted by the RCMP, for a hearing on John's visa application. After an hour with no decision made, the meeting was adjourned until June 2, by which time the bed-in would presumably be over.

Earlier that morning, fourteen-year-old student Jerry Levitan had brazenly searched out the Lennons' suite and, using a super-8 movie camera borrowed from his brother, filmed his encounter with the couple. Three excerpts from the silent (and occasionally out-of-focus) color footage have been broadcast on CBC.

RELEASE HISTORY

This footage was included in the 2000 CBC-TV special *The Passionate Eye: John & Yoko's Year of Peace,* which was released on DVD in 2002.

71a. Interview

J

Date: 26 May 1969
Time: afternoon
Location: King Edward Sheraton Hotel, Toronto
Interviewer: Jerry Levitan
Length: 21:42

John was impressed enough with Jerry Levitan's gumption to invite him back up to the suite that afternoon to record an interview for his school paper.

Despite being a starstruck teenage Beatle fan, Levitan holds his own as they chat about peace, suggesting the Lennons meet with prime minister Pierre Trudeau. John says they did send Trudeau an acorn to plant, to no avail. ("How much time does it take to stick your finger in the soil?") Jerry relates showing his copy of *Two Virgins* to his mother's coworker, who called it filth despite having a nudie calendar on the wall of his shop. "Give 'em their dirty pictures and we can get on with changing the world," suggests John.

Having found someone on his wavelength, John gives Jerry a copy of his and Yoko's new album, *Life*

with the Lions. When Levitan shares an outlandish theory about a hidden message in the "White Album's" running order, John doesn't condescend (as he undoubtedly would to an adult asking such a question), but relates stories of assembling the album and creating "Revolution 9," revealing that Yoko's "you become naked" contribution was dubbed in from a cassette.

Levitan wonders why the Beatles would let a square such as Glen Campbell broadcast their promo films (in April on his *Goodtime Hour*), but John appears both unaware and unconcerned. They speculate that perhaps Ed Sullivan's recent hipper image is down to having tried LSD, and they share their affection for Jerry Lewis comedies.

RELEASE HISTORY

2006: This interview was aired June 12 on KMYI-FM radio in San Diego and circulates from that broadcast. A five-minute edit provided the soundtrack for a 2007 animated short film, *I Met the Walrus.*

71b. Newsreel footage

J

Date: 26 May 1969
Time: 9:55 p.m.
Location: Malton Airport, Toronto
Length: 0:52

Apparently the Toronto solution was temporary, or else the Sheraton wasn't amenable to the likelihood of a weeklong media circus. Thus the Lennons only stayed overnight before traveling on to Montreal, flying out of Malton Airport around 9:55 p.m. and arriving at Dorval Airport. CBC-TV news cameras captured the cou-

ple boarding the plane, with Derek and Kyoko (and her balloon) in tow, along with some footage during the flight and their arrival in Montreal.

Another police escort accompanied the party to the Hôtel Reine-Elizabeth, where they checked in on the seventeenth floor and prepared for a weeklong "advertising campaign for peace."

RELEASE HISTORY

This silent footage circulates on video.

71c. Newsreel footage

J

Date: 27 May 1969
Location: room 1742, Hôtel Reine-Elizabeth, Montreal
Length: 4:40

These various interview clips all apparently stem from the first day of the bed-in. The first, lasting 1:20, is conducted by an unknown TV newsman. John and Yoko are lying in bed, Kyoko nestled between them, with several microphones pointed toward them. Kyoko seems to be enjoying the attention, and when the reporter asks Yoko how her daughter is reacting to the mayhem, she replies, "She knows what we're doing." "Don't I?" adds Kyoko.

A 2:13 clip, filmed by CBC-TV, has John explaining the significance of the acorns he's been sending to heads of state, Yoko further rationalizing Kyoko's presence, and John criticizing violent protest of any kind. Another 1:07 clip has John saying it's too early to compare this bed-in with the one in Amsterdam, and admitting that Beatles concerts were often surrounded by violence.

RELEASE HISTORY

This footage circulates on video.

72. TV documentary

J

Date: 29 May 1969
Time: evening
Location: room 1742, Hôtel Reine-Elizabeth, Montreal
Director: Norman Ross
Host: Stewart Klein
Interviewer: Ted Kavanau
Broadcast: 6 June 1969, 11:00–11:30 p.m. WNEW-TV, New York City *John & Yoko Lennon Have a Message for the World . . .*
Length: 26:50

On the third day of the bed-in, WNEW-TV in New York dispatched reporter Ted Kavanau and a film crew to Montreal. The result was a half-hour news special, full title *John & Yoko Lennon Have a Message for the World from Their Bed in the Queen Elizabeth Hotel in Montreal*. The crew arrived around dinnertime, capturing CFOX DJ Charles P. "Rodney" Chandler's 6:14 p.m. time check from his mobile radio studio in the hotel suite.

The show opens with John summarizing his position on violence, recommending that protesters think up peaceful alternatives to marching, which always seems to provoke further brutality. In the next scene, Derek Taylor hands John the telephone. He asks if it's Howard Smith, whose call they are expecting, but Derek says it's "Frank." It turns out to be a woman named Jackie, apparently calling from a radio station in Detroit. Over the speakerphone, she chats with "John F. Lennon," who reveals that he has applied for a visa at the U.S. embassy that morning. Jackie asks if he'll come to Windsor if he can't make it across the bor-

der, but John is noncommittal. Finally, he suggests hounding Capitol for copies of "The Ballad of John and Yoko," not officially released until June 4 in North America.

A live version of "Dizzy Miss Lizzy" (from Shea Stadium) is background to a montage of life at the bed-in, with members of the Montreal chapter of the International Society for Krishna Consciousness seated on the floor enjoying dinner while photographers and reporters hover around. Other visitors include Grant Fox and his wife and six-month-old daughter, who crawls happily across the bed. Fox was a U.S. Army deserter from Fort Dix, granted haven in Canada thanks to the American Deserters Committee.

This naturally leads to a discussion of war protests, with John espousing Gandhi's method of passive resistance. Yoko makes the infamous claim that if she had been Hitler's girlfriend, World War II might have been averted, feeling that a lack of communication led to the conditions allowing his rise to power. John challenges anyone to name a sustained attempt at changing things through peace, and someone mentions the U.S. civil rights movement. John points out how quickly that turned into chaos and rioting, and he thinks that "gimmicks and salesmanship" will prove more effective. Yoko reasons that if Coca-Cola (which she calls a "filthy product") can be branded into global consciousness via endless promotion, so can peace.

One journalist gets in front of the camera and is impolitely shoved aside, causing John to implore jokingly, "No violence, please, not in the bedroom!" This leads the reporter to whine about the whole event being a compromise, although he is unable to coherently explain why when asked directly by John, mumbling something about the media and the establishment. John and Yoko mock the poor guy, branding him a "snob," a "Puritan," and a "spinster poet"!

Amusingly enough, this is followed by DJ Chandler doing a couple of spots for Pepsi-Cola and Molson's Golden. Meanwhile, back in bed, John refuses to condemn the antiwar marches going on at college campuses across America, although he'd rather they use sex than violence, a tactic he recommended to the Campaign for Nuclear Disarmament in England: "Every day in the popular papers, they have bikini-clad girls. Get the CND girls in there. Use sex for peace." Ted Kavanau points out that John's philosophy isn't in line with either the mainstream or the radical revolutionaries. John responds that even he and Yoko had to break down barriers and destroy stereotypes (about "avant-garde artists" and "pop stars") when they first met, so he realizes that such breakthroughs will be needed on a worldwide level.

In the scenes that follow, a group chanting of the Hare Krishna mantra is led by the ISKCON visitors (described by the narration as "twelve Canadian Buddhists with shaved heads"), and a tuxedoed waiter delivers room-service dinner. Brief interviews with Derek Taylor and Capitol promo manager Richard Glenville-Brown conclude the special, with Kyoko grabbing Kavanau's microphone and pulling him onto a bed while jumping up and down.

RELEASE HISTORY

1996: Audio excerpts of this show (totaling 12:58) were released on the CD *Fab Four CD & Book Set*. Further portions were broadcast on *The Lost Lennon Tapes* radio series in 1989. The complete program circulates on video.

73. Radio interview   J

Date:	29 May 1969
Time:	evening
Location:	room 1742, Hôtel Reine-Elizabeth, Montreal (via telephone)
Interviewer:	Howard Smith
Broadcast:	29 May 1969 WABC-FM, New York City
Length:	23:29

Village Voice reporter Howard Smith was a passing acquaintance of Yoko's, having written about one of her "bag events" in New York several years earlier. It was therefore no problem for him to arrange a telephone interview with John and Yoko in Montreal, taped for playback later the same night on WABC radio.

John begins by describing the event in general terms, explaining that they are "selling this peace thing like soap" by talking to journalists and DJs virtually nonstop from ten each morning until ten at night. Smith asks why John wants to come to the United States, and John replies that he'd like to visit "the sources of power," including Washington, Moscow, and even the Pope! He also still hopes to deliver acorns to various world leaders in person, although he's hesitant to place any public pressure to force a meeting, particularly on Nixon.

Asked how the other Beatles view his peace campaign, John calls George "the most positive peacenik besides meself," Ringo "a sort of living acorn," and Paul "more intellectual about it, but he wants peace." Smith describes Ringo's reaction at a recent New York press conference (he wouldn't do the same things, but loves John for doing them), and mentions a new song dedicated to John's peace effort, Tom Paxton's "Crazy John." John is flattered and shares the news gleefully with Yoko.

To illustrate the power of positive thinking, John relates a story he'd seen recently on TV about a social experiment conducted on a class of students and their teachers. A few kids were chosen at random, after supposedly testing for exceptional abilities, and their teachers were told that by the end of the year, these particular students would show remarkable improvements. Of course, the teachers ended up giving those students more attention and positive encouragement, and they did end up at the top of their class. Smith is skeptical that this would translate to a peace campaign, but John feels that with continual reinforcement, he can indoctrinate the public to achieve anything they desire.

Still wary, Smith feels that John and Yoko's "hip, rich, rock-and-roll" image will dissuade anyone from listening, apart from those who are presumably already antiwar. John argues the point for a few minutes, insisting that if he shaved his beard, cut his hair, and looked like a clerk, it wouldn't make a difference. Smith isn't convinced, and after exchanging pleasantries with Yoko, tries to press the point with her. She responds with a lengthy tangent about how the visiting Krishna followers tried to get them to chant "Hare Krishna" rather than "peace," because the latter instantly calls to mind its opposite, "war," whereas the former transcends meaning.

The interview concludes with John discussing several Beatles-related issues, including the banning of "The Ballad of John and Yoko" and the next Beatles LP, which at that point was being held up by printing the book included with the package, but was scheduled for release in August. John finally has to beg off, because some "squares" from another radio station are due to call any minute, but invites Smith to call back on Saturday the thirty-first.

RELEASE HISTORY

This interview circulates in very good quality among collectors.

74. Radio interview   J

Date:	30 May 1969
Location:	room 1742, Hôtel Reine-Elizabeth, Montreal (via telephone)
Interviewer:	Howard Smith
Broadcast:	WABC-FM, New York City
Length:	9:35

Howard Smith took up John's invitation for a follow-up phone call the very next evening, enthusing about the enormous response the first interview had gotten when broadcast. Many listeners had phoned in with specific questions, and Smith put some of these to John in their second conversation.

Asked about his feelings on marching for peace, John notes that it's only when the demonstrations turn violent that they get noticed, which is obviously counterproductive. He calls the militant Black Power groups who raise a call to arms "madness . . . what the hell do they think they're gonna do after they've shot everyone? Y'know, and who's gonna control it then? All them people with guns that took over? It's gonna be great, isn't it?"

Returning to a theme from the previous day, Smith mentions that many listeners agreed with his suggestion that if John and Yoko presented themselves more conventionally, their message would reach a greater amount of people. John is leery, calling the length of his hair an "irrelevancy" and forswearing any claim to being a leader of any kind. Asked if he still writes, John says that he and Yoko will have books out in August. (These never surfaced, but may have included the proposed photo book of the You Are Here exhibit, a reissue of Yoko's *Grapefruit,* and perhaps even what became the booklet included in the *Wedding Album.*)

John tells people to write to their local newspapers rather than to him and Yoko if they want to do something constructive for peace. He goes on to claim that apart from aspirin, he hasn't ingested any drugs in a long time, but that his macrobiotic diet of brown rice and tea gets him just as high without any paranoia. Smith wonders how the Canadian press has been treating them, and John says that the British press are the most cynical anywhere, particularly regarding homegrown talent.

Finally, in discussing the film *Smile,* John hopes that they will be able to attend its screening in New York, which leads Smith to ask how his visa application is going. John wants to play it cool and wait for the process to work itself out rather than applying public pressure on the government to allow him in.

RELEASE HISTORY

This interview circulates in very good quality among collectors.

75. Radio interview   J

Date:	30 May 1969
Location:	room 1742, Hôtel Reine-Elizabeth, Montreal (via telephone)
Interviewer:	Tom Campbell, Bill Holley
Broadcast:	KYA-AM, San Francisco
Length:	10:00

John fielded this phone call from a Bay Area station on his own, answering questions from a pair of DJs and those submitted by listeners. He says that the goal of the bed-in is to sell peace "like you sell soap," and he thinks that it's the fourth day of the event. Miscalcula-tions by previous authors have thus dated this as a May 29 recording, but as noted earlier, the bed-in didn't officially begin until the Lennons' first full day in Montreal, the twenty-seventh. In addition, John describes sneaking out to visit the U.S. embassy "yesterday morning" to apply for a visa (which occurred on the twenty-ninth).

Bill Holley implores John to visit "the love city," San Francisco, should the visa be granted. John is noncommittal, naming New York City, Washington, DC, and Berkeley as other possible destinations. Holley mentions the march at People's Park that day, and

John relates "screaming like mad" for the demonstrators to remain peaceful (see the June entry for details).

Tom Campbell takes over with listeners' questions, but John is less than helpful about the nature of the Beatles' connection to their fan club magazine and the true meaning of "Hey Jude" ("anything you like, y'know"). He admits that he and Paul never had control of the Northern Songs catalog and were unable to prevent Dick James from selling out to the consortium from ATV.

Holley wonders why Billy Preston was given label credit on the "Get Back" single, and John praises his "funky piano solo," although he's perplexed that anyone would make a big deal of the credit: "It says 'with Billy Preston,' it doesn't say 'Billy Preston instead of the Beatles'!" Campbell asks about the latest Beatles single, and John explains that "The Ballad of John and Yoko" is simple reportage with no hidden message. He professes to enjoy "Old Brown Shoe" more for its sound than its lyrics.

Another listener question about film projects leads John to explain that the bed-in is being filmed: "It'll be an amazing film when you see the goings-on in the bedroom." Campbell leers, saying, "Oh, really?" but John clarifies that the goings-on consist of visitors in strange outfits, a radio station (CFOX 1470) setting up camp, and chanting Hare Krishna devotees. He speculates about distribution of the finished film, perhaps as a one-hour TV show, lamenting how hard it was to get *Two Virgins* released on his own record label.

John relates the whereabouts of the other Beatles and talks about the Moog synthesizer installed in George's house ("It's like living with HAL out of *2001*"), which gives him an opportunity to plug the two Zapple albums. He adds that the Beatles have finished an LP, "the rehearsal for a show which we never finished, so we got fed up and put the rehearsal out," and are halfway through recording another album, which they are taking a break from. He describes the book and film that will accompany the former project.

Asked about future plans, John says he's written a new song, "Give Peace a Chance," which he hopes to record as soon as possible. After some final words of encouragement for peace to sympathetic listeners, John wraps up the interview with a promise to visit San Francisco.

RELEASE HISTORY

1969: This interview was pressed on a blue vinyl 7-inch single, "The KYA 1969 Peace Talk." It was copied on the 1987 bootleg LP *Twice in a Lifetime*.

76. Radio interview   J

Date:	30 May 1969
Location:	room 1742, Hôtel Reine-Elizabeth, Montreal (via telephone)
Interviewer:	"Rosko" (Bill Mercer)
Broadcast:	WNEW-FM, New York City
Length:	13:52

This Friday was a particularly busy day for John on the phone. In addition to appearing on WABC, KPFA, and KYA, he fielded a phone call in the evening from WNEW's "Rosko," a hip DJ (real name Bill Mercer) who found everyone and everything to be "beautiful."

As the tape begins, John explains that he plans to use all his available funds to promote peace, since "money is a concept." Mercer wonders if John's attitude would be the same if he'd never achieved fame, and John says that he's always been peaceful despite an often malicious façade as a teenager. Mercer agrees that happiness is a simple principle, and John offers his latest slogans: "Give peace a chance, and remember love," suggesting WNEW should make a loop out of them to play between advertisements.

John says that he's been trying to stay optimistic in the face of skeptical questions but is reluctant to lecture or talk down to anyone, preferring open discourse and the free exchange of ideas. Mercer relates how WNEW's general manager, George Duncan, refused to ban or censor "The Ballad of John and Yoko," as many stations across the United States had. John responds with a nice Lennonism: "The only thing I'd ban is prejudged censorship." Calling himself one of Christ's fans, he feels that the mere inclusion of the word "Christ" is the only reason the song has been banned.

Timothy Leary takes the phone for a minute to chat with Mercer about the recent Supreme Court decision to repeal federal laws against marijuana possession. Mercer points out the hypocrisy of that judgment in light of the United States' continued refusal to grant John an entry visa. Leary's wife, Rosemary, offers a quick "peace unto you," and the phone is handed back to John, who asks for news of the People's Park march in Berkeley. Mercer has none to offer, and John hopes that all is well since his last bulletin an hour earlier. After a few more exchanges of "peace" and "Hare Krishna," Mercer bids good night to John, Yoko, and the Learys.

RELEASE HISTORY

This interview circulates in very good quality among collectors.

Date: 31 May 1969
Time: 5:00 p.m.–4:00 a.m.
Location: room 1742, Hôtel Reine-Elizabeth, Montreal
Producer: John Lennon, Yoko Ono

[A.] Give Peace a Chance—solo rehearsal (mono) (2:26)

[B.] Give Peace a Chance—group rehearsal (stereo) (1:51)

[C.] Give Peace a Chance—edit of basic take (mono) (1:32)

[D.] Remember Love—rough mix (stereo) (4:02)

[E.] Remember Love—RS? (4:00)

In the waning hours of May 30, once the press and public had been expelled from the suite, John, Yoko, and Derek rapped with Timothy and Rosemary Leary and their guest, *Rolling Stone* reporter Paul Williams. At one point, John grabbed his acoustic guitar and taught the others the song he planned to record the next day, "Give Peace a Chance."

Presumably it was up to Derek to arrange for recording equipment, and he did so through EMI in Canada, who contacted the owner of a local independent studio, André Perry. Perry, in turn, rented a four-track Ampex recorder from RCA and brought it up to the hotel early the next evening. While this and the film lights were being set up, John taught the song to the handful of people who were present, including Tommy Smothers, who doubled John's acoustic guitar part. John wrote out the words, such as they were, in black marker on a huge piece of posterboard so that everyone could sing along, and then opened the doors to allow as many people as possible to squeeze in.

In addition to John and Yoko, Tim and Rosemary Leary, Tommy Smothers, and Derek Taylor, several of the Krishna devotees were back, with a tambourine and drums to fortify the rhythm, as were Rabbi Abraham Feinberg and CFOX DJ Roger Scott. A strident New York voice heard on the early rehearsals (continually shouting "yeah!") has been identified variously as Allen Ginsberg (who is mentioned in the lyrics), Murray "The K" Kaufman (although he supposedly didn't arrive until Monday, June 2), or even Phil Spector—none of the three can be glimpsed in the footage of the recording session, however.

The earliest run-through (**A**) has John singing through the first three verses, with a few voices joining in tentatively on the choruses. It's likely that the final verse, which names many of the people in the room, was added at the last minute. A second rehearsal (**B**) from the original four-track tape (although it's mixed in narrow stereo) appeared on the *John Lennon Anthology* in 1998. This captures the end of another run-through, with John shouting "even Billy Graham!" before asking if anyone knows what an offbeat is. "An offbeat what?" quips Derek. John instructs people to clap "four-in-the-bar" on every beat, and he begins another rehearsal take, which fades out.

The final version of "Give Peace a Chance" was recorded in a single take around 11 p.m., with one microphone for John's vocal and guitar, one for Tommy Smothers, and two to capture the rest of the room. An edited version of this basic take (**C**) includes John's full count-in and four separate sections of the song, concluding with a round of applause. It reveals that the original song was played in C major (although the guitarists are playing D-shapes and were presumably tuned down a whole step); the single would be sped up considerably and subjected to overdubs (see the June 1 entry).

After most of the first incarnation of the Plastic Ono Band went home, André Perry remained behind to tape what would become the song's B-side, Yoko's "Remember Love." This was a similarly unpretentious work, with Yoko singing a simple melody on one track and John accompanying on a second track with acoustic fingerpicking. The rough mix (**D**) is in the original key of D major, while the single version (**E**) was again sped up slightly during postproduction.

RELEASE HISTORY

1969: **E** was released on a single worldwide. It's available on the 1997 CD reissue of *Unfinished Music No. 1: Two Virgins*.

1979: **A** was included on the vinyl bootleg *The Beatles vs. Don Ho* in good quality.

1989: Many of these recordings were broadcast in the radio series *The Lost Lennon Tapes*, in episodes 89-45 (**A**), 89-46 (**C**), and 89-47 (**D**).

1992: **A** and **C** were included on the vinyl bootleg *The Lost Lennon Tapes, Volume 24*.

1998: **B** was released on the John Lennon CD boxed set *Anthology*.

78. Studio session   J

Date: 1 June 1969
Location: Les Studios André Perry, Montreal
Producer: John Lennon, Yoko Ono

    [A.] Give Peace a Chance—"rough mix" (mono) (5:31)

    [B.] Give Peace a Chance—RS? (4:53)
    [C.] Give Peace a Chance—RS from take 1 (5:07)

As noted earlier, a bit of audio sweetening was needed to bring "Give Peace a Chance" up to a releasable standard. André Perry took it upon himself to transfer the song from four-track to eight-track back at his studio, and he called in a number of friends to add to the vocal choir, singing harmonies not present on the basic recording. Also added at some point was a heavy thumping backbeat throughout; some reports state that Ringo performed this back in London, although Perry denies it. A thick dose of tape delay enhanced the percussive effect, and the result was a single that was commercial enough to reach number 2 in the UK, and number 14 in the United States.

A so-called rough mix (**A**) aired on the radio series *The Lost Lennon Tapes* comes from the soundtrack of a promo film that documents the hotel recording session. It begins with some dialogue, apparently from dirty film soundtrack rather than a scratchy acetate (although it has echo added): John shouts, "Let's hear it for peace!" and someone exclaims, "Flagellation's for Capitol Records!" John invites people to join in on the verses. (". . . say what you like, y'know. It's on the wall . . . those bits aren't important, y'know, that's just to fill in.") And then he counts in. The song itself is merely a mono copy of the overdubbed final take, and the last 10 seconds revert to natural sound from the film soundtrack, as John calls for the camera lights to be shut off. The promo film soundtrack carries on for a further 33 seconds beyond the radio broadcast (the full clip runs 6:04), with John asking for the normal room lights to be turned on and adding the aside "What do you mean by 'normal,' Mr. Lennon?"

A shorter edit of this promo appears on the videos *John and Yoko: The Bed-in* and *The John Lennon Video Collection*. The documentary film *Imagine: John Lennon* includes a 1:20 composite of footage from the session with natural sound, including slightly different portions to the version broadcast on episode 89-46 of *The Lost Lennon Tapes* (see the May 31 entry).

The released version of the song (**B**) is in stereo, with handclaps and voices mixed left and right, John's vocal and guitar left of center, and the tambourine, Tommy Smothers's guitar, and overdubbed percussion centered. A remix on the *Lennon Legend* DVD (**C**) centers John's guitar and vocal and lets the multitrack play out a few seconds longer. For his embellishments to the recording, André Perry was rewarded with label credit for himself and his studio.

RELEASE HISTORY

1969: **B** was released on a single worldwide; U.S. copies of the single omitted John's count-in, which is evidently an edit piece mixed separately to the song. It's available on the CD *Lennon Legend*.

1989: **A** was broadcast on episode 89-48 of the radio series *The Lost Lennon Tapes*. It appears from that source on the 1992 vinyl bootleg *The Lost Lennon Tapes, Volume 24*.

2003: **C** was released on the soundtrack of the DVD *Lennon Legend*.

79. Interview   J

Date: 2 June 1969
Location: room 1742, Hôtel Reine-Elizabeth, Montreal
Interviewer: Fred Peabody
Length: 9:53

As the bed-in wound down, reporter Fred Peabody taped an interview with John for publication in *Concern* magazine. A ragged-voiced John says that despite people like "Al Crapp," reaction to the event has been immensely favorable. It's no wonder his voice is shot: by Derek Taylor's calculation, John had talked to three hundred radio stations over the course of the week.

John feels that the students who protest using violence are playing right into the hands of the establishment by giving them an obvious target and confirming stereotypes about "long-haired mobs." Peabody points out that it's no longer "cool" to be sentimental, but John finds nothing wrong with being unfashionable: "Square is not the opposite of hippie." He sings a bit of "When You're Smiling" to illustrate how having a peaceful attitude can persuade the people around you to do likewise.

Peabody asks whether John would fight a war under any circumstances, and John admits that even as a youngster, he'd planned to defect to southern Ireland if called up for military service. Asked what his vision of a peaceful political system is, John shudders at the thought of any kind of united world government: "Once they pooled their resources, we'd be finished." However, he can't come up with any alternate method of rule, offering up anarchy and tribalism as possibilities.

Realizing how idealistic this is all getting, Peabody wonders whether John has any tangible examples for the average peace-minded person to follow. John suggests sticking a poster in your window at home to advertise peace, and he counsels housewives to vote their conscience and workers to strike. He drives the message home with a simple reminder: "Just think of your children, y'know. Do you want them to be killed or don't you? And that's the choice we have in front of us. War or peace."

In two segments from this interview aired in 1990 on *The Lost Lennon Tapes,* John explains the philosophy behind "Revolution" and reveals that he began composing "The Ballad of John and Yoko" in Paris on March 20 prior to his wedding and completed the lyrics back in London early in April.

RELEASE HISTORY

1989: Much of this interview was broadcast on episode 89-48 of the radio series *The Lost Lennon Tapes,* chopped up into nine segments.

1990: Two further extracts were aired on episodes 90-07 and 90-13 of *The Lost Lennon Tapes.*

80. Location recordings J

Date: 26 May–2 June 1969
Location: room 1742, Hôtel Reine-Elizabeth, Montreal

[A.] **Radio Peace** (0:14)
[B.] **The Ballad of John and Yoko— a capella** (0:17)
[C.] **Get It Together** (1:44)
[D.] **Happiness Is a Warm Gun** (0:47)
[E.] **Because** (1:33)
[F.] **Oh Yoko!** (4:36)
[G.] **Give Peace a Chance—"last chance"** (0:26)
[H.] **Give Peace a Chance—"et cetera"** (0:18)

At various points during the bed-in, John and Yoko recorded musical improvisations and rudimentary run-throughs of various songs, usually accompanied by John's Gibson J-160E acoustic guitar, now adorned with his caricatures of the couple from both bed-ins.

A is a brief jingle for an underground radio station, with the couple singing "This Is Radio Peace" while John strums D and G chords. This snippet has traditionally been dated as March 26, from the Amsterdam event, but the book *Eight Arms to Hold You* pegs it as a probable Montreal recording. **B** is an excerpt from an unknown interview wherein John sings the chorus to the new Beatles single, tapping out the rhythm: "And each verse just says what we did."

C may or may not be John's attempt at writing a campaign song for Timothy Leary, who was pledging to run for governor of California at the time. Behind a C-major chord with descending bass line, John extemporizes lyrics, tossing in every slogan he can think of, in the vein of "Dig It": "Murray the K comes on Monday, Timothy Leary comes on Tuesday, John and Yoko come every day . . . kiss a cop for peace week, give peace a chance, remember love, Hare Krishna!" He injects the phrases "come together" and "get it together"; the former would be the basis of his eventual campaign song for Leary, which had a similar melody to the Kinks song "Drivin'." When Leary ended up running from the law rather than running for office, John appropriated the phrase "come together" for his own song.

The next two songs appear on the soundtrack of the video *John and Yoko: The Bed-in,* although as neither is synced to a visual performance, it's hard to say whether they were definitely recorded during the event. **D** finds John fingerpicking a pattern reminiscent of the intro to "Happiness Is a Warm Gun" as well as the bridge of "Julia." On top of this, he sings, "Mama, you're so beautiful this morning. I'd like to grab your weed." **E** is a relatively finished acoustic performance of "Because," with Yoko joining in on vocals, which is unfortunately largely buried under dialogue and natural sound from unrelated footage.

In the May 3 *New Musical Express,* John discussed "Because" as well as a second new song: "It's one I've written myself, and it's about Yoko, but I'll just change the word 'Yoko' to 'John,' and she can sing it about me." This was undoubtedly "Oh Yoko!" and indeed in the lengthy demo (**F**), Yoko sings along, inserting John's name in place of her own in the final chorus, as well as adding some lovely high harmonies. The song is mostly performed by John on his acoustic (in E major), with some alternate lyrics such as "in the middle of the sea I saw your name," and an unused "I want you, baby" bridge. In the background, Derek is apparently on the phone with Norman Seaman, Yoko's former manager in

New York. He suggests Seaman come to Canada where the Lennons will give a concert from a huge bed, and John stops singing for a moment to inject one of his lines from *A Hard Day's Night:* "Why don't we do the show right here?!"

In another interview excerpt (**G**), John plays and sings the chorus of "Give Peace a Chance," calling for one "last chance to give peace a chance folks, give chance a peace." This snippet presumably comes from June 2, the last day of the bed-in. Another rendition (**H**), this one captured on film, has John singing the refrain twice for a reporter, concluding with "et cetera, et cetera."

RELEASE HISTORY

1983: **A** was rebroadcast in a radio documentary, *John Lennon: A Celebration,* and subsequently bootlegged on the LP *Yin Yang.* It was copied on the CD-R *Vinyl to the Core.*

1989: Many of these recordings were broadcast in the radio series *The Lost Lennon Tapes,* in episodes 89-44 (**F**), 89-45 (**B, D,** and 59 seconds of **E**), and 89-48 (**G**).

1990: **D** and **E** were released on the home video *John and Yoko: The Bed-in.*

1991: **C** was broadcast on episode 91-11 of the radio series *The Lost Lennon Tapes.* The same year, **F** was included on the vinyl bootleg *The Lost Lennon Tapes, Volume 21,* and the following appeared on Howdy CDs, all taken from vinyl sources: **D** on *The 1968 Demos,* **F** on *My Love Will Turn You On,* and **G** on *Dreaming of the Past.*

1992: **D, E,** and **G** were included on the vinyl bootleg *The Lost Lennon Tapes, Volume 24,* with **E** being shortened to 37 seconds to include only the portion not buried beneath dialogue.

1993: **C** was included on the vinyl bootleg *The Lost Lennon Tapes, Volume 27.* **H** circulates on video.

81. TV documentary   J

Date:	26 May–2 June 1969
Location:	room 1742, Hôtel Reine-Elizabeth, Montreal
Director:	Carl Charlson
Host:	Patrick Watson
Broadcast:	8 June 1969, 10:00–11:00 p.m. CBC-TV *The Way It Is* #68
Length:	57:03

The CBC-TV news series *The Way It Is* dispatched a camera crew and anchorman Patrick Watson to cover John and Yoko's bed-in for an hour-long report titled "A Bedtime Story." Although the exact dates are unknown, the majority of the program seems to have been filmed on June 1, including visits from separatist Jacques-Larue Langlois, comedian Dick Gregory, and a gentleman who had been fasting for four days and walked all the way from Toronto to protest the war.

Also filmed that day were the events surrounding a "love-in" on Mount Royal promoted by CFOX, which had been broadcasting from the hotel all week. Things get out of hand when a large group of youngsters decides to stroll down the mountain and up to the seventeenth floor in hopes of an audience with John and Yoko. John is eventually able to placate the crowd by admitting fifteen-year-old Olga Naumenko, instructing her to lead the throng back up the hill peacefully, and handing her a bouquet of flowers to distribute.

The evening ended with Patrick Watson filming a lengthy interview at bedside. John explains how he built walls around himself during the years of Beatle-mania, which led to a period of depression and isolation at Kenwood after the tours ended. ("[I] played billiards with Ringo for nearly two years.") With Yoko's help, he now feels comfortable enough in his own skin to face the world and speak up for his beliefs. His confidence and optimism are evident when Watson challenges the notion that peace will be achieved in their lifetimes, and John replies, "I believe sincerely as soon as people want peace, and are aware that they can have it, they will have it. The only trouble is, they're not aware that they can get it."

Other visitors such as Tommy Smothers and Timothy Leary are also optimistic to some degree, but cartoonist Al Capp proves to be the least sympathetic adversary John and Yoko would face during the bedins. He was actually invited by CBC to "interview" the peaceniks for the benefit of the cameras, but clearly arrived with an agenda to ridicule rather than discuss the issue rationally.

Certainly it could be argued that the entire exercise of staying in bed for peace deserved ridicule, however sincere John and Yoko were, but Capp gets in curiously few satirical shots, preferring to take the low road. As John states his case calmly and Yoko struggles to get a word in, Capp utters such zingers as "Don't you think that being in bed is one thing, but you could go further, you could shower together?" "Good God, you've got to live with that [referring to Yoko]? I can see why you want peace. God knows, you can't have much," and "Whatever race you're the representative of, I ain't part of it! Now, maybe yours is the human race, and mine is something less hirsute."

In the end, John wins the battle by remaining placid even in the face of Capp calling his wife "Madame Nhu," but it's the genteel Derek Taylor who loses his temper, snapping at the cartoonist to "get out" and immediately apologizing when John chastises him. The surreal scene ends with Timothy Leary enthusiastically greeting a clearly uncomfortable Capp as John serenades him: "The way things are going, they're gonna crucify Capp."

RELEASE HISTORY

A very good copy of this black-and-white program circulates on video among collectors; colorized portions of it (primarily the Al Capp interview) appeared in the film *Imagine: John Lennon*. Large chunks of the soundtrack (the visits from Capp, Smothers, and Langlois, plus Patrick Watson's bedside interview) were released on the CD *Bedism*.

82. Documentary footage   J

Date: 24 May–3 June 1969
Location: London, Freeport, Toronto, Montreal, Ottawa
Length: 73:42

Although the Montreal bed-in was heavily documented by outside sources, John and Yoko naturally had their own film crew on hand and ended up with several hours of footage. This was edited down to feature-length in February 1970, but the result remained unreleased for twenty years. Cameraman Nick Knowland shot in full color and captured alternate angles of scenes seen in the WNEW and CBC-TV productions.

The film opens May 24 at London Airport as John, Yoko, and Kyoko (clutching a teddy bear) exit their white limo. This cuts to the Bahamas May 25 as the group boards Air Canada's flight for Toronto and then deals with customs and immigration upon their arrival. Once in Montreal on the morning of the twenty-seventh, room 1742 is prepared, and the various signs (REMEMBER LOVE, etc.) are created with black markers on posterboard.

Reporters are invited in for the opening press conference on the twenty-seventh and surround the bed with lights, cameras, and microphones. Roger Scott is heard on the soundtrack (but not seen at this point) interviewing John. This is followed by the Al Capp confrontation, with the camera staying almost exclusively on Capp. Visits from Dick Gregory and Tom Smothers are next, and likewise present alternate material and angles to *The Way It Is*. Similarly, some of the material from the WNEW special, filmed on the twenty-ninth, is seen from a different perspective.

On May 30, around 25,000 people in Berkeley, California, were participating in a protest march in support of the People's Park. Clashes with law enforcement in recent weeks had led to arrests, violence, and even deaths. To diminish the chances of that happening again, John and Yoko agreed to talk to Berkeley radio station KPFA via telephone. Their first remarkable conversation is captured in the film, with John counseling the protesters to simply disperse. Asked where exactly they should go, John at first says, "Anywhere . . . it's better than dying," but suggests staying in bed or going to Canada. He recommends singing "Hare Krishna" and ends up shouting in frustration down the phone, "You can make it, man! We can make it, together! We can get it together! Now, that's all!"

John concludes by declaring the phone line permanently open for their station and urges them to call back with an update. Later in the film we see one of the follow-up calls, this one decidedly less serious, as Yoko is asked if they are getting bedsores, and John declares it to be "kiss a cop for peace week."

A procession of visitors drops by the bedroom: a group of self-described revolutionaries, Rabbi Abraham Feinberg, delegates of the Beatles' U.S. fan club, Timothy Leary, a yoga-demonstrating swami, a hustling photographer, and DJ Murray the K. Some silent footage evidently from Freeport shows Kyoko swimming and playing with a starfish and John in the hotel, sporting a bathing cap.

Meanwhile, back in Montreal, the full clip of "Give Peace a Chance" is followed by John and Yoko enjoying room-service breakfast "on the seventh day" (probably June 2). Later that night, at 6:13 to be precise, CFOX DJ Chuck Chandler reenacts a broadcast "on our final night" for the benefit of the camera. In a very sweet and touching sequence, a clearly exhausted John and Yoko cuddle in bed and tease each other, reflecting on their remarkable week.

The next morning, they packed to leave for the capital, where they would attend a panel discussion on peace at the University of Ottawa. They arrived on the afternoon of June 3 via train and participated in the conference around 5 p.m. at Simard Hall. The film picks up with their underground journey two hours later (accompanied by Allen Klein) across the street. John says a few words to the crowd outside Tabaret Hall, and then he and Yoko are seen sleeping in the back of a car. University of Ottawa student president Allan Rock, who had arranged their appearance, drove them on a tour of the city, stopping at 24 Sussex Drive, the residence of Pierre Trudeau. Although the prime minister wasn't home, John left behind a flower and a note; in December, his luck would improve.

The film concludes with footage from the December filming of *Apotheosis 2* and the closing titles, filmed in February 1970 during editing.

From Ottawa, John and Yoko returned to Toronto via an overnight train. After sleeping in on the fourth, they traveled to Niagara Falls around 4 p.m. for a bit more filming (this can be seen in *Imagine: John Lennon*). On the fifth, their immigration hearing continued, but they were denied entry into the United States and flew back on a 9 p.m. flight to London (via Frankfurt, as they were obliged to take the first flight out before their temporary twelve-day visas expired).

RELEASE HISTORY

1990: This documentary was released on home video as *John and Yoko: The Bed-in.* Excerpts had previously been used in *Imagine: John Lennon* and other shows.

83. TV interview J

Date:	14 June 1969
Time:	evening
Location:	Stonebridge House, Wembley
Host:	David Frost
Broadcast:	10 July 1969, 8:30–10:00 p.m.
	syndicated (United States)
	The David Frost Show
Length:	26:08

By this time, the public could hardly be faulted for thinking that John was the only Beatle, so prevalent were his public appearances compared with his bandmates'. This evening, he and Yoko brought their peace campaign to America over the airwaves again, this time via David Frost's syndicated chat show, videotaped in London.

Declaring it "acorns for peace week," John, helped by Yoko and David, tosses acorns to various audience members. John holds up a copy of *Life with the Lions* and wishes the Queen a happy birthday. (June 14 was the official national holiday that year, although not Queen Elizabeth's actual date of birth.) Remembering their August 1968 appearance, Frost wonders if they're still knocking nails into wood, and Yoko presents him with one of her latest objects: "A box of smile." To his delight, Frost opens it to discover nothing more than a small mirror inside, reflecting his own smile back at him.

John explains how the nude *Two Virgins* cover seemed a natural idea at the time, and Frost jokes that it was interesting to note where distributors chose to place the price tag. Bragging that it's now selling for £10 on the black market, John says that while their bodies met on the cover of the LP, their minds met on the music, and this union inspired the album's title.

Frost cues up "Cambridge 1969" on a record player, and after playing a couple of excerpts, comments, "I can get all that in my backyard." John calls it "unfinished music" and compares it to the way young children express themselves without having a formalized method of communication. Frost points out that children don't market their "communication" to the general public, and John insists petulantly that youngsters dig the track, insinuating Frost is square.

To his credit, Frost carries on, flipping the disc over to play a bit of "No Bed for Beatle John," which he compares to plainsong and says "sounds rather nice." But he sensibly asks why they felt the need to immortalize such things on wax. Yoko responds that attempting to produce extraordinary works of art leads to competition, which leads to aggression and violence. Simpler and more mundane efforts, on the other hand, stress that "everybody is extraordinary . . . and everything that we do is beautiful."

After a commercial break, Frost asks for a definition of Bagism, which John explains in terms of his being confined in a "pop bag" and Yoko in an "avant-garde bag," from which they had to escape in order to communicate effectively. He points out that if people applying for jobs did so from within bags, they couldn't be discriminated against by their skin color, clothing, or hair length. He and Yoko try to get Frost to climb into a bag, but he skillfully changes the subject by asking whether Yoko has a special announcement to make. Since "it doesn't work," according to John, we never learn what this refers to.

John humorously describes the Vienna press conference. ("They were all sort of holding mics to this bag, y'know. And asking it how it felt, and was it glad to be here . . .") And he retells the story of his meeting with Yoko at the Indica Gallery, which he had already told on their last visit with Frost. He goes on to expound at length about the bed-ins and recycles many of the slogans, arguments, and themes familiar to anyone who had heard recent Lennon interviews.

While declaring that he's on their side, Frost is ultimately skeptical, calling their methods "marvelous idealism." John stresses that it's the people who have put leaders in charge, and thus it's the people who are responsible for any wars and violence that occur. Yoko calls Frost's "intellectual cynicism" dangerous, and John implores him to at least make an effort rather than sit back and accept war as inevitable.

RELEASE HISTORY

This show was rebroadcast on VH1's *Archives* series in March 1997. The original broadcast circulates in excellent quality on video.

84. Studio session   G

Date: ca. July 1969
Location: EMI Studios, London
Producer: George Harrison, Paul McCartney

[A.] Hare Krishna Mantra (3:32)

Members of the London branch of the International Society for Krishna Consciousness (ISKCON) first met up with George sometime in the spring of 1969, dining with him and Billy Preston, probably when George was producing Billy's LP in May. At the end of that month, John and Yoko had chanted along with other ISKCON devotees in Montreal, so it was natural that George would arrange for members of Camden's Radha Krsna Temple to record the most famous mantra for an Apple single.

George recorded the basic tracks (the Leslied guitar that opens the song, and the harmonium that provides the drone throughout) at Abbey Road in the first week of July, during time already booked for Beatles sessions. He overdubbed the bass guitar afterward, with Paul and Linda looking on. The vocals, tabla, bells, handclaps, and other percussion were supplied by the templegoers. Claims that Alan White played drums on the recording can be dismissed, as Alan has said he didn't meet any of the Beatles until September, when he was recruited into the Plastic Ono Band.

George also produced the single's B-side, "Prayer to the Spiritual Masters," which reportedly featured a contribution from Mal "Piano" Evans.

RELEASE HISTORY

1969: **A** was released on a single that reached number 11 in the UK charts but failed to chart in the United States. It was included on the 1971 Apple LP *The Radha Krsna Temple,* reissued on CD in 1993.

85. Studio session

Date: 1 July 1969
Time: 3:00–7:30 p.m.
Location: EMI Studio 2
Producer: George Martin

[A.] You Never Give Me Your Money—take 30 (mono) (5:57)

In the May 3 issue of *New Musical Express,* John revealed that "Paul and I are now working on a kind of song montage that we might do as one piece on one side." The first piece recorded for this medley was itself a collection of different song fragments, Paul's "You Never Give Me Your Money." Paul had written the song during his late-March trip to New York, contrasting his frustration over the financial squabbling at Apple with the freedom he felt with his new bride.

The Beatles recorded the basic track at Olympic on May 6, with Glyn Johns in the booth. Three reels were filled with thirty-six takes of the backing: George's Leslied guitar on track 1, Paul's piano on track 2, Ringo's drums on track 3, Paul's guide vocal on track 4, and John's low-pitched rhythm guitar on track 6. The best of these, take 30, was given a rough mix at the end of the session.

No further work was done as the group went their separate ways: Paul to Greece, Ringo to New York and the Bahamas, John to Montreal, George to Sardinia. When Paul returned to London June 17, he contacted George Martin about resuming Beatles sessions and reverting to the surefire *Pepper* formula: no Glyn Johns, no Olympic or Apple, no film crews, just Martin, Emerick, and Abbey Road. Martin duly cleared his schedule and studios 2 and 3 were block-booked for July and most of August.

At the end of June, Ringo and Maureen flew to France and John and Yoko drove across Scotland, but these were meant to be brief trips, and indeed, Ringo was back after a few days. Unfortunately, on July 1, John's driving skills got the better of him and he ran off the road and into a ditch; Yoko's injuries required a few days in the hospital, and naturally John stayed by her side, missing the first few Beatles sessions.

That same afternoon, Paul was back in Studio 2 retaping his lead vocal on track 4 of "You Never Give Me Your Money." A mono copy of the song as it stood at this point (**A**) has been bootlegged. It opens with some stray piano notes and ends with a bit of jamming in C major, followed by Glyn's "yeah" from the original session and some indecipherable dialogue.

RELEASE HISTORY

1978: **A** first surfaced on the vinyl bootleg *No. 3 Abbey Road N.W. 8* in very good quality and missing the piano notes at the start.

1991: **A** appeared from tape source on the CD *Unsurpassed Masters, Volume 5*, still missing the opening piano notes.

1994: **A** was included on the Vigotone CD *No. 3 Abbey Road N.W. 8* in slightly improved quality, and with the beginning intact, but running a bit fast.

86. Studio session

Date:	2 July 1969
Time:	3:00–9:30 p.m.
Location:	EMI Studio 2
Producer:	George Martin

[A.] Her Majesty—take 3 (mono) (0:23)
[B.] Golden Slumbers/Carry That Weight— take 1 (mono) (2:12)
[C.] Golden Slumbers/Carry That Weight— take 13 (mono) (3:10)

[D.] Her Majesty—edit of RS1 (0:22)
Mixed: 30 July 1969

Eager to be working again, Paul arrived early on July 2 to record a solo ditty for potential inclusion in the medley. "Her Majesty" had been written as far back as October 1968, and popped up in the January rehearsals at Apple. The composition hadn't gone any further since then, but Paul taped what there was of it in three takes, singing on one track while playing acoustic guitar on a second. A mono copy of take 3 has surfaced (**A**), ending with a strummed D-major chord. The song was released on *Abbey Road* in a rough stereo mix (**D**), preceded by a lengthy silence (see the July 30 entry for more details).

Once George and Ringo had arrived, the trio began taping a pair of songs that Paul had already been performing as one during the "Get Back" sessions. "Golden Slumbers" borrowed lyrics from a 1603 lullaby by playwright Thomas Dekker. "Carry That Weight" has been described as another comment on managerial and financial matters, but was written before Klein's arrival.

A charming scene on the *Anthology* DVD's bonus disc has Paul, George, Ringo, and George Martin at Abbey Road listening to a playback of the song's first take (**B** from reel E92839), which breaks down near the start of the "Carry That Weight" segment. After some debate, Martin convinces the others that the basic tracks consist of Ringo's drums, George's bass, and Paul's piano and lead vocal. All of this can be heard on the day's "best" take (**C**), including what sounds like a buried guide vocal, but is in fact George singing along far off-mic. The bootlegged recording suffers from a tape stretch that distorts the word "sluuuuumbers."

It's not clear which take this is: Mark Lewisohn reports that takes 13 and 15 were edited together the following day, with the result also called take 13, and that further overdubs were done to this edit. John Barrett's tape log indicates that takes 13 and 14 were to be edited, but has overdubs done to the original multitrack on July 3. There's no obvious edit point audible in the song, so perhaps they couldn't make up their minds which take was best but just chose to use take 13 in the end.

RELEASE HISTORY

1969: **D** was released on the LP *Abbey Road* and is available on EMI's CD of the same title.

1978: **A** and **C** first surfaced on the vinyl bootleg *No. 3 Abbey Road N.W. 8* in very good quality.

1991: **A** and **C** appeared from tape source on the CD *Unsurpassed Masters, Volume 5*.

1994: **A** and **C** were included on the Vigotone CD *No. 3 Abbey Road N.W. 8* in slightly improved quality, but with a glitch in **C** that removes a split-second of "Carry That Weight." Both tracks also run too fast.

2003: **D** was released on the soundtrack of the *Anthology* DVD.

87. Studio session

Date: 9 July 1969
Time: 2:30–10:15 p.m.
Location: EMI Studio 2
Producer: George Martin

[A.] Maxwell's Silver Hammer—take 5 (stereo) (3:46)

According to legend, John and Yoko made their conspicuous return to the studio this day, with a double bed being wheeled in for the recuperating (and once again expectant) Yoko. Recording began on Paul's "Maxwell's Silver Hammer" that afternoon, and although John later complained of being made to work on the song for a "hundred million" sessions, there's no evidence that he participated on the *Abbey Road* recording at all. Presumably he was referring to the tedious detail work on the song during the January sessions.

Basic tracks consisted of Paul on piano and guide vocal, George on bass, and Ringo on drums. The fifth of these takes (**A**) reveals that Paul still hasn't written lyrics for the third verse; he fills in the lines about "P.C. 31" with various mouth noises. Similarly, he vocalizes a solo during the instrumental chorus, cracking himself up with an overdramatic piano transition at one point. At the end, he asks for one more take, admitting that despite some "nice bits," there is room for improvement.

Presumably they took a break before continuing, as recordings resumed with take 11 and carried on through take 21. At the end of the session, acoustic guitar was overdubbed on the last of these takes during the final two choruses.

RELEASE HISTORY

1996: **A** was released on the CD *Anthology 3.*

88. Studio session

Date: 10 July 1969
Time: 2:30–9:30 p.m.
Location: EMI Studio 2
Producer: George Martin

[A.] Maxwell's Silver Hammer—RS13 (mono reduction) (3:41)
Mixed: 10 July 1969

More overdubs onto take 21, and again no discernible participation from John. Paul added some extra piano (bass notes and arpeggios) and George Martin played Hammond organ on the intro and transitions. Ringo clanged the anvil on the choruses, usurping Mal's previous role, and George threw in some Leslied electric guitar licks in various spots (the middles of verses, the solo, and final chorus). Finally, vocals were added: Paul's lead, double-tracked on the chorus, and backing vocals from Paul and George ("doo doo da doo doo" and "Maxwell must go free"), with Ringo joining in for the final "silver hammer, man."

Thirteen stereo mixes were prepared at day's end, and a mono copy of the last of these has surfaced (**A**). This opens with engineer Phil McDonald's remix announcement, followed by some stray piano and drum notes and Phil's "take 21" call from the previous day. At this point, the song still retains its opening drum fill and the D/F-sharp/Bm/D7/G passage, which would be chopped off just prior to final LP banding.

RELEASE HISTORY

1978: **A** first surfaced on the vinyl bootleg *No. 3 Abbey Road N.W. 8* in very good quality and missing the dialogue at the start.

1991: **A** appeared from tape source on the CD *Unsurpassed Masters, Volume 5,* still missing the opening dialogue.

1994: **A** was included on the Vigotone CD *No. 3 Abbey Road N.W. 8* in slightly improved quality, and with the beginning intact, but running a bit fast.

89. Studio session

Date: 11 July 1969
Time: 2:30 p.m.–midnight
Location: EMI Studio 2
Producer: George Martin

[A.] **Something—monitor mix of take 36 (mono)** (2:04)
[B.] **Something—take 37 (mono)** (5:38)

This session began with further additions to take 21 of "Maxwell's Silver Hammer": George overdubbed more lead guitar (on the choruses) and he and Paul added extra vocals to the final "silver hammer, man!" They then turned to a song started back in the spring, George's "Something."

After an aborted attempt in April, the basic track had been taped May 2 in thirty-six takes. The lineup was apparently Billy Preston on piano, Paul on bass, George on Leslied rhythm guitar, John on second rhythm guitar, and Ringo on drums. The last of these takes carried on for 7:48, well past the song proper into a tiresome jam. On May 5, Paul retaped his bass line, turning in a virtuoso performance, and George added a lead guitar part, including an equally outstanding solo. Organ was overdubbed on an unknown date by Billy Preston, presumably while George was working on Billy's *That's the Way God Planned It* album.

The song lacked vocals until this July 11 session, when George taped a lead vocal, manually doubling it for the choruses. A playback of take 36 (**A**) circulates from the CNN broadcast *The Music Room,* with the various tracks played in isolation.

The tape now filled, a reduction was done into take 37, freeing up two tracks by combining the piano and lead guitar onto track 1, and both vocals onto track 7. Track 2 contained drums, bass was on 5, rhythm guitar on 6, and organ on 8, with 3 and 4 open. A couple of minutes were also trimmed from the rambling coda, reducing the song's length to 5:32. This reduction take appears on bootleg (**B**) complete with Phil McDonald's take announcement. It was never used, however, as George would return to the original take 36 later in the week to redo the vocals, this time with some assistance from Paul.

RELEASE HISTORY

1978: **B** first surfaced on the vinyl bootleg *No. 3 Abbey Road N.W. 8* in very good quality.

1991: **B** appeared from tape source on the CD *Unsurpassed Masters, Volume 5;* it's also on the Vigotone CD *No. 3 Abbey Road N.W. 8* in slightly better quality, but running almost a half step too fast. The former release fades the song out, while the latter cuts off abruptly.

2003: **A** was aired May 5 on CNN's *The Music Room;* it appears on the CD-R *Unbootlegged 18.*

90. Studio session

Date: 18 July 1969
Time: 2:30–8:00 p.m.
Location: EMI Studio 3
Producer: George Martin

[A.] **Octopus's Garden—RS14** (2:48)
Mixed: 18 July 1969

[B.] **Octopus's Garden—RS from take 32 (#1)** (0:20)
[C.] **Octopus's Garden—RS from take 32 (#2)** (3:19)

Ringo's "Octopus's Garden" was the first of the pre-July recordings to be finished off for *Abbey Road.* On July 17, Paul added a second piano track (mostly bass notes). He and George then taped backing vocals, using a filter to produce an underwater effect during the guitar solo. Ringo added to the nautical theme by resurrecting the "Yellow Submarine" trick of blowing bubbles in water through a straw.

The next day, Ringo perfected his vocals (doubled with ADT on the bridges, but manually on the choruses) and added "sundry percussion" (drum fills before each chorus, heard in the left channel). The song was then mixed into stereo and, for some reason, mono. The latter was not a rough mix, since it was done seven times, but it was the only *Abbey Road* song to receive such treatment. The *Anthology* DVD remix (**B**) centers all the vocals, and the *Love* remix (**C**) adds elements from "Good Night," "Yellow Submarine," "Lovely Rita," "Polythene Pam," "Helter Skelter," and "Sun King."

RELEASE HISTORY

1969: **A** was released on the LP *Abbey Road* and is available on EMI's CD of the same title.

2003: **B** was released on the soundtrack of the *Anthology* DVD.

2006: **C** was released on the *Love* CD.

91. Studio session

Date: 21 July 1969
Time: 2:30–9:30 p.m.
Location: EMI Studio 3
Producer: George Martin

[A.] Come Together—take 1 (stereo) (3:37)

The final song John wrote for the Beatles, "Come Together," evolved out of a discarded campaign song for Timothy Leary, using a line from Chuck Berry's "You Can't Catch Me" as a springboard for John to free-associate twisted images from his current life and from old blues songs.

The backing was recorded in eight takes, using four-track tape. It consisted of Paul's rubbery bass line on track 1, George's chunky rhythm guitar on track 2, and Ringo's tom-heavy drums on track 3. On track 4,

John sang a live guide vocal, adding the "shoot me" handclaps and shaking a tambourine over the solo and coda. The first take (**A**) outlines the general concept of the song, with a few changes in lyric ("sideburns" would become "sideboard"). John's voice is in rough shape: He hasn't sung lead since "Give Peace a Chance," and his throat gives out entirely at one point. But he gives it his all, laughing his way through the last verse ("got to get some bobo") and enthusing "take it easy baby!" (and strangely, "Eartha Kitt, man!") toward the end.

The final take was copied over to eight-track tape, called take 9, at the end of the session, to allow for future additions.

RELEASE HISTORY

1996: **A** was released on the CD *Anthology 3*.

92. Studio session

Date: 17, 18, or 22 July 1969
Location: EMI Studio 3
Producer: George Martin

[A.] Oh! Darling—vocal overdub (mono) (9:43)

Second engineer Alan Parsons recalls Paul coming in early to several sessions in a row to redo his lead vocal for "Oh! Darling." The idea was to make his singing as rough and crude as possible, and by his fourth attempt on July 23, the trick had worked. According to Parsons, Paul attempted only one complete performance each day; thus this unreleased attempt (**A**) must come from one of the three previous sessions.

It apparently originates from the machine used to add tape delay to Paul's voice. As such, the beginning is extremely slow as the engineers adjust the speed, and thus the amount of delay. Computer manipulation allows us to decipher Paul's sluggish speech: "Well! It's too long, the delay. He says it's too long. Too long, mama! Too long! Delay! Delay. De-hello?" Once this is solved, Paul continues to test his microphone, setting

the levels of live vocal and playback in his headphones and the studio monitor. For several minutes, he babbles various nonsense, including a bit of Liverpool Institute's Latin motto and some of his recent lyrics ("money," "paper," "funny").

Finally the song is played back in his headphones, and he tries for a take, with a few lyrical differences to the finished product. The tape cuts out at the start of the second bridge. The CD *Studio Collection* syncs this alternate vocal to an OOPSed (and thus vocal-less) mix of the final *Abbey Road* version.

RELEASE HISTORY

1986: **A** first surfaced on the vinyl bootleg *Ob-La-Di, Ob-La-Da* in a 2:06 edit containing only the "song" portion.

1994: The final 8:26 of **A** appeared from tape source on the bootleg *The Ultimate Collection, Volume 1: Miscellaneous Tracks*.

2000: A slightly worse-quality but complete version of **A** was booted on the CD *Sink in the Can*.

93. Radio interview   P, G

Date: ca. 24 July 1969
Location: EMI Studio 2 (?)
Interviewer: Kenny Everett
Broadcast: 26 July and 13 September 1969 (?)
BBC Radio 1
Everett Is Here
Length: 4:00

In November 1968, Kenny Everett was given a new BBC Radio show, *Everett Is Here,* and a new Saturday morning slot. It took a surprisingly long time for him to acquire Beatles interviews for the series, but the recording of *Abbey Road* in London proved a good opportunity.

Paul had been recruited to provide jingles for two of Kenny's previous shows (see the mid-November 1967 and June 6, 1968, entries), and capitulated again. Finding a suitably dramatic chord progression at the piano (B, D, and E major with a constant B in the bass), Paul improvises a jingle: "Kenny Everett, Kenny Everett, Kenny Everett . . . is here." This soon mutates into "Can he have a ride, can he have a ride in your donkey?" This recording has been traditionally dated July 24, which makes some sense as Paul would have been at the piano that afternoon recording his demo of "Come and Get It" (see following entry).

A separate interview with George may be from the same date. The first segment has Kenny and George discussing high-fidelity recordings and facial hair. (George had started growing a beard in Sardinia.) This ends with Kenny's call "Send Lennon in! Actually, we'll have him next week. I've got him trapped into an interview," which points to a September 13 broadcast date. Kenny then plays the single "Hare Krishna Mantra" (released August 29 in the UK), quipping, "And that's just the first verse!" at the end.

George proceeds to plug the ISKCON's Rathayatra Festival, which he says is occurring "one-thirty on Sunday" at Hyde Park. A report in the *New Musical Express* indicated that the one-day event was due to take place on Saturday, July 26, and that Paul and George might attend. Perhaps hoping for a scoop, Kenny asks who will be there. George responds, "God . . . Lord Jagannath, and Krishna, and all the gang," and proceeds to quote a then-unreleased Bob Dylan song: "They're all gonna be there at that million-dollar bash!"

One assumes that this would have been broadcast July 26, but it seems to directly follow the September 13 material. Perhaps the festival was postponed, or perhaps Everett simply rebroadcast the original plug.

RELEASE HISTORY

These recordings circulate in fair quality among collectors and were included on the CD-R compilation *Attack of the Filler Beebs, Volume 4.*

94. Studio session   P

Date: 24 July 1969
Time: 2:30–3:30 p.m.
Location: EMI Studio 2
Producer: none

[A.] Come and Get It—take 1 (stereo) (2:26)

In June, it was announced that the Lovin Spoonful's ex-frontman John Sebastian would write the music for Ringo's film *The Magic Christian.* Whether this fell through or was just a rumor, in the end the task fell to Apple group the Iveys, rechristened Badfinger for the occasion. Paul agreed to produce a few of the soundtrack songs and contributed an original composition, "Come and Get It." The melody had come to him late one night at his Cavendish Avenue home, forcing him out of bed and down to his tape recorder to sketch out the song.

Rather than tape a simple demo at home, Paul recorded a one-man, one-take performance at EMI, while John watched from the control room and Phil McDonald manned the board. Using eight-track tape, Paul laid down a piano track and live vocal, then overdubbed a second vocal while shaking maracas. He filled up two further tracks with drums and bass, completing the demo. Amazingly, this multitracking, plus a single stereo remix, was done in a spare hour before George and Ringo showed up. A copy of the rough mix was taken away by Paul so that he could give it to Badfinger.

A fake stereo mix of this song (mono w/stereo echo) was prepared by Geoff Emerick for the *Sessions* album; this mixes out the second vocal/maraca track at the very end. It was used on *Anthology 3,* despite the fact that the multitracks and RS1 were readily available in the vault. Luckily, a true stereo copy surfaced in 1999.

RELEASE HISTORY

1983: An incomplete copy of **A** first appeared on the vinyl bootleg *File Under: Beatles,* taken from the "boardroom tape" (an off-line mono recording of a stereo mix prepared April 21, 1976). The full boardroom recording was finally booted from tape source in 2002 on the CD-R *As It Happened, Baby!*

1985: Geoff Emerick's fake stereo remix of **A** created for *Sessions* began to appear on vinyl bootlegs; it can be heard on Spank's CD of that title.

1996: Emerick's remix of **A** was officially released on *Anthology 3*.

1999: **A** appeared in excellent quality and true stereo from John Barrett's cassette material. It's been booted on the CDs *Another Sessions . . . Plus* and *Mythology, Volume 3*.

95. Studio session

Date: 24 July 1969
Time: 3:30–10:30 p.m.
Location: EMI Studio 2
Producer: George Martin

[A.] Ain't She Sweet (stereo) (2:05)

The main task this evening was to lay down a backing track for another of the medleys, pairing John's "Sun King" with his "Mean Mr. Mustard," the latter title dating back to Rishikesh and the former inspired by Fleetwood Mac's UK number 1 hit "Albatross." The recording was listed on the session sheet as "Part Two: Here Comes The Sun-King," perhaps because it formed the second part of the overall medley.

The Beatles played their standard instruments, with heavy tremolo on the guitars on "Sun King" and a distortion pedal on the bass for "Mean Mr. Mustard," and John sang a guide vocal. At one point, the E-C-B chord progression in "Mean Mr. Mustard" obviously

triggered off a spark of recognition, and John launched the band into the similarly patterned "Ain't She Sweet" (**A**).

While they probably haven't played it since 1961, they recall the song well, and it's marred only by John's gravelly vocal and hapless guitar solo. This performance sticks close to Gene Vincent's 1956 rendition rather than their own arrangement recorded for Polydor, although John tinkers with the lyrics: "I ask you very hydrofollicky." The song concludes with John's comment "I hope you liked that trip, boys."

Evidently they did, as it led to two more busked Vincent covers, "Who Slapped John?" and "Be-Bop-A-Lula," before the group returned to the task at hand, perfecting their own song by take 35. Overdubbing would continue the next day.

RELEASE HISTORY

1996: **A** was released on the CD *Anthology 3*.

96. Studio session

Date: 29 July 1969
Time: 2:30–10:45 p.m.
Location: EMI Studio 3
Producer: George Martin

[A.] Sun King/Mean Mr. Mustard—RS22 (3:37)
Mixed: 14 August 1969

[B.] Gnik Nus (0:55)

In two further sessions, on the twenty-fifth and twenty-ninth, the "Sun King/Mean Mr. Mustard" medley was completed. For "Sun King," organ, bongos, and maracas were added, along with two vocal tracks of rich harmonies for the nonsensical cod-Spanish lyrics. On "Mean Mr. Mustard," piano and tambourine were overdubbed, the former erasing one of the original guitar tracks. John sang a lead vocal, treated to ADT dur-

ing mixing, with Paul harmonizing in spots. To accommodate the song within the framework of the overall medley, John changed the name of Mr. Mustard's sister from Shirley to Pam, the protagonist of the song that would follow.

As the title suggests, "Gnik Nus" from the *Love* CD (**B**) is merely the vocal tracks for "Sun King" played backwards ("everybody's laughing, everybody's happy" in one channel is matched with "everybody's happy, everybody's laughing" in the other), overlaid with a tamboura drone.

RELEASE HISTORY

1969: **A** was released on the LP *Abbey Road* and is available on EMI's CD of the same title.

2006: **B** was released on the *Love* CD.

97. Studio session

Date: 30 July 1969
Time: 2:30–10:30 p.m.
Location: EMI Studio 3
Producer: George Martin

[A.] "Huge Melody"—RS2? (mono reduction) (15:36)
Mixed: 30 July 1969

[B.] Come Together—RS1 (4:16)
Mixed: 7 August 1969

[C.] Polythene Pam/She Came In through the Bathroom Window—RS32 (3:10)
Mixed: 14 August 1969

[D.] Come Together/Dear Prudence (4:45)

Work continued on "Come Together" July 22, with John retaping his lead vocal on track 4, Paul playing the "swampy" electric piano on track 5, and more electric guitar and maracas going on track 6. The next day, further vocal work was done, and Paul's harmony (on track 8) was perfected during the July 25 session. The final touch was some lead guitar for the end of the song, which was added July 30 on track 7. The song was mixed into stereo on August 7 (**B**); John's lead vocal was treated with ADT during the choruses. The *Love* CD includes a remix (**D**) that cross-fades into "Dear Prudence" and "Can You Take Me Back" near the end.

Meanwhile, work had been continuing on songs for the medley. To wrap the whole thing up, Paul had devised a rocking instrumental, similar to "Birthday" but with a much longer drum solo for Ringo and a prolonged two-chord workout to leave room for a guitar symposium. Seven takes of the basic guitars, bass, piano, and drums backing (with the drums taped in stereo, spread across two tracks of the tape) were recorded July 23 under the working title "Ending."

On the twenty-fifth, part three of the medley was recorded: John's "Polythene Pam" and Paul's "She Came In through the Bathroom Window." Both songs had been written in 1968 and rehearsed in January during the "Get Back" sessions. It took thirty-nine takes to perfect the backing of John on acoustic twelve-string guitar, Paul on bass, George on electric guitar, and Ringo on drums. The two songs were joined by a series of repeated D/A/E chords, with John counting out the bars. John and Paul each sang guide vocals on these takes, but overdubbed "proper" lead vocals at the end of the day, when the bass and drum performances were also redone.

The tape was filled on the twenty-eighth with over-

dubs of acoustic and electric guitar, acoustic and electric pianos, percussion, and more vocals. Much of this (the pianos, for instance) went unused, but a reduction was done to make room for the final vocal, guitar, and percussion overdubs on July 30. The track as released (**C**) has overdubs of backing vocals, tambourine, maracas, cowbell, a descending lead guitar line, and a "whip-crack" percussion effect.

The opening track for the medley, "You Never Give Me Your Money," received Paul's first bass overdub July 11 (on track 7). On the fifteenth, backing vocals and tambourine (on track 5) and chimes (on track 8 during the "magic feeling") were added. Paul also erased part of George's Leslied guitar on track 1 to manually double-track his lead vocal (on the second verse). With the tape now full, it was reduced into take 40 on July 30, and more backing vocals were overdubbed (behind "out of college, money spent").

The main task of the July 30 session was to create rough stereo mixes of all the bits and pieces and assemble them into a test edit (**A**), referred to as "The Long One" or "Huge Melody." The result ran nearly sixteen minutes and had "Her Majesty" inserted between "Mean Mr. Mustard" and "Polythene Pam," but after hearing the playback, Paul thought his song interrupted the flow of things. He instructed second engineer John Kurlander to remove "Her Majesty," which he did, tacking it on to the end of the reel after a bit of leader tape.

Mal Evans signed out the finished tape, took it to Apple for acetate cutting and returned it to Abbey Road the next day. Malcolm Davies, who cut the acetate, left in the 20-second gap and rough mix of "Her Majesty" at the end, and although it came as a surprise to Paul when hearing the disc, he liked the effect enough to have it duplicated exactly on the finished LP. Thus *Abbey Road* closes with a long silence, followed by the final D chord from the "Mean Mr. Mustard" rough mix, cross-faded with the rough mix of "Her Majesty." As the last chord of "Her Majesty" had been chopped off when piecing it into the test medley, it never made it to the album.

In fact, the tape box notes that the rough mix of "Her Majesty" was spliced straight from the end of the test reel into the master reel. Thus the mono dub we have of the July 30 test medley (**A**) must have been copied after this decision was made, as there is no sign of "Her Majesty," either in the middle or at the end. It opens with an "RS2" announcement (which is odd, as the rough mixes are labeled RS1 on the session sheet). Some points of interest that would later be mixed out include the organ passage that opens "Sun King," and some extra Scouse comments from John during the "Polythene Pam" guitar solo. ("Fab!

That's great! Real good, that. Real good.") "The End" is also at its original shorter length of 1:55; it would eventually be extended by editing to better accommodate the guitar solo overdubs.

RELEASE HISTORY

1969: **B** and **C** were released on the LP *Abbey Road* and are available on EMI's CD of the same title.

1991: **A** appeared from tape source on the CD *Unsurpassed Masters, Volume 5* in very good (yet distorted) quality, but running nearly a half step too slow.

1994: **A** was included on the Vigotone CD *No. 3 Abbey Road N.W. 8* at the correct speed, but with the released version of "Her Majesty" reinserted in its original slot.

2006: **D** was released on the *Love* CD.

98. Amateur footage

Date: ca. late July 1969
Location: Kinfauns and EMI Studios, London
Length: 7:06

These 8 mm home movies likely date from the last few days of July. The first, synchronized to a soundtrack of "Here Comes the Sun," depicts a pair of female fans visiting George at home in Esher. He stands on his front steps and obligingly autographs several photos before retreating inside. The fans are seen outside his gate, holding up their spoils and waving at the camera. This footage is traditionally dated July 29.

The second, synchronized to "Come Together," was apparently filmed during two separate days in the parking lot outside Abbey Road Studios. Each Beatle is seen arriving for *Abbey Road* sessions, usually dashing through the crowd of tourists and Apple Scruffs directly into the building. In one shot, George's hair is tied up in a topknot; comparison to a photo in the book *Waiting for the Beatles* seems to confirm the late July date. Both films are edited to repeat slightly, to better match the songs' lengths.

RELEASE HISTORY

This silent footage circulates among collectors in average quality.

99. Studio session   P

Date: 2 August 1969
Location: EMI Studios, London
Producer: Paul McCartney

[A.] Come and Get It—take 5 (2:19)
[B.] Come and Get It (2:19)

As instructed by composer/producer Paul McCartney, the Iveys re-created his demo of "Come and Get It" as closely as possible, right down to the piano/bass/drums/maracas instrumentation. The only embellishments were some Beatlesque vocal harmonies and a tambourine played by Paul.

An apparent outtake from this session (**A**) has Paul singing a guide vocal; it begins with a false start followed by Paul's "take 5" announcement and count-in. An alternate mix of this song, with no piano and different vocals, was prepared September 25 at Abbey Road for inclusion in the film *The Magic Christian.*

RELEASE HISTORY

1969: **B** was released on a single that reached number 4 in the UK and number 7 in the United States. In 1970, it was included on the Apple LP *Magic Christian Music,* which was reissued on CD in 1991.

2007: **A** was bootlegged on the double LP *Sessions.*

100. Studio session

Date: 4 August 1969
Time: 2:30–9:00 p.m.
Location: EMI Studio 2
Producer: George Martin

[A.] **Because—take 16 vocals (stereo)** (2:17)

[B.] **Because—take 16 instruments (stereo)** (1:10)

[C.] **Because—RS from take 16** (2:43)

As Ringo later put it, "We weren't sitting in the studio saying 'OK, this is it: last record, last track, last take.' " Nevertheless, August 1, 1969, was the last date on which all four Beatles began recording a song together—John's pun-filled and Beethoven-influenced "Because."

The backing took twenty-three attempts, with take 16 being "best"; George Martin played the main riff on a Baldwin electric harpsichord, a part doubled by John on electric guitar. Paul contributed bass, and Ringo kept time in their headphones on his hi-hat cymbal. What really lifted the song were its elaborate vocal harmonies, arranged by George Martin and sung by John, Paul, and George.

These filled three further tracks of the tape: one recorded on August 1 and two more on August 4, to produce nine voices in all. A bootlegged stereo mix isolating just the vocal tracks probably inspired a similar creation for *Anthology 3* (**A**). The bootlegged variation begins with the first lyric ("Because the world is round") and has some rhythm track leakage through the vocalists' headphones. The released mix begins a few seconds earlier (with the wordless vocal entrance), adds echo, and lessens the leakage by fading to silence between each line of vocal.

Conversely, a stereo mix of just the instruments (**B**) appears on the *Anthology* DVD; this has harpsichord left, bass centered, and guitar right. The *Love* CD has a mix (**C**) of the isolated vocals with added nature effects, ending with the final chord from "A Day in the Life" played backwards.

RELEASE HISTORY

1988: **A** surfaced on the vinyl bootleg *Ultra Rare Trax, Volume 5 & 6* in excellent quality. This appeared from tape source on the CDs *Not Guilty* and *Unsurpassed Masters, Volume 6,* running nearly a full half step too slow in both cases.

1996: A newly mixed version of **A** was released on the CD *Anthology 3,* including a bit more of the opening vocal than any bootlegged version.

2003: **B** was released on the soundtrack of the *Anthology* DVD.

2006: **C** was released on the *Love* CD.

101. Studio session

Date: 5 August 1969
Time: 2:30–6:30 p.m.
Location: EMI Studio 3
Producer: George Martin

[A.] **You Never Give Me Your Money—RS23** (3:57)
Mixed: 13 August 1969

After hearing the rough mix included in the "test medley," Paul decided that "You Never Give Me Your Money" needed a bit more work. Reduction take 40 and its additional vocal work were consigned to the reject pile. Instead, on July 31, Paul went back to take 30 and retaped some of his bass and piano work (the latter being a punch-in of "honky-tonk" sped-up piano for the "out of college" section).

On August 5, he prepared a four-track tape of sound-effects loops to be overlaid on the cross-fade between this song and "Sun King" during stereo mixing. The sounds of crickets and birds chirping and bells gently chiming proved an effective way to cover up the transition as well as providing atmosphere for the Sun King's entrance. The cross-fade was attempted August 14 and improved on the twenty-first.

RELEASE HISTORY

1969: **A** was released on the LP *Abbey Road* and is available on EMI's CD of the same title.

102. Studio session

Date: 5 August 1969
Time: 6:30–10:45 p.m.
Location: EMI Studio 2/Room 43
Producer: George Martin

[A.] **Because—take 16 (stereo)** (2:13)

[B.] **Because—RS2** (2:44)
Mixed: 12 August 1969

Thus far, George's Moog synthesizer had been used only at his home, to record the track "Under the Mersey Wall" for his *Electronic Sound* LP. In early August, he decided to bring it to Abbey Road and set it up in room 43, with the output connected by a mono cable that could reach to the control rooms of studios 2 and 3.

Each Beatle would get a turn to fiddle with the Moog, but for its inaugural use on August 5, it was George who played it, laying down overdubs to fill the two vacant tracks on take 16 of "Because." During the bridge, he played arpeggiated notes to match the harpsichord/guitar, and during the final verse, he double-tracked a hornlike part, playing the song's melody line. The song received its sole stereo mixes on August 12 and was ready for the album (**B**).

A unique mix created for the 1983 *Beatles at Abbey Road* presentation (**A**) isolates the vocal tracks for the song's first minute. Thereafter, all the instruments are present, in a different stereo mix (vocals separated more widely, bass mixed to the side, Moog split left and right).

RELEASE HISTORY

1969: **B** was released on the LP *Abbey Road* and is available on EMI's CD of the same title.

1983: The multimedia presentation *The Beatles at Abbey Road* included **A**. It can be heard from tape source on the bootleg CDs *Abbey Road Video Show* and *Turn Me On Dead Man: The John Barrett Tapes*.

103. Studio session

Date: 6 August 1969
Time: 2:30–11:00 p.m.
Location: EMI Studio 2/Room 43
Producer: George Martin

[A.] **Maxwell's Silver Hammer—edit of RS34/37** (3:24)
Mixed: 12 August 1969

The "Maxwell's Silver Hammer" multitrack had been filled July 11 with overdubs of extra guitar (on the choruses and solo) and vocals (on the final "silver hammer, man"). On August 6, Paul got his chance to play with George's new toy, adding Moog synthesizer passages to reduction copies, with take 27 being the best attempt. Stereo mixing was done that evening and again on the twelfth. Two days later, the song's final verse was remixed separately (to allow for the "wandering synth effect") as an edit piece, which was spliced into the previous best remix. The final touch was the removal of the song's opening four-bar passage, done August 25 during the LP's last session.

RELEASE HISTORY

1969: **A** was released on the LP *Abbey Road* and is available on EMI's CD of the same title.

104. Studio session

Date: 11 August 1969
Time: 2:30–11:30 p.m.
Location: EMI Studio 2
Producer: George Martin

[A.] **Oh! Darling—RS9** (3:24)
Mixed: 12 August 1969

[B.] **I Want You (She's So Heavy)—edit of RS8/10** (7:43)
Mixed: 20 August 1969

With the album nearing completion, simultaneous multi-studio sessions were necessary, reminiscent of the final few weeks of the "White Album." For instance, on August 8, Paul went into Studio 3 to add (unused) lead guitar and tambourine overdubs on "Oh! Darling" while John and Ringo were in Studio 2 working on "I Want You (She's So Heavy)". Both songs were completed on the eleventh, with Paul's song requiring only a new set of backing vocals (John's final contribution to a Beatles recording, incidentally) and final stereo mixing (**A**).

John's song was a bit more complicated. Recording had begun way back on February 22 at Trident, with Glyn Johns producing and Billy Preston contributing organ. Three reels were filled with thirty-five takes of the backing. John apparently sang live vocals with each of these, while reports that Paul sang on at least one take have proven hard to pin down. The supposed take has been bootlegged (on the LP *Rough Notes*), and while it's a decent vocal impression, the instrumental performance is less convincing. An apparent validation of this story appeared in Mark Lewisohn's *The Beatles Recording Sessions* only to disappear without explanation in his follow-up book, *The Complete Beatles Chronicle*.

In any case, the following day Glyn edited takes 9, 20, and 32 into what we'll call "master #1" and made an eight-track safety copy and a rough mono mix of this for John. During the Chris Thomas–helmed sessions, further overdubbing was done in EMI Studio 2. John and George began work at 1 a.m. on April 19, painstakingly adding a number of guitar parts on "master #1" and a reduction of this, called "take 1." George took home a rough stereo mix of the result.

On April 20, congas and Hammond organ were added to "take 1," and the song was probably deemed complete. But John saw his opportunity to add atmosphere to his megaguitar coda in August when George arrived with his Moog synthesizer. On the eighth, he generated a hailstorm of white noise, slowly building over the song's finale, while Ringo thumped out an extra backbeat. For an unknown reason (faulty memories?), these overdubs were done to "master #1" rather than "take 1."

Three days later, however, John, Paul, and George sang the "she's so heavy" vocal harmonies, going onto tracks 4 and 7 of "take 1." Not wanting to lose the Moog overdub, John then made a copy of "take 1" and edited the "she's so heavy" portions into "master #1," creating what we'll call "master #2" (following all this?).

On August 20, "take 1" was given eight stereo mixes, and "master #2" two more. These were edited together to produce the honest-to-God final master (**B**), with the splice occurring at 4:36 (between the words "she's" and "so"). This third and final "master" lasted 8:04, but John favored an abrupt climax, and the end was trimmed at a suitably dramatic moment. The song was still the longest ever released on a Beatles album, assuming you don't count "Revolution 9" as a song.

RELEASE HISTORY

1969: **A** and **B** were released on the LP *Abbey Road* and are available on EMI's CD of the same title.

105. Radio interview J

Date:	14 August 1969
Time:	afternoon
Location:	EMI Studio 2
Interviewer:	Kenny Everett
Broadcast:	20 and 27 September 1969, 10:00 a.m.–noon BBC Radio 1 *Everett Is Here*
Length:	3:39

Kenny Everett did indeed have John Lennon "trapped into" doing an interview, although John seemed less enthusiastic than on previous occasions. Kenny showed up during a mixing session and watched while stereo mixes of "Sun King/Mean Mr. Mustard" and an edit piece for "Maxwell's Silver Hammer" were prepared. John then took a break and joined Kenny on the studio floor; the interview was recorded in mono on EMItape (reel E93325) using Abbey Road's equipment.

John reveals that the LP in progress will be named after the studio's location and requests Gene Vincent's "Be-Bop-A-Lula," perhaps inspired by the Beatles' run-through on July 24. He specifically asks to hear "the real old [version] with the tape echo," and Kenny complies. Everett points out that those old recordings were done with a single microphone and notes that the Beatles seem to use on "millions of tracks," but John says that most of the basic backings are done as an ensemble.

We also learn that John plays old Beatles records at home to Yoko, since she isn't a "pop-picker," and that John knows only one joke (the first dirty joke he'd ever learned). He confirms that the next LP (*Get Back*) is finished and ready for release, because they "got fed up . . . so we just left it." Kenny compliments John on his patience at sessions, probably having noted the high take numbers on the songs being mixed. John explains that "Strawberry Fields Forever" was the most complicated Beatles recording, due to the numerous remakes.

Kenny finally let John "go back up the stairs and twiddle another tune," and took away the interview reel. Apparently he was unable to sneak out advance copies of the songs being mixed, but that didn't stop him from airing his own versions. Kenny was proficient at multitracking, harmonizing with himself several times to create a cappella jingles of pop songs. Several

Beatles-related examples of this have survived, including all three songs he heard that day. Despite brief exposure, the melodies must have been tattooed in his brain: For "Sun King," he sang his own cod-foreign lyrics, but "Maxwell's Silver Hammer" and "Mean Mr. Mustard" were both accurate reproductions.

A recording of the latter jingle was bootlegged in the early 1970s (on *Abbey Road Revisited* and other LPs) as a "studio outtake." Since Kenny used it as a bed for the interview, others have also surmised that it's part of the Beatles' version playing in the background on a monitor, but it's actually pure Kenny.

RELEASE HISTORY

These recordings circulate in fair quality among collectors and were included on the CD-R compilation *Attack of the Filler Beebs, Volume 4.*

106. Studio session

Date: 15 August 1969
Time: 2:30–5:30 p.m.
Location: EMI Studios 1 and 2
Producer: George Martin

[A.] Golden Slumbers/Carry That Weight—RS2 (3:08)
Mixed: 18 August 1969

[B.] Golden Slumbers/Carry That Weight—RS from take 17 (0:34)

After a reduction and overdubs on July 3, fourth, and thirtieth, the "Golden Slumbers"/"Carry That Weight" medley included drums on track 1, bass on track 2, piano on track 3, Paul's lead vocal on track 4, vocals from Paul, George, and Ringo on track 5, and Leslied guitar on track 6 (playing the C/G/A riff that ends the song). This much is heard on the test medley (see the July 30 entry).

On July 31, Paul retaped most of his "Golden Slumbers" lead vocal on track 4 (beginning at "smiles await you"). On track 7, a guitar solo (probably played by Paul) and extra drums were added to "Carry That Weight." That left track 8 free for George Martin to conduct a thirty-piece orchestra, playing his score, on August 15. This track was doubled with ADT during mixing three days later. The *Anthology* DVD remix (**B**) centers the drum track.

RELEASE HISTORY

1969: **A** was released on the LP *Abbey Road* and is available on EMI's CD of the same title.

2003: **B** was released on the soundtrack of the *Anthology* DVD.

107. Studio session

Date: 15 August 1969
Time: 7:00 p.m.–1:15 a.m.
Location: EMI Studio 1/2
Producer: George Martin

[A.] Something—monitor mixes of take 39 (mono) (2:55)

[B.] Something—RS10 (2:58)
Mixed: 19 August 1969

[C.] Something—RS from take 39 (#1) (2:58)
[D.] Something—RS from take 39 (#2) (3:30)

Rather than use the take 37 reduction mix of "Something" (see the July 11 entry), George opted to return to take 36 and redo his lead vocal performance on July 16.

Paul assisted with harmonies, and a bit of percussion was added. A new reduction into take 39 combined piano and lead guitar on track 1 and drums and percussion on track 2, placing bass on 5, Leslied guitar on 6, vocals on 7, and organ on 8. This freed up tracks 3 and 4 for George Martin's orchestral overdubs, and a rough mix of the song was done August 4 to assist him in preparing the score.

Martin conducted a twenty-one-piece ensemble August 15 in Studio 1, the same day that George nailed the final take of his guitar solo in Studio 2. With the song complete, it was mixed four days later and became George's first and well-deserved single A-side. A slight remix (**C**) appears on the *Anthology* DVD, while the *Love* remix (**D**) centers the bass, emphasizes the orchestra, and ends with elements from "Blue Jay Way" and "Nowhere Man." Also circulating is engineer Peter

Cobbin's re-creation (**A**) of a surround-sound mix session for the *Anthology* DVD, isolating various tracks.

RELEASE HISTORY

1969: **B** was released on the LP *Abbey Road* and is available on EMI's CD of the same title.

2003: **A** was aired May 5 on CNN's *The Music Room;* it appears on the CD-R *Unbootlegged 18.* The same year, **C** was released on the soundtrack of the *Anthology* DVD.

2006: **D** was released on the *Love* CD.

108. Studio session   P, R

Date: 17 August 1969
Location: EMI Studios, London
Producer: Paul McCartney

[A.] Que Sera, Sera (What Will Be, Will Be) (3:03)
[B.] The Fields of St. Etienne (3:09)

Although "Those Were the Days" and "Goodbye" had both been hits, Apple had a hard time finding a suitable song for Mary Hopkin's third single. Paul was originally scheduled to begin producing her second album after completion of the *Get Back* LP, but as that stretched into May and was superseded by *Abbey Road,* Mary's project took a backseat.

Eventually, Paul selected the oldie "Que Sera, Sera" for a potential single, much to Mary's displeasure. Perhaps as a compromise, the folkier "Fields of St. Etienne" was chosen as B-side. Paul produced both songs, with initial sessions at EMI around the middle of July (perhaps on Monday the fourteenth when no session for *Abbey Road* was held). Mary vacationed at home in Wales for a few days while Paul continued Beatles sessions. Another session was squeezed in on Sunday, August 17, as *Abbey Road* was winding down, and then Mary took off for a promotional trip to the United States. Final overdubs may have continued in her absence.

"Que Sera, Sera" (**A**) has a basic track of Paul playing acoustic guitar and Ringo drumming, with overdubs of Paul's bass and Leslied lead guitar and further drums from Ringo. "The Fields of St. Etienne" (**B**) has three acoustic guitars, at least one of which was presumably played by Paul. The bass and drums may also be played by Paul and Ringo; woodwinds and an unknown vocalist also provide accompaniment to Mary's double-tracked lead vocal.

The single was given a catalog number (Apple 16) and scheduled for release on September 12, but perhaps due to Mary's dissatisfaction with the choice of material, it came out only in France at the time. Another announcement suggested that "Fields of St. Etienne" would be the A-side, with an October 3 release date in the UK.

In the end, Mary switched producers for her third UK single, "Temma Harbour," not released until the following January. A belated U.S. release of **A** and **B** surfaced in June 1970, when "Que Sera, Sera" charted briefly, peaking at number 77.

RELEASE HISTORY

1969: **A** and **B** were released on a single in France only. Both were included on the 1972 compilation LP *Those Were the Days,* reissued on CD in 1995.

109. Studio session

Date: 18 August 1969
Time: 2:30–10:30 p.m.
Location: EMI Studio 2
Producer: George Martin

[A.] The End—take 7 w/final chord from A Day in the Life (stereo) (2:48)

[B.] The End—edit of RS4 (2:04)
Mixed: 21 August 1969

[C.] The End—RS from take 7 (0:33)

"The End" was nearly the end for the Beatles, being the penultimate song on their penultimate LP (in order of release). It was also completed during the penultimate overdub session for the album.

On August 5, the song had received its first vocal overdub, and two days later, more vocals were added, along with the guitar solos: Paul, George, and John trading two bars each three times in succession. Judging from the July 30 "test medley," this portion of the song originally lasted twenty-two bars, but was extended by editing to twenty-eight.

Careful examination of Paul's bass line reveals

that the final edit consists of three portions from the basic tracks:

bars 1 through 6
bar 9 through the fifth beat (eighth note) of bar 12
sixth beat of bar 4 through bar 22

Once this edit was done, the "love you" vocals and guitar solos were laid on top. More drums and bass were added August 8, a thirty-piece orchestra on the fifteenth, and piano on the eighteenth. The song was remixed that day and the next. At this stage, the song lasted 2:41, but editing on the twenty-first and twenty-fifth trimmed it to its final length. This may explain the strange edit points described above—perhaps the original edit simply repeated all twenty-two bars for a total length of forty-four.

On *Anthology 3*, a new and rather pointless variation (**A**) was created. This cuts in halfway through the second bar of Ringo's drum solo and obscures the drummer's shining moment by including the tambourine and guitar overdubs wisely mixed out of the original release. For no apparent reason, two bars are also chopped out just before the guitar solos, and the or-chestral overdub is brought up to maximum volume, overwhelming the delicate ending harmonies (and getting out of synch). To top off the madness, the final piano chord from "A Day in the Life" is tagged on, running backwards to a crescendo and then forward into silence. The *Anthology* DVD remix (**C**) has the orchestra mixed louder.

NOTE

A supposed "alternate mix" of this song appearing on the bootleg LP *Abbey Road Talks* and the CD *As It Happened, Baby!* sounds to me like a forgery created by editing.

RELEASE HISTORY

1969: **B** was released on the LP *Abbey Road* and is available on EMI's CD of the same title.

1996: **A** was released on the CD *Anthology 3*.

2003: **C** was released on the soundtrack of the *Anthology* DVD.

110. Studio session

Date: 19 August 1969
Time: 2:00 p.m.–4:00 a.m.
Location: EMI Studio 2/Room 43
Producer: George Martin

[A.] Here Comes the Sun—RS1 (3:04)
Mixed: 19 August 1969

[B.] Here Comes the Sun—RS from take 15 (0:28)
[C.] Here Comes the Sun—RS from takes 13 and 15 (4:18)

Started on a sunny day in May in Eric Clapton's garden as a release from the business tensions at Apple, and completed in Sardinia the following month, "Here Comes the Sun" was perhaps George's most impressive composition to date. Catchy and uplifting, with simple but evocative lyrics, George spent a lot of time perfecting the production, and the result is full of inspired touches.

Recording began way back on July 7, while John was still recuperating from his car crash. In thirteen takes, Ringo's drums, Paul's bass, and George's acoustic guitar and guide vocal were taped. George improved on his guitar track at the end of the session, and the next day the eight-track was filled with a fresh lead vocal and two sets of backing vocals from Paul and George. A reduction brought the song to take 15, which was roughly mixed into mono for George's listening pleasure.

On July 16, harmonium and handclaps were added, with further guitar parts overdubbed August 6 and eleventh. George Martin conducted a seventeen-piece orchestra playing his score on August 15, and four days later came the final touch: several Moog passages played by George on track 4 of the tape. The song was mixed (quite creatively) into stereo well past midnight. The *Anthology* DVD remix (**B**) centers the lead vocal and harmonium, while the *Love* remix (**C**) incorporates elements from "Within You Without You" and "Oh! Darling" and cross-fades with "The Inner Light."

On August 20, all four Beatles assembled at studio 2 for the last time as a group to oversee the master tape compilation for *Abbey Road*. The lineup before final editing and cross-fading (and side-swapping) looked like this (all versions as released unless otherwise noted):

SIDE A: Here Comes the Sun/Because/You Never Give Me Your Money (cross-fade not perfected at end)/Sun King/Mean Mr. Mustard/Polythene Pam/She Came In through the Bathroom Window/Golden Slumbers/Carry That Weight/ The End (unedited version—2:41)/Her Majesty

SIDE B: Come Together/Something/Maxwell's Silver Hammer (unedited version—3:31)/Octopus's Garden/Oh! Darling/I Want You (She's So Heavy)

RELEASE HISTORY

1969: **A** was released on the LP *Abbey Road* and is available on EMI's CD of the same title.

2003: **B** was released on the soundtrack of the *Anthology* DVD.

2006: **C** was released on the *Love* CD.

111. Amateur footage

Date: 22 August 1969
Location: Tittenhurst
Length: 0:31

With the album complete, a new batch of publicity photos was needed, if only to reflect the group's current hairstyles (since the last photo shoot, Ringo had grown a beard, and George a beard and mustache). John and Yoko had just moved into their Ascot estate, Tittenhurst, eleven days earlier, and it was chosen as a visually interesting (and convenient) location for the shoot.

Most of the photos show the foursome, rarely smiling, in various locations around the grounds and posing in the doorways, archways, and windows of the mansion. Yoko and Linda appear in a few of the shots, and luckily Linda brought along her color movie camera, filming the group in the day's third location, a patch of tall grass and wildflowers. The footage was unearthed twenty-five years later and made a poignant and fitting finale to the mammoth *Anthology* documentary.

RELEASE HISTORY

1996: This silent footage from Linda McCartney's private collection was seen for the first time in the *Anthology* home video documentary, slowed down and set to the Beatles' recording of "The End."

112. Home demo   J

Date: 24 August 1969 (?)
Location: Tittenhurst

   [A.] **Cold Turkey—demo take 1** (3:31)
   [B.] **Cold Turkey—demo take 1 w/guitar and vocal overdub** (3:35)
   [C.] **Cold Turkey—demo take 1 w/Yoko vocal overdub** (3:29)

By John's own admission, he and Yoko began snorting heroin sometime in 1968, "because of what the Beatles and their pals were doing to us." He claimed to be drug-free in numerous interviews in the spring of 1969, but his first serious attempt to kick the habit occurred soon after moving into Tittenhurst August 11. Having reportedly tied himself to a chair, John spent "thirty-six hours rolling in pain" and suffering through terrifying withdrawal symptoms.

In the spirit of sharing every part of his life with the public, John duly shaped the experience into a song, "Cold Turkey," and taped a home demo. The basic demo (**A**) has John's lead vocal and acoustic guitar joined by a second track of more guitar and occasional faint vocals. This recording was fleshed out by copying to a second tape and adding overdubs. One such attempt (**B**) has John harmonizing with himself on the chorus and playing some bassy acoustic guitar licks. Another (**C**) features Yoko's usual wordless vocalizing (and shouting "push PUSH me!"), which is quite appropriate in the context of the song, and would be imitated by John on the studio recording.

NOTE

The August 24 dating is based on a reference in *Q* magazine's chronology in their 1999 Beatles Collectors' Edition. For all I know, they could have plucked the date out of thin air, but as it's in the right time frame, I opted to include it here.

RELEASE HISTORY

1988: **B** was broadcast in episode 88-27 of the radio series *The Lost Lennon Tapes*. This source was used on the vinyl bootleg *The Lost Lennon Tapes, Volume 6* and the CD *Christmas Present*.

1989: **A** was broadcast in episode 89-24 of the radio series *The Lost Lennon Tapes*. It appears on the vinyl bootleg *The Lost Lennon Tapes, Volume 17* and (sped up considerably) on the CD *Gone from This Place*. The same year, **C** surfaced in episode 89-34; it was booted on the LP *The Lost Lennon Tapes, Volume 20* and the CD-R *Vinyl to the Core*.

2004: A slightly incomplete copy of **A** was released on the CD *Acoustic*.

113. Newsreel footage   J, G, R

Date: 31 August 1969
Time: evening
Location: Isle of Wight
Length: 0:17

A fortnight after the Woodstock Festival, a similar but smaller-scale three-day event was held on the Isle of Wight. The headliner on the final night was Bob Dylan, playing a set with the Band in his first live UK appearance in more than three years. Naturally, the Beatles wanted to attend, and while Paul stayed with Linda and their newborn daughter, Mary, the other three and their respective wives flew over by helicopter. Associated Press and Reuters newsreel cameras, aided by popping flashbulbs, picked out John, Yoko, George, Pattie, Ringo, and Maureen in the crowd of 200,000.

Dylan went on late, around 11 p.m., and played for just under an hour, disappointing many fans with his relatively shortened set. John and George visited with Bob backstage and he accepted their invitation to return to the mainland in the Apple-rented chopper. John later described the scene of his final meeting with Dylan, which occurred early the next morning at Tittenhurst: "He came over to our house with George after the Isle of Wight and when I had written 'Cold Turkey.' I was trying to get him to record. We had just put him on piano for 'Cold Turkey' to make a rough tape but his wife was pregnant or something and they left."

Presumably the "rough tape" John is referring to would be his home demo (see previous entry). John had also tried in vain to offer the song to his bandmates, assuming they would agree to record it for the next Beatles single. Such rejection from all sides must have helped sow the seeds for a decision John was gradually accepting as inevitable: a formal split from the band he had started twelve years earlier.

RELEASE HISTORY

The silent monochrome AP footage (0:11) was included in the video compilation *Beatles 1962 to 1970*. Reuters' silent color footage was included in BBC2's *Arena* documentary *Imagine "Imagine,"* aired September 20, 2003.

114. Studio session   G, R

Date: 5 September 1969
Location: Olympic Sound Studios, London
Producer: Denny Cordell, Leon Russell

[A.] Delta Lady (4:01)

American session musician Leon Russell was in England appearing in Joe Cocker's "Mad Dogs and Englishmen" tour. Cocker's producer, Denny Cordell, agreed to assist Russell in recording a self-titled LP, using Olympic Studios in London and a host of superstar British musicians.

One of the album's highlights was "Delta Lady," written by Russell about singer Rita Coolidge and already covered by Joe Cocker. On Russell's version, alongside Bill Wyman's bass, Steve Winwood's organ, and Eric Clapton's lead guitar, Ringo played drums and George vamped the rhythm on a Leslied guitar. "Delta Lady" was recorded between September 2 and fifth, but the two Beatles continued participating in sessions throughout the fall (see the October 1969 entry).

RELEASE HISTORY

1970: **A** was released on the LP *Leon Russell*, issued on CD several times. The 1991 compilation CD *Delta Lady* reportedly includes a version of this song with the fade extended by 14 seconds.

115. Speech

Date: 11 September 1969
Location: Tittenhurst
Length: 25:51

Several members of the Radha Krishna Temple had taken up residence on John's Ascot estate. When the seventy-three-year-old founder of the International Society for Krishna Consciousness, A. C. Bhaktivedanta Swami Prabhupada, made his first visit to London in September, he joined his disciples, living at Tittenhurst and setting up a temple on the grounds. A lengthy audio recording exists of John, Yoko, George, and the swami (and an unidentified American man) having a conversation about spiritual matters.

Prabhupada begins by asking what kind of philosophy they follow, and George says they've meditated on mantras given to them by the maharishi. Yoko wonders whether it's necessary to chant anything other than "Hare Krishna" if it's supremely powerful, and John asks if all mantras aren't just different names for the same god. Prabhupada likens it to needing a specific prescription to receive a particular medication. Yoko asks if it matters from whom you receive the mantra, and the swami replies that milk is neutral, but turns to poison when touched by a serpent's tongue. Yoko counters that milk is material, but a mantra is spiritual, and can't be spoiled.

John wants to know how to determine which guru to follow, noting that the maharishi sounded just as convincing as the swami. George feels it's best left to the devotee to choose from among the flowers whether he prefers roses or carnations. Prabhupada insists that you need to be a serious student, going so far as to recommend learning Sanskrit, since no English translation of the *Bhagavad Gita* can be authoritative.

George quotes the belief of another swami, Vivekananda, that books, temples, and other rituals are only secondary to Krishna perception anyway, and Prabhupada jokes, "Then why Vivekananda wrote so many books?" George illustrates his point with the story of someone in Rishikesh who went off to read the *Bhagavad Gita* as an excuse not to meditate, and opened it up to discover the advice "don't read books, meditate."

Having felt betrayed by the maharishi, John is still wary about deciding which spiritual master to follow: "We have to keep sifting through, like sand." Yoko sounds even more skeptical than her husband. George is more content to fashion his own philosophy by taking "pieces from here and there."

RELEASE HISTORY

1995: This recording was released in very good quality on the CD *Inside Interviews: Beatlemania.* A transcript also appeared in the 1981 book *Lennon '69: Search for Liberation.*

116. Interview

Date: 12 September 1969
Location: Apple Corps, London
Length: 38:37

John and Yoko's two latest films, *Self-Portrait* and *Mr. & Mrs. Lennon's Honeymoon,* had their premieres September 10 at the New Cinema Club in London's Institute of Contemporary Arts. Three earlier films, *Rape, Smile,* and *Two Virgins,* were also screened, but naturally all the media attention (scant though it was) focused on *Self-Portrait,* a fifteen-minute slow-motion film of John's John Thomas. A lengthy recording exists of John and Yoko talking with a number of print reporters (including Richard Williams of *Melody Maker,* and apparently others from *Disc and Music Echo, Rave,* and perhaps the *London Times*) two days after the premieres.

A number of topics are covered, beginning with lack of privacy, although John admits that if he really wanted to go unrecognized he could be a "bald, shaved man in the middle of India." He says that his only real friends are the other Beatles, close associates like Derek Taylor, Neil Aspinall, and Peter Brown, and people from Yoko's circle who are so busy trying to look cool they pretend the name Beatles doesn't impress them. Most hangers-on get their moment of near-glory and then drop off, but John confesses to being "a sucker for people" who has always been easily conned.

He says that while he's occasionally played with other musicians, playing with session men is a hassle, since he prefers simple rock-and-roll and when it comes to that, his bandmates are on his wavelength: "If I wanted to make a record, I'd choose the Beatles." Either John is lying through his teeth, or events beginning later that day led to a drastic change of mind. Asked about Brian Epstein, John says he doesn't think about him often, and has a "built-in resistance to sorrow," which basically amounts to not dwelling on anything painful. Primal therapy would change that drastically, as well.

More of the usual "people have the power to get peace" rap follows, and Yoko points out that violence can happen anywhere at any time, offering the example of their unexpected car crash. John says he'd love for Jesus or Buddha to come out of the sky and save everyone, but knows that everyone has to pitch in to instigate positive change in the world.

The discussion turns to *Self-Portrait,* and as Yoko takes a phone call, John tries to explain how it differs from an Andy Warhol film, leading to this bit of wisdom: "So that's the difference, y'know. Between a prick and a skyscraper." He compares his disdain for the avant-garde filmmaking elite to his hatred of the jazz purists who banned the Quarry Men from playing rock at his college and the Cavern, and his revenge is apparently to "let two hundred intellectuals sit there and watch a prick for three days."

Yoko returns and dismisses Warhol's films as camp, whereas theirs have a positive message of peace to spread (although how *Self-Portrait* achieves this is left undisclosed). John talk about *Smile* for a bit and reveals that they are working on documentaries of their Montreal bed-in and other trips, but "haven't got them together yet." In perhaps his most dubious comparison not made to Maureen Cleave, John insists earnestly that *Smile* is "a million years ahead of" Stanley Kubrick's *2001: A Space Odyssey.* His point seems to be that not every piece of art released needs to be a major event, and that if films were as disposable as TV programs, people would take them less seriously.

The sore point of money is raised, and John calls the Beatles' fortune a "myth," griping about how difficult it is to finance his own projects and break even, let alone make a profit. Complaining that Apple treats him and Yoko like second-class citizens, John describes a promo disc Kenny Everett prepared for an EMI sales conference that mentioned James Taylor and the Iveys but dared to ignore *Life with the Lions,* which outsold both artists in the United States and is "much more important than James Taylor's music, as far as I'm concerned." Saying he hasn't seen a paycheck in two or three years now that all their joint income goes directly into Apple, John suggests dividing their funds and having each Beatle receive what they earn directly.

Likening all of their projects to an ongoing diary, John says that the audience at the ICA screening was being filmed, and maybe on the next night of John and Yoko films in November, they'll show the audience a film of themselves watching films. Describing the *Wedding Album* track "John and Yoko," he is afraid that due to the lengthy delay in release, people will probably think it's a rip-off of the recent Serge Gainsbourg/Jane Birkin duet, "Je t'Aime . . . Moi Non Plus."

After more discussion of peace, John suggests that the Beatles have a backlog of compositions ready to record and have agreed to begin sessions again in January, when the *Get Back* album is due for release. Within twenty-four hours, John would be flying to Toronto and telling Allen Klein he was quitting the Beatles.

RELEASE HISTORY

2000: This interview was released as tracks 2–9 on the CD *Kaleidoscope Eyes.*

117. Concert   J

Date:	13 September 1969
Location:	Varsity Stadium, Toronto
Producer:	John Lennon, Yoko Ono

[A.] intro (1:36)
[B.] Blue Suede Shoes (2:13)
[C.] intro (0:10)
[D.] Money (That's What I Want) (3:00)
[E.] intro (0:26)
[F.] Dizzy Miss Lizzy (3:06)
[G.] intro (0:19)
[H.] Yer Blues (3:40)
[I.] intro (0:38)
[J.] Cold Turkey (3:03)
[K.] intro (0:32)
[L.] Give Peace a Chance (3:12)
[M.] intro (0:19)
[N.] Don't Worry Kyoko (Mummy's Only Looking for Her Hand in the Snow) (4:23)

[O.] intro (0:31)
[P.] John, John (Let's Hope for Peace) (11:23)
[Q.] outro (0:54)
Mixed: 25 September and 20 October 1969

Perhaps the only way to get John Lennon back onstage was to play to his impulsiveness, and Toronto promoter John Brower lucked out when he phoned Apple on the afternoon of September 12. He was merely calling to ask if John and Yoko would lend a bit of prestige to his Rock and Roll Revival festival concert the next day by flying in and perhaps introducing one of the acts. When John heard that the lineup included many of his idols (Little Richard, Chuck Berry, Jerry Lee Lewis, Gene Vincent, Bo Diddley), he could not resist, and made a startling counteroffer: I'll appear, but only if I can play.

Brower picked his jaw off the floor long enough to accept, and by 9 p.m. the flight and visa details were arranged. The only problem was finding a band on short notice. The other Beatles were probably ruled out (Ringo had just left the hospital; Paul was at home with his new baby; George was known to hate touring), so calls were placed to bassist Klaus Voormann, drummer Alan White, and Eric Clapton. The latter was not located until a telegram reached him the following morning, by which time Mal had rounded up the others for a 10 a.m. flight at London Airport.

The cold light of day caused John to have cold feet, but Clapton phoned and cursed at him until he gave in. A 3:15 p.m. departure was arranged, and the Plastic Ono Band was forced to choose a set list and rehearse it on their Air Canada flight. A motorcycle gang escorted the musicians' limo to Varsity Stadium, and less than twenty-four hours after accepting the gig, John found himself backstage trying to calm his nerves (puking and then reportedly snorting a line of cocaine).

The crowd roared its approval and held up lighters as the band took the stage, which must have bolstered John's confidence. With Allen Klein watching from the wings, and D. A. Pennebaker filming the proceedings, the Plastic Ono Band opened with three oldies, in keeping with the festival's theme. John threw himself into the performance, even doing his "Elvis legs" at one point! It was like Hamburg all over again, apart from the woman in the white bag with a microphone, adding shrieks and yelps to punctuate the numbers.

After a couple of songs, Yoko peeks out of the bag to hand John a cheat sheet with lyrics (on Bag Productions stationery). The oldies were familiar enough for John to wing the lyrics, but for "Yer Blues" and the brand-new "Cold Turkey" he needed to read along; the latter lacks the signature riff or any kind of organized ending, but comes off surprisingly well. With "Give Peace a Chance," it's back to ad-libbing the words; Eric Clapton joins in singing the chorus along with the crowd.

It was then time to hand the spotlight to Yoko, for what John later called "half rock and half madness." "Don't Worry Kyoko" would have been easy enough to learn, being a three-chord riff repeated ad infinitum. "John, John (Let's Hope for Peace)" is even simpler: Yoko singing variations of those words while John coaxes feedback from his amplifier, picking up the guitar and swinging it, fiddling with the knobs and toggles. The rest of the band are mostly spectators at this point, although White adds a few drum hits and Clapton helps out. John eventually sets his guitar down and lets Yoko "do her thing" while he watches, dances, imitates an airplane, and cradles her as she screams. One by one, the musicians leave the stage, with the guitar still buzzing away.

Newspapers reported that this portion of the act was roundly booed, but an audience tape that circulates proves John's claim that some were crying for more at the end. Certainly John was thrilled enough with his ability to conjure a band from thin air and have complete freedom to play and improvise that he duly informed Allen Klein he had decided to quit the Beatles.

RELEASE HISTORY

1969: The original mix of **A–Q** was released on the LP *Live Peace in Toronto 1969;* the 1995 CD featured a fresh stereo mix of the entire album, with a slightly longer version of **Q** and different levels on Yoko's vocals. The audience tape containing **A–P** was bootlegged in 1969, but is extremely rare. D. A. Pennebaker's footage of the concert is available on DVD as *Sweet Toronto*.

118. Promo clip   J

Date:	May–June and 13 September 1969
Location:	various
Director:	Jonas Mekas
Broadcast:	6 November 1969, 7:05–7:30 p.m.
	BBC1
	Top of the Pops

[A.] Cold Turkey (5:13)

Underground filmmaker Jonas Mekas began an ongoing relationship with John and Yoko when he visited their Montreal bed-in and filmed much of it using a silent handheld camera. He pared down the footage to a length of approximately five minutes and sent it to Apple for use in promoting the "Give Peace a Chance" single.

By the time the package reached John and Yoko, that single had come and gone, but they tried setting the music of "Cold Turkey" to the clip and found it fit like a glove. Mekas had employed a frenetic and fragmented cutting style that complemented the harrowing music well. John and Yoko supplemented the piece by splicing in some of their own footage from the Toronto Rock and Roll Revival concert.

The rest of the footage intercuts random images (clouds, traffic, a man pitching horseshoes) and printed slogans (TO YOKO + JOHN WITH LOVE; SING TOGETHER; POWER

TO THE WORKERS) with scenes from the bed-in, mostly from May 31 and June 1. These include the Al Capp skirmish, breakfast in bed, and the recording of "Give Peace a Chance." The finished film was aired once on *Top of the Pops* and then went into John and Yoko's film library, being screened in September 1971 at the Alexandra Palace in London, alongside promos for "The Ballad of John and Yoko," "Give Peace a Chance," and "Instant Karma!"

RELEASE HISTORY

1992: This promo was released on the home video *The John Lennon Video Collection.*

119. TV interview   J

Date:	15 September 1969
Location:	Apple Corps, London
Broadcast:	16 September 1969
	ITV
Length:	1:06

Following the concert in Toronto, most of the Plastic Ono Band entourage were chauffeured to a private estate owned by one Thor Eaton, where they spent the next day relaxing and touring the grounds in golf carts. On the fifteenth, the party flew back to London, and an ITV News crew filmed an interview with John and Yoko back at Apple Corps.

John explains how he was able to assemble the band quickly, now that rock musicians are resisting being segregated in bands in favor of gathering when-ever possible to jam and "howl." Asked whether this is the start of a solo performing career, John says he'll play it by ear and is reluctant to even label "Give Peace a Chance" a solo performance. The reporter asks for a definition of "howling," and Yoko calls it "an expression that's not so intellectualized as words," while John says it's merely "pure sound." The couple then proceed to demonstrate vocally.

RELEASE HISTORY

1996: The audio portion of this interview was released on the CD *Fab Four CD & Book Set,* with Yoko's howling demonstration excised. The footage also circulates on video.

120. Interview   G

Date:	mid-September 1969
Location:	Apple Corps, London
Interviewer:	Ritchie Yorke
Length:	32:55

Toronto *Globe and Mail* reporter and all-around rock journalist Ritchie Yorke sat down for a lengthy conversation with George at Apple around the middle of September, primarily to discuss *Abbey Road.* Edited highlights of their conversation have been published in various places, but a complete audio tape exists, reportedly from a broadcast on Pittsburgh radio station KQV.

George comments on each of the album's songs, naming "Because" as his favorite and singling out Ringo's unwittingly "cosmic" lyrics for "Octopus's Garden." He verifies that "Come Together" was the first song John worked on after recuperating from his car crash, and he marvels at John's ability to write songs that jump from one time signature to another organically, such as "All You Need Is Love." Of course, he also recounts the writing of his two contributions and says that "some people will hate" "Maxwell's Silver Hammer," presumably counting himself in that group.

He does have nice words for "Oh! Darling" and "Golden Slumbers," but skims over most of the medley songs, losing interest in the analysis and summing up the album as "very abstract." Yorke asks about the "White Album," and George admits it was a mistake releasing a double album, singling out "Revolution 9" and calling the LP too "heavy" to listen to in one sitting. He explains that a random phrase from a book, "gently weeps," inspired him to write a song about his guitar.

This leads to a discussion of Eric Clapton, whom George had recommended to John when the Plastic Ono Band was being recruited to play in Toronto. While Clapton enjoys the "self-torture" of being on the road, George is less enthusiastic and gives a protracted and astute history of the Beatles' stage career.

Their performance skills reached an apex in Hamburg and gradually stagnated as they became more famous and locked into a set list of the same dozen hit records. By the time they played Shea Stadium, they were performing merely to amuse themselves, as the audience had little interest in paying attention to the music. The controversies and violence of the 1966 tour soured George on touring for good, and no matter how much fans promise to behave if the Beatles would only play live, George remains unconvinced it could ever work again.

Brian's death is seen by George as just another turn of the karmic wheel, an inevitability that forced the group to begin paying attention to their finances, much to their dismay. George admits that, despite its altruistic beginnings, Apple has never been anything more than a company "to implement the whims of the Beatles," as Derek Taylor puts it. Derek pokes fun at George's latest such whim, "to take the worst minority religious cult in England and get a top thirty record with it in ten days." Clearly promoting the Radha Krishna Temple was proving a challenge for Apple's PR chief!

George talks about producing Jackie Lomax and then spends the last few minutes of the interview giving an uninterrupted monologue about his own interest in Indian culture and religion. He feels that some outside force was guiding him down the path of hearing and meeting Ravi Shankar, and concludes with the declaration that he is only "pretending" to be a Beatle, whereas his true purpose in life is to champion Indian music and Hinduism in the West.

RELEASE HISTORY

This interview circulates in excellent quality among collectors.

121. Studio session   P

Date:	18 September 1969
Location:	IBC Studios, London
Producer:	Mal Evans, Paul McCartney

[A.] Rock of All Ages (3:22)

Paul continued assisting at sessions for Badfinger's *Magic Christian* soundtrack recordings. According to some sources, he coproduced the basic tracks for the songs "Crimson Ship" and "Midnight Sun" and may have even played piano on them. He also assisted Mal Evans in producing the lovely ballad "Carry On till Tomorrow," which was scored for strings and conducted by George Martin.

Paul's most tangible contribution was to the B-side of "Come and Get It," a hard-driving rocker titled "Rock of All Ages." In addition to coproducing the song and assisting in its composition (uncredited), he plays the pounding piano track that features throughout. Paul even went so far as to sing a shared lead vocal track with Tom Evans, although this was probably meant as a guide vocal, and was erased by a second vocal from Tom. Paul's influence remains clear in the "I'm Down"–style shouting and Little Richard "woo's."

A Kenny Everett broadcast from the time of the single's release has Kenny pretending to phone Paul to uncover the truth.

KE (live): So, I rang him up anyway to find out if it was really him.
(dialing, ringing effects)
KE (on tape): Hullo?
KE (live): Ah. Is that really Paul McCartney?
KE (on tape): No, it's Mrs. Elsie Bladder. Why, is that Kenny Everett?
KE (live): No, it's Mildred Pratt!

RELEASE HISTORY

1969: **A** was released on the B-side of the single "Come and Get It." In 1970, it was included on the Apple LP *Magic Christian Music,* which was reissued on CD in 1991. The original single mix isolates Paul's piano in the right channel, while the mix used on the LP and CD centers the piano and fades nearly 10 seconds early.

122. Radio interview   P

Date:	19 September 1969
Location:	Apple Corps, London
Interviewer:	David Wigg
Broadcast:	21 and 28 September 1969, 3:00–4:00 p.m. BBC Radio 1 *Scene and Heard*
Length:	13:27

Paul's main contribution to *Abbey Road*'s promotion was this lengthy interview with David Wigg for *Scene and Heard.* Two excerpts totaling 7:40 were broadcast, but even more of the raw tape was included on the LP *The Beatles Tapes with David Wigg;* a photograph from the session also appears in the album's booklet.

Wigg begins by congratulating Paul on *Abbey Road* and asking which songs he likes best. Paul diplomatically chooses "Come Together," "Something," and "Because." Perhaps missing the wordplay inherent in the lyrics of the latter, Wigg questions the use of "blows my mind" and "turns me on" as passé, but Paul defends them, and adds that he likes "the whole of the long one" (the medley on side 2).

He relates having seen the lyrics to "Golden Slumbers" in a piano songbook belonging to his stepsister Ruth, and making up his own tune to the words, which "fitted with another bit of song I had, which is the verse in between it." Wigg asks about "Her Majesty," and Paul says he wrote it in Scotland "as a joke." This leads to a discussion of the royal family, and Paul recounts his experiences at the Royal Variety Performance and the MBE ceremony, explaining that the Beatles never accepted offers to perform at further Royal Variety shows because they didn't want to repeat past glories and invite comparisons.

After complaining about lack of privacy, Paul describes his three-week-old daughter, Mary, as "the best-looking baby you've ever seen . . . Just started her on cereal, took every drop!" Wigg wonders whether Paul will write a "Mary" song, and he reveals that one is already in the can ("Let It Be"), although it was written before Mary was born.

Paul insists that hangers-on usually end up falling off, and that true friends choose themselves by not insisting on special treatment. Wigg asks about the Beatles' declining image among the older generation (being hairy freaks, etc.), and Paul doesn't seem worried. He compares it to the switch from leather clothes to stage suits, when the Beatles had lost some fans who felt they'd sold out, but gained a great deal of new admirers.

Hitting a more tender spot, Wigg wonders how much control the Beatles have over Apple now that Allen Klein is in charge. Paul admits that he doesn't like "doing the business bit," but figures that someone has to do it. Wigg follows this up by passing along the news that the organizers of the Isle of Wight festival will ask the Beatles to headline the following year. Paul is reluctant to commit to the group ever appearing live again: "I just don't know what's gonna happen. It'll be all right, though."

One day later, during a meeting at Apple, Paul would get his answer. When Paul proposed undertaking an incognito tour of small clubs, John called him and his ideas "daft" and announced that he "wanted a divorce" from the Beatles. As the main purpose of the meeting that day was to sign a new royalty contract with Capitol, Klein, Paul, and Ringo (George was visiting his ailing mother in Liverpool) persuaded John not to spill the beans about his decision in public, as it would obviously jeopardize the deal. Everyone probably kept their fingers crossed that John would reconsider, but the fact remains that his only contributions to the Beatles' remaining group projects would be made from afar.

RELEASE HISTORY

1972: A unique 7-second segment of this interview (Paul talking about retirement) was broadcast on the BBC Radio documentary *The Beatles Story.*

1976: The rest of the interview was released on the LP *The Beatles Tapes with David Wigg,* later reissued on CD.

123. Newsreel footage   P

Date:	25 September 1969
Location:	London Pavilion
Broadcast:	25 September 1969
	BBC-TV
Length:	0:11

Proud parents Paul and Linda made one of their last public appearances this evening before retiring from the limelight for several months. The occasion was the UK premiere of the film *Midnight Cowboy,* and BBC News cameras caught Paul (and the back of Linda's head) arriving, alongside other stars such as Marty Feldman and Richard Harris.

RELEASE HISTORY

This silent color footage circulates on video among collectors.

124. Radio interview   R

Date: late September 1969
Location: Apple Corps, London
Interviewer: David "Kid" Jensen
Broadcast: 26 September 1969, 12:30–2:05 a.m.
Radio Luxembourg
Length: 16:44

The previous year, Paul had sat down for a song-by-song examination of the "White Album" for Radio Luxembourg. This time around, Ringo and John took on the same task for *Abbey Road,* recording separate interviews around the third week of September for broadcast on consecutive days.

First up was Ringo's chat with "Kid" Jensen, who opens the show by noting that many critics consider *Sgt. Pepper's Lonely Hearts Club Band* an apex of musical progression from which the Beatles have been declining. Ringo disagrees with this, feeling that progression doesn't have to involve hiring "a million-piece orchestra." Jensen reveals that "Come Together" will be released as a single in America, which is news to Ringo, who only knew of its flip side, "Something," being chosen. The idea to pull a single from the album was actually Allen Klein's, and it would end up being released in the UK as well, despite a general tradition of keeping LP and 45 releases separate in that country.

Ringo explains that his fragmented drum pattern in "Come Together" grew from experimentation when trying to find the right feel for the song. He calls "Something" his favorite track on the album, and goes on to recount the LP's lengthy evolution from the aftermath of *Get Back* sessions. Jensen wonders about the numerous comparisons that *Abbey Road* is drawing with *Revolver,* and Ringo doubts that they are much alike, although he admits he hasn't played the latter album in years.

The "happy-go-1920" "Maxwell's Silver Hammer" was "the hardest track on the album," according to Ringo (Paul is the only one who didn't share this feeling), apparently because it was difficult to get excited about after so many tedious sessions in January. Discussion of Ringo's straightforward rock style of drum-

ming is a prelude to "Oh! Darling," which Ringo compares to "Yer Blues." Naturally, the most in-depth introduction is for "Octopus's Garden," with Ringo recounting the trip that inspired its composition, and declaring that he can play anything on the piano as long as it's in C major.

The extended ending on "I Want You (She's So Heavy)" is explained by Ringo: "Usually, when we do a track, anyway, once we get to the end, we just play it and play it, just in case we get some magic. And I think we got a bit of magic in this one." Although Jensen tries to call it a Lennon/McCartney composition, Ringo stresses that it's all John's baby. Before "Here Comes the Sun," Jensen wonders why George has so many unrecorded numbers, and Ringo speculates that George shares his feeling about the difficulty of selling your own songs amid a raft of gems by "the other two."

Ringo's main comment about "Because" is to point out that it lacks percussion, and he has even less to say about side 2's medley, apart from pointing out who wrote which piece of it. He does talk about choosing a title for the LP, revealing that Paul came up with it after they had rejected random "found" titles along the lines of *Milk Bottle* or *Billy's Left Boot* (at one point, the working title was *Everest,* after the brand of cigarettes Geoff Emerick smoked). He also notes that the reason for the medley was John and Paul's habit of having "a thousand first verses" of songs floating around unfinished. Although "Her Majesty" is neither played nor mentioned by name, Ringo discloses that there is a surprise at the end, "our answer to 'God Save the Queen'!"

To wrap things up, Ringo says that their next LP, *Get Back,* will be out by Christmas, and he describes it as being rougher and less produced than *Abbey Road.* He doubts that there will be a new Beatles single by the end of the year, but jokes that they might dash off one called "Get Back, Kid Jensen."

RELEASE HISTORY

This interview circulates in fair quality among collectors from an off-line recording.

125. Radio interview   J

Date: late September 1969
Location: Apple Corps, London
Interviewer: Tony Macarthur
Broadcast: 27 September 1969, 12:30–2:05 a.m.
Radio Luxembourg
Length: 22:57

John's *Abbey Road* analysis was presided over by Tony Macarthur, who had conducted similar promotional interviews for *The Beatles* and *Life with the Lions,* and would do so again in December when *Live Peace in Toronto 1969* was released. The show opens with John explaining that "a spy in England" sent advance tapes of the album to the United States, and since "Something" generated the greatest airplay, it'll be pulled for a single, with "Come Together" possibly on the flip side.

He re-creates the "shoot me"/clapping effect from "Come Together" and says it was achieved with tape echo, not compression. Macarthur expresses the widely held opinion that "Something" is the most commercial song George has written, and John agrees, calling it "funky." "Maxwell's Silver Hammer," on the other hand, is a "typical McCartney sing-along." John admits he was recuperating from his accident while most of the song was taped, but doesn't sound too crushed about it, as Paul "really ground George and Ringo into the ground recording it."

"Oh! Darling" is described by Macarthur as a "'58 job," which leads to discussion of the Toronto Rock and Roll Revival. John runs down the lineups of the bill, the Plastic Ono Band, and its set list. Yoko points out that their set wasn't much of a revival, and John describes how they "ended up with a complete freakout with Yoko taking over." Macarthur wonders if the Plastic Ono Band will be a permanent ensemble, and John jokes that the lineup will be "flexible . . . 'cause it's plastic." As to future Beatles concerts, John is decidedly noncommittal, refusing to rule them out, but moaning about how much they have to live up to.

John has little to say about "Octopus's Garden" and thinks Ringo may have done some singing elsewhere on the album while John and Yoko were in the hospital (he did, on "Carry That Weight"). Introducing "I Want You (She's So Heavy)," John talks about the LP's use of Moog synthesizer, describing the various sounds it can produce and speculating that a future Plastic Ono Band concert might consist of just a Moog onstage playing preprogrammed music.

"Here Comes the Sun" reminds John of a Buddy Holly song, and he relates the genesis of "Because" from Yoko's playing the chords of "Moonlight Sonata" in reverse order. The song's intricate harmonies were chosen by George Martin after John requested "the alternative to thirds and fifths." He calls the medley "a good way of getting rid of bits of songs we'd had for years," and he reveals that all four of them contributed to composing the sections needed to link up the various song fragments.

After "You Never Give Me Your Money" ("[Paul]'s always on piano, you can't get him off"), John explains that the pseudo-foreign lyrics in "Sun King" were made up in the studio to embellish the repeat of the "Sun Riff." He says that while Paul knew a few words of Spanish from school, "chicka ferdy" was actually a Liverpool expression. Macarthur jokes that the song might be a hit in Brazil if pulled as a single and says that "Mean Mr. Mustard" reminds him, tempo-wise, of a *Revolver* track. John recalls that it was written in Rishikesh, with the title borrowed from a newspaper headline.

He compares "Polythene Pam" to "Not Fade Away" and "Summertime Blues," two songs that (in their original versions, anyway) were driven by briskly strummed acoustic guitars. Macarthur asks if "She Came In through the Bathroom Window" is about an event during an American tour; John says the title was conjured by Paul during his and John's visit to New York City in May 1968. White Trash's cover version of "Golden Slumbers"/"Carry That Weight" is heavily plugged, and when Macarthur describes "The End" as "a way to close the show," John blurts out, "What about 'Her Majesty'?" spoiling the surprise.

Nonetheless, the LP's finale is played "properly," with the full silence; after "Her Majesty," Macarthur reveals that Paul had played the song to him (presumably on his acoustic guitar rather than a demo) the previous November while setting tape levels for their "White Album" interview. John says that it was added as a joke, like the talking in the *Sgt. Pepper* runout groove that "everybody thought was something obscene."

RELEASE HISTORY

1984: Just over ten minutes of this interview was included on the vinyl bootleg *Abbey Road Talks*. The complete off-air recording circulates in good quality among collectors.

126. Studio session   J, R

Date: 28 September 1969
Location: Trident Studios, London
Producer: John Lennon, Yoko Ono

[A.] Cold Turkey—RS? (4:57)
Mixed: 29 September 1969

After the realization that he didn't need the Beatles to back him on "Cold Turkey" either onstage or on record, John wasted no time in reassembling the Plastic Ono Band to record the song for a single. Ringo deputized for Alan White on drums, but otherwise, the lineup of John's guitar, Klaus Voormann's bass, and Eric Clapton's guitar was reinstated. On September 25 at EMI studio 3, the song was recorded in twenty-six takes of backing and guide vocal. Although the final take, running 5:10, was selected as "best," John apparently opted for a remake three days later at Trident Studios, using the same musicians.

The best take from the Trident session (details

unknown) was mixed into stereo back at EMI on the twenty-ninth and pressed onto an acetate (**A**) that was aired on *The Lost Lennon Tapes*. This contains the basis of the released recording: guitars, bass, and drums, plus some guitar overdubs (at the very start and toward the middle and end). Most of John's lead vocals would later be rerecorded, although the moaning that enters at 3:25 was retained. This mix also includes some electric piano near the end (perhaps Yoko's contribution), which isn't audible in the final version. It ends cold without the brief backwards reprise added during final mixing (see the October 5 entry).

RELEASE HISTORY

1988: **A** was broadcast in episode 88-27 of the radio series *The Lost Lennon Tapes,* with the ending buried by narration. This source was used on the vinyl bootleg *The Lost Lennon Tapes, Volume 7,* with the ending spliced in from the released stereo mix.

1998: **A** appeared from the original acetate source on the bootleg CD *After the Remember,* with the ending intact.

127. Studio session   G, R

Date: September–October 1969
Location: Olympic Sound Studios, London
Producer: Denny Cordell, Leon Russell

[A.] **I Put a Spell on You** (4:05)
[B.] **Shoot Out on the Plantation** (3:06)
[C.] **Prince of Peace** (2:59)
[D.] **Pisces Apple Lady** (2:48)
[E.] **Roll Away the Stone** (3:05)
[F.] **(The New) Sweet Home Chicago** (3:06)
[G.] **Indian Girl** (4:04)
[H.] **(Can't Seem to) Get a Line on You** (4:23)

Sessions for Leon Russell's eponymous LP continued at Olympic, with Glyn Johns engineering, and George and Ringo sitting in occasionally. Of the tracks from the original album, it's likely that George plays electric guitar on **A**, **B**, **D**, and **E** and may play dobro or slide acoustic on **C**. Drumming is handled by Ringo on **B, D,** and **E,** while Charlie Watts drums on **A,** and **C** features percussion to which Ringo may contribute. Eric Clapton plays lead guitar on **C** and **E**.

Several outtakes from the original sessions, never mixed before in stereo, were included as bonus tracks on the 1993 CD reissue. "(The New) Sweet Home Chicago" apparently has Charlie Watts behind the kit, George on rhythm guitar, and Steve Winwood on electric piano. "Indian Girl" has George and Eric Clapton on acoustic guitars, Ringo on drums, and Klaus Voormann on bass. "(Can't Seem to) Get a Line on You" is the working title for "Shine a Light," a Jagger/Richards track from *Exile on Main St*. This take has Mick Jagger singing lead, Russell on piano, Ringo on drums, Bill Wyman on bass, and either Mick Taylor or Chris Stainton on slide guitar. As it concludes, Jagger comments, "That was quite nice."

RELEASE HISTORY

1970: **A–E** were released on the LP *Leon Russell*.

1993: The Gold CD reissue of *Leon Russell* included **A–E**, plus **F–H** as bonus tracks.

128. Radio promo   J

Date: ca. October 1969
Location: Apple Corps, London (?)

[A.] *Wedding Album* promo spot (0:25)

John and Yoko's third album, originally titled *The Wedding*, was to be released on the low-priced Zapple subsidiary label. Although it was complete by the beginning of May, production of the elaborate box of souvenirs that came with the album held release back until late October, by which time Zapple was defunct, a casualty of Allen Klein's cost-cutting measures.

To promote the LP, John and Yoko recorded a radio commercial, probably for airing on U.S. and Canadian stations. It begins with the couple delivering a brief pitch in sing-song voices: "This is John and Yoko here and we'd like you to listen to a bit of our *Wedding Album*—out soon on Apple. Peace! Good-bye!" This is followed by an extract from the track "John and Yoko."

RELEASE HISTORY

1989: This ad was rebroadcast in episode 89-02 of the radio series *The Lost Lennon Tapes*. The first 11 seconds (consisting of the new spoken material) appeared from this source on the vinyl bootleg *The Lost Lennon Tapes, Volume 14* later that year.

129. Studio session

Date: 2 October 1969
Time: 9:30–11:00 a.m.
Location: EMI Studios, Room 4
Producer: George Martin

[A.] Across the Universe—RS2 (3:46)
Mixed: 2 October 1969

As mentioned previously (see the February 4, 1968, entry), John had agreed to donate "Across the Universe" to a charity album for the World Wildlife Fund as soon as it was rejected from the sessions for a potential single. At the end of the January 7, 1969, session at Twickenham, the Beatles played back an acetate of the song to remind themselves how it went, as they were considering reviving it for the "Get Back" project.

That acetate presumably contains RM2 from February 8, 1968, as it incorporates the overdubs from that day (vocals, guitar, maracas, and piano). Interestingly, it already includes the animal sound effects; whether these were added during the original mono mixing or much later is unknown. This is probably the version that was slated for inclusion on the proposed *Yellow Submarine* EP, compiled March 13, 1969, but never issued.

At that stage, the song was still in its original key of D major, but George Martin prepared new stereo mixes the morning of October 2, speeding up the track a half step in pitch. Two mixes were done, one without sound effects and one with birds, children, and galloping horses. The effects match those on the acetate, although they are much longer at the beginning. This may be simply because the acetate wasn't played from the very start on January 7, or it may be that Martin redid them entirely. He placed the lead vocal, acoustic guitar, and tom-tom in the center, with tamboura and female backing vocals left and all February 8 overdubs right.

The result (**A**) was included on the charity LP, fittingly titled *No One's Gonna Change Our World*, compiled October 3 and very belatedly released on December 12 in the UK only. Americans had to buy an import or wait until the 1980 compilation LP *Rarities* to hear this mix of the song.

RELEASE HISTORY

1969: A was released in the UK on the various artists LP *No One's Gonna Change Our World*.

1978: A made its first appearance on a Beatles LP with the UK release of *Rarities*, available initially as part of a boxed set and in its own right the following year.

1980: The U.S. version of *Rarities* had a different lineup to its British counterpart, but included **A.**

1988: A was included on the compilation CD *Past Masters, Volume 2*.

130. Studio session   J, R

Date: 3 October 1969
Location: Studio A, Lansdowne Studios, London
Producer: John Lennon, Yoko Ono

[A.] Don't Worry Kyoko (Mummy's Only Looking for Her Hand in the Snow)— RS? (4:53)
Mixed: 5 October 1969

For the flip side of the latest Plastic Ono Band single, Yoko's new "song" from the Toronto gig was chosen to receive a studio treatment. The same format was followed, with Yoko letting loose on vocals while John and Eric Clapton played the E-G-A riff on slide guitars, Ringo did his best to keep time on drums, and Klaus Voormann played bass. The song was recorded in an unknown number of takes (it couldn't have taken many) at Lansdowne Studios, and was mixed into stereo two days later at EMI studio 2 by Geoff Emerick.

NOTE

This song appears from an acetate on the bootleg CD *Acetates and Alternates*, but offers nothing new apart from surface noise and reversed channels. Ditto the version of "Cold Turkey" on the same release.

RELEASE HISTORY

1969: A was released on the B-side of the "Cold Turkey" single. It was included on the 1971 LP *Fly* and is available on Rykodisc's 1997 CD reissue of that title.

131. Studio session J, R

Date: 5 October 1969
Time: 10:00 a.m.–10:00 p.m.
Location: EMI Studio 2
Producer: John Lennon, Yoko Ono

[A.] Cold Turkey—RS? (5:00)
Mixed: 5 October 1969

[B.] Cold Turkey—RS (5:00)

John probably finished off "Cold Turkey" on his own during this session, overdubbing a pair of new lead vocals (harmonizing with himself on the chorus) and adding more electric guitar. The final mix, engineered by Geoff Emerick, retained the narrow stereo picture of the earlier acetate, with only the guitar overdubs straying far from the center of the image. The recording was capped off by running the tape backwards for the final 3 seconds. A similar remix on the *Lennon Legend* DVD (**B**) pans John's lead vocal all over the place during the coda.

While the first Plastic Ono Band single had followed tradition by crediting "Give Peace a Chance" jointly to Lennon/McCartney, "Cold Turkey" was pointedly written by Lennon only.

RELEASE HISTORY

1969: **A** was released on a single that peaked at number 12 in the UK and struggled to reach number 30 in the United States. It's best found on the CD *Lennon Legend*.

2003: **B** was released on the soundtrack of the *Lennon Legend* DVD.

132. Studio session G

Date: 7 October 1969
Location: Morgan Studio, London
Producer: unknown

[A.] Exchange and Mart (4:15)
[B.] Spending All My Days (3:00)

Thanks to his friendship with Eric Clapton, George ended up participating in various projects with members of Cream, Blind Faith, and later Derek and the Dominoes. These two songs come from a solo session for an aborted solo album by Blind Faith's bassist, Rick Grech.

Both songs surfaced as bonus tracks on a German CD issue of Blind Faith's self-titled album, mislabeled as group recordings and with all four group members given composing credit. While Grech, Clapton, and Steve Winwood contributed, Alan White is on drums, not Ginger Baker.

"Exchange and Mart" is an instrumental jam, with Winwood on mandolin, White on drums, and Grech on violin. There are three guitars, one of which definitely sounds like Clapton and one buried in the center channel that could be George's contribution. The third guitar seems to be another Clapton overdub. Denny Laine reportedly participated in these sessions (he and White had played in a band called Wolf as teenagers), and may play the bass on this track.

"Spending All My Days" should never have seen the light of day, being sung and performed out of tune and completely unsynchronized. Winwood plays harpsichord, Grech sings (double-tracked, no less!) and plays bass, White drums, and Eric and George presumably play the two guitars (there's also a snare drum overdub).

RELEASE HISTORY

1986: **A** and **B** were included on the German CD reissue of the album *Blind Faith*.

133. Radio interview   G

Date: 8 October 1969
Location: Apple Corps, London
Interviewer: David Wigg
Broadcast: 12 and 19 October 1969, 3:00–4:00 p.m.
BBC Radio 1
Scene and Heard
Length: 16:59

David Wigg's string of solo Beatle interviews for *Scene and Heard* continued when he spoke with George for a second time. Their conversation opens with George putting his public persona in perspective, figuring that even though he's stuck with the tag "Beatle George" for the rest of his life, it's merely an irrelevancy compared with more eternal matters. Although being rich and famous comes with higher highs than the average lifestyle, George and his bandmates are also saddled with prodigious woes.

This leads George to one of his favorite topics: bitching about how much tax the government takes from his income. Throwing in a quote from "You Never Give Me Your Money," he declares that "it's illegal to keep the money you earn." He's quick to add that money doesn't equal happiness, however. George goes on to relate how he first encountered members of the Radha Krishna Temple at Apple and agreed to record the "Hare Krishna Mantra" single for them. He explains the purpose of chanting as a "method of becoming one with God" through repetition of holy words.

Wigg wonders if George accepts the stricter tenets of Krishna devotees, such as abstaining from drugs, alcohol, meat, and extramarital sex. He replies that he's a teetotaler and vegetarian, and claims that he hadn't been taking drugs even before his bust, but the police "seemed to bring it with them that day!" After imagining the BBC's legal department furiously snipping that portion of the tape, George explains that one needs a clean mind and body to get truly high, spiritually speaking.

The topic turns to *Abbey Road,* and Wigg gives George some stunningly backhanded compliments

about his two offerings on the album, dismissing all of George's earlier compositions with: "It's so unusual [for you] to contribute so much to an LP." George mutters that he wrote four songs that were just as good (if not as commercial) for the "White Album." Wigg misses the point, calling him a "late developer," and George says that there's no point comparing him with Lennon or McCartney, and that he has no control over whether his songs turn out accessible.

Asked what inspired "Something," his most celebrated love song, George gives the sterling endorsement: "Maybe Pattie. Probably." He passes on John's advice to finish writing a song as soon as possible after starting, describing a song (possibly "Dehra Dun") written in Rishikesh that still has only one verse completed. After telling the story of how he wrote "Here Comes the Sun," George chooses "Because" as his favorite song from *Abbey Road.* He enthuses about the song's three-part harmonies and sings a bit of "Yes It Is" to demonstrate an earlier example. George also praises Paul's talent for inventing pleasant melodies such as "Golden Slumbers," and he promotes "Octopus's Garden" as much more than the "fun" song for "little kids" Wigg paints it as.

Presumably after informing George of the offer for a live Beatles reunion at the next Isle of Wight festival (although it's not mentioned in the tape we have), Wigg asks for his opinion on a return to the concert stage. George is unsurprisingly less than enthusiastic, although he at least confesses to enjoying playing the guitar! The conversation comes full circle when George, realizing that he'll be forever tied to his bandmates, calls a spiritual split impossible, since "if you're listening, I'm the walrus, too!"

RELEASE HISTORY

1976: This interview was released on the LP *The Beatles Tapes with David Wigg,* later reissued on CD.

134. Radio interview   J

Date: 21 October 1969
Location: Apple Corps, London
Interviewer: David Wigg
Broadcast: 26 October 1969, 3:00–4:00 p.m.
BBC Radio 1
Scene and Heard
Length: 8:10

After recuperating from her second miscarriage in as many years, Yoko joined John on the peace campaign trail once again. On the twentieth, they remixed tapes of their Toronto concert; the same day, the "Cold Turkey" single and *Wedding Album* were released in America. They began promoting all these projects the following day by taping a second interview with David Wigg for *Scene and Heard.*

John rejects the notion of running for Parliament, figuring that the lack of regulation allows him to achieve more as a pop star than a politician. He claims to be happy with the state of their peace crusade, relating how even lorry and taxi drivers who encounter John and Yoko now flash a peace sign rather than a rude gesture! He goes on to describe the contents of the *Wedding Album,* calling the package of photos, cartoons, and press cuttings a family album, "but [from] a strange family." He also likens the "John and Yoko" track to "a very extreme" version of Stan Freberg's "John and Marsha."

Wigg asks about John's recent public request to have his share of Apple's income sent directly to him, through Bag Productions, and wonders if this signals a split from the other Beatles. John dismisses it as a "tax-business thing" and points out that since Yoko has never been a Beatle, any projects they do together have nothing to do with splitting the group. Perhaps sending out a public message to his bandmates, he suggests that Paul and George record albums of their own material, rather than simply donating excess songs to Mary Hopkin or Billy Preston.

In his recent interviews with Paul and George, Wigg had passed along the Isle of Wight festival organizers' invitation for the Beatles to reunite onstage at the 1970 event. Asked about this, John says he'd consider it carefully, but realizes what a letdown Dylan's recent appearance was for some people. He knows that the Beatles would be under even more pressure to turn in a spectacular performance: "They'll be expecting God to perform!" Yoko suggests holding an imaginary concert, since people already have expectations that will far exceed any reality.

Wigg asks what John wants for the future of the Beatles, and John's response reveals how much he's thinking of the group as a spent force. After a word of confidence in Allen Klein's ability to get the band the money it's due, John continues: "Whatever happens to the Beatles, so-called, we'll always be sort of friends, y'know. So all I want for the Beatles is their individual happiness. And whether that's in a collective form or not remains to be seen."

The interview concludes with a topic Wigg had also raised to Paul: the British public's general distaste for the current "long-haired, freaky" look the Beatles now have. John points out that they've always had longer hair than the average citizen, and that their once outrageous hair length from 1963 is considered acceptable in 1969. He admits that he has a hard time not judging people who look conservative exactly as they judge him, joking, "Would I let my daughter marry a short-haired man?"

RELEASE HISTORY

1976: 3:48 of this interview was released on the LP *The Beatles Tapes with David Wigg,* later reissued on CD. This release is taken from the unedited prebroadcast tapes. A fair-quality off-line tape of the original broadcast circulates among collectors; there is about a minute of overlap between the two sources.

135. Radio interview   J

Date:	ca. 22 October 1969
Location:	Apple Corps, London (via telephone)
Interviewer:	John Small
Broadcast:	26 October 1969
	WKNR-AM, Detroit
Length:	9:34

The full tale of the "Paul is dead" lunacy is told more fully in other books, but suffice it to say that a number of American college students and disc jockeys with too much time on their hands were able to expand a harmless diversion into a full-blown conspiracy theory within the course of ten days. The hotbed of media information on the rumor was Detroit radio station WKNR, whose DJ Russ Gibb had broadcast numerous "clues" phoned in by listeners. By October 21, the story was being picked up in New York City, and from there, it was a hop, skip, and a jump across the Atlantic.

Unfortunately, the protagonist, Mr. McCartney, was setting off to Glasgow en route to a vacation at his farm on the morning of the twenty-second, just as the story was breaking in London. Peter Brown phoned him that day to apprise him of the situation and ask for a statement. Paul gave him a one-liner borrowed from Mark Twain: "Rumors of my death have been greatly exaggerated." It made no difference, and for the next few days, the Apple phones would continue to ring off the hook.

Meanwhile, WKNR did its own investigating, with Russ Gibb speaking to Derek Taylor, who seemed slightly amused by it all, and taking a call from someone on the twenty-second who claimed to be Paul McCartney, but turned out to be Tony Bramwell. Around this time, WKNR's John Small got through to a bewildered John Lennon and recorded a phone conversation that, if nothing else, demonstrates that John could have had no hand in perpetrating any hoax.

John, apparently unaware that Paul had just left for Scotland, states that Paul can't be dead, as he's currently working on producing records for the Iveys and Mary Hopkin. He points out that Paul couldn't keep his wedding secret, and thus would hardly be able to pass away unnoticed. After throwing in some plugs for the "Cold Turkey" single, *Wedding Album,* and forthcoming *Live Peace in Toronto,* John expresses a wish to release a single a day and an LP every week, a sort of Plastic Ono Periodical.

Small asks if there's any significance in any of the "clues" on Beatles albums, and John confesses to not having boned up on all the clues, having just learned of the whole thing from that morning's paper. He describes the picture sleeve for the "Cold Turkey" single, a reproduction of the x-rays taken of his and Yoko's skulls, and realizes that it'll probably be more fuel for the fire. Since he doesn't have a habit of playing Beatles records backwards, John says he has no idea what they sound like in reverse.

John clearly isn't familiar with the "Billy Shears replacement" aspect of the rumor, as he expresses puzzlement as to how the *Abbey Road* cover could have been photographed with all four Beatles having their current looks: "What did we do, stuff him and shave

him? How could we do it? I don't understand what it's all about, y'know." He explains away Paul's bare feet on the cover as an example of Paul's odd sense of humor and says he didn't even notice at the time that Paul had removed his sandals. John's garb on the cover, described by the sleuths as ministerial, is described by its owner as merely "a nice Humphrey Bogart suit."

Dismissing the whole business as insane, John nevertheless concedes that it's great publicity for *Abbey Road.* He compares it to the rumors that James Dean might still be alive or that Bob Dylan had died after his 1966 motorcycle accident, although he feels those were more plausible.

RELEASE HISTORY

This interview and the other WNKR recordings mentioned above were included in a special originally broadcast October 26, 1969, and circulate in good quality from a 1978 re-airing on CKNW. It appears on the CD-R *Misshimmisshimmisshim.*

136. Radio interview   R

Date: 23 October 1969
Location: Apple Corps, London
Interviewer: Alex Bennett
Broadcast: WMCA, New York City
Length: 8:58

Being one of the largest radio stations in the country's largest market, WMCA could afford more than phone calls, and it sent one of its DJs, Alex Bennett, over to London, to report on the "Paul is dead" controversy. He arrived on the twenty-second, just as Paul was departing, and thus was forced to conduct interviews with secondary figures, including Derek Taylor, Neil Aspinall, *Abbey Road* cover photographer Iain Macmillan, half of Apple group Trash, and even Paul's tailor and barber!

Bennett's real coup was a brief interview with Ringo Starr, who had just arrived from Los Angeles with Neil the previous day and, like John, was caught unaware by the issue. Fittingly, the whole topic is disposed of expediently, with the ever-sensible Ringo proclaiming, "If people are gonna believe it, they're gonna believe it. I can only say it's not true." Bennett tosses

Ringo a few softball questions, allowing the drummer to expound on how nice it'd be to live on another planet, and to express wishes for peace and freedom on this one.

Ringo chats about his sons, admitting that they don't always let him join in when they are playing together. Bennett reminisces about the Beatles' 1965 Houston concert, which he had emceed, and at which Ringo had stepped on his hand while running offstage. He asks if Ringo was as frightened of the crowds as he looked that day, which leads to a recounting of Ringo's most harrowing experience, when he'd received death threats in Montreal in 1964. The conversation closes with Ringo's message to New York City: "Don't build up Central Park . . . it's the only bit of grass you've got!"

RELEASE HISTORY

The entire WMCA special, including this interview, circulates among collectors in fair quality from an off-air tape. It appears on the CD-R *Misshimmisshim misshim.*

137. Radio interview **P**

Date: 24 October 1969
Location: Campbeltown
Interviewer: Chris Drake
Broadcast: 27 October 1969, 10:00 p.m.–midnight
BBC Radio 2
Late Night Extra
Length: 3:24

After a few days, Paul agreed to speak with the BBC in hopes that people hearing his voice would see the light. Needless to say, it didn't work, but reporter Chris Drake drove out toward the remote farmhouse, walking the last two and a half miles after his car got bogged down.

Paul theorizes that the rumors have started because he has been avoiding the public eye lately, admitting that he used to do "an interview a week" just to keep his name in the headlines. Clearly he prefers keeping his personal life with his wife and newborn daughter quiet and completely private. Paul can see why this might lead people to suppose that he's no longer with us, but he makes it quite clear: "If the conclusion you reach is that I'm dead, then you're wrong. Because I'm alive and living in Scotland."

That taken care of, the rest of the interview focuses on the farm itself, which Paul concedes is "scruffy." He relates having been dubbed "the new Laird" when first meeting his neighbors, but says he'd hate to be thought of as a posh "squire of the district." Linda complains that their vacation is being ruined by the whole thing, when "everybody knows he's alive."

Finally, Paul says that with an album and film in the can, the Beatles have no more work in the near future, and that he may not even return to London until 1970. Which is pretty much what he proceeded to do.

RELEASE HISTORY

This circulates from two sources, both of which appear on the CD-R *Misshimmisshimmisshim*. The most complete is a poor-quality off-air tape, presumably from *Late Night Extra* or *The World at One;* this is missing the last few words from Linda. The second source is in slightly better quality and includes Drake's narration but only about half of the interview material; this comes from a rebroadcast on WMCA Radio's "Paul Is Dead" special.

138. Studio session **R**

Date: 27 October 1969
Time: 2:30–10:45 p.m.
Location: EMI Studio 3
Producer: George Martin

[A.] Night and Day—RS? (2:23)
Mixed: 27 October 1969

Judging from dialogue during the January "Get Back" sessions, Ringo had wanted to record a solo LP of standards for a long time, a project perhaps instigated by his performance on "Good Night" and his general love of the oldies his family used to sing at parties.

The album, working title *Ringo Starrdust,* began tentatively, with this single session for a song written by Cole Porter and specially arranged for Ringo by Chico O'Farrill. The backing was recorded this afternoon by a seventeen-piece band (saxes, trumpets, trombones, bass, piano, and drums), conducted by George Martin. After a break for dinner at 5 p.m., Ringo returned two hours later to tape his lead vocal.

His nervousness at taking the spotlight shows in his slightly shaky crooning, but he's clearly having a ball as he belts out the tune. At 9:30, the song was mixed into stereo and the first Ringo solo album was underway.

RELEASE HISTORY

1970: **A** was released on the LP *Sentimental Journey,* reissued on CD in 1995.

139. Promo clip

Date: ca. late October 1969
Location: various
Producer: Neil Aspinall
Broadcast: 13 November 1969, 7:05–7:50 p.m.
BBC1
Top of the Pops

[A.] Something (2:59)

Assembling promotional films for Beatles singles was becoming more and more difficult. For "Get Back" and "The Ballad of John and Yoko," the group had appeared together only via footage culled from the January sessions at Twickenham and Apple. By the end of October, there was no way the four could be assembled in front of the cameras for a performance or conceptual clip.

The idea behind the "Something" promo is simple and suitable: Each Beatle is seen outdoors at home with his respective spouse. George and Pattie appear in the backyard of Kinfauns, George looking solemn and Pattie smiling sweetly and sporting leather and fur coats. Ringo and Maureen ride mopeds around the grounds of Brookfields, the home they had purchased from Peter Sellers. A newly clean-shaven John strolls down the front steps at Tittenhurst with Yoko, the cou-

ple cloaked in black capes. Paul and Linda are seen on their Campbeltown farm, frolicking with their sheepdog Martha.

Paul looks particularly unkempt with scruffy facial hair, an undershirt, and Wellingtons. As he later recalled: "I was going through a hard period. I exhibited all the classic symptoms of the unemployed, the redundant man. First you don't shave, and it's not to grow a groovy beard, it's because you cannot be fucking bothered." The isolation from his bandmates was causing Paul to sink into depression and heavy drinking. Linda, by contrast, looks beautiful, as do Maureen, Yoko, and Pattie. An effective if telling promo, edited together by Neil Aspinall for its sole contemporary UK airing on *Top of the Pops* (November 13; Germany's *Beat Club* also broadcast the promo November 29).

RELEASE HISTORY

This clip first turned up complete in the *Private Reel* compilation, taken from Ringo's print. It now circulates in excellent quality on video thanks to its inclusion on a 1998 EPK distributed by Apple. A basically complete version (missing only the first few seconds) was included in the *Anthology* home video.

140. Newsreel footage   P

Date: late October 1969
Location: Campbeltown
Broadcast: CBS-TV (?)
Length: 1:30

Such was the curiosity over Paul's whereabouts and existence that many reporters took to trespassing on his farm. A team from *Life* magazine made the trek on foot and snapped photos of an angry Paul throwing a bucket of water at them. Paul quickly came to his senses and chased them down, offering an exclusive interview in exchange for destruction of the film documenting his outburst. The result was a cover story in the November 7 issue, with a clean-shaven and casually but smartly dressed Paul posing with Linda, Heather, and Mary.

In similar vein, a few days earlier a CBS television crew had driven across the moors in hopes of tracking down the reclusive Beatle. The footage they obtained was probably never aired, but circulates from the CBS News vaults. It shows an unshaven, shabbily attired Paul (looking much as he does in the "Something" promo) from afar, pacing around the mud in his gumboots with Martha. The crew got close enough to film Paul apparently agreeing to an off-camera interview, admonishing, "And don't try filming it, or you might get some trouble."

RELEASE HISTORY

This color footage circulates on video among collectors.

141. Radio interview

Date:	ca. late October 1969
Location:	Apple Corps, London
Interviewer:	Kenny Everett
Broadcast:	8 November 1969, 10:00 a.m.–noon
	BBC Radio 1
	Everett Is Here
Length:	4:29

In the beginning of November, John and Yoko were vacationing on a boat (and by some accounts, fasting in an attempt to kick their various addictions) with "Magic" Alex Mardas in Greece. While they were away, Kenny Everett broadcast this interview recorded back in London before their departure.

John shares his feelings on religion, with the wonderful turn of phrase "you can't say Christ was a flop," and compares the Beatles' followers to the Christian church (he never did learn). His point is that Christ's teachings (and Beatles music) remain just as valid as ever no matter the state of organized religion (or the record industry). He feels that every major artistic figure through history, from Beethoven to Keats to modern primitive painters, is trying to convey basically the same message through their works.

He goes on to compare the Woodstock and Isle of Wight festivals to spiritual revivals, with hundreds of thousands of people meeting for a peaceful, celebratory purpose. Although he wasn't at Woodstock, John passes along David Crosby's impression of the occasion, which was much more positive than some media portrayals. As for the Isle of Wight, John says it felt like being in church when he was young: "An amazing buzz, y'know. It's a big high." ("And a big hi to you," quips Kenny back in the studio.)

Comparing it to a contemporary rendition of "Amazing Grace," John feels that "Cold Turkey" is the latest in a series of progressive recordings stretching back to "Rain" and "Strawberry Fields Forever." He tries to explain the song's meaning to Kenny, using "I Want You (She's So Heavy)" as another example of his neoprimitive style of lyric writing.

RELEASE HISTORY

1999: The CD-R *Vinyl to the Core* included 2:43 of this interview from an off-air tape source, in good quality. The remainder circulates in poor quality.

142. Studio session

Date:	6 November 1969
Time:	7:00–10:00 p.m.
Location:	Wessex Sound Studios, London
Producer:	George Martin

[A.] Stormy Weather (stereo) (3:01)

The *New Musical Express* reported in its November 8 issue that Ringo had begun working on a solo LP that would include standards like "Night and Day," "Autumn Leaves," and "I'll Be Seeing You." In fact, only the first of these had been taped, and while the others may have been on a list of candidates, they have never surfaced and were probably never recorded or even arranged for the album.

One other reject was the Ted Koehler/Harold Arlen composition "Stormy Weather," which was recorded this evening on four-track tape at Wessex Studios. George Martin conducted an eighteen-piece ensemble consisting of saxophones, trumpets, trombones, piano, electric guitar, bass, and drums. Ringo then overdubbed his vocal over the backing, but as the song was never mixed for stereo at the time, it was presumably discarded as substandard rather quickly.

"Don't know why," as the song says, for it's a truly swinging rendition (arranger unknown), and the album could have used more pep. Ringo's singing is no more or less distinguished than elsewhere, and only gets more relaxed and polished as the song progresses, although an ill-advised bit of yodeling at the very end probably should have been mixed out.

RELEASE HISTORY

1999: An excellent copy of **A** first surfaced among John Barrett's cassette material. It's best found on the CD *Through Many Years*. The version on the CD-R *The Abbey Road Tape, Volume 2—Solo* is a split-second longer at the end but of worse quality.

143. Radio interview   J

Date: ca. mid-November 1969
Location: Tittenhurst
Interviewer: Wolfgang Frank
Broadcast: 12 December 1993
Radio Xanadu
Length: 3:34

Sometime after their return from Greece and India, John and Yoko were interviewed at their new home in Ascot by one Wolfgang Frank. This three-and-a-half-minute recording was chopped up into eight segments and padded out (with music and in-studio chat from Frank) to a one-hour special, broadcast in 1993.

John trots out his favorite quote of the era regarding a Beatles concert: "They expect Jesus and Buddha to come out and perform." Realizing that a new generation of adolescents is gradually replacing his, John says that he doesn't envy youth and can't wait to retire with Yoko to a little cottage in Cornwall. As far as he's concerned, newer "progressive" groups such as Fleetwood Mac and Jethro Tull are still basically playing rock-and-roll.

Although he used to write with Paul because they were always on the road together, John says they would eventually convene only for the "hard work" of finishing off each other's songs when an album deadline was approaching. When John reveals that he and Yoko vacationed in Greece, Frank asks how he can have the scruples to spend time in a country currently under martial law. John doesn't see it as that much different from "living in fascist Great Britain."

Amusingly, John offers tips on how to get people to finance avant-garde film projects, using the Austrian TV–funded *Rape* as an example. Apparently, he agreed to write "music" for its soundtrack, and the producers, expecting pop songs, signed the contract eagerly. Only then did they realize that his "music" would consist of "Radio Play," a piece of "unfinished music" consisting of someone snapping a radio dial back and forth.

Finally, John and Yoko discuss a visit to West Germany, agreeing to visit Munich first, being "the art center," and then Berlin. The visit, perhaps part of their planned peace campaign, never took place.

RELEASE HISTORY

This interview circulates in very good quality among collectors from the 1993 rebroadcast.

144. Newsreel footage   J

Date: 25 November 1969
Location: Apple Corps, London
Length: 0:57

Although it was probably a long time coming, the ever-mercurial John suddenly decided to return his MBE medal (officially the honor itself was nonrefundable). As early as September, he had Derek Taylor research the protocol involved, and he eventually dispatched his chauffeur Les Anthony to fetch the medal from Aunt Mimi's bungalow. On the morning of November 25, John set about typing up his reasons for the protest. He settled upon Britain's involvement in Nigeria's war with Biafra, its support of America's war with North Vietnam, and its lack of support for the chart success of "Cold Turkey."

Anthony delivered the letter and medal to Buckingham Palace, and John sat back and waited for the firestorm. None was forthcoming, as the British press were growing weary of John and Yoko's antics. His protest drew about a tenth of the coverage accrued when he received the MBE in the first place, although a press conference took place that afternoon at Apple, where he filmed an interview for the Reuters news agency.

The newsreel opens with stock footage of the Beatles at the palace and John and Yoko in Amsterdam before cutting to this brief sound bite from John at Apple. Although he professes staunch patriotism, he claims that "off the cuff" info from reporters about the truth behind the Biafra war has begun to cause him to be ashamed of being British. John's real reason for the public stunt (another plug for his yearlong peace campaign) is revealed at the end when he admits, "I could have done it privately, but the press would have found out anyway. You would have been here a week later instead. Less impact."

RELEASE HISTORY

This Reuters newsreel footage circulates on video among collectors.

145. Studio session

Date: 26 November 1969
Time: 7:00 p.m.–3:00 a.m.
Location: EMI Studio 2
Producer: Geoff Emerick, John Lennon

[A.] What's the New Mary Jane—RS5 (7:04)
[B.] What's the New Mary Jane—edit of RS4 into RS5 (?) (2:28)
Mixed: 26 November 1969

Casting around for material to generate a new Plastic Ono Band single, John dug up a couple of unreleased Beatles recordings begun in 1967 and 1968. The proposed A-side was "You Know My Name (Look Up the Number)," which would instead be saved for the next Beatles B-side (see the April 30 entry for details).

For the flip side, John chose an equally off-the-wall song, "What's the New Mary Jane," rejected during the "White Album" sessions. An acetate containing several versions documents some of the work done to the recording in this new session, which began with a new remix of the multitracks (RS4; see the August 14, 1968, entry).

A second remix from multitrack to stereo was done (**A**), this time with a simultaneous overdub: John, Yoko, and a group of friends (probably EMI and Apple employees) adding further vocals and noises. The tape opens with John instructing the ensemble to sing during the chorus rather than just listen. Amazingly, someone has to ask "Where's the chorus?" and John is obliged to point out the obvious. Engineer Mike Sheady announces "RS5" and take 4 is played back, beginning with some piano notes and John's count-in. Once the song begins, everyone adds another layer of vocals (Yoko bleating and John chuckling at some of the screaming already present on the tape) and various bells, horns, and whistles. John's "Let's hear it" comment at the end is largely buried by Yoko's new wailing.

The order of events becomes fuzzy at this point. As it wasn't a Beatles session, the recording was ignored in John Barrett's tape log. Our only source of information is Mark Lewisohn's *Recording Sessions,* which states that RS5 was edited and the result called RS6. Most likely, the tape was not physically spliced, but copied in pieces onto a new tape, since RS5 remained intact, as heard on the acetate.

Lewisohn's next entry is confusing: "Tape copying with simultaneous editing . . . of stereo remixes 4 into 5." This is most likely represented by **B,** which does seem to have two mixes playing simultaneously. Elements from both play side by side, but not synced up. ("Let's hear it" pops up while an earlier portion of the song continues.) Although it's not exactly edited, it does begin abruptly in mid-song.

The session ended with tape copies of RS4 and RS5, which appear together along with **B** on the aforementioned acetate. The Plastic Ono Band single was announced for a December 5 rush-release on Apple and then withdrawn just prior to the release date.

RELEASE HISTORY

1980: An acetate containing **A** was bootlegged on the 12-inch single *What a Shame Mary Jane Had a Pain at the Party.* It was copied on the CD-Rs *Vinyl to the Core* and *Acetate Collection,* running nearly a half step too fast.

2001: **B** first appeared in very good quality on the CD-R *Acetate Collection* at the correct speed.

146. Interview   J

Date: 27 November 1969
Location: Tittenhurst
Interviewer: Ken Zelig
Length: 5:28

Two days after John returned his MBE, reporter Ken Zelig visited him and Yoko at their home in Ascot and interviewed them about the event and the coming Christmas season. After recapping his reasons for the protest, John explains that he had to send out three copies of the letter, one to Queen Elizabeth, one to Harold Wilson, and "one to the something of the chancery" (secretary of the Central Chancery). Asked why he accepted the MBE in the first place, John admits bluntly that he was a hypocrite to do so and had in fact tossed the original letter into a pile of fan mail until Brian Epstein "and a few people" convinced him it would be in the Beatles' best interest to accept. Indeed, while rejecting such an offer would have been done in private, if the word had ever leaked, it would have meant career suicide.

Zelig asks what John and Yoko are doing about the wars in Vietnam and Biafra, and John insists that the peace movement is making progress, inasmuch as the Nixon administration has been forced into cranking out blatant propaganda claiming that a "silent majority" are in favor of the war. However, John isn't prepared to travel to the battlefield to prove his points: "We don't intend to be dead saints."

On a lighter note, Zelig elicits childhood memories relating to Christmas. John recalls feeling his stocking when he was about eight or nine and discovering his first harmonica, calling it "one of the great moments of my life." Yoko has fond memories of a lava lamp her family received one year. John names "Good King Wenceslas" as a favorite Christmas carol, which will come as no surprise to listeners of Beatles Christmas fan club discs, and says he and Yoko will spend the holiday together watching "all those terrible shows" on TV.

RELEASE HISTORY

1989–90: This interview was broadcast in seven segments in episodes 89-34, 89-52, 89-53, and 90-43 of the radio series *The Lost Lennon Tapes*.

147. Studio session   R

Date:	28 November 1969
Time:	8:30–11:00 p.m.
Location:	EMI Studio 2
Producer:	George Martin

[A.] Stardust—RS? (3:19)
Mixed: 28 November 1969

The working-title track for Ringo's solo project was the Hoagy Carmichael number "Stardust." It was arranged for the album by none other than Paul McCartney, MBE (with a major assist from George Martin). The backing was recorded November 7 at Wessex Sound Studios and consisted of strings, horns, piano, chimes, acoustic guitar, drums, and bass.

On the fourteenth, Ringo overdubbed his lead vocal at Trident and the song was given a rough stereo mix four days later at Abbey Road. On the twenty-eighth in Studio 2, a tape reduction was done to allow Ringo to record a second vocal track. This was done not for double-tracking purposes, but apparently to give two performances from which to choose. The overlap between the two can be heard at 1:00 into the song on the phrase "now my consolation." Final stereo mixing was done after the new overdub.

Although it was probably an inevitable choice given the title, Ringo's delivery of this song is goofy rather than sincere, with a shouted "aaaw, hit me!" going into the instrumental break.

RELEASE HISTORY

1970: **A** was released on the LP *Sentimental Journey,* reissued on CD in 1995.

148. Studio session   G

Date:	ca. November 1969
Location:	Trident and Apple Studios, London
Producer:	Doris Troy, George Harrison

[A.] Ain't That Cute (3:49)

New York–born R & B singer Doris Troy had appeared alongside John and George back in April 1965 on *Ready, Steady, Go!* In mid-1969, she was invited by friend and fellow singer Madeline Bell to record backing vocals for a session that turned out to be George Harrison producing Billy Preston's first LP. George and Doris got along well enough that she was signed to Apple as a solo artist in September.

Her first work for Apple was reportedly composing instrumental music for an animated film, *Timothy's Travels.* She and George soon cowrote a song, "Ain't That Cute," which he agreed to produce for her first Apple single. Sessions began in early November but were halted temporarily mid-month when Doris became ill. Although the lead guitar is often credited to Eric Clapton, it's actually played by Peter Frampton. Frampton also recalls that Berry Morgan played the drums, and while Ringo is usually attributed with this role, none of the press surrounding the single's release mentions his name.

Certainly George plays the rhythm guitar, including his first recorded slide work, and Klaus Voormann is on bass. Piano and electric organ are also present; it's possible Billy Preston overdubbed one or both of these upon his return to England in mid-December. George also produced the single's B-side, "Vaya Con Dios," but neither he nor Ringo plays on it. Sessions for a full LP would continue through the following spring and summer, with both George and Ringo participating.

RELEASE HISTORY

1970: **A** was released on a single, which failed to chart. It was included on the LP *Doris Troy,* reissued on CD in 1992.

149. Location recordings

Date: November–early December 1969
Location: various
Producer: Kenny Everett

[A.] The Beatles' Seventh Christmas Record (7:40)

As they had in 1968, the Beatles recorded their contributions to the final annual fan club Christmas disc individually and handed over the tapes to Kenny Everett. According to the sleeve notes, John's sections were recorded at Tittenhurst, Paul's at 7 Cavendish Avenue (he returned to London from Scotland around the third week of November), George's at 3 Savile Row, and Ringo's at his home in Surrey (before moving back to London December 5).

The disc is even more dispirited and unbalanced than the previous year's and is dominated by John and Yoko, with George showing up for a grand total of 6 seconds. It opens with John soliciting a Christmas greeting from persons unknown, and after an organ rendition of "The First Noël," we hear John and Yoko strolling through their garden, trying to ad-lib a conversation about Christmas. John wishes for some Corn Flakes "prepared by Parisian hands and . . . blessed by Hare Krishna Mantra."

More organ links to Paul's a cappella holiday tune, sung in various silly voices, which cuts to George's "Happy Christmas," the two words edited by Everett in the manner of a Hare Krishna chant. Ringo strums an acoustic guitar and offers an off-key ditty about "the coming sports day of our life," which has nothing to do with Christmas.

The *Abbey Road* rendition of "The End" quickly fades under more of John and Yoko's discussion, this time about Elizabethan high walls. Some tinkly music precedes Paul's main contribution, an acoustic guitar and vocal number that shows even less creativity than his 1968 jingle. He wishes everyone holiday tidings and reprises the song. An instrumental rendition of "Deck the Halls" serves as background for more of John and Yoko in the garden, with Yoko expounding about how wonderful the 1970s will be, and her husband teasing her and singing a bit of "Good King Wenceslas."

Moving inside Tittenhurst, the couple perform a lame series of impromptu duets, with John accompanying on Mellotron, playing a "waltz backing" loop at various speeds. Ringo is then heard repeating "Merry Christmas" faster and faster until the words are incomprehensible; the tape slows back down gradually to reveal he is now saying "Magic Christian." "Just a plug for the film, Ken, try and keep it on," he jokes, before offering a more sincere greeting.

This is followed by a skit with John and Yoko at the Mellotron playing the roles of a little boy and his mother discussing presents. A choir singing "The First Noël" fades up and closes out the recording, punctuated by a bit of laughter from Ringo. While the content of the recording was dissatisfying, at least it was shipped in a sleeve with a cute drawing by Zak Starkey on the back.

RELEASE HISTORY

1969: **A** was released on a flexi-disc, titled *The Beatles' Seventh Christmas Record,* mailed out to fan club members on December 19. It's available on the bootleg CD *The Ultimate Beatles Christmas Collection.*

150. TV interview   R

Date: 1 December 1969
Time: afternoon
Location: London
Interviewer: Tony Bilbow
Broadcast: 10 December 1969, 11:07–11:30 p.m.
BBC2
Line-Up
Length: 20:02

With *The Magic Christian* due to premiere in Britain on December 11, Ringo set about promoting it at the beginning of the month, filming a lengthy interview with Tony Bilbow for broadcast on BBC2's *Line-Up*. The movie was mentioned only tangentially over the course of the conversation, which took place in the back of Ringo's limousine and in a boat paddled by Tony and Ringo down the Thames.

The segment opens with Ringo descending the steps of 3 Savile Row, signing an autograph, and climbing in the back of a Mercedes limo, sporting a fur coat and a "Sink the Magic Christian" button on his hat. We then see said hat being blown into the Thames by a strong gust of wind. From there, the program cuts between car and boat footage every few minutes. Bits of "Her Majesty," "Yellow Submarine," and "Act Naturally" are heard on the soundtrack to link the various segments.

Ringo talks about the abrupt change of business strategy at Apple, largely due to Allen Klein's philosophy of trimming fat: "What we're really doing now is paying for when we opened it and played about. Because we used to keep everybody on forever, y'know, just because they were like a mate or a pal. They never did the jobs, but we used to keep them on . . . It's not a playground anymore." Admitting that the Beatles are too cowardly to handle the task, Ringo reveals that Peter Brown is in charge of firing people.

The Starr-man then launches into a bit of confused quasi-astronomy, first claiming that our solar system has fifty billion planets, and then reducing his estimate to five. His point is that there must be intelligent life out there, perhaps even on our own planet in a parallel dimension. He also enthuses sincerely about someone in America who is building a "time spaceship . . . purely on instructions from another planet" to allow travel to these alternate universes.

Having just alienated 95 percent of the nonhigh viewing audience, Ringo goes on to espouse the decriminalization of marijuana, feeling it's no more dangerous than drinking alcohol. He is also in favor of a lowered voting age, hoping to one day see a prime minister who is "black, beautiful, and twenty-six." Saying he was tired of the commute, Ringo discusses his imminent move back to London from the suburbs and chats about his family life.

Ringo relates a charming attempt to explain to one of his sons the dangers of sticking your finger in an electrical socket (his every reason being countered with

an inquisitive "Why?"). Zak was obviously destined for show business: When fans would stop by to visit Ringo, his young son assumed they were there to see him and posed happily for souvenir photos. Ringo says Zak doesn't quite understand his father's fame, but enjoys Beatles records and TV appearances, even though the sight of one daddy in the room and one on TV can be confusing!

Due to various childhood illnesses, Ringo missed the equivalent of several years' schooling, and he confesses that he is "intelligent but uneducated," with spelling being a particular bugbear. Finally, he talks about how acting in *Candy* had whetted his appetite for meatier roles, and how *The Magic Christian* was a suitable follow-up, as both films were based on novels by Terry Southern. Expressing disdain for "message films," Ringo yearns for straightforward Hollywood storytelling, reminiscing about playing a cowboy or pirate after seeing movies of those genres.

Although it probably didn't draw many people to the box office, this profile unquestionably demonstrates that Ringo was a down-to-earth guy caught up in some very unconventional times.

RELEASE HISTORY

This interview circulates among collectors on video in very good quality.

151. TV interview   J

Date:	2 December 1969
Location:	Tittenhurst
Producer:	Colin Clark
Host:	Desmond Morris
Broadcast:	30 December 1969, 10:30–11:30 p.m. ATV *Man of the Decade*
Length:	22:08

In hindsight, it's difficult to argue with the choice of John Lennon as one of the most influential figures of the 1960s. But it probably came as a shock at the time when anthropologist Desmond Morris selected John to stand alongside John F. Kennedy and Ho Chi Minh as one of three "men of the decade." The occasion was a TV documentary, with each of the show's three hosts presenting a twenty-minute segment on the person they had chosen.

Morris visited Tittenhurst on December 2 to film his interview with John, and the two convened a few days earlier to select archival newsreel and private footage to illustrate the story. This included the 1962 *People and Places* performance of "Some Other Guy" (seen without synchronized sound), the July 30, 1968,

"Hey Jude" session, making its TV debut, and the "Something" promo (both silent). John and Yoko also supplied footage of the Montreal bed-in from their then-unfinished documentary.

The bulk of the segment has John walking with Yoko around the grounds of Tittenhurst, expounding on a number of topics. Although Morris was asking questions, he remains unseen and unheard in the location footage, but adds commentary from a studio. Nick Knowland, John and Yoko's regular cameraman, was hired by ATV to shoot the interview, and a BBC camera crew was on hand to film the whole thing for their own documentary (see the December 6 entry).

John begins by dismissing his education as a waste of time, apart from learning how to read and write, and says that other musicians of his generation realized that success was possible without following the traditional route and subscribing to the values of the mainstream. Although he's describing his own voyage more so than that of society, John traces a development from early rock-and-roll's aggression through psychedelic bliss and back to cold hard reality again.

However, he doesn't seem to find reality all that frightening, or at least he goes out of his way to express extreme optimism for the future, citing the Woodstock and Isle of Wight festivals as well as the recent anti–Vietnam War Moratorium in Washington, DC. All of these, he points out, ended up being less violent than a typical Beatles concert, even though they involved greater numbers of young people.

Which is not to say John has any answers, as he admits he was unable to give specific advice to the protesters in Berkeley. He realizes that meditation and drugs were merely ways of coping with or escaping from the real struggles of existence, and he compares his personal relationship with Yoko to a plant that needs constant care and attention. Only by concentrating on improving such relationships and communicating freely will the world be able to live together in harmony.

The interview concludes with John waxing about how wonderful the next decade will be, reassuring skeptical viewers such as "Mrs. Grundy of South Birmingham-on-Toast" not to be afraid of a world run by people like him. "The sixties was just waking up in the morning, y'know. And we haven't even got to dinnertime yet. And I can't wait, y'know, I just can't wait. I'm so glad to be around. And it's just gonna be great and there's gonna be more and more of us." Such optimism would soon disappear from John's philosophy and remain absent for most of 1970.

RELEASE HISTORY

1980: The vinyl bootleg *Man of the Decade* included the soundtrack to this interview. The complete Lennon segment circulates on video in excellent quality.

152. Studio session   J

Date: 4 December 1969
Time: 7:00 p.m.–1:40 a.m.
Location: EMI Studio 2
Producer: John Lennon, Yoko Ono (?)

[A.] Item 1—RS? (4:06)
Mixed: 4 December 1969

John and Yoko were now turning out work at a prodigious pace, with two singles and three albums released in 1969. The amount of effort expended on each of these was another matter, and what was planned as their fourth "experimental" LP was recorded in a single evening at Abbey Road.

"Item 1" consisted of John, Yoko, Mal, Anthony Fawcett, and various studio engineers and staff sitting on the floor in a circle and trying to make one another laugh. "Item 2" was based on Yoko's "Whispering Piece" and featured everyone lining up to whisper a word or phrase into the microphone, each one building on the previous person's comments.

A BBC camera crew documented the occasion (see following entry), including recording of both items and playback of "Item 1" in the control booth. Among the names shouted out during "Item 1" are those of EMI employees Eddie Klein, Dave Harries, Francis Thompson, and Phil McDonald, some of whom, along with Geoff Emerick and Malcolm Davies, participated in the recording.

Stereo mixes were prepared of both "items" at the end of the session, and an acetate of at least part of "Item 1" (**A**) has been bootlegged. It makes for tedious, rather than uproarious, listening, and consists of several simultaneous tracks of laughter, shouting, and random percussion, awash with cavernous echo. Thankfully, John and Yoko decided against issuing the material, and John would stick to releasing only music for the rest of his LP career.

RELEASE HISTORY

1995: **A** was included on the bootleg CD *To Be Expected,* probably taken from Mal Evans's acetate auctioned at Sotheby's in August 1992.

153. TV feature   J

Date: 2–6 December 1969
Location: various
Host: David Dimbleby
Broadcast: 15 December 1969, 10:30–11:05 p.m.
BBC1
24 Hours: The World of John and Yoko
Length: 31:08

This "day in the life of the Lennons" BBC TV documentary was actually shot over the course of five consecutive days and gives a wonderful sense of how many projects the couple were involved in at any one time. Although the footage is rearranged nonchronologically, here is a rundown of which scenes were filmed on which day.

December 2 saw the BBC film their rival company ATV as Desmond Morris interviewed John for *Man of the Decade* (see earlier entry). We see Morris, strolling on the Tittenhurst grounds, pose a question, and we see part of John's answer (including two lines that overlap with the ATV broadcast). They are also seen chatting off the record in John's kitchen about the pomposity of politicians.

On December 3, John wore a lavender turtleneck sweater, which helps identify the footage from this date. In the morning, they are seen at home in their pajamas, lounging in bed and opening their mail (Yoko is also knitting a belated birthday gift for John). John reads out a hate letter concerning his return of the MBE, an article concerning a Welsh impostor who keeps booking hotel rooms under his name, and a rather chilling missive: Someone who claims to have contacted Brian Epstein via a Ouija board passes along the prediction that someone will attempt to assassinate John on March 6. John laughs it off: "Well, it's funny he never said anything to me in Athens."

John and Yoko are also seen at Tittenhurst seated near a picture window; John plays his Mellotron and wears a fake rubber nose. From there, they travel via limo to Apple, chatting with assistant Anthony Fawcett in the backseat. Topics include the amount of posters for their imminent "War Is Over" event and discussing plans for the following day. Their arrival at Apple and perusal of some photos are also captured, along with a BBC Radio producer's attempt to interview them as they leave Apple for a friend's house.

On December 4, filming followed a similar pattern (John wore black this day), beginning at Tittenhurst. While eating in bed, John makes a phone call to arrange a visit to Toronto, where he plans to sign the "Bag One" lithographs. Apparently some kind of exhibition was also planned, as Apple graphic designer John Kosh was sent in advance to check out a museum. John and Yoko are seen at home viewing a film print of the *People and Places* performance of "Some Other Guy" chosen for the *Man of the Decade* special. Scenes from that evening's EMI session (see the December 4 entry) for "Item 1" and "Item 2" are also included.

At Apple, in addition to providing some "routine signatures" for Peter Brown, John and Yoko are seen giving several interviews from their office. For an interview in the December 13 and twentieth issues of *New Musical Express,* John chats with Alan Smith about the futility of having to fight for space on Beatles albums. For Japanese radio, he and Yoko tape a message of peace and donate copies of various Plas-

tic Ono releases. For an interview with DJ Stuart Henry, they play word association with "fear," "insecurity," and "death."

But the lengthiest and juiciest segment is from a conversation with *New York Times* reporter Gloria Emerson, which turns into a replay of the Al Capp skirmish, only with a more formidable opponent. Emerson berates John and Yoko's peace events as self-promotional stunts, and John defends his tactics as more effective than "manifestos written by a lot of half-witted intellectuals" that go unread by the general public. John points out that "Give Peace a Chance" was sung by protesters at the recent antiwar moratorium in Washington, DC, but Emerson is unimpressed. Eventually, she interrupts Yoko and walks out: "Mrs. Lennon, we're boring each other, so I'll go away. Happily."

Some unused Apple footage from December 4 was included in a 2007 video file distributed online by Yoko. This begins with 43 seconds of John putting a copy of *Live Peace in Toronto* on his office turntable and playing the first track. Another 52-second clip has John explaining to a journalist that he and Yoko don't mind being attacked for having long hair or being nude, because it draws the fire away from their chief message of peace.

On the fifth, John and Yoko traveled to Suffolk to film *Apotheosis 2,* in which the ever-reliable Nick Knowland ascended in a balloon and filmed the Lennons on the ground, the countryside, and finally the clouds and sky. Scenes from this day include the Rolls-Royce driving through the snow, the setup and takeoff of the balloon, and John and Yoko checking in to the Bull Hotel in Long Melford that evening. Once in bed, they play a few rounds of a verbal game in the form "fortunately/unfortunately/in the end." From the morning of the sixth, they are also seen drinking tea in bed.

Voiceovers taped on an unknown date feature John talking about Yoko being his other half, and Yoko describing a rather paranoid dream.

RELEASE HISTORY

This documentary circulates on video in very good quality, minus any credits or introduction from the host. Brief outtakes of the "fortunately/unfortunately" sequence, along with other clips from this special, were included in the film *Imagine: John Lennon.* An audio extract of the outtake sequence (incomplete) was released on the John Lennon CD boxed set *Anthology* in 1998, misidentified as coming from the bed-in film. The other outtakes circulate from the 2007 video file.

154. TV interview   R

Date: 6 December 1969
Time: evening
Location: Studio 1, Wembley Studios
Host: David Frost
Broadcast: 6 December 1969, 11:10 p.m.–midnight
London Weekend Television
Frost on Saturday
Length: 17:59

In one of their few joint appearances to promote *The Magic Christian,* Ringo and Peter Sellers videotaped an appearance on one of David Frost's 3,400 BBC chat shows. Although it may exist in Frost's vaults, a video of the show has never been unearthed, and all we have to go by is a home-taped audio recording.

Peter remains serious for the first couple of minutes, explaining what the movie is about and why he made it, and then Spike Milligan's scene from the film is shown. Frost invites Spike to come out and join them, and the two former co-Goons are off and running, doing a series of characters, silly voices, and visual humor that dominate the next ten minutes and make it impossible for Frost to conduct any serious interviewing. At one point, Spike does an imitation of ventriloquist Peter Brough, who had appeared alongside Ringo and Spike on *Cilla* the previous year.

The Goonery translates badly on the circulating tape, due to the lack of visuals and shoddy sound quality. It also means that poor Ringo is relegated to the role of third wheel, although he and Peter get to sing a brief duet of "Octopus's Garden." Frost struggles to regain control, shouting to introduce another clip (the Sotheby's auction scene with John Cleese).

Keeping with the movie's theme, Frost asks whether money is the root of all evil, and Sellers agrees with Terry Southern's premise. At long last, Frost poses a question to Ringo (who jokes, "I'm on now?") about whether he enjoys being a millionaire. Ringo says he likes being able to buy houses, noting that he bought one from Sellers, who "made it before I did." Beatles fans who tuned in were probably disappointed, but *Goon Show* fans certainly got their fill.

RELEASE HISTORY

The audio portion of this interview circulates in fair quality from an off-air recording.

155. Concert   G

Date: 7 December 1969
Location: Fairfield Hall, Croydon
Producer: Jimmy Miller, Delaney Bramlett

[A.] Things Get Better (4:09)
[B.] intro (0:17)
[C.] Poor Elijah/Tribute to Robert Johnson (4:54)
[D.] intro (0:06)
[E.] Only You Know and I Know (4:07)
[F.] intro (0:33)
[G.] I Don't Want to Discuss It (5:24)
[H.] outro (0:09)
[I.] intro (0:04)
[J.] That's What My Man Is For (4:29)
[K.] intro (0:21)
[L.] Where There's a Will, There's a Way (4:55)
[M.] intro (0:04)
[N.] Coming Home (5:33)
[O.] intro (1:18)
[P.] Tutti-Frutti/The Girl Can't Help It/Long Tall Sally/Jenny Jenny (5:42)
[Q.] outro (0:12)

During George's October 1968 trip to Los Angeles, he was impressed by the performance of a husband-and-wife rock act, Delaney and Bonnie Bramlett. Together with their musician "friends" such as Leon Russell, Bobby Keys, Jim Price, Bobby Whitlock, Carl Radle, and Rita Coolidge, they recorded an LP, *The Original Delaney & Bonnie—Accept No Substitute,* which George tried to get released on Apple the following spring.

Although the deal fell through, the album was released in the United States on Elektra, and to support it, Delaney and Bonnie and Friends toured America as the opening act for Blind Faith. When the latter group fell apart, Eric Clapton decided to become a "friend" himself and rehearsed with Delaney and Bonnie at his Surrey home in November. An item in the October 11 *New Musical Express* reported that not only Clapton, but John Lennon, George Harrison, and an unnamed Rolling Stone were interested in joining Delaney and Bonnie's upcoming British tour.

In the end, George attended the opening night concert at the Albert Hall on December 1 and was impressed enough to go backstage and sign up. Packing a couple of guitars and provisions for the week, George joined the tour beginning the very next day, playing shows in Bristol, Birmingham, Sheffield, Newcastle,

Liverpool, and Croydon: two shows a night for six straight days. As it wasn't a Beatles show, and George was just another band member, he was able to enjoy performing live probably for the first time in six years.

Several shows were apparently recorded for LP release, including the Albert Hall concerts, and those in Bristol and Croydon, but it's not clear which songs are from which date. Certainly **F** and **O** stem from the final night of the tour (before the encore, the promoter announces that he'll "keep Croydon a swinging place for big shows"). During **P**, Delaney introduces all the band members: "Tex [Johnson], Bobby Keys, Jim Price, Bobby Whitlock, [Rita] Coolidge, Carl Radle, Jim Gordon, Dave Mason, Eric Clapton, and my beautiful honey [Bonnie]." No mention of George, so presumably the song itself comes from the Albert Hall.

On the rest of the album, George's playing is scarcely notable, with Clapton and Mason handling the lead and slide guitar playing. While George reportedly sang a few oldies such as "Everybody's Trying to Be My Baby" over the course of the tour (most likely in Liverpool), no recorded evidence has surfaced. On the LP sleeve, he is credited merely as "Mysterioso," a pseudonym previously used for his work on Cream and Jack Bruce releases.

RELEASE HISTORY

1970: **A**–**Q** were released on the LP *Delaney & Bonnie & Friends On Tour with Eric Clapton,* reissued on CD in 1989.

156. Studio session

Date:	8 December 1969
Time:	10:00 a.m.–12:15 p.m.
Location:	EMI Studio 2
Producer:	George Martin

[A.] Octopus's Garden—take 10 (stereo) (2:46)

In the same vein as 1965's *Music of Lennon & McCartney,* ITV's Yorkshire franchise produced a TV special celebrating the talents of George Martin. Titled *With a Little Help from My Friends,* it was videotaped on December 14 in Leeds and broadcast Christmas Eve and/or Boxing Day, depending on which region you viewed it from.

Assembling the Beatles to contribute a performance was out of the question at this point, but Ringo did agree to lip-sync his latest composition, "Octopus's Garden," for the benefit of the cameras. While the videotape of the show has never surfaced, the newly recorded track prepared at Abbey Road still exists. On December 2, George Martin and Geoff Emerick prepared two new stereo mixes from the Beatles' original multitrack of the song, labeled "version 1 + 2 respectively" in the tape log. RS2 retained only the original drum and rhythm guitar track on one channel and some of the vocals and bubbling effects on the second.

On December 8, this mix was copied onto a new two-track tape with simultaneous overdubs: on the music channel, fresh lead guitar, piano, and bass performances were added (by unknown musicians), while on the other channel, Ringo recorded a brand-new lead vocal. This took ten takes to perfect, and a 15-inches-per-second copy of the last of these was taken away by one Gordon Cox, presumably a member of the TV production team.

The extreme stereo separation reveals a few hidden details. In the music channel, Ringo's original guide vocal from the Beatles' session can be heard leaking through his drum mics (he sings the first verse three times). In the vocal channel, you can hear Ringo chuckle before the line "resting our head," and at one point the original lead vocal track used to double his voice on the bridges is faded up a couple of words too early.

RELEASE HISTORY

1999: After circulating among collectors for years, a poor-quality off-line recording of **A** was booted on the CD-R *Telecasts Four.* That same year, an excellent copy surfaced among John Barrett's cassette material and was booted in mono on the CD *Through Many Years.* The same year, the bootleg CD *More Masters* included a pseudo–stereo mix of **A,** made from the isolated vocal channel, faded between lines of lyrics to mute cross-leakage from the music channel.

2001: A true stereo but slightly inferior-quality copy of **A** appeared on the CD-R *The Abbey Road Tape, Volume 2—Solo.*

Date: ca. 10 December 1969
Location: Apple Corps, London
Length: 2:14

John and Yoko's cause of the week was the capital punishment case of James Hanratty, hanged by the state in 1962 for committing a murder of which his parents insisted he was innocent. On December 10, John and Yoko posed with Mr. and Mrs. Hanratty in their office, announcing their support and intention to produce a film about the case. In the photos, a large placard reading BRITAIN MURDERED HANRATTY can be spotted, and the following evening, John and Yoko attended the premiere of *The Magic Christian,* parading past the theater brandishing a banner bearing the same slogan.

The placard is visible in the background of this interview, filmed around this time in John and Yoko's Apple office. John explains that giving peace a chance literally means that—trying something nobody has attempted before. He expounds on another slogan he would later develop into a song, "power to the people," explaining that it's no use blaming the government for war when the general populace decides who the leaders are.

RELEASE HISTORY

2007: This footage appeared in a Christmas message released online by Yoko Ono.

Date: 10–12 December 1969
Location: Falkoner Theatre, Copenhagen
Broadcast: 27 February 1970
DR-TV
Beat '70: "The Original Delaney & Bonnie & Friends"

[A.] Poor Elijah/Tribute to Robert Johnson (4:56)
[B.] intro (0:15)
[C.] Don't Know Why (4:57)
[D.] intro (0:21)
[E.] Where There's a Will, There's a Way (4:42)
[F.] intro (0:32)
[G.] My Baby Specializes (4:10)
[H.] intro (0:04)
[I.] I Don't Want to Discuss It (5:33)
[J.] intro (0:08)
[K.] That's What My Man Is For (4:49)
[L.] intro (0:32)
[M.] Coming Home (1:08)

In addition to the remaining British dates, George agreed to travel with the Delaney and Bonnie and Friends tour to Denmark for three dates at the Falkoner Theatre in Copenhagen. Two of the shows (probably both houses from the final night, although it's uncertain) were videotaped for Danish TV and combined for broadcast the following February on the series *Beat '70.*

George stays relatively anonymous again, getting no more screen time than most of the other band members and taking no guitar or vocal solos. He alternates between playing his Gibson Les Paul (on **C** and **K**) and his psychedelically hued Fender Stratocaster (on the other numbers). Also taking part in this performance are Delaney (lead vocal and guitar) and Bonnie (lead vocal and tambourine) Bramlett, Eric Clapton (guitar and lead vocal on **C**), Jim Gordon (drums), Carl Radle (bass), Rita Coolidge (backing vocal, tambourine), Bobby Whitlock (organ), Bobby Keys (saxophone), and Jim Price (trumpet).

During the British leg of the tour, Dave Mason had handled the slide guitar duet with Eric Clapton on "Coming Home." Mason was unable to continue on to Denmark but taught George his part, launching a trademark that would permeate George's solo career. It was also during this stint that George got the idea to write a gospel song, using the Edwin Hawkins Singers' recent hit "Oh Happy Day" (and not a certain Chiffons tune) as inspiration. "My Sweet Lord" would be recorded by Billy Preston and the Hawkins Singers early the next year, but the author's version would become a chart-topper.

NOTE

The song list above matches the video I was able to obtain and cuts off midway through "Coming Home." The bootleg LP *Falconer* reportedly has the full version of that song, plus the show-closing Little Richard medley, and presumably those songs exist on the complete video as well. Another song reportedly from one of the Copenhagen concerts, "Only You Know and I Know," appears on the bootleg CD boxed set *Artifacts III*.

RELEASE HISTORY

1995: **A**–**K** were included on the bootleg CD *Songs I Forgot*. The show (taped in monochrome) also circulates on video in excellent quality.

158. Radio interview   J

Date:	early December 1969
Location:	Apple Corps, London
Interviewer:	Don Chandler
Broadcast:	*Pop Goes the Bulldog*
Length:	15:27

In this era of unrelenting peace salesmanship from John, it comes as a welcome and refreshing anomaly to hear him talk about music. And not his and Yoko's "Unfinished Music," for a change, but the history of British pop, for a radio documentary on that very topic. The interview, taped at his office in Apple's headquarters, is extremely well illustrated with excerpts of the songs and musical concepts John discusses.

Casting his mind back, John figures British pop has its roots in folk songs that migrated from country to country, mutating and evolving into skiffle in England and rhythm and blues and rockabilly in the United States. Although he used to imitate pop singers such as Johnny Ray and Frankie Laine, the first one to make an impact on John was Elvis Presley with "Heartbreak Hotel." When he first heard the artist and song name, John assumed it was another corny crooner peddling schlock. One listen convinced him otherwise, and Little Richard delivered the knockout blow with "Long Tall Sally": "After that, I just lost interest in everything else but rock-and-roll."

He compares Elvis's "Mystery Train" to skiffle songs such as "Railroad Bill," "Rock Island Line," and "Long Lost John," and he recounts the derision the Quarry Men faced when their repertoire switched from skiffle to electrified rock-and-roll. By the time they returned from the 1960 stint in Hamburg, the Beatles found it easy to stand out amid Liverpool's mass of genteel vocal groups with matching stage suits and pretentious lead singers.

In an astute bit of musical analysis, John explains how the "Mersey Beat" was created by British drummers who latched on to the heavy rhythms of piano and saxes in rock and R & B records rather than aping the swinging backbeat laid down by most American drummers. He points to the Dave Clark Five's records as the epitome of this sound. Nowadays, John feels that British rock has lost its way as an innovator, being mired in blues revivals and postpsychedelia.

The experimental side of Beatles music is traced from John Cage and Karlheinz Stockhausen through the tape loops in "Tomorrow Never Knows" and "A Day in the Life," which the interviewer calls "a terribly bold step." John downplays its achievement, insisting that "it's no secret we're gettin' from the hills . . . The Beatles are part of the movement, not *the* movement." He goes on to predict the imminent fusion of rock music and jazz from both ends of the continuum.

Asked the inevitable question about future Beatles concerts, John stresses how far apart they have drifted: "Whether we'll do anything together again is a . . . mute [sic] point." Although the concert in Toronto had whetted his appetite for live performances, he clearly doesn't want to be tied down again to a lengthy concert tour, preferring to play when and where he feels like it, with whoever is available. Within a few days, such an opportunity would present itself.

RELEASE HISTORY

This interview circulates among collectors in very good quality.

159. Radio interview

Date: early December 1969
Location: Apple Corps, London
Interviewer: Tony Macarthur
Broadcast: Radio Luxembourg
Length: 25:36

Along the lines of earlier profiles of the albums *The Beatles, Life with the Lions,* and *Abbey Road,* Radio Luxembourg's Tony Macarthur sat down for an in-depth examination of *Live Peace in Toronto 1969* with John and Yoko, discussing and then playing each track from the album.

After relating the events that led him to play at the Rock and Roll Revival, John says he has no interest in forming a permanent Plastic Ono Band, preferring to keep the lineup changeable. He also seems unenthusiastic about the prospect of any more Beatles concerts; clearly the negative response to Bob Dylan's set at the Isle of Wight has made him apprehensive about living up to heightened expectations (he also overestimates the Toronto crowd by a factor of five to ten!).

John explains that he used to sing "Blue Suede Shoes" with the Quarry Men before handing over the task to George, and he admits that he was nervous for the first couple of songs in Toronto. Songs such as "Money" and "Dizzy Miss Lizzy" were chosen not only because they were familiar favorites of John's, but were also easy for a newly formed band to pick up quickly. Macarthur asks if the concert was filmed, and John says that they obtained the rights to D. A. Pennebaker's film of their set, which they will "try and show" at some point.

Asked about the recently canceled Plastic Ono Band single, John gives the history of "You Know My Name (Look Up the Number)," saying that he'd thought it would make a good Christmas release, but that the other Beatles suddenly decided they wanted to release

the venerable recording on the B-side of "Let It Be," which is due out in January.

Introducing "Yer Blues," John remembers playing it with Eric Clapton previously, but incorrectly states that Clapton wasn't part of the *Rock and Roll Circus.* "Cold Turkey" was a brand-new song but easy enough to busk, even though Yoko was holding the lyric sheet just out of John's line of vision! He denies that the lyrics are strictly drug-related, saying he often writes a song around a title phrase he likes the sound of ("I'm a Loser" and "Day Tripper," for example) and that "cold turkey" can refer to any kind of pain or suffering.

After reiterating the logic behind returning his MBE, John says there will be another peace event around Christmas "which is a surprise" (the "War Is Over" poster campaign). Macarthur asks for an explanation of the subtitle "Mummy's Only Looking for Her Hand in the Snow," and Yoko is hardly forthcoming: "Well, why would anything be called anything, you know?" John explains that "John, John (Let's Hope for Peace)" was improvised, with the band playing against Yoko's vocal as though it were a lead saxophone or guitar, and claiming that the other musicians were "turned on" by the performance.

The show concludes with a description of the calendar included with the LP's first pressing, and John continues to plug Yoko's book *Grapefruit* even as Macarthur tries to sign off.

RELEASE HISTORY

This interview circulates among collectors in fair quality from an off-air recording. A bit of it was included on the 1976 vinyl bootleg *Away with Words,* and a good-quality extract was released on the 1999 CD *Man in the Clouds.*

160. Radio interview

Date: 12 December 1969
Location: Apple Corps
Interviewer: Harry Flower
Broadcast: South Africa
Length: 7:10

The plugging continued with an interview for a most unlikely outlet: South African radio, which had banned all Beatles records in the wake of the "bigger than Jesus" fiasco. John urges listeners to buy his new Plastic Ono Band album nonetheless and recounts how rapidly the Toronto gig came together. The interviewer,

one Harry Flower, points out that the ban has in fact been lifted, at least on one station, which is donating ninety minutes to promoting *Abbey Road.* John replies, "Let 'em do one on the Plastic Ono LP and I'll really thank 'em," and arranges for Flower to take a copy of the album back with him.

Discussing future plans, John mentions the *Get Back* album and film, due in January and February, respectively, and says that the Plastic Ono Band will also have a single out in January. ("I haven't recorded it yet.") He gives a sneak preview of the "War Is Over" poster event and an imminent visit to Toronto to arrange a peace festival. John then tries to recruit Bag Productions representatives in South Africa, offering any interested parties to write him in London, c/o Apple, 3 Savile Row.

John explains that they have already begun filming the Hanrattys' weekly public protests in Hyde Park but are waiting for a more professional documentarian to helm the project as director. On the fourteenth, the next of these protests took place at Speaker's Corner, with a "substitute John and Yoko" participating from

within the safety of a white bag. Apart from Yoko's exclamation at a UNICEF benefit (see the December 15 entry), little more was heard from the couple about the matter.

RELEASE HISTORY

This interview circulates among collectors in poor quality from an off-air recording.

161. Radio interview   R

Date:	15 December 1969
Location:	Apple Corps, London
Interviewer:	Kenny Everett
Broadcast:	25 December 1969, 10:00–10:15 a.m.
	BBC Radio 1
	Kenny Everett's Christmas Show
Length:	2:11

Each Christmas season, BBC Radio broadcast several charity appeals, including one in benefit of the British Wireless for the Blind Fund. This year, Ringo agreed to record the solicitation message at Apple, for airing in Kenny Everett's Christmas morning special.

Near the start of the broadcast, Kenny plays a teaser of the tape, telling Ringo to be patient for about

ten minutes. At fifteen past, Ringo delivers his loosely scripted plea, imploring listeners to send in donations and not "get stuck into your turkey and forget all about it." With some confusion about postal codes, Ringo reads out the fund's address twice, with Everett promising that Chris Denning will repeat the address yet again after the next record. Despite Ringo's participation, only £175 was raised for the cause.

RELEASE HISTORY

1998: A good-quality off-line copy of this recording was included on the bootleg CD *The Ultimate Beatles Christmas Collection.*

162. TV interview   J

Date:	15 December 1969
Location:	Apple Corps, London
Broadcast:	29 December 1969 (?)
	AVRO-TV
	Televiezer Magazine
Length:	3:10

Unveiling a plan that had been in the works for several months, John and Yoko's Christmas advertising blitz was launched in eleven major cities around the world beginning December 16. In each city, billboards, handbills, and posters were unveiled, declaring WAR IS OVER! in large type, with IF YOU WANT IT and HAPPY CHRISTMAS FROM JOHN & YOKO beneath.

A reporter from a Dutch TV news magazine filmed an interview with the couple at their Apple office the day they announced the campaign, seated conspicuously in front of a wall full of "War Is Over" posters in several languages. Calling it a part of their ongoing

peace crusade, John mentions that an ad agency is currently working on a similar antiracism promotion.

After naming the eleven cities, John is asked why war-torn places such as Saigon and Tel Aviv aren't among them. He says they had enough trouble getting posters distributed in London, and separates the cities into two groups: those where friends arranged the event (Tokyo, Amsterdam, Montreal, Toronto) and those where a publicity firm was hired for the task (Paris, Berlin, Rome, Athens). Apparently Apple was in charge of things in New York, and John laments, "It'll probably be the worst!" He reveals that about two thousand small posters will go up in each city, plus large billboards wherever possible, and concedes that he'll have to write a couple of hit songs to recoup his costs.

RELEASE HISTORY

This interview circulates among collectors on video.

Date: 15 December 1969
Location: Lyceum Ballroom, London
Producer: Geoff Emerick

[A.] **intro** (0:54)
[B.] **Cold Turkey** (6:35)
[C.] **intro** (1:41)
[D.] **Don't Worry Kyoko (Mummy's Only Looking for Her Hand in the Snow)** (14:02)
[E.] **outro** (1:30)

Toward the end of November, the organizers of a concert to benefit UNICEF announced that the Plastic Ono Band would be putting in an appearance at the event. This was news to John and Yoko, but they eventually agreed to perform, realizing it would be a chance to publicize their "War Is Over" poster campaign.

The core band members were contacted: Alan White, Klaus Voormann, and Eric Clapton. Fortune smiled on the Plastic Ono Band when Clapton unexpectedly showed up at the Lyceum with nearly the entire Delaney and Bonnie touring ensemble. Suddenly John and George would be performing in concert together for the first time in more than three years.

Assembled onstage in front of a huge "War Is Over" backdrop were John, George, Eric, and Delaney (guitars, with Eric playing George's psychedelic Fender Strat), Yoko (vocals), Bonnie Bramlett (tambourine), Alan White and Jim Gordon (drums), Billy Preston (keyboards), Klaus Voormann (bass), Bobby Keys (saxophone), Jim Price (trumpet), and hanger-on Keith Moon walloping White's floor tom. Also present were Bonzo Dog Band drummer Larry "Legs" Smith and Rascals drummer Dino Danelli, although it's unclear if they participated in the performance.

John and Yoko, dressed in white, each got a chance to sing their side of the latest Plastic Ono Band single. After a minute of microphone testing and feedback (**A**), John announces, "We'd like to do a number. This song's about pain." The band launches into a decent rendition of "Cold Turkey" (**B**), with Yoko at John's feet inside a white bag. More fiddling with mics and tuning (**C**), and then Yoko yells, "John! I love you! Britain! You killed Hanratty, you murderer!" receiving a smattering of startled applause.

"Don't Worry Kyoko" (**D**) reportedly lasted an epic forty minutes, and Geoff Emerick, recording the show on four-track tape, was forced to change reels midway through. Edits are audible at 1:38, 2:37, and 5:13, and there are undoubtedly others. The lyrics consist of "Hanratty!" and "Kyoko!" for the most part, and the only point of interest is a brief call-and-response between Yoko and the horn section. Toward the end, she repeats the phrase "Don't . . . Wor . . . reee" (which one journalist misheard as "War! Peace!"). Drummer Alan White, wondering how the hell to bring this eternal jam to an end, eventually plays faster and faster until the whole band is forced to come crashing down to earth. "Peace to you, baby!" exclaims Yoko as the crowd implausibly cries for more.

The fidelity of the recording is predictably muddy, given the volume of the stage level and the fact that Emerick had only four band tracks and two separate audience tracks to capture it all. He prepared stereo mixes on December 17, but John decided against releasing them at the time, feeling that the vocals weren't recorded well. On November 26, 1970, the day John and Yoko left for a visit to the United States, the four-track masters were copied.

It wasn't until the following October, during sessions for "Happy Xmas (War Is Over)" at the Record Plant East in New York, that John polished up the Lyceum recordings. Nicky Hopkins added electric piano to replace Preston's buried performance. It's probable John also touched up his vocals (the echo doesn't exactly match his singing in spots). The performance was scheduled to be released that Christmas as part of a *Live Jam* LP, but it was held back and packaged with John and Yoko's 1972 album *Some Time in New York City*. A Movietone newsreel capturing part of the Lyceum concert also exists.

RELEASE HISTORY

1972: **A–E** were released on the LP *Some Time in New York City,* on the "bonus album" *Live Jam*. It's also available on CD, although that source fades the crowd noise of **E** 8 seconds early.

164. Studio session

Date: mid-late December 1969
Location: London
Producer: George Harrison

[A.] All That I've Got (I'm Gonna Give It to You) (3:29)

In October, the single "Everything's All Right" was pulled from Billy Preston's debut Apple LP, but it failed to stir much interest. He was scheduled to return to England in the first week of November to record a new single, but work permit hassles delayed this visit until after the Delaney and Bonnie tour, which Billy had reportedly joined in Denmark (although he's not visible during the *Beat '70* telecast). With George producing again, the sessions produced at least two contenders; Billy's composition "Right Now" was considered but held back for his next album, *Encouraging Words*.

The song eventually chosen for the A-side was a number Billy cowrote with Doris Troy, "All That I've Got (I'm Gonna Give It to You)," very much in the vein of the soul-rock numbers on Billy's album. In addition to Billy's vocal, piano, and organ, the song features a horn section and tambourine. Ringo was recruited to play drums, and it's been reported that George contributed guitar, so perhaps he plays the bass (no lead or rhythm guitar is audible).

RELEASE HISTORY

1970: **A** was released on a single, which failed to chart in the UK and peaked at number 108 in the United States.

1993: **A** was included as a bonus track on Apple's CD reissue of *Encouraging Words*.

165. Press conference

Date: 17 December 1969
Location: Ontario Science Center, Toronto
Length: 53:26

On December 16, John and Yoko flew to Canada to launch what they hoped would be the beginning of "Year One A.P. (After Peace)," the latest and most grandiose phase of their antiwar campaign. Instead it would mark the end of their protest activities for a couple of years: Apart from the "War Is Over" poster event, none of the plans they announced to the media at a press conference the next day would take flight.

John opens the proceedings by reading the details of an international peace festival, to be held July 3–5 of the following year at Mosport Park, a speedway near Toronto. The proceeds from the concert would fund a peace committee, to be organized by Rabbi Abraham Feinberg with unclear aims. The question of whether the artists will be paid for their service is raised, with John repeatedly claiming the matter is unsettled: "We said we're gonna pay the musicians. Whether I'm included in that or not, I don't know . . . If I get the Beatles, I might have to pay 'em!"

Someone wonders whether John has tried to sell the other Beatles on performing concerts for peace, and he replies that he was able to get George for the UNICEF benefit and will try to "hustle" not only his bandmates, but the entire Apple roster, and even Elvis Presley, into playing at the peace festival. It's mentioned that Ringo is against touring, and John points out that George once opposed the idea, but had a great time on the road with Delaney and Bonnie and Friends. As for the Beatles' future, John claims that every album they've made since the end of touring could potentially have been their last, and that the situation is again up in the air.

Other proposed projects that never came to fruition were a peace ship to cruise international waters broadcasting messages of world harmony, and a peace vote, whereby "all the youth in the world" could choose peace or war, with the result being a sort of petition to demonstrate the will of the people to world leaders. Although a few reporters challenge the naivete of all these ideas, the general vibe is sympathetic, which is undoubtedly why John and Yoko chose to keep returning to Canada. (John readily admits he's scared to go to Vietnam, Biafra, or China, because "I don't wanna be a martyr.")

Asked what inspired their yearlong campaign, John describes receiving a conscience-nudging letter from filmmaker Peter Watkins: "It was like getting your call-up papers for peace." He also dismisses the notion that a neat haircut and smart suit would help get across his message: "Politicians do that. Now, how many members of the public are gullible to politicians, with the nice picture of the family, the dog, and a whore on the side?" He also refuses to be labeled as leader of a peace movement, calling such a role "dictatorship," but also not wanting to take the credit or blame for any results.

He has little problem assigning blame when it comes to drugs, claiming that users are not at fault, but rather it's the high-pressure society in which they live. John confesses that he took drugs when he felt hopeless but denies that having fame or money is a way of achieving hope: "We have exactly the same paranoias of everybody else, the same petty thoughts."

RELEASE HISTORY

Portions of this press conference were released on the CDs *John Lennon Forever, Rare Photos & Interview CD, Volume 2,* and *Inside Interviews: In My Life: John Lennon & Paul McCartney.* Footage from near the start was included in the CBC-TV documentary *A Visit for Peace,* which circulates on video (see the 17–22 December entry).

166. Radio interview   J

Date:	17 December 1969
Time:	evening
Location:	Ronnie Hawkins's Farm, Mississauga
Interviewer:	Howard Smith
Broadcast:	WABC-AM, New York City
Length:	86:47

Village Voice reporter Howard Smith was able to tape two phone interviews with John and Yoko during the Montreal bed-in. When they returned to North America in December, Smith was invited to travel up to Toronto for an in-person interview. It was conducted at a farmhouse on Mississauga Road on the outskirts of Toronto, where John and Yoko were staying as guests of rock musician Ronnie Hawkins. As the couple dined on stir-fried veggies and shrimp tempura, Smith taped their lengthy and rambling conversation.

Many of the topics, themes, and anecdotes are repeated elsewhere and are covered in other entries, including peace, the Hanratty case, Michael X, the MBE, reggae, and Bagism. Here are some of the other highlights:

- The stage for the international peace festival was going to be a giant bed.
- John and Yoko were approached to donate their time to a U.S. grapes boycott.
- The "War Is Over" poster event was previewed by one person in New York displaying the slogan on a sandwich board.
- John reveals that Ringo and George have both left the band for a few days each.
- One of the longtime Beatle associates fired by Klein was an "incompetent" and "nasty" guy who "gave it to the office girls," but the group could never bring themselves to sack him.
- Smith asks if John will charge admission to the peace festival, and he is unequivocal: "Oh sure, sure."
- After a ten-day rice diet in Greece, John relapsed in Bombay with curry and milkshakes: "It was like having every drug I've ever touched."
- Laying 90:1 odds against any more Beatles tours, John says he might be interested if Yoko, Billy Preston, Eric Clapton, and Elvis Presley played alongside the band.
- John thought Ringo's appearance on *Line-Up* (see the December 1 entry) was funnier than all of *The Magic Christian.*
- Yoko says that the 54 seconds John trimmed from "Revolution 9" was a pretty good part, and John says he wanted to couple "Revolution 1" and "Revolution 9" as a single but was vetoed.
- Although they didn't end up going, John and Yoko were penciled in to attend the MIDEM music business festival in Cannes the following January as Apple representatives; always eager for a gimmick, they decide to have another wedding ceremony while there.
- Asked what he listens to, John mentions recent discs by Johnny Winter and Lee Dorsey.
- John's had a faux-fur coat made out of human hair, which looks like "hundreds of Yoko's heads."

Smith was a good foil for John and Yoko because he let them speak their minds but also challenged their more outlandish ideas and tempered their daydreams with a dose of reality.

RELEASE HISTORY

This interview circulates in excellent quality among collectors.

Date:	18 December 1969
Time:	morning
Location:	Ronnie Hawkins's Farm, Mississauga
Length:	9:56

On their second morning in Toronto, John and Yoko taped a message for Japanese listeners, possibly for radio broadcast on the "peace network" they were assembling, although our source seems to be a two-sided acetate or single.

It opens with John and Yoko speaking a bit of Japanese to introduce their duet rendition of "Give Peace a Chance," accompanied by John's acoustic guitar; this lasts about a minute and ends with John repeatedly exclaiming "moshi-moshi."

The balance of the recording is Yoko talking in Japanese (which she admits is a bit rusty), while John plays acoustic guitar in the background, injecting another "moshi-moshi" at one point, and stopping briefly to answer the phone. He begins with some fingerpicking in A major, resembling a number of recent Lennon compositions, and segues into a rendition of a work in progress, "Make Love Not War" (which would become "Mind Games"), in C. Switching to the key of E, he plays a shuffle boogie and then the " 'Sun' riff" before detuning his low E string to D for a lengthy instrumental rendition of "Dear Prudence."

Yoko fills in Japanese fans on the plans for the peace festival and "Year One," urges correspondents to get to the point quickly, and says that she and John recently vacationed in India and escaped to Rome from there. Expressing a desire to return to Japan with John in 1970, Yoko says she's been telling John what a wonderful country it is, something that would have been difficult for him to gauge from the confines of the Tokyo Hilton in 1966.

RELEASE HISTORY

1985: This recording was included on the vinyl bootleg *Doll's House*.

1989: The rendition of "Give Peace a Chance," probably lifted straight from a copy of the bootleg, was broadcast on episode 89-48 of the radio series *The Lost Lennon Tapes*. It appears from that source on the 1992 vinyl bootleg *The Lost Lennon Tapes, Volume 24*.

167a. TV interview J

Date:	18 December 1969
Time:	afternoon
Location:	Ronnie Hawkins's Farm, Mississauga
Interviewer:	Nick Steed, Ken Cavanaugh
Broadcast:	18 December 1969
	CBC-TV
	CBC Weekday
Length:	7:56

Dressed in black from head to toe, John and Yoko met various reporters at Ronnie's farmhouse to elucidate upon their earlier press conference. For this CBC-TV interview, John and Yoko are seated at a table in front of one of the medium-size "War Is Over" posters, with a smaller one propped up in front of the microphones.

John explains why he doesn't feel the need to have short hair to get his message across, comparing it with how easily the "long-haired" early Beatles were able to succeed. Asked about Pierre Trudeau, John says the Canadian prime minister made a good impression on a visit to England and "does seem to be this side of the stone age." John encourages people to create their own peace posters and admits he has no more of an idea about whether the peace campaign will succeed than he did about the fate of the Beatles when they were playing at the Cavern Club.

RELEASE HISTORY

2006: This interview was included as a bonus feature on the DVD *Give Peace a Song*.

168. Newsreel footage

J

Date: 18 December 1969
Time: evening
Location: Ronnie Hawkins's Farm, Mississauga
Interviewer: Bob (?)
Length: 3:24

Sipping tea and smoking, John explains to "Bob" (an Associated Press reporter) why they've returned to Toronto for the latest leg of their peace campaign. He gets in plugs for the planned festival at "Monsoon Park" (Bob corrects this to Mosport Park) and the Beatles' next album and film, both scheduled for February release at this point.

John also holds up a copy of the Plastic Ono Band's *Live Peace in Toronto* LP, released December 16 in Canada. John had brought twenty copies of the album from London but surrendered twelve of these to customs at the airport to avoid paying duty fees. Bob ends the interview on a polite if slightly confused note: "Thank you very much, John. And you too, Ono."

RELEASE HISTORY

This color AP footage circulates on video among collectors.

169. TV interview

J

Date: ca. 18 December 1969
Time: evening
Location: Ronnie Hawkins's Farm, Mississauga
Length: 4:22

This interview with an unknown journalist was filmed during John and Yoko's stay at the farmhouse as the couple enjoyed a spot of tea, probably the same day as the Associated Press interview above.

John praises Canada for offering to help, complaining that most of the mail they get consists of "begging letters" that always seem to correspond to whatever is going on in the Lennons' life. ("We were married too, but my wife died and me leg fell off and me head went black.") Asked to define peace, John admits that he communicates in monosyllables and jingles, but sums it up with "Don't hurt people."

He talks about returning the MBE, claiming that he'd considered the move for a long time, but kept putting it off, akin to visiting the dentist. John also consid-

ers becoming a skinhead "in appearance only" should a new look be needed to publicize his cause. He and Yoko would come pretty close the following month, cropping off most of their hair while in Denmark.

The reporter brings up the "Cold Turkey" promotional film that "we just got from you," suggesting that he's with a TV station, perhaps the CBC network. John explains that the film was prepared by Jonas Mekas to go with "Give Peace a Chance," and he and Yoko express amazement at how well it synced up with "Cold Turkey" instead (both songs are around five minutes long).

RELEASE HISTORY

1995: A very small portion of this interview was released on the CD *Inside Interviews: In My Life: John Lennon & Paul McCartney*. The full clip circulates on video among collectors.

170. TV interview

J

Date: 20 December 1969
Time: evening
Location: University of Toronto
Broadcast: CBS-TV
Length: 4:59

During the Montreal bed-in, CBC Television had arranged for John and Yoko to meet with Al Capp and Dick Gregory, among others, filming the result for broadcast (and posterity). This time around, it was a U.S. network, CBS, that scheduled and filmed a sum-

mit with author and communication pundit Marshall McLuhan.

The conversation took place at the department of culture and technology at the University of Toronto, and while it lasted forty-five minutes, the only footage to surface from that day is a brief follow-up interview with a CBS reporter, with no sign of McLuhan. As the clip opens, the reporter is chatting with John about the *Abbey Road* album, revealing that he used to work in a film studio on that very road. After an edit, John comments on the "straight" lyrics to an unknown song of his. Once the cameraman is set, the actual interview commences.

Asked whether all the crusading will conflict with his art, John replies that art has no limits and that the reporter, the people watching at home, and the exercise of the interview itself are all art. John explains that each country has a prototypical reaction to the peace campaign and refers to a McLuhan comment about Canada's lack of a national identity. Generally speaking, the English refused to listen or take him and Yoko seriously. John isn't sure what the Americans' response has been but has a feeling it plays better in New York than in the Deep South.

After plugging the "War Is Over" poster event, John and Yoko offer a Christmas wish of "peace on earth." After a break to change film reels, John elaborates on this aspiration: "That implies no violence. No starving children. No violent minds, no violent households. No violence." The reporter points out what a monumental goal that is, but Yoko feels that in the age of instant communication, it'll take only a year or two to achieve.

RELEASE HISTORY

1996: A slightly incomplete audio copy of this interview was released on the CD *Fab Four CD & Book Set*. The complete color clip circulates on video from the CBS News vault.

171. TV interview   J

Date:	20 December 1969
Time:	10:15–11:15 p.m.
Location:	CBC Studio, Toronto
Interviewer:	Lloyd Robertson
Broadcast:	live
	CBC-TV
	CBC Weekend
Length:	11:13

John, Yoko, and Rabbi Abraham Feinberg were guests on the live news magazine *CBC Weekend,* with John even introducing the show specifically as "Peace Weekend."

Legislator Russell Doern, appearing via a linkup from Winnipeg, begins the segment by reading a letter from the premier of Manitoba asking John and Yoko to visit in 1970 to promote peace. John declares the offer "beautiful" and says he'll "definitely" be there for the province's 100th anniversary year. (The trip was never arranged.)

John explains yet again why he chose Canada rather than Vietnam or Biafra as a location for his peace crusade: "I don't want to be Mr. and Mrs. Dead Saint of 1970." Rabbi Feinberg is asked whether the whole enterprise is a waste of time, but he feels that the peace festival is a worthy and realistic project, as "it's intended to leap over the politicians and reach the people."

RELEASE HISTORY

Two brief segments of this show were rebroadcast in the 2000 CBC-TV special *The Passionate Eye: John & Yoko's Year of Peace,* which was released on DVD in 2002. The complete interview (minus the "Peace Weekend" intro) is included as a bonus feature on the 2006 DVD *Give Peace a Song.*

172. TV documentary   J

Date:	17–22 December 1969
Location:	various, Toronto
Broadcast:	CBC-TV
	A Visit for Peace
Length:	27:36

While not as extensive as *The Way It Is,* CBC-TV again produced a documentary covering John and Yoko's visit to Canada, specifically their six days in Toronto. It opens with footage of their arrival at the Ontario Science Center, followed by a lengthy segment of the press conference. The bulk of the show was filmed at Ronnie Hawkins's house one snowy day (probably the eighteenth).

A CBC reporter interviews John and Yoko, seated next to a Christmas tree holding a pair of stuffed white doves (supplied by Capitol of Canada "to make us feel at home"). John describes some of the ideas that led up to the "War Is Over" posters, such as a *War of the Worlds*–style hoax broadcast announcing that peace had been declared worldwide. He explains that they keep returning to Canada because people there take them seriously and offer assistance.

A brief interview clip with Rabbi Abraham Feinberg follows, and then John holds up the *Live Peace in Toronto* album, hoping that enough people will buy it to help pay for the peace campaign. He compares the situation to the financing of their films, which they had to pay for themselves and then try to recoup the money by finding distributors. After discussing the reasoning behind some of their unorthodox methods of protesting, John reveals that even his family considers him naive to hope for peace, but he feels "they don't know from Adam what's going on."

At this point the cameraman, evidently using a ten-minute reel, runs out of film. After a reload, John describes the search for meaning that followed the Beatles' massive success. After their final tour, John in particular sank into a depression that was lifted only by uniting with Yoko. He praises her optimism, intelli-

gence, and strength, and Yoko agrees that they are far more creative and prolific as a team.

John and Yoko are then seen riding a "Motoski" through the snow at Hawkins's farm and finally arriving at Union Station on the morning of the twenty-second with Anthony Fawcett and Ritchie Yorke to board the glass-enclosed observation car of the train that would take them to Montreal and Ottawa.

RELEASE HISTORY

This documentary circulates in excellent quality on video. The majority of the soundtrack was released on the CD *Bedism,* missing about five minutes (mostly narration, but including bits of the press conference and interview).

173. Press conference   J

Date: 22 December 1969
Location: Château Champlain, Montreal
Length: 0:22

En route to Ottawa, John and Yoko stopped over in Montreal for the day "just to say hello." For them, that meant holding a press conference at a local hotel, dressed in black and surrounded by "War Is Over"

posters. In this brief clip, John insists that if he preached to teenagers about drug use, it would fall on deaf ears but says "there's nothing like being straight."

RELEASE HISTORY

This color footage was included in the documentary *Imagine: John Lennon,* available on DVD.

174. Newsreel footage   J

Date: 23 December 1969
Time: 10:55 a.m.–noon
Location: Centre Block, Parliament Building, Ottawa
Length: 1:06

Long in the offing, John and Yoko's meeting with Canadian prime minister Pierre Trudeau was finally confirmed over the telephone on December 21. The Lennon entourage left Montreal via train the following night, arriving in Ottawa at 2 a.m. on the twenty-third. By 11 a.m., they were at the Parliament building, and flash-bulbs popped as the politician met the peace ambassadors. The tête-à-tête took place behind closed doors and lasted nearly an hour, but news cameras documented the before and after.

When John and Yoko finally emerge, a reporter asks what took so long. John seems oblivious, but Yoko says it was because they were all enjoying the conversation. John adds the oft-quoted sound bite "If all politicians were like Mr. Trudeau, there would be world peace."

John and Yoko also met with health minister John Munro for nearly two hours before flying back to Toronto and, from there, home to London.

RELEASE HISTORY

This newsreel footage was broadcast in the 2000 CBC-TV special *The Passionate Eye: John & Yoko's Year of Peace,* which was released on DVD in 2002.

174a. Interview

Date: 23 December 1969
Location: Toronto
Interviewer: Ritchie Yorke
Length: 0:24

In this interview with Toronto journalist Ritchie Yorke (later published in *Rolling Stone*), John makes it clear that he and the Beatles are no longer on the same page: "Paul did a good job in holding us together for a few years, while we were sort of undecided what to do, y'know. And I found out what to do, and it didn't really have to be with the Beatles. It could have been, if they want it, but it got that I couldn't wait for them to make up their mind about peace, or whatever. About committing themselves. It's the same as the songs. So I've gone ahead."

RELEASE HISTORY

1972: This interview was included in part twelve of the BBC Radio documentary *The Beatles Story*.

---

175. Speech

Date: 26–27 December 1969
Location: Tittenhurst
Length: 5:30

After returning to London for the Christmas holidays, John and Yoko recorded a radio message to promote the International Peace Festival in Canada. This may have been offered to a loose "peace network" of more than four hundred radio stations in the United States and thirty-five in Canada.

It begins with John's announcement that 1970 will be "year one" of a new era in peace, and reassurance that he and Yoko will return to Canada by July in time for the festival. To avoid any problems such as the violence at the recent Rolling Stones concert at Altamont Speedway, John implores listeners to start creating a peaceful climate. Yoko suggests that people hang bedsheets outside their windows as a white flag to "surrender to peace."

She goes on to relate that after the bed-in events, when they saw little immediate result, they began to believe all their doubters and sink into a depression. But toward the end of the year, particularly when they returned to Canada, they began to see the fruits of their labor borne. John once again stresses that people hold their fate in their own hands (thus the choice of "War Is Over If You Want It" for a slogan). He confides that they know all too well how easy it is to lose hope and try to numb the pain by escaping into hard drug use. John says not to fall for the desire to "turn on and drop out, man, 'cause you've gotta turn on and drop in. Or they're gonna drop all over you."

He and Yoko urge "hippies" to live up to their title and rather than turn their backs on the "unaware" establishment, to do their best to enlighten and edify the older generation. Yoko points out that remaining an exclusive faction by shunning people who have short hair will ultimately doom the peace movement. The message closes with another announcement of "Peace" and "Hope" year one, and a desire that the peace festival will start a worldwide trend.

RELEASE HISTORY

1970: This interview appeared on the vinyl bootleg *Get Back to Toronto,* issued on numerous labels with various lineups.

---

176. Speech

Date: late December 1969
Location: Apple Corps, London (?)
Length: 1:28

As a gesture of thanks, John agreed to record a promotional spot for Ronnie Hawkins's new single, "Down in the Alley." It was probably taped upon his return to London at the end of December and distributed to radio stations in February 1970 (a quote from the message appeared in ad copy for the single the week of February 28).

John explains that he knew Hawkins from his 1959 single "Forty Days" but had never met him until the visit to his farm. He recalls listening to a copy of Hawkins's latest recordings while signing his "Bag One" lithographs, and that "Down in the Alley" particularly caught his ear. At one point, John stops himself to interject, "I hope this isn't too long for a promo." Just in case it was, John recorded a separate message, lasting a mere 6 seconds, stating his name and introducing the song.

The two were coupled on a white-label single (Cotillion PRO-104/105), with the "Short Rap" on side 1 and the "Long Rap" on side 2. It didn't seem to help much, as "Down in the Alley" got little airplay and failed to reach the charts.

RELEASE HISTORY

1970: These recordings were released on a promotional single, *John Lennon on Ronnie Hawkins*. They've been copied on bootlegs such as *The Stereo Walk*.

1970: WILL YOU FORGIVE ME?

January 4   Paul, George, and Ringo's last task together in a recording studio for twenty-four years, adding overdubs to the song "Let It Be." John is still occupied in Denmark.

January 14   George purchases the Friar Park estate in Henley-on-Thames.

January 15   Bag One, an exhibition of John's lithographs, opens at the London Arts Gallery. More than half the etchings are confiscated by the police the following day as obscene and indecent material.

January 20   John and Yoko trade in their mop-tops for buzz cuts.

January 25   John and Yoko fly back to London from Denmark, with a brief stop in Paris due to fog.

January 26   Ringo and Maureen fly from London to Los Angeles.

January 29   Ringo attends the American premiere of his film *The Magic Christian* at the Four Star Theater, followed by a party at the Beverly Hills Hotel.

January 30   Ringo and Maureen attend an Elvis Presley show in Las Vegas, flying back to Los Angeles the following day.

February 1   Ringo and Maureen fly from Los Angeles to New York.

February 2   Ringo and Maureen fly from New York back to London.

February 4   John and Yoko hold a joint peace/black power ceremony on the rooftop of the Black Centre.

February 6   UK release of the Plastic Ono Band's "Instant Karma!"/"Who Has Seen the Wind?" single.

February 10   Paul begins recording sessions for his first LP at Morgan Studios around this date.

February 16   At Soho Street Studio, John and Yoko continue editing the raw footage of their Montreal bed-in.

February 20   U.S. release of the Plastic Ono Band's "Instant Karma!"/"Who Has Seen the Wind?" single.

February 26   U.S. release of *Hey Jude* (aka *The Beatles Again*) LP.

March 5   Newly pregnant Yoko checks into the London Clinic for medical observation, accompanied by John.

March 6   UK release of "Let It Be"/"You Know My Name (Look Up the Number)" single.

March 9   Yoko checks out of the London Clinic, followed closely by John.

March 11   U.S. release of "Let It Be"/"You Know My Name (Look Up the Number)" single.

March 12   George and Pattie move out of Kinfauns and into a mansion in Henley-on-Thames.

March 17   Ringo and Maureen attend Pattie Harrison's twenty-fifth birthday party, thrown by George at his new mansion in Henley-on-Thames.

March 27   UK release of Ringo's *Sentimental Journey* LP.

April 1   Final recording session for a Beatles album, overseen by Phil Spector and attended by Ringo.

Date: 3 January 1970
Time: 2:30 p.m.–12:15 a.m.
Location: EMI Studio 2
Producer: George Martin

[A.] I Me Mine—take 15 (intro) and take 16 (1:44)

[B.] I Me Mine—take 16 (1:44)

[C.] I Me Mine—RS1 (1:45)
Mixed: 5 January 1970

[D.] I Me Mine—RS from take 16 (2:19)

While Glyn Johns's completed *Get Back* LP mouldered on the shelf, editing of Michael Lindsay-Hogg's documentary film continued. After the final cut was completed in October 1969, it was decided to make the album a soundtrack companion to the film's theatrical release. To this end, Glyn was told to reconfigure the lineup to better reflect the film's contents. This meant dropping "Teddy Boy," which wasn't seen in the film, and adding a couple of songs that were, George's "I Me Mine" and John's "Across the Universe."

Glyn got to work on December 15 and twenty-first at Olympic and was able to add "Across the Universe" by preparing a new mix of the same recording recently released on the LP *No One's Gonna Change Our World* (see the February 4, 1968, entry). "I Me Mine" had never been captured on multitrack, so Paul, George, and Ringo convened at Abbey Road on January 3, 1970, to record the song from scratch, with George Martin at the helm and Glyn present (but Phil McDonald engineering). John was still in Denmark, but since he'd either mocked or ignored the song during its rehearsals at Twickenham, I'm sure his absence was seen as no great calamity by George.

The song was recorded in sixteen takes, with Ringo's drums on tracks 1 and 2 of the tape (combined and bounced across to track 8), Paul's bass direct-injected on track 3, and George's acoustic guitar on track 4. George also sang a guide vocal on each performance, and the trio jammed a two-minute "guitar bop piece" between takes 6 and 7.

Overdubs began with Paul's Hammond organ on track 6 and George's electric guitar (heard on the intro) on track 5. George then sang a lead vocal on track 1, doubling it for the bridge (joined by Paul) on track 2; both vocal tracks were combined and bounced across to track 7. That freed up track 1 for an electric piano overdub by Paul and track 2 for George's lead guitar riffs on the bridge. Paul and George then "dropped in" a pair of acoustic guitars on track 5. George redid the last half of his lead vocal on track 7 and finally sang an extra bit of lead vocal on track 2 at the song's climax.

Two days later, Glyn mixed the song into stereo (**C**), splicing some chat and the count-in from a different take onto the beginning of the song. ("All right. Are you ready, Ringo?" "Ready, George.") A rough copy of the song, with the original take 16 announcement and count-in (**B**) has also been bootlegged, ending with an inaudible comment from George. Both derive from the same basic mix, with tracks 4 and 5 left, 2 and 6 right, and 1, 3, 7, and 8 centered.

On *Anthology 3,* the song is preceded by some dialogue that actually fell before take 15, as George makes light of John's absence, pretending to be either Dozy or Beaky from the group Dave Dee, Dozy, Beaky, Mick, and Tich. The song is presented in a new mix (**A**), with track 2 left, track 5 right and the rest centered. The organ and electric piano are decreased in volume on this mix, and the lead guitar is brought to the fore.

Another remix (**D**) for *Let It Be . . . Naked* uses take 16, but with the last half of the song edited to repeat, as per Phil Spector's original mix (see the April 1 entry). Tracks 1 and 4 are mixed left, track 5 right, and everything else is centered, apart from the bridge vocals, which are split left and right.

RELEASE HISTORY

C was included on Glyn's second *Get Back* LP lineup (see January 1969 for full details).

1984: **B** surfaced on the vinyl bootleg *File Under: Beatles*. It's best found on the CD *Acetates*.

1996: **A** was released on the CD *Anthology 3*.

2003: **D** was released on the CD *Let It Be . . . Naked*.

Date: 4 January 1970
Time: 2:30 p.m.–4:00 a.m.
Location: EMI Studio 2
Producer: George Martin

[A.] Let It Be—RS? (3:48)
Mixed: 8 January 1970

[B.] Let It Be—RS1 (4:01)
Mixed: 26 March 1970

[C.] Let It Be—RS from edit of DDSI 31.64/31.65 and 4 Jan 70 overdubs (3:50)

While the Beatles were content to let the *Get Back* album speak for itself, with no overdubs and minimal editing, the songs pulled as singles were a different matter. As they would be subject to daily scrutiny via radio airplay, it was decided to polish them up a bit. With "Get Back" and "Don't Let Me Down," this merely meant editing two takes and vocal overdubs, respectively. Of the remaining numbers, "Let It Be" had "hit single" written all over it, but needed some repair work.

The original eight-track tape of take 27A, recorded January 31, 1969, probably looked like this:

track 1—lead vocal (Paul)
track 2—backing vocals (John and George)
track 3—organ (Billy Preston)
track 4—bass (John)
track 5—sync track for film crew
track 6—drums (Ringo)
track 7—lead guitar (George)
track 8—piano (Paul)

On April 30 of that year, George had erased track 7, replacing it with a fresh Leslied guitar performance. The result was added to Glyn's *Get Back* lineup, but close scrutiny revealed how inadequate John's original bass line was. During the January 4, 1970, session, Paul replaced track 4 with a bass performance of his own. Brass (scored by George Martin) was overdubbed on track 5, along with Paul's descending electric piano riffs.

The song was given a tape reduction into takes 28–30, with a simultaneous new overdub doubling the brass on track 5 and adding cellos at the end of track 2. Paul, George, and Linda (making her sole appearance on a Beatles recording) also triple-tracked some high harmonies (bouncing from track 7 to 4 and back to 7). Finally, track 4 received an overdub of George's lead guitar (non-Leslied, including a new solo), plus mara-

cas (Paul) and extra drums (Ringo) for the last half of the song. The eight-track tape now contained:

track 1—lead vocal and electric piano
track 2—old backing vocals and cellos
track 3—organ
track 4—new lead guitar, maracas, drums
track 5—double-tracked brass
track 6—bass and drums
track 7—new triple-tracked backing vocals and old lead guitar (April 30, 1969)
track 8—piano

A pair of stereo mixes concluded the session, and Glyn took away the tape but didn't slot the new mix into his LP lineup prepared the next day, apparently intending to keep the LP and single versions separate. Instead, a fresh stereo mix was done at Olympic on January 8 for the single. This mix (**A**) pans the backing vocals from left to right at the start and features George's April 1969 guitar performance from track 7, although a bit of the new guitar is used during the final verse, alongside the maracas and drums.

Phil Spector took a different approach when remixing his album version (**B**). The track 2 backing vocals are limited to the first chorus only, and track 7 is omitted entirely in favor of George's new guitar track. The song is also extended by an edit (from 3:08–3:21) that repeats a chorus. While the brass is overemphasized, the cellos, being on the end of the backing vocals track, are absent. Also notable is the lengthy tape delay applied to Ringo's cymbals in the second verse.

The remix (**C**) for *Let It Be . . . Naked* neither lets it be nor stands naked, using quite a bit of digital trickery. The majority of the song is take 27A from January 31, 1969, incorporating two January 4, 1970, overdubs: the new backing vocals and Paul's bass overdub. In addition, portions of take 27B (used in the film) are spliced in, specifically the third chorus and subsequent guitar solo (1:31–2:26) and the third verse and subsequent chorus (2:41–3:22). However, as Paul had sung "there will be no sorrow" on the third verse during take 27B, that line is replaced with take 27A's "speaking words of wisdom." Whew!

RELEASE HISTORY

1970: **A** was released on a single worldwide; it's available on the CDs *Past Masters, Volume 2, The Beatles 1967–1970* and *1*. **B** was included on the LP *Let It Be* and is on EMI's CD of that title.

2003: **C** was released on the CD *Let It Be . . . Naked*.

3. Press conference J

Date: 5 January 1970
Location: Ålborg
Length: 5:53

As mentioned earlier, while the other Beatles were finishing off recordings for the *Let It Be* soundtrack album, John was in Denmark with Yoko. In order to be with Kyoko over New Year's, they stayed with Yoko's ex-husband, Tony Cox, and his wife, Melinde. Naturally the local press wondered what would bring a Beatle to the Danish countryside, figuring there must be a reason deeper than family togetherness.

A press conference was held about a week into their stay to answer such questions, with both couples and Kyoko seated on a couch in front of a Christmas tree. Footage of the event circulates from a Danish TV broadcast and includes cutaways to footage of John and Yoko posing for photos in the snow outside Cox's farmhouse. John denies the rumor that he is there to purchase seventy acres of land, gives his usual peace spiel ("We're trying to prevent cancer and not cure it"), and praises the Danish landscape and people.

An audio recording, which may have been taped on the same occasion, has John participating in a group sing-along of a traditional Danish song, "O Kristelighed." Near the end, John encourages the ensemble by interjecting, "Come on, you cynics!" and concludes with an enigmatic "A.R.N. 1964."

While in Denmark, John made two important decisions: to withdraw his support for the International Peace Festival unless the promoters agreed not to charge admission (a practical impossibility), and to have his long hair whittled down to a mere inch, shorter than at any previous time in his adult life.

RELEASE HISTORY

1985: A 25-second excerpt of "O Kristelighed" appeared in very good quality on the vinyl bootleg *Both Sides*. A complete 2:33 rendition circulates in poor quality among collectors.

1995: The 3:20 press conference soundtrack was released on the CD *Inside Interviews: In My Life: John Lennon & Paul McCartney*. The color footage also circulates on video among collectors.

4. Location recording J

Date: January 1970
Location: Ålborg
Length: 0:08

As a gift for Tony Cox, John gave his host a cassette of his composing session for "She Said She Said" (see June 1966, #39). The tape was auctioned at Christie's April 30, 2002, along with a second tape consisting of John and Kyoko singing and improvising stories. Depending on which report you believe, this was recorded during the May 1969 bed-in or in January 1970 at the Danish farmhouse. In either case, it sold for £75,250; this short extract aired on the radio has John singing about "the end of the downtown lane."

Two further tapes from Cox's collection were auctioned the following year by MastroNet, both of similar content and taped in January 1970 at Ålborg. Although neither is circulating yet, the online auction catalog described them thusly:

"The first tape, Denmark III, is approximately 16 minutes long and begins with Kyoko strumming John's guitar. Yoko suggests to her daughter that she play something quiet, but John encourages, 'Oh, let her blow, let her blow.' Kyoko then sings the opening words of the Beatles' song 'Dear Prudence,' with John providing background chords. A few moments of awkwardness follow as John and Tony try to coax her to let John play. Tony, unable to mask his frustration, sums up the situation with a globally telling line, 'We're just all in a very delicate state.' John and Yoko nervously agree. Precocious and imaginative, Kyoko invents a song about blueberries, which John compliments as 'beautiful' and then goes on to explain how he tunes his guitar. The music continues and Kyoko asks John, 'What are you trying to do?' He responds, 'I'm just playing behind you . . . see one guitar goes like this [he strums the strings] and the other one always goes like this [he plays a few rock chords] so we don't play exactly the same, see. If you listen to the records, they all do that.' Several more minutes pass before Yoko says, 'Dinner's ready.' John, in his typical whimsical flair, quips to Yoko in a haughty voice, 'Said the queen! You interrupted a magnificent twirl of rhetoric!' What follows is a touching session of mother and daughter singing together. Yoko serenades Kyoko with a lullaby about the snow, which builds into an extemporaneous and rather personal melody. 'I like to be alone, I get tired of this nonsense . . . I'm not so happy because I don't want to be alone.' Kyoko adoringly echoes her words and John whistles in the background.

"Denmark IV, running a total of 30 minutes in length, contains a 13-minute intro of Tony playing the

Jew's harp, with barely audible banter in the background from John, Yoko and Kyoko. A further 17 minutes features John and Kyoko making up silly songs together. She calls one, 'The Radiant Bird,' which he playfully changes to 'The Radiant Beard.' Kyoko then names her next creation, 'The Radiant World of Natural,' and John takes on an announcer's voice to declare, 'The Radiant World of Natural by Kyoko Cox!' In between sections of Kyoko's fairy tale story, John suddenly rattles off a song consisting of a nonsensical list of words, 'Boys and bees and chimneys and trees and cheese and wax and cigarettes, oh!' The rhythmic beat of John's voice calls to mind his memorable singing and chanting on 'Give Peace A Chance.' When Kyoko's lyrics turn to princesses, wizards, tigers and a tale of a rolling stone, John cries, 'Whew hoo hoo hoo hoo, what a sad one.' The story about the rolling stone rolls on, with John remarking to Tony, 'Hmm, to whom it may concern!' in what appears to be a reference to the Rolling Stones. Tony and John laugh genuinely together and the cassette comes to an end."

A twenty-three-minute John/Kyoko recording along these lines has surfaced recently (on the CD-R *The BZ Auction Tape*), containing Kyoko improvising several songs backed by John's guitar and drum machine. John also sings a verse about Julian, and the two duet on "Yellow Submarine." I believe this to be a recording from July 1970 and not part of this batch of Danish recordings.

RELEASE HISTORY

This snippet from one of the first two tapes circulates as part of a 2002 BBC Radio report on the auction.

5. Studio session

Date:	8 January 1970
Time:	9:00–11:00 p.m.
Location:	Olympic Sound Studios, London
Producer:	Glyn Johns

[A.] For You Blue—RS1 (2:26)
Mixed: 25 March 1970

[B.] For You Blue—RS2 (?) (2:45)
[C.] For You Blue—RS from DDSI 25.46 and 8 Jan 70 vocal overdub (2:26)

After hearing Glyn's January 5 lineup for the *Get Back* LP, George decided to redo his lead vocal performance on "For You Blue." This was overdubbed during a mixing session this evening at Olympic, and George seemed to enjoy the task, tossing in various ad-libs over the solos ("Go, Johnny, go!") and ending with a smooth "rhythm and blues!"

Glyn remixed the song for stereo again that evening, and Malcolm Davies did likewise on February 28 back at Abbey Road. It's probably one of those two mixes (**B**) that was slotted into Glyn's final *Get Back* LP lineup; this mix uses George's new vocal overdub for the first and second verses, and the final line of the last verse.

Phil Spector's remix (**A**) is even sparser than Glyn's first attempt, omitting the acoustic guitar entirely after the intro and spreading the slide guitar, drums, and piano across the soundstage, with George's new vocal centered. The remix (**C**) for *Let It Be . . . Naked* leaves the acoustic guitar track up throughout the song and has the slide guitar and piano tracks swap channels.

On March 30, Spector prepared a loop of the song's instrumental verse and overlaid dialogue from the film soundtrack on top of it. It's not clear whether this was for promotional purposes or something for inclusion on the album, but it has yet to escape the vault.

RELEASE HISTORY

B was included on Glyn's second *Get Back* LP lineup with the beginning trimmed and one of the false starts and a laugh edited out. The Vigotone release mistakenly restores the excised material (see entry #1, January 1969, for details).

1970: **A** was released on the LP *Let It Be* and is on EMI's CD of that title.

2003: **C** was released on the CD *Let It Be . . . Naked*.

6. Studio session R

Date: 14 January 1970
Time: 2:30–5:30 p.m.
Location: Olympic Sound Studios, London
Producer: George Martin

[A.] Sentimental Journey—RS? (3:24)
Mixed: 20 February 1970

The title track of Ringo's LP marked his first collaboration with American producer Richard Perry, although they wouldn't meet for almost two years. Ringo had admired Perry's production of Tiny Tim's recent LP and invited him to work up a new arrangement of the 1945 hit "Sentimental Journey."

Perry recorded the backing in America in late 1969 using an interesting and eclectic instrumental lineup: guitar, bass, drums, piano, accordion, clarinets, saxophones, strings, autoharp, backing vocalists, and a "talking guitar" solo, perhaps played by Pete Drake (who would employ such a technique on George's and Ringo's next LPs).

On top of all this, Ringo recorded his lead vocal at Olympic Studios in London, double-tracking it for the first middle eight and inserting a dapper "let's go, now!" near the end. The song was mixed for the LP back at Abbey Road a month later.

RELEASE HISTORY

1970: **A** was released on the LP *Sentimental Journey,* reissued on CD in 1995.

7. Newsreel footage J

Date: 26 January 1970
Location: Hilton Paris hotel
Length: 1:36

Along with his lengthy tresses, John seemed to shed most of his 1969 optimism in Denmark, leaving it behind when he departed on January 25. His grandiose scheme for an international peace festival had been hastily abandoned, and his mood was probably dampened further by a blanket of fog that delayed him and Yoko overnight in Paris before they could return home.

A Paris correspondent for the Reuters news agency had the misfortune to film an interview with a rather surly John. Every line of questioning is a dead end: the reason for John's haircut ("I felt like it . . . why do you cut yours?"), his plans as a peace leader ("I'm not a leader—and I try not to make plans"), and the meaning of the Beatles' next single. ("What is this record about?" "Letting it be.")

RELEASE HISTORY

This color Reuters news clip circulates in very good quality on video.

8. Studio session J, G

Date: 27 January 1970
Time: 7:00 p.m.–4:00 a.m.
Location: EMI Studio 2
Producer: Phil Spector

[A.] Instant Karma! (We All Shine On)—RS4 (3:17)
Mixed: 27 January 1970

[B.] Instant Karma! (We All Shine On)—RS from take 10 (3:34)

"Ritten, Recorded, Remixed 27th Jan 1970." That bit of Apple ad copy tells the story of the Plastic Ono Band's most impressive single to date. John did indeed compose "Instant Karma!" on the morning of the twenty-seventh, using the upright piano at Tittenhurst to pound out the chord sequence. On the way to the studio, he decided that Phil Spector, in town to discuss the possibility of remixing the "Get Back" tapes, would be a perfect candidate to produce the song.

The story gets even better: According to Anthony Fawcett, John wanted to complete writing the song when he arrived at Apple and stopped off at a music store on the way to order a piano for immediate delivery to his office. Why he couldn't just go down and use the one in Apple's basement studio is a mystery, but the piano was duly delivered, and Abbey Road's familiar Studio 2 was hastily booked for a 7 p.m. starting time.

Phil Spector arrived, Klaus Voormann and Alan

White were contacted, and George deputized for Eric Clapton, bringing along Billy Preston. John and Phil were listed as coproducers on the session sheet, with Phil McDonald engineering. When the single was released, Spector got a well-deserved solo production credit.

According to Mark Lewisohn, the backing track was recorded in ten takes, with John on acoustic guitar, George on electric guitar, Klaus on bass, Alan on drums, and Billy on electric piano. Spector decided to strip these down to a minimum, accentuating the drums with wet reverberation and ditching the guitars in favor of a keyboard army: Klaus and John on electric piano and Alan and George playing a grand piano; according to the session sheet, a Hammond organ was also used. Mal Evans overdubbed chimes to emphasize certain words in the chorus ("moon," "stars," "sun").

John recorded his lead vocal, likewise slathered with cavernous echo, and playbacks convinced John that a vocal choir was needed to strengthen the chorus. As overdubs didn't even begin until midnight, the only place to recruit singers on the spur of the moment would be a nightclub, so Mal and Billy were dispatched to the nearby Hatchetts discotheque and returned with

a number of eager volunteers. Three tracks were filled with backing vocals "conducted" by George (even Allen Klein joined in!), plus handclaps and tambourine.

The song was remixed into stereo beginning at 3 a.m., and the reel of mixes was signed out by Mal to take to Apple for immediate mastering. By February 6, the first copies of the single were in British shops, and within a month of its composition, the song was in the top 30. John and George were so impressed with Spector's technique and skill, they not only handed over the "Get Back" tapes to him, but made plans to work with him on their respective first solo pop albums.

A remix (**B**) for the DVD *Lennon Legend* lets the song play through to its original ending, including a brief snatch of the Hammond organ apparently erased by other instruments.

RELEASE HISTORY

1970: **A** was released on a single that reached number 4 in the UK and number 3 in the U.S. charts. It's best found on the CD *Lennon Legend*.

2003: **B** was released on the soundtrack of the DVD *Lennon Legend*.

9. TV performance   R

Date:	27 January 1970
Location:	NBC Television Studio, Los Angeles
Producer:	Paul Keyes, Carolyn Raskin
Host:	Dan Rowan, Dick Martin
Broadcast:	23 February 1970, 8:00–9:00 p.m.
	NBC-TV
	Rowan & Martin's Laugh-In
Length:	4:57

The Beatles had all been faithful viewers of the U.S. sketch comedy *Laugh-In* after it was imported by the BBC in 1968, so when Ringo visited Los Angeles to attend the premiere of *The Magic Christian,* he was glad to tape a cameo appearance on the show.

It couldn't have taken long for Ringo to tape his eighteen segments, none of which last more than 30 seconds. In addition to introducing the show (as "Peter Sellers in the role of Ringo Starr"), Ringo appears on the show-closing "joke wall" and in painfully corny routines alongside cast members Dan Rowan, Arte Johnson, Ruth Buzzi, Alan Sues, Jo Anne Worley, Teresa Graves, Jeremy Lloyd, and guest star Carol Channing.

Ringo isn't given a chance to play any character other than himself, poking fun at his rock star image and generally acting as a straight man to zany one-liners. The show was telecast on BBC2 April 12.

RELEASE HISTORY

Ringo's appearance circulates on video in excellent quality, thanks to recent rebroadcasts.

10. Radio interview   J

Date: late January 1970
Location: Apple Corps, London
Interviewer: David Bellan
Broadcast: 28 May 1970, 2:15–2:30 p.m.
BBC World Service
Profile
Length: 14:12

David Bellan interviewed John and Yoko at Apple for this BBC World Service program sometime around the end of January (John says Ringo is away, and that he'll be seeing Paul later in the week). As the recently mixed "Instant Karma!" plays in the background, John talks about his meeting with Pierre Trudeau and the planned peace festival. ("At the moment there's all hell going on over there with different people organizing and disorganizing.") John also expresses his hopes for the new decade and discusses the peace campaign.

RELEASE HISTORY

This recording circulates in excellent quality thanks to its appearance on BBC Radio 6's website.

11. Studio session   J

Date: ca. January 1970
Location: Trident Studios, London
Producer: John Lennon

[A.] Who Has Seen the Wind? (2:01)

The flip side for the Plastic Ono Band's latest single was a joint John and Yoko composition, "Who Has Seen the Wind?" Most likely John wrote the melody and Yoko the lyrics, which resemble the sort of verse found in her book *Grapefruit.*

Yoko sings the opening verse a cappella and is joined by softly strummed guitar (John), harpsichord (arranger John Barham), flute (Yoko, according to one source), and tambourine (Mal Evans?). The result was swiftly mixed into stereo (guitar and harpsichord left, vocal centered, flute and tambourine right) for "instant" release.

RELEASE HISTORY

1970: **A** was released on the B-side of the "Instant Karma!" single. A mono mix was included on Rykodisc's 1997 CD issue of *Wedding Album.*

12. TV interview   R

Date: 26 January–1 February 1970
Location: Los Angeles
Interviewer: Sam Riddle
Broadcast: 7 March 1970, noon–12:30 p.m.
ABC-TV
Get It Together
Length: 6:39

The main purpose of Ringo's visit to America was to promote *The Magic Christian* and attend its January 29 U.S. premiere. Sometime before his return to England, Ringo filmed an interview for the Saturday morning TV pop-music series *Get It Together.*

Ringo denies any involvement in the "Paul is dead" hoax, though he does admit he can hear clues such as "I buried Paul" when people point them out. Riddle asks how large a family Ringo plans to have, and he jokes, "I'm not planning anything, God plans it. That's the way God planned it!" After some chat about fashion, Ringo describes the process that led up to the making of *The Magic Christian.* A clip from the film is introduced by Riddle as containing music written by Paul, and Ringo concurs, so he obviously assumed they would show a scene featuring "Come and Get It." Instead, a sequence set to Badfinger's "Carry On Till Tomorrow" is aired.

Afterward, Ringo clarifies the premise of the film, which is basically a modern parable about the effects of extreme greed. Asked to name his favorite movie stars, Ringo chooses Paul Newman, Steve McQueen, and Richard Burton. He has a harder time picking favorite musicians, but singles out "Something," "Come Together," and "Octopus's Garden" ("I gotta get a plug!") as highlights of *Abbey Road.*

RELEASE HISTORY

The audio portion of this interview circulates in good quality from an off-air recording.

13. TV interview

J

Date: 4 February 1970
Location: Black Centre, London
Interviewer: Peter Sissons
Broadcast: 4 February 1970, 10:00 p.m.
ITV
News at Ten
Length: 0:59

Leave it to John and Yoko to turn a haircut into a political demonstration. In a rather bizarre rooftop stunt this day, the couple exchanged locks of their hair with activist Michael X (aka Michael Abdul Malik), who in turn gave them a pair of bloodstained boxing trunks worn by Muhammad Ali. (Hey, I'm just reporting this stuff.) The plan was for Michael to auction off the hair to raise money for the Black Centre, a headquarters for various black power endeavors. John and Yoko would then auction off the trunks to raise money for their peace festival.

The exchange took place atop the building, with a handful of journalists present, including the ever-faithful ITV News, which filmed a brief interview with John and Yoko. After explaining that the new haircut was for the new year, John is asked whether this isn't "just another Lennon stunt." Of course it is, they gleefully admit, and John complains that he'd tried to keep the haircut private, hoping to travel unrecognized for a while, but the hairdresser had spilled the beans within three days.

RELEASE HISTORY

1996: The audio portion of this interview was released on the CD *Fab Four CD & Book Set*. The color footage circulates on video.

14. Radio interview

J

Date: 6 February 1970
Location: Apple Corps, London
Interviewer: David Wigg
Broadcast: 15 February 1970, 3:00–4:00 p.m.
BBC Radio 1
Scene and Heard
Length: 5:10

Although it had been four months since John asked for a "divorce" from the other Beatles, he was still reluctant, for whatever reason, to put a public end to the group. When he sat down for another interview with David Wigg, John sent out mixed signals about the group's fate.

In the plus column, he calls the group a good means of communicating and says he "wouldn't destroy it out of hand," but he also admits that the group now has no plans to record together until the *Let It Be* film and album are "sorted out." John says he plans to begin recording an LP with Yoko and Phil Spector in two weeks and understands that Paul is planning his own album.

Tellingly, John avows that the lull could signal "a rebirth or a death." Wigg finds the lack of group activity a novel situation, but John points out the lengthy

gap that preceded the release of *Sgt. Pepper.* John admits that the fights over naming a manager and the struggle to gain control of the Northern Songs catalog did cause a lot of friction, but stresses that he kept in touch with the other Beatles during his vacation in Denmark, sending them postcards and talking on the phone with George.

Wigg wonders how cautious John is in choosing the people and causes he's associated with. John defends Michael X and the parents of James Hanratty as sincere, saying he spent hours getting to know them and their positions. Wigg relates a threat he received after writing a *Daily Express* story about John's involvement in the Hanratty case, but John doesn't seem too concerned.

RELEASE HISTORY

1972: Portions of this interview were broadcast in the BBC Radio documentary *The Beatles' Story,* including 40 seconds not released on the LP noted below.

1976: 4:27 of this interview was released on the LP *The Beatles Tapes with David Wigg,* later reissued on CD.

15. TV interview J

Date: 7 February 1970
Time: evening
Location: Studio 1, Wembley Studios
Host: Simon Dee
Broadcast: 8 February 1970, 11:25 p.m.–12:15 a.m.
London Weekend Television
The Simon Dee Show
Length: 13:31

In their first television chat show appearance of 1970, John and Yoko brought along Michael X to give his cause a bit of airtime. The show's host, ex–disc jockey Simon Dee, had other ideas, preferring to chat with the eccentric couple rather than the more controversial activist.

After sending greetings to Julian and Kyoko, John praises previous guest George Lazenby, who had apparently gotten into a discussion of the questions surrounding President Kennedy's assassination. John compares the situation to James Hanratty's case and recommends having Hanratty's parents as guests. Dee wonders what evidence John can uncover that Scotland Yard missed, but John says the point is merely to open a public inquiry, since a private one suggested there may be more to the case than meets the eye.

The "Bag One" lithographs that John had finally signed in Canada went on display at the London Arts Gallery January 15. One day later, police arrived to confiscate eight of the prints as "indecent," a charge that would be dismissed in April. In the meantime, John expresses puzzlement at "the way they arrest pieces of paper with pen on." He compares the series of drawings to Picasso's erotic engravings and says that the images were published in a Danish newspaper without causing harm to society.

Dee asks why John and Yoko are preoccupied with

nudity, and John doesn't find it so abnormal, feeling that if any "average" person were subject to intense public scrutiny, their lives would seem "abnormal" as well. Yoko wishes that people would focus on their non-nude activities, and John patiently explains the reasoning behind the *Two Virgins* cover before steering the topic back to Michael X.

In a strangely uncomfortable moment, Dee introduces Michael but refuses to shake his hand ("because we met before the show"). "Racialism! I saw it," cries John, and Dee replies, "You've had your bit, OK?" Michael mentions how glad he is that John and Yoko have literally given of themselves (donating their hair) to support the Black Centre. Dee asks if the hair has been auctioned yet, and John says they are still deciding on an auction house, with Sotheby's already publicly turning them down because they "only sell art." John finds this hypocritical in light of their recent attempted sale of Napoleon's severed penis: "My hair is as arty as Napoleon's thingies!"

Michael talks about the aims of his organization and calls overtly racist MP Enoch Powell "a very strange kind of person" but "not a lunatic." John agrees that Powell is shrewd and proposes a Dick Gregory/ Enoch Powell showdown on Dee's program: "You'd be top of the polls for months." Asked what one thing he wants for black people in England, Michael replies simply, "Peace." Dee, not getting the answer he was looking for, asks for something tangible, but Michael is steadfast: "A chance to live in peace."

RELEASE HISTORY

The audio portion of this interview circulates in fair quality among collectors from an off-air tape.

16. Studio session G

Date: 7 February 1970
Location: Trident Studios, London
Producer: George Harrison

[A.] Govinda (4:43)

After the success of their first collaboration, George produced a second single for the Radha Krishna Temple early in 1970. As before, a traditional chant, "Govinda," was arranged by Mukunda Das Adkikary, and both traditional Eastern and modern Western in-

struments were blended to create a satisfying new sound.

The backing is provided by George's acoustic guitar, Klaus Voormann's bass, and drums that may well have been a Ringo contribution. Temple members supplied vocals, organ, flute, and bells, while EMI arranger John Barham scored and conducted a part for violins, violas, harp, and chimes that was probably overdubbed during the February 7 session.

The single's B-side, "Govinda Jai Jai," is a harmonium- and percussion-based chant that George produced but did not play on. George would go on to produce an entire album for the temple, but as it was released in 1971 and probably recorded well after March 1970, it falls outside the scope of this book.

RELEASE HISTORY

1970: **A** was released on a single that reached number 26 in the UK charts but failed to chart in the United States. It was included on the 1971 Apple LP *The Radha Krsna Temple,* reissued on CD in 1993.

17. Studio session R

Date:	10 February 1970
Time:	7:00–9:20 p.m.
Location:	EMI Studio 2
Producer:	George Martin

[A.] Dream—RS? (2:40)
Mixed: 20 February 1970

Johnny Mercer's "Dream" had actually been the fourth song started for *Sentimental Journey,* with the basic rhythm combo of electric guitar, bass, and drums being recorded at Trident the previous November 14. Ringo spent the rest of that session triple-tracking his mellow, low-register vocals, creating a sort of Starkey Brothers effect. A rough mix was prepared on the eighteenth by Geoff Emerick at EMI, and George Martin set about composing an orchestral arrangement.

This wasn't overdubbed until February 10, when Martin conducted a fifteen-piece band including trumpets, trombones, French horns, and vibes. The song was then mixed into stereo, with final mixing occurring ten days later.

RELEASE HISTORY

1970: **A** was released on the LP *Sentimental Journey,* reissued on CD in 1995.

18. TV performance J

Date:	11 February 1970
Time:	7:30–10:00 p.m.
Location:	Studio 8, Television Centre, London
Broadcast:	12 (**B**) and 19 (**A**) February 1970, 7:15–8:00 p.m.
	BBC1
	Top of the Pops

[A.] Instant Karma! (We All Shine On)—take 3 (3:26)
[B.] Instant Karma! (We All Shine On)—take 4 (3:37)

The recording and release of "Instant Karma!" was so swift that John and Yoko had no time to prepare a promotional film clip for broadcast on *Top of the Pops.* On February 5, the program aired a makeshift "promo" comprised of footage from the BBC's recent *24 Hours* documentary on John and Yoko, synchronized to the song.

Sometime the following week, John was persuaded to videotape a "live" performance of the song exclusively for *Top of the Pops.* Geoff Emerick created a fresh mono mix of the song, omitting John's lead vocal on the verses, at Abbey Road on the tenth. The next day, the Plastic Ono Band du jour arrived at BBC TV's studio. Four takes were required, with John playing upright piano and singing a live vocal, Alan White and Klaus Voormann miming their original roles, and Yoko, er, participating.

The video of take 3 (**A**) appears on the DVD *Lennon Legend;* John and Yoko sport black turtlenecks, while Mal Evans plays tambourine and Apple employee and future rock journalist BP Fallon joins in miming bass alongside Klaus. Yoko participates by knitting while seated on a stool and wearing a blindfold. Only a 2:07 portion of the audio for this take is circulating (the DVD audio substitutes a remix of the studio take).

For take 4 (**B**) John is wearing a paisley shirt, and he and Yoko have donned jean jackets with armbands reading "People for Peace." BP Fallon is now handling tambourine duties and Mal is nowhere to be seen. Yoko, meanwhile, has switched from knitting to holding up various cue cards (SMILE, PEACE, LOVE, HOPE, BREATHE). She also seems to be contributing vocally, but no live microphone is near enough to pick up her contribution.

There are slight lyrical differences between the two takes. In **A,** John sings "knock you right on the head" and "knock you right off your feet." In **B,** he omits the word "right" in both instances.

The 2:07 copy of **A** circulates on video from a December 9, 1980, rebroadcast on *Old Grey Whistle Test*. Its soundtrack has been bootlegged, slightly incomplete at either end, on the LP *Doll's House*, copied on the CD-R *Vinyl to the Core*. **B** was officially released on the home video *The John Lennon Video Collection* in 1992, and **A** (video only) on the DVD *Lennon Legend* in 2003. A black-and-white copy of the February 5 "promo" also circulates on video.

19. Radio interview   J

Date:	ca. 15 February 1970
Interviewer:	"Emperor Rosko" (Michael Pasternak)
Broadcast:	noon–1:00 p.m.
	BBC Radio 1
	Midday Spin
Length:	17:05

BBC disc jockey "Emperor Rosko" had spun records and emceed at the UNICEF benefit concert in December, and John and Yoko agreed to appear on his lunchtime show to answer questions sent in by listeners, and, of course, to promote "Instant Karma!"

We learn that John has no idea what joo-joo eyeballs are, that his and Yoko's hair hasn't been auctioned yet, and that he has a soft spot for gypsies. The Jackson Five's second hit, "ABC," was climbing the charts that week, and John sees the group as part of a legacy of prepubescent hitmakers dating back to Frankie Lymon and Stevie Wonder.

Many people wrote in wondering what Yoko's blindfolded card-holding performance on *Top of the Pops* was meant to represent (the "knitting" version not having aired yet). Yoko's explanation: "Well, I think the blindfold means to me like everybody in the world is like blind . . . the stool was like a grove, you know. And everybody's sitting on the grove blindfolded and trying their best, you know." Oh.

John reveals that he failed all his O-level exams and that he's a big fan of reggae music, having rehearsed in that style in Denmark. He says he's written a new song (perhaps "Across the Great Water" or "Make Love, Not War") that goes well with a reggae rhythm. Calling Paul's alleged death a rumor "started obviously by some madman in America," John clarifies that "I buried Paul" is in fact "cranberry sauce." As usual, he waffles on the issue of future live appearances by the Beatles, calling it a possibility but saying in the next breath that it's impossible to say whether it will happen.

One astute listener noticed the similarity between the musical progressions in "All You Need Is Love" and "Instant Karma!" and John admits that he was messing around with the chords of the former when composing the latter. Rosko wonders whether the UNICEF concert recording will ever be released, and John complains that the vocals weren't recorded right, although the massive backing group sounded fantastic. He figures that the market for "Cold Turkey" variations (studio, live in Toronto) won't be able to sustain the release of another version for a year or two.

Rosko complains that the stage volume at the show gave him a headache, and he compares Yoko's vocal performance to "a human clarinet." Yoko says she was trained to sing classical music, but secretly longed to sing pop songs. A few questions about peace follow, covering old ground, and finally Rosko asks John to name his favorite football players. He can come up with only names from his childhood, notably Albert Stubbins (who made it onto the *Sgt. Pepper* LP cover) and "Billy Little with the big kick."

RELEASE HISTORY

This interview circulates in good quality among collectors from an off-air tape.

20. Studio session   R

Date:	17 February 1970
Time:	10:00 a.m.–1:00 p.m.
Location:	EMI Studio 2
Producer:	George Martin
[A.]	I'm a Fool to Care—RS? (2:38)
Mixed:	20 February 1970

This Ted Daffan composition, once a hit for Les Paul and Mary Ford, was one of the lowlights of the *Sentimental Journey* LP. Klaus Voormann's arrangement throws in everything but the kitchen sink, and the overblown approach isn't helped by Ringo's lobotomized easy-listening vocal.

The song's backing was recorded at Abbey Road

Studio 2 on February 11, with Klaus conducting a fifteen-piece band consisting of brass, woodwinds, string bass, drums, and piano (the latter played by Billy Preston). Takes 19, 20, and 21 of this backing were spliced together to form a master take, also called "take 19". Ringo added his double-tracked lead vocal, a rough stereo mix was made, Klaus overdubbed acoustic guitar, and yet another stereo mix was created.

On the seventeenth, a tape reduction was done to make room for the addition of a fifteen-piece string ensemble conducted by Francis Shaw. The song's final stereo mixing occurred three days later, but all that work showed minimal results.

RELEASE HISTORY

1970: **A** was released on the LP *Sentimental Journey,* reissued on CD in 1995.

21. Studio session   R

Date: 18 February 1970
Time: 2:30–5:30 p.m.
Location: EMI Studio 2
Producer: George Martin

  [A.] Have I Told You Lately That I Love You—RS? (2:43)
  [B.] Let the Rest of the World Go By—RS? (2:53)
Mixed: 20 February 1970

If there's one thing worse than a 1970 rendition of a 1945 standard, it's a 1970 rendition done in a badly dated "go-go" pseudo-rock style. Such was the problem with Elmer Bernstein's arrangement of the Scott Wiseman composition "Have I Told You Lately That I Love You."

Its twenty-piece backing of drums, bass, electric guitar, piano, organ, horns, violin, and bird whistle (don't ask) was taped at Hollywood's A&M Studios on February 3 and sent overseas. Ringo recorded his lead vocal onto a simultaneous tape reduction February 9 at Abbey Road, perfecting it on the eighteenth. His singing is actually excellent on this number, perhaps his best performance on the album, which makes the embarrassing musical backing even more regretful.

An even older number, 1919's "Let the Rest of the World Go By," makes a mediocre LP closer. Les Reed conducted his own arrangement for a thirty-one-piece orchestra and nine vocalists on February 12, taping six takes in the key of B-flat and five more in C. It was decided that the lower key was more suitable for Ringo's range, so he overdubbed multitracked lead vocals onto take 6 that evening and on the eighteenth. Although he harmonizes with himself in spots, Ringo's performance is more workmanlike than heartfelt.

RELEASE HISTORY

1970: **A** and **B** were released on the LP *Sentimental Journey,* reissued on CD in 1995.

22. Studio session   R

Date: 19 February 1970
Time: 2:30–5:00 p.m.
Location: EMI Studio 2
Producer: George Martin

  [A.] Love Is a Many Splendoured Thing—RS? (3:05)
Mixed: 6 March 1970

More time was spent on "Love Is a Many Splendoured Thing" than any other track on Ringo's debut LP, and it was not time well spent. The Paul Webster/Sammy Fain standard had been newly arranged by Quincy Jones, who conducted a twenty-seven-piece orchestra at A&M Studios in Hollywood December 26, 1969.

Ringo added his lead vocal to this backing track during a January 14, 1970, session at Olympic but the result was rejected.

A remake began at Abbey Road February 3 with the taping of eight takes of a new backing track featuring a sixteen-piece ensemble (including bass, electric guitar, drums, piano, and congas), again conducted by Jones. Billy Preston added organ to the last of these takes, and Ringo overdubbed a lead vocal, with stereo mixing concluding the session. Ringo redid his vocal two days later, and on the seventeenth, a string section, conducted by Francis Shaw, was added.

The song was completed on the nineteenth with further overdubs: eight backing vocalists (who end up completely swamping Ringo's performance), two flutes, vibes, and more organ. Stereo mixing began on February 20 and was perfected by March 6, but the result is less than impressive.

RELEASE HISTORY

1970: **A** was released on the LP *Sentimental Journey,* reissued on CD in 1995.

23. Location recording   P

Date:	late December 1969–mid February 1970
Location:	7 Cavendish Avenue, London
Producer:	Paul McCartney

[A.]	**The Lovely Linda—RS?** (0:43)
[B.]	**Momma Miss America—RS?** (4:04)
[C.]	**Glasses/Suicide—RS?** (0:37)
Mixed:	21 February 1970

[D.]	**That Would Be Something—RS?** (2:37)
[E.]	**Valentine Day—RS?** (1:40)
Mixed:	22 February 1970

Paul had been nearly invisible since October 1969, remaining either on his farm in Scotland or at home in St. John's Wood, not speaking to the press, showing up at Apple, or appearing at public events. To occupy his time, he had been recording his first solo album on his newly installed home recording equipment.

As he later put it, the home tracks were recorded with a "Studer, one mike, and nerve." Indeed, although Paul received a Studer four-track recorder just before Christmas, he had but one microphone for input and no sound-level indicator or mixing board of any kind. This homegrown approach made it easy for the album to remain a secret for quite a while and allowed Paul to experiment with playing all the instruments himself.

His first recording, "The Lovely Linda" (**A**) was merely a couple of lines of melody sung to test the equipment, but it ended up opening the LP. Track 1 had the initial vocal and acoustic guitar performance, with Paul chuckling at the end. To this, he added a second acoustic guitar on track 2, book-slap percussion on track 3, and bass guitar on track 4.

Over the course of the next two months, Paul continued to amass home recordings, largely experimental in nature rather than fully composed songs. "That Would Be Something" was nothing more than a riff and a verse (**D**), written in Scotland the previous autumn. The acoustic guitar and vocal were laid down simultaneously. On the remaining three tracks went overdubs of tom-tom and cymbal, electric guitar, and then bass. The track features a false ending that cuts off rather abruptly.

"Momma Miss America" (**B**) was made up of two improvised instrumental pieces joined by an edit at 1:56; the first of these is announced by Paul as " 'Rock and Roll Springtime,' take one," and the song did bear that parenthetical adjunct to its title prior to release. Part 1 consists of drums, bass, tremeloed electric guitar, and piano, with the latter two tracks swapping places in the stereo image partway through. Part 2 has drums, bass, electric guitar, and a fourth track of acoustic guitar and then piano, mixed wild near the end, darting across the soundstage.

"Glasses" (**C**) was just as advertised: several tracks of wine glasses filled with different levels of water being rubbed to produce various pitches. As one of these tracks ends, it reveals what is apparently the recording underneath: Paul's piano performance of "Suicide," a song written as long ago as 1959 but never officially released in complete form. This recording would be joined to the song "Hot as Sun" with a hard edit (see the February 20 entry).

Finally, "Valentine Day" was presumably recorded or at least titled on February 14. This instrumental (**E**) was also improvised, with Paul playing drums, acoustic guitar, electric guitar, and a fourth track containing percussion and bass.

These home tapes were mixed into stereo at EMI Studio 2 on the dates noted above. **A, B,** and **C** had all been mixed into stereo at Morgan Studios earlier in the month, but those mixes were rejected. Other recordings begun at Cavendish Avenue were "Singalong Junk," "Junk," "Oo You," and "Teddy Boy," all of which would undergo further additions in the studio.

RELEASE HISTORY

1970: **A–E** were released on the LP *McCartney,* also available on CD.

24. Studio session

P

Date: 10–20 February 1970
Location: Morgan Studios, London
Producer: Paul McCartney

[A.] Oo You—RS? (2:48)
[B.] Teddy Boy—RS? (2:22)
[C.] Junk—RS? (1:54)
[D.] Kreen-Akrore—RS? (4:11)
Mixed: 10–20 February 1970

[E.] Singalong Junk—RS? (2:34)
Mixed: 21 February 1970

[F.] Hot as Sun—RS? (1:28)
Mixed: 24 February 1970

By the middle of February, Paul was not only continuing to tape new material at home, but supplementing these recordings with covert visits to Morgan Studios, booking the dates under the pseudonym Billy Martin.

Two of the songs begun at home, "Junk" and "Teddy Boy," had been written in Rishikesh and offered up to the Beatles for the "White Album" and "Get Back" projects, respectively. "Teddy Boy" began with acoustic guitar, bass, and two vocal tracks, one of Paul alone and one joined by Linda for harmonies.

Take 1 of "Junk" probably began as an acoustic guitar performance; Paul liked it enough that he retained the track and added piano, bass, and a second acoustic at home, calling the result "Singalong Junk." The second take of "Junk" consisted initially of two acoustic guitars, bass, and a lead vocal.

Also taped at his home studio were the first three tracks of "Oo You": bass, drums, and electric guitar. The song was copied over to eight-track at Morgan, and Paul came up with some rudimentary lyrics "one day after lunch." The recording (A) was finished that afternoon and includes a second electric guitar, tambourine, cowbell, lead vocal, and what sounds like a maraca but is in fact the rhythmic spritzing of an aerosol spray can!

"Teddy Boy," "Junk," and "Singalong Junk" were likewise transferred from four-track to eight-track at Morgan, and all three songs have an extra layer of audible tape hiss. Overdubs consisted of the following: drums, a bass drum, and clapping (**B**); brushed snare, bass drum, xylophone, and Paul's gorgeous harmony vocal (**C**); and Mellotron strings, drums, cymbal, and electric guitar (**E**). All four songs were mixed into stereo at Morgan, although "Singalong Junk" would be remixed at Abbey Road.

On the evening of February 17, Paul viewed an ATV documentary, *The Tribe That Hides from Man*, about the Kreen-Akrore tribe in Brazil. This inspired the track "Kreen-Akrore," which was supposed to re-create the atmosphere of a jungle hunt. Paul recorded the song (**D**) in two sections (the break falls at 1:55), laying down a pair of drum tracks first. For part one, he added piano, organ, and electric guitar, plus the sound of a bow and arrow shooting across the stereo image (at 1:00). He and Linda also overdubbed sped-up animal imitations, and the sound of a stampede was simulated by thumping on a guitar case. Part two has Paul and Linda's wordless vocals, some heavy breathing, a pair of electric guitars, and more organ.

One final song taped at Morgan was the instrumental "Hot as Sun" (**F**), whose tropical-flavored riff dated back to the Quarry Men's repertoire. After composing a contrasting section, Paul filled up the eight tracks by playing acoustic guitar, electric guitar, drums, a second acoustic, organ, maracas, bass, and bongos. The song would be joined to "Glasses"/"Suicide" after both recordings were remixed at Abbey Road.

RELEASE HISTORY

1970: **A–F** were released on the LP *McCartney,* also available on CD.

25. Studio session

P

Date: 22 February 1970
Time: noon–10:00 p.m.
Location: EMI Studio 2
Producer: Paul McCartney

[A.] Maybe I'm Amazed—RS? (3:49)
Mixed: 22 February 1970

[B.] Every Night—RS? (2:30)
Mixed: 24 February 1970

Despite two months of work thus far, the *McCartney* album was lacking in the "classic song" department. Having moved from Morgan Studios to Abbey Road on the twenty-first to begin remixing, Paul rectified the problem with a single session on the twenty-second, recording from start to finish two excellent numbers. The key difference was that both were fully realized compositions rather than slapped-together improvisations or experimental pieces.

The opening couplet of "Every Night" had been around since the "Get Back" sessions of January 1969, and Paul finished off the song during his Greek vacation a few months later, borrowing the refrain melody from "You Never Give Me Your Money." The recording (**B**) features three acoustic guitars, bass, and drums, and Paul's lead vocal, double-tracked in places ("resting my mind"). He also added electric guitar on the tape's eighth track, but it went unused in the mixing, done that night and perfected two days later.

"Maybe I'm Amazed" (**A**), a strong affirmation of his relationship with Linda, seemed an obvious choice to release as a single from the album, and indeed, a promo clip was prepared using Linda's photographs and aired in the UK and the United States. But Paul decided against releasing any single to support the LP, perhaps out of spite against Allen Klein, whose ABKCO would profit. Seven years later, when Paul could be assured the profits would go to MPL, the song was released as a live Wings single and reached the top 10.

Although he plays all the instruments himself, Paul manages to pull off an ensemble feel, as well as one of his best guitar solos ever. The eight tracks consist of piano, lead vocal, drums, bass, backing vocals (Paul and Linda), organ plus more vocals, lead guitar, and rhythm guitar.

RELEASE HISTORY

1970: **A** and **B** were released on the LP *McCartney*, also available on CD.

26. Studio session   R

Date:	24 February 1970
Time:	3:30–7:15 p.m.
Location:	EMI Studio 1
Producer:	George Martin

[A.] Blue Turning Grey Over You—edit of RS? (3:18)
Mixed: 24 February 1970

This Louis Armstrong hit, co-written by "Fats" Waller, was arranged for *Sentimental Journey* by Oliver Nelson and spanned several months of sessions. A demo take was recorded at EMI Studio 2 on November 28, 1969. On December 4, a 17-piece ensemble (trumpets, trombones, saxes, piano, bass, and drums) performed nine takes of a new backing track. Ringo added a lead vocal to this, ad-libbing some scat singing at the end ("I just lost myself there, child!") and the song was mixed into stereo.

More than two months later, Ringo added a second lead vocal during simultaneous tape reductions. Apparently Ringo was having a hard time with his new vocal, as seven stereo mixes were done using six of these reduction takes. Four of the mixes were assembled to produce the final master, and all the editing paid off to produce a lively and swinging performance.

RELEASE HISTORY

1970: **A** was released on the LP *Sentimental Journey*, reissued on CD in 1995.

27. Studio session   P

Date:	25 February 1970
Time:	11:30 a.m.–9:00 p.m.
Location:	EMI Studio 2
Producer:	Paul McCartney

[A.] Man We Was Lonely—RS1 (2:56)
Mixed: 25 February 1970

The last song recorded for *McCartney*, "Man We Was Lonely," was written toward the end of the sessions, with the verses composed February 25, perhaps during the one-hour lunch break between perfecting the backing track and beginning overdubs.

The basic track, probably acoustic guitar and a guide vocal, was perfected by take 12. Overdubs included bass guitar, bass drum, and two vocal tracks, with Linda duetting on the refrains. The "steel" electric guitar effect was produced by Paul playing his Telecaster with a drum peg. This was overdubbed twice, and during the sole stereo mix, these tracks were placed one in each channel, swapping places at the start and again at the end, in one of the album's few production effects.

Paul returned to Abbey Road for further playbacks and tape copying of the LP's master reel on March 16 and twenty-third, but otherwise he remained at home awaiting the scheduled April 17 release date and dreading the inevitable publicity tour. He later recalled: "I didn't want to do a press conference to launch the album because whenever I'd meet a journalist, they always floored me with one question: They'd say, 'Are you happy?' and it almost made me cry. I just could not say, 'Yes. I'm happy,' and lie through my teeth, so I stopped doing interviews." If only there were some way he could answer the inevitable questions without having to face reporters in person . . .

RELEASE HISTORY

1970: **A** was released on the LP *McCartney,* also available on CD.

28. Studio session   R

Date: ca. March 1970
Location: Island Studios, London
Producer: Stephen Stills, Bill Halverson

[A.] **To a Flame** (3:02)
[B.] **We Are Not Helpless** (4:12)

In addition to their work on the Doris Troy sessions, Ringo and Stephen Stills were well acquainted socially in late 1969. Stills purchased the Brookfields mansion from Ringo when he moved out in December. When Stills was in London to record his first solo LP, Ringo lent his sticks to a couple of numbers, credited on the sleeve merely as "Richie."

Neither song exactly taxed Ringo's drumming skills, requiring little more than simple backbeats and tom-tom patterns. "To a Flame" is an undistinguished mellow tune, featuring acoustic guitar, piano, and vibes. "We Are Not Helpless" is a bit more lively, with a gospel rave-up section toward the end. Stills probably plays the acoustic guitar, bass, pianos, and organs on this song.

Both songs include strings and horns, which may have been overdubbed later in America. A possible third song stemming from these sessions with Ringo, "As I Come of Age," wasn't released until the 1975 LP *Stills.* This may have been recorded much later, however.

RELEASE HISTORY

1970: **A** and **B** were released on the LP *Stephen Stills,* later reissued on CD. **A** was also released on the B-side of the hit single, "Love the One You're With."

29. Studio session   R

Date: 5 March 1970
Time: 10:00 a.m.–1:00 p.m.
Location: Morgan Studios, London
Producer: George Martin

[A.] **Whispering Grass (Don't Tell the Trees)—RS?** (2:34)
[B.] **Bye Bye Blackbird—RS?** (2:10)
Mixed: 6 March 1970

One evening in mid-February, Ringo and Maureen dined with the reclusive McCartneys at their Cavendish Avenue home. At the time, Paul was working on *McCartney* in Morgan Studios, and presumably he recommended the location to Ringo, who traveled there the following month to complete *Sentimental Journey.*

A pair of songs was recorded from start to finish on March 5 in a three-hour session. A demo of "Whispering Grass (Don't Tell the Trees)" had been taped February 9 at EMI Studio 2 to assist Ron Goodwin in creating a full arrangement. He conducted a thirty-six-piece orchestra this morning (brass, strings, bass, guitar, and drums). Ringo's neighbor Maurice Gibb conducted the same band (banjo, saxes, trumpets, piano, xylophone, strings, bass, and drums) in taping his own arrangement of "Bye Bye Blackbird."

Ringo then overdubbed his lead vocals on both songs, double-tracking his performance in places for "Bye Bye Blackbird." Both recordings were mixed into stereo at Abbey Road the following day.

RELEASE HISTORY

1970: **A** and **B** were released on the LP *Sentimental Journey,* reissued on CD in 1995.

30. Studio session R

Date: 6 March 1970
Time: 10:00 a.m.–noon
Location: Morgan Studios, London
Producer: George Martin

**[A.] You Always Hurt the One You Love—
RS?** (2:17)
Mixed: 6 March 1970

The *Sentimental Journey* sessions wrapped up with a song made popular by the Mills Brothers and newly arranged by John Dankworth, "You Always Hurt the One You Love." Ringo was present at De Lane Lea Studios February 25 as Dankworth conducted a twenty-piece ensemble (trumpets, saxes, drums, bass, guitar, flutes, and percussion). Ringo then added a double-tracked lead vocal and the song was mixed into stereo.

On March 6, in the LP's final session at Morgan Studios, Dankworth returned to play a saxophone solo, accompanied by some extra drumming. A piano track was also added, and the song was remixed the same evening at Abbey Road. Ringo turns in a decent but nonidiosyncratic performance of this tune, obviously a longtime favorite, as he quotes it during a January 1969 interview with David Wigg.

RELEASE HISTORY

1970: **A** was released on the LP *Sentimental Journey,* reissued on CD in 1995.

31. Radio interview G

Date: 11 March 1970
Time: 5:00–6:00 p.m.
Location: Studio H25, Aeolian Hall, London
Producer: Ted Beston
Interviewer: Johnny Moran
Broadcast: 30 March 1970, 4:31–5:15 p.m.
BBC Radio 1
The Beatles Today
Length: 24:40

When George arrived at BBC Radio's Aeolian Hall studios for the first time in more than five years, he sat down with *Scene and Heard* host Johnny Moran to tape an interview intended for that series. An hour later, there was enough entertaining material to produce a separate special for airing on Easter Monday. With the addition of several Beatles and Apple-related discs, twenty minutes of chat was stretched to fill a forty-five-minute slot.

The first topic is songwriting, with George recalling writing his first song, "Don't Bother Me," from his sickbed in Bournemouth. George's biggest hurdle was that John and Paul had a head start of several years, not to mention teamwork, which made it tough for George "to write some sort of crummy song and expect the Beatles to record it." Rather than submit the songs he was proudest of, he would choose ones he felt were easiest to communicate to the band.

To introduce Jackie Lomax's new single, "How the Web Was Woven," which George produced, he pokes fun at the song's authors, saying he knows which Matt Monro song they stole the melody from. George recounts his history with Billy Preston, from the Hamburg days through the Ray Charles performance where he was rediscovered. Although everyone had advised releasing "Everything's All Right" as a single, nobody bothered to buy it. "That's the Way God Planned It" also faced resistance from American R & B radio stations, who found it too "white," so George hopes that Billy's new single, "All That I've Got," will fare better.

Doris Troy's "Ain't That Cute" is also aired, with George describing how he and Doris cowrote the song in the studio, borrowing the chords from Leon Russell's "Delta Lady." George expresses interest in having an Apple house band, with people like Peter Frampton, to back various singers as well as releasing their own music. He mentions that members of the Temptations and Sam and Dave's backing group have played on Billy Preston's second Apple LP, currently in the works.

While he's influenced by everything he hears, George says he mainly listens to records by Bob Dylan, the Band, and Indian musicians. He feels that even if you don't understand the specifics of Eastern religion or philosophy, listening to spiritual music will have beneficial effects. The latest Radha Krishna Temple single, "Govinda," is prefaced by George's explanation that its title is another name for Krishna or God.

A lot of time is spent previewing the *Let It Be* album and film, which George says began as "a vague idea" of a TV show, the Beatles wanting to avoid another *Magical Mystery Tour* fiasco but not wanting to go the safe family entertainment route of Tom Jones, either. Although he "can't stand seeing" the finished product, George admits the documentary is instructive for anyone who wonders what a Beatles session is like.

He does praise the album's raw and immediate quality, calling it "the complete opposite to the sort of clinical approach that we've normally had." As Phil

Spector hasn't begun the reproduction, George describes the latest Glyn Johns lineup, saying that people will be familiar with "Don't Let Me Down" and that they break into Fats Domino numbers between songs (thinking of "I'm Ready," no doubt). He discusses "For You Blue," "I Me Mine," "The Long and Winding Road," "Across the Universe," "Dig a Pony," and "Dig It," and the latter three are played (from the World Wildlife LP and the unreleased Glyn Johns mixes).

Although he has a hard time recalling the title, George talks about *Sentimental Journey* and compares Paul's upcoming album to Eddie Cochran's one-man-band recordings. George says that over the summer, he hopes to record his own solo album, and that afterward the Beatles should be ready to record together. George's optimism is ironic, not only because of the perilous state of the band's unity, but because he was usually the least concerned with being a Beatle.

Joking that "Lennon's had his hair cut," George opines that 1970 will turn out to be great for the group, and that after doing solo albums, everyone will be refreshed and ready to record as a unit again. George ends on a surprisingly upbeat note: "I certainly, y'know, don't want to see the end of the Beatles. And I know I'll

do anything, y'know. Whatever Paul, John, Ringo would like to do, y'know, I'll—I'll do it. As long as we can all be free to be individuals at the same time . . . I think, y'know, that's just part of our life, y'know, is to be Beatles. And I'll play that game, y'know, as long as the people want us to."

RELEASE HISTORY

1970: Most of this interview was broadcast in the aforementioned documentary *The Beatles Today*. One minute and 5 seconds of unique material was aired on *Scene and Heard* March 15, and a further 42 seconds were included in the special *Let It Be*, broadcast May 23. All three BBC Radio shows circulate in fair to good quality among collectors from off-air tapes.

1984: Bits of the interview were included in the radio special *Sgt. Pepper's Lonely Hearts Club Band: A History of the Beatle Years 1962–1970* and were copied from that source on the CD-R *Vinyl to the Core*.

1999: The *Let It Be* broadcast of May 23, 1970, was included on the bootleg CD *Get Back 2nd Mix*.

32. Promo clip   R

Date: 15 March 1970
Time: 10:00 a.m.
Location: Talk of the Town, London
Producer: John Gilbert
Director: Neil Aspinall
Broadcast: 29 March 1970, 10:25–11:25 p.m.
London Weekend Television
Frost on Sunday

[A.] Sentimental Journey (3:19)

Ringo decided to film a promo clip for the title song, although it wasn't being released as a single, of his debut LP. Pulling out all the stops, Ringo and director Neil Aspinall concocted a production number to rival *Magical Mystery Tour*'s "Your Mother Should Know" sequence.

Chris Thomas prepared a new mono mix of "Sentimental Journey" at EMI Studio 3 on March 13, mixing out Ringo's main lead vocal track (but retaining his second vocal on the first middle eight). During filming, Ringo sang a live vocal on top of this, varying the lyrics slightly and responding to the applause at the end: "Thank you, thank you very much, you're too kind. Certainly wonderful."

The clip was filmed at the Talk of the Town nightclub, with an audience seated at tables surrounding

the stage. The backdrop was an enormous photographic blowup of the Dingle neighborhood in Liverpool where Ringo had grown up. In front of this, the Talk of the Town orchestra, conducted by George Martin, played along. Giant U.S. and UK flags were hung at either side of the stage above groups of male and female dancers, respectively, who joined Ringo onstage halfway through the number. As if this wasn't enough, near the end, backing singers Doris Troy, Madeline Bell, and Marsha Hunt descended from the ceiling on a huge platform.

The result was that any charm inherent in the sight of a pink bow tie–clad Ringo crooning into a handheld mic was overwhelmed by the spectacle surrounding him.

RELEASE HISTORY

This clip circulates among collectors in decent quality as part of Ringo's *Private Reel* collection. The soundtrack was first booted on the LP *Soldier of Love*, taken from its U.S. broadcast on *The Ed Sullivan Show*, May 17, 1970. It's best found on the vinyl bootleg *Richie & His Pals/Scouse the Mouse;* the CD *All Dried Up* fades out a few seconds early.

33. Radio interview   R

Date: 25 March 1970
Location: Apple Corps, London
Interviewer: David Wigg
Broadcast: 29 March and 5 April 1970, 3:00–4:00 p.m.
BBC Radio 1
Scene and Heard
Length: 8:10

The last of David Wigg's Beatle-era interviews was conducted with Ringo at Apple and broadcast in two consecutive editions of BBC Radio's *Scene and Heard.*

The first of these covers a variety of topics, beginning with "the soul brother," John Lennon, whose courage and convictions Ringo obviously admires: "He could jump off the Eiffel Tower and I'd approve it." Wigg asks how much influence Beatles wives have, and Ringo replies, "Some of them have more than others." Maureen's strength was speaking up for the British fans, evident in her advocating the Beatles to hold their proposed January 1969 concert in England when others were lobbying to travel abroad.

Ringo expresses great interest in branching out as a film actor, complaining that he's already been typecast as a light comedian. When his *Sentimental Journey* promotional duties are fulfilled, Ringo looks forward to setting up the entertainment center in his new home. Like John before him, Ringo had cut his hair fairly short toward the end of February, after several days of hesitation: "I was going through that looking in the mirror, saying 'Oh, I'll be all bald!'"

Calling himself "Mr. Show Business," Ringo describes the "Sentimental Journey" promo clip to Wigg, who asks if he's ever had dancing lessons. He recalls an aborted attempt at age eight when the sight of a roomful of girls frightened him away, joking, "I've been trying to get back ever since!" He blames the rumors of an imminent split on music journalists stirring up controversy, claiming that the Beatles are as united as ever and don't want to break up.

The April 5 segment is devoted to promoting *Sentimental Journey,* with Ringo relating the circumstances behind its recording and praising the quality and longevity of the songs from that era. He says that multiple arrangers were chosen to keep the project interesting and reveals that the title track and "Whispering Grass" are potential single contenders (in the end, no single was pulled from the LP). His preference is for "Whispering Grass," which is played to conclude the interview.

Another extract from the raw tape of this interview was released on the LP *The Beatles Tapes with David Wigg.* Wigg asks what the "most momentous moment" in the Beatles' career was, and Ringo chooses "Love Me Do" over more obvious choices such as having a number 1 hit or conquering America. "Just the idea of being on a bit of plastic . . . was really incredible. After all those years of playing, y'know."

RELEASE HISTORY

1976: All the material from the March 29 broadcast was included in fair quality on the vinyl bootleg *Away with Words.* A small excerpt of this and a forty-five-second unaired segment were released the same year on the LP *The Beatles Tapes with David Wigg,* later reissued on CD. Both the March 29 and April 5 broadcasts circulate from good-quality off-air tapes.

34. TV interview   R

Date: 29 March 1970
Time: 10:25–11:25 p.m.
Location: Studio 3, Wembley Studios
Host: David Frost
Broadcast: live
London Weekend Television
Frost on Sunday
Length: 2:44

To introduce the airing of the "Sentimental Journey" promo clip, Ringo made a brief live appearance on David Frost's latest chat/variety series. Although the original videotape reportedly still exists, all that circulates is a home recording of the audio content.

Explaining the concept behind the album, Ringo jokes that the songs were all learned from his parents when they would return drunk from visiting the pub. An awkward silence follows, which Ringo interrupts with "It went down better in the dressing room." He lists a few of the song titles and reveals that he plans to record an album of country songs as a follow-up.

Frost asks if the Beatles will ever appear onstage again as a group, and Ringo doubts it, but says that once everyone completes their solo albums, they might reunite for another Beatles LP. After Ringo describes what attracted him to its nightclub location, the promo is screened; by the time it ends, Ringo is evidently gone, as Frost begins to introduce a comedy sketch.

RELEASE HISTORY

This interview circulates in fair quality among collectors.

35. Open-end interview   R

Date:	ca. late March 1970
Location:	London (?)
Broadcast:	11 April 1970
	Radio Luxembourg
Length:	8:06

Returning to a form of promotion the Beatles had abandoned by 1965, Ringo recorded an open-ended radio interview discussing *Sentimental Journey*. It's not clear whether this was pressed on a disc or distributed on tape; our source is a broadcast on Radio Luxembourg's German-language service, and the DJ who "interviews" Ringo also has to translate the questions and responses to German for the benefit of the audience.

Each song from the first side of the LP is discussed and played in turn, so this may be only one-half of the full promo. Ringo explains that he wanted to do an LP of original compositions, but as he wrote only about one a year, he opted for the songs he grew up on before getting into rock-and-roll. "Sentimental Journey" was chosen as the title track because it has a similar connotation to *Starrdust* but isn't a ghastly pun. Ringo describes its arranger, Richard Perry, as "a young guy from LA," which the DJ helpfully translates as "Louisiana"!

Ringo contrasts the more modern approach of Perry with the big-band style of Chico O'Farrill, Count Basie's arranger, who had arranged "Night and Day" for the album. Ringo explains that he didn't play drums on the album because it would have taken too long for him to learn how to busk all those tunes along with a professional orchestra, and he reveals that some of the session musicians were "a bit heavy."

"Whispering Grass" was chosen because of Ringo's fondness for the Ink Spots' version, and he names it as his favorite song on the LP, thanks to film composer Ron Goodwin's atmospheric arrangement. As not only his friends, but friends of friends, have been "knocked out" by the album (what were they supposed to say?), Ringo feels it'll have a wide-ranging appeal. We also learn that the "plunkity" banjo in "Bye Bye Blackbird" was chosen by arranger Maurice Gibb after hearing a trad jazz band in a pub the night before Ringo asked him to contribute to the album.

Naturally, people suggested all their own favorite oldies when Ringo was selecting a track list, but he says he tried to stick with ones that he had a personal association with. One of the first albums Ringo owned contained Les Paul and Mary Ford's rendition of "I'm a Fool to Care," and he recounts how Klaus Voormann's arrangement didn't quite work until they replaced the session guitarist's performance with an overdub of Klaus himself playing the part.

"Stardust" was chosen because it was a renowned party piece of his stepfather, Harry, and Paul arranged it "because it was gonna be the title track." The interview concludes with a look at future plans: Paul's album is finished, George "has produced everyone around at the moment," John was going to start an album that week but had a cold, and Ringo plans to record an album of country songs next. There is no mention of future group projects.

RELEASE HISTORY

This interview circulates in good quality among collectors from an off-air tape.

36. Radio interview   R

Date:	31 March 1970
Time:	9:00–9:55 a.m.
Location:	Studio B9, Broadcasting House, London
Host:	Pete Murray
Broadcast:	live
	BBC Radio 2
	Open House
Length:	5:51

Continuing his *Sentimental Journey* press junket, Ringo appeared on the live BBC Radio request show *Open House* to read out listener's letters. He also chatted with host Pete Murray, who had previously introduced the Beatles on TV shows such as *Lucky Stars (Summer Spin)* and *Top of the Pops*. A homemade recording of the show's final twenty minutes exists, complete with music (not included in the timing above).

After Herb Alpert's "This Guy's In Love with You" is played, Ringo talks about each Beatle's solo album projects and says that maybe there will be another group album when they all have free time. He says he's been working a lot with George lately, has "been at Paul's," and sees John whenever he visits Apple. Ringo then reads out a request, which Murray introduces as Rufus Thomas's "Do the Funky Chicken."

Unfortunately, the wrong record is cued up, and what we hear is Mary Hopkin's latest Apple single, "Knock Knock Who's There?" Murray apologizes for the error, and after Ringo reads a request from a woman in Bolton, the Thomas track is played. Another listener is trying to get in touch with her former fellow nursing students from January 1964, and Ringo enthusiastically announces a familiar hit record from that period, "I Want to Hold Your Hand."

When it concludes, Ringo urges people not to live in the past but to buy his new album, "in your shops now." A request for the Ray Conniff Orchestra's "Melodie D'Amour" is honored, and Ringo gets in a hello to Zak and Jason while introducing a Boston Pops rendition of Ravel's "Bolero." One last request, for Joe Dolan's "You're Such a Good-looking Woman," closes out the show, and Murray wishes Ringo success with *Sentimental Journey* and the Beatles' next album, which Ringo adds will be out in "about two weeks."

Apple's plan at that stage was to release *Let It Be* on April 24 and push Paul's *McCartney* LP back to June 4, so the albums wouldn't be competing for shelf space. As far as Paul knew, his album was still penciled in for an April 17 release, and he had stuck to that schedule. The lack of communication between Paul and his bandmates was made plain this day when John and George wrote a letter explaining their reasons for the new release date.

Ringo was elected to hand-deliver the note to Paul and ended up bearing the full wrath of his fury at Allen Klein, Apple, and his impotence in overseeing his own career. As Ringo later testified, Paul "went completely out of control, shouting at me, prodding his fingers toward my face, saying, 'I'll finish you all now' and 'You'll pay!' He told me to put my coat on and get out."

A compromise was reached where Paul would be allowed to retain his original release date and *Let It Be* would be delayed for the umpteenth time, to May 8. The following day, steps would be taken that alienated Paul even further from the Beatles.

RELEASE HISTORY

This interview circulates among collectors from a poor-quality off-air recording.

37. Studio session

Date:	1 April 1970
Time:	7:00 p.m.–2:00 a.m.
Location:	EMI Studio 1
Producer:	Phil Spector
[A.]	**The Long and Winding Road—edit of RS10/13** (3:35)
[B.]	**I Me Mine—edit of RS11/12** (2:24)
[C.]	**Across the Universe—RS13** (3:43)
Mixed:	2 April 1970

The Beatles' recording career stumbled to a halt this evening during a session with one Beatle participating under the control of a producer chosen by two of the other Beatles, all without the knowledge of the fourth Beatle. Thus far, Phil Spector had done his job quietly and efficiently, remixing and piecing together most of the *Let It Be* album in a week of sessions at the end of March in Abbey Road's Room 4.

Come April Fool's Day, Spector decided to build his "Wall of Sound" around three remaining numbers: one each by John, Paul, and George. Arrangers Richard Hewson, Brian Rogers, and John Barham had composed new scores that would be added by a thirty-five-piece orchestra, a fourteen-piece choir, and Ringo, who

sat in on drums for all the overdubs but whose contribution is generally inaudible.

The first task was to make tape reductions of each song. For "Across the Universe," this was easy enough, and the four-track take 8 was copied onto three tracks of a new eight-track tape, omitting both sets of backing vocals (female fans and Beatles). Overdubs consisted of cellos, violas, acoustic guitars, and harp on tracks 4 and 6, violins on track 5, trumpets, trombones, and Ringo's drums on 6 and 8, and the choir on 7 and 8. The final mix (**C**) slowed the song down from the key of D to C-sharp.

"The Long and Winding Road" used the same January 26 take that Glyn had chosen; the original eight tracks contained Paul's lead vocal, his piano, John's bass, George's guitar, Billy Preston's electric piano, two tracks for Ringo's drums, and one for the backing vocal mic, which went unused. Spector reduced the seven to five by combining one drum track with the bass, and the electric piano with the guitar (this track was largely unused in the final mix). Contrary to some reports, he did not erase Paul's vocal track to make room for more strings, but did mix out Paul's half-spoken vocal on the second bridge.

The controversial overdubs were as follows: strings

on track 6, brass and Ringo's drums on track 7, and the choir on track 8. Two stereo mixes were joined together the next day (the edit is at 1:26) to create the finished master (**A**).

The last song was "I Me Mine," which Spector had already extended by editing take 16 after the first 1:20 to jump back and repeat the middle eight and remainder of the song. This edit was reduced as follows: tracks 1 (electric piano) and 6 (organ) were combined, as were tracks 2 (lead guitar and end vocal) and 4 (acoustic rhythm guitar). This freed up track 4 for brass and Ringo's drums, and track 6 for strings. The song was mixed and edited (**B**) along with the other two on April 2, concluding Spector's work on *Let It Be.*

Test pressings of the album were sent out to all four Beatles, and Paul was aghast at what he heard. He fired off an angry letter to Allen Klein and Phil Spector on April 14. It reveals that Paul had actually considered adding orchestration to "The Long and Winding Road," no great shock to anyone who's heard his latter-day performances of the song. What he objected to was having it done behind his back and in a most un-Beatlesque fashion, far less tasteful than any George Martin arrangement.

He demanded "strings, horns, voices and all added noises . . . be reduced in volume," "vocal and Beatle instrumentation . . . be brought up in volume," and "harp . . . be removed completely at the end of the song and original piano notes to be substituted" (they are actually there but buried). None of the changes were made, which isn't surprising given the state of relations between Paul and the others at the time.

Remember Paul's dilemma about how to promote the *McCartney* LP without facing the press? A compromise solution was found when a series of questions was devised for Paul to answer, which would be distributed to the press in printed form, with review copies of the album. Who came up with the questions? According to Paul's authorized biography, *Many Years from Now,* Peter Brown did. According to Peter Brown's unauthorized Beatle biography, *The Love You Make,* Paul came up with the questions.

Whatever the case, Paul chose to answer in terms not much stronger than those John had given in dozens of interviews already about the Beatles' shaky future:

Q: Are you planning a new album or single with the Beatles?

A: No.

Q: Is this album a rest away from Beatles, or start of solo career?

A: Time will tell. Being a solo album means it's "the start of a solo career" . . . and not being done with the Beatles means it's a break. So it's both.

Q: Is your break with the Beatles, temporary or permanent, due to personal differences, or musical ones?

A: Personal differences, business differences, musical differences, but most of all because I have a better time with my family. Temporary or permanent? I don't know.

Q: Do you foresee a time when Lennon-McCartney becomes an active songwriting partnership again?

A: No.

None of this was exactly news to anyone who hadn't had their head buried in the sand the last few months, but because it was Paul's first public proclamation in nearly six months, it was taken as a declaration of independence. On April 10, the headlines screamed: "Paul Is Quitting the Beatles."

RELEASE HISTORY

1970: **A**–**C** were released on the LP *Let It Be* and are on EMI's CD of that title.

APPENDIX A:
MASTER NEWSREEL LIST FOR THE YEARS 1966–1970

When it came to newsreel and TV news footage, I opted only to give entries to items I was actually able to view (or could verify were circulating). However, there is obviously a lot more film of the Beatles out there waiting to be plundered for use in future documentaries. To assist you in identifying which events were filmed, and by which company, here is an index compiled by scouring the written databases for the archives of the Associated Press (AP), the British Broadcasting Corporation (BBC), Independent Television News (ITN), the National Broadcasting Company (NBC), British Pathé (PATHE), and Reuters Newsagency (REU).

I wasn't able to gain access to ABC or CBS's archives and have omitted some minor companies (Universal, Movietone) who infrequently covered the Beatles, as well as most non-UK or -U.S. sources. Also note that Reuters tended to supply footage to ITN and NBC, while the BBC relied on AP, so overlapping clips may reside in more than one archive. Where possible, I've given the approximate length of the footage as noted in the database (compare the timings to individual entries to see how much is circulating); "C" indicates color footage.

1966:

Jan 21	George marries Pattie Boyd	BBC (0:18)
Jan 22	George and Pattie wedding press conference	AP (0:55), BBC (1:28), ITN (0:59), PATHE, REU (1:47)
Feb 8	George and Pattie leave for Barbados honeymoon	BBC (0:26)
Feb 25	George and Pattie return from Barbados	BBC (0:16)
Feb 28	Cavern Club shuts down	BBC (1:04)
May 2	Fans in New York queue for tickets	BBC (0:24)
Jun 23	London Airport departure for Germany	BBC (0:26)
	Beatles arrive in Munich	BBC (0:24), REU (1:01)
Jun 26	Fans in Hamburg	AP (1:28)
	Beatles arrive in Hamburg, Castle Tremsbuttel	PATHE
	Concert at Ernst Merck Halle, Hamburg	REU (1:37)
Jun 28	Protesters in Tokyo	BBC (0:53)
Jun 30	Beatles arrive in Tokyo	AP (1:11), REU (1:09)
	Tokyo fans, protesters, press conference	AP (5:20)
	Tokyo press conference	AP (12:16), NBC (12:41)
	Fans outside Budokan	REU (0:57)
Jul 1	Fans in Tokyo	AP (5:20)
Jul 3	Beatles leave Tokyo for Manila	REU (1:05)
Jul 4	Concert at Manila Stadium	REU (1:10)
Jul 5	Beatles arrive in New Delhi	AP (0:38)
Jul 8	London Airport return from India	BBC (1:23), ITN (2:05), PATHE (0:45), REU (1:46)
	London Airport interview	REU (2:14)
Jul 23	Cavern Club reopens	PATHE
Aug 6	Brian Epstein New York press conference	AP (1:50), BBC (1:10), NBC (1:47)
Aug 11	KKK spokesman in Memphis	BBC (0:58)
	London Airport departure for United States	BBC (1:36)
	Beatles change planes in Boston	AP (1:30), BBC (0:26)
	Beatles arrive in Chicago	NBC (1:21)
	Beatles arrive in Chicago, press conference	AP (1:23), BBC (0:24)
	Chicago press conference	REU (1:42)
Aug 15	Washington, DC, press conference	BBC (1:55)
Aug 17	Concert at Toronto Maple Leaf Gardens	REU (1:17)
Aug 22	Fan—Warwick Hotel ("Sprout of a new generation")	AP (3:13)
	Fans outside Warwick Hotel	AP (1:13)
	New York press conference	AP (18:40), NBC (2:16)
	New York "junior press conference"	AP (1:33)
Aug 23	Concert at Shea Stadium	BBC (0:32), REU (0:48)
Aug 24	Beatles arrive in Los Angeles	NBC (0:20)
	Los Angeles press conference	NBC (C/24:25)
Sep 13	John films *How I Won the War* in Celle	REU (0:49)
Sep 29	Yoko Ono's "Cut Piece" in London	PATHE
Nov 8	Brian Epstein denies split rumor	REU (1:42)

1967:

May 25	John's psychedelic Rolls-Royce	PATHE (0:49)
Jun 19	Paul admits taking LSD	ITN (2:12)
Jul 24	Julian's gypsy caravan	PATHE (0:57)
Jul 31	John and Paul return from Greece	BBC (0:14)
Aug 20	Ringo visits Jason in the hospital	BBC (0:16), ITN (1:18)
Aug 24	Beatles attend the maharishi lecture at Hilton	BBC (2:18)
Aug 25	Beatles leave for Bangor via rail	BBC (1:20), ITN (0:45), REU (1:36)
	Beatles arrive in Bangor	REU (1:04)
Aug 26	Beatles in Bangor w/maharishi	AP (0:49), BBC (0:21), REU (1:20)
	Maureen and Jason leave the hospital	BBC (0:21)
Aug 27	Reactions to Brian Epstein's death	AP (1:30), BBC (1:01), REU (1:47)
Sep 15	Filming *Magical Mystery Tour* in Newquay	REU (1:02)
Oct 17	Arrival at Brian Epstein's memorial service	ITN (0:28)
Oct 18	*How I Won the War* premiere	BBC (1:13), ITN (0:41), NBC (2:05), REU (2:00)
Dec 4	John at Jonathan Hague exhibition	REU (1:14)
Dec 5	Apple Boutique opens in Baker Street	AP (C/1:37), PATHE (1:20)

1968:

Jan 4	Paul and George attend *Mulberry Bush* premiere	REU (1:48)
Jan 7	George departs for India	BBC (0:11)
Jan 10	George at EMI Bombay	BBC (0:27), REU (C/0:45)
Jan 24	Mia Farrow and maharishi depart for India	BBC (C/0:16)
Jan 25	John and George attend fashion show	PATHE (1:03)
Feb 15	John and George depart for India	ITN (0:22)
Feb 16	John and George arrive in New Delhi	BBC (0:22), REU (1:23)
Feb 17	John and George at Rishikesh camp	BBC (C/0:22), REU (1:21)
Feb 18	Ringo and Paul depart for India	AP (0:48)
	John and George at Rishikesh camp	BBC (C/2:06)
	Ringo and Paul's departure, John and George at camp	ITN (2:00)
Feb 19	Ringo and Paul arrive in New Delhi	AP (1:20), REU (C/2:16)
Feb 20	Beatles in New Delhi and Rishikesh	REU (C/1:39)
Feb 21	Beatles at Rishikesh camp	AP (1:26), BBC (C/0:26), REU (2:40)
Mar 26	Paul and Jane return from India	AP (0:35), BBC (2:06)
May 14	John and Paul New York press conference	AP (2:09), NBC
May 16	John and Paul return from United States	BBC (C/0:18)
Jul 1	John and Yoko open *You Are Here* exhibit	REU (C/1:18)
Jul 8	*Yellow Submarine* press preview	BBC (C/0:17), ITN (0:38)
Jul 17	*Yellow Submarine* premiere	AP (1:13), BBC (C/0:18), REU (C/2:08)
Jul 31	Apple Boutique closes	AP (1:34), BBC (C/1:07), REU (C/1:39)
Aug 11	John and Yoko at fashion show	PATHE
Oct 19	John and Yoko at Marylebone Court	BBC (C/0:29), ITN (0:11), NBC (C/0:48), REU (C/1:31)
Nov 28	John at Marylebone Court	BBC (C/0:21), REU (C/0:54)

1969:

Mar 4	Paul and Linda at *Isadora* premiere	REU (1:55)
Mar 12	Paul marries Linda Eastman	AP (0:49), BBC (C/3:47), ITN (3:08), PATHE, REU (C/1:26)
	Paul and Linda interview at home	REU (C/1:07)
Mar 18	George and Pattie en route to court	BBC (C/0:21)
	George and Pattie leave court	ITN (0:19)
Mar 20	John and Yoko at Le Bourget, Paris	REU (C/1:10)
Mar 25	John and Yoko Amsterdam press conference	AP (1:56), ITN (3:40)
Mar 27	John and Yoko in Amsterdam	REU (C/1:02)
Mar 31	George and Pattie at Marylebone court	BBC (C/0:26)
Apr 1	John and Yoko return from Amsterdam	BBC (C/0:22), ITN (0:59)
May 16	Ringo leaves on the *QEII*	AP (1:34)
May 27	John and Yoko Montreal press conference	AP (0:59), REU (1:32)
Aug 31	John, George, and Ringo at Isle of Wight concert	AP (1:23), BBC (C/5:04), REU (C/1:15)
Sep 15	John and Yoko "howl" at Apple	AP (1:04), ITN (1:05)
Sep 25	Paul and Linda at *Midnight Cowboy* premiere	BBC (C/0:30), REU (C/2:05)
Nov 25	John returns MBE	REU (2:19)
Dec 11	*The Magic Christian* premiere	REU (C/0:50)
Dec 15	WAR IS OVER billboard in Times Square	AP (C/1:15)
Dec 17	John and Yoko Toronto press conference	REU (1:13)
Dec 18	"Lennon on Peace" in Toronto	AP (C/3:24)
Dec 23	John and Yoko on meeting Pierre Trudeau	BBC (C/0:45), REU (1:28)

1970:

Jan 16	John's lithographs confiscated in London	BBC (C/1:57)
Jan 26	John and Yoko interview in Paris	REU (C/1:36)
	Ringo arrives in Los Angeles	NBC (C/4:16)
Jan 29	John's lithographs go on display in New York	AP (C/2:41)
Feb 4	John and Yoko donate hair to Michael X	AP (C/1:00), ITN (1:02)

APPENDIX B:
JOHN LENNON'S HOME TAPES 1966–1969

These recordings all originate from John's personal tape archive and most were aired during the 1988–1992 syndicated radio series *The Lost Lennon Tapes*. As I couldn't narrow down the recording dates to within a month or two, I've compiled them all here in an appendix.

[A.]	**Chi-Chi's Cafe**	(3:24)
[B.]	**Daddy's Little Sunshine Boy**	(0:27)
[C.]	**Down in Cuba**	(2:05)
[D.]	**Pedro the Fisherman**	(1:05)
[E.]	**Breakdown**	(1:46)
[F.]	**Stranger in My Arms**	(3:33)
[G.]	**Mellotron Music #1**	(1:29)
[H.]	**Mellotron Music #2**	(0:28)
[I.]	**Mellotron Music #3**	(0:20)
[J.]	**Mellotron Music #4**	(1:47)
[K.]	**Mellotron Music #5**	(1:43)
[L.]	**Julia—instrumental**	(2:51)
[M.]	**Julia—vocal overdub take 1**	(3:20)
[N.]	**Julia—vocal overdub take 2**	(2:54)
[O.]	**Woman Is the Nigger of the World**	(0:54)
[P.]	**I Want You**	(5:45)
[Q.]	**The Maharishi Song**	(3:09)

The first batch of five recordings stems from the period between the end of touring and the start of John's relationship with Yoko, when he had a lot of free time on his hands. Perhaps too much, as anyone who has listened to these tapes can attest. They feature John in his music room at Kenwood, usually with Ringo to lend a hand, playing various rhythmic and instrumental settings on his Mellotron and ad-libbing over the top.

Latin rhythms brought to mind a nightclub spoof (**A**), a nonsensical rhumba (**C**), and a folk song (**D**). The latter appears on side B of a tape with various "Strawberry Fields Forever" demos and tells the tale of Pedro, a fisherman from Bristol "with not a fish to fash." "Chi-Chi's Cafe" is actually an assembly of various fragments from many tapes assembled by the *Lost Lennon* producers and stars the Jolly Jumping Pally Poodles, Mr. Tommy Cartwright, and Woody the Woodburn crooning various absurd ditties. "Down In Cuba" has John introducing a swinging trio of "bass, maracas, and bass" who "do their utty" to entertain the clientele.

Another fragment (**B**) has John prompting Ringo to sing "Daddy's Little Sunshine Boy" a cappella, while the "Breakdown" (**E**) features the pair as a music-hall duo trading one-liners. (John: "Have you got a minute for an old-timer?" Ringo: "No, I've got an hour for a young man, though!")

These are clearly only a sampling from a wealth of John/Ringo home tapes. The log of John's tape archive includes notations on various reels such as "JOHN & RINGO MESSING AROUND," "JOHN W/MELLOTRON," "JOHN & RINGO + WOMEN," and "JOHN CLOWNS AROUND." Doug Sulpy has written about several such tapes that are not in wide circulation. One is a 14:30 compilation of twenty-one segments, three of which have been bootlegged ("Lucy from Littletown" on *Revolution*, plus **C** and **D** above). Another has ten minutes of John and Ringo playing records and chatting with Julian (possibly from the same tape as **F–K**); a third contains fifteen minutes of their tomfoolery, including two snippets used in **A**.

Sulpy has also heard four more portions of John's Mellotron improvisations (totaling 10:17), none of which have vocals. Further examples of these (**F–K**) stem from side A of a cassette with "Strawberry Fields" demo overdubs on the flip side. The only one with vocals is "Stranger in My Arms," which has John ad-libbing soppy romantic lyrics over a Mellotron vamp. The others are tough to sit through, being reminiscent in places of both the incidental music for *Magical Mystery Tour* and George's *Electronic Sound* LP.

Two other cassettes from the summer of 1968 document John's attempts to perfect a demo of "Julia," a song first recorded in a looser arrangement during the May sessions at Kinfauns. The first tape lasts 4:42 and opens with John setting up the microphone, dealing with feedback, and grabbing his acoustic guitar. After a count-in, he begins an instrumental take that must have proved unsatisfactory, as it's cut off during the second verse and erased by a second attempt. Only this latter take (**L**), which is complete, has been bootlegged; it matches the structure of the released studio version.

On a second cassette, John played back the instrumental backing (**M**, including some of the aborted take) and overdubbed a lead vocal. Another overdub take that follows (**N**) has John trying to sing and play along, but it proves too much for him, as he swaps the last two verses, plays bum notes, and gives up vocally toward the end.

The final set of recordings probably comes from the late spring of 1969; all three are relatively low-fidelity and feature John playing slide guitar and singing, accompanied by Yoko. This very early arrangement of "Woman Is the Nigger of the World" (**O**) has quite a different melody, but the same lyrics that would be expanded when John returned to the song three years later. The title is based on a phrase of Yoko's that had been around since at least late 1968 (see the December 12, 1968, entry for *Rood Wit Blauw*).

"I Want You" (**P**) is an improvised dialogue between the two lovers, sung over John's bluesy scales and riffs. It's hardly romantic, though, with lines such as "I want you on the floor and I want you on the rack" and "Yoko, you better lose some weight"! Of far greater interest is "The Maharishi Song" (**Q**), in which John looks back with a mixture of disgust and whimsy at his experience in Rishikesh a year previously. Nobody escapes his scalpel, not the guru (whom Yoko amusingly labels "a sex maniac"), his yes-men and hangers on, or the naive and starstruck disciples. Only John himself comes out looking clever: "Me, I took it for real. I wrote six hundred songs about how I feel. I felt like dying and crying and committing suicide, but I felt creative. And I thought, 'What the hell's this got to do with what that silly little man's talking about?'"

Also on these 1969 reels are pieces titled "Do You Remember?" (a line used in "I Want You"), "The Dream We Dream Together" (another of Yoko's aphorisms later used in the song "Now or Never"), and "Why Do We Always Have To . . ."

RELEASE HISTORY

1988: The radio series *The Lost Lennon Tapes* aired several of these recordings, in episodes 88-12 (**B**), 88-33 (**C**), and 88-48 (**A** and **M**). In addition, **L** appeared as background music beneath narration in several episodes throughout the series. The vinyl bootleg series of *The Lost Lennon Tapes* on Bag Records included **A** (volume 11), **B** (volume 2), and **C** (volume 10). All three appear from this source on the CD-R *Vinyl to the Core.*

1989: The radio series *The Lost Lennon Tapes* aired several of these recordings, in episodes 89-35 (**O**), 89-37 (**Q**), and 89-41 (**N**).

1991: **P** was broadcast in episode 91-04 of the radio series *The Lost Lennon Tapes.* The same year, **D** was aired in episode 91-32; it appeared from this source on the vinyl bootleg *The Lost Lennon Tapes, Volume 31,* later issued on CD. Also that year, a clean but mediocre-quality version of **L** was bootlegged on the CD *Unsurpassed Demos,* and very good copies of **M, N, P,** and **Q** appeared on the CD *The 1968 Demos.*

1993: **O** was bootlegged on the CD boxed set *Christmas Present.*

1994: The bootleg CD *Revolution* included **F–I** and **M,** all from tape source. **M** was also longer than any previous appearance, as it included the false start. The same year, **E, J,** and **K** were booted on the CD *The Lost Pepperland Reel,* also from tape source.

GLOSSARY

Acetate: A disc cut for demonstration purposes, in a very limited number of copies

Backing track: The first layer of a recording to be taped (usually just instruments, perhaps with a guide vocal)

Beeb: Short for the BBC (British Broadcasting Corporation)

Breakdown: A performance of a song that doesn't make it to the end for whatever reason

CD(-R): A (recordable) compact disc

Demo: A rough recording used to demonstrate a song to another artist or to an arranger or producer

Double-tracking: Recording the same vocal or instrumental performance on two separate tracks of the tape to give a fuller, but not identical, sound

Duophonic: Capitol Records' method of giving a mono recording "fake" stereo sound (see Rechanneling)

EP: A 7-inch 45 RPM extended-play record, usually with two songs per side

EQ: Equalization; manipulation of sonic frequencies to achieve a certain sound (heavy bass, bright treble, warm midrange)

Fabs: Another collective moniker for the Beatles (short for "Fab Four")

LP: A 12-inch 33 RPM long-playing record album

Macca: Nickname for Paul McCartney

Mix: To combine various tracks of a tape (usually two, four, or eight in the Beatles' case) down to a two-channel (for stereo) or one-channel (for mono) recording

Monitor mix: A rough external recording for reference purposes, made by pointing a microphone at the studio speakers during playback

OOPS: Acronym for Out of Phase Stereo. A method of isolating the material in a stereo recording that is not common to both channels (anything not in the middle)

Outfake: A recording that is not what it seems, usually passing off a song as something new by manipulating the sound

Outtake: A performance of a song (or scene in a film) not used in creating the final product

Overdub: To add new sound to an existing tape

RM, RS: Remix from multitrack tape to mono or stereo

Rechanneling: A method of producing pseudostereo from a mono source by reducing bass frequencies in one channel and treble in the other

Reduction: A method of combining many tracks on one tape to a lesser number of tracks on a second tape, freeing space for further overdubs

Rhythm track: see Backing track

Rough mix: A mix for reference purposes, or to provide the artist with a quick unpolished copy of their work

Track: A segment (usually a complete song) of an album. Also, a division of magnetic recording tape into discrete, simultaneously recordable segments (twin-track, four-track, eight-track, and so on)

SELECTED BIBLIOGRAPHY

THE HOLY TRINITY:

The Beatles Anthology by the Beatles
The Beatles: Recording Sessions by Mark Lewisohn
The Complete Beatles Chronicle by Mark Lewisohn

GENERAL INFORMATION/BIOGRAPHIES:

The Beatles by Hunter Davies
The Beatles at the BBC by Kevin Howlett
The Beatles Forever by Nicholas Schaffner
Beatles Gear by Andy Babiuk
John Lennon in My Life by Pete Shotton and Nicholas Schaffner
John Lennon: One Day at a Time by Anthony Fawcett
Lennon by Ray Coleman
The Man Who Made the Beatles: An Intimate Biography of Brian Epstein by Ray Coleman
McCartney by Chris Salewicz
Paul McCartney: Many Years from Now by Barry Miles
Shout!: The True Story of the Beatles by Philip Norman
Waiting for the Beatles: An Apple Scruff's Story by Carol Bedford
With a Little Help from my Friends: The Making of "Sgt. Pepper" by George Martin with William Pearson
Yesterday: My Life with the Beatles by Alistair Taylor

DISCOGRAPHICAL DETAILS:

All Together Now by Harry Castleman and Walter J. Podrazik
The Beatles: An Illustrated Record by Roy Carr and Tony Tyler
The Beatles Price Guide for American Records by Perry Cox and Joe Lindsay
The Beatles' Story on Capitol Records by Bruce Spizer
The Beatles: The Ultimate Recording Guide by Allen J. Wiener
Beatles Undercover by Kristofer Engelhardt
Do You Want to Know a Secret? by L.R.E. King
Drugs, Divorce, and a Slipping Image (and *Get Back*) by Doug Sulpy and Ray Schweighardt
Eight Arms to Hold You by Chip Madinger and Mark Easter
Every Little Thing by William McCoy and Mitchell McGeary
Fixing a Hole by L.R.E. King
The 910's Guide to the Beatles' Outtakes by Doug Sulpy
Not For Sale by Belmo
You Can't Do That: Beatles Bootlegs & Novelty Records by Charles Reinhart

MUSICAL ANALYSIS:

The Art & Music of John Lennon by John Robertson
The Beatles as Musicians: "Revolver" through the "Anthology" by Walter Everett
A Day in the Life: The Music and Artistry of the Beatles by Mark Hertsgaard
Tell Me Why: A Beatles Commentary by Tim Riley

FILMS/PHOTOGRAPHS:

Beatles at the Movies by Roy Carr
The Beatles Files by Andy Davis
The Making of the Beatles' "Magical Mystery Tour" by Tony Barrow
Richard Lester and the Beatles by Andrew Yule

QUOTES:

A Hard Day's Write by Steve Turner
Beatles in Their Own Words, edited by Barry Miles
Beatlesongs by William J. Dowlding
John Lennon in His Own Words, edited by Barry Miles
Lennon Remembers: The "Rolling Stone" Interviews by Jann Wenner
Paul McCartney in His Own Words by Paul Gambaccini

TIMELINES:

The Beatles: A Day in the Life by Tom Schultheiss
The Beatles: A Diary by Barry Miles
The Beatles: An Illustrated Diary by Har V. Fulpen
The Beatles London by Piet Schreuders, Mark Lewisohn, and Adam Smith
The Beatles: 25 Years in the Life by Mark Lewisohn

TOURS:

The Beatles Live! by Mark Lewisohn
Ticket to Ride: The Extraordinary Diary of the Beatles' Last Tour by Barry Tashian

PERIODICALS:

Beatlefan, Beatles Book Monthly, Beatlology, Belmo's Beatleg News, Goldmine, Good Day Sunshine, Illegal Beatles, Mojo, Musician, New Musical Express, The 910, Q, Rolling Stone, Strawberry Fields Forever

DISCOGRAPHY

1 (CD: Apple/Capitol CDP 7243 5 9325 2 8)

The 1968 Demos (bootleg CD: Howdy HR-4)

1989 Beatleg News Christmas Record (bootleg EP: WS01-A/B)

The A.M. Tape (CD-R: No Label Records NLR 0001)

Abbey Road (CD: Parlophone CDP 7 46446 2)

Abbey Road Revisited (bootleg LP: CBM 3907)

Abbey Road Talks (bootleg LP: Nebulous Records ALTSW-383)

The Abbey Road Tape, Volume 1 (CD-R: Unicorn UC-082)

The Abbey Road Tape, Volume 2—Solo (CD-R: Unicorn UC-084)

Abbey Road Video Show (bootleg CD: Strawberry STR 020)

Acetate Collection (CD-R: Unicorn UC-087)

Acetates (bootleg CD: Yellow Dog YD 009)

Acetates: double-disc version (bootleg CD: Yellow Dog YD 080/081)

Acoustic (CD: Capitol 7243 8 7442924)

After the Remember (bootleg CD: Masterfraction MFCD 008/009)

"All You Need Is Love" (CD single: Parlophone CDR 5620)

Another Flaming Pie (CD-R: No Label Records NLR 9714)

Another Sessions . . . Plus (bootleg CD: Vigotone VT-180)

Another Tracks of "Magical Mystery Tour" (bootleg CD: Sweet Zapple SZ-015/016)

Anthology 2 (CD: Apple CDP 7243 8 34448 2 3)

Anthology 3 (CD: Apple CDP 7243 8 34451 2 7)

Anthropology (CD-R: Silent Sea SS005)

Arrive without Aging (bootleg CD: Vigotone VT-6869)

Arrive without Travelling (bootleg LP: Vigotone VIGO 69)

As It Happened, Baby! (CD-R: RAR/Darthdisc)

As Nature Intended (bootleg CD: Vigotone VT-122)

*Atlanta*Munich*Seattle* (bootleg CD: Spank SP 145)

Attack of the Filler Beebs, Episode 3 (CDR: Silent Sea Productions SS003)

Attack of the Filler Beebs, Episode 2 (CD-R: Silent Sea Productions SS002)

Attack of the Filler Beebs, Volume 4 (CD-R)

Away with Words (bootleg LP)

Back-Track (bootleg CD: BT 6267 2)

Back-Track, Part 2 (bootleg CD: BT 6368-2)

Back-Track, Part 3 (bootleg CD: BT 6369-2)

Beatle Talk (LP: Great Northwest Music Co. GNW-4007)

Beatle Views (LP: BV 1966)

The Beatles (CD-EP: Capitol C2-15867)

The Beatles (CD: Parlophone CDP 7 46443/4 2)

The Beatles (LP: Apple PMC 7067/68)

The Beatles 1962–1966 (CD: Apple CDP 7 97036 2 2)

The Beatles 1962–1966 (LP: Apple PCSP 717)

Beatles '66: Munich · San Francisco (bootleg CD: Odeon MO 1966)

Beatles 4 Ever (bootleg LP: Beat Riff Records)

Beatles at Shea Stadium Described by Erupting Fans (LP: Audio Journal AJ1)

The Beatles Broadcast Collection, Trailer 2 (bootleg CD: Yellow Dog YD 076/077)

The Beatles Canadian Press Conference (CD: ISBN 0 9515255 6 5)

The Beatles Talk with Jerry G. (LP: Backstage BSR-1165)

The Beatles Talk with Jerry G., Volume 2 (LP: Backstage BSR-1175)

Beatles Tapes: The Beatles in the Northwest (CD: Jerden JRCD 7006)

The Beatles Tapes with David Wigg (CD: Polydor 42284 7185-2)

The Beatles Tour: The Great Takeover (bootleg LP: Wizardo WRMB 502)

The Beatles vs. Don Ho (bootleg LP: Melvin MM08)

Bedism (CD: Dressed To Kill)

The Best of Tobe Milo (bootleg LP: Tobe Milo 10Q 1/2)

Blackpool Night Out '64—Upgraded (CD-R: Unicorn UC-088)

Blind Faith (CD: RSO 825 094-2)

Both Sides (bootleg LP: MIW Records 8)

Brave New World (CD: Capitol CDP 7 91246 2)

Bravo Beatles Britztournee (bootleg CD: MBE 002 6621/2)

The British Are Coming (LP: Silhouette SM-10013)

Budokan '66 (bootleg LP: L 4342)

The BZ Auction Tape (CD-R)

Candlestick Park: Big Events of '66 (bootleg CD: Masterdisc MDCD-007)

Candlestick Park, San Francisco '66 (bootleg LP: Beatlive BR 001)

Casualties (bootleg LP: Capitol SPRO-9469)

Celluloid Rock (bootleg CD: Yellow Dog YD 006)

Christmas Present (bootleg CD: White Fly WF 001/1-3)

Cilla 1963–1973 The Abbey Road Decade (CD: Zonophone 7243 8 57053 2 8)

A Collection of Beatles Oldies (LP: Parlophone PMC 7016)

Complete North American Tour 1966 (bootleg CD: Misterclaudel mccd-074)

Control Room Monitor Mixes (bootleg CD: Yellow Dog YD 032)

Cornology, Volume 2—The Outro (CD: EMI 7 99597 2)

Crossroads (CD: Polydor 835 261-2)

A Day in the Life (bootleg CD: Yellow Dog YD 2001)

Delaney & Bonnie & Friends On Tour with Eric Clapton (CD: Atco 33326-2)

Die Beatles In Deutschland 1966! (bootleg CD: Invasion Unlimited IU 9647-1)

Die Beatles In Essen (CD)

Die Goldenen OTTO-Sieger 1966 (7-inch flexi disc)

Dig It! (bootleg CD: Condor 1987)

Doll's House (bootleg LP: Maidenhead MHR JET 909-1)

Don't Touch That Dial 2 (CD: Jumbo TJLCD 1966A)

Doris Troy (CD: Apple CDP 7 98701 2)

Down In Havana (CD-R: Unicorn UC-068)

Dreaming of the Past (bootleg CD: Howdy CD 555-01)

Electronic Sound (CD: Apple ZAPPLE 02)

EMI Outtakes (bootleg LP: 1374)

Encouraging Words (CD: Apple CDP 7 81279 2)

Fab Four CD & Book Set (CD: Mastertone 8016)

The Fab Four On Tour (CD: Dynamic Images)

Fanthology (bootleg CD: Yellow Dog YD 067/68)

File Under: Beatles (bootleg LP: Gnat GN70075-1)

Five Nights in a Judo Arena (bootleg CD: Swingin' Pig TSP CD-011)

Five Nights in a Judo Arena (bootleg LP: De Weintraub 426)

Fly (CD: Rykodisc RCD 10415/16)

"Free as a Bird" (CD single: Apple C2 7243 8 58497 2 5)

From Beatles in Memphis 1966 (bootleg CD: Misterclaudel mccd-075)

From Kinfauns to Chaos (bootleg CD: Vigotone VT-183/4)

From Me to You (bootleg CD: Roaring Mouse DPRO-79971)

From the Blue Angel (CD: Edsel EDCD 422)

George Harrison Welcome to Japan 1967 Interview (LP: Wax Records GH TALK 001 LP)

"Get Back" (CD single: Parlophone CDR 5777)

Get Back—The Glyn Johns Final Compilation (bootleg CD: Vigotone VT-182)

Get Back 2nd Mix—The Real to Reel Collection (bootleg CD: Strawberry STR 006)

Get Back John Barrett's Reel (bootleg CD: JB-03001)

The "Get Back" Journals (bootleg CD: Vigotone 101/108)

Get Back to Toronto (bootleg LP: CBM 209)

The Golden Beatles (CD: Overseas 30CP-56)

Gone from This Place (bootleg CD: Vigotone VT-CD 01)

Gone Tomorrow Here Today (bootleg CD: Repro-Man RPM 100)

Goodnight Vienna (bootleg LP: Dakota DR 6975)

The Gospel According To: The Beatles (LP: Baktabak BAK 2108)

"Hello Goodbye" (CD single: Parlophone CDR 5655)

"Hello Goodbye" (single: Capitol 2056)

"Hey Jude" (CD single: Parlophone CDR 5722)

Hey Jude (LP: Apple SW 385)

Historic Interviews, Volume 2 (cassette)

I Apologize (LP: Sterling Productions 8895-6481)

Imagine . . . All the Outtakes (bootleg CD: Vigotone VT-119)

"In the First Place" (CD single)

Indian Rope Trick (bootleg LP: Beat 1)

Inside Interviews: Beatlemania (CD: Laserlight 12 678)

Inside Interviews: In My Life: John Lennon & Paul McCartney (CD: Laserlight 12 676)

Inside Interviews: Talk Downunder: Sydney to Seattle (CD: Laserlight 12 680)

Is This What You Want? (CD: Apple 7 97581 2)

It Was Twenty Years Ago Today (bootleg LP: "TMOQ")

It's All in the Mind Y'Know (bootleg CD: Beat CD 017)

It's Not Too Bad (bootleg CD: Pegboy 1008)

James Taylor (CD: Apple CDP 7 97577 2)

Japan 1966 (bootleg CD: Masterdisc MDCD 010/011)

Jewels and Binoculars (bootleg CD: Vigotone VT-192/217)

John Lennon Forever (CD: Laserlight 12 593)

Johnny Moondog (bootleg LP: Boxtop KOK-1-5832)

Kaleidoscope Eyes (CD: Delta 46076)

The KYA 1969 Peace Talk (single: KYA 1969)

"Lady Madonna" (CD single: Parlophone CDR 5675)

Last Live Show (bootleg LP: TMOQ 71012)

Lennon & McCartney Songbook (CD: Connoisseur Collection VSOP CD 150)

Lennon Legend (CD: Parlophone 8 21954 2)

Leon Russell (CD: DCC/Shelter GZS-1049)

Let It Be (CD: Parlophone CDP 7 46447 2)

Let It Be . . . Naked (CD: Apple CDP 7243 5 95713 2 4)

Life with the Lennons (bootleg EP: Tobe Milo 4Q 13/14)

The Little Red Album (bootleg LP: SAPCOR 38)

Live at the Circus Crone (bootleg LP: Fabulous Four Records L 30157)

Live in Europe & US TV Casts (bootleg LP: CBM 3571)

Live in Paris 1964 and in San Francisco 1966 (bootleg CD: Pyramid RFT CD 002)

Live Peace in Toronto 1969 (CD: Apple CDP 7 90428 2)

Live: Make as Much Noise as You Like! (CD-R: FLO 006)

Liverpool Sound Collage (CD: Hydra LSC01)

Lost and Found (bootleg CD: Quarter Apple PCS 7287)

The Lost Lennon Tapes, Volume 1 (bootleg LP: Bag 5073)

The Lost Lennon Tapes, Volume 2 (bootleg LP: Bag 5074)

The Lost Lennon Tapes, Volume 3 (bootleg LP: Bag 5075)

The Lost Lennon Tapes, Volume 4 (bootleg LP: Bag 5076)

The Lost Lennon Tapes, Volume 6 (bootleg LP: Bag 5078)

The Lost Lennon Tapes, Volume 7 (bootleg LP: Bag 5079)

The Lost Lennon Tapes, Volume 8 (bootleg LP: Bag 5080)

The Lost Lennon Tapes, Number 9 (bootleg LP: Bag 5081)

The Lost Lennon Tapes, Volume 10 (bootleg LP: Bag 5082)

The Lost Lennon Tapes, Volume 13 (bootleg LP: Bag 5085)

The Lost Lennon Tapes, Volume 14 (bootleg LP: Bag 5086)

The Lost Lennon Tapes, Volume 17 (bootleg LP: Bag 5089)

The Lost Lennon Tapes, Volume 18 (bootleg LP: Bag 5090)

The Lost Lennon Tapes, Volume 20 (bootleg LP: Bag 5092)

The Lost Lennon Tapes, Volume 21 (bootleg LP: Bag 5093)

The Lost Lennon Tapes, Volume 24 (bootleg LP: Bag 5096)

The Lost Lennon Tapes, Volume 27 (bootleg LP: Bag 5099)

The Lost Lennon Tapes, Volumes 30–32 (bootleg CD: Bag 5102/3/4)

The Lost Pepperland Reel (bootleg CD: Vigotone VT-132)

Love (CD: Capitol 0946 3 79810 2 3)

LS Bumblebee (bootleg LP: CBM 3626)

Magic Christian Music (CD: Apple CDP 7 97579 2)

Magical Mystery Tour (CD: Parlophone CDP 7 48062 2)

Magical Mystery Tour (CD-EP: Capitol C2-15865/6)

Magical Mystery Tour (LP: Capitol SMAL 2835)

Magical Mystery Tour (LP: Horzu SHZE 327)

Man of the Decade (bootleg LP: MOTD 1269)

Mary Jane (bootleg LP: TMOQ MJ 543)

McCartney (CD: Capitol CDP 7 46611 2)

McGough & McGear (CD: EMI CDP 7 91877 2)

Miscellaneous Tracks (bootleg CD: Yellow Dog YD 2005)

More Masters (bootleg CD: Roaring Mouse DPRO-7997 4/5/6)

My Love Will Turn You On (bootleg CD: Howdy CD 555-02)

Mythology, Volume 2 (bootleg CD: Strawberry 011-014)

Mythology, Volume 3 (bootleg CD: Strawberry 015-018)

Night Ride (CD-R: FLO 005)

No One's Gonna Change Our World (LP: EMI Starline SRS 5013)

No. 3 Abbey Road NW 8 (bootleg CD: Vigotone VT-116)

Not For Sale (bootleg CD: Condor 1986)
Not For Sale (bootleg LP: NEMS MOP 910)
Not Guilty (bootleg CD: Condor 1989)
Nothing but Aging (bootleg LP: Vigotone VT-LP-68)
Nothing Is Real (bootleg LP: NEMS BUD 280)

Ob-La-Di, Ob-La-Da (bootleg LP: Thames LG 3301)
Off White (bootleg LP: Hawk Records WHT 868)

"Paperback Writer" (CD single: Parlophone CDR 5452)
Past Masters, Volume 2 (CD: Parlophone CDP 7 90044 2)
The Paul Jones Collection, Volume 3: Come into My Music Box (CD: RPM RPM183)
Pepperland (CD-R: Silent Sea SS007-008)
The Peter Sellers Tape (bootleg CD: Masterdisc MDCD001 or Spank SP-104)
Post Card (CD: Apple CDP 7 97578 2)
Posters, Incense, and Strobe Candles (bootleg CD: Vigotone VIGO 109)
Primal Colours (bootleg CD: Masterdisc MDCD 009)

The Radha Krsna Temple (CD: Apple CDP 7 81255 2)
Rare Photos & Interview CD, Volume 1 (CD: MasterTone Multimedia Ltd. JG 001-2)
Rare Photos & Interview CD, Volume 2 (CD: MasterTone Multimedia Ltd. JG 002-2)
Rare Photos & Interview CD, Volume 3 (CD: MasterTone Multimedia Ltd. JG 003-2)
Rare Tracks (bootleg CD: Red Square RS 02)
Rarities (LP: Capitol SHAL-12060)
"Real Love" (CD single: Apple C2 7243 8 58544 2 2)
Real Stereo, Album 2 (bootleg CD: Master of Orange MOO-10007)
Reel to Real Sessions (bootleg CD: Strawberry STR 019)
Revolution (bootleg CD: Vigotone VT-116)
Revolver (CD: Parlophone CDP 7 46441 2)
Revolver (LP: Parlophone PMC 7009)
Richie & His Pals / Scouse the Mouse (bootleg LP: Wibble Records WR71982)
Rolling Stones Rock and Roll Circus (CD: ABKCO 1268-2)
Rumitape and More (bootleg CD: JAP-1)

The Scaffold at Abbey Road 1966–1971 (CD: EMI 7243 496435 2 9)
Sentimental Journey (CD: Apple CDP 7 98615 2)
Sessions (bootleg CD: Spank SP-103)
Sessions (bootleg LP: ST 12373/4)
Sgt. Pepper Deluxe (CD-R: Purple Chick PC-122/126)
Sgt. Pepper's Lonely Hearts Club Band (CD: Parlophone CDP 7 46442 2)
Sgt. Pepper's Lonely Hearts Club Band (LP: Parlophone PMC 7027)
Shea! / Candlestick Park (bootleg CD: Spank SP-109)
Shea, the Good Old Days (bootleg LP: CBM 2315)
Singing the Blues (bootleg LP: King Records MLK 003)
Singles Collection (The London Years) (CD: ABKCO 1218-2)
Sink in the Can (CD-R: Snottebel Myr 640707)
Soldier of Love (bootleg LP: Contra Band TB-1022)
Some Time in New York City (CD: Capitol CDP 7 46782/3 2)
Songs for a Tailor (CD: Polydor 85 242-2)
Songs I Forgot (bootleg CD: Planet 1005)

The Songs Lennon and McCartney Gave Away (LP: EMI NUT 18)
Spicy Beatles Songs (bootleg LP: TMOQ 71076)
Stephen Stills (CD: Atlantic 7202-2)
The Stereo Walk (bootleg LP: B4)
Strawberry Fields Forever (bootleg CD: Condor 1988)
Strawberry Fields Forever (bootleg LP: NEMS Clue 9)
"Strawberry Fields Forever" (CD single: Parlophone CDR 5570)
Strawberry Lane (CD-R: Silent Sea SS069-070)
Studio Outtakes (bootleg EP: Tobe Milo 4Q 11/12)

Talkology, Volume 2 (CD: TY002)
Telecasts Four (CD-R: Silent Sea SS 022)
That's the Way God Planned It (CD: Capitol CDP 7 97580 2)
Thirty Days (bootleg CD: Vigotone VT-218/34)
Those Were the Days (CD: Apple 7243 8 30197 2 4)
Through Many Years (bootleg CD: Vigotone VT-181)
Timeless (CD: Overseas 30CP-104)
Timeless II (CD: Overseas 30CP-76)
To Be Expected (bootleg CD: Strawberry SAMPLER001)
Tragical History Tour (bootleg LP: Sapcor 37)
Troubador (CD: Epic/Legacy E2K 46986)
Turn Me On Dead Man: The John Barrett Tapes (bootleg CD: Vigotone VT-178/179)
Twice in a Lifetime (bootleg LP: B-7)

The Ultimate Beatles Christmas Collection (bootleg CD: Vigotone VT-172/173)
The Ultimate Collection, Volume 1: Miscellaneous Tracks (bootleg CD: Yellow Dog YDB 103)
The Ultimate Collection, Volume 1: TV Appearances (bootleg CD: Yellow Dog YDB 102)
The Ultimate Collection, Volume 3: Studio Sessions, 1965–66 (bootleg CD: Yellow Dog YDB 303)
The Ultimate Collection, Volume 2: Live, Live, Live (bootleg CD: Yellow Dog YDB 201)
Ultra Rare Trax, Volume 1 (bootleg CD: The Swingin' Pig TSP CD-001)
Ultra Rare Trax, Volume 2 (bootleg CD: The Swingin' Pig TSP CD-002)
Ultra Rare Trax, Volume 3 (bootleg CD: The Swingin' Pig TSP CD-025)
Ultra Rare Trax, Volume 5 & 6 (bootleg LP: The Swingin' Pig TR 2191 S)
Una Sensazionale Intervista Dei Beatles (EP: Apple DPR-108)
Unbootlegged 1 (CD-R: No Label Records NLR 0101)
Unbootlegged 18 (CD-R: No Tapo Records NTR 0405)
Unfinished Music No. 1: Two Virgins (CD: Rykodisc RCD 10411)
Unfinished Music No. 1: Two Virgins (LP: Apple APCOR 2)
Unfinished Music No. 2: Life with the Lions (CD: Rykodisc RCD 10412)
Unfinished Music No. 2: Life with the Lions (LP: Zapple 01)
Unsurpassed Demos (bootleg CD: Yellow Dog YD 008)
Unsurpassed Masters, Volume 3 (bootleg CD: Yellow Dog YD 003)
Unsurpassed Masters, Volume 4 (bootleg CD: Yellow Dog YD 004)
Unsurpassed Masters, Volume 5 (bootleg CD: Yellow Dog YD 005)

Unsurpassed Masters, Volume 6 (bootleg CD: Yellow Dog YD 012)

Unsurpassed Masters, Volume 7 (bootleg CD: Yellow Dog YD 013)

Upgraded Collection—Highlights (bootleg CD: Fool On Hog Hill FHH CDH001)

Video 1 (CD-R: RAR007)

Vinyl to the Core (CD-R)

Wedding Album (CD: Rykodisc RCD 10413)

We'd Like to Carry On (CD-R: JFC-005)

West Coast Invasion (CD: One Way OW 10848)

What a Shame Mary Jane Had a Pain at the Party (bootleg 12-inch single: R8028)

White Sessions (CD-R: Silent Sea SS011-014)

Yellow Submarine (CD: Parlophone CDP 7 46445 2)

"Yellow Submarine" (CD single: Parlophone CDR 5493)

Yellow Submarine Songtrack (CD: Apple CDP 7243 5 21481 2 7)

Yer Blues (bootleg CD: Library 2329)

"Yesterday" . . . And Today (LP: Capitol T-2553 + ST-2553)

Yin Yang (bootleg LP: BAG 5071)

SONG, SHOW, AND FILM TITLE INDEX

ABOUT THE AUTHOR

John C. Winn has studied the Beatles' recordings for more than thirty years, and has written six books and numerous articles about the band's musical output. He was born in Berkeley, California, and currently lives in Vermont, surrounded by thousands of Beatles CDs, LPs, cassettes, DVDs, books, and magazines. His favorite album is *Revolver*.